2003

www.relaischateaux.com

L.U.C - A proud watchmaking tradition

L.U.C Quattro. Chronometer, 4 spring barrels, 9½-day power-reserve, "Geneva Seal"

www.chopard.com

The L.U.C collection is exclusively available at selected watch specialists and Chopard Boutiques worldwide

1 • RÉGIS BULOT
International President

2 • JEAN-LOUIS BOTTIGLIERO
Chief Executive Officer

3 • MICHEL ROUX
The Waterside Inn

4 • ROBERT GAGNON
L'Auberge Hatley

5 • SANTI SANTAMARIA
Can Fabes

6 • JAUME TAPIES
El Castell de Ciutat

7 • PHILIPPE CAZAUDEHORE
Cazaudehore et la Forestière

8 • B. DE GASTINES-CACHART
Château de Curzay

9 • JEAN-ANDRÉ CHARIAL
Oustau de Baumanière

10 • DAVID GARRETT
The Point

11 • MICHEL ROSTANG
Restaurant Michel Rostang

12 • FREDRIK ASPEGREN
The Cellars Hohenort

13 • BILL BENNETT
Langdon Hall

14 • MIWAKO FUJIMOTO
Göran Kadan

15 • MICHEL GAUL
La Gaichel

16 • CHRISTIAN GERMAIN
Château de Montreuil

17 • PHILIPPE GOMBERT
Château de la Treyne

18 • PATRICK HENRIROUX
La Pyramide

19 • MALCOLM LEWIS
Longueville Manor

20 • JEAN-MICHEL LORAIN
La Côte Saint-Jacques

21 • FLORIAN MOOSBRUGGER
Gasthof Post

22 • THIERRY NAIDU
Château de la Chèvre d'Or

23 • CORRADO NEYROZ
Hôtel Hermitage

24 • PATRICK O'CONNELL
The Inn at Little Washington

25 • ROLAND PIERROZ
Hôtel Rosalp

26 • DANIELA SAUTER
Brandenburger Hof

27 • JACQUES THOREL
L'Auberge Bretonne

28 • MICHEL TROISGROS
Maison Troisgros

Editorial

Dear Friends,

Men and women with a passion for hospitality and pampering... Men and women devoted to catering for discerning guests... That's what we, the members of the Relais & Châteaux Association, stand for.

To support and encourage the activities of all our members, to continuously raise the quality of our services and to highlight what sets us apart as upscale, charming and refined hotels, the President and the Board of Directors, chosen from our very own ranks, have placed their faith in a team headed by our Chief Executive Officer, Jean-Louis Bottigliero.

With the backing of the Board members, we keep an ever-watchful eye on the quality standards of the Association's member properties in all four corners of the globe. We also supervise its marketing activities which draw on products that have found favour with our guests, for instance our gift certificates in euro which have proved popular with European travellers and the new gift certificates in US dollars just launched in North America.

Offering special moments means fully satisfying those who have placed their trust in us and honour us with their presence.
All we have to do is continue cultivating what makes us different, the difference that has been elevated to a benchmark.

Bon voyage!

Régis Bulot
INTERNATIONAL PRESIDENT

The hallmark of an "A. Lange & Söhne" is not just a prestigious name, it is also 150 years of exquisite Saxon watchmaking artistry.

(Hellmut Wempe)

A. LANGE & SÖHNE

Lange 1 in 18 k gold.

Exquisite Timepieces & Jewelry · Est. 1878

Hamburg Berlin Hanover Düsseldorf Dortmund Frankfurt Mannheim Stuttgart Bremen Nuremberg Leipzig Dresden Cologne Kampen/Sylt London Madrid Paris Vienna New York MS Europa
Head Office Germany: ✆+49 (0)40/33 44 8-0, Fax +49 (0)40/33 18 40 www.wempe.com **New York** 700, Fifth Avenue ✆+1 212/397 90 00 **Paris** 16, Rue Royal ✆+33 (0)1/42 60 21 77 **London** 135, New Bond Street ✆+44 (0)20/74 93 22 99 **Vienna** Kärntner Str. 41 ✆+43 (0)1/512 33 22 **Madrid** Serrano, 58 ✆+34 91/426 22 26

Table of Contents

Useful Information

	page
Gift Certificates Relais & Châteaux	3 & 612
Luxury Alliance	4
Practical advice	7
How to make a reservation?	9
Gift Certificates and Relais & Châteaux special Lys offers	11
Calendar of Relais & Châteaux-Silversea gourmet cruises	40
Ecole des Chefs	436
Internet: www.relaischateaux.com	352
Relais & Châteaux partners	665

Index

Alphabetic index of Relais & Châteaux	13
Alphabetic index of Relais Gourmands	29
New properties 2003	36
Index of properties by country	629
Theme-based index: sports & leisure, fitness & beauty, meeting facilities	629

Relais & Châteaux properties

FRANCE

Alsace/Lorraine	145	Paris	51
Brittany/Normandy/Pas-de-Calais	85	Paris Region	71
Burgundy/Franche-Comté	155	Provence	199
French Riviera/Corsica	221	Savoy/Mont Blanc	185
Loire Valley	103	The Greater South-West	117
Lyon/Rhône Valley	169		

Please refer to next page for an index of our properties around the world

More infos on **www.relaischateaux.com**

NESPRESSO : UN CERTAIN ART DE VIVRE

Ceux qui comptent parmi les amateurs de café le savent déjà : choisir Nespresso, c'est avoir la garantie d'un espresso incomparable jour après jour, tasse après tasse. Le secret ? Une sélection de cafés des meilleures origines, conditionnés dans une capsule renfermant hermétiquement une dose individuelle de café fraîchement moulu. Et, pour s'adapter à cette capsule, un système exclusif équipant une gamme de machines signée en partenariat avec les plus grands noms de l'espresso. Il suffit de se préparer un espresso pour en être convaincu. La pression élevée (19 bars) de la machine et le calibrage précis de la température de l'eau révèlent un espresso à l'arôme incomparable et à la mousse onctueuse. Simple, pratique, rapide et propre, le système Nespresso a été conçu pour offrir un confort d'utilisation inégalé. Plus d'effort, ni d'erreur. Votre espresso est parfait, à chaque fois.

NESPRESSO

Amsterdam Barcelona Bruxelles Düsseldorf Lausanne London
Milano New York Paris Sydney Tel Aviv Tokyo Wien Zürich

www.nespresso.com

Table of Contents (continued)

Relais & Châteaux Properties

EUROPE
MIDDLE EAST

Austria	335	Liechtenstein	257
Belgium	241	Lithuania	355
Czech Republic	332	Luxembourg	241
Denmark	355	Malta	440
Dubai	479	Netherlands	241
France	51	Norway	355
Germany	297	Portugal	443
Greece (Crete)	476	Slovenia	350
Iceland	355	Spain	443
Ireland	393	Sweden	355
Israel	479	Switzerland	257
Italy	401	Turkey	479
Lebanon	479	United Kingdom	367

AMERICA

Argentina	619	French West Indies	607
Barbados	607	Mexico	607
Bermuda	607	Puerto Rico	607
Brazil	619	United States	553
Canada	537	Uruguay	619
Colombia	619	Virgin Islands	607
Ecuador	619		

AFRICA
INDIAN OCEAN

Morocco	486	South Africa	489
Mauritius	489	Tanzania	489
Namibia	489	Zimbabwe	489
Seychelles	489		

ASIA
OCEANIA

Australia	512	New Zealand	512
Indonesia	516	South Korea	521
Japan	521		

More info on **www.relaischateaux.com**

"Who can provide you with the key to 800 of the most luxurious hotels and restaurants on the planet?"

Introducing the new **Relais & Châteaux Gift Certificate**, available in US dollars. Accepted around the world at all Relais & Châteaux and select Leading Hotels of the World. For more information, call (1) (212) 856 0115 (USA) or (44) (0)20 7978 5842 (UK).

Luxury Alliance

Whether your dream holiday includes a luxurious hotel or resort, a celebrated restaurant, a distinctive train journey, a romantic cruise or an exotic adventure tour, turn to the Luxury Alliance, the source for your extraordinary travel lifestyle.
Subscribe to our e-newsletter with the latest on our special offers, by completing the enclosed response card or visit
www.luxury-alliance.com

FINE COUNTRY HOUSE HOTELS AROUND THE GLOBE

With renowned establishments in more than 50 countries, the 459 Relais & Châteaux are loyal to the quality charter established almost 50 years ago, encompassing the famed Five "C's" : Courtesy, Charm, Character, Calm and Cuisine.

LUXURY SETS THEM APART. LEADING HOTELS BRINGS THEM TOGETHER

For more than 70 years, The Leading Hotels of the World have symbolized the ultimate in luxury hospitality. Experience this tradition of excellence at nearly 400 hotels and resorts worldwide.

WWW.LUXURY-ALLIANCE.COM
THE SOURCE FOR YOUR EXTRAORDINARY TRAVEL LIFESTYLE

THE WORLD'S BEST LARGE-SHIP CRUISE LINE

Voted "Best Large-Ship Cruise Line" by *Travel + Leisure* readers for a record seventh consecutive year, Crystal Cruises combines large ship spaciousness and comfort with impeccable, highly-personalized service.

THE DEFINING ELITE LUXURY CRUISE EXPERIENCE

Silversea goes above and beyond to achieve the distinction of being the World's Best Small Ship Cruise Line.

THE MOST ROMANTIC ADVENTURE IN THE WORLD

Orient-Express invites you to experience the journey of a lifetime combining nostalgia, discovery, romance and fine dining. Choose from many expertly crafted journeys in Europe, UK, Asia or Australia.

Abercrombie & Kent, Inc.

THE FIRST NAME IN LUXURY ADVENTURE TRAVEL

Extraordinary journeys to more than 100 countries on all seven continents. Escorted programs and independent, custom-tailored itineraries let you travel wherever, whenever and however you choose.

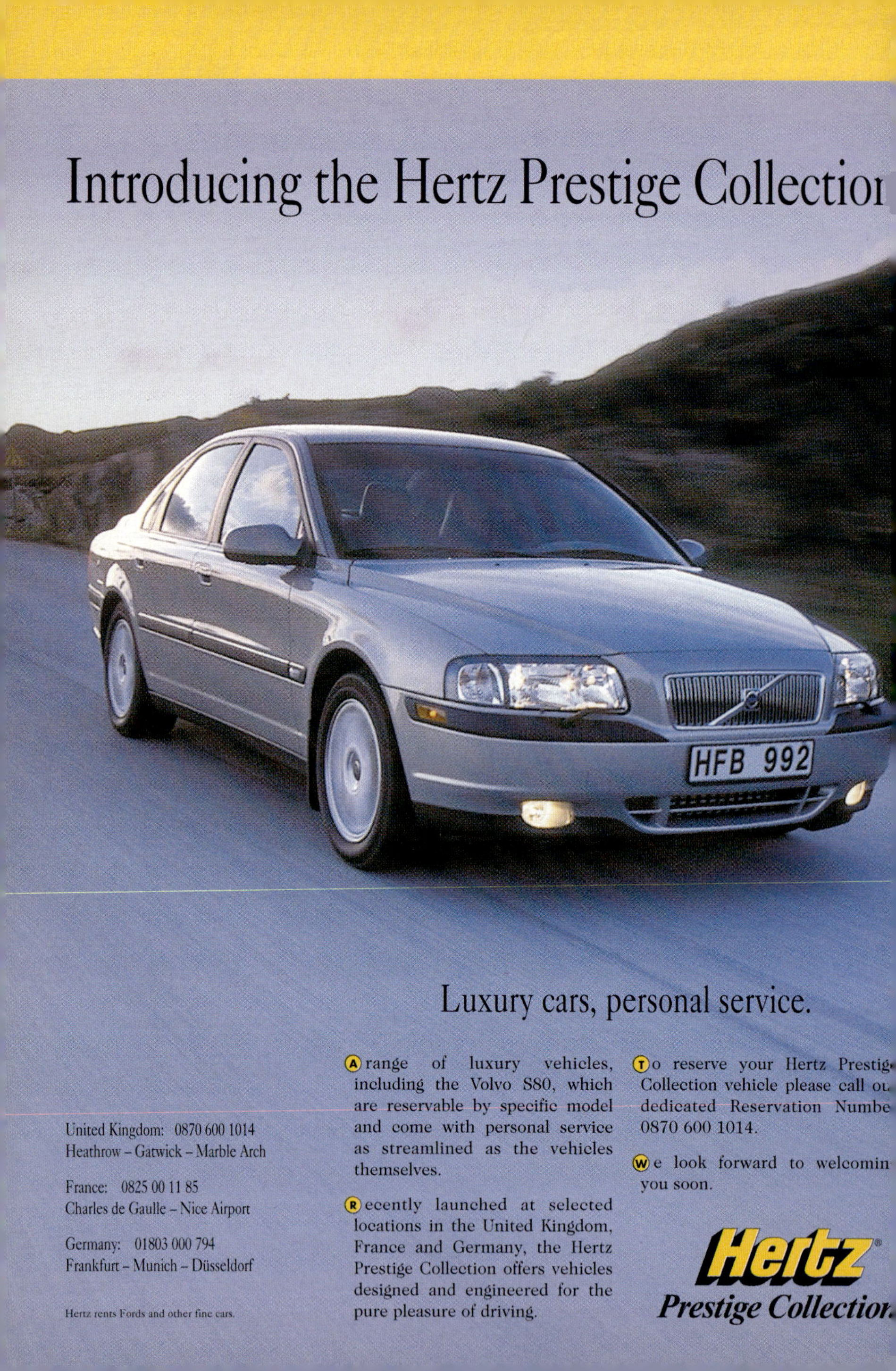

Introducing the Hertz Prestige Collection

Luxury cars, personal service.

United Kingdom: 0870 600 1014
Heathrow – Gatwick – Marble Arch

France: 0825 00 11 85
Charles de Gaulle – Nice Airport

Germany: 01803 000 794
Frankfurt – Munich – Düsseldorf

Hertz rents Fords and other fine cars.

A range of luxury vehicles, including the Volvo S80, which are reservable by specific model and come with personal service as streamlined as the vehicles themselves.

R ecently launched at selected locations in the United Kingdom, France and Germany, the Hertz Prestige Collection offers vehicles designed and engineered for the pure pleasure of driving.

T o reserve your Hertz Prestige Collection vehicle please call our dedicated Reservation Number 0870 600 1014.

W e look forward to welcoming you soon.

Practical advice

Reservation terms

The reservation terms (payment of a deposit, indication of your credit card number...) will be given to you directly by the individual member properties or by our central reservation office.
Each property has its own terms and conditions for cancelling or changing a stay. They will be stipulated to you when you make your reservation.
The rates given are merely by way of information and vary between the high and the low seasons.
They are given on each page in the local currency and in euros for some countries.

Offer a dream with Relais & Châteaux

● The collection of Gift Certificates (pages 3 and 612) and special Lys offers (pages 43 et 663) are a simple and elegant way of offering dreams à la carte either as a personal or corporate gesture.
● Wedding list: your friends will be happy to contribute to your dream trip with Relais & Châteaux.
Information and documentation on **(33) (0)1 45 72 90 00**.

Conference & Reception

Relais & Châteaux will be happy to assist you in organising your seminars, conferences and receptions (details on pages 629 to 659).

Welcome Trophy

For 15 years Relais & Châteaux and Moët & Chandon have awarded the Welcome Trophy to two properties which have distinguished themselves through the excellence of their welcome and their service.
This award is based on the guest comment forms completed by the Relais & Châteaux guests around the world.
In the Guide they are indicated by this symbol:

WELCOME TROPHY 2003
RESTAURANT MICHEL ROSTANG (P. 055)   **HOTEL SCHLOSS SEEFELS** (P. 349)

It's love on both sides

Reverso Gran'Sport Lady

One side times your life to a second; the other offers you diamonds, a second time-zone, and the sun and the stars. The Reverso Gran'Sport for women houses a complicated movement reflecting all the beauty of the watchmaker's art. It makes turning the pivoting case a more entertaining sport than ever.

JAEGER-LeCOULTRE

For your free copy of the Manufacture's book of Timepieces, please contact your local retailer or Jaeger-LeCoultre Switzerland, tel. +41 21 845 02 02. www.mjlc.com. Dials reversed for photo.

Information and Reservations

By Internet

www.relaischateaux.com
(immediate reservation online).

By telephone

EUROPE

	TELEPHONE
France	0 825 32 32 32*
Germany, Austria Benelux, Switzerland United Kingdom, Sweden	00 800 2000 00 02*
Italy	(39) 055 239 6168
Spain	(34) 901 100 105*
Other European countries	(33) (0) 1 45 72 96 50

AMERICA

	TELEPHONE
USA - Canada	(1) 800 735 2478*
Canada (French-speaking)	(1) 866 390 0090*
Argentina	(54) 11 5555 8040
Brazil	(55) (11) 3256 2811

ASIA-OCEANIA

	TELEPHONE
Japan	(81) 3 3475 6876
Australia	(61) 2 9299 2280

OTHER COUNTRIES

	TELEPHONE
	(33) (0) 1 45 72 96 50

*Toll-free numbers: Free calls   *0,15 €/mn.   *0,033 €/mn.

By GDS (Travel Agents)

Relais & Châteaux properties are accessible with the code «WB» in the following GDS: Amadeus, Apollo/Galileo, Worldspan and Sabre.
To consult and download these codes: **www.relaischateaux.com** (travel agency section).

The gift of Relais & Châteaux

The Relais & Châteaux gift certificates and Lys Packages are the perfect formula for everlasting memories -- Courtesy, Charm, Character, Calm and Cuisine.

These gift certificates and packages open the door to a world of romance and dreams without restraint...

Gift certificates are available in US dollars or euros, and are accepted at all 459 Relais & Châteaux establishments worldwide.

RELAIS & CHÂTEAUX GIFT CERTIFICATES AND FORFAITS LYS

For more information, call (1) (212) 856 0115 (USA) or (44) (0)20 7978 5842 (UK), or visit www.relaischateaux.com

Alphabetic index of properties

 An exceptional property featuring the highest level service, amenities and furnishings.

 The refined comfort of a magnificent residence.

 A beautiful property with a high level of comfort, of the «relais de campagne» type.

 Relais Gourmands. Restaurants known for their excellent cuisine.

Properties	Country			Page
Abbaye de Sainte Croix	France	⚜		215
Abbaye La Pommeraie	France	⚜		153
Abtei (Hotel)	Germany	⚜		300
Ada Hotel	Turkey	⚜		481
Aerie (The)	Canada	⚜		550
Akelaŕe (Restaurant)	Spain		◉	454
Albereta et Rest. G. Marchesi (L')	Italy	⚜	◉	410
Albergo (Hotel)	Lebanon	⚜		482
Albergo Giardino	Switzerland	⚜		284
Alpenhof Murnau	Germany	⚜		330
Alpes Hôtel du Pralong	France	⚜		195
Ambasciata (Ristorante)	Italy		◉	419
Ambassadeurs (Les)	France		◉	53
American Colony Hotel (The)	Israel	⚜		484
Anaga (Hotel)	Japan	⚜		522
Antica Osteria del Ponte	Italy		◉	408
Apicius	France		◉	60
Arlberg Hospiz	Austria	⚜		337
Arnsbourg (L')	France		◉	149
Arpège (L')	France		◉	63
Arzak (Restaurante)	Spain		◉	456
Asaba	Japan	⚜		529
Auberge Bretonne (L')	France	⚜	◉	100
Auberge de Noves	France	⚜		210
Auberge des Templiers	France	⚜	◉	75
Auberge du Bois Prin	France	⚜		187
Auberge du Moulin Hideux	Belgium	⚜		250
Auberge du Père Bise	France	⚜	◉	190

More info on www.relaischateaux.com

KRUG PAR PIERRE BONNEFILLE

GRAND VIN DE CHAMPAGNE

L'ABUS D'ALCOOL EST DANGEREUX POUR LA SANTÉ, CONSOMMEZ AVEC MODÉRATIO

Properties	Country			Page
Auberge du Raisin	Switzerland	⚜	⬢	273
Auberge du Soleil	United States	⚜		597
Auberge et Clos des Cimes	France	⚜	⬢	175
Auberge Hatley	Canada	⚜	⬢	541
Auberge La Regalido	France	⚜		207
Aureole	United States		⬢	557
Bagatelle (Restaurant)	Norway		⬢	362
Ballylickey Manor House	Ireland	⚜		395
Barbizon (Restaurant)	Belgium		⬢	245
Bardet (Jean) - Château Belmont	France	⚜	⬢	106
Bareiss (Restaurant)	Germany		⬢	323
Bas-Bréau (Hôtellerie du)	France	⚜		74
Bas Rupts et Chalet Fleuri	France	⚜		146
Bécasse (La)	Japan		⬢	524
Bellevue (Hotel)	Italy	⚜		404
Berasategui (Martin) - Restaurante	Spain		⬢	455
Bergerie (La)	Luxembourg		⬢	251
Bernardin (Le)	United States		⬢	560
Biras Creek	Virgin Islands	⚜		611
Blackberry Farm	United States	⚜		579
Blanc (Georges)	France	⚜	⬢	167
Blantyre	United States	⚜		565
Bodysgallen Hall	United Kingdom	⚜		385
Bondoux (Jean-Paul) (Restaurant)	Argentina		⬢	625
Bonne Etape (La)	France	⚜	⬢	222
Borgo Paraelios	Italy	⚜		433
Bottaccio di Montignoso (Il)	Italy	⚜		422
Bourgogne (La)	Uruguay		⬢	624
Boyer «Les Crayères»	France	⚜	⬢	81
Brandenburger Hof (Hotel)	Germany	⚜		303
Bras (Michel)	France	⚜	⬢	130
Bretagne et sa Résidence (Le)	France	⚜	⬢	97
Bruderholz (Restaurant)	Switzerland		⬢	258
Buckland Manor Hotel	United Kingdom	⚜		381
Buerehiesel (Restaurant)	France		⬢	151
Bülow Residenz	Germany	⚜		305
Burg Schlitz	Germany	⚜		301
Burg Wernberg (Hotel)	Germany	⚜		317
Burghotel Hardenberg	Germany	⚜		308
Bushmans Kloof Wilderness Reserve	South Africa	⚜		500
Cabro d'Or (La)	France	⚜		212
Cagnard (Le)	France	⚜		232

More info on www.relaischateaux.com

Properties	Country			Page
Cala del Porto (Hotel)	Italy	⚜		431
Calandre (Ristorante Le)	Italy		♥	416
Cala Rossa (Grand Hôtel de)	France	⚜		237
Cala Sant Vicenç (Hotel)	Spain	⚜		475
Can Fabes	Spain		♥	463
Canoe Bay	United States	⚜		588
Cardinale et sa Résidence (La)	France	⚜		200
Carré des Feuillants	France		♥	67
Casa de Carmona	Spain	⚜		449
Casa Medina	Colombia	⚜		621
Casa Velha do Palheiro	Portugal	⚜		444
Cashel House Hotel	Ireland	⚜		397
Castel Clara	France	⚜		96
Castel Marie-Louise	France	⚜		101
Castello del Sole	Switzerland	⚜		283
Cazaudehore et «La Forestière»	France	⚜		73
Cellars-Hohenort (The)	South Africa	⚜		510
Centenaire (Hôtel du)	France	⚜	♥	125
Cerf (Restaurant du)	Switzerland		♥	271
Certosa di Maggiano (Hotel)	Italy	⚜		426
Chalet d'Adrien	Switzerland	⚜		279
Chalet du Mont d'Arbois	France	⚜		193
Champs-Elysées (Restaurant)	Mexico		♥	609
Chapel (Alain)	France	⚜	♥	171
Chapelle Saint-Martin (La)	France	⚜		120
Charlie Trotter's	United States		♥	584
Charlotte Inn (The)	United States	⚜		573
Château Cordeillan-Bages	France	⚜	♥	133
Château d'Adoménil	France	⚜		147
Château d'Audrieu	France	⚜		90
Château de Castel-Novel	France	⚜		122
Château de Codignat	France	⚜		173
Château de Courcelles	France	⚜		83
Château de Curzay	France	⚜		113
Château de Faverges-de-la-Tour	France	⚜		182
Château de Feuilles	Seychelles	⚜		491
Château de Germigney	France	⚜		163
Château de la Chèvre d'Or	France	⚜	♥	236
Château de la Treyne	France	⚜		126
Château de Locguénolé	France	⚜	♥	95
Château de Marçay	France	⚜		105
Château de Mercuès	France	⚜		129

Properties	Country			Page
Château de Montcaud	France	⚜		203
Château de Montreuil	France	⚜		86
Château de Noirieux	France	⚜		104
Château de Noizay	France	⚜		108
Château de Puy Robert	France	⚜		124
Château de Riell	France	⚜		143
Château de Rochegude	France	⚜		201
Château de Roumégouse	France	⚜		128
Château de Trigance	France	⚜		223
Château d'Igé	France	⚜		165
Château du Sureau	United States	⚜	●	600
Château du Domaine St-Martin	France	⚜		233
Chateau Yering	Australia	⚜		513
Chaumière (La)	France	⚜		89
Cheneaudière (Hostellerie La)	France	⚜	●	152
Chewton Glen	United Kingdom	⚜		375
Chibois (Jacques) - Bastide St-Antoine	France	⚜	●	230
Cigogne (Hôtel de la)	Switzerland	⚜		268
Clearwater Lodges	South Africa	⚜		504
Clos (Hostellerie Le)	France	⚜		77
Clos de la Violette	France		●	217
Clos St. Denis	Belgium		●	246
Club de Cavalière (Le)	France	⚜		225
Cobblers Cove	Barbados	⚜		615
Côte St-Jacques (La) (Jean-Michel Lorain)	France	⚜	●	156
Coutanceau (Richard) (Restaurant)	France		●	119
Crillon-le-Brave (Hostellerie de)	France	⚜		202
Crocodile (Au)	France		●	150
Cybele Forest Lodge and Spa	South Africa	⚜		498
Daniel	United States		●	559
Darroze (Hélène)	France		●	65
Da Vittorio (Ristorante)	Italy		●	409
De Snippe (Hôtel)	Belgium	⚜		242
Débarcadère (Hostellerie du)	Switzerland	⚜		269
Deidesheimer Hof (Hotel)	Germany	⚜		320
Der Bär (Hotel)	Austria	⚜		343
Deuring Schlössle	Austria	⚜	●	336
Domaine d'Auriac	France	⚜		142
Domaine de Bassibé	France	⚜		137
Domaine de Châteauneuf	France	⚜		219
Domaine de Châteauvieux	Switzerland	⚜	●	267
Domaine de la Bretesche	France	⚜		99

Properties	Country			Page
Domaine des Hauts de Loire	France	⚜	◉	109
Dominik (Hotel)	Italy	⚜		413
Don Alfonso 1890	Italy		◉	437
Duchessa Isabella (Hotel)	Italy	⚜		420
Eau à la Bouche (Hôtel L')	Canada	⚜	◉	543
Eden Rock	French West Indies	⚜		613
El Castell de Ciutat	Spain	⚜		458
El Cenador de Salvador	Spain	⚜		451
«El Montiboli» (Hotel)	Spain	⚜		469
Ellerman House	South Africa	⚜		509
Elounda Mare Hotel	Greece (Crete)	⚜		477
Engø Gård	Norway	⚜		363
Enoteca Pinchiorri	Japan		◉	531
Enoteca Pinchiorri (Restaurant)	Italy		◉	421
Ermitage Am See	Switzerland	⚜		261
Espérance (L')	France	⚜	◉	157
Estalagem Casa Melo Alvim	Portugal	⚜		445
Everest	United States		◉	585
Falsled Kro	Denmark	⚜	◉	357
Farlam Hall Hotel	United Kingdom	⚜		388
Faugeron (Restaurant)	France		◉	54
Fearrington House (The)	United States	⚜		578
Ferme St-Siméon (La)	France	⚜		88
Fortaleza do Guincho	Portugal	⚜		448
French Laundry (The)	United States		◉	595
Frênes (Hostellerie Les)	France	⚜		209
Fürstenhof Celle	Germany	⚜		306
Gagnaire (Pierre)	France		◉	57
Gaichel (La)	Luxembourg	⚜		253
Gallia Palace Hotel	Italy	⚜		429
Gary Danko	United States		◉	598
Gasthof Post	Austria	⚜		338
Gastonian Inn	United States	⚜		582
Gavroche (Le)	United Kingdom		◉	368
Gidleigh Park	United Kingdom	⚜	◉	378
Gill (Restaurant)	France		◉	87
Girasol	Spain		◉	466
Glenapp Castle	United Kingdom	⚜		389
Glendorn	United States	⚜		575
Goldener Hirsch Inn	United States	⚜		591
Gôra Kadan	Japan	⚜		530
Gran Hotel Son Net	Spain	⚜		474

More info on www.relaischateaux.com

Properties	Country			Page
Grand Cœur (Le)	France	⚜		197
Grand Véfour (Le)	France		☙	69
Grande Roche	South Africa	⚜	☙	503
Grandhotel Schönegg	Switzerland	⚜		282
Gravetye Manor	United Kingdom	⚜		374
Greuze (Restaurant)	France		☙	164
Grüner Baum (Hotel)	Austria	⚜		348
Guérard (M.) «Les Prés d'Eugénie»	France	⚜	☙	138
Gutshaus Stolpe	Germany	⚜		302
Gygax (Nik) - Gasthof Löwen	Switzerland		☙	264
Hacienda Na Xamena (Hotel)	Spain	⚜		471
Hambleton Hall	United Kingdom	⚜		383
Hameau Albert 1ᵉʳ (Le)	France	⚜	☙	188
Hartwell House	United Kingdom	⚜		372
Hastings House	Canada	⚜		549
Hatta Fort Hotel	Dubai	⚜		485
Haus Paradies (Hotel)	Switzerland	⚜	☙	292
Hautes Rives (Hôtel)	France	⚜		135
Hautes Roches (Les)	France	⚜		107
Heinitzburg (Hotel)	Namibia	⚜		511
Hermitage (Hotel)	Italy	⚜		403
Hiramatsu (Restaurant)	Japan		☙	527
Hof Van Cleve	Belgium		☙	244
Hoffmeister (Hotel)	Czech Republic	⚜		333
Hohenhaus (Hotel)	Germany	⚜		314
Holt (Hotel)	Iceland	⚜		364
Home Hill	United States	⚜		571
Home Ranch (The)	United States	⚜		592
Homestead Inn	United States	⚜	☙	563
Horai	Japan	⚜		525
Horizons and Cottages	Bermuda	⚜		616
Horned Dorset Primavera (The)	Puerto Rico	⚜		610
Hostellerie Alpenrose	Switzerland	⚜		276
Hubertus (Hotel)	Austria	⚜	☙	344
Hunter's - Tsala	South Africa	⚜		501
Imba Matombo Lodge	Zimbabwe	⚜		494
Inn at Little Washington (The)	United States	⚜	☙	577
Inn at Manitou (The)	Canada	⚜		544
Inn at Sawmill Farm (The)	United States	⚜		572
Inverlochy Castle	United Kingdom	⚜		390
Jagdhof Glashütte (Hotel)	Germany	⚜		315
Jardin des Sens (Le)	France	⚜	☙	205

Properties	Country			Page
Jean Georges	United States		✤	561
Johann Lafer's Stromburg	Germany	⚜	✤	316
Jules César (Hôtel)	France	⚜		206
Kasteel Wittem	Netherlands	⚜		254
Kattegat Gastronomi	Sweden	⚜	✤	358
Kauri Cliffs	New Zealand	⚜		515
Kendov Dvorec	Slovenia	⚜		351
Kingsbrae Arms	Canada	⚜		538
Kinnaird	United Kingdom	⚜		391
Knob Hill Inn	United States	⚜		590
Krägga Herrgård	Sweden	⚜		359
Kunststuben (Restaurant)	Switzerland		✤	262
Kur-und Sporthotel Dollenberg	Germany	⚜		325
Kwandwe Private Game Reserve	South Africa	⚜		505
La Collegiata (Hotel)	Italy	⚜		425
Lafarque (Hostellerie)	Belgium	⚜	✤	249
Lake Placid Lodge	United States	⚜		567
Lameloise	France	⚜	✤	162
Landgut Luxnachmühle (Hotel)	Austria	⚜		339
Landhaus Ammann (Hotel)	Germany	⚜		307
Landhaus "Zu den Rothen Forellen"	Germany	⚜		309
Langdon Hall	Canada	⚜		545
Las Balsas (Hosteria)	Argentina	⚜		627
Le Divellec - La Cuisine de la Mer	France		✤	61
Leijontornet & Victory Hotel	Sweden	⚜	✤	361
Lemuria Resort	Seychelles	⚜		492
Léon de Lyon	France		✤	177
Levernois (Hostellerie de)	France	⚜	✤	161
Lion d'Or (Grand Hôtel du)	France	⚜	✤	112
Little Beaver Creek Ranch	Canada	⚜		547
Little Nell (The)	United States	⚜		593
Locanda l'Elisa	Italy	⚜		424
Loges de l'Aubergade (Les)	France	⚜	✤	131
Loiseau (Bernard) - La Côte d'Or	France	⚜	✤	159
Londolozi Private Game Reserve	South Africa	⚜		497
Longueville House	Ireland	⚜		396
Longueville Manor	United Kingdom	⚜		379
Lucknam Park	United Kingdom	⚜		380
Lumière	Canada		✤	548
Maisons de Bricourt	France	⚜	✤	91
Mallory Court	United Kingdom	⚜		382
Manoir aux Quat' Saisons (Le)	United Kingdom	⚜	✤	371

More info on www.relaischateaux.com

Properties	Country			Page
Manoir de Lan-Kerellec	France	⚜		92
Manoir «Inter Scaldes»	Netherlands	⚜	◉	255
Marine Hermanus (The)	South Africa	⚜		508
Marlfield House	Ireland	⚜		399
Mas de Torrent	Spain	⚜		460
Mas des Herbes Blanches (Le)	France	⚜		213
Matahari Beach Resort & Spa	Indonesia	⚜		519
Mayflower Inn (The)	United States	⚜		564
Meadowood Napa Valley	United States	⚜		596
Melograno (Il)	Italy	⚜		439
Meridiana (La)	Italy	⚜		418
Métropole (Le)	France	⚜		235
Middlethorpe Hall	United Kingdom	⚜		386
Mikuni	Japan		◉	532
Mirage - Garden Hotel & Spa (La)	Ecuador	⚜		622
Mizpe-Hayamim	Israel	⚜		483
Morrison House	United States	⚜		576
Moulin de l'Abbaye	France	⚜		123
Moulin de la Gorce (Au)	France	⚜		121
Moulin de Mougins (Le)	France	⚜	◉	229
Moulin des Ramiers (Le)	Belgium	⚜		248
Neichel (Restaurant)	Spain		◉	467
Newport House	Ireland	⚜		398
Nomades (Les)	United States		◉	587
Oasis (Restaurant L')	France		◉	228
Old Drovers Inn	United States	⚜		566
Ombremont	France	⚜	◉	194
Orangerie (L')	United States		◉	603
Orfila (Hotel)	Spain	⚜		450
Orsi (Pierre) (Restaurant)	France		◉	179
Oustau de Baumanière	France	⚜	◉	211
Pamushana	Zimbabwe	⚜		495
Paradise Hotel Jeju	South Korea	⚜		533
Parc Victoria (Le)	France	⚜		139
Park Hotel Weggis	Switzerland	⚜		263
Parkhotel Sonnenhof	Liechtenstein	⚜		295
Parkhotel Villa Grazioli	Italy	⚜		434
Pas de l'Ours (Hostellerie du)	Switzerland	⚜		277
Patina Restaurant	United States		◉	604
Pellicano (Il)	Italy	⚜		432
Peregrino (Hotel el)	Spain	⚜		457
Pescatore (Restaurant dal)	Italy		◉	417

Properties	Country			Page
Petit Nice-Passédat (Le)	France	⚜	☻	216
Pflaums Posthotel Pegnitz	Germany	⚜		319
Phébus (Hostellerie Le)	France	⚜		214
Pic	France	⚜	☻	183
Pinsonnière (La)	Canada	⚜		539
Pitcher Inn (The)	United States	⚜		570
Plage (Hôtel de la)	France	⚜		93
Plaisance (Hostellerie de)	France	⚜		134
Planters Inn	United States	⚜		581
Plettenberg (The)	South Africa	⚜		502
Point (The)	United States	⚜		568
Pont de Brent (Le)	Switzerland		☻	274
Posada de la Casa del Abad	Spain	⚜		452
Posada de los Pájaros - Spa & Hotel	Argentina	⚜		626
Post Hotel	Canada	⚜		546
Posta Vecchia (La)	Italy	⚜		435
Poularde (Hostellerie La)	France	⚜	☻	174
Prieuré (Le)	France	⚜		208
Prince Maurice (Le)	Mauritius	⚜		493
Pyramide (La)	France	⚜	☻	181
Pyrénées (Les)	France	⚜	☻	140
Quartier Français (Le)	South Africa	⚜		507
Quinta das Lagrimas (Hotel)	Portugal	⚜		447
Rancho de San Juan	United States	⚜		594
Rancho Valencia Resort	United States	⚜		605
Ravet (Bernard) (L'Ermitage de)	Switzerland	⚜	☻	272
Read's	Spain	⚜		473
Relais Borgo San Felice (Hotel)	Italy	⚜		427
Relais de la Poste	France	⚜	☻	136
Relais Il Falconiere	Italy	⚜		428
Réserve (La)	France	⚜		141
Réserve de Beaulieu (La)	France	⚜	☻	234
Résidence de la Pinède	France	⚜		226
Residenz Heinz Winkler	Germany	⚜	☻	331
Rheinhotel Fischerzunft	Switzerland	⚜	☻	259
Richelieu (Le)	France	⚜		118
Robin (Bernard) - Le Relais	France		☻	111
Rochat (Philippe) - Rest. de l'Hôtel de Ville	Switzerland		☻	270
Rodat (El)	Spain	⚜		467
Rosa Alpina	Italy	⚜		414
Rosa dos Ventos (Hotel e Fazenda)	Brazil	⚜		623
Rosalp (Hôtel)	Switzerland	⚜	☻	278

More info on www.relaischateaux.com

Properties	Country			Page
Rostang (Michel) - Restaurant	France		⊙	55
Royal Champagne	France	⚜		79
Ryland Inn (The)	United States		⊙	562
Saint-Paul (Le)	France	⚜		231
Saint-Roch (Hostellerie)	Belgium	⚜		247
San Pietro (Hotel)	Italy	⚜		438
San Román de Escalante (Hotel)	Spain	⚜		453
San Ysidro Ranch	United States	⚜		601
Sant Pau (Restaurant)	Spain		⊙	462
Santa Marta (Hotel)	Spain	⚜		461
Santabbondio	Switzerland		⊙	287
Savoy (Guy) - Restaurant	France		⊙	59
Schloss Dürnstein (Hotel)	Austria	⚜		345
Schloss Hubertushöhe	Germany	⚜		304
Schloss Hugenpœt (Hotel)	Germany	⚜		311
Schloss Seefels (Hotel)	Austria	⚜		349
Schloss Wilkinghege (Hotel)	Germany	⚜		310
Schlosshotel Chastè	Switzerland	⚜		293
Schlosshotel Igls	Austria	⚜		342
Schlosshotel Lerbach	Germany	⚜	⊙	313
Schwarzmatt (Hotel)	Germany	⚜		327
Schwarzwald - Hotel Adler	Germany	⚜		326
Schwarzwaldstube (Restaurant)	Germany		⊙	324
Seeger's	United States		⊙	583
Seehotel Siber	Germany	⚜		328
Seiryuso	Japan	⚜		528
Shamrock (Hostellerie)	Belgium	⚜		243
Sharrow Bay Country House	United Kingdom	⚜		387
Sheen Falls Lodge	Ireland	⚜		394
Sherman House (The)	United States	⚜		599
Singita Private Game Reserve	South Africa	⚜		496
Sole di Ranco (Il)	Italy	⚜	⊙	407
Sønderho Kro	Denmark	⚜		356
Sorriso (Al)	Italy	⚜	⊙	405
Sources des Alpes (Les)	Switzerland	⚜		281
Splügenschloss (Hotel)	Switzerland	⚜		260
Sporthotel Singer	Austria	⚜		340
Stadt Hamburg (Hotel)	Germany	⚜		299
Steirereck (Restaurant)	Austria		⊙	346
Stikliai Hotel	Lithuania	⚜		365
Stock Hill Country House	United Kingdom	⚜		376
Sultan Palace	Tanzania	⚜		490

Properties	Country			Page
Summer Lodge	United Kingdom	⚜		377
Table des Guilloux (La)	Luxembourg		◉	252
Taubenkobel	Austria	⚜	◉	347
Talvo (Jöhris) (Restaurant)	Switzerland		◉	289
Tante Claire (La)	United Kingdom		◉	369
Thoresta Herrgård	Sweden	⚜		360
Toiny (Le)	French West Indies	⚜		614
Top Hotel Hochgurgl	Austria	⚜		341
Torre del Remei	Spain	⚜		459
Torre del Visco (La)	Spain	⚜		465
Tosen Goshobo	Japan	⚜		523
Triple Creek Ranch	United States	⚜		589
Trois Tilleuls & Spa (Les)	Canada	⚜		540
Troisgros (La Maison)	France	⚜	◉	172
Tru	United States		◉	586
Tswalu Kalahari Reserve	South Africa	⚜		499
Tugu Bali (Hotel)	Indonesia	⚜		517
Verniaz et ses chalets (La)	France	⚜		186
Veyrat (Marc) - Auberge de l'Eridan	France	⚜	◉	189
Veyrat (Marc) - La Ferme de mon Père	France	⚜	◉	191
Victoria (Hôtel)	Switzerland	⚜		275
Vieux Castillon (Le)	France	⚜		204
Vieux Logis (Le)	France	⚜		127
Vieux Manoir au Lac (Le)	Switzerland	⚜		266
Vigny (Hôtel De)	France	⚜		56
Vila Bled (Hotel)	Slovenia	⚜		353
Villa (La)	France	⚜		239
Villa Abbazia	Italy	⚜		415
Villa Belrose (La)	France	⚜		227
Villa Del Quar (Hotel)	Italy	⚜		412
Villa Fiordaliso	Italy	⚜		411
Villa Florentine	France	⚜		180
Villa Gallici	France	⚜		218
Villa Hammerschmiede (Hotel)	Germany	⚜		322
Villa La Massa	Italy	⚜		423
Villa Margherita	Switzerland	⚜		285
Villa des Orangers (La)	Morocco	⚜		487
Villa Principe Leopoldo & Residence	Switzerland	⚜		288
Villino	Germany	⚜		329
Vineyard at Stockcross (The)	United Kingdom	⚜		373
Wald & Schlosshotel Friedrichsruhe	Germany	⚜	◉	321
Walserhof (Hotel)	Switzerland	⚜	◉	294

More info on www.relaischateaux.com

Properties	Country			Page
Walther (Hotel)	Switzerland	⚜		291
Waterloo House	Bermuda	⚜		617
Waterside Inn (The)	United Kingdom	⚜	◉	370
Wauwinet (The)	United States	⚜		574
Wenger (Georges)	Switzerland	⚜	◉	265
White Barn Inn	United States	⚜	◉	569
Wickaninnish Inn (The)	Canada	⚜		551
Woodlands Resort & Inn	United States	⚜	◉	580
Xara Palace (The)	Malta	⚜		441
Ynyshir Hall	United Kingdom	⚜		384
Zur Traube (Hotel Restaurant)	Germany	⚜	◉	312

More info on www.relaischateaux.com

Alphabetical Index of Relais Gourmands

Fine hospitality has always been a hallmark of the members of Relais & Châteaux. The most important celebrities in world gastronomy are associated under the Relais Gourmand label. Spread over 20 countries, each one of them is an international culinary benchmark without in any way neglecting the spirit of his own culture.

Thanks to their excellent setting, service, wine cellar and cuisine, the Relais Gourmands boast all the qualities of creativity and refinement needed to fulfil your every wish.

More information on: www.relaisgourmands.com

Properties	Country	Town	Page
Akelaŕe (Restaurant)	Spain	San Sebastián	454
Albereta et Rest. G. Marchesi (L')	Italy	Erbusco-Franciacorta	410
Ambasciata (Ristorante)	Italy	Quistello-Mantova	419
Ambassadeurs (Les)	France	Paris	53
Antica Osteria del Ponte	Italy	Cassinetta di Lugagnano	408
Apicius	France	Paris	60
Arnsbourg (L')	France	Baerenthal	149
Arpège (L')	France	Paris	63
Arzak (Restaurante)	Spain	San Sebastián	456
Auberge Bretonne (L')	France	La Roche-Bernard	100
Auberge des Templiers	France	Boismorand	75
Auberge du Père Bise	France	Talloires	190
Auberge du Raisin	Switzerland	Cully	273
Auberge et Clos des Cimes	France	St-Bonnet-le-Froid	175
Auberge Hatley	Canada	North Hatley	541
Aureole	United States	New York	557
Bagatelle (Restaurant)	Norway	Oslo	362
Barbizon (Restaurant)	Belgium	Jezus-Eik	245
Bardet (Jean) - Château Belmont	France	Tours	106
Bareiss (Restaurant)	Germany	Baiersbronn-Mitteltal	323
Bécasse (La)	Japan	Osaka	524
Berasategui (Martin) - Restaurante	Spain	Lasarte-Oria	455
Bergerie (La)	Luxembourg	Geyerschaff	251
Bernardin (Le)	United States	New York	560
Blanc (Georges)	France	Vonnas	167
Bondoux (Jean-Paul) (Restaurant)	Argentina	Ayacucho, Buenos Aires	625

GAGGENAU

VOUS ASPIREZ A CUISINER SANS ODEURS NI FUMÉES ?

Le vario aérateur télescopique est une hotte révolutionnaire. Car il aspire les fumées, vapeurs et graisses de cuisson à l'endroit même où elles sont émises, son efficacité est exceptionnelle. Son bras télescopique, pivotable et réglable en hauteur, permet une aspiration directe juste au-dessus de la casserole ou de la poêle dans un silence record. Au repos, il s'encastre totalement dans le plan de travail et ne prend aucune place.

Vous voulez en savoir plus sur les appareils encastrables Gaggenau ?
Venez visiter sur rendez-vous une
de nos Galeries d'exposition :

PARIS - Tél. 01 58 05 20 20 - STRASBOURG – Tél. 03 88 59 66 20
LYON - Tél. 04 78 54 82 99 - MARSEILLE - Tél. 04 91 95 91 91
Service consommateurs - Tél. 01 49 48 24 22
Ou notre site Internet : www.gaggenau.com

GAGGENAU, LA DIFFERENCE

Properties	Country	Town	Page
Bonne Etape (La)	France	Château-Arnoux	222
Bourgogne (La)	Uruguay	Punta del Este	624
Boyer «Les Crayères»	France	Reims	81
Bras (Michel)	France	Laguiole	130
Bretagne et sa Résidence (Le)	France	Questembert	97
Bruderholz (Restaurant)	Switzerland	Basel	258
Buerehiesel (Restaurant)	France	Strasbourg	151
Calandre (Ristorante Le)	Italy	Sarmeola di Rubano, Padova	416
Can Fabes	Spain	Sant Celoni	463
Carré des Feuillants	France	Paris	67
Centenaire (Hôtel du)	France	Les Eyzies-de-Tayac	125
Cerf (Restaurant du)	Switzerland	Cossonay-Ville	271
Champs-Elysées (Restaurant)	Mexico	Ciudad de México	609
Chapel (Alain)	France	Mionnay	171
Charlie Trotter's	United States	Chicago	584
Château Cordeillan-Bages	France	Pauillac	133
Château de la Chèvre d'Or	France	Eze-Village	236
Château de Locguénolé	France	Hennebont	95
Château du Sureau	United States	Oakhurst	600
Cheneaudière (Hostellerie La)	France	Colroy-la-Roche	152
Chibois (Jacques) - Bastide St-Antoine	France	Grasse	230
Clos de la Violette	France	Aix-en-Provence	217
Clos St. Denis	Belgium	Kortessem	246
Côte St-Jacques (La) (Jean-Michel Lorain)	France	Joigny	156
Coutanceau (Richard) (Restaurant)	France	La Rochelle	119
Crocodile (Au)	France	Strasbourg	150
Daniel	United States	New York	559
Darroze (Hélène)	France	Paris	65
Da Vittorio (Ristorante)	Italy	Bergamo	409
Deuring Schlössle	Austria	Bregenz	336
Domaine de Châteauvieux	Switzerland	Peney-Dessus	267
Domaine des Hauts de Loire	France	Onzain	109
Don Alfonso 1890	Italy	S. Agata Sui Due Golfi	437
Eau à la Bouche (Hôtel L')	Canada	Sainte-Adèle	543
Enoteca Pinchiorri	Japan	Tokyo	531
Enoteca Pinchiorri (Restaurant)	Italy	Firenze	421
Espérance (L')	France	St-Père-sous-Vézelay	157
Everest	United States	Chicago	585
Falsled Kro	Denmark	Falsled	357
Faugeron (Restaurant)	France	Paris	54
French Laundry (The)	United States	Yountville	595
Gagnaire (Pierre)	France	Paris	57
Gary Danko	United States	San Francisco	598

Properties	Country	Town	Page
Gavroche (Le)	United Kingdom	London	368
Gidleigh Park	United Kingdom	Chagford	378
Gill (Restaurant)	France	Rouen	87
Girasol	Spain	Moraira	466
Grand Véfour (Le)	France	Paris	69
Grande Roche	South Africa	Paarl	503
Greuze (Restaurant)	France	Tournus	164
Guérard (M.) «Les Prés d'Eugénie»	France	Eugénie-les-Bains	138
Gygax (Nik) - Gasthof Löwen	Switzerland	Thörigen	264
Hameau Albert 1er (Le)	France	Chamonix	188
Haus Paradies (Hotel)	Switzerland	Ftan	292
Hiramatsu (Restaurant)	Japan	Tokyo	527
Hof Van Cleve	Belgium	Kruishoutem	244
Homestead Inn	United States	Greenwich	563
Hubertus (Hotel)	Austria	Filzmoos	344
Inn at Little Washington (The)	United States	Washington	577
Jardin des Sens (Le)	France	Montpellier	205
Jean Georges	United States	New York	561
Johann Lafer's Stromburg	Germany	Stromberg	316
Kattegat Gastronomi	Sweden	Torekov	358
Kunststuben (Restaurant)	Switzerland	Küsnacht	262
Lafarque (Hostellerie)	Belgium	Pepinster - Goffontaine	249
Lameloise	France	Chagny	162
Le Divellec - La Cuisine de la Mer	France	Paris	61
Leijontornet & Victory Hotel	Sweden	Stockholm	361
Léon de Lyon	France	Lyon	177
Levernois (Hostellerie de)	France	Beaune	161
Lion d'Or (Grand Hôtel du)	France	Romorantin-Lanthenay	112
Loges de l'Aubergade (Les)	France	Puymirol	131
Loiseau (Bernard) - La Côte d'Or	France	Saulieu	159
Lumière	Canada	Vancouver	548
Maisons de Bricourt	France	Cancale	91
Manoir aux Quat' Saisons (Le)	United Kingdom	Great Milton	371
Manoir «Inter Scaldes»	Netherlands	Kruiningen Yerseke	255
Mikuni	Japan	Tokyo	532
Moulin de Mougins (Le)	France	Mougins	229
Neichel (Restaurant)	Spain	Barcelona	467
Nomades (Les)	United States	Chicago	587
Oasis (Restaurant L')	France	La Napoule	228
Ombremont	France	Le Bourget-du-Lac	194
Orangerie (L')	United States	Los Angeles	603
Orsi (Pierre) (Restaurant)	France	Lyon	179
Oustau de Baumanière	France	Les-Baux-de-Provence	211

Properties	Country	Town	Page
Patina Restaurant	United States	Los Angeles	604
Pescatore (Restaurant dal)	Italy	Mantova	417
Petit Nice-Passédat (Le)	France	Marseille	216
Pic	France	Valence	183
Pont de Brent (Le)	Switzerland	Brent/Montreux	274
Poularde (Hostellerie La)	France	Montrond-les-Bains	174
Pyramide (La)	France	Vienne	181
Pyrénées (Les)	France	St-Jean-Pied-de-Port	140
Ravet (Bernard) (L'Ermitage de)	Switzerland	Vufflens-le-Château	272
Relais de la Poste	France	Magescq	136
Réserve de Beaulieu (La)	France	Beaulieu-sur-Mer	234
Residenz Heinz Winkler	Germany	Aschau	331
Rheinhotel Fischerzunft	Switzerland	Schaffhausen	259
Robin (Bernard) - Le Relais	France	Bracieux	111
Rochat (Philippe) - Rest. de l'Hôtel de Ville	Switzerland	Crissier	270
Rosalp (Hôtel)	Switzerland	Verbier	278
Rostang (Michel) - Restaurant	France	Paris	55
Ryland Inn (The)	United States	Whitehouse	562
Sant Pau (Restaurant)	Spain	Sant Pol de Mar	462
Santabbondio	Switzerland	Sorengo-Lugano	287
Savoy (Guy) - Restaurant	France	Paris	59
Schlosshotel Lerbach	Germany	Bergisch Gladbach	313
Schwarzwaldstube (Restaurant)	Germany	Baiersbronn-Tonbach	324
Seeger's	United States	Atlanta	583
Sole di Ranco (Il)	Italy	Ranco Varese	407
Sorriso (Al)	Italy	Soriso	405
Steirereck (Restaurant)	Austria	Wien	346
Table des Guilloux (La)	Luxembourg	Schouweiler	252
Taubenkobel	Austria	Schützen/Gebirge	347
Talvo (Jöhris) (Restaurant)	Switzerland	St Moritz/Champfèr	289
Tante Claire (La)	United Kingdom	London	369
Troisgros (La Maison)	France	Roanne	172
Tru	United States	Chicago	586
Veyrat (Marc) - Auberge de l'Eridan	France	Veyrier-du-Lac	189
Veyrat (Marc) - La Ferme de mon Père	France	Megève	191
Wald & Schlosshotel Friedrichsruhe	Germany	Friedrichsruhe-Zweiflingen	321
Walserhof (Hotel)	Switzerland	Klosters	294
Waterside Inn (The)	United Kingdom	Bray	370
Wenger (Georges)	Switzerland	Le Noirmont	265
White Barn Inn	United States	Kennebunkport	569
Woodlands Resort & Inn	United States	Summerville	580
Zur Traube (Hotel Restaurant)	Germany	Grevenbroich	312

New properties 2003

Welcome to the 24 properties joining the Relais & Châteaux Association this year.

Hélène Darroze
4, rue d'Assas
75006 Paris
France   p. 65

Domaine de la Bretesche
44780 Missillac
France   p. 99

Hostellerie de Plaisance
Place du Clocher
33330 Saint-Emilion
France   p. 134

Hostellerie Le Phébus
Route de Murs - Joucas
84220 Gordes
France   p. 214

Domaine de Châteauneuf
83860 Nans-les-Pins
France   p. 219

La Bergerie
Maison 1
L-6251 Gevershaff
Luxembourg   p. 251

Park Hotel Weggis
Hertensteinstrasse 34
CH-6353 Weggis
Switzerland p. 263

Domaine de Châteauvieux
16 ch. de Châteauvieux
CH-1242 Peney-Dessus
Switzerland p. 267

Restaurant du Cerf
Rue du Temple 10
CH-1304 Cossonay-Ville
Switzerland p. 271

Chalet d'Adrien
Chem. des Creux - CH-1936 Verbier
Switzerland p. 279

Landhaus "Zu den Rothen Forellen"
Marktplatz 2,
D-38871 Ilsenburg
Germany p. 309

Taubenkobel
Hauptstrasse 27-33
A-7081 Schützen/Gebirge
Austria p. 347

Engø Gård
GML. Engovei 25, BP 104
N-3145 Tjøme
Norway p. 363

The Vineyard at Stockcross
Newbury - Berkshire RG20 8JU
United Kingdom p. 373

Hotel Cala del Porto
Via del Pozzo
I-58040 Punta Ala
Italy p. 431

Casa de Carmona
Plaza de Lasso, 1
E-41410 Carmona
Spain p. 449

Hotel el Peregrino
Crta. Pamplona a Logroño - Km 23
E-Puente la Reina
Spain p. 457

El Rodat
Ctra. al Cabo de la Nao S/N
E-03730 Jávea - Spain p. 467

Read's
E-07320 Santa Maria del Cami
Spain p. 473

Kwandwe Private Game Reserve
Private Bag X27
Benmore 2010
South Africa p. 505

Kauri Cliffs
5955 Matauri Bay Road
Matauri Bay
New Zealand p. 515

Restaurant Hiramatsu
5-15-13 Minamiazabu
Minato-ku, 106-0047 Tokyo
Japan p. 527

Home Hill
703 River, Plainfield
New Hampshire 03781
United States   p. 571

 Tru
676 North Saint Clair
Chicago - Illinois 60611
United States   p. 586

A journey above and beyond all expectations…

SILVERSEA®

VOTED WORLD'S BEST

Travel + Leisure 4 Years   **Condé Nast** 6 Consecutive Years   **Robb Report** 3 Consecutive Years
Telegraph Travel Awards, UK 2 Consecutive Years

Fascinating cultures. Meaningful discoveries. New insights. The magic of the most longed for destinations unfolds before you from your private veranda.

Welcome aboard the very special ships of Silversea — voted world's best by prestigious publications, travel associations and most notably, past guests. Here gracious hosts greet you by name and always remember your personal preferences. With every detail cared for in advance — including an extensive selection of fine wines and spirits, and all gratuities — you're free to relax and enjoy the journey.

On every Silversea voyage experience the culinary mastery of *La Collection du Monde* — 30 signature dishes created exclusively for Silversea by Relais & Châteaux – Relais Gourmands master chefs.

Join international Relais & Châteaux guest chefs on select voyages for the ultimate culinary exploration featuring regionally inspired cuisine, artful culinary demonstrations and a grand gala dinner.

2003 CULINARY ARTS SERIES VOYAGES
Featuring Relais & Châteaux – Relais Gourmands Master Chefs

AFRICA
VOYAGE 2302
Dubai to Dubai — March 16 – 23

CANADA & THE COLONIAL COAST
VOYAGE 4324
New York City to Montréal — Sept 20 – 29

VOYAGE 4327
New York City to Nassau — Oct 16 – 26

THE CARIBBEAN
VOYAGE 1301
Fort Lauderdale to Colón — Jan 3 – 12

VOYAGE 4305
Acapulco to Colón — March 28 – Apr 6

EUROPE
VOYAGE 3322
Rome to Cannes — July 23 – 29

VOYAGE 3324
Barcelona to Venice — Aug 5 – 14

VOYAGE 1326
Paris to Lisbon — Aug 7 – 17

VOYAGE 1333
Barcelona to Lisbon — Oct 1 – 11

THE FAR EAST, CHINA & JAPAN
VOYAGE 2314
Singapore to Singapore — July 19 – 26

VOYAGE 3337
Kuala Lumpur to Hong Kong — Nov 28 – Dec 10

SOUTH AMERICA
VOYAGE 3302
Valparaíso to Buenos Aires — Jan 20 – Feb 5

VOYAGE 3302B
Ushuaia to Buenos Aires — Jan 28 – Feb 5

Past guests of Relais & Châteaux enjoy a $300 per suite shipboard credit
($150 per guest) on all 2003 voyages. Ask for offer code R&C 1

For more information or a complimentary brochure visit **www.silversea.com** or call toll-free in the U.S. 800-722-9955 or in the U.K. +44 (0) 870-333-7030.

En route to freedom!

Relais & Châteaux and Hertz present the Forfait Lys Liberté – available at over 70 enchanting hotels in France. The Liberté opens the doors to your dreams, your car and your hotel -- all at attractive rates*.

For more information, call **(1) (212) 856 0115 (USA)** or **(44) (0)20 7978 5842 (UK)** or visit **www.relaischateaux.com**

*From 410 € (2002 price) for a Category C car rental (Renault Megane or equivalent) for 2 days, 1 night, with unlimited mileage, one hotel night in a double room, breakfast and dinner for 2 persons (beverages excluded).

Forfait Lys Liberté Relais & Châteaux.
Charming trips, with room and Hertz car included.

www.hertz.com

Collection New Man
Automne-Hiver 2002
Aix en Provence
Catalogue sur demande 02 41 71 50 00
Boutique accessoires on line : www.newman.fr

Des vêtements conçus comme des voyages

Regions of France

France

■ Paris	51	■ Alsace/Lorraine	145
■ Paris Region	71	■ Burgundy/Franche-Comté	155
■ Brittany/Normandy/ Pas-de-Calais	85	■ Lyon/Rhône Valley	169
■ Loire Valley	103	■ Savoie/Mont Blanc	185
		■ Provence	199
■ The Greater South-West	117	■ French Riviera/Corsica	221

More info on www.relaischateaux.com

Northwest France

Northeast France

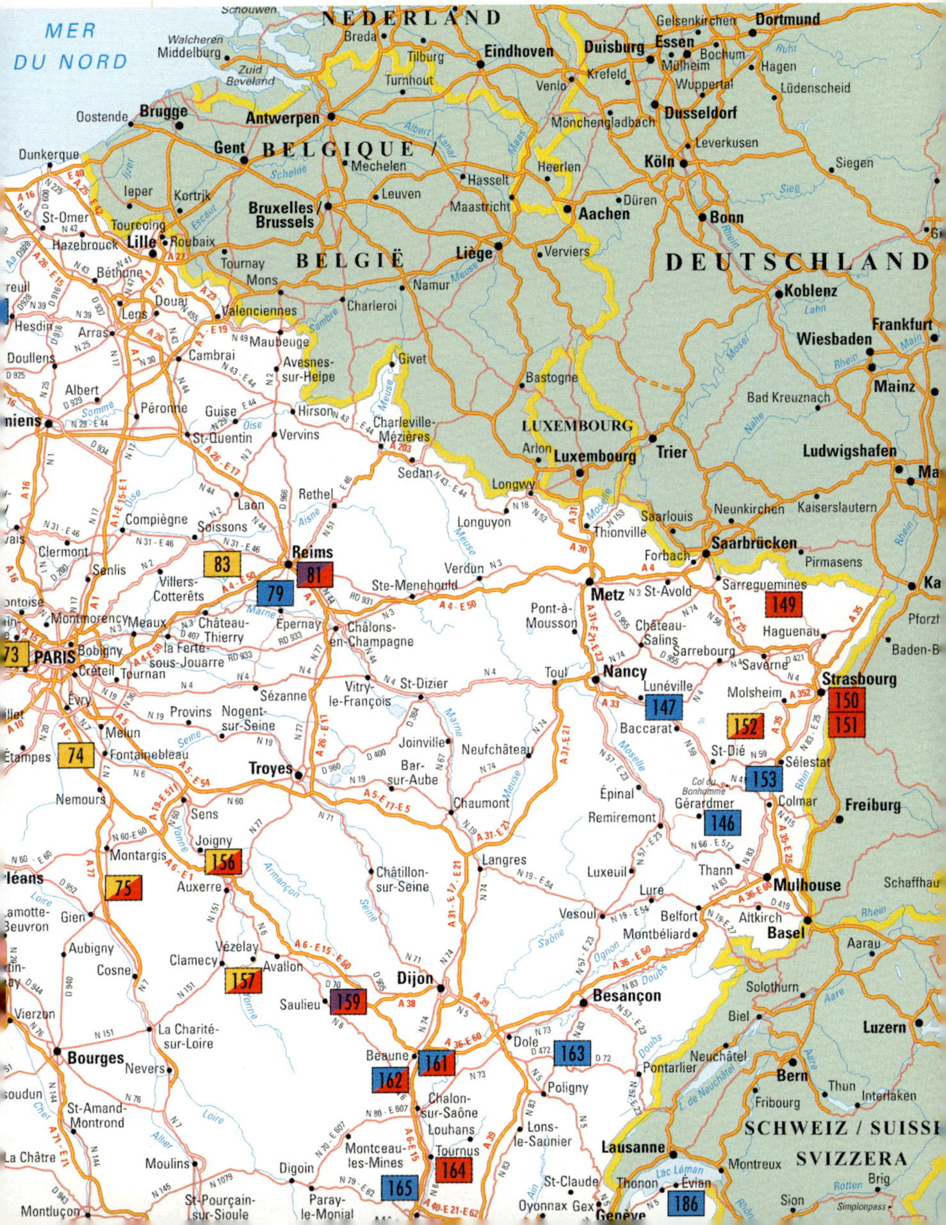

Southwest France

Southeast France

Relais & Châteaux Worldwide Now in Paris!

A special boutique la Maison des Relais & Chateaux... Discover 459 unique hotels and gourmet restaurants, reservations and gift certificates, Dream à la carte!

MAISON DES RELAIS & CHÂTEAUX
33, boulevard Malesherbes 75008 Paris
Tel: (33) (0)1 45 72 90 00

Paris

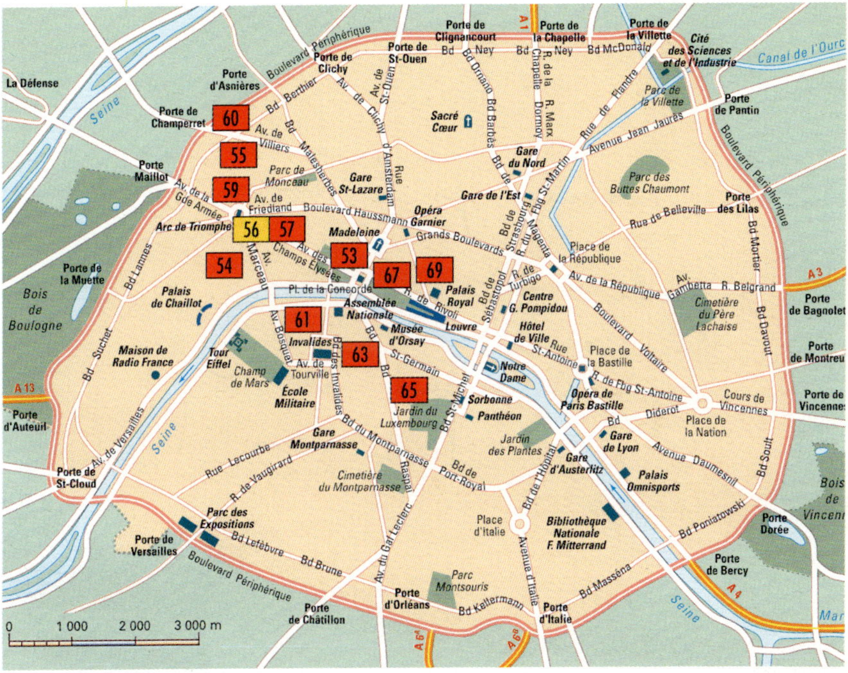

France

Properties	Relais & Châteaux	Relais Gourmands	Page
Ambassadeurs (Les)		⊛	53
Apicius		⊛	60
Arpège (L')		⊛	63
Carré des Feuillants		⊛	67
Darroze (Hélène)		⊛	65
Faugeron (Restaurant)		⊛	54
Gagnaire (Pierre)		⊛	57
Grand Véfour (Le)		⊛	69
Le Divellec - La Cuisine de la Mer		⊛	61
Rostang (Michel) - Restaurant		⊛	55
Savoy (Guy) - Restaurant		⊛	59
Vigny (Hôtel de)	⚜		56

More info on www.relaischateaux.com

* I don't see time passing,
  I look at my watch.

BLANCPAIN

MANUFACTURE DE HAUTE HORLOGERIE

*Je ne regarde pas le temps qui passe,
je regarde la montre.* *

Guy Savoy

★★★
Guy Savoy, Chef, Paris.

The world's thinnest
and only self-winding Tourbillon
with one week power reserve.
Water-resistant to 100 meters.

Boutiques Blancpain
8, rue de la Paix F-75002 Paris Tel.: +33 1.42.92.08.88
25, rue du Fbg Saint Honoré F-75008 Paris Tel.: +33 1.53.43.08.80
29, La Croisette F-06400 Cannes Tel.: +33 4.93.38.11.11

Blancpain - Switzerland - www.blancpain.com

Les Ambassadeurs

SINCE 1977

10, place de la Concorde
75008 Paris
France

Tel. : (33) 01 44 71 16 16
Fax : (33) 01 44 71 15 02
ambassadeurs@relaischateaux.com

France

The former ballroom of this XVIIIth century private mansion overlooking the place de la Concorde has become the restaurant Les Ambassadeurs. In this temple of elegance and excellent taste, Chef Dominique Bouchet invites you to taste his refined culinary creations, such as «la charlotte de crabe et tomate, crémeux au jus de carapaces» or «le millefeuille au chocolat Manjari, compote de pommes cuites à la façon Tatin». Superb wine list.

Private function rooms. Jacket and tie required.

Access: Hôtel de Crillon. At the angle of the rue Boissy-d'Anglas and the place de la Concorde.

Airports: Paris Orly (Intl) 15 km, Paris Ch. de Gaulle (Intl) 25 km
Train station: Saint-Lazare 1 km

Owner: Société du Louvre
General Manager: Philippe Krenzer
Open all year
Currency: Euro (€)
Rates: Menus 62-135 € s.i.
Carte 145 € s.i. (wine included)
Dogs: not allowed
Accepted cards: AE, DC, JCB, MC, VS

Dominique Bouchet

More info on www.relaischateaux.com/ambassadeurs

Restaurant Faugeron

France
SINCE 1979

52, rue de Longchamp
75116 Paris
France

Tel. : (33) 01 47 04 24 53
Fax : (33) 01 47 55 62 90
faugeron@relaischateaux.com

Gerlindé Faugeron welcomes guests to one of the finest restaurants in Paris with exquisite charm and courtesy. Her husband, Henri, has been delighting gourmet palates for years with innovative culinary masterpieces such as «œuf coque à la purée de truffes» and «jarret de veau de lait de Corrèze à la moutarde violette». As for the wine waiter, Jean-Claude Jambon, he was recently voted the best «sommelier» in the world.

Access: From Etoile, take avenue Kléber and the rue de Longchamp.

Airports: Paris Orly (Intl) 15 km, Paris Ch. de Gaulle (Intl) 25 km

Owner: Henri Faugeron
Weekly closing: Saturday and Sunday
Annual closing:
In August and from Dec. 23rd to January 3rd
Currency: Euro (€)
Rates: Menus
lunch 54 € s.i.
dinner 114 € s.i.
Carte 130-150 € s.i.
Dogs: not allowed
Accepted cards: AE, JCB, MC, VS

Henri Faugeron

More info on www.relaischateaux.com/faugeron

Restaurant Michel Rostang

SINCE 1982

20, rue Rennequin
(corner rue Gustave-Flaubert)
75017 Paris • France

Tel. : **(33) 01 47 63 40 77**
Fax : (33) 01 47 63 82 75
rostang@relaischateaux.com

France

Brochettes de langoustines au romarin», «risotto de homard et petit épeautre», «canette de Bresse "Miéral" au sang» and the dazzling finale : «tarte chaude au chocolat amer». Virtuoso chef Michel Rostang, a Dauphinois who has become an honorary Parisian, creates a veritable symphony of flavours, elevating gourmet cuisine to its highest level. This elegant restaurant's wine list is truly exceptional.

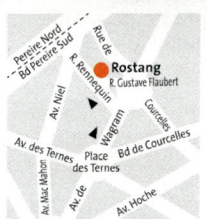

Access: From Etoile, take av. de Wagram and the 2nd left (rue Rennequin) after place des Ternes.

Airports: Paris Orly (Intl) 15 km, Paris Ch. de Gaulle (Intl) 25 km
Train station: Saint-Lazare 4 km

Owner: Michel Rostang
Weekly closing: Saturday (lunch), Sunday, Monday (lunch)
Annual closing: 1st fortnight in August
Currency: Euro (€)
Rates: Menus 120 € s.i. 60 € s.i. (week lunch) Carte 104-119 € s.i.
Dogs: allowed
Accepted cards: AE, DC, JCB, MC, VS

Michel Rostang

More info on www.relaischateaux.com/rostang

Hôtel de Vigny

France
SINCE 1993

9-11, rue Balzac
75008 Paris
France

Tel. : (33) 01 42 99 80 80
Fax : (33) 01 42 99 80 40
vigny@relaischateaux.com

Just a stone's throw from the Champs-Elysées, this elegant hotel is the perfect combination of tradition, tranquillity and elegance. It has simply everything to tempt you to Paris from breakfast served in one of the charming guest rooms, the aromatic teas and other treats to be savoured in front of an open fire in the mahogany-panelled lounge to the culinary delights that await you in the Art Deco bar restaurant.

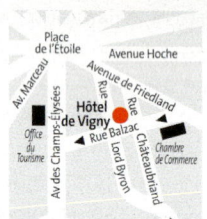

Access: At the top of the Champs-Elysées, via rue Washington and rue Chateaubriand.

Airports: Paris Orly (Intl) 15 km, Paris Ch. de Gaulle (Intl) 25 km
Train station: Saint-Lazare 5 km

Owner: SA de Vigny
General Manager: Charles Bourdin
Open all year
Currency: Euro (€)
Rates: Carte 35-58 € s.i.
26 rooms: starting at 350 € s.i.
11 suites: starting at 515 € s.i.
Breakfast: starting at 21 € s.i.
Dogs: allowed
Accepted cards: AE, DC, JCB, MC, VS

More info on www.relaischateaux.com/vigny

Pierre Gagnaire

SINCE 1997

6, rue Balzac
75008 Paris
France

Tel. : (33) 01 58 36 12 50
Fax : (33) 01 58 36 12 51
gagnaire@relaischateaux.com

France

After establishing an excellent reputation in the provinces, Pierre Gagnaire has opened an elegant restaurant in Paris. This talented chef, renowned for his innovative contemporary cuisine, has been hailed as authentic, curious and modern. Inspired creations such as «pigeon Gauthier cuit au sautoir, aux bâtons de cannelle, côtes de blettes terre de Sienne, à la fondue de cèpes» will delight gourmet guests.

Place de l'Etoile nearby.

Access: At the top of the Champs-Elysées, by the rue Washington and the rue Chateaubriand.

Airports: Paris Orly (Intl) 15 km, Paris Ch. de Gaulle (Intl) 25 km
Train station: Saint-Lazare 5 km

Owner: CFCG SARL
General Manager: Ch. Gagnaire
Weekly closing: Saturday and Sunday lunch
Annual closing: One week in Spring, one week at All Saints' Day, from July 14th to 31st, lunch in August
Currency: Euro (€)
Rates: Menus 80-183 € s.i. Carte 150 € s.i.
Accepted cards: AE, DC, MC, VS

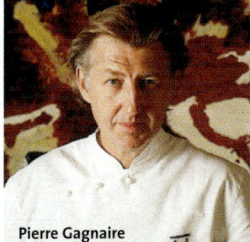

Pierre Gagnaire

More info on www.relaischateaux.com/gagnaire

Restaurant Guy Savoy

SINCE 1989

18, rue Troyon
75017 Paris
France

Tel. : (33) 01 43 80 40 61
Fax : (33) 01 46 22 43 09
savoy@relaischateaux.com

France

For Guy Savoy, who apprenticed with Troisgros, the word impossible does not exist. He has mastered the intricacies of French gastronomic tradition. This virtuoso chef's creations are audacious and inventive: his «soupe d'artichaut à la truffe noire, brioche feuilletée aux champignons et truffe» and the «bar en écailles grillées aux épices douces» are masterpieces. The wine cellar is a treasure trove of exceptional vintages. New decor by Jean-Michel Wilmotte.

Access: From Etoile, take avenue de Wagram; rue Troyon to the 2nd left.

Airports: Paris Orly (Intl) 15 km, Paris Ch. de Gaulle (Intl) 25 km

Owner: Guy Savoy
Weekly closing: Saturday (lunch), Sunday and Monday
Annual closing: August, Christmas and New Year's Eve celebrations
Currency: Euro (€)
Rates: Menu «Prestige» 186 € s.i.
Menu «Festin» 229 € s.i.
Carte 160 € s.i.
Dogs: allowed
Accepted cards: AE, DC, JCB, MC, VS

Guy Savoy

More info on www.relaischateaux.com/savoy

Apicius

SINCE 1987

122, avenue de Villiers
75017 Paris
France

Tel. : (33) 01 43 80 19 66
Fax : (33) 01 44 40 09 57
apicius@relaischateaux.com

Gourmets flock to this elegant restaurant, named after the famous gourmet of Roman times, to savour Jean-Pierre Vigato's inspired cuisine. The menu is a celebration of pure flavours, offering «foie gras de canard poêlé en aigre-doux aux radis noirs confits» and «pigeon de ferme désossé et farci de vieux jambon et champignons». Savour the sublime «soufflé au chocolat noir», a veritable delight.

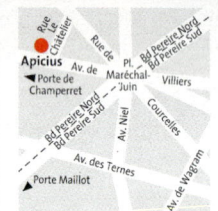

Access: From Etoile, av. Mac-Mahon, av. Niel, to the left of place du Maréchal-Juin, av. de Villiers.

Airports: Paris Orly (Intl) 15 km, Paris Ch. de Gaulle (Intl) 25 km

Owner: Jean-Pierre Vigato
Weekly closing: Saturday and Sunday
Annual closing: From August 1st to 30th
Currency: Euro (€)
Rates: Menu tasting 104 € s.i.
Carte starting at 76 € s.i.
130 € s.i. (wine included)
Dogs: allowed
Accepted cards: AE, DC, JCB, MC, VS

More info on www.relaischateaux.com/apicius

Le Divellec «La Cuisine de la Mer»

SINCE 1976

107, rue de l'Université
75007 Paris
France

Tel. : (33) 01 45 51 91 96
Fax : (33) 01 45 51 31 75
ledivellec@relaischateaux.com

France

This elegant restaurant, decorated in the style of a luxury yacht, is «moored» on the Invalides esplanade. Virtuoso chef Jacques Le Divellec stands at the helm, creating superb seafood cuisine with subtle Mediterranean accents. Gourmet guests will be enchanted by his «homard à la presse avec son corail» and «huîtres spéciales frémies à la laitue de mer». These culinary marvels are accompanied by the finest vintages.

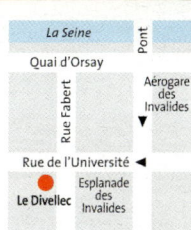

Access: At the corner of rue de l'Université and the Esplanade des Invalides.

Airports: Paris Orly (Intl) 15 km, Paris Ch. de Gaulle (Intl) 25 km
Train station: Invalides 0,3 km

Owner: Jacques Le Divellec
Weekly closing: Saturday and Sunday
Annual closing: August
Currency: Euro (€)
Rates: Menus 50-65 € s.i. (lunch only)
Carte 84-107 € s.i.
Dogs: not allowed
Accepted cards: AE, DC, JCB, MC, VS

Jacques Le Divellec

More info on www.relaischateaux.com/ledivellec

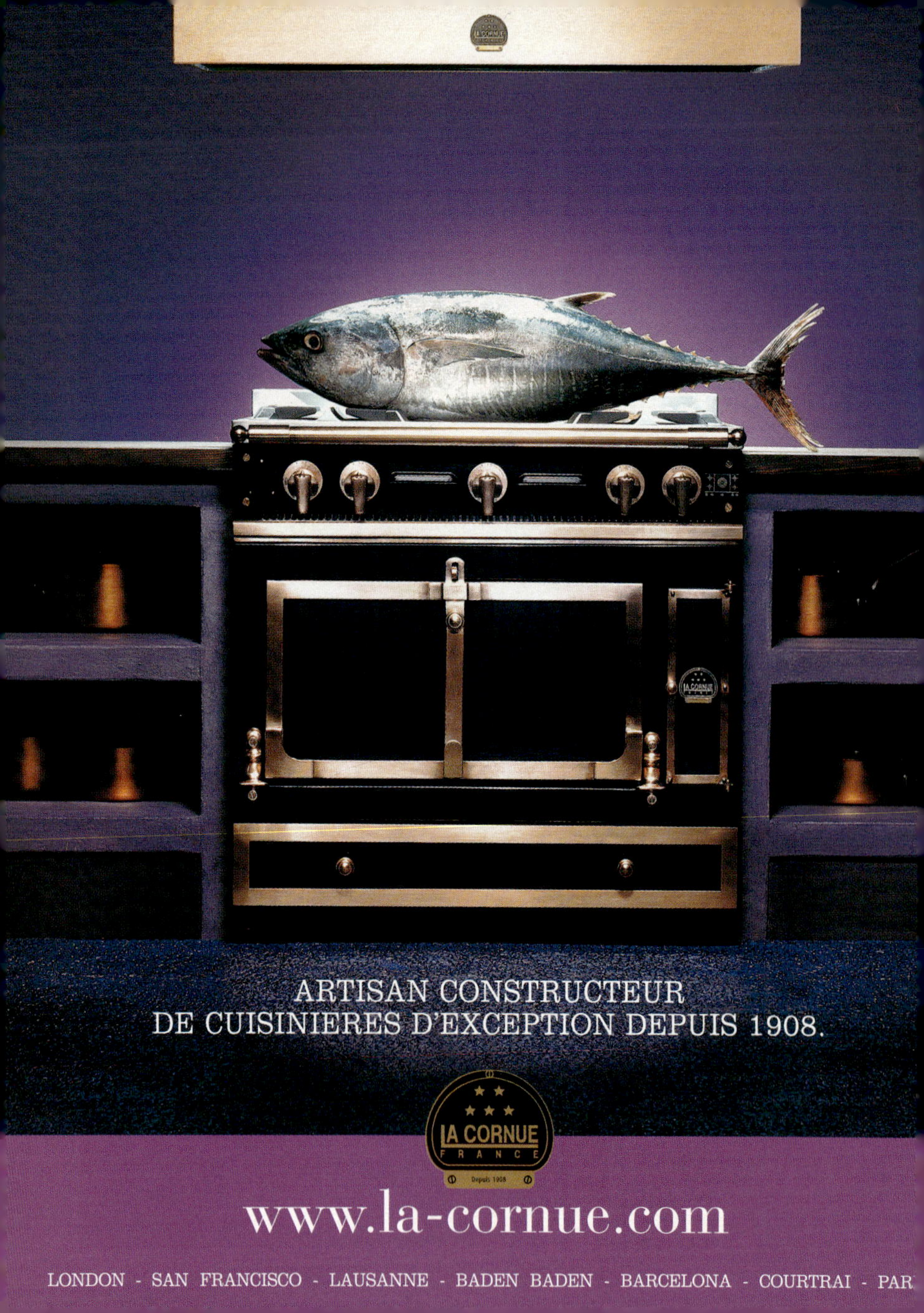

ARTISAN CONSTRUCTEUR
DE CUISINIERES D'EXCEPTION DEPUIS 1908.

www.la-cornue.com

LONDON - SAN FRANCISCO - LAUSANNE - BADEN BADEN - BARCELONA - COURTRAI - PAR

L'Arpège

SINCE 1999

84, rue de Varenne
75007 Paris
France

Tel. : (33) 01 45 51 47 33
Fax : (33) 01 44 18 98 39
arpege@relaischateaux.com

France

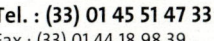

Alain Passard, the rôtisseur, imbues his vegetarian cuisine with his fiery artistic skills. In his vegetable dishes he presents an array of aromas where precision and attention to detail culminate in the most unexpected love match of flavours. The wine cellar is full of excellent organic wines, the perfect accompaniment to his «green» cuisine.

Access: From the esplanade des Invalides, take boulevard des Invalides, then rue de Varenne.

Airports: Paris Orly (Intl) 15 km, Paris Ch. de Gaulle (Intl) 25 km
Train station: Paris-Montparnasse 2 km

Owner: Alain Passard
Weekly closing: Saturday and Sunday
Open all year
Currency: Euro (€)
Rates: Carte 152-183 € s.i.
Dogs: allowed
Accepted cards: AE, DC, JCB, MC, VS

Alain Passard

More info on www.relaischateaux.com/arpege

The world is changing.
Blink and you´ll miss it.

Navigation Technologies is a world leader in the creation, maintenance and supply of high-quality digital navigable maps. Detailed research carried out by our field team of geographers enables us to offer our customers amongst the most comprehensive and up-to-date range of digital maps available. From the earliest beginnings of in car navigation, the industry has chosen NAVTECH maps as a preferred solution. The majority of nav-equipped vehicles carry our maps - more than a million drivers in Europe alone. This position allows us to work with OEMs on the future of intelligent motoring. The research and development collaboration encompasses projects on Voice Recognition, ADAS, and Real Time Traffic Information.

We drive the roads you drive.

Call our hotline for more information: +49 (0) 61 96 - 58 93 00 · www.navtech.com

Hélène Darroze

SINCE 2003

4, rue d'Assas
75006 Paris
France

Tel. : (33) 01 42 22 00 11
Fax : (33) 01 42 22 25 40
darroze@relaischateaux.com

France

Hélène, from the southwest of France, remains faithful to the simple and authentic flavours of products. The foie gras and poultry come from the Landes, the beef from Chalosse, the salmon from the Adour river and the milk-fed lamb from the Basque Country. Whilst upholding the values inherited from her childhood, she cleverly combines them with imagination and mischievousness, always listening to her emotions when cooking and displaying a real, particularly feminine, sensitivity.

Access: From boulevard Saint-Germain, take boulevard Raspail. At place Deville, take rue d'Assas.

Airport: Paris Orly (Intl) 30 km
Train station: Paris-Montparnasse 1 km

Owner/General Manager: Hélène Darroze
Weekly closing: Sunday, Monday
Open all year
Currency: Euro (€)
Rates: Menus 69 (lunch) - 110 € s.i.
Carte 46-95 € s.i.
Dogs: allowed
Accepted cards: AE, MC, VS

Hélène Darroze

More info on www.relaischateaux.com/darroze

Carré des Feuillants

SINCE 1991

14, rue de Castiglione
75001 Paris
France

Tel. : (33) 01 42 86 82 82
Fax : (33) 01 42 86 07 71
feuillants@relaischateaux.com

France

On the site of the former Feuillants convent located between place Vendôme and the Tuileries Gardens, Alain Dutournier delights guests with his inventive cuisine. Open to ever changing tastes, he does his utmost every instant to guarantee guests an exceptional dining experience. The cellar beneath the restaurant is well stocked with rare vintages, some of which are for sale for consumption off the premises.
Private salons.

Access: From the Opera, rue de la Paix, pl. Vendôme; from the Concorde, rue Royale, rue St-Honoré.

Airports: Paris Orly (Intl) 15 km, Paris Ch. de Gaulle (Intl) 25 km

Owner: Alain Dutournier
Weekly closing: Saturday and Sunday
Annual closing: August
Currency: Euro (€)
Rates: Menus 58 € s.i. (lunch) 138 € s.i.
Carte 105 € s.i.
Dogs: allowed (on a leash)
Accepted cards: AE, DC, JCB, MC, VS

Alain Dutournier

More info on www.relaischateaux.com/feuillants

Le Grand Véfour

SINCE 1986

17, rue de Beaujolais
75001 Paris
France

Tel. : (33) 01 42 96 56 27
Fax : (33) 01 42 86 80 71
vefour@relaischateaux.com

France

The XVIIIth century decor of this elegant restaurant, resplendent with gilt-edged mirrors and chandeliers, was once admired by Bonaparte, Victor Hugo, Colette, Malraux and Cocteau. Guy Martin carries on the gourmet tradition of Le Grand Véfour, with his sublime «ravioles de foie gras à l'émulsion de crème truffée», «tourte d'artichauts et légumes confits» and «sorbet aux amandes amères», served with the finest French wines.

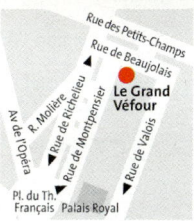

Access: In the Palais-Royal gardens.

Airports: Paris Orly (Intl) 15 km,
Paris Ch. de Gaulle (Intl) 25 km

Owner: S.H. Concorde
General Manager: Guy Martin
Weekly closing: Friday evening, Saturday and Sunday
Annual closing: Easter, August and from December 25th to 31st
Currency: Euro (€)
Rates: Menu 73 € s.i. (lunch)
Carte 150-180 € s.i.
Dogs: not allowed
Accepted cards: AE, DC, JCB, MC, VS

Guy Martin

More info on www.relaischateaux.com/vefour

Paris Region

France

Properties	Nearest major city	Relais & Châteaux	Relais Gourmands	Page
Auberge des Templiers	Montargis	⚜	◉	75
Bas-Bréau (Hôtellerie du)	Fontainebleau	⚜		74
Boyer «Les Crayères»	Reims	⚜	◉	81
Cazaudehore et «La Forestière»	St-Germain-en-Laye	⚜		73
Château de Courcelles	Soissons	⚜		83
Clos (Hostellerie Le)	Verneuil-sur-Avre	⚜		77
Royal Champagne	Epernay	⚜		79

More info on www.relaischateaux.com

Cazaudehore et «La Forestière»

SINCE 1973

1, av. Kennedy
78100 St-Germain-en-Laye
(Yvelines) • France

Tel. : **(33) 01 30 61 64 64**
Fax : (33) 01 39 73 73 88
cazaudehore@relaischateaux.com

France

From this charming residence, nestling amidst rose gardens and forest groves, visitors can stroll along tranquil bridle paths to the Château de Saint-Germain-en-Laye where Louis XIV was born. «La Forestière», an idyllic rustic haven, offers exquisitely comfortable guestrooms, innovative cuisine, an exceptional wine cellar and cigar humidor. Enjoy lunch beneath the scented arbours in spring or dine beside a log fire in autumn.

(Other activities P. 629)

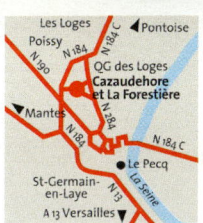

Access: From Paris, A13, 2nd exit, then RN 186 towards Saint-Germain, N 184 towards Pontoise.

Airports: Paris Orly (Intl) 35 km, Paris Ch. de Gaulle (Intl) 45 km
Train station: Saint-Germain-en-Laye 1,5 km

Owner/General Manager: Philippe Cazaudehore
Weekly closing: Rest.: Monday (except holidays)
Open all year
Currency: Euro (€)
Rates: Menus week lunch 48 € s.i. (wine included) dinner/week-end 61 € s.i. (wine included)
Carte 70-80 € s.i.
25 rooms: off-season 178 € s.i. season 198 € s.i.
5 suites: off-season 240 € s.i. season 260 € s.i.
Breakfast: 15 € s.i.
Dogs: allowed (extra cost 25 € s.i.)
Golf: 2 km
Accepted cards: AE, DC, JCB, MC, VS

More info on www.relaischateaux.com/cazaudehore

France — SINCE 1960

Hôtellerie du Bas-Bréau

22, rue Grande
77630 Barbizon
(Seine-et-Marne) • France

Tel. : **(33) 01 60 66 40 05**
Fax : (33) 01 60 69 22 89
basbreau@relaischateaux.com

This secluded hunting lodge, surrounded by a sea of greenery on the outskirts of Fontainebleau forest, is an oasis of comfort and tranquillity. Once a favourite retreat for the artists of the Barbizon school, the lodge's tastefully decorated rooms were more recently enjoyed by Emperor Hiro-Hito. A truly idyllic spot in which to savour gourmet cuisine and fine wines served in elegant crystal and silverware.

(Other activities P. 629)

Access: From Paris or Lyon, take motorway A6, exit Fontainebleau, towards Barbizon (8 km).

Airports: Paris Orly (Intl) 40 km, Paris Ch. de Gaulle (Intl) 80 km
Train station: Fontainebleau 10 km

Owners: Jean-Pierre and Dominique Fava
General Manager: Tino Malchiodi
Open all year
Currency: Euro (€)
Rates: Menus 74 € s.i., Week lunch 53 € s.i. Carte 100 € s.i.
12 rooms: 140-350 € s.i.
8 suites: starting at 410 € s.i.
Breakfast: 18 € s.i.
Dogs: allowed (extra cost)
Golf: Cély 5 km
Accepted cards: AE, MC, VS

More info on www.relaischateaux.com/basbreau

Auberge des Templiers

SINCE 1954

Les Bezards
45290 Boismorand
(Loiret) • France

Tel. : (33) 02 38 31 80 01
Fax : (33) 02 38 31 84 51
templiers@relaischateaux.com

France

This former post house, beautifully restored by the Dépée Family 50 years ago, was one of the first Relais & Châteaux. Savour a superb «marbré d'asperges vertes au foie gras à la vinaigrette d'huile de truffes» and enjoy prestigious wines in the restaurant overlooking a magnificent park full of hundred-year-old oaks. Explore the Loire châteaux, the beautiful Sologne forests and the vineyards of Sancerre and Pouilly.

(Other activities P. 629)

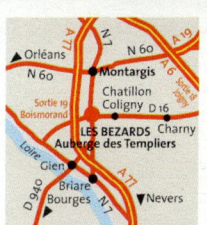

Access: From Paris, A6 - at Dordives, then take A77 towards Nevers, exit N° 19 Boismorand (3 km auberge).

Airports: Paris Orly (Intl) 100 km, Vimory 20 km
Helipad: N 47° 48' E 02° 44' 43"
Train station: Nogent/Vernisson 5 km

Owners: Dépée Family
Annual closing: 3 weeks in February
Currency: Euro (€)
Rates: Menus 55 € s.i. (lunch) 70-115 € s.i.
Carte 80-110 € s.i.
22 rooms: 125-240 € s.i.
8 suites: starting at 270 € s.i.
Breakfast: 15 € s.i.
Dogs: allowed
Golf: 2 to 25 km
Accepted cards: AE, DC, JCB, MC, VS

More info on www.relaischateaux.com/templiers

Hostellerie Le Clos

SINCE 1975

98, rue de la Ferté-Vidame - BP 323
27133 Verneuil-sur-Avre Cedex
(Eure) • France

Tel. : (33) 02 32 32 21 81
Fax : (33) 02 32 32 21 36
leclos@relaischateaux.com

France

This authentic Norman manor, with its impressive slate-roofed turrets and magnificent red brick façade, lies in a fortified village built by King Henry I in the early XIIth century. The old-fashioned living room and the guest-rooms filled with tasteful antique furniture are imbued with historic charm, while the dining room is decorated in stunning trompe l'œil. Superb cuisine is enhanced by an excellent wine list.

Hunting. (Other activities P. 629)

Access: From Paris, A12/A13 towards Dreux and N12 until Verneuil; stay on N12 and turn right at the 1st light.
Airports: Paris Ch. de Gaulle (Intl) 110 km, Paris Orly (Intl) 110 km
Train station: Verneuil-sur-Avre 0,5 km

Owners: Colette and Patrick Simon
Weekly closing: Restaurant: Monday noon, Tuesday noon (except holidays), Monday evening (from Jan. 19th to March 10th and from Nov. 1st to Dec. 15th)
Annual closing: From January 1st to 19th and from December 15th to 31st
Currency: Euro (€)
Rates: Menus 33-70 € s.i. Menu-carte 49 € s.i. half-board (week-end and holidays)
4 rooms: 149-183 € s.i.
6 suites: starting at 205 € s.i.
Breakfast: 15 € s.i.
Dogs: allowed (extra cost) **Golf:** 7 km
Accepted cards: AE, DC, JCB, MC, VS

More info on www.relaischateaux.com/leclos

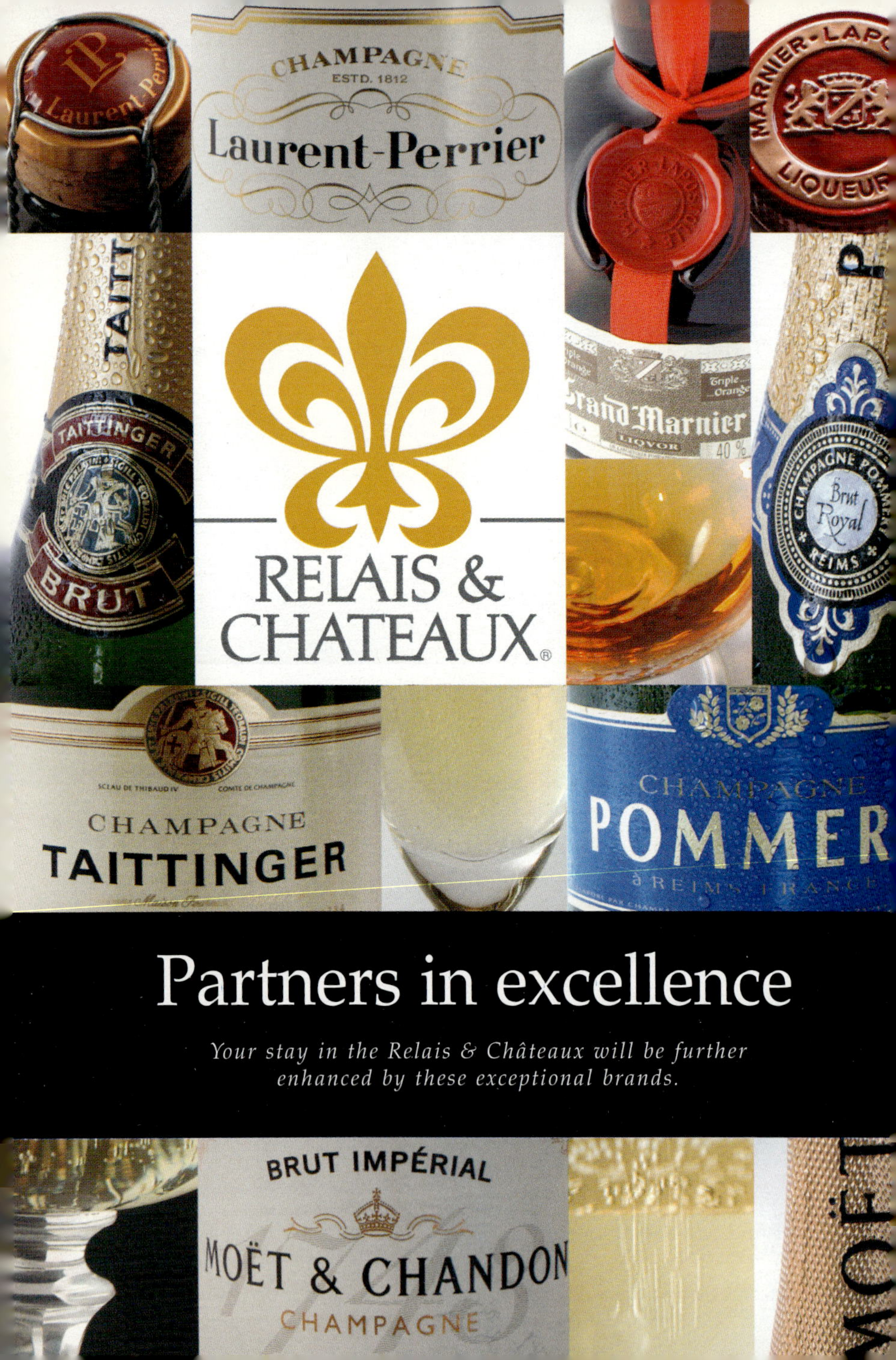
CHAMPAGNE
ESTD. 1812
Laurent-Perrier
RELAIS &
CHATEAUX
Grand Marnier
CHAMPAGNE
TAITTINGER
CHAMPAGNE
POMMERY
Partners in excellence
Your stay in the Relais & Châteaux will be further enhanced by these exceptional brands.
BRUT IMPÉRIAL
MOËT & CHANDON
CHAMPAGNE

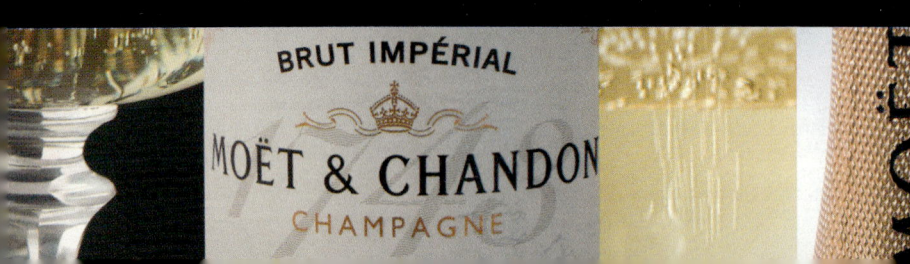

Royal Champagne

SINCE 1975

51160 Champillon-Epernay
(Marne) • France

Tel. : (33) 03 26 52 87 11
Fax : (33) 03 26 52 89 69
royalchampagne@relaischateaux.com

France

This former coach inn celebrates the very best of Champagnes with more than 200 exceptional varieties and vintages of bruts and rosés. The cuisine matches the quality of the cellar. The guestrooms offer breathtaking vistas of the vineyards and the Marne valley. The ideal retreat for champagne enthusiasts who want to visit vineyards and wineries of grand Champagne houses.

Visits of wine cellar and vineyard, historical sites, walks in the National Park. (Other activities P. 629)

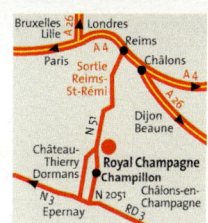

Access: From Paris: exit the A4 or A26 at Reims, exit St-Rémi, N51 towards Epernay, then towards Champillon, N2051. From Troyes: leave the A26 at Châlons, exit St-Gibrien.
Airports: Paris Orly (Intl) 130 km, Paris Ch. de Gaulle (Intl) 130 km
Helipad: N 49° 05' 34" E 3° 58' 35"
Train station: Epernay 7 km

Owner: Provital S.A.
General Manager: Andrea Ricci
Weekly closing: Restaurant: Monday noon
Annual closing: From January to March
Currency: Euro (€)
Rates: Menus 38 € s.i. (lunch except Sunday) 55-90-125 € s.i. Carte 65-125 € s.i.
20 rooms: 210-280 € s.i.
5 suites: 320-360 € s.i.
Breakfast: 18 € s.i.
Dogs: allowed (extra cost) **Golf:** 25 km
Accepted cards: AE, DC, JCB, MC, VS

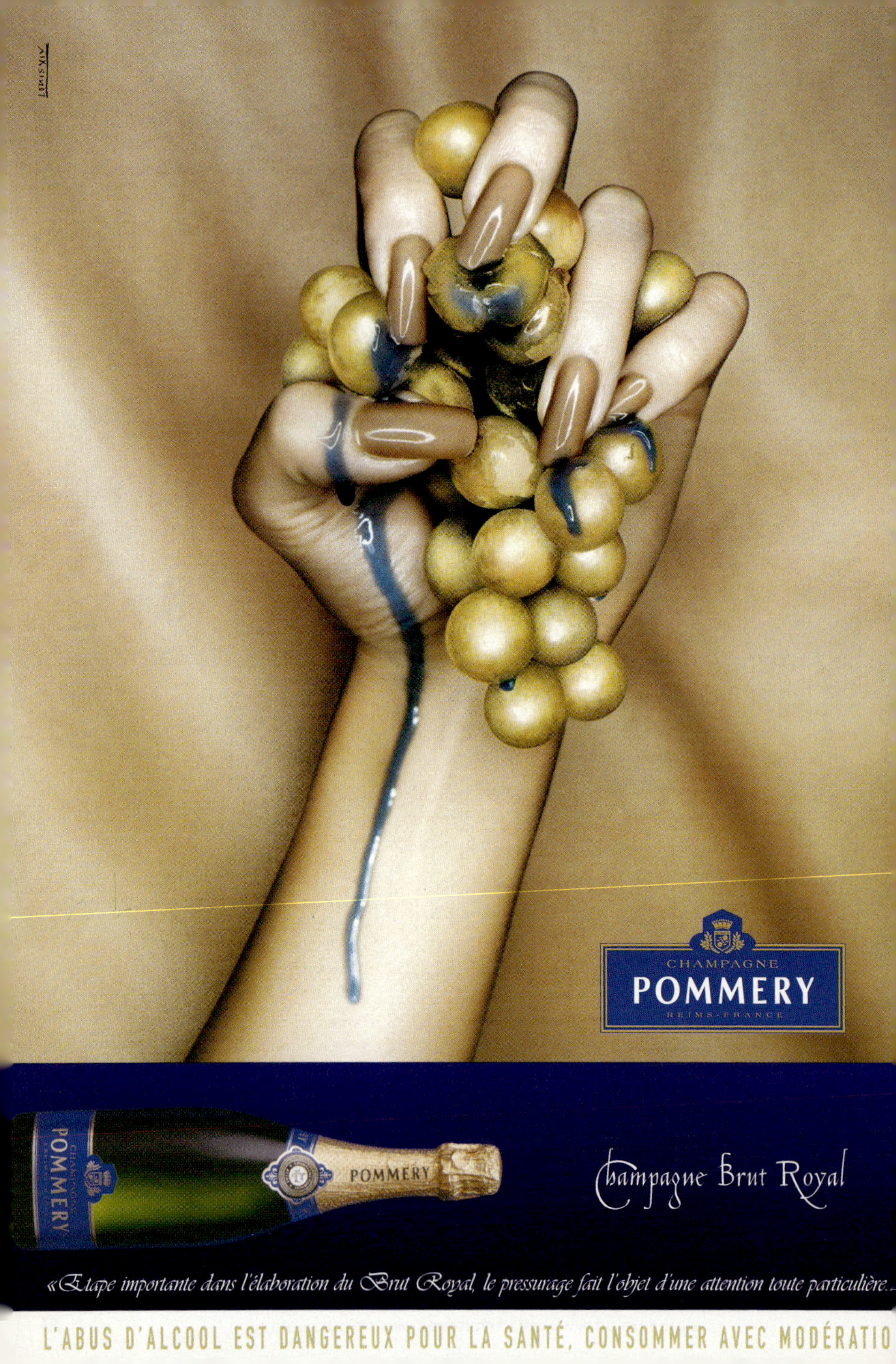

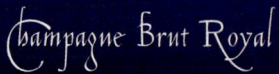

Champagne Brut Royal

«Étape importante dans l'élaboration du Brut Royal, le pressurage fait l'objet d'une attention toute particulière...»

L'ABUS D'ALCOOL EST DANGEREUX POUR LA SANTÉ, CONSOMMER AVEC MODÉRATIO

Boyer «Les Crayères»

SINCE 1984

64, bd Henry-Vasnier
51100 Reims
(Marne) • France

Tel. : (33) 03 26 82 80 80
Fax : (33) 03 26 82 65 52
crayeres@relaischateaux.com

France

Gérard and Elyane Boyer welcome you to an elegant turn-of-the-century residence set in English-style parkland. Blending tradition, comfort and refinement, the Boyers have created a luxurious gourmet retreat, where guests can relax in sumptuous rooms and savour superb cuisine. The «filets de rouget de roche grillés, sauce au thym, petite galette de pommes de terre dorées et ail doux caramélisé» is simply sublime.

(Other activities P. 629)

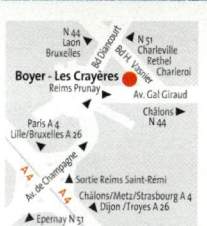

Access: A4 or A26, exit 25, towards Châlons-en-Champagne, Reims-Prunay.

Airports: Paris Charles de Gaulle (Intl) 130 km, Paris Orly (Intl) 140 km
Helipad: N 49° 14' 52" E 04° 02' 90"
Train station: Reims 1 km

Owners: X. Gardinier Family
General Manager: Elyane Boyer
Weekly closing: Rest.: Monday and Tuesday
Annual closing: From Dec. 23rd to January 13th
Currency: Euro (€)
Rates: Carte 115-130 € s.i.
16 rooms: 248-360 € s.i.
3 suites: 360-435 € s.i.
Breakfast: 23 € s.i.
Dogs: allowed (extra cost) **Golf:** Gueux 5 km
Accepted cards: AE, DC, JCB, MC, VS

More info on www.relaischateaux.com/crayeres

Château de Courcelles

SINCE 1993

02220 Courcelles-sur-Vesle
(Aisne) • France

Tel. : (33) 03 23 74 13 53
Fax : (33) 03 23 74 06 41
courcelles@relaischateaux.com

France

Cross the threshold of this magnificent XVIIth century château, set in the midst of enchanting parkland, and you will understand why Racine, La Fontaine, les Dumas, father and son, and Jean Cocteau (who designed the staircase banister) fell under its spell. Its secret ? Friendly service, comfortable, individually styled rooms and exquisite haute cuisine accompanied by a long list of exceptional champagnes.
Jogging course. (Other activities P. 629)

Access: Paris, pte de la Chapelle A1 exit Soissons, N2 Soissons, N31 Reims, Braine, Courcelles is 3 km away.

Airports: Paris Ch. de Gaulle (Intl) 100 km, Reims 40 km
Helipad: N 49° 20' 17" E 3° 34' 8"
Train station: Soissons 15 km

Owner: Bernard Anthonioz
General Manager: Jean-Philippe Fourier
Open all year
Currency: Euro (€)
Rates: Menus 40-75 € s.i. Carte 45-80 € s.i.
11 rooms: 150-285 € s.i.
9 suites: 285-335 € s.i.
Breakfast: 15 € s.i.
Dogs: allowed (extra cost)
Golf: de l'Ailette 18 km
Accepted cards: AE, DC, JCB, MC, VS

More info on www.relaischateaux.com/courcelles

Brittany - Normandy Pas-de-Calais

France

Properties	Nearest major city	Relais & Châteaux	Relais Gourmands	Page
Auberge Bretonne (L')	La Roche-Bernard	⚜	◉	100
Bretagne et sa Résidence (Le)	Vannes	⚜	◉	97
Castel Clara	Belle-Ile-en-Mer	⚜		96
Castel Marie-Louise	Nantes	⚜		101
Château d'Audrieu	Caen	⚜		90
Château de Locguénolé	Hennebont	⚜	◉	95
Château de Montreuil	Montreuil-sur-Mer	⚜		86
Chaumière (La)	Honfleur	⚜		89
Domaine de la Bretesche	La Baule	⚜		99
Ferme St-Siméon (La)	Honfleur	⚜		88
Gill (Restaurant)	Rouen		◉	87
Maisons de Bricourt	Cancale	⚜	◉	91
Manoir de Lan-Kerellec	Lannion	⚜		92
Plage (Hôtel de la)	Douarnenez	⚜		93

More info on www.relaischateaux.com

France

Château de Montreuil

SINCE 1982

4, chaussée des Capucins
62170 Montreuil-sur-Mer
(Pas-de-Calais) • France

Tel. : (33) 03 21 81 53 04
Fax : (33) 03 21 81 36 43
montreuil@relaischateaux.com

This beautiful manor house, secluded behind elegant ramparts, offers comfortable rooms opening out onto exquisite landscaped gardens. In this atmosphere of bucolic charm, you will be enchanted by Christian Germain's cuisine, a delicious concoction of light sauces made with fresh local ingredients and garden vegetables and herbs. After sampling one of the fine wines you will find it hard to leave this earthly paradise.

(Other activities P. 629)

Access: Opposite the Roman citadel of Montreuil-sur-Mer; from north first right, from south 3rd left.

Airports: Paris Ch. de Gaulle (Intl) 180 km, Lille 120 km
Train station: Etaples 15 km

Owners: Christian and Lindsay Germain
Weekly closing: Hotel/Rest.: Monday
Rest. only: Tuesday at lunch from September 9th to May 5th, Thursday at lunch
Annual closing: From mid-Dec. to end of January
Currency: Euro (€)
Rates: Menu lunch 34 € s.i. (except Sunday and bank holidays) Menu-carte 55-75 € s.i.
13 rooms: 155-210 € s.i.
300-380 € s.i. (half board 2 p.)
1 suite: 350 € s.i. (half board 2 p.)
Breakfast: 15 € s.i.
Dogs: allowed (extra cost) **Golf:** 3 nearby
Accepted cards: AE, DC, JCB, MC, VS

More info on www.relaischateaux.com/montreuil

Restaurant Gill

SINCE 2001

8-9, quai de la Bourse
76000 Rouen
(Seine-Maritime) • France

Tel. : **(33) 02 35 71 16 14**
Fax : (33) 02 35 71 96 91
gill@relaischateaux.com

France

On the quays not far from the Cathedral, discover the superb residence of Gill and Sylvie Tournadre who will delight your palates with inventive dishes made with the best Normandy products in a bright elegant decor. Savour the «pigeon à la rouennaise avec ses raviolis de foie gras», «sole de Dieppe accompagnée de crème façon normande» and «dos de cabillaud rôti avec pommes, oignons confits et sauce de cidre».

Access:
Motorway A13: exit Oissel N 22 towards Rouen centre. Take fast lane for 10 km. Cross the Seine river via the Corneille bridge. Turn left.
Go 200 m: the restaurant is on the right.
Airport: Paris Ch. de Gaulle (Intl) 120 km
Train station: Rouen 2 km

Owner/Chef: Gilles Tournadre
General Manager: Sylvie Tournadre
Weekly closing: Sunday, Monday
Annual closing: From January 2nd to 8th, from April 13th to 28th and from August 4th to 26th
Currency: Euro (€)
Rates: Menus 40 € s.i. (week)
Carte 80-110 € s.i.
Dogs: allowed
Accepted cards: AE, DC, MC, VS

Gilles Tournadre

More info on www.relaischateaux.com/gill

France

La Ferme Saint-Siméon

SINCE 1964

Rue Adolphe-Marais
14600 Honfleur
(Calvados) • France

Tel. : (33) 02 31 81 78 00
Fax : (33) 02 31 89 48 48
simeon@relaischateaux.com

This beautifully restored farm was the favourite retreat of XIXth century painters such as Monet, Sisley, Courbet, Boudin and Jongkind, who were enchanted by the ethereal light reflected in its estuary. The charm of bygone days still lingers on in the farm's tastefully decorated rooms. Savour delicious seafood and regional cuisine, relax in the elegant Italian palace decor of the spa or visit the picturesque port of Honfleur.

Beauty centre, bio-sauna face and body treatments, special terrace service. (Other activities P. 629)

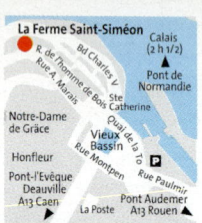

Access: From Paris A14, A13, A29, exit 3. Cross Honfleur then take D513 by the coast.

Airports: Deauville (Intl) 10 km, Paris Ch. de Gaulle (Intl) 190 km
Helipad: N 49° 25' 32" E 000° 13' 09"
Train station: Deauville 12 km

Owners: Boelen Family
Weekly closing: Restaurant: Monday all day, Tuesday noon
Open all year
Currency: Euro (€)
Rates: Menus 52 € s.i. (week lunch) 98 € s.i. Carte 69-79 € s.i.
25 rooms: 150-450 € s.i. **4 suites:** 750-850 € s.i.
Breakfast: 20 € s.i.
Dogs: allowed in some rooms **Golf:** 10 km
Accepted cards: AE, JCB, MC, VS

More info on www.relaischateaux.com/simeon

La Chaumière

SINCE 1993

Route du Littoral
14600 Honfleur-Vasouy
(Calvados) • France

Tel. : (33) 02 31 81 63 20
Fax : (33) 02 31 89 59 23
chaumiere@relaischateaux.com

France

The Seine meets the sea at the foot of this magnificent half-timbered «chaumière» so typical of the Normandy region. Lie beneath the ancient oak-beamed ceilings and enjoy the bucolic charm of its eight cosy guestrooms, each individually decorated. The garden terrace is an idyllic setting in which to savour simple, traditional cuisine prepared with fresh ingredients from the sea and the surrounding countryside.

Private access to the beach, terrace service, forest walks, sailing, fishing, polo nearby. (Other activities P. 629)

Access: From Paris A14, A13, A29, exit 3. Cross Honfleur then take D513 by the coast.

Airports: Deauville (Intl) 10 km, Paris Ch. de Gaulle (Intl) 190 km
Train station: Deauville 10 km

Owners: Boelen Family
Weekly closing: Restaurant: Tuesday and Wednesday at lunch
Annual closing: From January 5th to 31st
Currency: Euro (€)
Rates: Menus 29-58 € s.i. Carte 38-53 € s.i.
8 rooms: 150-230 € s.i.
1 suite: 400 € s.i.
Breakfast: 15 € s.i.
Dogs: allowed in some rooms
Golf: 6 km
Accepted cards: AE, JCB, MC, VS

More info on www.relaischateaux.com/chaumiere

Château d'Audrieu

SINCE 1977

France

14250 Audrieu
(Calvados) • France

Tel. : (33) 02 31 80 21 52
Fax : (33) 02 31 80 24 73
audrieu@relaischateaux.com

Gaiety and elegance are the two words which automatically spring to mind to describe this magnificent XVIIIth century chateau, a listed building set amongst exquisite French gardens and parkland. Louis XV and Louis XVI wainscoting, period fireplaces and furniture give a personal touch to the ancestral home of Gérard and Irène Livry-Level. Superb, innovative cuisine enhanced by an excellent wine list.

(Other activities P. 629)

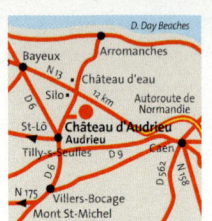

Access: Express way N 13 Caen-Bayeux, exit Loucelles, Audrieu, D158 b.
Airports: Paris Ch. de Gaulle (Intl) 250 km, Caen 12 km
Train stations: Caen, Bayeux 15 km
Owners: Livry-Level Family
Weekly closing: Restaurant: Monday all day, Tuesday, Wednesday, Thursday, Friday for the lunch (except seminars). Limited menu for guests on Monday evening in the season
Annual closing: From December 15th to February 14th
Currency: Euro (€)
Rates: Menus 45-84 € s.i. Carte 61-84 € s.i.
19 rooms: 115-260 € s.i.
10 suites: 263-410 € s.i.
Breakfast: Continental 15 € s.i. Buffet 22 € s.i.
Dogs: allowed (extra cost) except rest.
Golf: 15 km
Accepted cards: AE, MC, VS

More info on www.relaischateaux.com/audrieu

Maisons de Bricourt

SINCE 1989

1, rue Du Guesclin
35260 Cancale
(Ille-et-Villaine) • France

Tel. : (33) 02 99 89 64 76
Fax : (33) 02 99 89 88 47
bricourt@relaischateaux.com

France

Three idyllic retreats await you in the picturesque Saint-Malo region. Enjoy rustic elegance at «Les Rimains», a cottage facing the Cancale oyster beds and dine at «Le Château Richeux», the sea-front bistrot «Le Coquillage» overlooking Mont-Saint-Michel bay. Savour Olivier Rœllinger's gourmet specialities : «saint-pierre retour des Indes» and «homard aux saveurs de l'île aux épices» in his childhood home, an XVIIIth century «malouinière».

(Other activities P. 629)

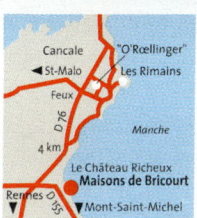

Access: From Rennes, N137 via Saint-Malo. Taxi service between the three residences.

Airports: Dinard 20 km, Rennes 70 km
Train station: St-Malo 14 km

Owner: Olivier Rœllinger
Weekly closing: Rest.: Tuesday and Wednesday
Open all year
Currency: Euro (€)
Rates: Le Relais Gourmand Menu 82 € s.i. (lunch) Carte 80 € s.i. Le Coquillage 26-44 € s.i.
16 rooms: 114-274 € s.i.
3 suites: 152-305 € s.i.
Breakfast: 16 € s.i.
Dogs: allowed (extra cost)
Golf: 3 km
Accepted cards: AE, DC, JCB, MC, VS

More info on www.relaischateaux.com/bricourt

Manoir de Lan-Kerellec

France — SINCE 1983

Allée centrale de Lan-Kerellec
22560 Trébeurden
(Côtes-d'Armor) • France

Tel. : **(33) 02 96 15 00 00**
(33) 02 96 15 47 47
Fax : (33) 02 96 23 66 88
lankerellec@relaischateaux.com

This XIXth century Breton manor, lovingly restored and decorated by Luce Daubé, lies on the Côte de Granit rose within walking distance of fine sand beaches. The guestrooms all overlook the sea while the cruiseliner-style dining-room offers superb panoramic views of the coast and the local islands. Savour Loire wines and imaginative cuisine prepared with fresh ingredients from the sea and surrounding countryside.

Whirlpool, strolling on the islands. (Other activities P. 629)

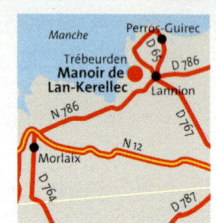

Access: Lannion, D 65 Trébeurden, towards «Les Plages»/Perros-Guirec, before village exit.

Airports: Brest (Intl) 80 km, Lannion 7 km
Train station: Lannion 10 km

Owners: Luce and Gilles Daubé
Weekly closing: Rest.: Monday noon, Tuesday noon
Annual closing: From January 1st to mid-March and from mid-November to December 31st
Currency: Euro (€)
Rates: Menus 40-65 € s.i. Carte 40-70 € s.i. (Wednesday to Sunday) **Breakfast:** 13-19 € s.i.
16 rooms: 90-300 € s.i.
3 suites: starting at 320 € s.i.
Dogs: allowed (extra cost)
Golf: St-Samson 5 km, several golf courses 50 km
Accepted cards: AE, DC, JCB, MC, VS

More info on www.relaischateaux.com/lankerellec

Hôtel de la Plage

SINCE 1971

29550 Sainte-Anne-la-Palud
(Finistère Sud) • France

Tel. : (33) 02 98 92 50 12
Fax : (33) 02 98 92 56 54
laplage@relaischateaux.com

France

Contemplate the fiery splendour of a Breton sunset from the windows of this charming hotel, which has been welcoming guests with family-style hospitality since the 1920's. Savour excellent regional cuisine, prepared with the local fishermen's catch of the day. After an invigorating stroll along the sandy shore, the soothing sound of the waves will lull you to sleep in your cosy guestroom.

(Other activities P. 629)

Access: From Rennes, N165, exit Quimper Nord, D39 until Plonevez-Porzay, D61 towards Ste-Anne-la-Palud.
Airports: Brest (Intl) 80 km, Quimper 25 km
Train station: Quimper 20 km
Owners/General Managers: Anne and Jean Milliau Le Coz
Weekly closing: Rest.: Tuesday and Wednesday for lunch (low season, except group)
Annual closing: From beginning November to the end of March
Currency: Euro (€)
Rates: Menus 45-85 € s.i. Carte 50-90 € s.i.
26 rooms: 145-260 € s.i.
4 suites: 206-260 € s.i.
Breakfast: 14 € s.i.
Dogs: allowed (extra cost) except rest.
Golf: 35 km
Accepted cards: AE, DC, MC, VS

More info on www.relaischateaux.com/laplage

L'ESPRIT DE TONGE

SOLID OAK FURNITURE - BATHROOMS - CUSTOM MADE FURNITURE
KITCHENS - PAINTINGS - **GIFTS AND ARTICLES FOR THE HOUSE**
FABRICS FOR CURTAINS - DRESSING - **TURNKEY REALISATIONS**

Catalogue upon request to **S.A. de Tonge** D. 35 - 06560 Valbonne (send 5 Euros by check)

PARIS
75116
152, Avenue de Malakoff
(Porte Maillot)
Tél. 01 45 02 14 02
Ouvert de 10ʰ à 19ʰ

SAINT TROPEZ
83990
4, Avenue Foch
(Place des Lices)
Tél. 04 94 97 26 71
Ouvert de 10ʰ à 13ʰ et de 15ʰ à 19ʰ

CANNES
06400
93, Rue d'Antibes
Tél. 04 93 39 20 00
Ouvert
de 10ʰ à 19ʰ

VALBONNE
06560
810, Route de la Valmasque
(entre Mougins et Antibes)
Tél. 04 93 95 80 00
Ouvert de 9ʰ à 19ʰ

Château de Locguénolé

SINCE 1970

Route de Port-Louis
56700 Hennebont
(Morbihan) • France

Tel. : (33) 02 97 76 76 76
Fax : (33) 02 97 76 82 35
locguenole@relaischateaux.com

France

These beautiful XIXth century castle and XVIIIth century manor stand in luxuriant parkland stretching 2 km along a scenic bay. Historic furniture, wood panelling and tapestries recall the splendour of bygone days. The cuisine pays tribute to Breton produce and local seafood. Savour the «carpaccio de homard fumé, vinaigrette aux aromates, tartine de pince aux herbes et foie gras» enhanced by a superb wine list.

Boarding pontoon. 120-hectare grounds, fitness course. (Other activities P. 629)

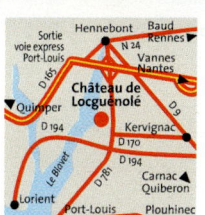

Access: From Nantes, Rennes or Quimper exit Port-Louis on the high-speed route exit n° 40; then 3 km.
Airports: Nantes (Intl) 160 km, Lorient 15 km
Helipad: N 47° 46' 14" W 03° 17' 04
Train station: Lorient 10 km

Owner: Alyette de la Sablière
General Manager: Bruno de la Sablière
Weekly closing: Rest.: Monday evening from October 1st to April 30th (except for groups and holidays), Monday to Friday for lunch (except. for groups and holidays)
Annual closing: From January 2nd to February 7th
Currency: Euro (€)
Rates: Menus 49-89 € s.i. Carte 58-85 € s.i.
24 rooms: 115-275 € s.i. **4 suites:** 260-395 € s.i.
Breakfast: 16-24 € s.i.
Dogs: allowed (extra-cost) **Golf:** 16 km
Accepted cards: AE, DC, JCB, MC, VS

More info on www.relaischateaux.com/locguenole

Castel Clara

SINCE 1982

Goulphar, Belle-Ile-en-Mer
56360 Bangor
(Morbihan) • France

Tel. : (33) 02 97 31 84 21
Fax : (33) 02 97 31 51 69
castelclara@relaischateaux.com

This hotel, perched above the spectacular coast of Belle-Ile-en-Mer, offers breathtaking views of the ocean and the cliffs of Goulphar. It combines the charm of unspoiled natural surroundings with the height of luxury and refinement. The rooms with their muted colours are an oasis of tranquility, the seafood cuisine as invigorating as the climate. Stroll on the heather-covered hills or relax in the thalassotherapy institute.

Thalassotherapy. (Other activities P. 629)

Access: From Port-Maria Quiberon, 45 min. crossing. At the Palais, towards Goulphar (8 km).

Airports: Nantes (Intl) 150 km, Lorient 45 km
Train station: Auray 35 km

Owner: SNHPET
General Manager: Guillaume Goumy
Annual closing: From Nov. 15th to Feb. 15th
Currency: Euro (€)
Rates: Menus 27-59 € s.i. Carte 43-70 € s.i.
26 rooms: 107-261 € s.i.
14 suites: 167-540 € s.i.
Breakfast: 13 € s.i. buffet 23 € s.i.
Dogs: allowed extra cost (except rest.)
Golf: 7 km
Accepted cards: AE, DC, MC, VS

Le Bretagne et sa Résidence

SINCE 1976

13, rue Saint-Michel
56230 Questembert
(Morbihan) • France

Tel. : (33) 02 97 26 11 12
Fax : (33) 02 97 26 12 37
bretagne@relaischateaux.com

France

In this charming ivy-clad manor in the picturesque town of Questembert, Georges Paineau and his son-in-law Claude Corlouer create culinary masterpieces of extraordinary colour and flavour. Savour superb «turbot rôti aux étrilles écrasées, salpicon de légumes», exquisite «dos de cabillaud en croûte d'herbes au poivre de Setchuan» or try the «poitrine de pigeon laquée à la sauge». After your meal, retire to a pretty guestroom.

Fishing, hiking. Cooking and painting classes. (Other activities P. 629)

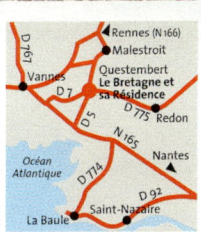

Access: From Nantes, take the N165, cross the «La Vilaine» river, D139, follow signs.

Airports: Nantes (Intl) 80 km, Lorient 60 km
Helipad: N 47° 39' 37" W 002° 26' 46"
Train station: Questembert 1 km

Owner: Georges Paineau
Weekly closing: Monday all day, Tuesday noon, Wednesday noon (except August)
Annual closing: 3 weeks in January
Currency: Euro (€)
Rates: Menus 35-70-98 € s.i. Carte 58-99 € s.i.
6 rooms: 88-149 € s.i.
3 suites: 183-213 € s.i.
Breakfast: 17 € s.i.
Dogs: allowed (extra cost)
Golf: 15 km
Accepted cards: AE, JCB, MC, VS

More info on www.relaischateaux.com/bretagne

Domaine de la Bretesche

SINCE 2003

44780 Missillac
(Loire-Atlantique) • France

Tel. : (33) 02 51 76 86 96
Fax : (33) 02 40 66 99 47
bretesche@relaischateaux.com

France

On the borders of the Pays Breton and the Loire valley, in the Brière nature reserve, an immense, 200-ha domain where the forest borders on a park with rhododendrons and the fairways of a beautiful 18-hole golf course. Across from a splendid 15th century château on the banks of a pond, the restaurant and rooms are housed in magnificent bright stone buildings set around a flower-filled courtyard.

(Other activities P. 629)

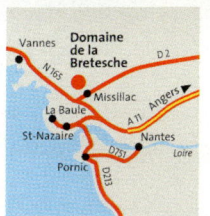

Access: Motorway A11, via Nantes. N 165 towards Vannes. Exit Missillac - La Bretesche.
Airport: Nantes (Intl) 55 km
Helipad: N 47° 30' 18'' W 02° 10' 04''
Train station: La Baule 30 km

Owner: Alain Besse
General Manager: Christophe Delahaye
Weekly closing: Restaurant: Sunday evening (from October 15th to April 15th), Monday, Tuesday noon (except dinners in July/August)
Annual closing: Rest.: from Nov. 12th to 22nd Hotel/Rest.: from January 17th to March 7th
Currency: Euro (€)
Rates: Menus 40-75 € s.i. Carte 56-77 € s.i.
24 rooms: 120-230 € s.i. **7 suites:** 230-295 € s.i.
Breakfast: 15 € s.i.
Dogs: allowed (hotel only, extra cost) **Golf:** 100 m.
Accepted cards: AE, DC, JCB, MC, VS

More info on www.relaischateaux.com/bretesche

L'Auberge Bretonne

SINCE 1994

2, place Du Guesclin
56130 La Roche-Bernard
(Morbihan) • France

Tel. : (33) 02 99 90 60 28
Fax : (33) 02 99 90 85 00
aubbretonne@relaischateaux.com

France

This beautiful inn, lovingly restored by Solange and Jacques Thorel, is no longer a secret gourmet refuge. Today reservations must be made in advance if you wish to savour the extraordinary «homard rôti au citron et au poivre, un blini de blé noir» and exquisite «baba trempé à la chartreuse jaune, une crème glacée à la vanille». After enjoying one of the superb vintages, retire to a bright, comfortable guestroom.

Fishing, flying club. (Other activities P. 629)

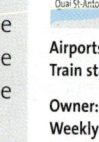

Access:
From Paris, A11 via Chartres, Angers, Nantes N165 towards Vannes.

Airports: Nantes (Intl) 60 km, Rennes 90 km
Train station: La Baule 27 km

Owner: Jacques Thorel
Weekly closing: Rest.: Thursday all day, Monday, Tuesday and Friday lunch
Annual closing: Rest.: from January 5th to 25th and from November 13th to December 8th
Currency: Euro (€)
Rates: Menus 30-125 € s.i. Carte 55-80 € s.i.
8 rooms: 76-229 € s.i.
Breakfast: 14 € s.i.
Dogs: allowed (extra cost)
Golf: 10 km
Accepted cards: AE, DC, JCB, MC, VS

More info on www.relaischateaux.com/aubbretonne

Castel Marie-Louise

SINCE 1969

1, avenue Andrieu
44500 La Baule
(Loire-Atlantique) • France

Tel. : (33) 02 40 11 48 38
Fax : (33) 02 40 11 48 35
marielouise@relaischateaux.com

France

This beautiful XIXth century manor is set amidst a flower-filled park opposite the loveliest beach in Europe. It enjoys a charming setting where the emphasis is on fine dining and hospitality. The tastefully decorated rooms with their fine antique furniture are an oasis of tranquility. An imaginative cuisine, with the very best in regional products, is further enhanced by the sommelier's favourites. Wonderful wine cellar.

Biking, tennis, watersports, thalasso centre nearby, hiking trails, cooking classes. (Other activities P. 629)

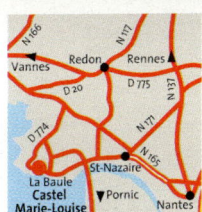

Access: From Nantes, N165 towards St. Nazaire then N171, exit La Baule. La Baule Ouest, Castel at the seaside, close to the casino.

Airports: Nantes (Intl) 60 km, La Baule 4 km
Train station: La Baule 4 km

Owners: Desseigne-Barrière Family
General Manager: Arnaud Bamvens
Weekly closing: Rest.: lunch, except Sunday (low season)
Annual closing: From mid-Nov. to mid-Dec.
Currency: Euro (€)
Rates: Menus 41-80 € s.i. Carte 61-122 € s.i.
29 rooms: 145-430 € s.i.
2 suites: 320-500 € s.i.
Breakfast: 18 € s.i.
Dogs: allowed (extra cost 10 €) except rest.
Golf: Saint-Denac 6 km
Accepted cards: AE, DC, JCB, MC, VS

More info on www.relaischateaux.com/marielouise

Loire Valley

Properties	Nearest major city	Relais & Châteaux	Relais Gourmands	Page
Bardet (Jean) - Château Belmont	Tours	✤	●	106
Château de Curzay	Poitiers	✤		113
Château de Marçay	Chinon	✤		105
Château de Noirieux	Angers	✤		104
Château de Noizay	Amboise	✤		108
Domaine des Hauts de Loire	Blois	✤	●	109
Hautes Roches (Les)	Tours	✤		107
Lion d'Or (Grand Hôtel du)	Romorantin	✤	●	112
Robin (Bernard) - Le Relais	Chambord		●	111

More info on www.relaischateaux.com

Château de Noirieux

France — SINCE 1995

26, route du Moulin
49125 Briollay
(Maine-et-Loire) • France

Tel. : (33) 02 41 42 50 05
Fax : (33) 02 41 37 91 00
noirieux@relaischateaux.com

This elegant château, framed by luxuriant foliage and rhododendron bushes, offers picturesque views across the river Loir. After strolling through the winter garden or reclining in front of an elegant fireplace in the lounge, retire to a sumptuous Louis XIII or Regency guestroom hung with superb works of art. Savour refined seasonal dishes accompanied by fine wines and exceptional vintages from the Loire region.

(Other activities P. 629)

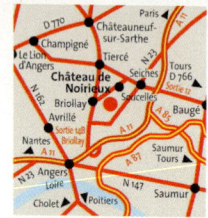

Access: From Paris, Le Mans and Saumur A 11, exit 14 Tiercé, D 52 to Briollay, then D 109. From Nantes, Angers, A 11, exit 14B Tiercé, D 52 to Briollay, then D 109.
Airports: Nantes (Intl) 89 km, Paris Orly (Intl) 280 km **Train station:** Angers-St Laud 15 km
Helipad: N 47° 34' 32" W 000° 28' 04"

Owner: Michael Shen
General Managers: Anja and Gérard Côme
Weekly closing: Hotel/Rest.: Sunday evening, Monday (Nov. to mid-April); Rest.: Monday, Tuesday (mid-April to Oct. 31st, except residents)
Annual closing: From Feb. 16th to March 20th and from November 2nd to 27th
Currency: Euro (€)
Rates: Menus 49-62-92 € s.i. Carte 70-85 € s.i.
18 rooms: 165-315 € s.i. **1 suite:** 315 € s.i.
Breakfast: 19 € s.i.
Dogs: allowed (extra cost) **Golf:** 25 km
Accepted cards: AE, DC, JCB, MC, VS

More info on www.relaischateaux.com/noirieux

Château de Marçay

SINCE 1976

37500 Marçay-Chinon
(Indre-et-Loire) • France

Tel. : (33) 02 47 93 03 47
Fax : (33) 02 47 93 45 33
marcay@relaischateaux.com

France

The twin towers of this magnificent XVth century château, which lies near Chinon where Joan of Arc met King Charles VII, soar above a landscape that once enchanted François Rabelais. The château's tastefully decorated rooms, which blend wood panelling, sumptuous materials and period furniture, also offer every modern comfort. The refined cuisine is enhanced by an excellent selection of fine wines and Loire vintages.

(Other activities P. 629)

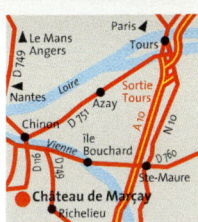

Access:
A10, exit Sainte-Maure towards Chinon Sud, then D 116, village of Marçay.
Airport: Tours 60 km

Helipad: N 47° 06' 17" E 000° 13' 16"
Train station: Chinon 6 km

Owner: Philippe Mollard
General Manager: Bernard Beteille
Weekly closing: Rest.: Monday noon, Tuesday noon, Thursday noon
Annual closing: From mid-January to mid-March
Currency: Euro (€)
Rates: Menus 46 € s.i. (lunch) 75 € s.i.
Carte 55-65 € s.i.
30 rooms: 114-246 € s.i.
4 suites: 280 € s.i.
Breakfast: 18 € s.i.
Dogs: allowed **Golf:** Roiffé St-Hilaire 20 km
Accepted cards: AE, DC, JCB, MC, VS

More info on www.relaischateaux.com/marcay

Jean Bardet - Château Belmont

France — SINCE 1990

57, rue Groison
37100 Tours
(Indre-et-Loire) • France

Tel. : (33) 02 47 41 41 11
Fax : (33) 02 47 51 68 72
bardet@relaischateaux.com

This white Touraine stone residence, set amidst landscaped gardens, provides an idyllic refuge for gourmets and nature lovers all year round. Sophie Bardet welcomes guests with charming hospitality, showing them to their spacious, bright guestroom, while her husband Jean prepares exquisite seasonal cuisine. Savour divine desserts, excellent wines and the extraordinary «"assiette verte" de légumes primeurs de Jean Bardet».

Jogging, table tennis. (Other activities P. 629)

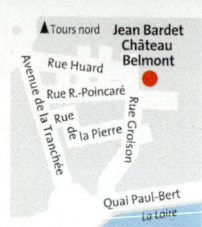

Access: A10 Tours-Nord, towards the centre, av. Maginot, av. de la Tranchée, 2nd left.

Airports: Paris Orly (Intl) 250 km, Tours 2 km
Train station: Tours 1 km

Owners: Sophie and Jean Bardet
General Manager: Jean Bardet
Weekly closing: Restaurant: Saturday noon, Monday noon, Tuesday noon
Hotel/Restaurant: Sunday evening, Monday (from January 2nd to March 31st and from November 1st to December 31st)
Open all year
Currency: Euro (€)
Rates: Menus 60-130 € s.i. Carte 84-107 € s.i.
16 rooms: 115-229 € s.i.
5 suites: 283-351 € s.i.
Breakfast: 20 € s.i.
Dogs: allowed **Golf:** 12 km
Accepted cards: AE, DC, JCB, MC, VS

More info on www.relaischateaux.com/bardet

Les Hautes Roches

SINCE 1991

86, quai de la Loire
37210 Rochecorbon
(Indre-et-Loire) • France

Tel. : (33) 02 47 52 88 88
Fax : (33) 02 47 52 81 30
hautesroches@relaischateaux.com

France

On the banks of the Loire river, the last wild river of Europe and in the heart of the Vouvray vineyards, this former monastery is a symbol of the Val de Loire style with its troglodyte rooms. The lounges and dining-rooms are located in this charming XVIIIth century castle with its tuff walls. Enjoy the cuisine with its savoury fish dishes and fine regional wines, served in summer on the terrace overlooking the river.

Bicycle touring, visit of cellars and castles, hiking in the vineyard... (Other activities P. 629)

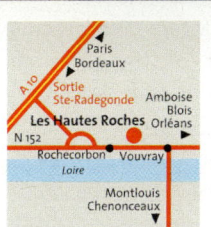

Access: From Paris, A10 exit Tours Nord, Sainte-Radegonde; then left towards Vouvray.

Airports: Paris Orly (Intl) 220 km, Tours 8 km
Train station: Tours St-Pierre-des-Corps 7 km

Owner: Philippe Mollard
General Manager: Didier Edon
Annual closing: From the end of January to mid-March
Currency: Euro (€)
Rates: Menus 56-70 € s.i. Carte 55-68 € s.i.
15 rooms: season 125-250 € s.i.
off-season 125-210 € s.i.
Breakfast: 16 € s.i.
Dogs: allowed
Golf: 15 km
Accepted cards: AE, DC, JCB, MC, VS

More info on www.relaischateaux.com/hauteroches

France

Château de Noizay

SINCE 1992

Route de Chançay
37210 Noizay
(Indre-et-Loire) • France

Tel. : (33) 02 47 52 11 01
Fax : (33) 02 47 52 04 64
noizay@relaischateaux.com

This elegant XVIth century residence, in the heart of the Loire châteaux and the Vouvray vineyards, was used as a refuge by the protestants during the Amboise conspiracy in 1560. The splendour of bygone days has been authentically recreated here. The lavishly decorated rooms with period furniture testify to this. The cuisine follows the seasons and is enhanced by a fine wine cellar with Vouvray and other Loire wines.

Hot-air balloon, helicopter, visit of cellars and castles (Other activities P. 629)

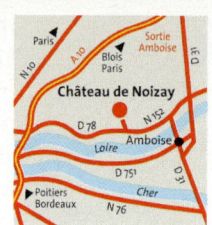

Access:
A10 exit N18 Amboise/Château-Renault, D31 towards Amboise, N152 towards Vouvray-Tours, D78 Noizay.

Airports: Paris Ch. de Gaulle (Intl) 230 km, Tours 18 km
Helipad: N 47° 25' 19" E 000° 53' 30"
Train station: St-Pierre-des-Corps 15 km

Owner/General Manager: François Mollard
Annual closing: From mid-January to mid March
Currency: Euro (€)
Rates: Menus 40-52-65 € s.i.
Carte 55-75 € s.i.
19 rooms: 130-260 € s.i.
Breakfast: 17 € s.i.
Dogs: allowed (extra cost)
Golf: Ardrée 28 km
Accepted cards: AE, DC, MC, VS

More info on www.relaischateaux.com/noizay

Domaine des Hauts de Loire

SINCE 1967

Route de Herbault
41150 Onzain
(Loir-et-Cher) • France

Tel. : (33) 02 54 20 72 57
Fax : (33) 02 54 20 77 32
hauts-loire@relaischateaux.com

France

This magnificent hunting lodge, built in 1860 by the famous publisher Panckoucke, is secluded in tranquil parkland. Relish the calm of a cosy guestroom with painted beams, then savour exquisite gourmet delicacies such as «salade d'anguille croustillante à la vinaigrette d'échalote» or «pigeonneau du vendômois au jus de presse», accompanied by superb local wines. Visit the Loire valley by hot-air balloon or helicopter.

Visit of cellars and castles. (Other activities P. 629)

Access: From Paris, A10 exit Blois, then N152 towards Tours. At the bridge of Chaumont towards Onzain.
Airports: Paris Orly (Intl) 200 km,
Paris Ch. de Gaulle (Intl) 220 km, Tours 40 km
Helipad: N 47° 30' 26" E 1° 08' 47"
Train station: Onzain 4 km

Owners: Bonnigal Family
General Manager: Pierre-Alain Bonnigal
Weekly closing: Rest.: Monday and Tuesday (except bank holidays)
Annual closing: From Dec. 1st to February 20th
Currency: Euro (€)
Rates: Menus 60 € s.i. (Lunch) 80-115 € s.i.
Carte 80-100 € s.i.
25 rooms: 110-265 € s.i. **10 suites:** 310-430 € s.i.
Breakfast: 20 € s.i.
Dogs: not allowed **Golf:** 15 km
Accepted cards: AE, DC, JCB, MC, VS

More info on www.relaischateaux.com/hauts-loire

Marc et Cécile H. restaurateurs.
60 couverts par jour. 3 toques toute l'année.

Hôtels

Restaurants

Centres de loisirs

Quand on travaille dans la restauration ou l'hôtellerie, ce qu'on cherche avant tout c'e[st] le confort de ses clients et une cuisine de qualité. C'est pourquoi Antargaz, premi[er] distributeur indépendant de propane et de butane en France, livre à chacun et en tou[te] sécurité l'énergie nécessaire pour la cuisson, l'eau chaude et le chauffage, même da[ns] les endroits les plus reculés. Ainsi, où que vous soyez, Antargaz vous apporte l'énerg[ie] et les conseils à la hauteur de votre hospitalité. **www.antargaz.fr** ou **3615 antarga[z]**

Bernard Robin – Le Relais

SINCE 1990

1, av. de Chambord
41250 Bracieux
(Loir-et-Cher) • France

Tel. : **(33) 02 54 46 41 22**
Fax : (33) 02 54 46 03 69
robin@relaischateaux.com

France

Bernard Robin has chosen to show-case his culinary creations in this picturesque residence near the Loire châteaux. Robin's «anguille de Loire fumée, copeaux de foie gras de canard à la croque au sel» and «géline de Touraine rôtie à la broche et truffée sous la peau» are veritable masterpieces, while the «lièvre à la royale» is simply sublime. The cellar is a treasure trove of local vintages, the service is impeccable and the hospitality unparalleled.

Hunting in Sologne, hot-air balloon, Loire castles. (Other activities P. 629)

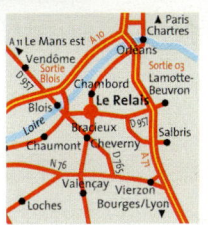

Access: From Paris, A10, exit Chambord-Mer, Bracieux on the road to Cheverny.

Airports: Paris Ch. de Gaulle (Intl) 180 km, Tours 80 km
Helipad: N 47° 33' 30" E 1° 32' 22"
Train station: Blois 20 km

Owner: Bernard Robin
Weekly closing: Tuesday and Wednesday
Annual closing:
From Dec. 20th to end of January
Currency: Euro (€)
Rates: Menus 42-84 € s.i. Carte 54-84 € s.i.
Dogs: allowed
Golf: Cheverny 9 km, Bich 15 km
Accepted cards: AE, DC, JCB, MC, VS

Bernard Robin

More info on www.relaischateaux.com/robin

Grand Hôtel du Lion d'Or

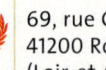

SINCE 1978

69, rue Georges-Clemenceau
41200 Romorantin-Lanthenay
(Loir-et-Cher) • France

Tel. : (33) 02 54 94 15 15
Fax : (33) 02 54 88 24 87
liondor@relaischateaux.com

This beautiful Renaissance manor is a perfect illustration of French art de vivre. Didier Clément, one of the great chefs of his generation, creates gourmet dishes of high culinary delight using forgotten products with names like: rocambole, graine de paradis, angélique... Rare and subtle dishes accompanied by superb Loire wines. Exquisitely comfortable rooms and lounges around a patio full of serenity.

Loire castles, bicycle touring. (Other activities P. 629)

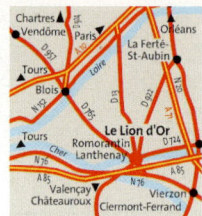

Access: From Paris, A10 then A71 towards Bourges, exit Salbris then D724. From Clermont-Ferrand : A71 then A85 towards Tours, exit Romorantin.

Airports: Paris Orly (Intl) 170 km, Paris Ch. de Gaulle (Intl) 200 km
Train station: Romorantin 1 km

Owners: Colette and Alain Barrat, Marie-Christine and Didier Clément
Annual closing: From Feb. 17th to March 27th and from November 24th to December 4th
Currency: Euro (€)
Rates: Menus 79-115 € s.i. Carte 98-120 € s.i.
13 rooms: 155-350 € s.i.
3 suites: 230-430 € s.i.
Breakfast: 19 € s.i.
Dogs: allowed
Golf: 3 courses less than 30 minutes away
Accepted cards: AE, DC, MC, VS

More info on www.relaischateaux.com/liondor

Château de Curzay

SINCE 1996

86600 Curzay-sur-Vonne
(Vienne) • France

Tel. : (33) 05 49 36 17 00
Fax : (33) 05 49 53 57 69
curzay@relaischateaux.com

France

Built in 1710, the Château de Curzay is set in the heart of an immense parkland on the banks of a river. The individually decorated rooms, the terrace with its majestic cedars, the pool in the shade of the XIIth century towers and the light, innovative cuisine offer you a haven of calm and serenity and a superb culinary experience. Nearby, you can discover the Futuroscope and the Marais Poitevin.

(Other activities P. 629)

Access: A10, exit 30. Poitiers south. N11, towards Niort-Lusignan; at Coulombiers, towards Jazeneuil. From Niort, A10 exit 31 towards Lusignan, in Rouillé towards Sanxay.
Airport: Poitiers 25 km
Helipad: N 46° 29' 04" E 000° 02' 55"
Train station: Poitiers 25 km

Owners: Brigitte de Gastines-Cachart and Eric Cachart
General Manager: Eric Cachart
Annual closing: From January to April, November, December
Currency: Euro (€)
Rates: Menus 35-86 € s.i. Carte 45-76 € s.i.
20 rooms: 145-275 € s.i.
2 suites: 310 € s.i.
Breakfast: starting at 15 € s.i.
Dogs: allowed (extra cost)
Golf: 10 km
Accepted cards: AE, DC, MC, VS

More info on www.relaischateaux.com/curzay

CRÉATEUR D'AUTOMOBILES

Live the difference.

RENAULT préconise elf The official fuel consumption figures in mpg (l/100km) for the 3.0 V6 dCi are: Urban 23.5 (12.0),

RENAULT VEL SATIS

Naturally, the new Vel Satis boasts everything you'd expect of an executive saloon –an outstandingly powerful and flexible engine choice including what 'Fleet World' described as "the most refined and responsive diesel we've ever tested". But with the Vel Satis, Renault has also redefined luxury motoring with an exceptionally roomy cabin that's 13cms taller than the class average. While its revolutionary Trigonal rear suspension system simply means more comfort and less noise. All of which makes for a sumptuously different take on luxury, whichever way you look at it.

For more details call 0800 072 3373 or visit www.renault.co.uk

Extra Urban 41.5 (6.8), Combined 32.5 (8.7). The official CO_2 emission is 232g/km.

The Greater South-West

France

Properties	Nearest major city	Relais & Châteaux	Relais Gourmands	Page
Bras (Michel)	Rodez	✽	✽	130
Centenaire (Hôtel du)	Sarlat	✽	✽	125
Chapelle Saint-Martin (La)	Limoges	✽		120
Château Cordeillan-Bages	Bordeaux	✽	✽	133
Château de Castel-Novel	Brive	✽		122
Château de la Treyne	Souillac	✽		126
Château de Mercuès	Cahors	✽		129
Château de Puy Robert	Brive	✽		124
Château de Riell	Perpignan	✽		143
Château de Roumégouse	Rocamadour	✽		128
Coutanceau (Richard) (Restaurant)	La Rochelle		✽	119
Domaine d'Auriac	Carcassonne	✽		142
Domaine de Bassibé	Pau	✽		137
Guérard (M.) «Les Prés d'Eugénie»	Pau	✽	✽	138
Hauterive (Hôtel)	Bordeaux	✽		135
Loges de l'Aubergade (Les)	Agen	✽	✽	131
Moulin de l'Abbaye	Périgueux	✽		123
Moulin de la Gorce (Au)	Limoges	✽		121
Parc Victoria (Le)	Saint-Jean-de-Luz	✽		139
Plaisance (Hostellerie de)	Bordeaux	✽		134
Pyrénées (Les)	Biarritz	✽	✽	140
Relais de la Poste	Dax	✽	✽	136
Réserve (La)	Albi	✽		141
Richelieu (Le)	La Rochelle	✽		118
Vieux Logis (Le)	Périgueux	✽		127

More info on www.relaischateaux.com

Le Richelieu

France — SINCE 2001

44, avenue de la Plage
17630 La Flotte-en-Ré
(Charente-Maritime) • France

Tel. : (33) 05 46 09 60 70
Fax : (33) 05 46 09 50 59
richelieu@relaischateaux.com

The sea stretches as far as the eye can see beyond the terrace and large lawn. Le Richelieu, named after the Cardinal who resisted the threat of the French Protestants, is sheltered by La Flotte-en-Ré harbour jetty. Nestling between green vegetation and the sea, small white houses offer relaxation in a refined, gentle, luminous setting. Thalassotherapy facilities on the premises.

(Other activities P. 629)

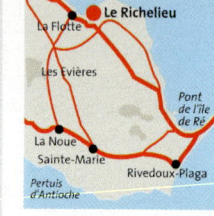

Access: From Paris- Motorway A10, exit 33 towards La Rochelle/île de Ré. Trunk road 11 to La Rochelle then towards île de Ré.
On île de Ré towards La Flotte.
Airports: Bordeaux (Intl) 200 km, La Rochelle 8 km
Train station: La Rochelle 20 km

Owners: Gendre Family
Annual closing: From the beginning of January to the beginning of February
Currency: Euro (€)
Rates: Menus 50-65 € s.i. Carte 25-50 € s.i.
34 rooms: 125-400 € s.i.
6 suites: 370-500 € s.i.
Breakfast: 20 € s.i.
Dogs: allowed
Golf: 20 km
Accepted cards: AE, MC, VS

More info on www.relaischateaux.com/richelieu

Restaurant Richard Coutanceau

SINCE 1988

Plage de la Concurrence
17000 La Rochelle
(Charente-Maritime) • France

Tel. : **(33) 05 46 41 48 19**
Fax : (33) 05 46 41 99 45
coutanceau@relaischateaux.com

France

Virtuoso chef Richard Coutanceau is capable of drawing the most subtle flavours from seafood. His «tartare de langoustines aux huîtres spéciales», «homard breton à la coque ou en millefeuille» are extraordinary, while the «bar de ligne rôti sur sa peau croustillée au parfum de basilic et à la tomate confite» is a culinary masterpiece. The exceptional cellar includes a 19-year-old Pineau blanc which is served with dessert.
(Other activities P. 629)

Access: From Paris, A 10 exit 33; N11, La Rochelle city centre, follow the sign «La Plage».

Airports: Bordeaux (Intl) 200 km, La Rochelle 5 km
Train station: La Rochelle 2 km

Owner: Richard Coutanceau
Weekly closing: Sunday
Open all year
Currency: Euro (€)
Rates: Menus 38-73 € s.i.
Carte 44-57 € s.i.
Dogs: allowed
Golf: 12 km
Accepted cards: AE, DC, JCB, MC, VS

Richard Coutanceau

More info on www.relaischateaux.com/coutanceau

France

La Chapelle Saint-Martin

SINCE 1973

Nieul-près-Limoges
87510 Nieul
(Haute-Vienne) • France

Tel. : (33) 05 55 75 80 17
Fax : (33) 05 55 75 89 50
chapelle@relaischateaux.com

Only minutes from the ceramic capital of Limoges, you will discover this formerly private residence in its verdant property surrounded by 100-year-old trees. The lovely view on the ponds endows the rooms with a pastoral light. You will appreciate the spacious lounges and the dining-rooms decorated with old paintings. In the heartland of porcelain, you will savour the «milk-fed veal» served with a wide selection of Bordeaux vintages.

Water-skiing and sailing (on the lake), hunting... (Other activities P. 629)

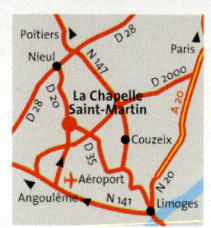

Access: From Limoges, towards Angoulême N 141, airport, 4 km after, on D 20. From Paris exit 28.
Airport: Limoges (Intl) 4 km
Helipad: N 45° 53' 589" E 001° 10' 724"
Train station: Limoges 10 km

Owners: Dudognon Family
General Manager: Gilles Dudognon
Weekly closing: Restaurant: Sunday evening (from October 30th to April 1st), Monday all day, Tuesday noon, Wednesday noon
Annual closing: Restaurant: January
Currency: Euro (€)
Rates: Menus 39-66 € s.i. Carte 49-75 € s.i.
9 rooms: 105-198 € s.i.
4 suites: 229 € s.i.
Breakfast: 13 € s.i.
Dogs: allowed (except rest.) **Golf:** 15 km
Accepted cards: AE, DC, MC, VS

More info on www.relaischateaux.com/chapelle

Au Moulin de la Gorce

SINCE 1991

87800 La Roche-l'Abeille
(Haute-Vienne) • France

Tel. : (33) 05 55 00 70 66
Fax : (33) 05 55 00 76 57
moulingorce@relaischateaux.com

France

Pastoral calm, bucolic charm, fishing… no wonder the writer Jean Giraudoux cherished this part of the countryside. Enjoy an idyllic stay in one of the charming rooms, each named after a flower. The cuisine is like the property: warm, full or character and rich in bourgeois tradition. Excellent wine list.

(Other activities P. 629)

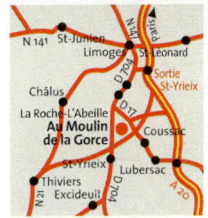

Access: From Paris, towards Brive-Toulouse, exit St-Yrieix, D 704 La Roche-l'Abeille.

Airport: Limoges (Intl) 40 km
Train station: Limoges 30 km

Owners: Isabelle and Pierre Bertranet
Weekly closing: Monday noon, Tuesday noon, Wednesday noon (except holidays and from April to October)
Annual closing: From Nov. 12th to Dec. 4th and from January 2nd to April 2nd
Currency: Euro (€)
Rates: Menu-carte 39-62 € s.i.
Menu tasting 75 € s.i.
9 rooms: 68-150 € s.i.
1 suite: 206 € s.i.
Breakfast: 13 € s.i.
Dogs: allowed
Golf: 30 km
Accepted cards: AE, DC, MC, VS

More info on www.relaischateaux.com/moulingorce

Château de Castel-Novel

France • SINCE 1965

19240 Varetz
(Corrèze) • France

Tel. : **(33) 05 55 85 00 01**
Fax : (33) 05 55 85 09 03
novel@relaischateaux.com

How could you fail to be enchanted by this elegant XVth century «castel»? French writer Colette once fell under its spell and moved in as lady of the manor. And when you experience the comfort and tranquil charm of the guestrooms and the idyllic park, you'll understand why. Traditional cuisine, prepared with fresh ingredients from the Limousin countryside, is complemented by Cahors, Bergerac and vintage Bordeaux.

Walking paths on the property. (Other activities P. 629)

Access: From Paris, A 10, then A 71 and A 20 exit Vierzon until Brive, exit Brive nord, Varetz by D 901.

Airports: Bordeaux (Intl) 160 km, Brive 5 km
Helipad: N 45° 11' E 001° 27'
Train station: Brive 12 km

Owners: Albert and Christine Parveaux
Weekly closing: Restaurant: lunches from Monday to Friday
Annual closing: End of October to beg. of May
Currency: Euro (€)
Rates: Menus 42-80 € s.i. Carte 60 € s.i.
32 rooms: 140-250 € s.i.
5 suites: 300-330 € s.i.
Breakfast: 15 € s.i.
Dogs: allowed
Golf: 3 holes on the premises
18 holes at 10 km and 25 km
Accepted cards: AE, DC, JCB, MC, VS

More info on www.relaischateaux.com/novel

Moulin de l'Abbaye

SINCE 1981

1, route de Bourdeilles
24310 Brantôme-en-Périgord
(Dordogne) • France

Tel. : (33) 05 53 05 80 22
Fax : (33) 05 53 05 75 27
moulin@relaischateaux.com

France

A romantic market town, Brantôme truly merits its accolade of the «Venice of the Périgord». It was also home to the abbot of the same name, the author of the book *La Vie des dames galantes*. On the banks of the river Dronne, the Moulin de l'Abbaye, the Maison du Meunier and the Maison de l'Abbé guarantee a stay steeped in history, full of charm and freshness. Quality cuisine in the Moulin restaurant; on the riverside terrace or in the «Fil de l'Eau», its delightful fisherman's bistro.

Visit to museums, prehistoric caves and castles. (Other activities P. 629)

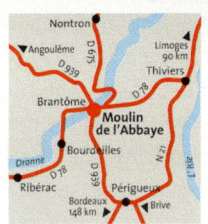

Access: D 939 between Angoulême and Périgueux. In Brantôme, direction «l'Abbaye».

Airports: Bordeaux (Intl) 120 km, Périgueux 25 km, Bergerac 70 km
Train station: Angoulême-TGV 50 km

Owner: S.A. Moulin de l'Abbaye
General Managers: Bernard and Yvette Dessum
Weekly closing: Restaurant: lunch
(except weekends and bank holidays)
Annual closing: From November 2nd to April 30th
Currency: Euro (€)
Rates: Menus 45-80 € s.i. Menu-carte 65 € s.i.,
«Au Fil de L'Eau» 22-27 € s.c.
16 rooms: 170-200 € s.i. **3 suites:** 245-280 € s.i.
Breakfast: 17 € s.i.
Dogs: allowed **Golf:** 25 km
Accepted cards: AE, DC, JCB, MC, VS

More info on www.relaischateaux.com/moulin

France — SINCE 1988

Château de Puy Robert

Route de Valojoulx
24290 Montignac-Lascaux
(Dordogne) • France

Tel. : (33) 05 53 51 92 13
Fax : (33) 05 53 51 80 11
puyrobert@relaischateaux.com

This elegant neo-Renaissance château, which lies en route to Lascaux, makes an idyllic stopping place. The tiny boudoir, hidden in a turret overlooking the park, is simply one of the most romantic guestrooms imaginable. Savour inventive seasonal cuisine, prepared with the very best regional ingredients, and sample one of the excellent local vintages. Ideally located for visiting the region's famous prehistoric sites.

Visit to many castles, historic villages and caves. (Other activities P. 629)

Access: From Paris, A10 then A71 and A20, Brive, N89 le Lardin St-Lazare, Montignac.

Airports: Bordeaux (Intl) 175 km, Brive 37 km
Helipad: N 45° 3' 8" E 1° 9' 50"
Train station: Brive 37 km

Owner: Albert Parveaux
General Managers: Christine Le Bihan and Denis Petrel
Weekly closing: Restaurant: week lunch
Annual closing: From mid-October to the beginning of May
Currency: Euro (€)
Rates: Menus 37-75-123 € s.i. Carte 55-76 € s.i.
33 rooms: 122-256 € s.i.
5 suites: 256-326 € s.i.
Breakfast: 15 € s.i.
Dogs: allowed
Golf: 28 km
Accepted cards: AE, DC, JCB, MC, VS

More info on www.relaischateaux.com/puyrobert

Hôtel du Centenaire

SINCE 1983

24620 Les Eyzies-de-Tayac
(Dordogne) • France

Tel. : (33) 05 53 06 68 68
Fax : (33) 05 53 06 92 41
centenaire@relaischateaux.com

France

This elegant residence, set on the picturesque banks of the Vézère, where the painters of the Lascaux caves once fished, is a haven of calm offering bright, comfortable rooms. The beautiful Dordogne countryside is the perfect place to savour Roland Mazère's inventive cuisine, based on regional and seasonal produce. Gourmets will be enchanted by his exquisite «terrine chaude de cèpes, risotto aux truffes».

Eyzies Prehistoric museum, Lascaux caves, and Sarlat. (Other activities P. 629)

Access: At the intersection of D 47 (Périgueux-Sarlat) and D 706.

Airports: Bordeaux (Intl) 170 km, Périgueux 40 km
Train station: Les Eyzies 1 km

Owners: Mazère-Scholly Family
Weekly closing: Restaurant: Monday noon, Tuesday noon, Wednesday noon and Friday noon
Annual closing: From Nov. to beginning of April
Currency: Euro (€)
Rates: Menus 60-90-110 € s.i.
38 € s.i. (lunch except Sunday and holidays)
Carte 61-91 € s.i.
20 rooms: 137-228 € s.i.
4 suites: 260-381 € s.i.
Breakfast: 20 € s.i.
Dogs: allowed
Golf: 20 km
Accepted cards: AE, DC, MC, VS

More info on www.relaischateaux.com/centenaire

Château de la Treyne

France — SINCE 1993

46200 Lacave
(Lot) • France

Tel. : (33) 05 65 27 60 60
Fax : (33) 05 65 27 60 70
treyne@relaischateaux.com

This magnificent château (built in the XIVth and XVIIth centuries) overlooks the Dordogne and blends the authenticity of the past with the comfort and quality of a landmarked site. Its French gardens extend into a 300-acre forest. Michèle Gombert has mastered the art of fine living, offering luxurious rooms, breakfast beneath the hundred-year-old cedars and dinner in the Louis XIII salon or on the riverside terrace.

Discovery of the châteaux of the Dordogne valley by helicopter, hot-air ballon. (Other activities P. 629)

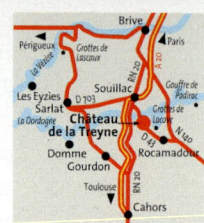

Access: A20, exit 55 south of Souillac, D43, towards Lacave (6 km); Pinsac, after the bridge over the Dordogne.

Airports: Toulouse (Intl) 180 km, Brive 40 km
Helipad: N 44° 51' 01" E 01° 31' 38"
Train station: Souillac 6 km

Owner: Michèle Gombert
General Manager: Philippe Bappel
Weekly closing: Restaurant: from Tuesday to Friday for lunch
Annual closing: From Nov. 16th to December 20th and from January 6th to April 4th
Currency: Euro (€)
Rates: Menus 45 € s.i. (lunch) 65-100 € s.i. Carte 60-95 € s.i. **Breakfast:** 15 € s.i.
14 rooms: 160-320 € s.i. **2 suites:** 440 € s.i.
Dogs: allowed **Golf:** 10 km
Accepted cards: AE, DC, JCB, MC, VS

More info on www.relaischateaux.com/treyne

Le Vieux Logis

SINCE 1955

24510 Trémolat
(Dordogne) • France

Tel. : **(33) 05 53 22 80 06**
Fax : (33) 05 53 22 84 89
vieuxlogis@relaischateaux.com

France

Henry Miller was so enchanted by this XVIIth century Carthusian monastery of Perigord that he came to spend a week and ended up staying a month. You'll understand why when you discover this idyllic haven filled with birdsong and the babbling of the garden brook. Seasonal cuisine in the former tobacco drying room or under the linden trees. Regional restaurant at the «Bistrot du Logis».

(Other activities P. 629)

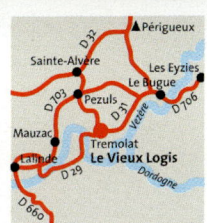

Access:
From Bordeaux, follow Sarlat D660; from Paris, Périgueux (N89) Le Bugue.
Airports:
Bordeaux (Intl) 120 km, Bergerac 32 km
Helipad: N 44° 52' 566" E 000° 49' 732"
Train station: Trémolat 1 km

Owner: Bernard Giraudel
Weekly closing: Rest.: lunch from February 27th to June 14th and from Sept. 16th to January 26th (except weekend and bank holidays)
Dinner on Tuesday and Wednesday (except from April 15th to October 15th)
Annual closing: From Jan. 27th to February 26th
Currency: Euro (€)
Rates: Menus 30-45-60-75 € s.i. Carte 50-70 € s.i.
19 rooms: 146-245 € s.i. **7 suites:** 310 € s.i.
Breakfast: 15 € s.i
Dogs: allowed **Golf:** 20 km
Accepted cards: AE, DC, MC, VS

More info on www.relaischateaux.com/vieuxlogis

France — SINCE 1966

Château de Roumégouse

Route de Rocamadour, Rignac
46500 Gramat
(Lot) • France

Tel. : (33) 05 65 33 63 81
Fax : (33) 05 65 33 71 18
roumegouse@relaischateaux.com

This elegant residence, which lies on the Compostella pilgrimage route, is set amidst unspoiled natural surroundings. Luce and Jean-Louis Lainé have decorated their guestrooms in styles ranging from Louis XIV to Napoleon III and their impeccable taste is reflected in the dining rooms which serve local cuisine. Enjoy a candlelit dinner on the exquisite flowered terrace overlooking the Rocamadour plateau.

Flight over Rocamadour in hot air balloon, Padirac abyss. (Other activities P. 629)

Access: From Gramat, follow signs on N140. A20 exit Gramat.

Airports: Toulouse (Intl) 170 km, Brive 60 km
Helipad: N 44° 48' 01" E 001° 41' 21"
Train station: Gramat 5 km

Owners: Luce and Jean-Louis Lainé
Weekly closing: Rest.: Monday noon, Tuesday, Wednesday noon, Thursday noon
Annual closing: From beginning November to Easter
Currency: Euro (€)
Rates: Menus 31-60 € s.i. Carte 60-72 € s.i.
13 rooms: 120-195 € s.i.
2 suites: starting at 225 € s.i.
Breakfast: 13 € s.i.
Dogs: allowed
Golf: 30 km
Accepted cards: AE, DC, MC, VS

More info on www.relaischateaux.com/roumegouse

Château de Mercuès

SINCE 1959

46090 Mercuès
(Lot) • France

Tel. : (33) 05 65 20 00 01
Fax : (33) 05 65 20 05 72
mercues@relaischateaux.com

France

For twelve centuries, the château at Mercuès was the summer residence of the bishops of Cahors. Today the guestrooms, opening onto a breathtaking vista of vineyards, valleys and French gardens, have lost none of their feudal grandeur. In this kingdom of «foie gras», truffles and wine, the cuisine is rich and generous. Meanwhile, Georges Vigouroux's vintage Cahors age to perfection in the cathedral-like vaults of the cellar.

(Other activities P. 629)

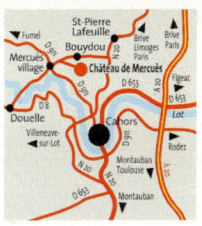

Access: Paris, Limoges, Souillac, Cahors via the A20. Paris, Bordeaux, Montauban, Cahors via the A10, A62, A20. From Cahors to Mercuès take the D 911.

Airport: Toulouse (Intl) 102 km
Helipad: N 44° 29' 75" E 01° 24' 04"
Train station: Cahors 10 km

Owner: Georges Vigouroux
General Manager: Bernard Denegre
Weekly closing: Rest.: Monday (all day), Tuesday, Wednesday and Thursday noon
Annual closing: From November 1st to Easter
Currency: Euro (€)
Rates: Menus 50-88 € s.i. Carte 60-85 € s.i.
22 rooms: 150-250 € s.i.
8 suites: 260-400 € s.i.
Breakfast: 15 € s.i.
Dogs: allowed (hotel only) **Golf:** 30 km (9 holes)
Accepted cards: AE, DC, JCB, MC, VS

More info on www.relaischateaux.com/mercues

Michel Bras

France — SINCE 1994

Route de l'Aubrac
12210 Laguiole
(Aveyron) • France

Tel. : (33) 05 65 51 18 20
Fax : (33) 05 65 48 47 02
bras@relaischateaux.com

On the heights of the Aubrac plateau, the Bras family home is fashioned in a spirit of total harmony with the landscape: a world of plants, stone and luminosity. The cuisine of Michel and Sébastien is inspired by this locality and reveals to their guests unsuspected flavours such as in the «gargouillou de jeunes légumes», the «pièce de bœuf fermier Aubrac» or even the «biscuit au chocolat coulant». Rare wines.

(Other activities P. 629)

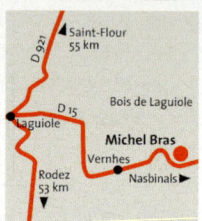

Altitude: 1225 metres.
Access: From Laguiole, towards Aubrac. 5.5 km turn left, follow «Michel Bras» signs.

Airports: Clermont-Ferrand (Intl) 170 km, Rodez 60 km
Helipad: N 44° 44' E 2° 55' 5''
Train station: Rodez 60 km

Owners: Ginette and Michel Bras
Weekly closing: Hotel: Monday (except in July-August) Rest.: Monday (all day), Tuesday and Wednesday for lunch
Annual closing: From November 1st to April 7th
Currency: Euro (€)
Rates: Menus 45-85-135 € s.i. Carte 76-137 € s.i.
15 rooms: 183-320 € s.i.
Breakfast: 20 € s.i.
Dogs: allowed (extra cost)
Golf: 9 holes at 10 km
Accepted cards: AE, DC, JCB, VS

More info on www.relaischateaux.com/bras

Les Loges de l'Aubergade

SINCE 1987

52, rue Royale
47270 Puymirol
(Lot-et-Garonne) • France

Tel. : (33) 05 53 95 31 46
Fax : (33) 05 53 95 33 80
aubergade@relaischateaux.com

France

A blessed place in a blessed region. A modern medieval architecture with the monastery and the dining and sitting rooms marked by the talent of decorator Jacques Garcia. And the cuisine! Michel Trama blends culinary tradition with modern innovation. You will never become weary of «papillote de pomme de terre au fumet de truffes». Havana cigar passion.

ULM, smokers' lounge. (Other activities P. 629)

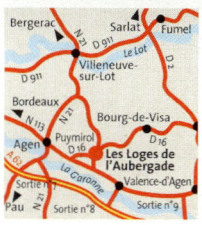

Access: From Toulouse, A62 exit Valence-d'Agen, towards Golfech/Lamagistère via the N113 then D20, D248. From Bordeaux, A62 exit Agen, towards Toulouse via the N113 to Lafox then D16.
Airports: Toulouse (Intl) 90 km, Bordeaux (Intl) 165 km
Train station: Agen 15 km

Owners: Mr and Mrs Trama
Weekly closing: Sunday evening, Monday, Tuesday noon (low season) Monday noon (season)
Annual closing: February holidays
Currency: Euro (€)
Rates: Menus 54-108 € s.i.
Carte 53-84 € s.i. **Breakfast:** 18 € s.i.
10 rooms: 145-267 € s.i.
Dogs: allowed (extra cost) **Golf:** 10 km
Accepted cards: AE, DC, JCB, MC, VS

More info on www.relaischateaux.com/aubergade

Luxurious Privacy by Train

Discover a new perspective on **luxury travel in France**.

For the first time ever, the exceptional beauty of France can be enjoyed from **aboard a private train**.

Encounter the most spectacular areas and the diversity of this beautiful country from this unique and refined environment.

Along the way, celebrate French traditions and culture, savour the legendary food and wine and enjoy exclusive entry to châteaux and museums.

One departure per week **for 22 privileged guests...**

For information and brochures:
www.frenchrailcruise.fr
France : +33-(0)5 56 00 64 64 - UK : +44-(0)20 7978 5842
USA : 1-800-438 7245 or 1-800-782 2424 - CANADA : 1-800-361 72

Château Cordeillan-Bages

SINCE 1991

Route des Châteaux
33250 Pauillac
(Gironde) • France

Tel. : **(33) 05 56 59 24 24**
Fax : (33) 05 56 59 01 89
cordeillan@relaischateaux.com

France

This 17th century Carthusian monastery combines the spirit of land and estuary and enchants with both its authenticity and modernity. Savour exquisite regional dishes with Pauillac lamb, accompanied by one of the thousands of Bordeaux from the cellar. The Ecole du Bordeaux offers wine-tasting courses. In the heart of Médoc, culture and pleasure are all the same.

(Other activities P. 629)

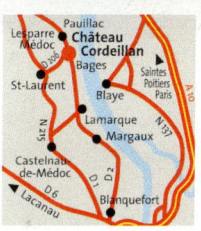

Access: A10 towards Mérignac, bypass exit 7, N215 St-Laurent, D206 Pauillac, or directly D2.
Airport: Bordeaux (Intl) 45 km
Helipad: N 45° 11' 29" O 000° 45' 12"
Train station: Pauillac 2 km

Owner: Jean-Michel Cazes
General Manager: Thierry Marx
Weekly closing: Rest.: Saturday noon, Monday, Tuesday noon
Annual closing: From Dec. 15th to January 31st
Currency: Euro (€)
Rates: Menus 50 € s.i. (at noon except on Sundays) evenings 85 € s.i. Carte 60-85 € s.i. Special menu for guests on Monday evening: 45 € s.i. **Breakfast:** 15-20 € s.i.
25 rooms: 126-265 € s.i. **4 suites:** 282-400 € s.i.
Dogs: allowed **Golf:** 4 courses 20-35 km
Accepted cards: AE, DC, JCB, MC, VS

Thierry Marx

More info on www.relaischateaux.com/cordeillan

France

SINCE 2003

Hostellerie de Plaisance

Place du Clocher
33330 Saint-Emilion
(Aquitaine) • France

Tel. : (33) 05 57 55 07 55
Fax : (33) 05 57 74 41 11
plaisance@relaischateaux.com

Gérard and Chantal Perse uphold the excellent traditions of savoir-vivre in the mediaeval town of Saint-Emilion. Acquired in 2001, the Plaisance has been faithfully restored to its 18th century origins. The panoramic terrace offers a wonderful view. The entire property is graced with an elegance which turns the Hostellerie into an exceptional setting, set off by a residence with four suites in the Château Pavie.

Visits of castles. (Other activities P. 629)

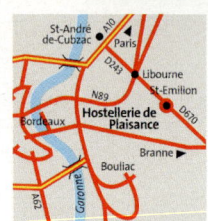

Access:
From Bordeaux, towards Libourne N 89, exit Libourne - Bergerac. Towards St-Emilion via D 670.
From Paris, A 10, exit St-André-de-Cubzac. Towards Libourne - St-Emilion via D 243.
Airport: Bordeaux (Intl) 35 km
Train station: Libourne 8 km

Owners: Chantal and Gérard Perse
Annual closing:
Hotel: from January 1st to February 12th
Restaurant: from January 2nd to February 12th
Currency: Euro (€)
Rates: Menus 31-80 € s.i. Carte 65-97 € s.i.
16 rooms: 120-260 € s.i.
3 suites: 330 € s.i.
Breakfast: 15 € s.i.
Dogs: allowed (extra cost) **Golf:** 30 km
Accepted cards: AE, DC, JCB, MC, VS

More info on www.relaischateaux.com/plaisance

Hôtel Hauterive

SINCE 1978

3, place Camille-Hostein
33270 Bouliac
(Gironde) • France

Tel. : (33) 05 57 97 06 00
Fax : (33) 05 56 20 92 58
stjames@relaischateaux.com

France

Inspired by tobacco driers, Jean Nouvel has designed the hotel buildings and swimming pool. From this exceptional setting overlooking Bordeaux and the Garonne, you will enjoy the quiet of the vineyards and the surrounding park. The sun-soaked cuisine is accompanied by the best wines in the region. There are two further temptations: the «Bistroy» open to the world and the «Espérance» (village cafe and rotisserie).

(Other activities P. 629)

Access:
A 10, exit Toulouse/Bayonne, leave beltway at exit 23, towards Bouliac.

Airport: Bordeaux (Intl) 10 km
Train station: Bordeaux St-Jean 5 km

Owner: Hauterive - St James - S.A.
General Manager: Jean-Claude Borgel
Open all year
Currency: Euro (€)
Rates: Menu 70 € s.i. Carte 76 € s.i.
Café de l'Espérance 24 € s.i.
Le Bistroy 30 € s.i.
15 rooms: 185-200 € s.i.
3 suites: 270-300 € s.i.
Breakfast: 15-18 € s.i.
Dogs: allowed
Golf: 15 km
Accepted cards: AE, DC, MC, VS

More info on www.relaischateaux.com/stjames

Relais de la Poste

France • SINCE 1999

24, avenue de Maremne
40140 Magescq
(Landes) • France

Tel. : **(33) 05 58 47 70 25**
Fax : (33) 05 58 47 76 17
poste@relaischateaux.com

A stone's throw from the vast beaches of the Landes, this former post house on the road to Santiago de Compostela upholds a family tradition. The rooms with their contemporary décor and furniture look onto a spacious, tranquil park. Jean Coussau's cuisine draws on the seasonal flavours and aromas of the rich Landes region featuring dishes like «saumon de l'Adour», «asperges des sables», «foie gras de canard chaud aux raisins» or game and mushrooms. Superb collection of Armagnacs.

Thermal baths, beach. (Other activities P. 629)

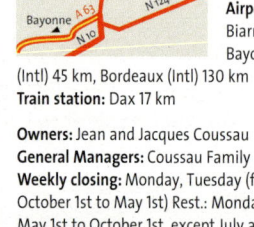

Access: From Bordeaux, towards Bayonne, San Sebastian via A10, exit 10 Magescq.
Airports: Biarritz Bayonne Anglet (Intl) 45 km, Bordeaux (Intl) 130 km
Train station: Dax 17 km

Owners: Jean and Jacques Coussau
General Managers: Coussau Family
Weekly closing: Monday, Tuesday (from October 1st to May 1st) Rest.: Monday (from May 1st to October 1st, except July and August)
Annual closing: From Nov. 12th to December 20th
Currency: Euro (€)
Rates: Menus 53-69 € s.i. Carte 60-70 € s.i.
10 rooms: 126-185 € s.i.
2 suites: 200-230 € s.i.
Breakfast: 11-14 € s.i.
Dogs: allowed **Golf:** 20 km (18 holes)
Accepted cards: AE, DC, VS

Jean Coussau

More info on www.relaischateaux.com/poste

Domaine de Bassibé

SINCE 1980

32400 Segos
(Gers) • France

Tel. : (33) 05 62 09 46 71
Fax : (33) 05 62 08 40 15
bassibe@relaischateaux.com

France

Earthen red tiles and elegant white façades gleaming in the afternoon sun, sylvan green ivy creepers framing the shutters: the colours of this spacious, picturesque residence appear to have been lifted from an artist's palette. Dinner, served in the old wine press or beneath the plane trees, features the rich traditional cuisine of the Gers region enhanced by excellent local wines: Madiran, Jurançon and Tursan.

Low season: reservation required for lunch.
Visit to wineries and vineyards. (Other activities P. 629)

Access: Bordeaux-Pau-Spain: 35 km north of Pau, 8 km south of Aire-s/ Adour; D260 Segos.

Airports: Bordeaux (Intl) 150 km, Pau 32 km
Helipad: N 43° 37' 65" E 0° 15' 88"
Train station: Pau 35 km

Owners: Olivier and Sylvie Lacroix
Weekly closing: Tuesday, Wednesday and lunchs
Annual closing: From beginning of January to the end of March
Currency: Euro (€)
Rates: Menu-carte 41 € s.i.
10 rooms: 125 € s.i.
7 suites: 190 € s.i.
Breakfast: 11 € s.i.
Dogs: allowed
Golf: 7 km
Accepted cards: AE, DC, MC, VS

More info on www.relaischateaux.com/bassibe

Michel Guérard «Les Prés d'Eugénie»

France — SINCE 1968

40320 Eugénie-les-Bains
(Landes) • France

Tel. : (33) 05 58 05 06 07
Fax : (33) 05 58 51 10 10
guerard@relaischateaux.com

In the past century, Empress Eugénie was extremely fond of this elegant colonial hamlet where the white palace, «Les Prés», the «Couvent des Herbes» and the «Ferme aux Grives» gracefully court each other in balmy gardens of magnolias and verbena. Today, Christine and Michel Guérard delight guests with a rare symphony of herb gardens, climbing roses, magic springs, exotic fragrances, exquisite guestrooms and delicious flavours which distil a refined «Art de vivre».

Ferme Thermale®, Fitness and Mineral water Spa, Beauty Centre, Cuisine Minceur Active®, vegetable and herb gardens, vineyard, Maison Marine®. (Other activities P. 629)

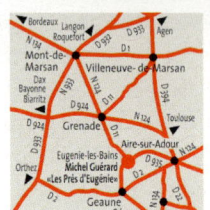

Access: From Bordeaux A63, RN134-Mont-de-Marsan; N124 towards Grenade-sur-Adour.
Airports: Bordeaux (Intl) 150 km, Pau 45 km
Train station: Dax TGV 70 km

Owners: Christine and Michel Guérard
General Manager: Olivier Pollard
Weekly closing: Rest. Gastronomique: lunch and Monday evening (except on the eve of bank holidays, bank holidays and high season)
Annual closing: From January 5th to March 27th and from December 1st to 19th
Currency: Euro (€)
Rates: Grande Cuisine Gourmande 115-160 € s.i. (evening) Carte 100-140 € s.i. Auberge Ferme aux Grives 40 € s.i. **Breakfast:** 28 € s.i.
30 rooms: 260-370 € s.i. **10 suites:** 380-490 € s.i.
Dogs: allowed in Couvent (extra cost)
Accepted cards: AE, DC, MC, VS

More info on www.relaischateaux.com/guerard

Le Parc Victoria

SINCE 1996

5, rue Cepé
64500 Saint-Jean-de-Luz
(Pyrénées-Atlantiques) • France

Tel. : (33) 05 59 26 78 78
Fax : (33) 05 59 26 78 08
parcvictoria@relaischateaux.com

France

Just a stone's throw from the beach, this 19th century private manor house offers tranquillity in 17 elegantly furnished rooms and suites, Art Deco furniture and contemporary bathrooms. It looks onto a spacious park with ancient trees. Simply add the gourmet delights to be enjoyed in the dining room or beside the swimming pool and the pleasures of the nearby coast. The perfect formula for delightful holidays.
Thalassotherapy (500 m). (Other activities P. 629)

Access: A 63, exit Saint-Jean-de-Luz nord; turn right after the 4th traffic light.

Airport: Biarritz Bayonne Anglet (Intl) 15 km
Train station: Saint-Jean-de-Luz 0,5 km

Owner: Roger Larralde
General Manager: Richard Perodeau
Weekly closing: Restaurant: Tuesday
Annual closing:
Hotel: from November 15th to March 15th
Restaurant: from November 1st to April 1st
Currency: Euro (€)
Rates: Menus 35-66 € s.i. Carte 53-68 € s.i.
9 rooms: 152-240 € s.i.
8 suites: 238-394 € s.i.
Breakfast: 14 € s.i.
Dogs: allowed (extra cost)
Golf: 2 km
Accepted cards: AE, DC, JCB, MC, VS

More info on www.relaischateaux.com/parcvictoria

Les Pyrénées

France — SINCE 1988

19, place du Général-de-Gaulle
64220 St-Jean-Pied-de-Port
(Pyrénées-Atlantiques) • France

Tel. : (33) 05 59 37 01 01
Fax : (33) 05 59 37 18 97
pyrenees@relaischateaux.com

Anne-Marie and Firmin Arrambide welcome guests to the elegant rooms of this former coach inn set in one of the most beautiful villages in the Basque country. Les Pyrénées is renowned for its refined cuisine and gourmets will not fail to appreciate this talented chef's innovative creations. Savour «petits poivrons farcis à la morue», a remarkable «saumon frais de l'Adour grillé à la béarnaise» and superb wines.

(Other activities P. 629)

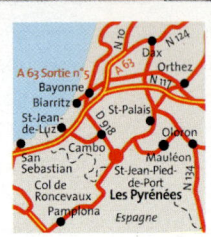

Access: From Bordeaux A 63, exit n° 5 at Bayonne, D 932 Cambo-les-Bains, D 918.

Airports: Biarritz Bayonne Anglet (Intl) 50 km, Bordeaux (Intl) 240 km
Train station: St-Jean-Pied-de-Port 0,5 km

Owners: Mr and Mrs Firmin Arrambide
Weekly closing: Monday evening (from Nov. to March) Tuesday (from Sept. 20th to June 30th)
Annual closing: From January 5th to 28th and from November 20th to December 22nd
Currency: Euro (€)
Rates: Menus 39-88 € s.i. Carte 70 € s.i.
18 rooms: 92-150 € s.i.
3 suites: 199-213 € s.i.
Breakfast: 15 € s.i.
Dogs: allowed
Golf: 50 km
Accepted cards: AE, DC, MC, VS

Firmin Arrambide

More info on www.relaischateaux.com/pyrenees

La Réserve

SINCE 1973

Route de Cordes
81000 Albi
(Tarn) • France

Tel. : (33) 05 63 60 80 80
Fax : (33) 05 63 47 63 60
reservealbi@relaischateaux.com

France

This lovely residence near Albi, on the banks of the Tarn, is a haven of greenery. Air-conditioned and tastefully-decorated guestrooms overlook a park, pond, river and swimming pool. The dining-room and terrace dominating the Tarn offer an idyllic setting for savouring a dutifully regional cuisine, or a «pool» luncheon. You will have the time to leisurely explore the magnificent city of Albi.

Toulouse-Lautrec Museum, Ste-Cécile Cathedral, St-Salvy Romanesque cloister, Gaillac wineries, bastide tour. (Other activities P. 629)

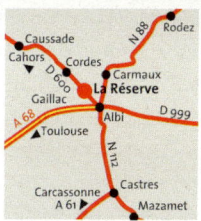

Access: From Toulouse A68 until Albi. At the Albi exit, D600 towards Cordes.
Airports: Toulouse (Intl) 78 km, Albi 8 km

Helipad: N 43° 56' 51" E 2° 07' 47"
Train station: Albi Madeleine 2 km

Owner: SARL J. Rieux and Cie
General Manager: Hélène Hijosa-Rieux
Weekly closing: Rest.: Tuesday (all day) and 2 lunches a week
Annual closing: From November 1st to April 30th
Currency: Euro (€)
Rates: Menus 32-50 € s.i. Carte 45-60 € s.i.
23 rooms: 130-280 € s.i.
1 suite: 360 € s.i.
Breakfast: 15 € s.i.
Dogs: allowed (extra cost)
Golf: 2 courses 6 and 12 km
Accepted cards: AE, DC, JCB, MC, VS

More info on www.relaischateaux.com/reservealbi

France — SINCE 1970

Domaine d'Auriac

Route de Saint-Hilaire, B.P. 554
11009 Carcassonne
(Aude) • France

Tel. : (33) 04 68 25 72 22
Fax : (33) 04 68 47 35 54
auriac@relaischateaux.com

Carcassonne: 2000 years of history. With its fragrant park and only minutes away from the medieval city, the Domaine d'Auriac combines comfort with splendid regional cuisine and fine wines from the legendary vineyards. Swimming pool, tennis and 18-hole golf are ideal for relaxing; abbeys and Cathar sites will immerse you in history from the beautiful gourmet Aude region to the foot of the Cévennes and Pyrénées.

(Other activities P. 629)

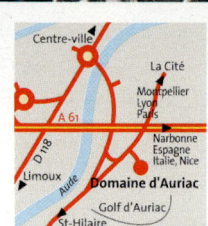

Access: A61, exit Carcassonne ouest, towards «centre-ville» and centre hospitalier.
Airports: Carcassonne-Salvaza (Intl) 7 km, Toulouse (Intl) 100 km, Perpignan (Intl) 100 km
Helipad: N 43° 11' 507" E 002° 20' 175"
Train station: Carcassonne 4 km

Owner: Bernard Rigaudis
General Manager: Anne-Marie Rigaudis
Weekly closing: Off-season: Sunday ev., Monday Season: rest. Tuesday, Wednesday, Friday noon
Annual closing: From Jan. 2nd to Feb. 3rd, from April 27th to May 5th and from Nov. 16th to 24th
Currency: Euro (€)
Rates: Menus 47-73 € s.i. Carte 61-74 € s.i.
26 rooms: 109-421 € s.i.
Breakfast: 18 € s.i.
Dogs: allowed (extra cost) **Golf:** 18 holes
Accepted cards: AE, DC, JCB, MC, VS

More info on www.relaischateaux.com/auriac

Château de Riell

SINCE 1972

Molitg-les-Bains
66500 Prades
(Pyrénées-Orientales) • France

Tel. : (33) 04 68 05 04 40
Fax : (33) 04 68 05 04 37
riell@relaischateaux.com

France

Perched like a grandiose and elegant eyrie opposite the snow-capped peak of Mont Canigou, the Château de Riell guards the portals to the wild Catalan region. This intimate, comfortable haven, echoing with the sound of Pablo Casals's cello and Flamenco guitars, is an idyllic setting in which to savour noble vintages and delicious, sun-drenched cuisine. Its thermal baths endow you with an exquisite sense of well-being.

Thermal baths, hunting, climbing... (Other activities P. 629)

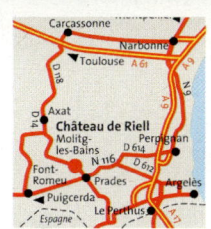

Access: A 9 exit Perpignan South, towards Prades/Andorra; in Prades, towards Molitg-les-Bains (7 km)

Airport: Perpignan (Intl) 45 km
Train station: Prades 7 km

Owner: Biche Barthélémy
Annual closing: From November 3rd to March 31st
Currency: Euro (€)
Rates: Menu 39 € s.i. (week lunch)
Menu-carte 61 € s.i. (dinner, Sunday and holidays)
19 rooms: 157-267 € s.i.
3 suites: 298-336 € s.i.
Breakfast: 16 € s.i.
Dogs: allowed except rest. (extra cost 16 €)
Golf: 15 km (9 holes) - 45 km
Accepted cards: AE, DC, JCB, MC, VS

More info on www.relaischateaux.com/riell

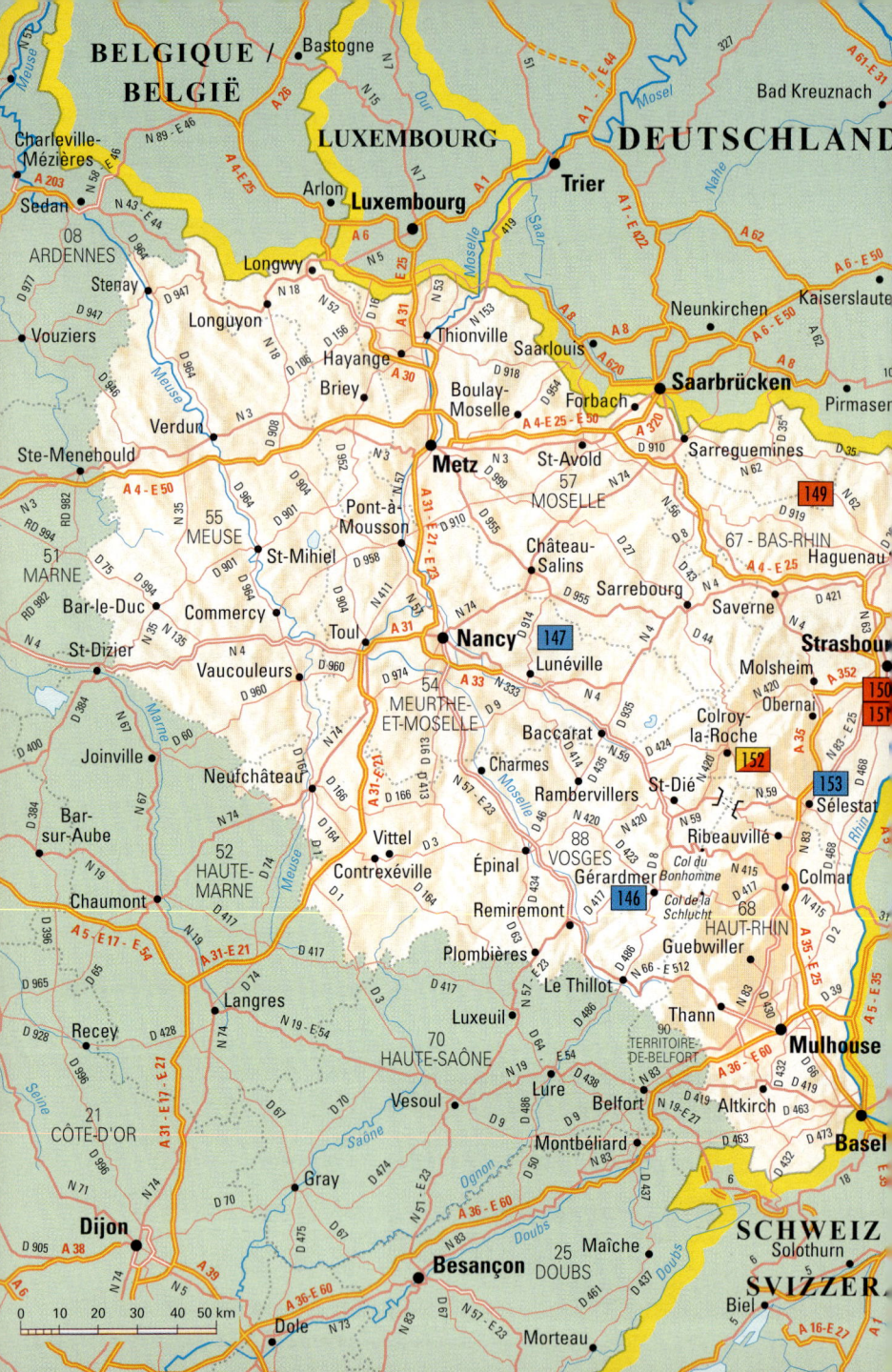

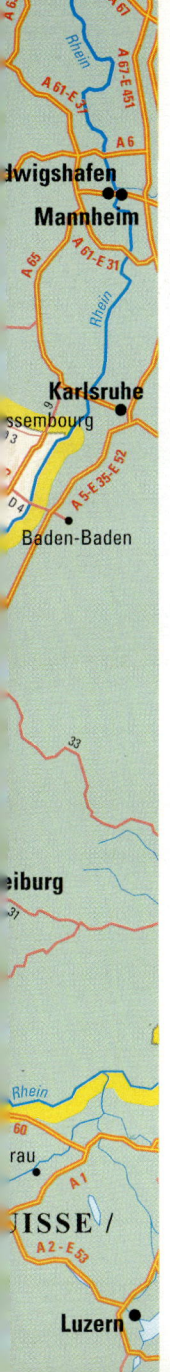

Alsace - Lorraine

France

Properties	Nearest major city	Relais & Châteaux	Relais Gourmands	Page
Abbaye La Pommeraie	Sélestat	✦		153
Arnsbourg (L')	Bitche		☻	149
Bas Rupts et Chalet Fleuri	Colmar	✦		146
Buerehiesel (Restaurant)	Strasbourg		☻	151
Château d'Adoménil	Lunéville	✦		147
Cheneaudière (Hostellerie La)	Sélestat	✦	☻	152
Crocodile (Au)	Strasbourg		☻	150

More info on www.relaischateaux.com

France — SINCE 2002

Bas Rupts et Chalet Fleuri

88400 Gérardmer
(Vosges) • France

Tel. : (33) 03 29 63 09 25
Fax : (33) 03 29 63 00 40
basrupts@relaischateaux.com

Close to Gérardmer, in the Vosges foothills, is the setting of a beautiful property consisting of two buildings, one of them being a huge flower-decked chalet. Between fir trees and waterfalls, delightful, comfortable rooms decorated in the traditional Austrian style. The owner and chef, Michel Philippe, now assisted by his daughter, Sylvie, knows how to welcome you. Guests feel very much at home here.
(Other activities P. 629)

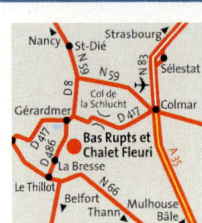

Access: 3 km from Gérardmer, towards La Bresse.

Airport: Strasbourg (Intl) 100 km
Train station: Remiremont 25 km

Owner: Michel Philippe
General Manager: Sylvie Philippe-Witdouck
Open all year
Currency: Euro (€)
Rates: Menus 30-90 € s.i. Carte 58-75 € s.i.
22 rooms: 135-170 € s.i.
2 suites: 235 € s.i.
Breakfast: 13-17 € s.i.
Dogs: allowed
Golf: 50 km
Accepted cards: AE, MC, VS

More info on www.relaischateaux.com/basrupts

Château d'Adoménil

SINCE 1990

Rehainviller
54300 Lunéville
(Meurthe-et-Moselle) • France

Tel. : (33) 03 83 74 04 81
Fax : (33) 03 83 74 21 78
adomenil@relaischateaux.com

France

When the Duke of Lorraine created his own «petit Versailles» he built it in Lunéville. Standing close by in a spacious park, the Château d'Adoménil possesses the same architectural elegance. As the Lorraine light glints on the wood panelling and antique furniture of the château's interior, swans and mallards glide around the moat outside. Refined cuisine is enhanced by a rare Côtes-de-Toul or a fruity Gewurztraminer.

(Other activities P. 629)

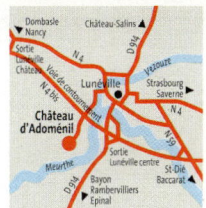

Access: Nancy, exit Lunéville Château, N4, take a right turn at the Lunéville sign (3 km).

Airport: Louvigny 55 km
Train station: Lunéville 8 km

Owner: Michel Million
Weekly closing: Sunday evening (except from April 15th to Nov. 1st), Monday and Tuesday noon
Annual closing: From January 2nd to 31st
Currency: Euro (€)
Rates: Menus 41-79 € s.i. Carte 67-75 € s.i.
7 rooms: 140-165 € s.i.
5 suites: 200-210 € s.i.
Breakfast: 15 € s.i.
Dogs: allowed
Golf: practice on the premises
Accepted cards: AE, DC, JCB, MC, VS

More info on www.relaischateaux.com/adomenil

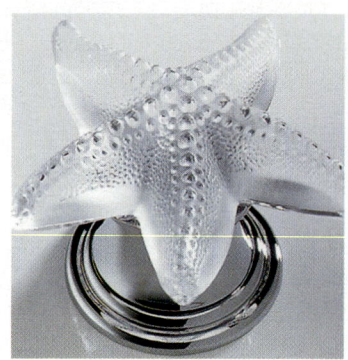

Cristal de LALIQUE

PARIS • LYON • CANNES • GENEVA • UNITED KINGDOM • GERMANY • SPAIN • USA
To get a list of the registered JCD Créations dealers, please contact us
Tel: +33 (0) 3 22 60 20 80 - Fax: +33 (0) 3 22 26 41 01 - Email: contact@thg.fr
Internet: www.thg.fr

L'Arnsbourg

SINCE 2000

18, Untermuhlthal
57230 Baerenthal
(Moselle) • France

Tel. : (33) 03 87 06 50 85
Fax : (33) 03 87 06 57 67
arnsbourg@relaischateaux.com

France

An exceptional forest residence in a magical glade, in the heart of the Northern Vosges. Cathy Klein, a charming hostess who keeps her (blue) eyes on everything, and her brother, Jean-Georges, are one of the most brilliant culinary duos around today. Their style? It is based on lightness and freshness. They conjure up dishes which surprise and seduce. Just one example «grillade de foie de canard au citron confit».

Hunting, fishing. (Other activities P. 629)

Access: From Paris, Strasbourg or Germany, take the A 4, exit Haguenau. Towards Sarreguemines N 62. At Philippsbourg, towards Baerenthal. In Baerenthal, take D 87 towards Zinsviller (4 km).
Airport: Strasbourg (Intl) 70 km
Train station: Niederbronn 15 km

Owners: Klein Family
General Managers: Cathy and Jean-Georges Klein
Weekly closing: Tuesday and Wednesday
Annual closing: January, 1st fortnight in September
Currency: Euro (€)
Rates: Menus 52-115 € s.i.
Carte 99-124 € s.i.
Dogs: allowed
Golf: 15 km
Accepted cards: AE, DC, JCB, MC, VS

Jean-Georges Klein

More info on www.relaischateaux.com/arnsbourg

Au Crocodile

France — SINCE 1984

10, rue de l'Outre
67000 Strasbourg
(Bas-Rhin) • France

Tel. : (33) 03 88 32 13 02
Fax : (33) 03 88 75 72 01
crocodile@relaischateaux.com

Time passes but the Crocodile remains faithful to French culinary traditions. Culinary enthusiasts, Monique and Emile Jung are devoted to cultivating the art of surprising refined palates. They cordially invite you to embark on a delightful journey to the land of flavours and enjoy their poetic adaptations to the changing seasons. Luxury, tranquillity and epicurean voluptuousness are the terms that spring to mind!

Museums, cathedral, Christmas market, astronomical clock. (Other activities P. 629)

Access: From Paris, Colmar and Germany, A4, exit place des Halles, city centre, parking Kléber.

Airport: Strasbourg (Intl) 13 km
Train station: Strasbourg 1 km

Owners: Monique and Emile Jung
Weekly closing: Sunday and Monday except holidays
Annual closing: From July 6th to 28th and from December 24th to January 5th
Currency: Euro (€)
Rates: Menus 58 € s.i. (week lunch) 116 € s.i. Carte 75-108 € s.i.
Dogs: allowed
Golf: 10 km
Accepted cards: AE, DC, JCB, MC, VS

Emile Jung

More info on www.relaischateaux.com/crocodile

Restaurant Buerehiesel

SINCE 1985

4, parc de l'Orangerie
67000 Strasbourg
(Bas-Rhin) • France

Tel. : **(33) 03 88 45 56 65**
Fax : (33) 03 88 61 32 00
buerehiesel@relaischateaux.com

France

This elegant country house in the Orangerie park is an idyllic setting in which to enjoy superb gourmet cuisine. Antoine and Viviane Westermann's culinary talent and their intelligent use of local produce have placed their restaurant at the peak of gastromomic excellence. Savour «poulet de Bresse cuit comme un Baeckeoffe», «brioche caramélisée à la bière, glace à la bière et poire rôtie» and enjoy fine Alsatian wines.

European Parliament, museums, cathedral, astronomical clock, Palais de l'Europe, Alsatian vineyards. (Other activities P. 629)

Access: From the A4 - exit 51, towards the Palais de l'Europe, via av. des Vosges and allée de la Robertsau.

Airport: Strasbourg (Intl) 13 km
Train station: Strasbourg 5 km

Owner: Antoine Westermann
Weekly closing: Tuesday and Wednesday
Annual closing:
From December 31st to January 21st
and from July 29th to August 20th
Currency: Euro (€)
Rates: Menus 100-132 € s.i.
Business menu 52 € s.i. (week lunch)
Carte 85-110 € s.i.
Dogs: allowed
Golf: 10 km
Accepted cards: AE, DC, MC, VS

Antoine Westermann

More info on www.relaischateaux.com/buerehiesel

Hostellerie La Cheneaudière

France — SINCE 1975

67420 Colroy-la-Roche
(Bas-Rhin) • France

Tel. : (33) 03 88 97 61 64
Fax : (33) 03 88 47 21 73
cheneaudiere@relaischateaux.com

Nestling between Alsace and the Vosges mountains, this picturesque residence features calm, comfortable rooms with breathtaking views of the mountains and forests. After relaxing in the sauna, whirlpool or indoor pool, guests can choose between two restaurants, one offering gourmet cuisine, the other regional specialities. Enjoy «tartare de saumon frais d'Ecosse», «filet de chevreuil en habit de choux verts» and prestigious wines. Discovery weeks.

(Other activities P. 629)

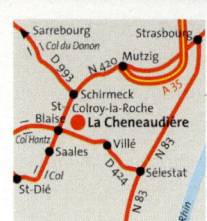

Access: From Strasbourg, towards St-Dié via the col, divided highway towards Schirmeck, then St-Blaise-la-Roche, church on the left.

Airports: Strasbourg (Intl) 45 km, Mulhouse Bâle 107 km
Train station: St Blaise-la-Roche 5 km

Owners: A. and M. François
General Managers: Bossée and François Families
Open all year
Currency: Euro (€)
Rates: Menus Rest. «Les Princes de Salm» 110 € s.i.
Rest. «Les Pastoureaux» 38 € s.i.
22 rooms: 130-260 € s.i.
7 suites: 330-420 € s.i.
Breakfast: 14 € s.i. buffet 19 € s.i.
Dogs: allowed (extra cost)
Golf: Rhinau 45 km
Accepted cards: AE, DC, MC, VS

More info on www.relaischateaux.com/cheneaudiere

Abbaye La Pommeraie

SINCE 1992

8, avenue du Maréchal-Foch
67600 Sélestat
(Bas-Rhin) • France

Tel. : (33) 03 88 92 07 84
Fax : (33) 03 88 92 08 71
pommeraie@relaischateaux.com

France

The Hostellerie Abbaye de Pommeraie, once part of a Cistercian abbey, awaits you in the heart of the finest vineyards. You can be sure of a warm Alsatian welcome and will be thrilled with the attentive service of your hosts, by the elegant, spacious rooms looking onto the old town or garden and by the cuisine which in both the Prieuré and the Apfelstuebel does full justice to the flavours and products of the region.
(Other activities P. 629)

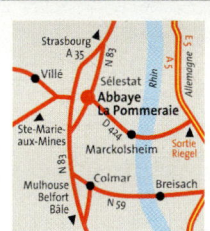

Access: From Strasbourg, towards Colmar via the A35 and N83, exit Sélestat, then follow signs.

Airports: Strasbourg (Intl) 40 km, Colmar 15 km
Train station: Sélestat 0,8 km

Owners: Christiane and Pascal Funaro
Weekly closing: Rest. «Le Prieuré»: Sunday evening and Monday noon
Open all year
Currency: Euro (€)
Rates: Menu 47 € s.i. (wine included) Carte 51-66 € s.i. Winstub 26 € s.i.
10 rooms: 132-193 € s.i.
4 suites: 239-310 € s.i.
Breakfast: 14 € s.i.
Dogs: allowed (extra cost)
Golf: 20 km
Accepted cards: AE, DC, MC, VS

More info on www.relaischateaux.com/pommeraie

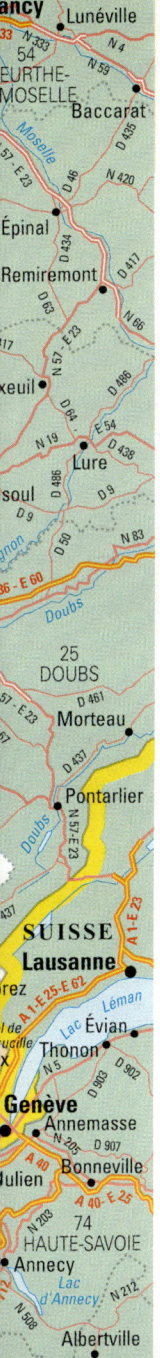

Burgundy Franche-Comté

France

Properties	Nearest major city	Relais & Châteaux	Relais Gourmands	Page
Blanc (Georges)	Mâcon	✦	✦	167
Château de Germigney	Besançon	✦		163
Château d'Igé	Mâcon	✦		165
Côte St-Jacques (La) (J.-M. Lorain)	Joigny	✦	✦	156
Espérance (L')	Vézelay	✦	✦	157
Greuze (Restaurant)	Tournus		✦	164
Lameloise	Chagny	✦	✦	162
Levernois (Hostellerie de)	Beaune	✦	✦	161
Loiseau (Bernard) - La Côte d'Or	Saulieu	✦	✦	159

More info on www.relaischateaux.com

La Côte Saint-Jacques

France — SINCE 1977

14, faubourg de Paris
89300 Joigny
(Yonne) • France

Tel. : (33) 03 86 62 09 70
Fax : (33) 03 86 91 49 70
lorain@relaischateaux.com

Nestling on the banks of the river Yonne, the Côte Saint-Jacques is the ideal setting for people looking for quiet and unspoilt nature, creative and emotive cuisine, a family welcome and the warmth and sophistication of a property where relaxation comes naturally. Whilst you enjoy the unique decor of the restaurant and rooms overlooking the river, your children will be pampered in a specially designed room.

Cooking classes, playroom for children, boat trips. (Other activities P. 629)

Access: From Paris, exit Joigny (A6) n°18 or Sens (A5); from Lyon, exit Joigny Migennes (A6) n°19.

Airports: Paris Orly (Intl) 120 km, Branches 30 km
Helipad: N 47° 59' 32" E 3° 22' 27"
Train station: Joigny 2 km

Owners: Michel and Jean-Michel Lorain
Annual closing: From January 6th to February 5th
Currency: Euro (€)
Rates: Menu 68 € s.i. (2 glasses of wine included) week lunch, menu 99 € s.i. lunch, menu 134 € s.i. lunch-dinner, carte 95-135 € s.i.
23 rooms: 131-270 € s.i.
9 suites: 320-475 € s.i.
Breakfast: 17-26 € s.i.
Dogs: allowed
Golf: 18 and 33 km
Accepted cards: AE, DC, JCB, MC, VS

More info on www.relaischateaux.com/lorain

L'Espérance

89450 St-Père-sous-Vézelay
(Yonne) • France

Tel. : (33) 03 86 33 39 10
Fax : (33) 03 86 33 26 15
esperance@relaischateaux.com

France

SINCE 1977

Born in the village, Marc Meneau is thoroughly versed in the flavours of his region. At the foot of the «eternal hill», in an extremely comfortable and warm setting, you will be able to breathe in and savour creamy peas, carrots foie gras, the best poulardes de Bresse. A superb wine list. Charming rooms in the heart of leafy countryside with many rivers.
Climbing. (Other activities P. 629)

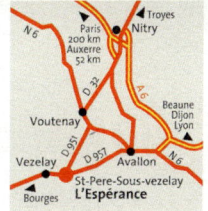

Access: From Paris, take the A6 to exit Nitry, D 944 - D 32 towards Vézelay; at Voutenay, take the N6.

Airports: Paris Orly (Intl) 180 km, Auxerre 50 km
Helipad: N 47° 27' 784" E 003° 46' 285"
Train station: Avallon 13 km

Owner: Marc Meneau
Weekly closing:
Restaurant: Tuesday (off-season),
Tuesday noon (season), Wednesday noon
Annual closing: February
Currency: Euro (€)
Rates: Menus 84-130 € s.i.
167 € s.i. (weekend and bank holidays)
Carte 91-137 € s.i..
21 rooms: 167-228 € s.i.
6 suites: starting at 275 € s.i.
Breakfast: 26 € s.i.
Dogs: allowed
Accepted cards: AE, DC, JCB, MC, VS

More info on www.relaischateaux.com/esperance

Bernard Loiseau - La Côte d'Or

21210 Saulieu
(Côte-d'Or) • France

Tel. : **(33) 03 80 90 53 53**
Fax : (33) 03 80 64 08 92
loiseau@relaischateaux.com

France

SINCE 1975

Gourmets flock to this idyllic country haven to savour the culinary marvels created by Bernard Loiseau. Drawing subtle flavours from the best local produce, Loiseau has a fine eye for detail and each dish is an artistic masterpiece. Savour the superb «blanc de volaille fermière lardé de truffes et le foie gras chaud de canard au jus de truffe», accompanied by an excellent local wine. Elegant guestrooms in a fine Burgundian residence, with a beautiful garden.

Burgundy wineries, Morvan park. Castles, abbaye de Fontenay, shop, billiards. (Other activities P. 629)

Access: From Paris, A6, exit Avallon or Bierre. From Dijon or Lyon, A38 - A6, exit Pouilly-en-Auxois.
Airports: Paris Orly (Intl) 200 km, Dijon 70 km
Train station: Montbard 40 km

Owner: Bernard Loiseau S.A.
General Manager: Dominique Loiseau
Open all year
Currency: Euro (€)
Rates: Menus 124 € s.i. (except dinner on weekend) 116-182 € s.i. Carte 130-175 € s.i.
20 rooms: week, off-season 125-195 € s.i. weekend, season 195-300 € s.i.
12 suites: week, off-season 230-350 € s.i. weekend, season 325-430 € s.i.
Breakfast: 17-28 € s.i.
Dogs: allowed
Golf: Chailly 25 km
Accepted cards: AE, DC, JCB, MC, VS

More info on www.relaischateaux.com/loiseau

Hostellerie de Levernois

SINCE 1991

Route de Combertault, Levernois,
21200 Beaune
(Côte-d'Or) • France

Tel. : (33) 03 80 24 73 58
Fax : (33) 03 80 22 78 00
levernois@relaischateaux.com

France

This picturesque residence, set in a park of oaks, cedars and weeping willows, offers a variety of bright, comfortable rooms. Lulled by the sound of the river splashing against the ancient water-wheel, guests will enjoy undisturbed peace in this idyllic country haven. Savour gourmet cuisine, featuring delicacies such as «petits escargots de Bourgogne en cocotte lutée», and choose from more than 800 excellent vintages.

(Other activities P. 629)

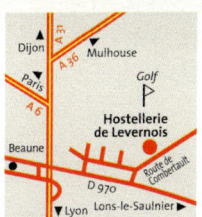

Access: From Lyons-Paris, exit 24-1 Beaune-Chagny; D970 towards Lons-le-Saunier; Levernois, signs «Jean Crotet».

Airport: Dijon 50 km
Helipad: N 46° 59' 47" E 004° 53' 01"
Train station: Beaune 5 km

Owner: SA Hostellerie Levernois
General Manager: Christophe Crotet
Weekly closing: Sunday evenings, Tuesday, Wednesday at lunch (from Oct. 31st to April 1st)
Annual closing: From Dec. 1st to January 3rd
Currency: Euro (€)
Rates: Menus 23-30 € s.i.(week lunch) 104 € s.i.
Carte 69-99 € s.i.
15 rooms: 168-335 € s.i.
1 suite: 260-298 € s.i.
Breakfast: 19 € s.i.
Dogs: allowed **Golf:** 100 m
Accepted cards: AE, DC, MC, VS

More info on www.relaischateaux.com/levernois

Lameloise

France — SINCE 1990

36, place d'Armes
71150 Chagny
(Saône-et-Loire) • France

Tel. : (33) 03 85 87 65 65
Fax : (33) 03 85 87 03 57
lameloise@relaischateaux.com

The Lameloise family has been established on the picturesque square of Chagny for over a hundred years now in a beautiful XVth century house with gleaming wooden floors. Their renowned cuisine is inspired by Burgundy tradition, and the «raviolis d'escargots de Bourgogne dans leur bouillon d'ail doux» and «pigeonneau rôti à l'émiettée de truffes» are culinary masterpieces. The cellar is a treasure trove of fine vintages.
(Other activities P. 629)

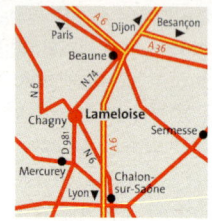

Access: From Lyon, A6 exit Chalon-Nord, RN 6, Chagny, near the post office; from Paris, A6 exit Beaune.

Airports: Lyon St-Exupéry (Intl) 150 km, Dijon 50 km
Train station: Chagny 1 km

Owner: Jacques Lameloise
Weekly closing: Restaurant: Tuesday and Thursday at lunch, Wednesday
Hotel: Wednesday
Annual closing: From December 18th to January 23rd
Currency: Euro (€)
Rates: Menus 85-115 € s.i.
Carte 75-105 € s.i.
16 rooms: 125-260 € s.i.
Breakfast: 20 € s.i.
Dogs: allowed
Golf: 15 km
Accepted cards: AE, DC, JCB, MC, VS

More info on www.relaischateaux.com/lameloise

Château de Germigney

Rue Edgar-Faure
39600 Port-Lesney
(Jura) • France

Tel. : (33) 03 84 73 85 85
Fax : (33) 03 84 73 88 88
germigney@relaischateaux.com

France

SINCE 1999

This XVIIIth century manor was built amidst a landscape of forests and lakes. The comfortably restored rooms have been redesigned by the interior designer, Roland Schön. An eclectic decoration, combining contemporary and Napoleon III styles. In the restaurant, you will succumb to the Franche-Comté products prepared in yellow Jura wine, alongside the light savours of the Mediterranean.

Climbing, hot-air balloon. (Other activities P. 629)

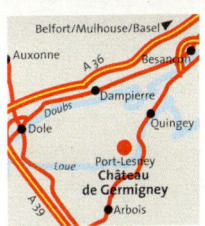

Access: From Paris: A6, A36, A39 exit Dole, D472 towards Villers-Farlay, Mouchard, N83. From Lyon: A39 towards Bourg-en-Bresse, exit Pontarlier, N83 towards Besançon. From Basel: A35, A36, exit Besançon, N83 towards Lons-le-Saunier.
Airports: Geneva (Intl) 120 km, Dijon 100 km
Train station: Mouchard 1 km

Owners: Roland and Verena Schön
General Managers: Vanessa and Arnauld Baert
Weekly closing: Restaurant: Tuesday
Annual closing: From January 1st to 31st and from February 16th to March 6th
Currency: Euro (€)
Rates: Menus 22 € s.i. (week lunch) 31-77 € s.i. Carte 38-57 € s.i.
16 rooms: 110-215 € s.i.
4 suites: 200-275 € s.i.
Breakfast: 16 € s.i.
Dogs: allowed **Golf:** 30 km (18 holes)
Accepted cards: AE, DC, MC, VS

More info on www.relaischateaux.com/germigney

Restaurant Greuze

France — SINCE 1978

Rue Albert-Thibaudet
71700 Tournus
(Saône-et-Loire) • France

Tel. : (33) 03 85 51 13 52
Fax : (33) 03 85 51 75 42
greuze@relaischateaux.com

Restaurant Greuze, named after the renowned XVIIIth century painter, has become a fashionable rendez-vous for gourmets and celebrities. For a quarter of a century, Jean Ducloux, one of the highest stars in the firmament of French gastronomy, has perpetuated culinary tradition with his «pâté en croûte Alexandre Dumaine», «quenelles de brochets Racouchot» and «poulet de Bresse sauté Jean Ducloux». Savour superb vintage Burgundies.

Saint-Philibert Abbey, Greuze museum, Solutré museum. (Other activities P. 629)

Access: Motorway A6, exit Tournus; near the Saint-Philibert Abbey.

Airports: Lyon St-Exupéry (Intl) 100 km, Dijon 80 km
Train station: Tournus 1 km

Owner: Jean Ducloux
Annual closing: From November 17th to December 10th
Currency: Euro (€)
Rates: Menus 45-91 € s.i.
Carte starting at 46 € s.i.
Dogs: allowed
Golf: 15 km
Accepted cards: AE, DC, JCB, MC, VS

Jean Ducloux

More info on www.relaischateaux.com/greuze

Château d'Igé

SINCE 1972

71960 Igé
(Saône-et-Loire) • France

Tel. : (33) 03 85 33 33 99
Fax : (33) 03 85 33 41 41
ige@relaischateaux.com

France

Set in the heart of the Mâcon vineyards, a region rich in Romanesque architecture, the Château d'Igé, fortified in 1235, displays its feudal towers in the midst of a beautiful garden. You will enjoy a warm welcome, charming rooms, the refined cuisine of the chef featuring mainly local specialities and a tranquil and authentic setting. Flower-filled terrace. Regional Burgundy wines. A veritable haven!

1 h 45 from Paris by the TGV. Romanesque church tours, visit of Cluny, Cormatin, Tournus, Lamartine tour, Solutré, caves, walks, the wine trail, tasting. (Other activities P. 629)

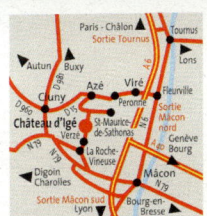

Access: From Lyon, A 6 exit Mâcon south, N 79 towards Moulins, Montceau, exit La Roche-Vineuse, towards La Roche-Vineuse, Verzé, Igé. A 40 exit Mâcon center.
Airport: Lyon St-Exupéry (Intl) 90 km
Train station: Mâcon Loche 12 km

Owner: Françoise Germond-Lieury
Weekly closing: Restaurant: all lunch from Monday to Thursday (except bank holidays)
Annual closing: From December 1st to March 1st
Currency: Euro (€)
Rates: Menus 35-46-54-69 € s.i.
Carte 34-57 € s.i.
8 rooms: 91-142 € s.i.
6 suites: 172-206 € s.i.
Breakfast: 14 € s.i.
Dogs: allowed (extra cost)
Golf: 12 km
Accepted cards: AE, DC, MC, VS

More info on www.relaischateaux.com/ige

Georges Blanc

SINCE 1972

01540 Vonnas
(Ain) • France

Tel. : (33) 04 74 50 90 90
Fax : (33) 04 74 50 08 80
blanc@relaischateaux.com

France

In Vonnas one of the most flower-bedecked villages in France, the Blanc's Inn has existed since 1872. In the Bresse region, Georges Blanc's cuisine blends authentic tradition and innovation throughout the seasons. In this unique setting, you will enjoy the warm welcome of the Blanc family and its team. On the nearby market square, another restaurant «L'Ancienne Auberge», upholds traditional family-style cuisine.

Museums, hiking, tours, Bresse Farms. (Other activities P. 629)

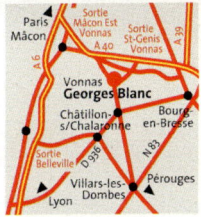

Access: 1 h from Geneva beween Bourg-en-Bresse and Mâcon. Exits Vonnas on A40 linking A6 and A39.
Airport: Lyon St-Exupéry (Intl) 80 km
Helipad: N 46° 13' 120" E 4° 59' 030"
Train station: Mâcon Loché 20 km

Owner: Georges Blanc
Weekly closing: Rest.: Wednesday noon, Monday and Tuesday (except holidays)
Annual closing: From January 2nd to February 1st
Currency: Euro (€)
Rates: Menus 105-240 € s.i. Carte 120 € s.i.
L'Ancienne Auberge 26 € s.i.
21 rooms: 135-310 € s.i.
9 suites: 340-530 € s.i.
Breakfast: 23 € s.i.
Dogs: allowed
Golf: 12 km
Accepted cards: AE, DC, JCB, MC, VS

More info on www.relaischateaux.com/blanc

Lyon
Rhône Valley

France

Properties	Nearest major city	Relais & Châteaux	Relais Gourmands	Page
Auberge et Clos des Cimes	St-Etienne	⚜	◉	175
Chapel (Alain)	Lyon	⚜	◉	171
Château de Codignat	Clermont-Ferrand	⚜		173
Château de Faverges-de-la-Tour	La Tour-du-Pin	⚜		182
Léon de Lyon	Lyon		◉	177
Orsi (Pierre) (Restaurant)	Lyon		◉	179
Pic	Valence	⚜	◉	183
Poularde (Hostellerie La)	St-Etienne	⚜	◉	174
Pyramide (La)	Lyon	⚜	◉	181
Troisgros (La Maison)	Roanne	⚜	◉	172
Villa Florentine	Lyon	⚜		180

More info on www.relaischateaux.com

*126 prestigious "Grands Crus"
commit themselves to sharing their values
in the same respec
of the Charter that binds them*

Honorary members
Château Cheval Blanc
Château Mouton Rothschild
Château d'Yquem

Members
Château Angélus
Château Balestard la Tonnelle
Château Bastor-Lamontagne
Château Beau Séjour Bécot
Château Beaumont
Château Beauregard
Château Belgrave
Château Beychevelle
Château Bouscaut
Château Branaire-Ducru
Château Brane-Cantenac
Château Broustet
Château Camensac
Château Canon
Château Canon-la-Gaffelière
Château Cantemerle
Château Cantenac Brown
Château Cap de Mourlin
Château Carbonnieux
Château Chasse-Spleen

Château Citran
Château Clarke
Château Clerc Milon
Château Climens
Château Clinet
Château Cos d'Estournel
Château Cos Labory
Château Coufran
Château Croizet-Bages
Château d'Angludet
Château d'Armailhac
Château Dassault
Château Dauzac
Château de Chantegrive
Château de Fieuzal
Château de France
Château de Lamarque
Château de Malle
Château de Rayne Vigneau
Château Doisy-Védrines
Château Dufort-Vivens
Château du Tertre
Château Ferrande
Château Ferrière
Château Figeac
Château Fonplégade

Château Fonréaud
Château Fourcas-Dupré
Château Fourcas-Hosten
Château Franc-Mayne
Château Gazin
Château Giscours
Château Grand Mayne
Château Grand-Puy Ducasse
Château Greysac
Château Gruaud Larose
Château Guiraud
Château Haut-Bages Libéral
Château Haut-Bailly
Château Haut-Bergey
Château Kirwan
Château L'Evangile
Château La Cabanne
Château La Conseillante
Château La Couspaude
Château La Croix de Gay
Château La Dominique
Château La Gaffelière
Château La Lagune
Château La Louvière
Château La Pointe
Château La Tour Blanche

Château La Tour Carnet
Château La Tour de By
Château La Tour Figeac
Château Labégorce
Château Lafaurie-Peyraguey
Château Lafon-Rochet
Château Lagrange
Château Langoa Barton
Château Larcis Ducasse
Château Larmande
Château Larrivet-Haut-Brion
Château Lascombes
Château Latour-Martillac
Château Léoville Barton
Château Léoville Poyferré
Château Les Carmes Haut-Brion
Château Les Ormes de Pez
Château Lynch-Bages
Château Lynch-Moussas
Château Malartic-Lagravière
Château Malescasse
Château Malescot St-Exupery
Château Marquis d'Alesme
Château Marquis de Terme
Château Maucaillou
Château Monbrison

Château Nairac
Château Olivier
Château Pape Clément
Château Pavie
Château Pavie Decesse
Château Petit Village
Château Phélan Ségur
Château Pichon Longueville
Château Pichon Longueville
   Comtesse de Lalande
Château Picque Caillou
Château Pontet-Canet
Château Poujeaux
Château Prieuré-Lichine
Château Rahoul
Château Rauzan Gassies
Château Rauzan-Ségla
Château Sigalas-Rabaud
Château Siran
Château Smith Haut Lafitte
Château Suduiraut
Château Talbot
Château Troplong Mondot
Clos Fourtet
Domaine de Chevalier
Vieux Château Certan

Union des Grands Crus de Bordeaux

10, cours du XXX Juillet F-33000 Bordeaux - Fax : +33 (0)5 56 51 64 12
Internet : ugcb.net

Alain Chapel

SINCE 1973

01390 Mionnay
(Ain) • France

Tel. : (33) 04 78 91 82 02
Fax : (33) 04 78 91 82 37
chapel@relaischateaux.com

France

Enjoy exquisite hospitality at this elegant country house, set in the picturesque village of Mionnay. Alain Chapel's renowned concept of taste, based on blending regional tradition with refined gourmet techniques, is today perpetuated by Suzanne Chapel and chef Philippe Jousse. Savour «soufflé léger aux noisettes et thym frais, sorbet au citron de Menton» and other sublime specialities accompanied by fine wines.

Pérouges (medieval city), ornithological park. (Other activities P. 629)

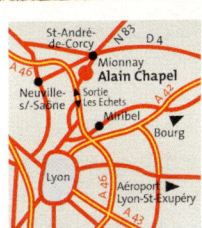

Access: Take the A 46 beltway - exit Les Echets, towards Villars-les-Dombes, N 83.
Airport: Lyon St-Exupéry (Intl) 25 km

Train station: Lyon Part-Dieu 20 km

Owners: Chapel Family
General Manager: Suzanne Chapel
Weekly closing: Monday and Tuesday all day, Thursday at lunch
Annual closing: January
Currency: Euro (€)
Rates: Menus 96-115-130 € s.i. Carte 96 € s.i. Week lunch 60 € s.i. (Wednesday, Friday)
12 rooms: 107-130 € s.i.
Breakfast: 15 € s.i.
Dogs: allowed (extra cost)
Golf: 2 km
Accepted cards: AE, DC, JCB, MC, VS

More info on www.relaischateaux.com/chapel

La Maison Troisgros

France — SINCE 1966

Place de la Gare
42300 Roanne
(Loire) • France

Tel. : (33) 04 77 71 66 97
Fax : (33) 04 77 70 39 77
troisgros@relaischateaux.com

The Troisgros Family, today Michel and Marie-Pierre, perpetuate French gastronomic tradition with flair. Savour their «écrevisses en court-bouillon de petits légumes aigres-doux». Enjoy the infinitely subtle cuisine, the superb wine cellar and the very comfortable modern rooms. There is also «Le Central» next door: a cafe-grocery that proposes dishes combining tradition and fancy and many take-away delicacies.

(Other activities P. 629)

Access: From Paris, A 6 - exit South Chalon, towards Paray-le-Monial and Roanne. From Paris, A 71 - exit Saint-Germain Laval.
From Lyon, N 7 towards Roanne.
Airports: Lyon St-Exupéry (Intl) 110 km, Roanne 6 km
Train station: Roanne 0,1 km

Owners: Marie-Pierre and Michel Troisgros
Weekly closing: Tuesday and Wednesday
Annual closing: February school holidays and first half of August
Currency: Euro (€)
Rates: Menus 130-160 € s.i.
Carte 140 € s.i. Le Central 30 € s.i.
13 rooms: 155-280 € s.i.
5 suites: 340-380 € s.i.
Breakfast: 24 € s.i.
Dogs: allowed (extra cost)
Golf: 2 km
Accepted cards: AE, DC, JCB, MC, VS

Michel Troisgros

More info on www.relaischateaux.com/troisgros

Château de Codignat

SINCE 1975

Lezoux
63190 Bort-l'Etang
(Puy-de-Dôme) • France

Tel. : **(33) 04 73 68 43 03**
Fax : (33) 04 73 68 93 54
codignat@relaischateaux.com

France

This XVth century château, 20 minutes away from the Vulcania Park, with its red-tiled roof and medieval turrets offer superb views across the Auvergne volcanos. The past's grandeur is reflected in the guestrooms' antique furniture, tapestries and four poster-beds while modern comforts include splendid «trompe l'œil» bathrooms and private whirlpools. After a helicopter tour of Romanesque churches and Auvergne castles, enjoy a romantic dinner by candlelight.

Karting, flight over volcanos in private plane, riding school. Vulcania Park, the trail of Auvergne's castles, Romanesque churches. (Other activities P. 629)

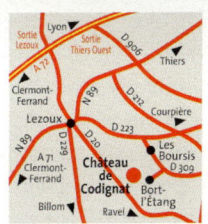

Access:
From Clermont-Ferrand, motorway towards Lyon, exit 1 Lezoux, towards town centre, and follow Courpière Road, towards Bort-l'Etang.
Airport: Clermont-Ferrand (Intl) 20 mn
Helipad: N 45° 46' 981" E 003° 24' 754"
Train station: Lezoux 4 km

Owners: Monique Barberan and Guy Vidal
General Managers: Guy Vidal and Denis Lesage
Annual closing: From Nov. 3rd to March 20th
Currency: Euro (€)
Rates: Menus 48-65-90 € s.i.
Carte starting at 80 € s.i.
15 rooms: 150-310 € s.i. 335-455 € s.i.
(half board - 2 pers.) **4 suites:** 320-450 € s.i.
500-600 € s.i. (half board - 2 pers.)
Breakfast: 14 € s.i.
Dogs: allowed (welcome) **Golf:** 35 km
Accepted cards: AE, DC, MC, VS

More info on www.relaischateaux.com/codignat

Hostellerie La Poularde

France — SINCE 1974

42210 Montrond-les-Bains
(Loire) • France

Tel. : (33) 04 77 54 40 06
Fax : (33) 04 77 54 53 14
poularde@relaischateaux.com

True to its post house origins, La Poularde's rooms are decorated in a fusion of traditional and contemporary style. Virtuoso chef Gilles Etéocle, recipient of the «Meilleur Ouvrier de France» award, creates a gastronomic symphony of flavours. Exquisite seasonal culinary delights are enhanced by the sommelier, elected Best French Sommelier.

Castle visit, museums, walks, thermal baths, casino, œnological evenings (pairing wine and food). (Other activities P. 629)

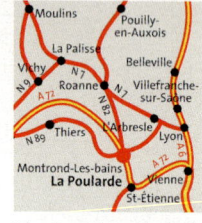

Access: From Saint-Etienne, A 72 towards Clermont-Ferrand, exit N°7 Montrond-Montbrison. **Airports:** Saint-Etienne (Intl) 8 km, Lyon St-Exupéry (Intl) 70 km

Owners: Gilles and Monique Etéocle
Weekly closing: Hotel: Sunday (from November 1st to April 30th), Monday
Rest.: Sunday evening (from November 1st to April 30th), Monday and Tuesday noon
Annual closing: From January 2nd to 22nd and from August 3rd to 19th
Currency: Euro (€)
Rates: Menus 45 € s.i. (lunch), 60-108 € s.i. (week-end) Carte 95-110 € s.i.
7 rooms: 78-117 € s.i. **7 suites:** 123-229 € s.i.
Breakfast: 16 € s.i.
Dogs: allowed **Golf:** Forez 3 km
Accepted cards: AE, DC, JCB, MC, VS

Gilles Etéocle

More info on www.relaischateaux.com/poularde

Auberge et Clos des Cimes

SINCE 1997

Place de l'Eglise
43290 St-Bonnet-le-Froid
(Haute-Loire) • France

Tel. : (33) 04 71 59 93 72
Fax : (33) 04 71 59 93 40
cimes@relaischateaux.com

France

Between Velay and Vivarais, prolong your stay in one of these lovely comfortable rooms overlooking valleys and mountains. Then meet Régis whose cuisine reflects the magnificent natural surroundings. Savour the «ragoût aux lentilles vertes du Puy et œuf fumé», «brochette "Margaridou"» and «agneau en croûte de foin de cistre». Michelle, his wife, will suggest the fine Rhone valley wines of Condrieu and Hermitage.
Mountain-biking. (Other activities P. 629)

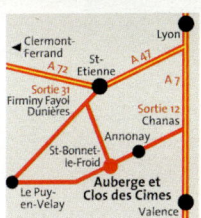

Altitude: 1125 metres.
Access: From Lyon: A 7 south, exit Chanas-Annonay, Le-Puy-en-Velay From Clermont-Ferrand: A 47 towards St-Etienne, exit n°31, then Dunières. In Dunières towards St-Bonnet-le-Froid.
Airport: Lyon St-Exupéry (Intl) 100 km
Train station: St-Etienne 50 km

Owner: Régis Marcon
General Managers:
Michèle Marcon, François Lofficial
Weekly closing: Monday evening (March, April, November and December), Tuesday, Wednesday
Annual closing: From November 15th to Easter
Currency: Euro (€)
Rates: Menus 75-110 € s.i.
Carte 70-105 € s.i.
12 rooms: 135-211 € s.i.
Breakfast: 16 € s.i.
Dogs: allowed **Golf:** 15 and 30 km
Accepted cards: AE, MC, VS

Régis Marcon

More info on www.relaischateaux.com/cimes

Carreaux

Arts de la table

Salles de bains

Wellness

My House of Villeroy & Boch

Tout ce qu'il faut pour un bel intérieur :
équipements de salles de bains, carreaux,
accessoires d'intérieur, et arts de la table.

Villeroy & Boch Arts de la Table
5, avenue des Morillons
F-95140 Garges les Gonesse

www.villeroy-boch.fr

Léon de Lyon

SINCE 1985

1, rue Pléney (corner of the rue du Plâtre)
69001 Lyon
(Rhône) • France

Tel. : (33) 04 72 10 11 12
Fax : (33) 04 72 10 11 13
leon@relaischateaux.com

France

Recently, a new dining room has added to the standing of the restaurant. Jean-Paul Lacombe continues to conjure up refined and enhanced Lyonnaise cuisine that is both imaginative and light. A superb wine cellar that boasts the finest regional appellations: Beaujolais, Côtes-du-Rhône and Burgundy. Various regional collections adorn the walls of the restaurant; sixty old paintings depict the theme of the kitchen boy.

Opera, traboules visit, Canuts Museum, Basilica of Fourvière.
(Other activities P. 629)

Access: On the peninsula, toward place des Terreaux, before the plaza (at the corner of the rue du Plâtre).

Airport: Lyon St-Exupéry (Intl) 20 km
Train station: Lyon Part-Dieu 2 km

Owners: Fabienne and Jean-Paul Lacombe
Weekly closing: Sunday and Monday
Annual closing: From August 3rd to 25th
Currency: Euro (€)
Rates: Menus 55 € s.i. (lunch) 95-130 € s.i.
Carte 91 € s.i.
Dogs: allowed
Golf: 20 km
Accepted cards: AE, JCB, MC, VS

Jean-Paul Lacombe

More info on www.relaischateaux.com/leon

Porsche a choisi **Mobil 1** www.porsche.com

Porsche Cayenne
La forêt noire libère enfin son secret

Restaurant Pierre Orsi

SINCE 1981

3, place Kléber
69006 Lyon
(Rhône) • France

Tel. : (33) 04 78 89 57 68
Fax : (33) 04 72 44 93 34
orsi@relaischateaux.com

France

In an ancient manor close to the Tête-d'Or park, Pierre Orsi, «Meilleur Ouvrier de France», has been conjuring up imaginative cuisine fully in tune with the seasons since 1975. Against a sumptuous backdrop, Geneviève Orsi enthusiastically describes specialities like «foie gras chaud de canard poêlé sur nid d'épinards» and «marinière de loup et rouget au basilic». Fine selection of Mâcon-Clessés and French vintages.

Theme nights, lounges. Visits to the vaulted cellar. (Other activities P. 629)

Access: Near the Tête d'Or-park, the Cité Internationale, and the Part-Dieu railway station.

Airports: Lyon St-Exupéry (Intl) 20 km, Lyon-Bron 10 km
Train station: Lyon Part-Dieu 1 km

Owner: Pierre Orsi
General Manager: Geneviève Orsi
Weekly closing: Sunday and Monday
Open all year
Currency: Euro (€)
Rates: Menus 43 € s.i. (lunch) 60-77-107 € s.i. Carte 60-84 € s.i.
Dogs: allowed
Golf: 20 km
Accepted cards: AE, JCB, MC, VS

Pierre Orsi

More info on www.relaischateaux.com/orsi

France — SINCE 1996

Villa Florentine

25-27, montée Saint-Barthélemy
69005 Lyon
(Rhône) • France

Tel. : (33) 04 72 56 56 56
Fax : (33) 04 72 40 90 56
florentine@relaischateaux.com

This splendid villa, offering sublime panoramic views of Lyon, certainly lives up to its name. Everything from its elegant façade to its sunny rooms, furnished with a mixture of Renaissance refinement and contemporary Italian design, has a sumptuous Florentine feel to it. Savour refined cuisine and superb Rhône vintages at the restaurant «Les Terrasses de Lyon», while contemplating the city lights twinkling below.

Visits : Fourvière basilica, St-Jean cathedral, Gallo-Roman museum... (Other activities P. 629)

Access: From the Saône docks (Old Lyon), go to the gare Saint-Paul, then follow signs to the basilique Fourvière.

Airports: Lyon St-Exupéry (Intl) 25 km, Lyon-Bron 10 km
Train station: Lyon Part-Dieu 5 km

Owners: Giorgi Family
General Manager: Annie Blancardi
Open all year
Currency: Euro (€)
Rates: Menus 53-69-100 € s.i. (except holidays) Carte 28-55 € s.i
20 rooms: 230-762 € s.i.
8 suites: 382-762 € s.i.
Breakfast: 20 € s.i.
Dogs: allowed in some rooms (extra cost)
Golf: 15 km
Accepted cards: AE, DC, JCB, MC, VS

More info on www.relaischateaux.com/florentine

La Pyramide

SINCE 1999

14, bd Fernand-Point
38200 Vienne
(Isère) • France

Tel. : (33) 04 74 53 01 96
Fax : (33) 04 74 85 69 73
pyramide@relaischateaux.com

France

«Il n'y a de restaurant que Point. Un point, c'est tout», to paraphrase a famous Sacha Guitry quotation. Yet, for Patrick Henriroux inheriting the restaurant does not signify simply continuing a famous tradition but innovating it as well. A stay at La Pyramide remains an unforgettable experience. The superb cuisine of the South of France and the Dauphiné region is a delight. Savour «moelleux de dormeurs à l'artichaut cru comme en Provence». Then, retire to one of the extremely charming guestrooms: the best way to know the hotel.

Horseback riding. (Other activities P. 629)

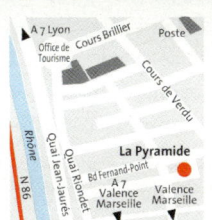

Access: From Vienne, follow signs for «Pyramide». Do not follow signs for «centre ville».

Airport: Lyon St-Exupéry (Intl) 30 km
Train station: Vienne 2 km

Owners: Pascale and Patrick Henriroux
Weekly closing: Rest.: Tuesday and Wednesday
Annual closing: February
Currency: Euro (€)
Rates: Menus 80-115 € s.i. Carte 107 € s.i.
20 rooms: 135-200 € s.i.
4 suites: 235-320 € s.i.
Breakfast: 16-19 € s.i.
Dogs: allowed (extra cost)
Golf: 25 km
Accepted cards: AE, DC, JCB, MC, VS

More info on www.relaischateaux.com/pyramide

France · SINCE 1983

Château de Faverges-de-la-Tour

38110 Faverges-de-la-Tour
(Isère) • France

Tel. : (33) 04 74 97 42 52
Fax : (33) 04 74 88 86 40
faverges@relaischateaux.com

Guests will be enchanted by this elegant residence set amidst a sea of greenery in the picturesque Dauphiné countryside. They will also be impressed by the Tournier family's warm welcome and generous hospitality. The cosy bedrooms are bright and comfortable, the lounges grand and tastefully decorated. Dinner, served in the candlelit splendour of the vaulted cellars, is a feast of regional cuisine and fine Savoy wines.

Hot-air ballooning... (Other activities P. 629)

Access: From Geneva A43 (by Annecy), exit St-Genix/Giers. From Lyon A43 (by St-Exupéry), exit La Tour-du-Pin.

Airport: Lyon St-Exupéry (Intl) 42 km
Helipad: N 45° 35' 26" E 005° 32' 09"
Train station: La Tour-du-Pin 10 km

Owners: Tournier Family
General Manager: Christophe Bricaud
Annual closing: From October to May
Currency: Euro (€)
Rates: Menus 48-60-75 € s.i.
Carte 50-70 € s.i.
34 rooms: 165-360 € s.i.
2 suites: 460-500 € s.i.
Breakfast: 15-20 € s.i.
Dogs: allowed (extra cost)
Golf: private (9 holes)
Accepted cards: AE, DC, JCB, MC, VS

More info on www.relaischateaux.com/faverges

Pic

SINCE 1973

285, avenue Victor-Hugo
26000 Valence
(Drôme) • France

Tel. : (33) 04 75 44 15 32
Fax : (33) 04 75 40 96 03
Auberge du Pin : (33) 04 75 44 53 86
pic@relaischateaux.com

France

Granddaughter of André, daughter of Jacques, Anne Pic upholds tradition with flair, revealing the true nature of products. Enjoy the «pigeon en croûte de noix» and the «filet de loup au caviar» of this innovative hundred-year-old restaurant. The chef's husband David warmly welcomes guests, suggesting vintages from the fine cellar. Minutes away, the Auberge du Pin offers the charms of a simpler Provence-style cuisine.

Discovery of the Drôme and of the Ardèche, visit to wine cellars. (Other activities P. 629)

Access: From Lyon or Marseille, A 7, exit Valence S; towards city centre V.-Hugo, follow signs.
Airports: Lyon St-Exupéry (Intl) 100 km, Valence 10 km
Helipad: N 44° 54' 56" E 4° 58' 07"
Train station: Valence 1 km

Owners: David and Anne Pic-Sinapian
Weekly closing: Rest.: Tuesday (from November to March), Sunday evening and Monday
Auberge du Pin: Wednesday (from Oct. to May)
Annual closing: Rest.: From January 1st to 23rd
Currency: Euro (€)
Rates: Menus 49 € s.i. week lunch (drinks incl.) 100-130 € s.i. Carte 75-130 € s.i.
Auberge du Pin 28 € s.i.
12 rooms: 130-280 € s.i. **3 suites:** 200-350 € s.i.
Breakfast: 16-20 € s.i.
Dogs: allowed (extra cost) **Golf:** 10 km
Accepted cards: AE, DC, JCB, MC, VS

Anne-Sophie Pic

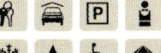

More info on www.relaischateaux.com/pic

Savoie Mont Blanc

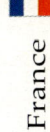

France

Properties	Nearest major city	Relais & Châteaux	Relais Gourmands	Page
Alpes Hôtel du Pralong	Courchevel	⚜		195
Auberge du Bois Prin	Chamonix	⚜		187
Auberge du Père Bise	Annecy	⚜	◉	190
Chalet du Mont d'Arbois	Megève	⚜		193
Grand Cœur (Le)	Méribel	⚜		197
Hameau Albert 1ᵉʳ (Le)	Genève	⚜	◉	188
Ombremont	Chambéry	⚜	◉	194
Verniaz et ses chalets (La)	Evian	⚜		186
Veyrat (M.) - Auberge de l'Eridan	Annecy	⚜	◉	189
Veyrat (M.) - La Ferme de mon Père	Megève	⚜	◉	191

More info on www.relaischateaux.com

La Verniaz et ses chalets

SINCE 1960

Av. d'Abondance, Neuvecelle-Eglise
74500 Evian-les-Bains
(Haute-Savoie) • France

Tel. : (33) 04 50 75 04 90
Fax : (33) 04 50 70 78 92
verniaz@relaischateaux.com

Nestling between the lake and the mountains above Evian, La Verniaz is an ensemble of old Alpine houses and chalets secluded in beautiful floral parkland. Many of the spacious, individually styled rooms have their own private balcony set amidst the trees. The inventive and generous cuisine, featuring a traditional woodfire «Rôtisserie» and delicious fish freshly caught from Lake Geneva, is enhanced by fine Savoy wines.
Water sports. (Other activities P. 629)

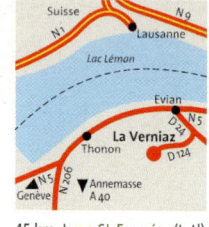

Altitude: 550 m.
Access: In Evian, across from the landing stage, avenue d'Abondance, the Neuvecelle-Eglise roundabout.
Airports: Geneva (Intl) 45 km, Lyon St-Exupéry (Intl) 200 km
Train station: Evian 2 km

Owners: Verdier Family
Weekly closing: Rest.: Monday and Tuesday (except dinner for residents) (except holidays and July-Aug.)
Annual closing: From mid-Nov. to mid-Feb.
Currency: Euro (€)
Rates: Menus 35-70 € s.i. Carte 45-75 € s.i.
30 rooms: 105-195 € s.i. (winter)
130-220 € s.i. (summer)
2 suites/5 chalets: starting at 220 € s.i. (winter) starting at 250 € s.i. (summer)
Breakfast: 14 € s.i.
Dogs: allowed (extra cost) **Golf:** 2 km
Accepted cards: AE, DC, JCB, MC, VS

More info on www.relaischateaux.com/verniaz

Auberge du Bois Prin

SINCE 1987

69, chemin de l'Hermine
Les Moussoux
74400 Chamonix Mont-Blanc
(Haute-Savoie) • France

Tel. : (33) 04 50 53 33 51
Fax : (33) 04 50 53 48 75
boisprin@relaischateaux.com

France

Serene vistas of the Mont-Blanc. Denis Carrier moves between his vegetable garden and kitchen, nurtures vegetables and flowers which are lovingly presented to guests in his deliciously inventive recipes brimming over with the most enchanting flavours. The Bois Prin team epitomises freshness and good humour. You will love the mountains, wines and the cuisine in this beautiful chalet. Skiing and hiking close to the hotel.

Climbing, parapenting, mountaineering. (Other activities P. 629)

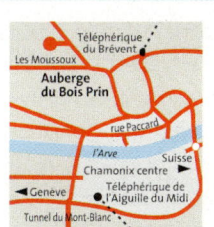

Altitude: 1100 metres.
Access: Highway - exit Chamonix south, follow signs to the hotel, towards Les Moussoux.
Airports: Geneva (Intl) 83 km, Annecy 94 km
Train station: Chamonix 1 km

Owners: Carrier Family
General Manager: Denis Carrier
Weekly closing: Rest.: Monday at lunch and Wednesday at lunch
Annual closing: From April 22th to May 7th and from October 27th to November 27th
Currency: Euro (€)
Rates: Menus 28-69 € s.i. Carte 47-66 € s.i.
11 rooms: 107-224 € s.i.
Breakfast: 13 € s.i.
Dogs: allowed (extra cost)
Golf: 3 km
Accepted cards: AE, DC, MC, VS

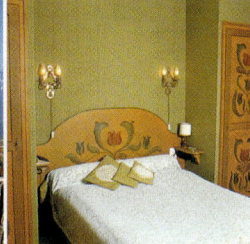

More info on www.relaischateaux.com/boisprin

Le Hameau Albert Ier

France • SINCE 2000

119, impasse du Montenvers, BP 55
74402 Chamonix
(Haute-Savoie) • France

Tel.: (33) 04 50 53 05 09
Fax: (33) 04 50 55 95 48
albert@relaischateaux.com

The Carrier family has reigned over the Hameau Albert Ier hotel in Chamonix since its 1903 creation. Authenticity, welcome, tradition and gastronomy are master words here from the rooms and chalets in the park to Pierre Carrier's creations. Savour «filet d'ombre et miel de bourgeons de sapin», «boudin de la maison, carti à la chirve». Wine list with over 20000 bottles. In the Hameau's farmhouse, the typical restaurant «La Maison Carrier».

Climbing, kayaking. (Other activities P. 629)

Altitude: 1000 m.
Access: A40 Lyon-Geneva, Chamonix. Enter at Chamonix north, towards Swiss Argentière, 2nd road on the right.
Airports: Geneva (Intl) 80 km, Annecy 80 km
Train station: Chamonix 0,5 km

Owners: Pierre and Martine Carrier
Weekly closing: Albert Ier: Wednesday, Thursday noon. La Maison Carrier: Monday
Annual closing: Hotel: from Nov. 12th to Dec. 3rd. Albert Ier: from May 11th to 27th and from Nov. 2nd to Dec. 4th. La Maison Carrier: from June 2nd to 17th and from Nov. 12th to December 16th
Currency: Euro (€)
Rates: Menus 49-129 € s.i. Carte 80-110 € s.i. La Maison Carrier 25-40 € s.i. **Breakfast:** 14 € s.i.
39 rooms: 136-381 € s.i. **3 suites:** 381-686 € s.i.
Dogs: allowed **Golf:** 4 km
Accepted cards: AE, DC, JCB, MC, VS

More info on www.relaischateaux.com/albert

Auberge de l'Eridan-Marc Veyrat 🇫🇷

SINCE 1991

13, vieille route des Pensières
74290 Veyrier-du-Lac
(Haute-Savoie) • France

Tel. : (33) 04 50 60 24 00
Fax : (33) 04 50 60 23 63
veyrat@relaischateaux.com

France

Beautiful mansion in a flower-decked park on the edge of Lake Annecy, where the charm of 12 rooms contributes to the poetry of the place. Marc Veyrat, the plant magician, blends forgotten aromas of the Alpine pastures with an exceptional cuisine: the «escalope de foie chaud au pain d'épice aux huit arômes» or the «coquilles Saint-Jacques et ris de veau au petit lait de coquelicot» are an invitation to discover new flavours.

(Other activities P. 629)

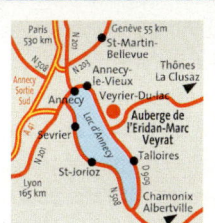

Access: Exit Annecy south towards the city centre, the left shore is Veyrier-du-Lac (direction Thônes). At the first roundabout in Veyrier, turn right 2 times.
Airports: Geneva (Intl) 50 km, Annecy 5 km
Train station: Annecy 4 km

Owner: Marc Veyrat
Weekly closing: Monday and Tuesday all day, Wednesday noon (except July and August)
Annual closing: From mid-November to the beginning of May
Currency: Euro (€)
Rates: Menus 205-295 € s.i. Carte 76-99 € s.i.
9 rooms: 450-650 € s.i.
2 suites: 587-709 € s.i.
Breakfast: 60 € s.i.
Dogs: allowed (extra cost) **Golf:** 3 km
Accepted cards: AE, DC, JCB, MC, VS

More info on www.relaischateaux.com/veyrat

Auberge du Père Bise

SINCE 1973

Route du Port
74290 Talloires
(Haute-Savoie) • France

Tel. : (33) 04 50 60 72 01
Fax : (33) 04 50 60 73 05
bise@relaischateaux.com

Perpetuating a hundred-year-old family culinary tradition, Sophie Bise reinvents gourmet pleasures with dishes such as the «tatin de pommes de terre, truffes et foie gras». The warm welcome, the comfort of the guestrooms which overlook a lake with the purest water in Europe and the fine wine cellar with its rare vintages all make the Auberge du Père Bise the ideal place to relax and enjoy the dolce vita.

(Other activities P. 629)

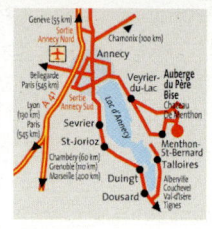

Access: Exit motorway South or North, Annecy centre east bank, Veyrier-du-Lac, Talloires, first roundabout turn right.

Airports: Geneva (Intl) 55 km, Annecy 18 km
Helipad: N 45° 50' 23" E 006° 12' 41"
Train station: Annecy 13 km

Owners: Charlyne and Sophie Bise
Weekly closing: Tuesday noon, Friday noon
Annual closing: From mid-Dec. to March 22nd
Currency: Euro (€)
Rates: Menus 76-110-140 € s.i.
Carte 91-130 € s.i.
25 rooms: 230-275 € s.i.
9 suites: 385-460 € s.i.
Breakfast: 17-22 € s.i.
Dogs: allowed (extra cost)
Golf: 2 km
Accepted cards: AE, DC, JCB, MC, VS

More info on www.relaischateaux.com/bise

La Ferme de mon Père

SINCE 2001

367, route de Crêt
74120 Megève
France

Tel. : (33) 04 50 21 01 01
Fax : (33) 04 50 21 43 43
monpere@relaischateaux.com

France

Marc Veyrat has rebuilt a genuine mountain farmhouse whose floor opens onto a live cowshed. 5 guest rooms and 3 suites offer an amazing decoration which allies the sun of ceramics and the authenticity of wood to ensure cosiness. Savour a superb cuisine full of flavours: the two foies gras (one cold with fig purée and the other warm with fragrant myrrh) and «nuggets savoyards de poulet, arôme de cacahuète».
(Other activities P. 629)

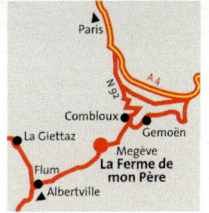

Access: From Paris: motorway A 40, exit Sallanches, Megève (11 km) From South: exit Albertville.

Airports: Geneva (Intl) 65 km, Annecy 60 km
Train station: Sallanches 10 km

Owner/Chef: Marc Veyrat
Weekly closing: Monday, Tuesday, Wednesday noon, Thursday noon, Friday noon
Annual closing: From the end of April to the end of november
Currency: Euro (€)
Rates: Menus 220-298 € s.i. Carte 300 € s.i.
5 rooms: 457-792 € s.i.
3 suites: 762-1830 € s.i.
Breakfast: 60 € s.i.
Dogs: allowed
Golf: 2 km
Accepted cards: AE, DC, MC, VS

Marc Veyrat

More info on www.relaischateaux.com/monpere

Pas facile d'investir en ce moment!

Pas pour tout le monde.
Tu connais la Banque **Sanpaolo** ?

Le groupe Sanpaolo, créé en 1563 durant la Renaissance italienne,
est aujourd'hui, au premier plan des banques européennes.
La **Banque Sanpaolo** s'adresse avant tout à une clientèle
de particuliers et d'entreprises recherchant un contact
privilégié. Parce qu'elle offre compétence et réactivité
et qu'elle est régulièrement récompensée pour ses qualités
de gestion (Victoire 2001 des Sicav de « La Tribune »,
Trophée d'Or 2001 « Le Revenu », meilleur OPCVM 2001
« La Vie Financière »), vous gagnerez à connaître la **Banque Sanpaolo**.

Contactez nous : **www.sanpaolo.fr** ou **01 47 54 47 77**

BANQUE
SANPAOLO
Un de vos amis y est déjà

52, avenue Hoche - 75008 Paris - GROUPE SANPAOLO IMI

Chalet du Mont d'Arbois

SINCE 1992

447, chemin de la Rocaille
74120 Megève
(Haute-Savoie) • France

Tel. : (33) 04 50 21 25 03
Fax : (33) 04 50 21 24 79
montarbois@relaischateaux.com

France

Set high above Megève and reflecting the spirit of luxury and Savoyard heritage, the hotel and its new Noémie chalet provide comfort, peace and well-being. Private golf course, skiing, «indoor-outdoor» pool, spa and beauty studio. The menu highlights the Rothschild and Savoyard culinary traditions. Minutes away, enjoy the same welcoming spirit of the Taverne with its old wood decor. Cellar with vintage Bordeaux.

Beauty salon and fitness, carriage rides. (Other activities P. 629)

Altitude: 1350 metres.
Access: From Paris, motorway exit Sallanches, Megève (11 km). From the south, exit Albertville.
Airports: Geneva (Intl) 65 km, Annecy 60 km
Owners: B. and N. de Rothschild
General Manager: Alexandre Faix
Annual closing: From mid-October to mid-Dec. and from mid-April to mid-June
Currency: Euro (€)
Rates: Menus 46-107 € s.i. Carte 69-84 € s.i.
La Taverne du Mont d'Arbois 42 € s.i.
25 rooms: 193-634 € s.i. (summer)
276-833 € s.i. (winter)
7 suites: (for 2 to 6 pers.) 629-3648 € s.i. (summer) 1000-3648 € s.i. (winter)
Breakfast: 23 € s.i.
Dogs: allowed **Golf:** 300 m (private)
Accepted cards: AE, DC, MC, VS

More info on www.relaischateaux.com/montarbois

Ombremont

France · SINCE 2000

RN 504
73370 Le Bourget-du-Lac
(Savoie) • France

Tel. : (33) 04 79 25 00 23
Fax : (33) 04 79 25 25 77
ombremont@relaischateaux.com

Overlooking the Bourget lake, this romantic turn-of-the-century villa is at the heart of a park a hundred years old. The sunny rooms with fresh-cut flowers are warmly personalised and have every modern comfort. The regional cuisine gives more than its due to fish. Savour the «cannellonis de lavaret fumé» and «filet de perche rôti à l'huile de poivrons rouges». Savoy wines have pride of place.

Kayaking. (Other activities P. 629)

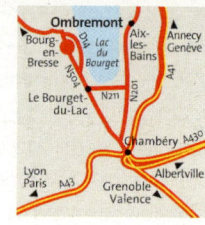

Access: From Chambéry, follow signs to Le Bourget-du-Lac, then RN 504 towards Belley, Bourg-en-Bresse (2 km).

Airports: Lyon St-Exupéry (Intl) 75 km, Geneva (Intl) 100 km, Chambéry 4 km
Train station: Chambéry 10 km

Owner: Jean-Pierre Jacob
Weekly closing: Rest.: Monday, Tuesday noon, Thursday noon
Annual closing: From the beginning of November to the beginning of May
Currency: Euro (€)
Rates: Menus 49 € s.i. (lunch, except Sunday) 130 € s.i. Carte 90-120 € s.i.
12 rooms: 150-228 € s.i.
5 suites: 245-320 € s.i.
Breakfast: 14 € s.i.
Dogs: allowed (extra cost)
Golf: 10 km
Accepted cards: AE, DC, JCB, MC, VS

Jean-Pierre Jacob

More info on www.relaischateaux.com/ombremont

Alpes Hôtel du Pralong

SINCE 1975

Route de l'Altiport, B.P. 13
73121 Courchevel 1850 Cedex
(Savoie) • France

Tel. : (33) 04 79 08 24 82
Fax : (33) 04 79 08 36 41
pralong@relaischateaux.com

France

In Courchevel, in the heart of the Three Valleys, this comfortable residence offers great skiing, hospitality and French tradition. The spacious rooms with light wood panelling encourage guests to relax in discreet luxury. On the hotel doorstep, a ski lift will carry you up to the Olympic slopes. Unwind in the large indoor pool, saunas, hammam, Jacuzzi and massage rooms. The cuisine is sophisticated and appetising.

All winter and mountain sports. (Other activities P. 629)

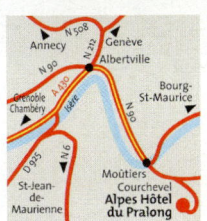

Altitude: 1850 m.
Access: From Albertville, towards Moûtiers and Courchevel 1850, towards Altiport for about 1.5 km.

Airports: Lyon St-Exupéry (Intl) 160 km, Geneva (Intl) 160 km
Train station: Moûtiers 25 km

Owner: EURL du Pralong
G. Managers: Albert and Christine Parveaux
Annual closing: From mid-April to mid-Dec.
Currency: Euro (€)
Rates: Menus lunch 50 € s.i. dinner 70 € s.i. Carte 75 € s.i.
56 rooms: half-board/pers. 180-405 € s.i.
8 suites: half-board/pers. 415-650 € s.i.
Breakfast: included
Dogs: allowed
Accepted cards: AE, DC, JBC, MC, VS

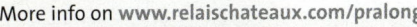

More info on www.relaischateaux.com/pralong

Le Grand Cœur

SINCE 1966

73550 Méribel
(Savoie) • France

Tel. : (33) 04 79 08 60 03
Fax : (33) 04 79 08 58 38
grandcoeur@relaischateaux.com

France

This authentic Savoyard chalet, nestling at the foot of the slopes in the centre of Méribel, is tastefully decorated with fine wood panelling, sumptuous fabrics and embroidery. After an invigorating day on the slopes, unwind in the sauna, hammam or whirlpool, sip apéritifs at the piano bar or recline in front of a roaring fire. Savour exquisite candlelit meals at one of the most sought-after restaurants in Méribel.

Snowmobiling, hangliding, parapenting, walks, dog sleighing, snow shoeing, skating, bowling, swimming-pool. (Other activities P. 629)

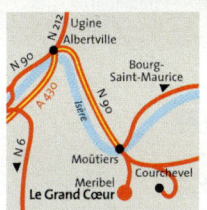

Altitude: 1400 metres.
Access: From Lyon, A 43 towards Chambéry, Albertville, N 90 Moûtiers, D 90 Méribel.

Airports: Lyon St-Exupéry (Intl) 190 km, Chambéry 80 km
Train station: Moûtiers 18 km

Owner: Sogeco S.A.
General Managers: Mr. and Mrs. Edouard Ruchti
Annual closing:
From April 7th to December 12th
Currency: Euro (€)
Rates: Menus 40-65 € s.i. Carte 45-75 € s.i.
35 rooms: (half board/pers.) 140-265 € s.i.
5 suites: (half board/pers.) 285-455 € s.i.
Breakfast: buffet included
Dogs: allowed (extra cost)
Accepted cards: AE, DC, JCB, MC, VS

More info on www.relaischateaux.com/grandcoeur

43
HAUTE-LOIRE
Allier
Loire
Langogne
Thueyts
07
ARDÈCHE
Privas
Le Pouzin
Baix
200
Loriol
Crest
Die
26
DRÔME
Aubenas
Montélimar
Dieulefit
Joyeuse
Viviers
Rhône
A 7 - E 15
48
LOZÈRE
Villefort
Les Vans
Bourg-
St-Andéol
Valréas
Nyons
Ardèche
Florac
St-Ambroix
Bollène
201
Rochegude
Pont-
St-Esprit
Vaison-
la-Romaine
Séderon
La Grand-
Combe
Bagnols-sur-Cèze
203
Orange
202
Crillon-
le-Brave
Alès
St-Jean-
du-Gard
Sault
Carpentras
Anduze
Gard
Uzès
Castillon-
du-Gard
Villeneuve-
lès-Avignon
84 - VAUCLUSE
Le Vigan
30
GARD
204
208
Avignon
Montfavet
209
Gordes
213
214
Apt
Ganges
Noves
210
Cavaillon
Bonnieux
St-Martin-
de-Londres
Nîmes
Beaucaire
Tarascon
St-Rémy-de-Prov.
Sommières
Fontvieille
Les Baux-de-Prov.
Cadenet
Hérault
207
211
Durance
Pertuis
Gignac
St-Gilles
Arles
212
215
Salon-de-P.
217
Montpellier
205
Lunel
206
218
Aix-
en-Proven
34
HÉRAULT
Aigues-
Mortes
Étang
de Vaccarès
Grand Rhône
13 - BOUCHES-
DU-RHÔNE
Berre-
l'Étang
Palavas
Le Grau-
du-Roi
Istres
Étang
de Berre
Marignane
Stes-Maries-
de-la-Mer
Martigues
Bassin
de Thau
Sète
Port-
St-Louis
Carro
Aubagn
Marseille
216
Le Cap-d'Agde
Golfe
du Lion
La Ciota
MER MÉDITERRANÉE
0
10
20
30
40
50 km

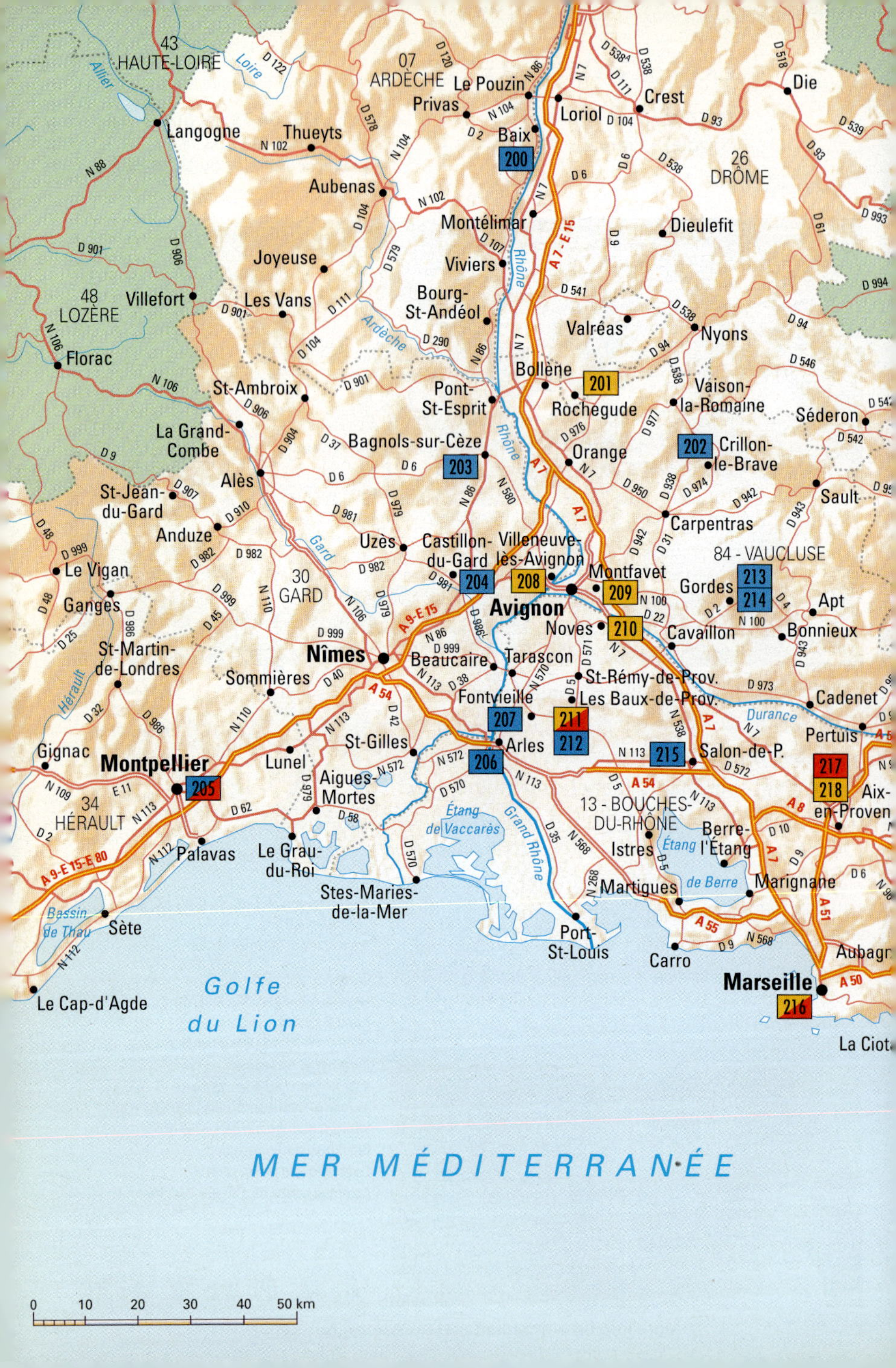

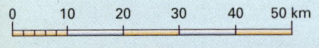

Provence

France

Properties	Nearest major city	Relais & Châteaux	Relais Gourmands	Page
Abbaye de Sainte Croix	Salon-de-Provence	⚜		215
Auberge de Noves	Avignon	⚜		210
Auberge La Regalido	Arles	⚜		207
Cabro d'Or (La)	Arles	⚜		212
Cardinale et sa Résidence (La)	Montélimar	⚜		200
Château de Montcaud	Orange/Avignon	⚜		203
Château de Rochegude	Orange	⚜		201
Clos de la Violette	Aix-en-Provence		⬤	217
Crillon-le-Brave (Hostellerie de)	Avignon	⚜		202
Domaine de Châteauneuf	Aix-en-Provence	⚜		219
Frênes (Hostellerie Les)	Avignon	⚜		209
Jardin des Sens (Le)	Montpellier	⚜	⬤	205
Jules César (Hôtel)	Arles	⚜		206
Mas des Herbes Blanches (Le)	Avignon	⚜		213
Oustau de Baumanière	Arles	⚜	⬤	211
Petit Nice-Passédat (Le)	Marseille	⚜	⬤	216
Phébus (Hostellerie Le)	Avignon	⚜		214
Prieuré (Le)	Avignon	⚜		208
Vieux Castillon (Le)	Nîmes/Avignon	⚜		204
Villa Gallici	Aix-en-Provence	⚜		218

More info on www.relaischateaux.com

La Cardinale et sa Résidence

France — SINCE 1954

Résidence de la Cardinale
Quartier Serre Petoux
07250 Le Pouzin
(Ardèche) • France

Tel. : (33) 04 75 85 80 40
Fax : (33) 04 75 85 82 07
cardinale@relaischateaux.com

This ancient residence and estate was one of the first Relais & Châteaux. Situated on the River Rhône at the foot of the Ardèche mountains, it has 10 comfortable, charming guestrooms with their own terraces. The warm hospitality and considerate service of this famous establishment is renowned. A reflection of the sunny climate, the food is generous and pays tribute to tasty local produce. Excellent wine cellar with rare vintages.

Go-carting, visits of prehistoric sites and caves, Gorges de l'Ardèche, vineyards visits. (Other activities P. 629)

Access: A 7, exit Loriol-sur-Drôme, right towards Le Pouzin (N 104). In Le Pouzin towards Le Teil (N 86). After the roundabout, go straight for 1500 m, then turn right (entrance of la Résidence).
Airports: Lyon St-Exupéry (Intl) 150 km, Valence 30 km
Train station: Montélimar 20 km

Owner: S.A. La Nouvelle Cardinale
General Manager: Frank Wegener
Weekly closing: Rest.: Monday, Tuesday (from October to April)
Annual closing: From Nov. to the beg. of December and from the beg. of January to mid-February
Currency: Euro (€)
Rates: Menus 30-69 € s.i. Carte 46-84 € s.i.
6 rooms: 159-219 € s.i.
4 suites: 289-329 € s.i.
Breakfast: 16 € s.i.
Dogs: allowed (extra cost) **Golf:** 25 km
Accepted cards: AE, DC, MC, VS

More info on www.relaischateaux.com/cardinale

Château de Rochegude

SINCE 1967

26790 Rochegude
(Drôme) • France

Tel. : (33) 04 75 97 21 10
Fax : (33) 04 75 04 89 87
rochegude@relaischateaux.com

France

This magnificent XIIth century fortress, once the summer residence of the Marquis de Rochegude, towers majestically above the Côtes-du-Rhône and its sumptuously furnished, air-conditioned rooms offer superb vistas of the vineyards. Unwind in the green haven of its 25-acre park, recline by the pool or enjoy the tennis courts. Delicious meals, served in the medieval armoury, are enhanced by the finest regional wines.

Theme-based stays according to the season: truffles, olive oil. (Other activities P. 629)

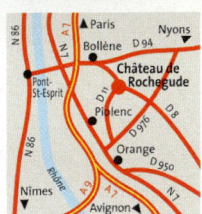

Access: A7, exit Bollène, towards Carpentras (D8), follow signs for Relais & Châteaux.
Airports: Marseille (Intl) 110 km, Avignon 45 km
Helipad: N 44° 14' 49" E 004° 49' 38"
Train station: Orange 15 km

Owner: S.A.R.L. Abbaye de Bouchet
General Manager: André Chabert
Weekly closing: Sunday evening, Monday and Tuesday at lunch (low season)
Annual closing: From mid-Nov. to mid-Dec.
Currency: Euro (€)
Rates: Menus 35-99 € s.i. Carte 60-85 € s.i.
24 rooms: 170-350 € s.i.
3 suites: 350-550 € s.i.
Breakfast: 18 € s.i.
Dogs: allowed (extra cost)
Golf: Putting green on the premises 10 km
Accepted cards: AE, DC, JCB, MC, VS

More info on www.relaischateaux.com/rochegude

France

Hostellerie de Crillon-le-Brave

SINCE 1995

Place de l'Eglise
84410 Crillon-le-Brave
(Vaucluse) • France

Tel. : (33) 04 90 65 61 61
Fax : (33) 04 90 65 62 86
crillonbrave@relaischateaux.com

This elegant residence, perched above the village roofs, welcomes you into a green haven secluded behind tall, ochre walls. Its rooms, bathed in the scent of clematis and jasmine wafting up from the Italian-style gardens, offer stunning views across the vineyards to the Mont Ventoux, once cherished by Mistral and Cézanne. Enjoy sun-drenched cuisine and regional wines beneath the fig trees or in the vaulted dining-room.

(Other activities P. 629)

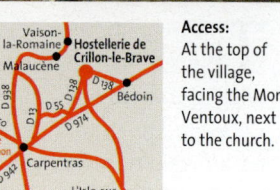

Access: At the top of the village, facing the Mont Ventoux, next to the church.

Airports: Marseille (Intl) 100 km, Avignon 40 km
Train station: Avignon 30 km

Owner: S.A. Hostellerie de Crillon-le-Brave
General Manager: David Candillon
Weekly closing: Rest.: for lunch for the week
Annual closing: From January 2nd to March 13th
Currency: Euro (€)
Rates: Menus 67 € s.i. Menu (lunch) 26 € s.i. Carte 50-75 € s.i. Le Bistrot 35-45 € s.i.
24 rooms: 156-280 € s.i.
8 suites: 280-540 € s.i.
Breakfast: 17 € s.i.
Dogs: allowed (extra cost)
Golf: 30 km
Accepted cards: AE, DC, MC, VS

More info on www.relaischateaux.com/crillonbrave

Château de Montcaud

SINCE 1996

Route d'Alès
(4 km from Bagnols-sur-Cèze)
Combe 30200 Sabran
(Gard) • France

Tel. : (33) 04 66 89 60 60
Fax : (33) 04 66 89 45 04
montcaud@relaischateaux.com

France

The sound of local festivals is barely discernible in this haven of well-being and light. Tastefully decorated rooms open onto peaceful parkland, and guests spend calm, serene days lounging by the pool, playing tennis or strolling through the rose garden. Dine al fresco on the patio of a charming farmhouse and savour superb cuisine which pays tribute to the sea and the Provençal markets. Excellent Côtes-du-Rhône.

(Other activities P. 629)

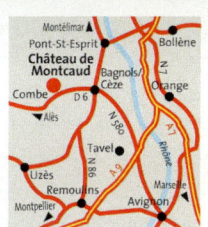

Access: A7 from the south, exit Avignon Sud, A7 from the north, exit Bollène, A9 from the south, exit Remoulins. Continue towards Bagnols-sur-Cèze then D6 towards Alès.
Airports: Marseille (Intl) 120 km, Avignon 40 km
Helipad: N 44° 10' 23" E 004° 34' 19"
Train station: Avignon 33 km

Owners: Family Baur, S.A. Classics Hôtels
General Managers: Anne and Rudy W. Baur
Weekly closing: «Les Jardins de Montcaud» : lunch, «Le Bistrot»: weekend
Annual closing: From Jan. 1st to April 11th and from Nov. 2nd to Dec. 31st **Currency:** Euro (€)
Rates: Menus 57-85 € s.i. Carte 60-90 € s.i. Bistrot 25 € s.i. **Breakfast:** buffet 19 € s.i.
22 rooms: 175-320 € s.i. **7 suites:** 320-575 € s.i.
Dogs: allowed (extra cost) **Golf:** 22 km
Accepted cards: AE, DC, JCB, MC, VS

More info on www.relaischateaux.com/montcaud

Le Vieux Castillon

France — SINCE 1982

Castillon-du-Gard
30210 Remoulins
(Gard) • France

Tel. : (33) 04 66 37 61 61
Fax : (33) 04 66 37 28 17
vieuxcastillon@relaischateaux.com

Between Nîmes and Avignon, close to the Cévennes national park, the Camargue and the Alpilles, this hilltop hamlet offers breathtaking vistas of the Ventoux valley. With its magnificent patios, medieval architecture and honey-coloured stone terraces set in the heart of a Provençal village, Le Vieux Castillon is a truly unique domain. Enjoy musical evenings, sun-drenched cuisine and an exceptional selection of Côtes-du-Rhône.

(Other activities P. 629)

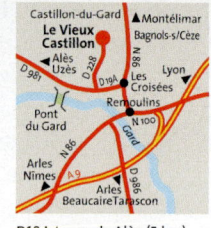

Access: From Paris, Marseille or Montpellier, A9 exit Remoulins. From Remoulins, N86 towards Montélimar then to the left, at Croisées, D19A towards Alès (5 km).
Airports: Marseille (Intl) 110 km, Nîmes 27 km
Train station: Avignon 25 km

Owners: Walser Family
General Manager: Patrick Walser
Weekly closing: Restaurant: Monday noon and Tuesday noon
Annual closing: Beg. of January to mid. February
Currency: Euro (€)
Rates: Menus 46 € s.i. (week. lunch) 75-99 € s.i. (dinner and week-end) Carte approx. 97 € s.i.
32 rooms: 198-283 € s.i.
2 suites: 308 € s.i.
Breakfast: 15 € s.i.
Dogs: allowed
Golf: 15 km
Accepted cards: AE, DC, JCB, MC, VS

More info on www.relaischateaux.com/vieuxcastillon

Le Jardin des Sens

SINCE 1995

11, avenue Saint-Lazare
34000 Montpellier
(Hérault) • France

Tel. : (33) 04 99 58 38 38
Fax : (33) 04 99 58 38 39
jardinsens@relaischateaux.com

France

Jacques and Laurent Pourcel's refined cuisine, which pays tribute to rich Mediterranean flavours and the regional produce of Languedoc, is a veritable festival for the senses. The Pourcel's exquisite creations are accompanied by superb wines carefully selected by Olivier Chateau. Enjoy a true gourmet experience in the glass-fronted dining-room overlooking the beautiful garden, then retire to a charming guestroom.
(Other activities P. 629)

Access: City centre, then «Le Corum» (Convention centre), Nîmes road, then avenue St-Lazare.

Airports: Montpellier (Intl) 5 km, Nîmes 60 km
Train station: Montpellier 1 km

Owners: Jacques and Laurent Pourcel, Olivier Chateau
Weekly closing: Rest.: Sunday, Monday noon, Wednesday noon
Annual closing: Rest.: From January 2nd to 20th
Currency: Euro (€)
Rates: Menus 46 € s.i. (week lunch) 90-122 € s.i. Carte 120 € s.i.
12 rooms: 170-250 € s.i.
2 suites: 300-450 € s.i.
Breakfast: 20 € s.i.
Dogs: allowed **Golf:** 10 km
Accepted cards: AE, MC, VS

More info on www.relaischateaux.com/jardinsens

France

Hôtel Jules César

SINCE 1968

9, boulevard des Lices - BP 116
13631 Arles Cedex
(Bouches-du-Rhône) • France

Tel. : (33) 04 90 52 52 52
Fax : (33) 04 90 52 52 53
julescesar@relaischateaux.com

This sumptuous XVIIth century Carmelite convent, converted into a luxury hotel, is bathed in an aura of charm and serenity. Today the cloister, the elegant chapel, a protected historical site, still echoes with the strains of heavenly music when it hosts private classical and baroque concerts. Gourmets seek out the Cloître and the Lou Marquès, renowned for their delicious regional specialities and outstanding wine lists.

Hunting in Camargue, deep-sea fishing... (Other activities P. 629)

Access: From Nîmes, highway A54 - exit n°5, towards bd G.-Clemenceau then bd des Lices.

Airports: Marseille (Intl) 80 km, Nîmes-Arles 25 km
Train station: Arles 1,2 km

Owners: Michel and Jacqueline Albagnac
General Manager: Arnaud Sehebiade
Annual closing: From the beginning of November to December 23rd
Currency: Euro (€)
Rates: Menus 36-72 € s.i. Carte 50-75 € s.i.
49 rooms: 198-215 € s.i.
5 suites: starting at 382 € s.i.
Breakfast: 15-25 € s.i.
Dogs: allowed (extra cost)
Golf: 20-25 km
Accepted cards: AE, DC, JCB, MC, VS

More info on www.relaischateaux.com/julescesar

Auberge La Regalido

SINCE 1970

Rue Frédéric-Mistral
13990 Fontvieille
(Bouches-du-Rhône) • France

Tel. : (33) 04 90 54 60 22
Fax : (33) 04 90 54 64 29
regalido@relaischateaux.com

France

In a tiny village immortalised by Alphonse Daudet, this picturesque old mill cloaked in twining ivy and flowers appears to have sprung to life from an artist's palette. Many of its charming rooms, named after flowers and herbs, possess private terraces with enchanting views across the old village roofs. If you're seeking the authentic flavour of Provence, look no further than La Regalido's delicious regional cuisine.

Moulin de Daudet, local products. (Other activities P. 629)

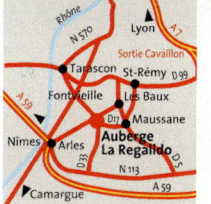

Access: On A59, exit Arles N°7. From Lyon, A7, exit Cavaillon, towards St-Rémy, Maussane and Fontvieille.

Airports: Marseille (Intl) 90 km, Nîmes-Arles 30 km
Train station: Arles 10 km

Owners: Michel Family
Weekly closing: Restaurant: Monday all day, Tuesday noon, Saturday noon
Annual closing: From beginning of January to the end of February
Currency: Euro (€)
Rates: Menus 46-61 € s.i. Carte 53-69 € s.i.
15 rooms: 137-290 € s.i.
Breakfast: 8-15-19 € s.i.
Dogs: allowed (extra cost)
Golf: Les Baux-Mouriès 10 km
Accepted cards: AE, DC, JCB, MC, VS

More info on www.relaischateaux.com/regalido

France

Le Prieuré

SINCE 1959

7, place du Chapitre
30400 Villeneuve-lès-Avignon
(Gard) • France

Tel. : **(33) 04 90 15 90 15**
Fax : (33) 04 90 25 45 39
leprieure@relaischateaux.com

You will be totally enchanted by this elegant XIVth century priory, secluded in a secret garden decorated with rose bowers and a Provençal pergola. The ambience of «elegant idleness» praised by the writer Colette imbues its spacious, comfortable guestrooms and shaded patios as the evening breeze wafts the scent of flowers past the tables. Superb sun-gorged cuisine is complemented by excellent Côtes-du-Rhône.

(Other activities P. 629)

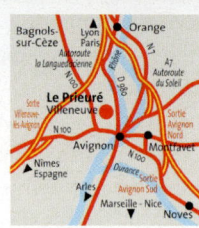

Access: From Paris or Spain: A7, exit Villeneuve, Roquemaure. From Nice or Marseille: A7, exit Avignon Sud, towards Avignon-Nîmes-Villeneuve.
Airports: Marseille (Intl) 78 km, Avignon 12 km
Train station: Avignon 7 km

Owners: Mille Family
General Manager: François Mille
Weekly closing: Rest.: Tuesday, Wednesday (except July, August) and May 1st
Annual closing: From Nov. 2nd to March 13th
Currency: Euro (€)
Rates: Menus 36-58-82 € s.i.
Carte 40-80 € s.i.
26 rooms: 95-215 € s.i.
10 suites: 245-295 € s.i.
Breakfast: 15 € s.i.
Dogs: allowed, in room only **Golf:** 12 km
Accepted cards: AE, DC, JCB, MC, VS

More info on www.relaischateaux.com/leprieure

Hostellerie Les Frênes

SINCE 1981

645, avenue des Vertes-Rives
84140 Avignon-Montfavet
(Vaucluse) • France

Tel.: (33) 04 90 31 17 93
Fax: (33) 04 90 23 95 03
lesfrenes@relaischateaux.com

France

In this beautiful 19th century bourgeois residence, a warm welcome by the Biancone family is always guaranteed. Tucked under trees, the annexes look onto lovely old woods. The guest and bathrooms are all luxuriously furnished. The restaurant «Le Jardin des Frênes» invites you to discover its gourmet cuisine which draws its sophistication from Provencal products. Relax in the spa and superb heated swimming pool.

Spa. (Other activities P. 629)

Access: A7, exit Avignon south, towards Avignon, exit n°8. A9, exit Tavel towards Avignon, towards Marseille, exit n°8. Montfavet, at the church, turn right at the traffic light.
Airports: Marseille (Intl) 75 km, Avignon 3 km
Train station: Avignon 5 km

Owners: Biancone Family
General Manager: Hervé Biancone
Weekly closing: Restaurant: for the lunch
Annual closing: From November to mid-April
Currency: Euro (€)
Rates: Menus 54-69-82 € s.i. Carte 58-91 € s.i.
16 rooms: 206-400 € s.i.
2 suites: starting at 535 € s.i.
Breakfast: 16 € s.i.
Dogs: allowed
Golf: Châteaublanc 3 km, Grand Avignon 5 km
Accepted cards: AE, DC, JCB, MC, VS

More info on www.relaischateaux.com/lesfrenes

Auberge de Noves

France — SINCE 1954

Domaine du Devès
Route de Châteaurenard
13550 Noves
(Bouches-du-Rhône) • France

Tel. : (33) 04 90 24 28 28
Fax : (33) 04 90 24 28 00
noves@relaischateaux.com

Encased in a lovingly maintained, wooded 15-hectare park, this resplendent, peaceful manor looked after by the Lalleman Family for three generations, has an irresistible magical air of enchantment. The serene setting, elegant rooms, delicious Provençal cuisine, varied choice of wines, fragrant air and swimming pool all majestically express the quality of life.

Visit to antique dealers in Provence towns and villages: on request. (Other activities P. 629)

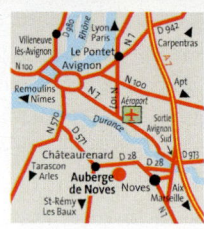

Access: By A7, exit Avignon South, then towards Aix, Marseille, then towards Châteaurenard.

Airports: Marseille (Intl) 65 km, Avignon 7 km
Helipad: N 43° 52' 87" E 004° 53' 02"
Train station: Avignon TGV 12 km

Owners: Lalleman Family
Weekly closing: Rest.: Monday, Tuesday lunch (low season) and Saturday lunch
Annual closing: From November 3rd to December 21st
Currency: Euro (€)
Rates: Menus 39 € s.i. (lunch) 74-90 € s.i. Carte 72-95 € s.i.
19 rooms: 199-282 € s.i. **4 suites:** 365 € s.i.
Breakfast: 18 € s.i.
Dogs: allowed **Golf:** nearby
Accepted cards: AE, DC, JCB, MC, VS

More info on www.relaischateaux.com/noves

Oustau de Baumanière

SINCE 1958

13520 Les-Baux-de-Provence
(Bouches-du-Rhône) • France

Tel. : (33) 04 90 54 33 07
Fax : (33) 04 90 54 40 46
oustau@relaischateaux.com

France

This XIVth century farmhouse, imbued with traditional Provençal charm, is set in idyllic natural surroundings straight out of a Cézanne painting. Jean-André Charial perpetuates the culinary traditions of his grandfather, Raymond Thuilier, and gourmet guests will be delighted by his «raviolis de truffes aux poireaux» and «gigot d'agneau en croûte», enhanced by superb wines. Enjoy exquisite hospitality and spacious rooms.

(Other activities P. 629)

Access: From the North, A7 exit Avignon South, towards Noves, then St-Rémy-de-Provence, Les Baux. From the Southeast, A7 exit Salon towards Arles N113, D5 Maussane-les-Baux.
Airports: Marseille (Intl) 60 km, Nîmes 45 km
Helipad: N 43° 44' 8" E 004° 47' 7"
Train station: Avignon 25 km

Owners: Charial Family
G. Managers: Jean-André and Geneviève Charial
Weekly closing: Hotel: Wednesday; Rest.: Wednesday and Thursday at lunch from Nov. 1st to March 31st
Annual closing: From the beginning of January to the beginning of March
Currency: Euro (€) **Breakfast:** 19 € s.i.
Rates: Menus 84-138 € s.i. Carte 110-130 € s.i.
17 rooms: 240-260 € s.i. **13 suites:** 385-420 € s.i.
Dogs: allowed (extra cost) **Golf:** 3 and 10 km
Accepted cards: AE, DC, JCB, MC, VS

More info on **www.relaischateaux.com/oustau**

La Cabro d'Or

SINCE 1969

13520 Les-Baux-de-Provence
(Bouches-du-Rhône) • France

Tel. : (33) 04 90 54 33 21
Fax : (33) 04 90 54 45 98
cabro@relaischateaux.com

If you are seeking an elegant country stopover on the way to L'Oustau de Baumanière, you will be enchanted by the pure simplicity and the ambience of total liberty at the Cabro d'Or. Set amidst luxuriant foliage overlooking a landscape of olive trees, its comfortable rooms open onto an exceptional garden. The Mediterranean cuisine draws its inspiration from regional produce and the hotel garden's herbs and vegetables.

(Other activities P. 629)

Access: From the North: A 7 exit Avignon South, towards Noves, then St-Rémy-de-Provence, Les Baux.
Airports: Marseille (Intl) 60 km, Nîmes-Arles 45 km
Helipad: N 43° 44' 8" E 004° 47' 7"
Train station: Avignon 25 Km

Owners: Charial Family
G. Managers: Jean-André and Geneviève Charial
Weekly closing: Hotel: Monday evening from Oct. 15th to March 15th Restaurant: Monday from Oct. 15th to March 15th, Tuesday lunch all year
Annual closing: From Nov. 11th to Dec. 20th
Currency: Euro (€)
Rates: Menus 46-70 € s.i. Carte 61-76 € s.i.
23 rooms: 125-215 € s.i.
8 suites: 240-330 € s.i.
Breakfast: 13 € s.i.
Dogs: allowed (extra cost 8 €) **Golf:** 2 km
Accepted cards: AE, DC, MC, VS

More info on www.relaischateaux.com/cabro

Le Mas des Herbes Blanches

SINCE 1976

Joucas
84220 Gordes
(Vaucluse) • France

Tel. : (33) 04 90 05 79 79
Fax : (33) 04 90 05 71 96
masherbes@relaischateaux.com

France

This sun-drenched, traditional Provence farmhouse lies tucked away in the heart of the Garrigue. Far removed from the hustle and bustle of the festivals, this tranquil location is the ideal spot to unwind, savour imaginative Mediterranean cuisine and appreciate a wine list brimming over with Côtes-du-Rhône whilst taking in breath-taking views of the Luberon landscape.

(Other activities P. 629)

Access: A7, exit Cavaillon, towards Apt (D 2). In Coustellet, towards Gordes, roundabout before Gordes, towards Joucas (D 102).

Airports: Marseille (Intl) 85 km, Avignon 40 km
Helipad: N 43° 56' 08" E 005° 14' 39"
Train station: Avignon 40 km

Owners: Paul and Evelyne Juillard
Annual closing: From January 4th to March 7th
Currency: Euro (€)
Rates: Menus 42-73 € s.i. Carte 65-80 € s.i.
13 rooms: 167-288 € s.i.
6 suites: 284-434 € s.i.
Breakfast: 18 € s.i.
Dogs: allowed (extra cost)
Golf: Saumane 23 km
Accepted cards: AE, DC, MC, VS

More info on www.relaischateaux.com/masherbes

France

Hostellerie Le Phébus

SINCE 2003

Route de Murs
Joucas
84220 Gordes
(Vaucluse) • France

Tel. : (33) 04 90 05 78 83
Fax : (33) 04 90 05 73 61
phebus@relaischateaux.com

Between Gordes and Roussillon, in the heart of the garrigue, a sun-drenched building, erected over remains dating back to the Templars, offers its guests the pleasures of a 4-hectare park and the charm of a setting decked out in the colours of Provence. Here, in Lubéron, the Mediterranean determines the flavours of the cuisine and atmosphere. The inn has a large swimming pool and some suites boast their own private one.

(Other activities P. 629)

Access: Motorway A7, exit Cavaillon. Towards Apt (D2). At Coustellet, towards Gordes, Joucas (D102).

Airports: Marseille (Intl) 85 km, Avignon 35 km
Helipad: N 43° 55' 45'' E 005° 15' 29''
Train station: Avignon 40 km

Owners: Mathieu Family
General Manager: Richard Mathieu
Weekly closing:
Restaurant: lunch from Monday to Friday
Annual closing: From October 20th to April 7th
Currency: Euro (€)
Rates: Menus 38-90 € s.i. Carte 60-95 € s.i.
18 rooms: 120-229 € s.i.
8 suites: 228-580 € s.i.
Breakfast: 15-18 € s.i.
Dogs: allowed (extra cost) **Golf:** 20 km
Accepted cards: AE, MC, VS

More info on www.relaischateaux.com/phebus

Abbaye de Sainte Croix

SINCE 1977

Route du Val-de-Cuech, D 16
13300 Salon-de-Provence
(Bouches-du-Rhône) • France

Tel. : (33) 04 90 56 24 55
Fax : (33) 04 90 56 31 12
saintecroix@relaischateaux.com

France

This magnificent XIIth century abbey, set amidst gardens of lavender and rosemary, has been lovingly restored and the monks' cells converted into luxury suites and guestrooms. You will be enchanted by the superb Romanesque architecture, the beautiful vaulted ceilings and the delightfully rustic furniture. Dine on the restaurant's panoramic terrace and savour Provençal cuisine and excellent local vintages.

(Other activities P. 629)

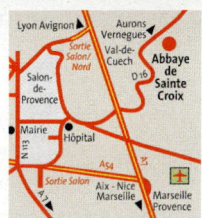

Access: From Aix, Marseille, Lyon and Avignon: A7. From Montpellier and Arles: A54. First exit to Salon. In Salon, follow the signs.

Airport: Marseille (Intl) 30 km
Helipad: N 43° 39' 05" E 005° 07' 59"
Train station: Salon-de-Provence 5 km

Owners: Bossard Family
General Managers: Catherine Bossard and Monique Morel
Weekly closing: Restaurant: week lunch (off-season, except bank holidays)
Annual closing: From the beginning of November to mid-March
Currency: Euro (€)
Rates: Menus 60-76-88-105 € s.i. Carte 76 € s.i.
21 rooms: 165-285 € s.i.
4 suites: 410-440 € s.i.
Breakfast: 22 € s.i.
Dogs: allowed (except rest.) **Golf:** 10 km
Accepted cards: AE, DC, JCB, MC, VS

More info on www.relaischateaux.com/saintecroix

France — SINCE 1975

Le Petit Nice-Passédat

Anse de Maldormé
Corniche J.-F.-Kennedy
13007 Marseille
(Bouches-du-Rhône) • France

Tel. : (33) 04 91 59 25 92
Fax : (33) 04 91 59 28 08
passedat@relaischateaux.com

The Passédat Family welcomes you to its two Greek villas with their luxurious rooms overlooking the Mediterranean. Gérald Passédat creates a contemporary cuisine with specialities from Marseille: «anémones en beignets», «rouleaux de langoustines», very rare «cigales de mer», «sept desserts» for gourmets. Discover the very fine wine list.

Water sports, thalassotherapy nearby. (Other activities P. 629)

Access: From Marseille, exit E/N motorway, towards the beach via the Kennedy corniche «hauteur 160».
Airport: Marseille (Intl) 25 km
Train station: Saint-Charles 4 km
Owners: Passédat Family
General Managers: Gérald and Sidonie Passédat
Weekly closing: Rest.: Sunday, Monday from Jan. 1st to the end of April and from the beg. of Oct. to the end of Dec. (except bank holidays) Sunday noon, Monday noon from May to Oct.
Open all year
Currency: Euro (€)
Rates: Menus 59 € s.i. (lunch, drinks included) 85-130-170 € s.i. Carte 100-150 € s.i.
13 rooms: 190-490 € s.i. **3 suites:** 610-790 € s.i.
Breakfast: 10-25 € s.i.
Dogs: allowed (extra cost) **Golf:** 10 km
Accepted cards: AE, DC, JCB, MC, VS

Gérald Passédat

More info on www.relaischateaux.com/passedat

Clos de la Violette

SINCE 2001

10, avenue de la Violette
13100 Aix-en-Provence
(Bouches-du-Rhône) • France

Tel. : (33) 04 42 23 30 71
Fax : (33) 04 42 21 93 03
violette@relaischateaux.com

France

Overlooking Aix, you will enjoy the immense charm of this restaurant with its indoor garden and appreciate the delicate subtle cuisine of Jean-Marc Banzo. With genuine Mediterranean flair, this imaginative chef is always striving to create perfect culinary delights using only the finest regional produce. Savour «petits farcis de légumes provençaux au jus d'agneau» and «pigeon fermier en "sanguette paysanne"».

(Other activities P. 629)

Access: From city centre, follow signs for «Parking Pasteur» then «Villa Gallici» (the Clos de la Violette is next door).

Airport: Marseille (Intl) 25 km
Train station: Marseille 25 km

Owners: Jean-Marc and Brigitte Banzo
Weekly closing: Monday noon, Wednesday noon, Sunday
Annual closing: From August 6th to 21st
Currency: Euro (€)
Rates: Menus 54 € s.i. (lunch) Carte 60-90 € s.i. «Ballade gourmande» 107 € s.i.
Dogs: not allowed
Golf: 5 km
Accepted cards: AE, VS

Jean-Marc Banzo

More info on www.relaischateaux.com/violette

Villa Gallici

France

SINCE 1996

Av. de la Violette
13100 Aix-en-Provence
(Bouches-du-Rhône) • France

Tel. : (33) 04 42 23 29 23
Fax : (33) 04 42 96 30 45
gallici@relaischateaux.com

This country house overlooking Aix is bathed in the soft Provençal light so often depicted by Cézanne. Set amidst an elegant Florentine garden, where cypress trees are reflected in a luxurious pool, it offers sumptuous rooms with terraces and private gardens. Linger over an aperitif in the shade of the plane trees, then savour traditional Provençal cuisine accompanied by the finest Bordeaux, Burgundies and Aix wines.

Gymnastic. Sainte-Victoire mountain, promenade «Cézanne footsteps», the Alpilles, the Luberon. (Other activities P. 629)

Access: From the city centre, follow the yellow signs.

Airport: Marseille (Intl) 25 km
Train station: Aix-en-Provence 4 km

Owner: Villa Gallici s.a.s.
General Manager: Bruno Bazi
Weekly closing: Restaurant closed at noon and Monday evening (low season)
Annual closing: Rest.: from Nov. 24th to Dec. 14th
Currency: Euro (€)
Rates: Hotel restaurant (reserved for guests)
Carte 60-90 € s.i.
18 rooms: 270-480 € s.i.
4 suites: 540-585 € s.i.
Breakfast: 27 € s.i.
Dogs: allowed (extra cost)
Golf: 5 km
Accepted cards: AE, DC, JCB, MC, VS

More info on www.relaischateaux.com/gallici

Domaine de Châteauneuf

SINCE 2003

83860 Nans-les-Pins
(Var) • France

Tel. : (33) 04 94 78 90 06
Fax : (33) 04 94 78 63 30
chateauneuf@relaischateaux.com

France

At the foot of the Sainte-Baume range (a pilgrimage destination and one of the finest belvederes in Provence), Châteauneuf is a splendid 18th century country house, set in the heart of a park adjacent to a magnificent 18-hole golf course. The restaurant and the upscale facilities match the priviliged environment. Luxury is omnipresent but discreet, elegance its lifestyle. A site devoted to beauty.
Vineyards, winetasting. (Other activities P. 629)

Access: A8, exit St-Maximin, take N 560 towards St-Zacharie/Marseille for 8 km. At the stop sign turn right, then follow signs for 400 m. Entry on the left.
Airports: Marseille (Intl) 70 km, Toulon 80 km
Helipad: N 43° 23' 44'' E 5° 46' 29''
Train station: Aix-en-Provence TGV 60 km

Owner: SARL Hôtel du Domaine de Châteauneuf
General Manager: Georges Cremilleux
Weekly closing: Rest.: week lunch (except holidays)
Annual closing: From January 2nd to February 27th and from November 3rd to December 18th
Currency: Euro (€)
Rates: Menus 43-60 € s.i. Carte 53-65 € s.i.
26 rooms: 119-329 € s.i. **4 suites:** 230-569 € s.i.
Breakfast: 17 € s.i.
Dogs: allowed (extra cost) **Golf:** on the premises
Accepted cards: AE, DC, JCB, MC, VS

More info on www.relaischateaux.com/chateauneuf

French Riviera Corsica

Properties	Nearest major city	Relais & Châteaux	Relais Gourmands	Page
Bonne Etape (La)	Sisteron	⚜	♥	222
Cagnard (Le)	Nice	⚜		232
Cala Rossa (Grand Hôtel de)	Porto-Vecchio	⚜		237
Château de la Chèvre d'Or	Nice/Monaco	⚜	♥	236
Château de Trigance	Draguignan	⚜		223
Château du Domaine St-Martin	Nice	⚜		233
Chibois (J.) - Bastide St-Antoine	Grasse	⚜	♥	230
Club de Cavalière (Le)	Le Lavandou	⚜		225
Métropole (Le)	Nice	⚜		235
Moulin de Mougins (Le)	Cannes	⚜	♥	229
Oasis (Restaurant L')	Cannes		♥	228
Réserve de Beaulieu (La)	Monte-Carlo	⚜	♥	234
Résidence de la Pinède	St-Tropez	⚜		226
Saint-Paul (Le)	Nice	⚜		231
Villa (La)	Calvi	⚜		239
Villa Belrose (La)	St-Tropez	⚜		227

More info on www.relaischateaux.com

La Bonne Etape

France · SINCE 1971

Chemin du Lac
04160 Château-Arnoux
(Alpes-de-Haute-Provence) • France

Tel. : (33) 04 92 64 00 09
Fax : (33) 04 92 64 37 36
bonneetape@relaischateaux.com

The Gleizes's innovative cuisine is inspired by the subtle aromas of the Haute-Provence region. Their «agneau de Sisteron» with all its preparations and the «crème glacée au miel de lavande» are veritable works of art. Excellent regional wines. Retire to one of the 18 tastefully decorated rooms to prolong this gourmet stay. According to your fancy, simple cuisine «Au Goût du Jour». Walks in the fragrant garrigues.

(Other activities P. 629)

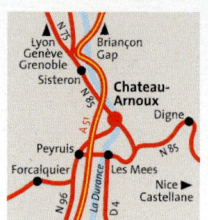

Access: A 51 from North: exit Château-Arnoux; from South: exit Aubignosc, follow Château-Arnoux then «La Bonne Etape».
Airports: Marseille (Intl) 120 km, Nice (Intl) 160 km
Helipad: N 44° 05' 17" E 6° 00' 36"
Train station: Marseille 120 km

Owners: Pierre and Jany Gleize
Weekly closing: From November to March: Rest.: Monday and Tuesday; Hotel: Monday Au Goût du Jour: Monday and Tuesday at lunch
Annual closing: From Jan. 3rd to February 12th and from November 25th to December 10th
Currency: Euro (€)
Rates: La Bonne Etape Menus 37-98 € s.i. Carte 60 € s.i. Au Goût du Jour 22 € s.i.
10 rooms: 138-198 € s.i.
8 suites: 168-298 € s.i.
Breakfast: 14 € s.i.
Dogs: allowed **Golf:** 18 km
Accepted cards: AE, DC, JCB, MC, VS

More info on www.relaischateaux.com/bonneetape

Château de Trigance

SINCE 1966

83840 Trigance
(Var) • France

Tel. : **(33) 04 94 76 91 18**
Fax : (33) 04 94 85 68 99
trigance@relaischateaux.com

France

Set at the entrance to the Gorges du Verdon, this XIth century fortress built by the Saint-Victor monks offers breathtaking views of the Provençal landscape. Trigance flourished in the Middle Ages during the reign of the Demandolx, whose coat of arms still adorns the magnificent medieval rooms, furnished with four-poster beds, oak chests and tapestries. A candlelit dinner in the vaulted cellar is a magical experience.

Historical and botanic paths, rafting on the Verdon river. (Other activities P. 629)

Altitude: 800 metres.
Access: A8 exit n°36 Le Muy-Draguignan, D54 then D955 towards Castellane. After Comps, 8 km on the left.
Airports: Nice Côte d'Azur (Intl) 100 km, Toulon 120 km
Train station: Les Arcs-Draguignan 50 km

Owners: Thomas Family
Weekly closing: Rest.: Tuesday at lunch (low season)
Annual closing: From Nov. 1st to March 22nd
Currency: Euro (€)
Rates: Menus 35-45-60 € s.i. Carte 50 € s.i.
8 rooms: 110-160 € s.i.
2 suites: 180 € s.i.
Breakfast: 13 € s.i.
Dogs: allowed
Golf: 20 km
Accepted cards: AE, DC, JCB, MC, VS

More info on www.relaischateaux.com/trigance

Le Club de Cavalière

SINCE 2000

83980 Le Lavandou
(Var) • France

Tel. : (33) 04 98 04 34 34
Fax : (33) 04 94 05 73 16
cavaliere@relaischateaux.com

France

This ochre provençal villa near Lavandou overlooks the Mediterranean, as you have always imagined it. Surrounded by umbrellas pines, bougainvillea, and exotic gardens, the hotel with its private beach, the rooms and bungalows with private balconies combine to offer you an idyllic stay in the land of the cicadas. Savour the refined Mediterranean cuisine in the restaurant with its superb view of the bay of Cavalière.

Polo, jet ski, boat trips, water gymnastics, parascending. (Other activities P. 629)

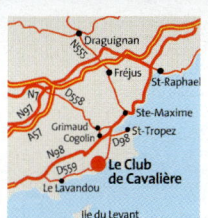

Access: A7 motorway: Aix-en-Provence, A50 Toulon-Hyères. Le Lavandou, Cavalière. From Nice, A57 Hyères, Le Lavandou, Cavalière.
Airports: Marseille (Intl) 90 km, Nice Côte d'Azur (Intl) 120 km, Toulon 18 km
Train station: Toulon 42 km

Owner: Sogeco S.A.
General Managers: Marielle and Edouard Ruchti
Annual closing: From September 30th to May 1st
Currency: Euro (€)
Rates: Menus 40-65 € s.i. Carte 45-75 € s.i.
38 rooms: 290-520 € s.i.
4 suites: 470-585 € s.i.
Breakfast: buffet included
Dogs: allowed (extra cost)
Golf: 18 km
Accepted cards: AE, DC, JCB, MC, VS

More info on www.relaischateaux.com/cavaliere

France

Résidence de la Pinède

SINCE 1987

Plage de la Bouillabaisse - B.P. 105
83992 Saint-Tropez
(Var) • France

Tel. : (33) 04 94 55 91 00
Fax : (33) 04 94 97 73 64
pinede@relaischateaux.com

This opulent white villa is set next to its own private beach overlooking the Citadelle, the gulf and the magnificent St-Tropez peninsula. Constantly embellished by its owners, this sumptuous Côte d'Azur paradise is ideally located near the world's most famous fishing village. Relax on the shaded terrace and enjoy delightfully flavoursome cuisine while contemplating a truly magical landscape.

Water sports, private beach. (Other activities P. 629)

Access: A8, exit Le Muy, towards Ste-Maxime; Saint-Tropez, left after the 1st light 50 m coast side.

Airports: Nice Côte d'Azur (Intl) 100 km, Toulon 55 km
Train station: St-Raphaël 38 km

Owners: Delion Family
Annual closing: From October 6th to April 17th
Currency: Euro (€)
Rates: Menus 52-122 € s.i. Carte 114 € s.i.
36 rooms: 255-820 € s.i.
4 suites: starting at 500 € s.i.
Breakfast: 23-35 € s.i.
Dogs: allowed (extra cost)
Golf: 5-10 km
Accepted cards: AE, DC, MC, VS

More info on www.relaischateaux.com/pinede

Villa Belrose

SINCE 1999

Boulevard des Crêtes
83580 Gassin
(Var) • France

Tel. : (33) 04 94 55 97 97
Fax : (33) 04 94 55 97 98
belrose@relaischateaux.com

France

From its lofty setting, surrounded by lush greenery, this beautiful villa with its pure lines offers a panoramic view of the gulf of Saint-Tropez, the port and the village. The restaurant with its outstanding terrace invites you to savour Mediterranean cuisine. A luxurious beauty centre will welcome you in an exclusive setting designed to promote relaxation, comfort and well-being.

Deep-sea fishing, go-carting, water sports. Beauty Treatment Centre «La Prairie». (Other activities P. 629)

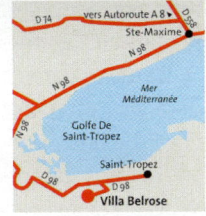

Access: A 8 exit Le Muy, towards Ste-Maxime, St-Tropez, follow the route along the sea-coast and the signs for «La Villa Belrose».

Airports: Nice Côte d'Azur (Intl) 100 km, Toulon 55 km
Train station: St-Raphaël 30 km

Owner: Thomas Althoff
General Manager: Robert-Jan van Straaten
Annual closing: From October 28th to March 13th
Currency: Euro (€)
Rates: Menus 45-85 € s.i. Carte 52-85 € s.i.
36 rooms: 140-645 € s.i.
2 suites: 600-2250 € s.i.
Breakfast: 21-27 € s.i.
Dogs: allowed (extra cost)
Golf : 15 km (18 holes)
Accepted cards: AE, DC, MC, VS

More info on www.relaischateaux.com/belrose

Restaurant L'Oasis

SINCE 2001

6, rue Jean-Honoré-Carle
06210 La Napoule
(Alpes-Maritimes) • France

Tel. : (33) 04 93 49 95 52
Fax : (33) 04 93 49 64 13
oasis@relaischateaux.com

Three brothers, Stéphane, François and Antoine, united by the same passion, sharing the same creativity and skills. La Napoule's famous restaurant welcomes you in a flamboyant patio with an enchanting garden or on the verandas of the conservatory. The cuisine is deeply rooted in the Mediterranean region, with some oriental nuances and pays tribute to the very best of flavours.

(Other activities P. 629)

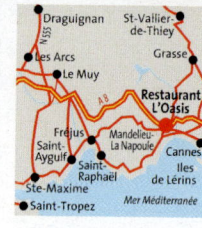

Access: Via motorway A 8: exit 40, follow signs for port of La Napoule. L'Oasis is across from port. Via the coast: across from entrance to port of La Napoule.
Airport: Nice Côte d'Azur (Intl) 30 km
Train station: La Napoule 0,5 km

Owners: Stéphane and François Raimbault
Weekly closing : Sunday evening, Monday (from mid-October to mi-March), Monday noon
Annual closing : From January 6th to February 5th
Currency: Euro (€)
Rates: Menus 42-115 € s.i.
Carte 76-114 € s.i.
Dogs: allowed
Golf: 1 km
Accepted cards: AE, DC, MC, VS

The Raimbault brothers

More info on www.relaischateaux.com/oasis

Le Moulin de Mougins

SINCE 1995

Quartier Notre-Dame-de-Vie
06250 Mougins
(Alpes-Maritimes) • France

Tel. : **(33) 04 93 75 78 24**
Fax : (33) 04 93 90 18 55
mougins@relaischateaux.com

France

Roger Vergé has transformed this picturesque mill into a paradise of French gastronomy. Guests will be enchanted by this virtuoso chef's «chartreuse de frais légumes de printemps à l'ail doux confit et huile de basilic», and «poupeton de fleur de courgette à la truffe noire de Valréas et son jus crémeux», accompanied by rare wines. There are 7 guestrooms for those who wish to prolong their stay in this kingdom of pleasure.

Cooking classes. (Other activities P. 629)

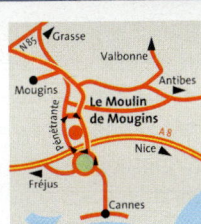

Access: A 8, feeder Cannes/Mougins. 1st roundabout, thruway Grasse/Mougins, exit «Mougins-Centre» turn right.

Airport: Nice Côte d'Azur (Intl) 30 km
Train station: Cannes 15 km

Owners: Roger and Denise Vergé
General Manager: Denise Vergé
Weekly closing: Restaurant: Monday
Annual closing: From January 1st to 10th and from December 1st to 31st
Currency: Euro (€)
Rates: Menus 45 € s.i. (lunch) 90-120 € s.i.
Carte 90-130 € s.i.
3 rooms: 140-190 € s.i.
4 suites: 300-330 € s.i.
Breakfast: 15 € s.i.
Dogs: allowed (extra cost)
Golf: 2 km
Accepted cards: AE, DC, MC, VS

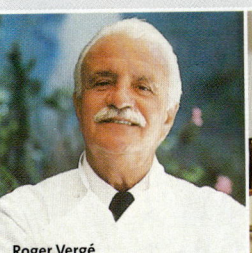

Roger Vergé

More info on www.relaischateaux.com/mougins

Bastide Saint-Antoine-Jacques Chibois

France — SINCE 2000

48, avenue Henri-Dunant
06130 Grasse
(Alpes-Maritimes) • France

Tel. : (33) 04 93 70 94 94
Fax : (33) 04 93 70 94 95
saintantoine@relaischateaux.com

This elegant XVIIIth country provençal house near Grasse overlooks the Bay of Cannes in the shade of its thousand-year-old olive tree park. From the tranquillity of the tastefully decorated sumptuous rooms with their balconies, you will then savour the delicious cuisine of Jacques Chibois who will delight your palate with a veritable symphony of new flavours such as «fraîcheur de fraises à l'huile d'olive vanillée et olives confites». Excellent wine list.
Bowling pitch. (Other activities P. 629)

Access: After exiting the Cannes motorway, towards Grasse centre. After the tunnel, towards St-Antoine/St-Jacques, then first on the right.
Airport: Nice Côte d'Azur (Intl) 30 km
Train station: Cannes 13 km

Owner: Jacques Chibois
General Manager: Patrice Dubois
Open all year
Currency: Euro (€)
Rates: Menus 47 € (lunch) s.i. 107-135 € s.i. Carte 95 € s.i.
8 rooms: 164-295 € s.i.
3 suites: 339-434 € s.i.
Breakfast: 21 € s.i.
Dogs: not allowed **Golf:** 2 km
Accepted cards: AE, DC, JCB, MC, VS

More info on www.relaischateaux.com/saintantoine

Le Saint-Paul

SINCE 1992

86, rue Grande
06570 Saint-Paul-de-Vence
(Alpes-Maritimes) • France

Tel. : (33) 04 93 32 65 25
Fax : (33) 04 93 32 52 94
stpaul@relaischateaux.com

France

Set in the heart of the famous medieval village of Saint-Paul-de-Vence, this XVIth century bourgeois home offers elegantly decorated rooms bathed in the scent of lavender. Choose between two dining rooms, one with a magnificent vaulted ceiling and frescos, the other set around a fountain. Alternatively, enjoy a romantic candlelit dinner on the flower-covered terrace, savouring Provençal cuisine beneath the stars.

Maeght Foundation, art galleries, tourist excursions. (Other activities P.629)

Access: A8, exit Cagnes-sur-Mer, towards Vence then La Colle-sur Loup/Saint-Paul.

Airport: Nice Côte d'Azur (Intl) 15 km
Train station: Cagnes-sur-Mer 10 km

Owner: Olivier Borloo
Open all year
Currency: Euro (€)
Rates: Menus 45 € s.i. (week lunch)
65-82 € s.i. Carte 70 € s.i.
15 rooms: 170-300 € s.i.
4 suites: 260-580 € s.i.
Breakfast: 20 € s.i.
Dogs: allowed (extra cost)
Golf: 12 km
Accepted cards: AE, MC, VS

More info on www.relaischateaux.com/stpaul

France — SINCE 1974

Le Cagnard

Rue Sous Barri, Haut de Cagnes
06800 Cagnes-sur-Mer
(Alpes-Maritimes) • France

Tel. : (33) 04 93 20 73 21
Fax : (33) 04 93 22 06 39
cagnard@relaischateaux.com

In the heart of the Riviera this 13th century residence is perched like a jewel in a crown on the ramparts of the Grimaldi fort. It offers simply breathtaking views. Each room (once the setting for the chivalrous romance between Nicolette and Aucassin) is imbued with the poetic spirit of Modigliani, Fujita and the famous Renoir who all fell completely in love with this unique place. Guard room with painted, coffered ceiling. Renowned, inspired cuisine.

Visit to the village and Grimaldi fort, Chagall, Matisse, Picasso, Maeght museums, Renoir house, Biot glassworks. Private beaches. (Other activities P. 629)

Access: A8 exit 47, or RN 98, towards city centre, follow signs for «Haut de Cagnes-Bourg médiéval». In the village, turn right after «Planastel» car-park, in rue Xavier Blanc (narrow lane).
Airport: Nice Côte d'Azur (Intl) 8 km
Train station: Cagnes-sur-Mer 1,5 km

Owners: Mr and Mrs Félix Barel
General Manager: Françoise Laroche
Weekly closing: Restaurant: Tuesday at lunch, Thursday at lunch
Annual closing: Restaurant: from the beginning of November to mid-December
Currency: Euro (€)
Rates: Menus 54 € s.i. (lunch) 64-84 € s.i.
Carte 69-91 € s.i. **Breakfast:** 15 € s.i.
20 rooms: 137-244 € s.i. **5 suites:** 290-396 € s.i.
Dogs: allowed (extra cost) **Golf:** 8 km Mougins
Accepted cards: AE, DC, JCB, MC, VS

More info on www.relaischateaux.com/cagnard

Le Château du Domaine St Martin

SINCE 1970

Avenue des Templiers - BP 102
06142 Vence Cedex
(Alpes-Maritimes) • France

Tel. : **(33) 04 93 58 02 02**
Fax : (33) 04 93 24 08 91
stmartin@relaischateaux.com

France

This former residence of the Templar Knights, nestling amidst olive trees just a few steps from the Matisse Chapel, offers a superb panoramic view across 100 kilometres of hills and Mediterranean coastline. The guestrooms are havens of calm and the flavoursome cuisine is enhanced by the finest Provence wines. Magnificent heated overflow swimming pool.

20 mn from the sea, museums, galleries. (Other activities P. 629)

Access: A8, exit Cagnes-sur-Mer; Vence, follow Autres directions, Col de Vence-Coursegoules.
Airport: Nice Côte d'Azur (Intl) 20 km
Helipad: N 43° 43' 50" E 7° 6' 40"
Train station: Nice 25 km

Owner: S.A.H. Eden Roc
General Manager: Philippe Perd
Annual closing: From mid-November to the beginning of February
Currency: Euro (€)
Rates: «La Commanderie» : 42 € s.i. (lunch week) 69-92 € s.i. Carte 94-126 € s.i. «L'oliveraie» : 54-90 € s.i. (lunch)
34 rooms: 235-790 € s.i.
6 suites: 915-2290 € s.i.
Breakfast: 22-30 € s.i.
Dogs: not allowed **Golf:** 20 km
Accepted cards: AE, DC, JCB, MC, VS

More info on www.relaischateaux.com/stmartin

La Réserve de Beaulieu

France — SINCE 1999

5, bd du Général-Leclerc
06310 Beaulieu-sur-Mer
(Alpes-Maritimes) • France

Tel. : (33) 04 93 01 00 01
Fax : (33) 04 93 01 28 99
reservebeaulieu@relaischateaux.com

Elegance, refinement, a gentle way of life and comfort are the watch-words which best describe the decor of this splendid Florentine residence where tradition and renewal have been so skilfully blended. In the restaurant, savour the delicious Mediterranean dishes such as «la bohémienne de grosses langoustines au doux amer de Campari». A sumptuous pool heated to 30° all year round. Discover the hotel's new boutique as well as its Maria Galland health and beauty centre.

Water sports, private harbor, shop. (Other activities P. 629)

Access: From Nice or from Monaco: follow the seacoast towards Beaulieu.
Airport: Nice Côte d'Azur (Intl) 15 km
Train station: Beaulieu 0,5 km
Owners: Delion Family
General Manager: Jean-Claude Delion
Open all year
Currency: Euro (€)
Rates: Menus 46-88-130 € s.i.
Carte 76-122 € s.i.
27 rooms: low season 183-634 € s.i.
high season 504-1260 € s.i.
10 suites: low season 916-1050 € s.i.
high season 1165-1940 € s.i.
Breakfast: 21-27 € s.i.
Dogs: allowed (extra cost)
Golf: Mont-Agel 12 km (18 holes)
Accepted cards: AE, DC, MC, VS

More info on www.relaischateaux.com/reservebeaulieu

Le Métropole

SINCE 1979

15, bd du Maréchal-Leclerc
06310 Beaulieu-sur-Mer
(Alpes-Maritimes) • France

Tel. : (33) 04 93 01 00 08
Fax : (33) 04 93 01 18 51
metropole@relaischateaux.com

France

This opulent gold and white villa, built in the style of an Italian palace, is set in magnificent gardens opening onto a private beach and pier. Guests will discover elegance, discretion and comfort and enjoy the luxury of the sumptuous pool heated to 30° all year round. Dine on the terrace beneath a beautiful white canopy, savouring superb regional cuisine which brings out the full splendour of seasonal produce.

(Other activities P. 629)

Access: From Nice or Monaco, follow the coast towards Beaulieu.

Airport: Nice Côte d'Azur (Intl) 15 km
Train station: Beaulieu 0,3 km

Owner: S.A. Hôtel Métropole
General Manager: Jean Rauline
Annual closing: From October 20th to Dec. 20th
Currency: Euro (€)
Rates: Menus 72-86 € s.i. Carte 70-100 € s.i.
35 rooms: half board - 2 pers. 280-710 € s.i.
5 suites: half board - 2 pers. 580-1120 € s.i.
Breakfast: 22 € s.i.
Dogs: allowed (extra cost)
Golf: Mont-Agel 18 km
Accepted cards: AE, DC, JCB, MC, VS

   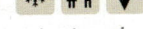

More info on www.relaischateaux.com/metropole

Château de La Chèvre d'Or

France — SINCE 1956

Moyenne corniche, rue du Barri
06360 Eze-Village
(Alpes-Maritimes) • France

Tel. : (33) 04 92 10 66 66
Fax : (33) 04 93 41 06 72
chevredor@relaischateaux.com

Perched between the mountains and the Mediterranean in the medieval village of Eze, the Château de la Chèvre d'Or has a superb view. The elegant rooms are set in the village. Its three restaurants offer a choice of cuisine suited to every fancy: «La Chèvre d'Or», gastronomic restaurant with its fine vintages and collection of cognacs and armagnacs, minutes away, «Le Grill du Château» and Italian-style «L'Oliveto».

Bowling pitch, ping-pong, tennis (500 m). (Other activities P. 629)

Access: From Nice (A8), exit La Turbie, Moyenne corniche towards Eze-Village.
Airport: Nice Côte d'Azur (Intl) 12 km
Train station: Monaco 8 km
Owner: S.C.I. La Chèvre d'Or
General Manager: Thierry Naidu
Weekly closing: Gastronomic restaurant: Wednesday (off-season)
Annual closing: From Nov. 23th to March 4th
Currency: Euro (€)
Rates: Menus 60 € s.i. (week lunch) 75 € s.i. (lunch) 130 € s.i. Carte 100-140 € s.i. Grill du Château 40 € s.i. Oliveto 32 € s.i.
26 rooms: 260-750 € s.i.
8 suites: 570-2450 € s.i.
Breakfast: 24-25 € s.i.
Dogs: allowed **Golf:** 7 km
Accepted cards: AE, DC, JCB, MC, VS

Grand Hôtel de Cala Rossa

SINCE 1993

20137 Porto-Vecchio
(Corse) • France

Tel. : (33) 04 95 71 61 51
Fax : (33) 04 95 71 60 11
calarossa@relaischateaux.com

France

Tucked away in a lush private park, the Grand Hôtel de Cala Rossa enjoys a wonderful location on a superb, fine sandy beach. Ideal both for family holidays and romantic stays. The cuisine does more than justice to divine seafood flavours without in any way neglecting regional products and autumn delights. Equipped with a magnificent spa, Cala Rossa invites you to come and explore Corsica at any time of the year.

Windsurfing, biking, boat trips, private hunting. (Other activities P. 629)

Access: 7 km north of Porto Vecchio, towards Bastia.

Airports: Figari (Intl) 35 km, Bastia Poretta (Intl) 90 km
Helipad: N 41° 37' 37" E 009° 20' 37"

Owners: Canarelli Family
General Manager: Patricia Biancarelli
Annual closing: From the beginning of January to the beginning of April
Currency: Euro (€)
Rates: Menus 43-84 € s.i. Carte 69-107
42 rooms: 215-550 € s.i.
6 suites: 365-720 € s.i.
Breakfast: 30 € s.i.
Dogs: not allowed
Golf: Spérone 40 km
Accepted cards: AE, DC, JCB, MC, VS

More info on www.relaischateaux.com/calarossa

La Villa

Chemin de Notre-Dame-de-la-Serra
20260 Calvi
(Corse) • France

Tel. : (33) 04 95 65 10 10
Fax : (33) 04 95 65 10 50
lavilla@relaischateaux.com

France

SINCE 1995

This elegant residence, part Corsican monastery, part Roman villa, is set in the picturesque hills of Calvi between the sea and the mountains. La Villa's exquisite guestrooms, sunny sitting rooms and flower-covered terraces are an open invitation to la dolce vita and the cuisine is a festival of Corsican flavours. Discover the forests of Bonifato, the Scandola nature reserve and the stunning views across Calvi Bay.

Trips, fitness. (Other activities P. 629)

Access: Notre-Dame-de-la-Serra lane. By plane: Calvi Ste-Catherine airport 7 km away. By sea: connections with Cie SNCM from Marseille, Nice, Toulon, arrival in Calvi and L'Ile-Rousse.
Airports: Calvi (Intl) 7 km, Bastia (Intl) 95 km
Train station: Calvi 2 km

Owner: Jean-Pierre Pinelli
Annual closing: From January 2nd to March 31st
Currency: Euro (€)
Rates: Carte 53-91 € s.i.
25 rooms: 300-570 € s.i.
28 suites: 510-1400 € s.i.
Breakfast: 23 € s.i.
Dogs: not allowed
Golf : 10 km (6 holes)
Accepted cards: AE, DC, JCB, MC, VS

More info on www.relaischateaux.com/lavilla

Benelux

Properties Belgium	Nearest major city	Relais & Châteaux	Relais Gourmands	Page
Auberge du Moulin Hideux	Bouillon	⚜		250
Barbizon (Restaurant)	Brussel		◉	245
Clos St. Denis	Tongeren		◉	246
De Snippe (Hôtel)	Bruges	⚜		242
Hof Van Cleve	Gent		◉	244
Lafarque (Hostellerie)	Liège	⚜	◉	249
Moulin des Ramiers (Le)	Namur	⚜		248
Saint-Roch (Hostellerie)	Liège	⚜		247
Shamrock (Hostellerie)	Oudenaarde	⚜		243

Luxembourg				
Bergerie (La)	Echternach		◉	251
Gaichel (La)	Arlon	⚜		253
Table des Guilloux (La)	Luxembourg		◉	252

Netherlands				
Kasteel Wittem	Maastricht	⚜		254
Manoir «Inter Scaldes»	Middelburg	⚜	◉	255

More info on www.relaischateaux.com

Belgium

SINCE 1991

Hotel De Snippe

53, Nieuwe Gentweg
B-8000 Bruges
(Flandre-occidentale) • Belgium

Tel. : (32) (050) 33 70 70
Fax : (32) (050) 33 76 62
desnippe@relaischateaux.com

Set in the heart of Bruges, the «Venice of Northern Europe», this magnificent hotel was once the mayor's residence. Its beautiful XVIIIth century decor has been lovingly restored by Luc and Francine Huysentruyt, and the stylish rooms have been designed to ensure utmost comfort. After a romantic stroll by the «Lac d'Amour» or a visit to one of the famous local museums, enjoy refined cuisine in the elegant winter garden.

(Other activities P. 629)

Access: Towards the city-centre. After the belfry, to the right.

Airports: Ostende (Intl) 30 km, Brussels (Intl) 100 km

Owners: Luc and Francine Huysentruyt
Weekly closing: Hotel: Sunday (from Nov. to Easter) Rest.: Sunday and Monday noon
Annual closing: From January 19th to February 13th and 2 weeks in the end of November
Currency: Euro (€)
Rates: Menus 50-66 € s.i. Carte 87 € s.i.
3 rooms: starting at 145 € s.i.
5 suites: starting at 195 € s.i.
Breakfast: included
Dogs: allowed **Golf:** Knokke-Le Zoute 16 km, Damme-Sijsele 10 km
Accepted cards: AE, DC, MC, VS

More info on www.relaischateaux.com/desnippe

Hostellerie Shamrock

SINCE 1976

Ommegangstraat, 148
B-9680 Maarkedal
Belgium

Tel. : (32) (055) 21 55 29
Fax : (32) (055) 21 56 83
shamrock@relaischateaux.com

Belgium

Bathed in soft, hazy sunlight, this elegant English-style manor, set in a somptuous park designed by the famous landscape artist J. Wirtz, would not look out of place in an Impressionist painting. This idyllic country retreat is the perfect setting in which to enjoy Claude De Beyter's innovative cuisine, flavoured with herbs from his own garden. The Shamrock is ideally situated near Bruges, Belœil and Gand.
Hiking in the woodlands. (Other activities P. 629)

Access: From Renaix, towards Oudenaarde (N 60), follow Muziekbos.

Airport: Brussels (Intl) 50 km
Train station: Oudenaarde 12 km

Owners: Livine and Claude De Beyter
Weekly closing: Monday, Tuesday
Annual closing: From July 15th to August 1st
Currency: Euro (€)
Rates: Menus 61-93 € s.i. Carte 60-85 € s.i.
4 rooms: 170-190 € s.i.
1 suite: 220 € s.i.
Breakfast: included
Dogs: not allowed
Golf: 15 km
Accepted cards: AE, DC, MC, VS

More info on www.relaischateaux.com/shamrock

Hof Van Cleve

Belgium

SINCE 2000

Riemegemstraat, 1
B-9770 Kruishoutem
Belgium

Tel. : (32) (09) 383 58 48
Fax : (32) (09) 383 77 25
vancleve@relaischateaux.com

In the Flemish Ardennes countryside 20 km from Gent, this rural farmhouse decorated with contemporary paintings performs a wonderful symphony of natural flavours interpreted by chef Peter Goossens. Nature is omnipresent. The recently renovated property offers you exceptional moments. Excellent wine card and old spirits as well as cigar card. Heaven for the most demanding palates.

(Other activities P. 629)

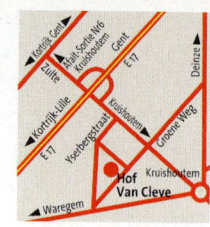

Access: Motorway E17 Lille-Courtrai (Kortrijk)-Anvers (Antwerpen), exit n°6 for Kruishoutem. Follow signs to Kruishoutem, after 1 km on the right, follow the signs.
Airports: Brussels (Intl) 60 km, Lille-Lesquin 40 km
Train station: Waregem 8 km

Owner: Peter Goossens
Weekly closing: Sunday and Monday
Annual closing: From Dec. 24th to January 10th, 1 week at Easter and 3 weeks in August
Currency: Euro (€)
Rates: Menus 150-250 € s.i. Carte 125-300 € s.i.
Dogs: not allowed
Golf: 5 km
Accepted cards: AE, DC, MC, VS

Peter Goossens

More info on www.relaischateaux.com/vancleve

Restaurant Barbizon

SINCE 1964

95, Welriekendedreef
B-3090 Jezus-Eik (Overijse)
(Brabant) • Belgium

Tel. : (32) (02) 657 04 62
Fax : (32) (02) 657 40 66
barbizon@relaischateaux.com

Belgium

For forty-five years, this elegant mansion near Brussels has welcomed gourmets from around the world. After studying with Troisgros and Chapel, Alain Deluc has created his own culinary masterpieces such as «raviolis aux truffes et céleris rave, émulsion gourmande», «thon et sa grosse langoustine rôtie, jus court au citron vert et coriandre», and «pigeon de vendée, croquant aux épices, miel et verjus». Enjoy fine wines, cigars and old Armagnacs.

Visits: Church of Notre-Dame-au-Bois, arboretum of Tervuren...
(Other activities P. 629)

Access: From Brussels, E411, towards Namur, exit n° 2 to Jezus-Eik Hœilaart, then take a right turn.

Airports: Brussels (Intl) 12 km, Namur 40 km
Helipad: N 50° 47' 318'' E 004° 28' 122''
Train station: Groenendaal 5 km

Owner: Alain Deluc
Weekly closing: Tuesday and Wednesday
Annual closing: From January 6th to 29th and from July 15th to August 6th
Currency: Euro (€)
Rates: Menus 36 € s.i.(week lunch) starting at 46 € s.i. Carte 62-99 € s.i.
Dogs: allowed
Golf: Tervuren 9 km
Accepted cards: AE, MC, VS

Alain Deluc

More info on www.relaischateaux.com/barbizon

Clos St. Denis

Belgium — SINCE 1995

Grimmertingenstraat 24
B-3724 Kortessem
(Limburg) • Belgium

Tel. : (32) (012) 23 60 96
Fax : (32) (012) 26 32 07
stdenis@relaischateaux.com

This magnificent XVIIth century farm-house, overlooking a picturesque courtyard, is decorated with oak panelling, Louis XIII furniture and sumptuous tapestries. An idyllic setting in which to savour Christian Denis's gourmet compositions. Enjoy «fantaisie de homard et de pommes de terre aux truffes du Périgord», «ravioli de foie d'oie, crème légère de truffes noires», accompanied by a vintage from the superb wine list.

Access: Motorway E40 dir. Louvain. At Louvain, take A2 - (E314) dir. Genk. At Lummen take A13 (E313) dir. Hasselt - Liège. At Hasselt take exit 29 dir. Tongeren N20 - (13 km).
Airport: Brussels (Intl) 95 km
Helipad: L 50° 49' 27" l 005° 25' 52"
Train station: Tongres 5 km

Owners: Denise and Christian Denis
Weekly closing: Tuesday and Wednesday
Annual closing: From April 7th to 15th, from July 16th to 30th and from December 28th to January 4th
Currency: Euro (€)
Rates: Menus 95-130 € s.i.
Carte 95-130 € s.i.
Dogs: not allowed
Accepted cards: AE, DC, MC, VS

Christian Denis

More info on www.relaischateaux.com/stdenis

Hostellerie Saint-Roch

SINCE 1982

Rue du Parc - Vallée de l'Ourthe
B-4180 Comblain-la-Tour
(Liège) • Belgium

Tel. : (32) (04) 369 13 33
Fax : (32) (04) 369 31 31
saintroch@relaischateaux.com

Belgium

This beautiful residence, formerly a post house, is set in the heart of a magnificent valley, and its flower-bedecked terrace looks out over the River Ourthe. Lovingly restored by owners Francis and Nicole Dernouchamps, the Saint-Roch offers an intimate atmosphere and peaceful rooms decorated with period furniture. Enjoy exceptional hospitality, superb seasonal cuisine and an outstanding selection of wines and brandies.

(Other activities P. 629)

Access: From Liege, towards «Luxembourg», motorway E25, exit Sprimont n°45, after Sprimont; towards Chanxhe, after the bridge over the Ourthe, follow signs «Hostellerie St-Roch» to the left.
Airports: Brussels (Intl) 110 km, Liege Bierset 30 km
Train station: Comblain-la-Tour 0,5 km

Owners: Mr and Mrs Dernouchamps-Cawet
Weekly closing: Hotel: Monday and Tuesday (except July-August) Rest.: Monday and Tuesday (Tuesday in July-August)
Annual closing: From January 3rd to March 10th
Currency: Euro (€)
Rates: Menus 32-64 € s.i. Carte 50-75 € s.i.
7 rooms: 150-170 € s.i.
8 suites: starting at 215 € s.i.
Breakfast: included
Dogs: allowed (extra cost)
Golf: 18-28 km (5 golf courses)
Accepted cards: AE, DC, MC, VS

More info on www.relaischateaux.com/saintroch

Le Moulin des Ramiers

Belgium — SINCE 1999

31-32, rue Basse
B-5332 Crupet
Belgium

Tel. : (32) (083) 699 070
Fax : (32) (083) 699 868
ramiers@relaischateaux.com

Set amidst the luxuriant foliage of Wallonie, the Ramiers is one of the great tables of Belgium thanks to the renowned talent and warm welcome of its hosts, Jeanine and André Fieuw. In this XVIIIth century mill, transformed into a hotel, you will appreciate the beamed ceilings of the superb rooms elegantly decorated with china, pewter, and baroque furniture. As for the restaurant, you will enjoy the classically-inspired yet contemporary cuisine of the chef, the owners' son, Hugues.

(Other activities P. 629)

Access: From E 411, exit 19 Spontin, Crupet 7 km away. From N 4, exit Assesse, Crupet 6 km away.

Airports: Gosselies (Intl) 50 km, Brussels (Intl) 78 km
Helipad: N 50° 20' 98" E 004° 57' 33"
Train station: Assesse 6 km

Owners: André and Jeanine Fieuw
Weekly closing: Monday evening and Tuesday, Monday all day (from nov. 1st to april 30th)
Annual closing: From January 6th to 17th, from March 3rd to 21st and from June 30th to July 10th (restaurant only)
Currency: Euro (€)
Rates: Menus 35-48-68 € s.i. Carte 46-69 € s.i.
6 rooms: starting at 116 € s.i.
Breakfast: 12 € s.i.
Dogs: allowed (extra cost)
Golf: 16 km (18 holes)
Accepted cards: AE, DC, MC, VS

More info on www.relaischateaux.com/ramiers

Hostellerie Lafarque

Chemin des Douys 20
B-4860 Pepinster - Goffontaine
(Liège) • Belgium

Tel. : (32) (087) 46 06 51
Fax : (32) (087) 46 97 28
lafarque@relaischateaux.com

Belgium

SINCE 1991

Victor Hugo once wrote «On a clear day, under a blue sky, the Vesdre Valley sometimes resembles a ravine, sometimes a garden, but always a paradise». Hosts Michel and Agnès Lafarque invite you to stay in their elegant 1920's house set in such a garden. This idyllic country haven is the perfect place to enjoy gourmet cuisine – «dos de loup de mer au raisiné», «mousse glacée à l'ananas confit» – fine wines and «joie de vivre».

Spa. (Other activities P. 629)

Access:
Motorway E 42, exit Pepinster RN61 towards Chaudfontaine; hotel indicated at Goffontaine. Motorway «des Ardennes» E 25, exit n° 45, towards Pepinster.
Airports: Brussels (Intl) 100 km, Liege Bierset 30 km
Helipad: N 50° 34' E 5° 46'
Train station: Verviers 10 km

Owners: Michel and Agnès Lafarque
Weekly closing: Monday and Tuesday
Annual closing: From March 10th to 30th and from September 1st to 15th
Currency: Euro (€)
Rates: Menus 65-75 € s.i. Carte 68-87 € s.i.
5 rooms: starting at 135 € s.i.
3 suites: starting at 200 € s.i.
Breakfast: 13 € s.i
Dogs: not allowed
Golf: Gomzé 15 km
Accepted cards: AE, DC, MC, VS

More info on www.relaischateaux.com/lafarque

Belgium

Auberge du Moulin Hideux

SINCE 1960

B-6831 Noirefontaine
(Luxembourg) • Belgium

Tel. : (32) (061) 46 70 15
Fax : (32) (061) 46 72 81
hideux@relaischateaux.com

Nestling in the picturesque Semois valley, this XVIIIth century millhouse has been an idyllic country inn for the past 50 years. When you discover its cosy ambience, its comfortable rooms, spacious tennis courts and indoor heated pool, you will understand why the Auberge du Moulin Hideux became the very first Relais de Campagne outside France. Enjoy romantic strolls through the forest and excellent regional cuisine.

Walks in the woodlands. (Other activities P. 629)

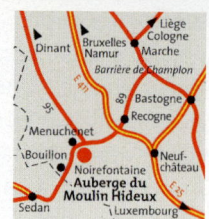

Access: From Brussels or Luxembourg, E411, exit 25, towards Bouillon; from Paris, A4 Reims towards Liège.

Airports: Luxembourg (Intl) 95 km, Brussels (Intl) 160 km
Train station: Libramont 20 km

Owners: Charles and Martine Lahire
Weekly closing: Restaurant: Wednesday and Thursday for lunch (March to June only)
Annual closing: From Dec. 1st to March 15th
Currency: Euro (€)
Rates: Menus 60-75 € s.i. 100 € s.i. with wine
Carte 50-87 € s.i.
9 rooms: starting at 200 € s.i.
3 suites: starting at 240 € s.i.
Breakfast: included
Dogs: allowed (extra cost) **Golf:** 40 km
Accepted cards: AE, DC, MC, VS

More info on www.relaischateaux.com/hideux

La Bergerie

SINCE 2003

Maison 1
L-6251 Geyershaff
Luxembourg

Tel. : **(352) 79 04 64**
Fax : (352) 79 07 71
bergerie@relaischateaux.com

Luxembourg

A sheep has been kept as the emblem of this former sheep farm now converted into a magnificent residence. Following in his father's footsteps, Thierry Phal and his wife, Josette, continue to offer welcoming and impeccable service. The cuisine, always disciplined, full of flavours and excellence: «palette de foie gras d'oie et de canard aux cinq saveurs», «symphonie de noix de coquilles Saint-Jacques», «pigeonneau des Landes grillé en crapaudine».

(Other activities P. 629)

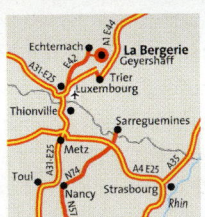

Access: From Strasbourg, motorway A 4-E 25, towards Metz. After Metz, motorway A 31-E 25, towards Luxembourg airport. Motorway A 1-E 44, exit 13, E 42, Echternach then Geyershaff.
Airport: Luxembourg (Intl) 30 km
Train station: Luxembourg 30 km

Owner: Claude Phal
General Manager: Thierry Phal
Weekly closing: Lunch week, Sunday evening, Monday
Annual closing: From January 15th to February 15th
Currency: Euro (€)
Rates: Carte 80-120 € s.i.
Dogs: allowed
Golf: 10 km
Accepted cards: AE, DC, MC, VS

Thierry Phal

More info on www.relaischateaux.com/bergerie

Luxembourg

La Table des Guilloux

SINCE 1997

17-19, rue de la Résistance
L-4996 Schouweiler
Luxembourg

Tel. : (352) 37 00 08
Fax : (352) 37 11 61
guilloux@relaischateaux.com

Gourmets flock to Pierrick and Lysiane Guilloux's picturesque country house to savour some of the finest cuisine in Luxembourg. Discover a sublime «tournedos de morue fraîche poêlée, purée grand-mère», a remarkable «queue de bœuf farcie au foie gras» and a superb «turbot rôti aux échalotes confites». Heavenly desserts and a wonderfully eclectic wine list complete this extraordinary gastronomic experience.

Access: From the airport: motorway towards Brussels, exit Bertrange. After Dippach, towards Schouweiler. From France: towards Brussels, exit Bertrange.
Airport: Luxembourg (Intl) 12 km
Train station: Luxembourg 12 km

Owners: Pierrick and Lysiane Guilloux
Weekly closing: Monday, Tuesday and Saturday at lunch
Annual closing: From August 1st to 15th and from December 23rd to January 5th
Currency: Euro (€)
Rates: Menus 40-50 € s.i.
Carte 37-50 € s.i.
Dogs: allowed

Pierrick Guilloux

More info on www.relaischateaux.com/guilloux

La Gaichel

SINCE 1971

L-8469 Gaichel/Eischen
Luxembourg

Tel. : (352) 39 01 29
Fax : (352) 39 00 37
gaichel@relaischateaux.com

Luxembourg

Since 1852, this elegant rose-coloured residence has preserved the tradition of family hospitality and fine living. La Gaichel's comfortable guestrooms open out onto pretty balconies overlooking a country stream meandering through 35 acres of luxuriant parkland. The hotel is also renowned as a gourmet retreat where guests can dine al fresco on the beautiful garden terrace or enjoy the refined ambience of the restaurant.

(Other activities P. 629)

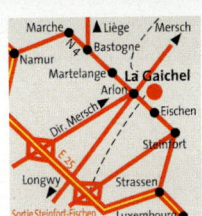

Access: From Belgium, E411, E25 exit Arlon, «autres directions» sign, then towards Mersch, Gaichel. From Luxembourg (via the motorway): exit Steinfort, Eischen, Gaichel.
Airports: Luxembourg (Intl) 25 km, Brussels (Intl) 185 km
Train station: Arlon 4 km

Owners: Michel and Claudine Gaul-Jacquemin
Weekly closing: Sunday evening, Monday, Tuesday noon
Annual closing: From January 5th to February 6th and from August 17th to 28th
Currency: Euro (€)
Rates: Menus 40-90 € s.i. Carte 52-73 € s.i.
13 rooms: 110-145 € s.i.
Breakfast: included
Dogs: not allowed
Golf: on the premises (9 holes)
Accepted cards: AE, MC, VS

More info on www.relaischateaux.com/gaichel

Kasteel Wittem

Wittemer Allée 3
NL-6286 AA Wittem
(Limburg) • Netherlands

Tel. : (31) (043) 4501208
Fax : (31) (043) 4501260
wittem@relaischateaux.com

SINCE 1980

"Discover the history of the Netherlands at this magnificent medieval castle, surrounded by an ancient moat and a picturesque park. Kasteel Wittem certainly lives up to its motto «Hospitality and Aptitude». You will find this impeccable service everywhere from the elegant rooms of the castle to the suites in the donjon. Enjoy a country luncheon on the terrace by the moat and a divine candlelit dinner in the restaurant.

Walks, biking, thermal baths (8 km). (Other activities P. 629)

Access: E25, exit Maastricht, N278 towards Vaals; E314, exit N281, towards Vaals, Maastricht.

Airports: Brussels (Intl) 130 km, Amsterdam Schiphol (Intl) 200 km
Train station: Maastricht 17 km

Owners: Ritzen Family
General Managers: Peter and Marc Ritzen
Open all year
Currency: Euro (€)
Rates: Menus 60-90 € s.i.
Carte 60-73 € s.i.
10 rooms: 160-185 € s.i.
2 suites: 230 € s.i.
Breakfast: 17 € s.i.
Dogs: not allowed
Golf: 7 km
Accepted cards: AE, DC, JCB, MC, VS

More info on www.relaischateaux.com/wittem

Manoir «Inter Scaldes»

Zandweg 2
NL-4416 NA Kruiningen Yerseke
(Zeeland) • Netherlands

Tel. : (31) (113) 381753
Fax : (31) (113) 381763
scaldes@relaischateaux.com

SINCE 1988

Netherlands

This magnificent manor, with its picturesque thatched roof and English-style gardens, is set near one of the most beautiful deltas in Europe. Here, Jannis Brevet creates seafood dishes such as you have never tasted before. His «homard au sauterne» is extraordinary and the «Saint-Jacques en coquilles lutées à la truffe» divine. Enjoy heavenly desserts and superb wines, then retire to an elegant guestroom.
Hunting... (Other activities P. 629)

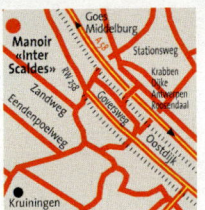

Access: From Anvers, A 12, then A 58 towards Vlissingen, exit n°33 Yerseke/Hansweert to the left, third way to the left.

Airport: Brussels (Intl) 100 km
Helipad: N 51° 27' 24'' E 04° 01' 17''
Train station: Kruiningen 5 km

Owners: J.P. and C.S. Brevet
Weekly closing: Rest.: Monday and Tuesday (except residents)
Annual closing: 2 weeks in February
Currency: Euro (€)
Rates: Menus 74-99 € s.i.
Carte 68-127 € s.i.
12 suites: 165-230 € s.i.
Breakfast: 18 € s.i.
Dogs: allowed (extra cost)
Golf: 11 km
Accepted cards: AE, DC, MC, VS

Jannis Brevet

More info on www.relaischateaux.com/scaldes

Switzerland
Liechtenstein

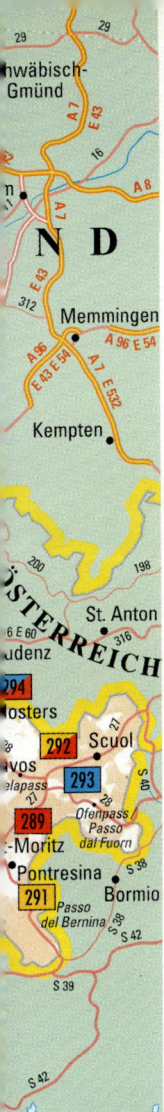

Properties Switzerland	Nearest major city	Relais & Châteaux	Relais Gourmands	Page
Albergo Giardino	Locarno	⚜		284
Auberge du Raisin	Lausanne	⚜	●	273
Bruderholz (Restaurant)	Basel		●	258
Castello del Sole	Locarno	⚜		283
Cerf (Restaurant du)	Lausanne		●	271
Chalet d'Adrien	Verbier	⚜		279
Cigogne (Hôtel de la)	Genève	⚜		268
Débarcadère (Hostellerie du)	Lausanne	⚜		269
Domaine de Châteauvieux	Genève	⚜	●	267
Ermitage Am See	Zürich	⚜		261
Grandhotel Schönegg	Zermatt	⚜		282
Gygax (Nik) - Gasthof Lowen	Bern		●	264
Haus Paradies (Hotel)	Scuol	⚜	●	292
Hostellerie Alpenrose	Gstaad	⚜		276
Kunststuben (Restaurant)	Zürich		●	262
Park Hotel Weggis	Lucerne	⚜		263
Pas de l'Ours (Hostellerie du)	Crans-Montana	⚜		277
Pont de Brent (Le)	Montreux		●	274
Ravet (Bernard) (L'Ermitage de)	Morges	⚜	●	272
Rheinhotel Fischerzunft	Schaffhausen	⚜	●	259
Rochat (Ph.) - Rest. de l'Hôtel de Ville	Lausanne		●	270
Rosalp (Hôtel)	Martigny	⚜	●	278
Santabbondio	Lugano		●	287
Schlosshotel Chastè	Scuol	⚜		293
Sources des Alpes (Les)	Sion	⚜		281
Splügenschloss (Hotel)	Zürich	⚜		260
Talvo (Jöhri's) (Restaurant)	St Moritz		●	289
Victoria (Hôtel)	Montreux	⚜		275
Vieux Manoir au Lac (Le)	Bern	⚜		266
Villa Margherita	Lugano	⚜		285
Villa Principe Leopoldo & Resid.	Lugano	⚜		288
Walserhof (Hotel)	Davos	⚜	●	294
Walther (Hotel)	St Moritz	⚜		291
Wenger (Georges)	La Chaux-de-Fonds	⚜	●	265

Liechtenstein

Parkhotel Sonnenhof	St. Gallen	⚜		295

Equivalent in euros for information only (rate of 2/07/01). Application of the exchange rate valid on the day of transaction.

More info on www.relaischateaux.ch

Switzerland

Restaurant Bruderholz

SINCE 1977

Bruderholzallee 42
CH-4059 Basel
Switzerland

Tel. : **(41) (061) 361 82 22**
Fax : (41) (061) 361 82 03
bruderholz@relaischateaux.com

On the residential hillside of Bruderholz overlooking Basel, Pierre Buess welcomes you in his splendid restaurant with its floral gardens. In the kitchen, Jean-Claude Wicky will create a veritable feast for your senses with his symphony of flavours, inspired by French culinary tradition. Savour «feuilleté à la truffe noire du Périgord» or «canard nantais au vinaigre de noix et miel de châtaignes». Superb vintages.

Contemporary Art Museum, Tinguely Museum, Puppen Museum, Kunst Museum, Sacher Foundation (music), Beyeler Foundation. (Other activities P. 629)

Access: From the Basel train station, follow signs for «Bruderholz».

Airport: Basel (Intl) 5 km
Train station: Basel 5 km

Owner: Pierre Buess
Weekly closing: Sunday and Monday
Open all year
Currency: Swiss franc (CHF)
Rates: Menus 88-190 CHF s.i. - 58-125 €
Carte 45-95 CHF s.i. - 30-62 €
Dogs: allowed
Golf: Hagenthal 6 km
Accepted cards: AE, DC, MC, VS

Jean-Claude Wicky

More info on www.relaischateaux.com/bruderholz

Rheinhotel Fischerzunft

SINCE 1984

Rheinquai 8
CH-8202 Schaffhausen
Switzerland

Tel. : (41) (052) 632 05 05
Fax : (41) (052) 632 05 13
fischerzunft@relaischateaux.com

Switzerland

Relax on the waterside terrace of this splendid XVIIth century estate, set on the picturesque banks of the Rhine, and enjoy idyllic surroundings and complete tranquillity. The supremely comfortable guestrooms are bathed in natural light. Virtuoso chef André Jaeger has blended European gourmet tradition with Asiatic inspiration and his innovative menus, enhanced by the finest vintages, are a veritable feast for the senses.

(Other activities P. 629)

Access: From Zurich, green signs to St-Gallen, Winterthur. Highway exit Schaffhausen.

Airport: Zurich (Intl) 40 km
Train station: Schaffhausen 2,5 km

Owner: André Jaeger
Weekly closing: Rest.: Monday, Tuesday (from January 8th to March 31st)
Open all year
Currency: Swiss franc (CHF)
Rates: Menus 168-195 CHF s.i. - 110-128 €
Carte 65-76 CHF s.i. - 43-50 €
10 rooms: 190-440 CHF s.i. - 125-289 €
Breakfast: included
Dogs: allowed (extra cost)
Golf: 20 km
Accepted cards: AE, DC, MC, VS

André Jaeger

More info on www.relaischateaux.com/fiserzunft

Switzerland

Hotel Splügenschloss

SINCE 1986

Splügenstrasse 2/Genferstrasse
CH-8002 Zürich
Switzerland

Tel. : (41) (01) 289 99 99
Fax : (41) (01) 289 99 98
splugenschloss@relaischateaux.com

A magnificent townhouse, your residence in the heart of Zurich, in a quiet location, close to the lakeside promenade, the elegant Bahnhofstrasse, the Tonhalle and the opera house. Charming, individually appointed rooms for business clients and connoisseurs who appreciate the warm hospitality of the Stump/Öhrbom family. Savour inventive and light French/Swiss cuisine at the Schloss-restaurant.

Museums, concerts, opera, theatre. (Other activities P. 629)

Access: From central station, follow Limmatquai, Quai-Brücke, then General-Guisan-Quai. Turn right at Rentenanstalt, then Jenatschstrasse.
Airport: Zurich (Intl) 6 km
Train station: Hauptbahnhof 2 km

Owners: Stump/Öhrbom Family
Open all year
Currency: Swiss franc (CHF)
Rates: Menus 65-110 CHF s.i. - 43-72 €
Carte 75-250 CHF s.i. - 49-164 €
48 rooms: 295-580 CHF s.i. - 196-386 €
2 suites: starting at 695 CHF s.i. - 463 €
Breakfast: included
Dogs: allowed (extra cost)
Golf: 3 km
Accepted cards: AE, DC, JCB, MC, VS

More info on www.relaischateaux.com/splugenschloss

Ermitage Am See

SINCE 2000

Seestrasse 80
CH-8700 Küsnacht
(Zürich) • Switzerland

Tel. : (41) (01) 914 42 42
Fax : (41) (01) 914 42 43
ermitage@relaischateaux.com

Switzerland

Near Zurich, in the heart of a picturesque landscape of lakes and forests, the Ermitage offers you the charm of its comfortable rooms with a spectacular view on the lake. Between two strolls through the vineyards, enjoy a romantic candlelight dinner savouring a subtile and refined cuisine served with the excellent regional wines. Visit an unusual site: the Fraumünster church with its stained glass windows by Chagall.

Museums. Private limousine on request. (Other activities P. 629)

Access: Zurich, place «Bellevue», follow signs to Rapperswil via the Seestrasse (N17), continue for about 7 km.

Airport: Zürich (Intl) 15 km
Train station: Küsnacht ZH 1 km

Owner: Hotel Ermitage Am See AG
General Managers: Lisbeth and Kurt Schmid
Open all year
Currency: Swiss franc (CHF)
Rates: Menus 62-150 CHF s.i. - 41-99 €
Carte 95-136 CHF s.i. - 62-89 €
20 rooms: 195-410 CHF s.i. - 128-270 €
6 suites: 510-780 CHF s.i. - 335-513 €
Breakfast: carte 25 CHF s.i. - 16 €
Dogs: allowed (extra cost)
Golf : 10 km
Accepted cards: AE, DC, MC, VS

More info on www.relaischateaux.com/ermitage

Switzerland

Restaurant Kunststuben

SINCE 1992

Seestrasse 160
CH-8700 Küsnacht
(Zürich) • Switzerland

Tel. : **(41) (01) 910 07 15**
Fax : (41) (01) 910 04 95
kunststuben@relaischateaux.com

Gourmets flock to this elegant restaurant near Zurich to savour Horst Petermann's inspired cuisine. A master of precise timing, Petermann draws the most exquisite flavours from his ingredients and dazzles guests with his repertoire of culinary innovation. Savour «les écrevisses pates rouges et le mille-feuille aux artichauts et truffes noires», «le cochon de lait au chutney d'abricots sauce aux épices» and the finest Swiss and French wines.

C.G. Jung Institute. (Other activities P. 629)

Access: Zurich, place Bellevue, towards Rapperswil via the Seestrasse.

Airport: Zurich (Intl) 15 km
Train station: Küsnacht 0,2 km

Owners: Horst and Iris Petermann
Weekly closing: Sunday and Monday
Annual closing: 2 weeks in February and 3 weeks mid-August
Currency: Swiss franc (CHF)
Rates: Menus 78 CHF (lunch) s.i. - 51 €
135-195 CHF s.i. - 89-128 €
Carte 36-85 CHF s.i. - 24-56 €
Dogs: allowed (no extra cost)
Golf: 3 km
Accepted cards: AE, DC, MC, VS

Horst Petermann

More info on www.relaischateaux.com/kunststuben

Park Hotel Weggis

SINCE 2003

Hertensteinstrasse 34
CH-6353 Weggis
Switzerland

Tel. : **(41) (041) 392 05 05**
Fax : (41) (041) 392 05 28
weggis@relaischateaux.com

Switzerland

In a shady park, on the banks of Lake Lucerne, the two light buildings with their balconies and turrets of the Park Hotel, offer upscale facilities in an enchanting setting enhanced by a wellness centre, three restaurants and a vinotheque. The splendid view of the lake (with a private beach) and the Central Swiss Alps, the understated, elegant décor all testify to a very special lifestyle.

(Other activities P. 629)

Access: On the motorway A4-E41, exit Küssnacht am Rigi. Follow Road 2 for 0.5 km. Then Road 2B for 6.8 km.

Airport: Zurich (Intl) 65 km
Train station: Küssnacht am Rigi 8 km

Owner: Aldopark AG
General Manager: Peter Kämpfer
Weekly closing: Restaurant Annex: Tuesday
Currency: Swiss franc (CHF)
Rates: Menus 78-100 CHF s.i. - 51-66 €
Carte 95-125 CHF s.i. - 62-82 €
34 rooms: 320-520 CHF s.i. - 210-342 €
9 suites: 500-1100 CHF s.i. - 329-723 €
Breakfast: 25-45 CHF s.i. - 16-30 €
Dogs: allowed (hotel, extra cost)
Golf: 8 km
Accepted cards: AE, DC, MC, VS

More info on www.relaischateaux.com/weggis

Nik Gygax - Gasthof Löwen

Switzerland

SINCE 2001

Langenthalstrasse 1
CH-3367 Thörigen
(Bern) • Switzerland

Tel. : (41) (062) 961 2107
Fax : (41) (062) 961 1672
lowen@relaischateaux.com

Not far from the splendid baroque town of Solothurn, between Bern and Basel, the village of Thörigen is home to the culinary talent of Nik Gygax. His preference goes to poultry dishes «canard de Challans laqué au miel de pissenlit» and meat dishes in general. Dishes on his menu include Simmental beef, Emmental milk-fed veal and Sisteron lamb. His wife Gabi's warm welcome is a prelude to her husband's generous cuisine.

(Other activities P. 629)

Access: A1: Wangen a/A - Herzogenbuchsee - Thörigen
A1: Kirchberg - Herzogenbuchsee - Thörigen (from Bern)

Airports: Zürich (Intl) 70 km, Bern Belp 30 km
Train station: Herzogenbuchsee 2 km

Owner: Nik Gygax
Weekly closing: Sunday and Monday
Annual closing: From September 21st to October 12th
Currency: Swiss franc (CHF)
Rates: Menus 130-180 CHF s.i. - 85-118 €
Carte 28-70 CHF s.i. - 18-46 €
Dogs: allowed
Golf: 18 km
Accepted cards: AE, DC, MC, VS

More info on www.relaischateaux.com/lowen

Georges Wenger

SINCE 1998

2, rue de la Gare
CH-2340 Le Noirmont
(Jura) • Switzerland

Tel. : (41) (032) 957 66 33
Fax : (41) (032) 957 66 34
wenger@relaischateaux.com

Switzerland

In the region of Swiss watch making, Georges Wenger and his wife invite you to come and share the flavours of a place which imparts its rounded character to contemporary cuisine inspired by tradition. The rooms invite you to relax in a tranquil and refined setting offering every possible comfort. Sumptuous wine cellar.
Climbing, ice-skating. (Other activities P. 629)

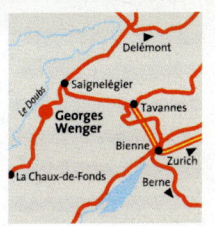

Altitude: 1000 m.
Access: From Geneva, A1 dir. La Chaux-de-Fonds, then N18 dir. Bâle.

Airports: Berne Belp (Intl) 80 km, Zurich (Intl) 100 km
Train station: Le Noirmont 0,3 km

Owners: Georges and Andrea Wenger
Weekly closing:
Restaurant: Monday and Tuesday
Annual closing:
From December 23rd to January 23rd
Currency: Swiss franc (CHF)
Rates: Menus 95-190 CHF s.i. - 62-125 €
Carte 90-130 CHF s.i. - 59-85 €
1 room: 270 CHF s.i. - 178 €
4 suites: 300-380 CHF s.i. - 197-250 €
Breakfast: included
Dogs: allowed (extra cost)
Golf: 5 km
Accepted cards: AE, DC, JCB, MC, VS

More info on www.relaischateaux.com/wenger

Switzerland

Le Vieux Manoir au Lac

SINCE 1969

Rue de Lausanne 18
CH-3280 Murten-Meyriez
(Fribourg) • Switzerland

Tel. : (41) (026) 678 61 61
Fax : (41) (026) 678 61 62
vieuxmanoir@relaischateaux.com

This beautiful manor is set in a romantic park overlooking the tranquil waters of Lake Morat. Its spacious guestrooms, tastefully decorated with period furniture, offer vistas of idyllic green countryside stretching away to the horizon. Seasonal cuisine, prepared with the finest local produce, is enhanced by an exceptional Vully wine. Take a bicycle tour or experience the wonders of outdoor opera.

Private beach, water sports, vineyard visits. Art and culture : Open air Opera Festival, the «Jeudis du Vieux Manoir». (Other activities P. 629)

Access: From the north, towards Bern/Neufeld, exit Murten/Morat. From the south, N12, exit Fribourg Nord.

Airports: Berne Belp (Intl) 30 km, Zurich (Intl) 120 km, Geneva (Intl) 120 km
Train station: Morat 1 km

Owner: Annelise Leu
General Manager: Michael Gähler
Annual closing: From mid-Dec. to mid-Feb.
Currency: Swiss franc (CHF)
Rates: Menus 75-130 CHF s.i. - 49-85 €
Carte 80-110 CHF s.i. - 53-72 €
23 rooms: 390-470 CHF s.i. - 256-309 €
10 suites: 510-580 CHF s.i. - 335-381 €
Breakfast: included
Dogs: allowed (extra cost)
Golf: 5 between 8 and 40 km
Accepted cards: AE, DC, MC, VS

More info on www.relaischateaux.com/vieuxmanoir

Domaine de Châteauvieux

SINCE 2003

16 ch. de Châteauvieux
CH-1242 Peney-Dessus
Switzerland

Tel. : (41) (022) 753 15 11
Fax : (41) (022) 753 19 24
chateauvieux@relaischateaux.com

Switzerland

In the former outbuildings of the Château de Peney, close to Geneva, Philippe Chevrier reunites his love of the beautiful and the good. In a tranquil setting, he prepares a cuisine constantly in pursuit of perfection: «porcelet de la ferme d'Ormalingen rôti et laqué aux fèves avec un jus réduit à la sarriette»; «homard breton rôti entier sur risotto à la truffe blanche d'Alba» and, when in season, game birds and animals...

(Other activities P. 629)

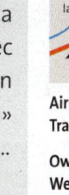

Access: Motorway E 25 - E 62. Exit Bernex. Follow Chancy, Aire-la-Ville and Peney-Dessus.

Airport: Geneva 8 km
Train station: Satigny 2 km

Owner/General Manager: Philippe Chevrier
Weekly closing: Restaurant: Sunday, Monday
Annual closing: From December 23rd to January 6th, from April 20th to 28th and from July 27th to August 11th
Currency: Swiss franc (CHF)
Rates: Menus 86-210 CHF s.i. - 57-138 €
Carte 170-280 CHF s.i. - 112-184 €
17 rooms: 285-395 CHF s.i. - 187-260 €
Breakfast: included
Dogs: allowed
Golf: 15 km
Accepted cards: AE, DC, MC, VS

Philippe Chevrier

More info on www.relaischateaux.com/chateauvieux

Switzerland — SINCE 1989

Hôtel de la Cigogne

17, place Longemalle
CH-1204 Genève
Switzerland

Tel. : (41) (022) 818 40 40
Fax : (41) (022) 818 40 50
cigogne@relaischateaux.com

In the heart of Geneva, a short stroll from the lake and old town, the Hôtel de la Cigogne enjoys an ideal setting. The character of the magnificently furnished rooms and suites coupled with the elegance of the salon lend this turn-of-the-century residence its special charm. Beneath its elegant glass roof, the restaurant offers gourmet cuisine enhanced by an exceptional wine list featuring the very best vintages.

Wellness and fitness centre 100 m away... (Other activities P. 629)

Access: From the Paris motorway, Annemasse, Geneva-Vallard, city centre before the Mont-Blanc bridge, turn left.

Airport: Geneva (Intl) 8 km
Train station: Cornavin 1 km

Owner: René Favre
General Manager: Philippe Vuillemin
Open all year
Currency: Swiss franc (CHF)
Rates: Menus 65-110 CHF s.i. - 43-72 €
Carte 75-115 CHF s.i. - 49-76 €
43 rooms: 460 CHF s.i. - 302 €
9 suites: 780-890 CHF s.i. - 513-585 €
Breakfast: included
Dogs: allowed (extra cost) except rest.
Golf: 8 km
Accepted cards: AE, DC, MC, VS

More info on www.relaischateaux.com/cigogne

Hostellerie du Débarcadère

SINCE 1983

Chemin du Crêt 7
CH-1025 St-Sulpice-Lausanne
(Vaud) • Switzerland

Tel. : (41) (021) 694 33 33
Fax : (41) (021) 691 50 79
debarcadere@relaischateaux.com

Switzerland

The Kluvers' elegant hotel, set on the picturesque banks of Lake Geneva, is renowned for its exceptional hospitality. Its comfortable rooms, resplendent with pastel walls and rustic furniture, offer superb panoramic vistas of the lake and the winter garden is a sheer delight. Enjoy generous cuisine featuring salmon trout, char and perch from the lake, accompanied by fine wines from Switzerland and France.

Trips, water sports, jogging, museums. (Other activities P. 629)

Access: From the highway, towards Lausanne sud, exit Saint-Sulpice.

Airport: Geneva (Intl) 40 km
Train station: Lausanne 5 km

Owners: Tony and Caroline Kluvers
Weekly closing: Saturday noon and Sunday from October to March
Annual closing: From Dec. 20th to January 20th
Currency: Swiss franc (CHF)
Rates: Menus 105-141 CHF s.i. - 69-93 €
Carte 25-95 CHF s.i. - 16-62 €
12 rooms: 197-420 CHF s.i. - 130-276 €
3 suites: 300-520 CHF s.i. - 197-342 €
Breakfast: 23 CHF s.i. - 15 €
Dogs: allowed (extra cost)
Golf: 20 km
Accepted cards: AE, MC, VS

More info on www.relaischateaux.com/debarcadere

Switzerland — SINCE 1998

Rest. de l'Hôtel de Ville - Ph. Rochat

1, rue d'Yverdon
CH-1023 Crissier
(Vaud) • Switzerland

Tel. : (41) (021) 634 05 05
Fax : (41) (021) 634 24 64
hoteldeville@relaischateaux.com

This elegant restaurant near Lausanne is a temple of gastronomy where chef Philippe Rochat delights gourmet palates with his exquisite culinary masterpieces and fine wines. The «chartreuse de pointes d'asperges vertes aux morilles à la fricassée de grenouilles» is excellent, the «canard nantais cuit rosé au vin de Brouilly» superb and the «conversation tiède de fraises des bois, glace à la vanille» simply divine.

Numerous museums (Olympique 5 km, the Hermitage 6 km away). (Other activities P. 629)

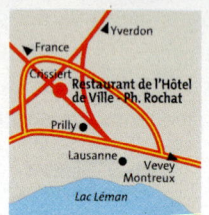

Access: 5 km from Lausanne, motorway exit Crissier, take direction Crissier centre.

Airports: Geneva (Intl) 50 km, Lausanne 5 km
Train station: Lausanne 5 km

Owner: Philippe Rochat
Weekly closing: Sunday and Monday
Annual closing: Last week of July, first two weeks of August and two weeks at Christmas
Currency: Swiss franc (CHF)
Rates: Menus 240-260 CHF s.i. - 158-171 €
Carte 50-100 CHF s.i. - 33-66 €
Dogs: allowed
Golf: 5 km
Accepted cards: AE, DC, MC, VS

Philippe Rochat

More info on www.relaischateaux.com/hoteldeville

Restaurant du Cerf

SINCE 2003

Rue du Temple 10
CH-1304 Cossonay-Ville
(Vaud) • Switzerland

Tel. : (41) (021) 861 26 08
Fax : (41) (021) 861 26 27
ducerf@relaischateaux.com

Switzerland

Original flavours and aestheticism are the order of the day here. In a mediaeval dining room with contemporary décor, Carlo Crisci lovingly conjures up dishes which are true works of art, creations constantly updated to the seasons often based on wild herbs and roots. The epitomy of excellence and refinement. Savour «foie gras en gelée de vino santo» or «pigeon de Racan en vessie parfumé à la flouve».

Access: On the motorway Lausanne Yverdon-les-Bains A 1-E 23, exit Cossonay. On the outskirts of the village turn right, towards old town, restaurant parallel to the Temple.
Airport: Geneva (Intl) 60 km
Train station: Cossonay 2,5 km

Owner/General Manager: Carlo Crisci
Weekly closing: Sunday, Monday
Annual closing: From December 23th to January 2nd and the three last weeks of July
Currency: Swiss franc (CHF)
Rates: Menus 155-215 CHF s.i. - 102-141 €
Carte 111-165 CHF s.i. - 73-108 €
Dogs: allowed
Accepted cards: AE, MC, VS

Carlo Crisci

More info on www.relaischateaux.com/ducerf

L'Ermitage de Bernard Ravet

Switzerland — SINCE 2002

Route du Village
CH-1134 Vufflens-le-Château
(Vaud) • Switzerland

Tel. : (41) (0) 21 804 68 68
Fax : (41) (0) 21 802 22 40
lermitage@relaischateaux.com

Tastefully and elegantly refurbished, this beautiful XVIIIth century property of Bernard and Ruth Ravet, located 15 minutes from Lausanne, offers a holiday setting which is tantamount to a lifestyle in the Vaud region. Originally from Burgundy, Bernard Ravet offers gourmets the very best from his repertoire: «marinière d'écrevisses au pistou de basilic», «canard fermier doré et confit au miel de châtaignier».

(Other activities P. 629)

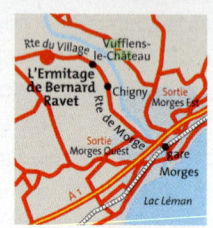

Access:
From Geneva: exit Morges. Follow signposts «Vufflens-Chigny». From Lausanne: exit Morges west. Follow signposts «Vufflens-Chigny».
Airport: Geneva (Intl) 55 km
Train station: Vufflens 0,5 km

Owner/General Manager: Bernard Ravet
Weekly closing: Sunday and Monday
Annual closing: Three weeks in August, three weeks at Christmas
Currency: Swiss franc (CHF)
Rates: Menus 160-198 CHF s.i. - 105-130 €
Carte 168-200 CHF s.i. - 110-132 €
6 rooms: 350-400 CHF s.i. - 230-263 €
3 suites: 450-580 CHF s.i. - 296-381 €
Breakfast: included
Dogs: allowed
Golf: 25 km
Accepted cards: AE, DC, MC, VS

Bernard Ravet

More info on www.relaischateaux.com/lermitage

Auberge du Raisin

SINCE 1991

1, place de l'Hôtel-de-Ville
CH-1096 Cully
(Vaud) • Switzerland

Tel. : **(41) (021) 799 21 31**
Fax : (41) (021) 799 25 01
raisin@relaischateaux.com

Switzerland

In this elegant old Swiss inn, Adolfo Blokbergen creates innovative gourmet cuisine, drawing the most subtle flavours from his ingredients. You will be enchanted by his superb «île flottante à l'émulsion d'asperges vertes au caviar» and her «grillade d'écrevisses en cappucino». The cellar, filled with Swiss, French and Californian vintages, includes famous white wines from the Lavaux vineyard.
Museums, walks, beach. (Other activities P. 629)

Access: From Lausanne, exit Belmont; at Lutry towards Villette; 2 km later, towards Cully.

Airports: Geneva (Intl) 70 km, Sion 80 km
Train station: Cully 1 km

Owner: Jean-Jacques Gauer S.A.
General Managers: Mr and Mrs A. Blokbergen
Open all year
Currency: Swiss franc (CHF)
Rates: Menus 89-198 CHF s.i. - 59-130 €
Carte 79-160 CHF s.i. - 52-105 €
7 rooms: 320 CHF s.i. - 210 €
2 suites: 450-550 CHF s.i. - 296-362 €
Breakfast: 15 CHF s.i. - 10 €
Dogs: allowed (extra cost)
Golf: 8 km
Accepted cards: AE, DC, MC, VS

Adolfo Blokbergen

More info on www.relaischateaux.com/raisin

Le Pont de Brent

SINCE 1991

CH-1817 Brent/Montreux
(Vaud) • Switzerland

Tel. : (41) (021) 964 52 30
Fax : (41) (021) 964 55 30
brent@relaischateaux.com

Switzerland

Talented Norman chef Gérard Rabaey, now accepted as an honorary Vaudois, welcomes gourmets to this picturesque residence above Montreux. Rabaey's inventive French cuisine is prepared with the finest local produce. Savour: «morilles farcies sur truffes, poireaux et asperges vertes», «rougets aux choux nouveaux, sabayon au poivron», «éventail à la rhubarbe, glace noix et miel». The cellar is a treasure trove of Swiss and French vintages.

Walks and trips (château of Chillon). (Other activities P. 629)

Access: Motorway N9, exit Montreux West, towards Blonay-Brent, go through the village.

Airport: Geneva (Intl) 100 km
Train station: Montreux 3 km

Owner: Gérard Rabaey
Weekly closing: Sunday and Monday
Annual closing: From December 22nd to January 6th and from July 13th to August 4th
Currency: Swiss franc (CHF)
Rates: Menus 190-230 CHF s.i. - 125-151 €
Carte 130-220 CHF s.i. - 85-145 €
Dogs: allowed
Golf: 15 km
Accepted cards: MC, VS

Gérard Rabaey

More info on www.relaischateaux.com/brent

Hôtel Victoria

CH-1823 Glion
(Vaud) • Switzerland

Tel. : **(41) (021) 962 82 82**
Fax : (41) (021) 962 82 92
victoria@relaischateaux.com

SINCE 1975

Switzerland

This splendid residence, set in a beautiful park on a hillside sloping down to Lake Geneva, benefits from an invigorating climate all year round. The morning sun bathes the spaciously comfortable guestrooms with soft light and guests can contemplate the lake and the snow-capped peaks from a private balcony. Enjoy hunting, fishing or hiking, then savour inventive, light cuisine and excellent Swiss and French wines.

Excursions, boat trips on Lake Geneva, shop. (Other activities P. 629)

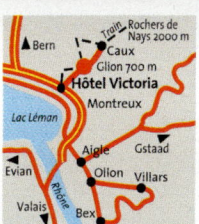

Altitude: 700 metres.
Access: Motorway exit Montreux, towards the Lake for 500 m, Caux Glion.

Airport: Geneva (Intl) 85 km
Train station: Glion 150 m

Owner: Toni Mittermair
Open all year
Currency: Swiss franc (CHF)
Rates: Menus 65-85 CHF s.i. - 43-56 €
Carte 50-100 CHF s.i. - 33-66 €
50 rooms: 250-370 CHF s.i. - 164-243 €
9 suites: 450-600 CHF s.i. - 296-395 €
Breakfast: included
Dogs: allowed (extra cost)
Golf: 18 km, private practice
Accepted cards: AE, DC, MC, VS

More info on **www.relaischateaux.com/victoria**

Switzerland

Hostellerie Alpenrose

CH-3778 Schönried-Gstaad
(Berne) • Switzerland

SINCE 1979

Tel. : **(41) (033) 744 67 67**
Fax : (41) (033) 744 67 12
alpenrose@relaischateaux.com

This enchanting chalet is in the heart of the skiing and hiking area near Gstaad-Saanen. The spacious rooms with pinewood panelling, whirlpools and fireplaces, offer a superb view of the glaciers. You will appreciate the hotel's extreme comfort, the warm welcome of the owners and the serenity of the majestic natural setting. Enjoy the specialities of Alpenrose by candlelight or before a crackling fire.

Cross-country, Menuhin Music Festival, UBS Tennis Open, polo, vintage carrallye, hot-air balloon. (Other activities P. 629)

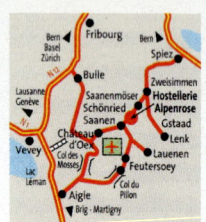

Altitude: 1200 metres.
Access: From Geneva, Lausanne, N 12 exit Bulle, then Saanen, towards Zweisimmen. From Berne heading towards Interlaken, exit Wimmis, towards Gstaad.
Airports: Geneva (Intl) 120 km, Zurich (Intl) 150 km
Train station: Schönried 0,7 km

Owners: Carole and Michel von Siebenthal
Weekly closing: Rest.: Monday, Tuesday noon
Annual closing: From mid-Oct. to mid-December
Currency: Swiss franc (CHF)
Rates: Menus 110-150 CHF s.i. - 72-99 €
Carte 25-120 CHF s.i. - 16-79 €
14 rooms: 220-490 CHF s.i. - 145-322 €
4 suites: 450-700 CHF s.i. - 296-460 €
Breakfast: included
Dogs: allowed (extra cost) **Golf:** 3,5 km
Accepted cards: AE, DC, MC, VS

More info on www.relaischateaux.com/alpenrose

Hostellerie Du Pas de L'Ours

SINCE 1997

Rue du Pas de l'Ours
CH-3963 Crans-Montana
(Valais) • Switzerland

Tel. : (41) (027) 485 93 33
Fax : (41) (027) 485 93 34
pasdelours@relaischateaux.com

Switzerland

This charming chalet, set in the heart of a renowned ski resort, blends modernity and traditional elegance. The guestrooms, all equipped with fireplaces and private whirpools, look out across idyllic natural surroundings and a wide range of sporting activities lie just outside your door. With impeccable service, traditional cuisine and fine wines, how could your stay at the Pas de l'Ours be anything but exceptional?

(Other activities P. 629)

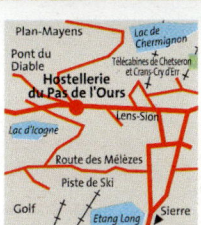

Altitude: 1500 m.
Access: Rhône motorway, exit Sierre towards Crans-Montana via Chermignon, then follow signs.
Airports: Geneva (Intl) 180 km, Sion 25 km
Train station: Sierre 15 km

Owner: Bestenheider Family
G. Manager: Severine Bestenheider-Reynaud
Weekly closing: Restaurant: Sunday night, Monday and Tuesday noon (in the low season)
Annual closing: One month in spring and one month in autumn
Currency: Swiss Franc (CHF)
Rates: Menus 65-145 CHF s.i. - 43-95 €
Carte 80-120 CHF s.i. - 53-79 €
9 suites: starting at 350 CHF - s.i. 230 €
Breakfast: included
Dogs: allowed (extra cost) **Golf:** 500 m
Accepted cards: AE, DC, MC, VS

More info on www.relaischateaux.com/pasdelours

Switzerland

Hôtel Rosalp

SINCE 1980

Route de Médran
CH-1936 Verbier
(Valais) • Switzerland

Tel. : (41) (027) 771 63 23
Fax : (41) (027) 771 10 59
rosalp@relaischateaux.com

This picturesque chalet, set in the heart of the Verbier ski resort, is the perfect place to enjoy the superb culinary creations of Roland Pierroz, recently voted «Chef of the Year». Savour «foie gras poêlé à la vinaigrette d'asperges et cage de pomme de terre croustillante», accompanied by one of the cellar's 65000 fine wines, then retire to a cosy guestroom.

(Other activities P. 629)

Altitude: 1500 metres.
Access: From Lausanne, Martigny - Gd-St-Bernard; at Sembrancher towards Verbier (200 m after central square).
Airports: Geneva (Intl) 200 km, Sion 50 km
Train station: Martigny 28 km

Owner: Roland Pierroz
Annual closing: End of April to beg. of July and end of Sept. to beg. of Dec.
Currency: Swiss franc (CHF)
Rates: Menus 175-200 CHF s.i. - 115-132 €
Carte 95-140 CHF s.i. - 62-92 €
18 rooms: summer 340-400 CHF s.i. - 224-263 €
winter 460-500 CHF s.i. - 302-329 €
3 suites: starting at 810 CHF s.i. - 533 €
Breakfast: 25 CHF s.i. - 16 €
Dogs: allowed (extra cost)
Golf: 3 km
Accepted cards: AE, DC, MC, VS

Roland Pierroz

More info on www.relaischateaux.com/rosalp

Chalet d'Adrien

SINCE 2003

Chemin des Creux
CH-1936 Verbier
(Valais) • Switzerland

Tel. : (41) (027) 771 62 00
Fax : (41) (027) 771 62 24
adrien@relaischateaux.com

Switzerland

In the heart of the ski area of the Four Valleys, a majestic setting for this elegant and tranquil property: the Chalet d'Adrien overlooks Verbier and boasts a truly breathtaking view of the Grand Combin. Elegant and warm décor, personalised treatments in the intimate and welcoming spa, upscale quality restaurants: the service here testifies to an unequivocal love of detail, absolute authenticity and exclusivity.

(Other activities P. 629)

Altitude: 1700 m.
Access: Motorway A9-E62. Exit Montreux. Road 9 towards Martigny. Road 21-E27 towards Col du Gd-St-Bernard. Follow Sembrancher, Verbier and towards Savoleyres.
Airports: Geneva (Intl) 200 km, Sion 50 km
Train station: Martigny 27 km

Owner: Brigitte de Turckheim-Cachart
General Manager: Eric Cachart
Annual closing: From end of April to beginning of July and from beg. of Sept. to beg. of December
Currency: Swiss franc (CHF)
Rates: Menus 95-200 CHF s.i. - 62-131 €
Carte 59-140 CHF s.i. - 39-92 €
19 rooms: 300-650 CHF s.i. - 197-427 €
6 suites: 700-900 CHF s.i. - 460-592 €
Breakfast: 25 CHF s.i. - 16 €
Dogs: allowed (extra-cost) **Golf:** 1 km
Accepted cards: AE, DC, MC, VS

More info on www.relaischateaux.com/adrien

Les Sources des Alpes

SINCE 1990

CH-3954 Leukerbad
(Valais) • Switzerland

Tel. : (41) (027) 472 20 00
Fax : (41) (027) 472 20 01
sources@relaischateaux.com

Switzerland

This idyllic haven of peace and calm is set in the picturesque splendour of the Valais Alps. A recent winner of the «Best Swiss Health Farm» award, this elegant XIXth century hotel offers spacious, sunny rooms with superb vistas of the surrounding countryside. Relax in the thermal baths, enjoy a hydrotherapy session or a rejuvenating mud treatment, then savour light, inventive cuisine and seafood specialities.

(Other activities P. 629)

Altitude: 1412 m.
Access: From Lausanne, highway towards Simplon-Brig to Sion, Sierre, then Susten.

Airports: Geneva (Intl) 200 km, Sion 40 km
Train station: Leuk 15 km

Owner: Aquawell S.A.
General Managers: Marianne and Marco Colombo
Annual closing:
From November 23rd to December 18th
Currency: Swiss franc (CHF)
Rates: Menus 50-150 CHF s.i. - 33-99 €
Carte 30-160 CHF s.i. - 20-105 €
22 rooms: 450-550 CHF s.i. - 296-362 €
8 suites: 630-850 CHF s.i. - 414-559 €
Breakfast: included
Dogs: allowed (extra cost) except restaurant and thermal bath **Golf:** 22 km, 40 km
Accepted cards: AE, DC, JCB, MC, VS

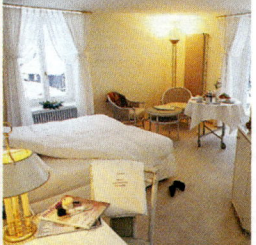

More info on www.relaischateaux.com/sources

Switzerland

SINCE 1995

Grandhotel Schönegg

CH-3920 Zermatt
(Valais) • Switzerland

Tel. : (41) (027) 966 34 34
Fax : (41) (027) 966 34 35
schonegg@relaischateaux.com

After being picked up at the station by the hotel car, guests are whisked up into the mountains to this picturesque chalet where flower-filled balconies offer stunning views of the Matterhorn. Enjoy an invigorating day on the ski slopes, then relax in a sauna before enjoying a romantic candlelit dinner. Impeccable service, refined cuisine and exceptional Valais wines will make your stay unforgettable.

(Other activities P. 629)

Altitude: 1620 metres.
Access: In Täsch, leave your car in the parking lot then train or taxi (10-15 mn) to Zermatt (hotel shuttle).
Airports: Geneva (Intl) 234 km, Sion 73 km
Helipad: N 46° 01' 49" E 07° 45' 20"
Train station: Zermatt 0,3 km

Owners: Mary-José Metry-Julen Family
Annual closing: Hotel: from April 23rd to May 23rd and from October 5th to November 28th
Rest.: from April 1st to July 1st
and from September 15th to December 15th
Currency: Swiss franc (CHF)
Rates: Menus 65-75 CHF s.i. - 43-49 €
Carte 50-120 CHF s.i. - 33-79 €
34 rooms: 250-530 CHF s.i. - 164-348 €
2 suites: 420-770 CHF s.i. - 276-506 €
Breakfast: included
Dogs: allowed (extra cost)
Accepted cards: AE, DC, JCB, MC, VS

More info on www.relaischateaux.com/schonegg

Castello del Sole

SINCE 1985

Via Muraccio 142,
CH-6612 Ascona
(Tessin) • Switzerland

Tel. : (41) (091) 791 02 02
Fax : (41) (091) 792 11 18
castellosole@relaischateaux.com

Switzerland

This residence is a haven of peace in 20 acres of luxuriant parkland with a private beach on Lake Maggiore offering many sporting activities. Enjoy Italian and French cuisine served at the «Locanda Barbarossa» and in the «Tre Stagioni» restaurant, accompanied by Merlot wines from the estate. Relax in the piano bar and inner courtyards on fine summer nights. Pavilion with luxurious, air-conditioned junior-suites and suites.

(Other activities P. 629)

Access: From Lucern, N2, towards Bellinzona, exit Bellinzona sud, towards Locarno.

Airports: Lugano (Intl) 40 km, Milan Malpensa (Intl) 110 km
Train station: Locarno 5 km

Owner: Terreni alla Maggia SA
General Manager: Simon V. Jenny
Annual closing: From Oct. 26th to March 27th
Currency: Swiss franc (CHF)
Rates: Menus 70-90 CHF s.i. - 46-59 €
Carte 45-130 CHF s.i. - 30-85 €
64 rooms: 520-680 CHF s.i. - 342-447 €
15 suites: 750-1600 CHF s.i. - 493-1052 €
Breakfast: included
Dogs: not allowed **Golf:** Driving-range, private putting green, Ascona golf course 2 km
Accepted cards: AE, DC, JCB, MC, VS

More info on www.relaischateaux.com/castellosole

Albergo Giardino

Switzerland — SINCE 1990

Via Segnale 10
CH-6612 Ascona
(Tessin) • Switzerland

Tel. : (41) (091) 785 88 88
Fax : (41) (091) 785 88 99
giardino@relaischateaux.com

The exquisitely romantic guestrooms in this Mediterranean country home are bathed in the scent of flowers wafting up from the exotic gardens. Enjoy an aperitif by the water-lily covered pond, then choose between refined gourmet cuisine at the Ristorante Aphrodite or more traditional Italian fare at the Osteria. Relish excellent Tessin wines and enjoy open-air performances beneath the stars at the «Teatro Giardino».

(Other activities P. 629)

Access: Motorway N2 via Gotthard, towards Bellinzona, exit South Bellinzona, towards Locarno.

Airports: Lugano (Intl) 40 km, Milan Malpensa (Intl) 110 km
Helipad: N 46° 09' 39" E 08° 52' 43"
Train station: Locarno 5 km

Owner: Albergo Giardino S.A.
General Manager: Franz Reichhof
Annual closing: From mid-Nov. to mid-March
Currency: Swiss franc (CHF)
Rates: Menus 65-150 CHF s.i. - 43-99 €
Carte 65-150 CHF s.i. - 43-99 €
54 rooms: starting at 680 CHF s.i. - 453 €
18 suites: starting at 790 CHF s.i. - 527 €
Breakfast: included
Dogs: allowed (40 CHF - 26 € s.i./day) **Golf:** 1 km
Accepted cards: AE, DC, MC, VS

More info on www.relaischateaux.com/giardino

Villa Margherita

SINCE 1986

CH-6935 Bosco Luganese
(Tessin) • Switzerland

Tel. : (41) (091) 611 51 11
Fax : (41) (091) 611 51 10
margherita@relaischateaux.com

Switzerland

Overlooking Lugano, from your comfortable room, you will have a splendid view over the famous landscape of Ticino's southern lakes. The villa offers an open-air and a covered pool with salt water at 32° amidst the lawns of a wonderful park. Garden lovers will adore the green alleyways. In the garden restaurant, surrounded by Mediterranean vegetation, you will be served delicious regional dishes and excellent wines.

Massage. (Other activities P. 629)

Access: From the N2, exit Lugano north, towards Ponte Tresa, right at the 1st light after roundabout towards Cademario.

Airports: Lugano (Intl) 6 km, Milan Malpensa (Intl) 80 km
Train station: Lugano 7 km

Owners: Herzog and Poretti Families
General Manager: Margherita Poretti-Herzog
Annual closing: From October 26th to Easter
Currency: Swiss franc (CHF)
Rates: Menus 76-98 CHF s.i. - 50-64 €
Carte 40-98 CHF s.i. - 26-64 €
26 rooms: 376-540 CHF s.i. - 247-355 €
7 suites: starting at 564 CHF s.i. - 371 €
Breakfast: included
Dogs: allowed (extra cost) except rest.
Golf: Magliaso 10 km
Accepted cards: AE, DC, MC, VS

More info on www.relaischateaux.com/margherita

Santabbondio

SINCE 2001

Via Fomelino 10,
CH-6924 Sorengo-Lugano
(Tessin) • Switzerland

Tel. : (41) (091) 993 23 88
Fax : (41) (091) 994 32 37
santabbondio@relaischateaux.com

Switzerland

Martin Dalsass and his wife, Lorena, have been in Sorengo near Lugano, an almost Italian part of Ticino, since 1985. Their culinary delights are enhanced by the warm and charming atmosphere of the restaurant, set in an attractive garden with a romantic terrace. Martin Dalsass's cuisine reflects this: simple, refined and tasteful. His dishes change daily according to market availability and his whim.

(Other activities P. 629)

Access: Motorway exit Lugano south. Three traffic lights still left heading towards the airport; towards Montagnola at the 4th traffic light; turn right after 80 meters.
Airports: Lugano (Intl) 2,5 km, Milan Malpensa (Intl) 70 km
Train station: Sorengo 0,3 km

Owners: Martin and Lorena Dalsass
Weekly closing: Sunday, Monday
Annual closing: First two weeks of January
Currency: Swiss franc (CHF)
Rates: Menus 55-174 CHF s.i. - 36-114 €
Carte 100-145 CHF s.i. - 66-95 €
Dogs: not allowed
Golf: 5 km
Accepted cards: AE, DC, MC, VS

Martin Dalsass

More info on www.relaischateaux.com/santabbondio

Switzerland — SINCE 2000

Villa Principe Leopoldo & Residence

Via Montalbano, 5
CH-6900 Lugano
(Tessin) • Switzerland

Tel. : (41) (091) 985 88 55
Fax : (41) (091) 985 88 25
leopoldo@relaischateaux.com

This magnificent villa, built for Prince Leopold Von Hohenzollern in 1868, is set on the beautiful Collina d'Oro, overlooking the sparkling waters of Lake Lugano. The splendours of the Belle Epoque are still evident in the luxurious suites and the sumptuous drawing room decorated with marble fireplaces and works of art. Enjoy traditional Swiss hospitality and savour refined cuisine enhanced by superb Piemontese wines.

Climbing, mountain-biking. (Other activities P. 629)

Access: Leave motorway at Lugano south, towards Lago. Turn left at first traffic lights, towards Ponte Tresa. At second traffic lights, turn left and follow hotel signs.
Airport: Lugano (Intl) 5 km
Train station: Lugano 3 km

Owner: Leopoldo Hotels and Restaurants SA
General Manager: Maurice R.L. Urech
Open all year
Currency: Swiss franc (CHF)
Rates: Menus 62-130 CHF s.i. – 41-85 €
Carte 26-75 CHF s.i. - 17-49 €
71 rooms: 470-795 CHF s.i. - 310-523 €
4 suites: 1100-1950 CHF s.i. - 725-1282 €
Breakfast: included
Dogs: allowed (extra cost)
Golf: 5 km
Accepted cards: AE, DC, JCB, MC, VS

More info on www.relaischateaux.com/leopoldo

Restaurant Jöhri's Talvo

SINCE 1994

Via Gunels 15
CH-7512 St. Moritz/Champfèr
(Grisons) • Switzerland

Tel. : (41) (081) 833 44 55
Fax : (41) (081) 833 05 69
talvo@relaischateaux.com

Switzerland

On the edge of Saint-Moritz, this fine XVIIth century Graubünden house with its sunny terrace, decorated porch and wooden shutters is the meeting place of all enlightened gourmets. Roland and Brigitte Jöhri's infectious good humour creates an ideal setting in which to enjoy the delicious combination of French gastronomy and regional specialities. Open all day with a wide variety of dishes and a heavenly wine list.

(Other activities P. 629)

Access: From Italy, Silvaplana, towards St-Moritz, follow signs to Suvretta/Champfèr.

Airports: Zurich (Intl) 180 km, Samedan 10 km
Train station: St-Moritz 1 km

Owners: Roland and Brigitte Jöhri
Weekly closing: Monday (except holidays and season) and Tuesday (summer)
Annual closing: From mid-April to mid-June and mid-October to mid-December
Currency: Swiss franc (CHF)
Rates: Menus 78-228 CHF s.i. - 51-150 €
Carte 80-100 CHF s.i. - 53-66 €
Dogs: not allowed
Golf: nearby
Accepted cards: AE, DC, MC, VS

Roland Jöhri

More info on www.relaischateaux.com/talvo

Place it as you like & put your music on display

Why let your favourite CDs disappear into an anonymous black box? Put your music on display – and place it exactly where you want it. BeoSound 9000 offers more placement options than any other music system. Place it vertically, horizontally, upright or lying down. On the wall or on its stand. The control panel and the text in the display will of course adapt to your choice. BeoSound 9000: CD, radio, digital music via BeoLink®

Find your nearest Bang & Olufsen store at www.bang-olufsen.com

BANG & OLUFSEN

BeoSound 9000

Hotel Walther

SINCE 1993

CH-7504 Pontresina
(Grisons) • Switzerland

Tel. : (41) (081) 839 36 36
Fax : (41) (081) 839 36 37
walther@relaischateaux.com

Switzerland

This magnificent baroque manor, perched at 1800 metres in the Engadine mountains, is set amidst some of the most stunning Swiss countryside. With its modern comfort and the warm hospitality of its owners, Hotel Walther offers you perfectly relaxing holidays in summer as in winter. The light, inventive cuisine which changes with the seasons is accompanied by the finest Swiss, French and Italian vintages.

In summer: tennis lessons and accompanied hiking. In winter: accompanied alpine and cross-country skiing. (Other activities P. 629)

Altitude: 1800 metres.
Access: 8 km from St-Moritz.

Airports: Zurich (Intl) 220 km, Samedan 6 km
Train station: Pontresina 1 km

Owners: Walther Family
General Managers: Thomas and Anne-Rose Walther
Annual closing: From April 21st to June 13th and from Oct. 5th to December 18th
Currency: Swiss franc (CHF)
Rates: Menus 65-100 CHF s.i. - 43-66 €
Carte 60-90 CHF s.i. - 39-59 €
64 rooms: 390-640 CHF s.i. - 256-421 €
9 suites: half board 560-970 CHF s.i. - 368-638 €
Breakfast: included
Dogs: allowed (extra cost) **Golf:** 6 km
Accepted cards: AE, DC, MC, VS

More info on www.relaischateaux.com/walther

Hotel Haus Paradies

Switzerland — SINCE 1986

CH-7551 Ftan
(Grisons) • Switzerland

Tel. : (41) (081) 861 08 08
Fax : (41) (081) 861 08 09
paradies@relaischateaux.com

In the clear air of Engadine with its beautiful green or snow-covered meadows, this hotel lives up to its name. 24 elegant rooms offer a unique view of an imposing mountain landscape. Culinary delights are to be had in the starred gourmet restaurant «La Bellezza». The cosy library and the Eden Garden are relaxing oases. Nature, art and culture are in complete harmony. Full range of leisure activities.

Cross-country skiing, skiing, sledging, snow-shoeing, mountaineering, mountain-biking, breakfast in the mountains, fitness, guided art tours. (Other activities P. 629)

Altitude: 1650 metres.
Access: From Landeck (A), exit Scuol. From Verina tunnel and from St. Moritz, exit Ardez (mountain road for 5 km).
Airports: Zurich (Intl) 210 km, Samedan 50 km
Train station: Scuol 5 km

Owners: Paradies Touristic A.G. (Rahe and Schmittner Families)
G. Managers: Waltraud and Eduard Hitzberger
Annual closing: From the beg. of April to the end of May and from the end of October to mid-Dec.
Currency: Swiss franc (CHF)
Rates: Menus 63-198 CHF s.i. - 41-130 €
Carte 65-140 CHF s.i. - 43-92 €
10 rooms: 240-460 CHF s.i. - 158-302 €
14 suites: 545-1250 CHF s.i. - 358-822 €
Breakfast: 25 CHF s.i. - 16 €
Dogs: allowed (except restaurant) **Golf:** 15 km
Accepted cards: AE, DC, MC, VS

More info on www.relaischateaux.com/paradies

Schlosshotel Chastè

SINCE 1997

CH-7553 Tarasp Sparsels
(Grisons) • Switzerland

Tel. : (41) (081) 861 30 60
Fax : (41) (081) 861 30 61
chaste@relaischateaux.com

Switzerland

This picturesque Engadin house, covered in snow throughout winter and bedecked with flowers in summer, is a tribute to the finest Swiss woodwork. Cross its charming threshold and discover a cosy ambience in which your attentive hosts, the Pazellers, do their utmost to ensure your well-being. An invigorating stroll through the idyllic countryside will whet your appetite for the Pazellers' delicious traditional cuisine.

(Other activities P. 629)

Altitude: 1440 metres.
Access: From Zurich via the Davos region, Flüela pass in summer or Klosters-Vereina tunnel in winter, exit before Scuol. From Landeck, last exit at Scuol then towards Vulpera Tarasp.
Airports: Zurich (Intl) 210 km, Samedan 50 km
Train station: Scuol 6 km

Owners: Daniela and Rudolf Pazeller
Weekly closing: Rest.: Monday and Tuesday
Annual closing: From April 6th to May 28th and from October 19th to December 20th
Currency: Swiss franc (CHF)
Rates: Menus 65-120 CHF s.i. - 43-79 €
Carte 45-80 CHF s.i. - 30-53 €
13 rooms: 280-340 CHF s.i. - 184-224 €
8 suites: 350-550 CHF s.i. - 230-362 €
Breakfast: 18-22 CHF s.i. - 12-14 €
Dogs: allowed (except rest.) extra cost
Golf: 6 km
Accepted cards: AE, DC, MC, VS

More info on www.relaischateaux.com/chaste

Switzerland

Hotel Walserhof

SINCE 1999

Landstrasse 141
CH-7250 Klosters
(Grisons) • Switzerland

Tel. : (41) (081) 410 29 29
Fax : (41) (081) 410 29 39
walserhof@relaischateaux.com

A stay at the Walserhof means vast fields of snow in winter and long sunny walks in summer. In this beautiful mountain chalet, Beat Bolliger will show you the full extent of his talent. Savour his «mille-feuille de volailles fumées au foie de canard» or his «truite aux écailles de pommes de terre sur lentilles», traditional seasonal dishes, spiced with the chef's modernist touch. Fine international wine cellar.

Climbing, parapenting, sleighing, skating. (Other activities P. 629)

Access: From Zurich, N3 towards Chur, exit Landquart, towards Davos.

Airport: Zurich (Intl) 160 km
Train station: Klosters 0,1 km

Owners: Beat and Gabi Bolliger
General Manager: Beat Bolliger
Annual closing: From April 21st to June 21st and from October 19th to December 4th
Currency: Swiss franc (CHF)
Rates: Menus 75-175 CHF s.i. - 49-115 €
Carte 75-180 CHF s.i. - 49-118 €
9 rooms: 220-460 CHF s.i. - 145-302 €
6 suites: 420-950 CHF s.i. - 276-625 €
Breakfast: 24 CHF s.i. - 16 €
Dogs: allowed (extra cost)
Golf: 10 km (18 holes)
Accepted cards: AE, DC, MC, VS

More info on www.relaischateaux.com/walserhof

Parkhotel Sonnenhof

SINCE 1979

Mareestrasse, 29
FL-9490 Vaduz
Liechtenstein

Tel. : (423) 239 02 02
Fax : (423) 239 02 03
sonnenhof@relaischateaux.com

Liechtenstein

This elegant hotel is set in luxuriant parkland overlooking the picturesque town of Vaduz and its medieval castle. The comfortable guestrooms open onto terraces or balconies, with stunning vistas of the Rhine Valley, the vineyards and the Swiss Alps. Relax in the swimming pool, solarium and sauna before savouring seasonal specialities and fine wines in the candlelit dining room. Golf courses nearby.
(Other activities P. 629)

Access: From Zurich, motorway towards Chur, exit Vaduz/Liechtenstein, towards Schloss Vaduz.

Airports: Altenrhein (Intl) 35 km, Zurich (Intl) 120 km
Train station: Buchs 12 km

Owners: Emil Real Family
Annual closing:
From December 21st to January 13th
Currency: Swiss franc (CHF)
Rates: Menus 90-170 CHF s.i. - 59-112 €
Carte 78-120 CHF s.i. - 51-79 €
17 rooms: 360-450 CHF s.i. - 237-296 €
12 suites: 460-620 CHF s.i. - 302-408 €
Breakfast: included
Dogs: allowed in room only (extra cost)
Golf: 20 km
Accepted cards: AE, DC, JCB, MC, VS

More info on www.relaischateaux.com/sonnenhof

Germany

Properties	Nearest major city	Relais & Châteaux	Relais Gourmands	Page
Abtei (Hotel)	Hamburg	⚜		300
Alpenhof Murnau	München	⚜		330
Bareiss (Restaurant)	Baiersbronn		◉	323
Brandenburger Hof (Hotel)	Berlin	⚜		303
Bülow Residenz	Dresden	⚜		305
Burg Schlitz	Waren	⚜		301
Burg Wernberg (Hotel)	Regensburg	⚜		317
Burghotel Hardenberg	Göttingen	⚜		308
Deidesheimer Hof (Hotel)	Mannheim	⚜		320
Fürstenhof Celle	Hannover	⚜		306
Gutshaus Stolpe	Greifswald	⚜		302
Hohenhaus (Hotel)	Eisenach	⚜		314
Jagdhof Glashütte (Hotel)	Siegen	⚜		315
Johann Lafer's Stromburg	Mainz/Wiesbaden	⚜	◉	316
Kur-und Sporthotel Dollenberg	Strassburg	⚜		325
Landhaus Ammann (Hotel)	Hannover	⚜		307
Landhaus «Zu den Rothen Forellen»	Wernigerode	⚜		309
Pflaums Posthotel Pegnitz	Nürnberg	⚜		319
Residenz Heinz Winkler	München	⚜	◉	331
Schloss Hubertushöhe	Berlin	⚜		304
Schloss Hugenpœt (Hotel)	Düsseldorf	⚜		311
Schloss Wilkinghege (Hotel)	Münster	⚜		310
Schlosshotel Lerbach	Köln	⚜	◉	313
Schwarzmatt (Hotel)	Freiburg im Breisgau	⚜		327
Schwarzwald - Hotel Adler	Zürich	⚜		326
Schwarzwaldstube (Restaurant)	Baiersbronn		◉	324
Seehotel Siber	Konstanz	⚜		328
Stadt Hamburg (Hotel)	Hamburg	⚜		299
Villa Hammerschmiede (Hotel)	Karlsruhe	⚜		322
Villino	Lindau	⚜		329
Wald & Schlosshotel Friedrichsruhe	Heilbronn	⚜	◉	321
Zur Traube (Hotel Restaurant)	Düsseldorf	⚜	◉	312

More info on www.relaischateaux.com/de

Bon voyage.

www.mastercard.com

Please inquire about exclusive MasterCard® values by calling
Relais & Chateaux reservations, or visit our web site.

Hotel Stadt Hamburg

SINCE 1979

Strandstrasse 2
D-25980 Westerland/Sylt
(Schleswig-Holstein) • Germany

Tel. : (49) (04651) 8580
Fax : (49) (04651) 858220
stadthamburg@relaischateaux.com

Germany

Imagine 40 kilometres of fine sand beaches, a stunning natural landscape of billowing dunes and an invigorating climate. This elegant XIXth century residence set on a picturesque island in the North Sea offers idyllic surroundings and supreme comfort. Its charming rooms, decorated with country house furniture and flowers are havens of calm. Enjoy romantic walks along the shore and savour delightful regional cuisine.

Water sports, pool pavilion and Shiseido beauty salon. (Other activities P. 629)

Access: From Hamburg, A 7 Flensburg, B 199 Niebüll, a 45 min. crossing.

Airports: Hamburg Fuhlsbüttel (Intl) 240 km, Westerland 2 km
Train station: Westerland 0,5 km

Owner: Harald Hentzschel
General Manager: Bernd Knochenhauer
Open all year
Currency: Euro (€)
Rates: Menus 39-79 € s.i. Carte 24-37 € s.i.
48 rooms: single 108-170 € s.i.
double 170-275 € s.i.
24 suites: 295-340 € s.i.
Breakfast: 17 € s.i.
Dogs: allowed (except restaurant)
Golf: 5 km
Accepted cards: AE, DC, MC, VS

More info on www.relaischateaux.com/stadthamburg   299

Hotel Abtei

Germany — SINCE 1994

Abteistrasse 14
D-20149 Hamburg
Germany

Tel. : (49) (040) 442905
Fax : (49) (040) 449820
abtei@relaischateaux.com

This elegant residence, set in a wonderfully calm street near the Außenalster, is imbued with the splendour and charm of the past. The guestrooms and suites are tastefully decorated with careful attention to detail. On sunny days, guests can enjoy a cup of tea in the beautiful private garden. The «Prinz Frederick» restaurant offers fine, classical cuisine accompanied by excellent wines.

Polo, sailing. (Other activities P. 629)

Access: In Hamburg, follow signs to «Zentrum, Hauptbanhof, Außenalster».

Airport: Hamburg Fuhlsbüttel (Intl) 5 km
Train station: Dammtor 2 km

Owners: Petra and Fritz Lay
General Manager: Tanja Schultz
Weekly closing: Restaurant: Sunday and Monday
Annual closing: One week in summer and from December 24th to 26th
Currency: Euro (€)
Rates: Menus 40-80 € s.i.
Carte 20-28 € s.i.
9 rooms: 180-250 € s.i.
2 suites: 250-270 € s.i.
Breakfast: 16 € s.i.
Dogs: allowed (extra cost) except restaurant
Golf: 17 km
Accepted cards: AE, MC, VS

More info on www.relaischateaux.com/abtei

Burg Schlitz

SINCE 2002

D-17166 Hohen Demzin
(Mecklenburg-Vorpommern)
Germany

Tel. : (49) (03996) 12700
Fax : (49) (03996) 127070
schlitz@relaischateaux.com

Germany

Built in 1823, the immense and splendid neo-classical building of Burg Schlitz is a true architectural treasure in the region of Mecklenburg-Western Pomerania. The setting offers the double attraction of upscale accommodation (period furniture and superb Parisian and Berlin tapestries) and 80 hectares of woodlands interspersed with fountains, obelisks and other sculptural monuments.
Archery, horseback riding... (Other activities P. 629)

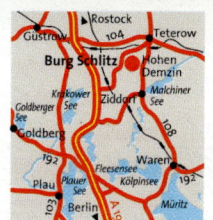

Access: Motorway E 55 (A 19): exit Linstow, left turn at each of 3 «T» intersections on B 180 dir. Teterow.

Airport: Berlin Tegel (Intl) 170 km
Helipad: N 53° 42' 06'' E 12° 32' 55''
Train station: Teterow 9 km

Owners: Mathias Stinnes and Elisabeth Schrader
General Managers: Maja and Thomas Kilgore
Weekly closing: Monday
Open all year
Currency: Euro (€)
Rates: Menus 39-79 € s.i. Carte 14-38 € s.i.
14 rooms: 210-230 € s.i.
6 suites: 250-750 € s.i.
Breakfast: 15 € s.i.
Dogs: allowed (small) **Golf:** 15 km
Accepted cards: AE, DC, MC, VS

More info on www.relaischateaux.com/schlitz

Germany

Gutshaus Stolpe

SINCE 2001

Dorfstraße 37,
D-17391 Stolpe bei Anklam
(Mecklenburg-Vorpommern)
Germany

Tel. : (49) (039721) 5500
Fax : (49) (039721) 55099
stolpe@relaischateaux.com

Gutshaus Stolpe is situated in the heart of a listed estate dating back to the XIXth century surrounded by a park with old established trees. The estate lies above the river Peene which flows into the nearby Baltic Sea. Most of the rooms are furnished with beautiful antiques. The guest is free to choose between elegant rooms in the main building or rooms in the annex with its Mediterranean flair.

Steambath, wine tasting, horse-drawn carriage tours... (Other activities P. 629)

Access: From Hamburg: A19 exit Güstrow, then B104 to Stavenhagen, and B194 to Demmin, and B110 to Stolpe via Jarmen. From Berlin: A11 exit Prenzlau, B109 to Anklam, then B110 to Stolpe.
Airports: Berlin Tegel (Intl) 170 km, Heringsdorf 25 km
Helipad: N 53° 52' 21" E 013° 33' 54"
Train station: Anklam 7 km

Owners: Kurt and Jutta Stürken
General Manager: Kathrin Wirth-Ueberschär
Weekly closing: Restaurant: Monday
Annual closing: From January 6th to 26th
Currency: Euro (€)
Rates: Menus 40-80 € s.i. Carte 13-28 € s.i.
27 rooms: 125-155 € s.i. **6 suites:** 160-355 € s.i.
Breakfast: included
Dogs: allowed (extra cost) **Golf:** 25 km
Accepted cards: AE, MC, VS

More info on www.relaischateaux.com/stolpe

Hotel Brandenburger Hof

SINCE 1995

Eislebener Strasse 14
D-10789 Berlin (Wilmersdorf)
Germany

Tel. : (49) (030) 21405-0
Fax : (49) (030) 21405-100
brandenburger@relaischateaux.com

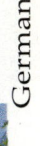

Germany

This magnificient turn-of-the-century manor house is located in a quiet street near the Kurfürstendamm. The interior of the house leaves an impression of timeless elegance and a certain artistic ambition. Many of the rooms, fitted out in the Bauhaus style, overlook the winter garden, an oasis of greenery for unforgettable moments. The restaurants: «Der Wintergarten» is open for you all year round and «Die Quadriga» proposes classical grande cuisine.

Massages, Kanebo beauty suite. Limousine service, own box office. (Other activities P. 629)

Access: Berliner Ring (A 110) exit «Wilmersdorf», then «Kurfürstendamm», 4 km to «Gedächtniskirche».
Airports: Berlin-Tegel (Intl) 12 km, Berlin Schönefeld (Intl) 20 km
Train station: Zoologischer Garten 1 km

Owner: Daniela Sauter
General Manager: Markus Otto Graf
Weekly closing: Restaurant «Die Quadriga»: Saturday, Sunday
Annual closing: Restaurant «Die Quadriga»: from Jan. 1st to 12th and July 14th to August 17th
Currency: Euro (€)
Rates: Menus 70-90 € s.i. Carte 25-38 € s.i.
78 rooms: single 165-245 € s.i.
double 240-280 € s.i. **4 suites:** 450 € s.i.
Breakfast: included
Dogs: allowed (extra cost) except rest. **Golf:** 12 km
Accepted cards: AE, DC, JCB, MC, VS

More info on www.relaischateaux.com/brandenburger

Germany · SINCE 2000

Schloss Hubertushöhe

Robert-Koch-Str. 1
D-15859 Storkow
(Brandenburg) • Germany

Tel. : (49) (033678) 430
Fax : (49) (033678) 43100
hubertushoehe@relaischateaux.com

60 km from Berlin, on the banks of the magnificent Storkow lake, the hotel awaits you like an oasis of calm and greenery. This splendid turn-of-the-century house, decorated in period style, offers luxurious and refined services. Surrounded by century-old trees in the 5 ha park of the castle, you will enjoy exceptional moments. The charm and the natural environs make Hubertushöhe a perfect place to stay.
Boat hire. (Other activities P. 629)

Access: By car from Berlin or Potsdam on the A12, exit at Storkow, cross Rieplos, at Storkow follow signs to Beeskow.

Airport: Berlin-Schönefeld (Intl) 30 km
Helipad: N 52° 14' 207'' O 013° 58' 139''
Train station: Storkow 0,5 km

Owner: Reemtsma C. Fab GmbH
General Manager: Jörg Steinhäuser
Weekly closing: Monday
Annual closing: January
Currency: Euro (€)
Rates: Menus 40-75 € s.i.
Carte 25-32 € s.i.
18 rooms: 128-345 € s.i.
4 suites: 260-440 € s.i.
Breakfast: included
Dogs: allowed (extra cost)
Golf: 10 km, 2 courses
Accepted cards: AE, DC, MC, VS

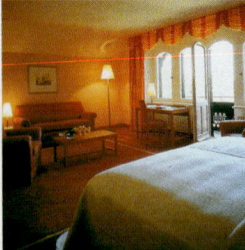

More info on www.relaischateaux.com/hubertushohe

Hotel Bülow Residenz

SINCE 1997

Rähnitzgasse 19
D-01097 Dresden
(Sachsen) • Germany

Tel. : (49) (0351) 800 30
Fax : (49) (0351) 800 3100
bulow@relaischateaux.com

Germany

The elegant facade of the Bülow Residenz, built in 1730, is a marvel of palatial architecture. This luxury hotel, set in the very heart of Dresden, combines the splendour of bygone days with the utmost in modern comfort. Delicious seasonal cuisine, served in the beautiful courtyard or at the «Caroussel» restaurant, features regional specialities enhanced by the finest French and German vintages.

(Other activities P. 629)

Access: From the airport, take Königsbrücker Landstrasse, towards the city centre.
At Albertplatz, 2nd on the right (Königstrasse), to Palaisplatz, turn left (Heinrichstrasse) and again left (Rähnitzgasse).
Airport: Klotzsche (Intl) 10 km
Train station: Neustadt 1 km

Owner: Horst Bülow
General Manager: Ralf J. Kutzner
Open all year
Currency: Euro (€)
Rates: Menus 32-76 € s.i. Carte 35-49 € s.i.
25 rooms: single 170 € s.i. double 210 € s.i.
5 suites: 260-380 € s.i.
Breakfast: 15 € s.i.
Dogs: allowed (extra cost)
Golf: 12 km
Accepted cards: AE, DC, MC, VS

More info on www.relaischateaux.com/bulow

Germany — SINCE 1978

Fürstenhof Celle

Hannoversche Strasse 55/56
D-29221 Celle
(Niedersachsen) • Germany

Tel. : (49) (05141) 2010
Fax : (49) (05141) 201120
furstenhof@relaischateaux.com

In the magnificent delta of the Lüneburg Heath, 20 minutes away from Hanover, you will be enchanted by this fine Baroque manor built in 1670. Culinary diversity in the restaurant Endtenfang, one of Germany's finest gourmet restaurants, run by a master chef inspired by French cuisine, a bistro, the Palio, with authentic Tuscan cuisine and personal hospitality enthuse the most demanding guests.

Tennis, biking, theme dinners, theatre, castles, museums, excursions to the heath land, stallion shows at the Celle stud farm. (Other activities P. 629)

Access: From the South, A 7 exit Celle. From the North, A 7 exit Soltau-South.

Airport: Hanover (Intl) 40 km
Train station: Celle 1 km

Owners: Grafen Hardenberg Families
General Manager: Carsten K. Rath
Weekly closing: Rest.: Sunday and Monday (except bank holidays and during trade fairs)
Open all year
Currency: Euro (€)
Rates: Menus 80-90 € s.i. Carte 22-35 € s.i.
71 rooms: 175-190 € s.i.
5 suites: 240-265 € s.i.
Breakfast: included
Dogs: allowed (extra cost) except restaurant
Golf: 8 km
Accepted cards: AE, DC, MC, VS

More info on www.relaischateaux.com/furstenhof

Hotel Landhaus Ammann

SINCE 1987

Hildesheimer Strasse 185
D-30173 Hannover
(Niedersachsen) • Germany

Tel. : (49) (0511) 830818
Fax : (49) (0511) 8437749
ammann@relaischateaux.com

Germany

This charming hotel is a heaven of peace in the centre of Hanover, situated between the Eilenriede forest and the Herrenhauser baroque gardens. It offers elegant guestrooms with Louis XVI furniture. Make the most of the summer, dining on the partially covered patio or new open-air terrace. This refined establishment will appeal to those who adore fine cuisine and wines.

Water sports. (Other activities P. 629)

Access: A 7 exit «Hannover-Anderten», B 65 exit «Hannover-Döhren», turn right towards center.

Airport: Hanover (Intl) 25 km
Train station: Hauptbahnhof 2,5 km

Owner: Ammann GmbH
General Manager: Helmut Ammann
Open all year
Currency: Euro (€)
Rates: Menus 50-89 € s.i.
Carte 13-32 € s.i.
12 rooms: single 115-170 € s.i.
double 135-195 € s.i.
2 suites: 275 € s.i.
Breakfast: included
Dogs: allowed (except restaurant)
Golf: 5 km
Accepted cards: AE, DC, JCB, MC, VS

More info on www.relaischateaux.com/ammann

Burghotel Hardenberg

Germany — SINCE 2000

Im Hinterhaus 11a
D-37176 Nörten-Hardenberg
(Niedersachsen) • Germany

Tel. : (49) (05503) 9810
Fax : (49) (05503) 981666
hardenberg@relaischateaux.com

Ten minutes from Göttingen, this exclusive hotel is located in an authentic half-timbered, 18th century residence. A cultivated but altogether relaxed atmosphere gives visitors the impression they are the personal guests of Count Hardenberg. The restaurant Novalis is famed for its refined cuisine and superb wine list. Lush forests, rolling hills and a 36-hole golf course, what better setting to unwind and relax.

Banquet in the fortress ruins, incentives, outdoor activities. (Other activities P. 629)

Access: BAB 7 exit Nörten-Hardenberg, go towards Nörten-Hardenberg. Turn left after the service station, turn right after the church, the hotel is 1 km away.
Airports: Frankfurt (Intl) 250 km, Hannover 100 km
Helipad: N 51° 45' 37" O 009° 02' 57"
Train station: Nörten-Hardenberg 1 km

Owner: Carl Graf von Hardenberg
General Manager: Ralf O. Leidner
Weekly closing:
Rest. «Novalis»: Sunday, Monday
Rest. «Keilerschänke»: Tuesday, Wednesday
Annual closing: December 24th
Currency: Euro (€)
Rates: Menus 22-64 € s.i. Carte 34-47 € s.i.
43 rooms: 100-300 € s.i.
1 suite: 230-350 € s.i.
Breakfast: included
Dogs: allowed (extra cost) except rest. **Golf:** 5 km
Accepted cards: AE, DC, MC, VS

More info on www.relaischateaux.com/hardenberg

Landhaus «Zu den Rothen Forellen»

SINCE 2003

Marktplatz 2,
D-38871 Ilsenburg
Germany

Tel. : (49) (039452) 93 93
Fax : (49) (039452) 93 99
forellen@relaischateaux.com

Germany

The Landhaus, restored in 1995, is situated close to the Hochharz mountains nature reserve, in the small, historic town of Ilsenburg. It dates back to 1574 and is close to a trout-filled lake. Its excellent cuisine and absolute tranquil setting will satisfy the most exacting demands. The spa, with its sauna and beauty centre, and the children's space make it the ideal place for rest and relaxation.

(Other activities P. 629)

Acess: From the south, motorway A 7, exit Rhüden, B 82 Goslar then B 6 Ilsenburg. From the east, motorway A 395, exit Bad Harzburg. Follow B 6 Ilsenburg.
Airport: Hannover (Intl) 100 km
Train station: Ilsenburg 1 km

Owners/General Managers:
Reinhard and Heidemarie Prause
Open all year
Currency: Euro (€)
Rates: Menus 25-85 € s.i. Carte 12-28 € s.i.
51 rooms: 125-200 € s.i.
1 suite: 240 € s.i.
Breakfast: included
Dogs: allowed (extra cost)
Golf: 15 km
Accepted cards: AE, DC, JCB, MC, VS

More info on www.relaischateaux.com/forellen

Hotel Schloss Wilkinghege

Germany — SINCE 1992

Steinfurter Strasse 374
D-48159 Münster
(Nordrhein-Westfalen) • Germany

Tel. : (49) (0251) 213045
Fax : (49) (0251) 212898
wilkinghege@relaischateaux.com

This romantic Renaissance château, set in the heart of the magnificent Westphalian countryside, combines modern comfort with a unique historical ambience. Rediscover XVIth century splendour beneath its beautiful white stucco ceilings, as you relax in the elegant rooms hung with silk tapestries and decorated with period furniture. The contemporary cuisine is accompanied by excellent white wines and vintage Bordeaux.

Biking. (Other activities P. 629)

Access: A1, towards Bremen, exit Münster North, towards centre, left at the 2nd light after the exit towards Kinderhaus.

Airports: Münster (Intl) 20 km, Düsseldorf (Intl) 120 km
Train station: Münster 5 km

Owners: Lubert and Rembert Winnecken
Annual closing: From December 24th to 25th
Currency: Euro (€)
Rates: Menus 59-73 € s.i. Carte 25-32 € s.i.
22 rooms: single 95-165 € s.i.
double 140-305 € s.i.
13 suites: 180-250 € s.i.
Breakfast: included
Dogs: allowed (extra cost) except restaurant
Golf: on the premises (18 holes)
Accepted cards: AE, DC, JCB, MC, VS

More info on www.relaischateaux.com/wilkinghege

Hotel Schloss Hugenpœt

SINCE 1975

August Thyssen Strasse 51
D-45219 Essen (E-Kettwig)
(Nordrhein-Westfalen) • Germany

Tel. : (49) (02054) 12040
Fax : (49) (02054) 120450
hugenpoet@relaischateaux.com

Germany

This magnificent Renaissance castle, nestling in the picturesque Ruhr valley between Dusseldorf and Essen, is surrounded by a sea of forest greenery. Guests will be enchanted by the castle's historical ambience, while gourmets will appreciate the superb cuisine inspired by the finest French traditions. The remarkable cellar, stocked with more than 300 vintages, features some of the finest German wines.

Private concerts. Sports club with personal training... (Other activities P. 629)

Access: Take the Rat.-Breitscheid exit at the Breitscheid interchange (A3/A52), towards Essen. Take the B227 towards Velbert, then towards E.-Kettwig.
Airport: Düsseldorf (Intl) 18 km
Train station: Essen 2 km

Owner: Michael Lübbert
Open all year
Currency: Euro (€)
Rates: Menus 70-90 € s.i.
Carte 23-35 € s.i.
21 rooms: 180-255 € s.i.
4 suites: 325-450 € s.i.
Breakfast: included
Dogs: allowed (extra cost) except restaurant
Golf: Oefte 5 km
Accepted cards: AE, DC, JCB, MC, VS

More info on www.relaischateaux.com/hugenpoet

Hotel Restaurant «Zur Traube»

Germany

SINCE 1984

Bahnstrasse 47
D-41515 Grevenbroich
(Nordrhein-Westfalen) • Germany

Tel. : (49) (02181) 68767
Fax : (49) (02181) 61122
zurtraube@relaischateaux.com

Behind the magnificent façade of this XIXth century residence lies an elegant dining room renowned as one of Germany's finest restaurants. Gourmets will marvel at Dieter Kaufmann's creative flair and be enchanted by this virtuoso chef's inventions, inspired by traditional French cuisine. The exceptional cellar features over 30000 vintages and guests can prolong their stay in a stylish room, named after a famous wine.

(Other activities P. 629)

Access: From Dusseldorf, A46 towards Aachen, exit 13, towards the city centre.

Airports: Düsseldorf (Intl) 35 km, Cologne 35 km
Train station: Grevenbroich 0,5 km

Owners: Dieter and Elvira Kaufmann
Weekly closing: Sunday and Monday
Annual closing: From December 23rd to January 15th and July 16th to August 6th
Currency: Euro (€)
Rates: Menus 43-100 € s.i.
Carte 30-43 € s.i.
4 rooms: 179-205 € s.i.
2 suites: starting at 245 € s.i.
Breakfast: included
Dogs: not allowed
Golf: 2 km
Accepted cards: AE, MC, VS

More info on www.relaischateaux.com/zurtraube

Schlosshotel Lerbach

SINCE 1994

Lerbacher Weg
D-51465 Bergisch Gladbach
(Nordrhein-Westfalen) • Germany

Tel. : (49) (02202) 2040
Fax : (49) (02202) 204940
lerbach@relaischateaux.com

Germany

The Schlosshotel Lerbach nestles amongst rolling hills in a breathtakingly beautiful park. Its individually styled, elegant rooms and suites create the impression of a stately country home. With its motto «where dreams come true», this grand manor with its romantic flair is home to one of Germany's best restaurants, the aromatic gourmet cuisine of starred chef Dieter Müller.

Concerts, biking, picnic in the park, hot-air balloon. (Other activities P. 629)

Access: A4, towards Olpe, exit Gladbach-Bensberg then Bergisch-Gladbach centre.

Airport: Cologne-Bonn 25 km
Helipad: O 7° 9' 15" N 50° 58' 50"
Train station: Bergisch Gladbach 3 km

Owners: Thomas H. Althoff and Kurt Wagner
General Manager: Hinrik Dollmann
Open all year
Currency: Euro (€)
Rates: Menus 58-125 € s.i. Carte 35-46 € s.i.
42 rooms: 200-300 € s.i.
12 suites: 425-1350 € s.i.
Breakfast: included
Dogs: allowed (extra cost)
Golf: 5 km
Accepted cards: AE, DC, MC, VS

More info on www.relaischateaux.com/lerbach

Hotel Hohenhaus

SINCE 1990

D-37293 Herleshausen-Holzhausen
(Hessen) • Germany

Tel. : (49) (05654) 9870
Fax : (49) (05654) 1303
hohenhaus@relaischateaux.com

Nestling in a wooded valley, just a few miles from Eisenach, the birthplace of Bach and Luther, this elegant family manor offers comfortable guestrooms, decorated in a contemporary style. Relax in the indoor pool where wide bay windows overlook acres of unspoilt countryside, then enjoy an aperitif in front of a roaring fire. Savour seasonal specialities of the region accompanied by a vast collection of German wines.

Ergometer. (Other activities P. 629)

Access: From Bad Hersfeld, A4 towards Eisenach, exit Herleshausen, or Wildeck-Obersuhl, B400.
Airports: Erfurt (Intl) 80 km, Frankfurt (Intl) 180 km
Helipad: N 51° 02' 25" E 010° 04' 48"
Train station: Herleshausen 5 km

Owner: Hohenhaus GmbH
General Manager: Hannes Horsch
Weekly closing: Rest.: Sunday evening, Monday and Tuesday noon
Annual closing: From January 7th to 31st
Currency: Euro (€)
Rates: Menus 70-95 € s.i. Carte 28-51 € s.i.
26 rooms: single 115-165 € s.i. double 185-215 € s.i.
Breakfast: 18 € s.i.
Dogs: allowed (extra cost) except restaurant
Golf: 10 and 45 km
Accepted cards: AE, DC, JCB, MC, VS

More info on www.relaischateaux.com/hohenhaus

Hotel Jagdhof Glashütte

SINCE 2002

Glashütter Str. 20
D-57334 Bad Laasphe-Glashütte
(Nordrhein-Westfalen) • Germany

Tel. : (49) (02754) 3990
Fax : (49) (02754) 399 222
jagdhof@relaischateaux.com

Germany

In the hills of Wittgenstein, an idyllic manor house is set in a breathtaking landscape of meadows, rippling streams and conifers. It is the epitomy of excellent hospitality and joy of living. The decor is both refined and opulent and relaxation is a foregone conclusion thanks to its beauty centre. Young and light gourmet cuisine is enhanced by an excellent wine list at the «Ars Vivendi».

Fishing... (Other activities P. 629)

Access: A45 exit n° 21 Siegen Netphen towards Siegerlandhalle, then B54 towards Limburg and Bad Laasphe. In Netphen-Deutz towards Feudingen, in Volkholz right towards Glashütte.
Airport: Frankfurt (Intl) 120 km
Helipad: N 50° 55' 06'' O 08° 17' 00''
Train station: Feudingen 4 km

Owner/General Manager: Edmund Dornhöfer
Weekly closing: Rest. «Ars Vivendi»:
Sunday and Monday
Annual closing: Rest. «Ars Vivendi»:
from Jan. 21th to 29th and from August 5th to 27th
Currency: Euro (€)
Rates: Menus 25-83 € s.i. Carte 27-66 € s.i.
19 rooms: 196-246 € s.i.
10 suites: 256-346 € s.i.
Breakfast: 15 € s.i.
Dogs: allowed (extra cost)
Golf: 30 km
Accepted cards: AE, DC, JCB, MC, VS

More info on www.relaischateaux.com/jagdhof

Johann Lafer's Stromburg

Germany — SINCE 1997

D-55442 Stromberg
(Rheinland-Pfalz) • Germany

Tel. : **(49) (06724) 93100**
Fax : (49) (06724) 931090
johannlafer@relaischateaux.com

Joie de vivre and a perfect treat! This is the daily offering for the guests of Johann Lafer and his team! Not only is the excellence of the cuisine and wine cellar a source of pure delight, but the friendly atmosphere and exceptional hospitality will also contribute to the pleasures of a stay at this establishment, run by Germany's number one television chef, located in the vicinity of a magnificent winegrowing region.

Cooking school, golf school, helicopter tours, boat trips, hot air ballooning. (Other activities P. 629)

Access: A 61 - Cologne - Ludwigshafen, exit Stromberg, follow the «Johann Lafers Stromburg» signs for 1 kilometre.

Airport: Frankfurt (Intl) 75 km
Train station: Bingen 9 km

Owners: Silvia Buchholz-Lafer, Johann Lafer
General Manager: Silvia Buchholz-Lafer
Weekly closing:
Restaurant «Le Val d'Or»: Monday
Open all year
Currency: Euro (€)
Rates: Menus 59-105 € s.i. Carte 28-34 € s.i.
13 rooms: 149-225 € s.i.
1 suite: 409 € s.i.
Breakfast: 15 € s.i.
Dogs: allowed (extra cost)
Golf: 1 km
Accepted cards: AE, DC, JCB, MC, VS

More info on www.relaischateaux.com/johannlafer

Hotel Burg Wernberg

SINCE 2000

Schlossberg 10
D-92533 Wernberg-Köblitz
(Bayern) • Germany

Tel. : (49) (09604) 939 0
Fax : (49) (09604) 939 139
burgwernberg@relaischateaux.com

Germany

This XIIth century historical site in Bavaria, fully restored with all the modern comforts, offers you a romantic and unique setting for your stay. Perched on a hill and flanked by feudal turrets, the castle will astound you with its gothic rooms, its gourmet restaurant Kastell, its regional restaurant Burgkeller and its elegant salons.

Hunting, biking. (Other activities P. 629)

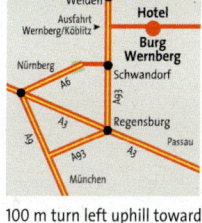

Access: From the A93, take the Wernberg-Köblitz exit in the direction of Wernberg-Köblitz centre. After the yellow church turn right, after 100 m turn left uphill towards the castle.
Airports: Munich Franz Josef Strauss (Intl) 180 km, Nuremberg 85 km **Train station:** Wernberg 1,5 km

Owners: Conrad Family
General Manager: Arwed and Régine Sparber
Weekly closing: Rest.«Kastell»:
Monday and Tuesday
Annual closing: Rest. «Kastell»:
From January 2nd to 28th
Currency: Euro (€)
Rates: Menus 31-98 € s.i. Carte 10-35 € s.i.
25 rooms: 135-195 € s.i. **5 suites:** 220-325 € s.i.
Breakfast: 15 € s.i.
Dogs: allowed (extra cost) **Golf:** 10 km
Accepted cards: AE, MC, VS

More info on www.relaischateaux.com/burgwernberg

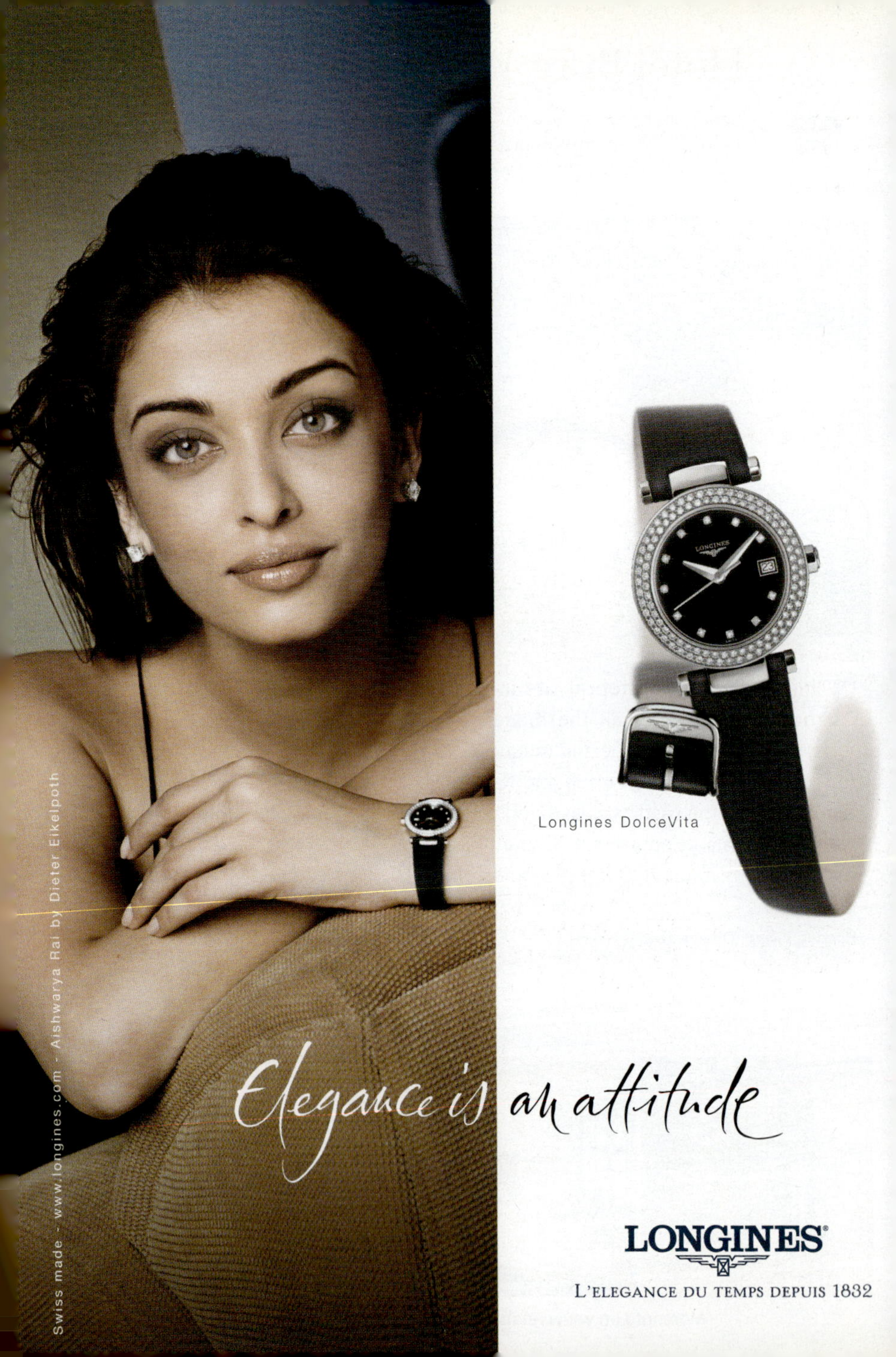

Longines DolceVita
Elegance is an attitude
LONGINES
L'ELEGANCE DU TEMPS DEPUIS 1832
Swiss made - www.longines.com - Aishwarya Rai by Dieter Eikelpoth

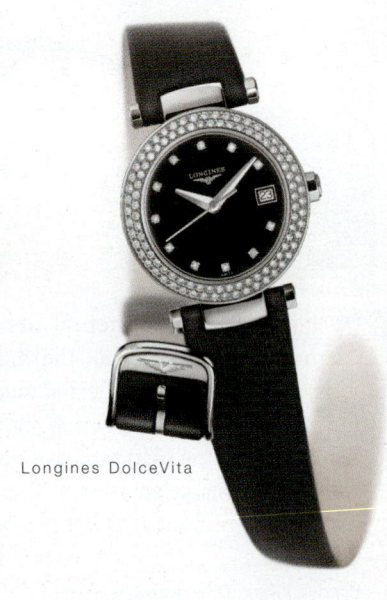

Pflaums Posthotel Pegnitz

SINCE 1981

Nürnberger Strasse 8-16
D-91257 Pegnitz
(Bayern) • Germany

Tel. : (49) (09241) 7250
Fax : (49) (09241) 80404
pflaums@relaischateaux.com

Germany

No other hotel in Europe can better personify the links associating one family for the past three hundred years with landscapes, art, culture and a coaching inn. Its extraordinary, hospitable atmosphere venerates the memory of Richard Wagner. A Mecca of comfort, high-class cuisine and excellent wines. Golf and fly-fishing.

Art and Design Gallery, free car transfer to the Bayreuth Festival Hall and the Nuremberg Toy Trade Fair, art gallery, Modern Art museum, billiards, polo, fly fishing, beauty salon 24 hours a day. (Other activities P. 629)

Access: Take the A3 from Frankfurt to the Nuremberg interchange, then follow the A9 towards Berlin. Take the Pegniz exit after 5 km.

Airports: Nuremberg (Intl) 57 km, Bayreuth 27 km
Helipad: N 49° 45' 48'' E 11° 54' 34''
Train station: Pegnitz 2 km

Owners: Andreas and Hermann Pflaum
General Manager: Andreas Pflaum
Open all year
Currency: Euro (€)
Rates: Menus 30-84 € s.i. Carte 14-28 € s.i.
25 rooms: 145-300 € s.i.
25 suites: 300-920 € s.i.
Breakfast: 18 € s.i.
Dogs: allowed (extra cost)
Golf: 9 km (27 holes)
Accepted cards: AE, DC, MC, VS

More info on www.relaischateaux.com/pflaums

Germany

Hotel Deidesheimer Hof

SINCE 1993

Am Marktplatz
D-67146 Deidesheim
(Rheinland-Pfalz) • Germany

Tel. : (49) (06326) 96870
Fax : (49) (06326) 7685
deidesheimer@relaischateaux.com

You will be received in a Renaissance manor overlooking the most romantic market square in the region - a temple of tranquillity as confirmed by the many famous names in the Golden Book. The executive chef serves tasty regional dishes in the «Weinstube St. Urban» whereas in the gourmet restaurant «Schwarzer Hahn» he pays fitting tribute to classical French cuisine. Exquisite wine cellar.

Cooking classes, wine tasting... (Other activities P. 629)

Access: From Bad Dürkheim or Neustadt, follow the wine route (B 271) to Deidesheim.
Airport: Frankfurt (Intl) 90 km
Train station : Deidesheim 0,5 km

Owners: Hahn Family
Weekly closing: «Schwarzer Hahn»: Sunday and Monday, from January 1st to 30th and from June 29th to August 21st
Annual closing: From January 1st to 3rd
Currency: Euro (€)
Rates: Menus 38-95 € s.i. Carte 13-32 € s.i.
24 rooms: single 95-165 € s.i.
double 130-180 € s.i.
4 suites: 210-270 € s.i.
Breakfast: 12 € s.i.
Dogs: allowed (extra cost)
Golf: 10 km
Accepted cards: AE, DC, MC, VS

More info on www.relaischateaux.deidesheimer

Wald und Schlosshotel Friedrichsruhe

SINCE 1965

D-74639 Friedrichsruhe-Zweiflingen
(Baden-Württemberg) • Germany

Tel. : (49) (07941) 60870
Fax : (49) (07941) 61468
waldschloss@relaischateaux.com

Germany

Three elegant residences await you, nestling in a magnificent 7-acre park. Combining the charms of an unusual habitat and exquisite menus, Prince Zu Hohenlohe-Œhringen's former summer palace and hunting pavillion have become one of Germany's most renowned gourmet retreats. Savour sublime fish and game specialities and extraordinary desserts and discover the excellent Verrenberg, a wine from the estate's vineyard.

Jogging, aquagymnastics, exercise therapy, various castles and museums, open-air festivals Jagsthausen and Schwäbisch Hall, hot air ballooning, wine tasting, archery, table tennis, helipad. (Other activities P. 629)

Access: A6 exit Öhringen; cross the town, then follow signs for Friedrichsruhe (6 km).

Airport: Stuttgart (Intl) 80 km
Train station: Öhringen 6 km

Owner: Fürst Kraft zu Hohenlohe-Œhringen
General Manager: Lothar Eiermann
Open all year
Currency: Euro (€)
Rates: Menus 41-102 € s.i. Carte 23-38 € s.i.
27 rooms: 160-235 € s.i.
16 suites: 266-390 € s.i.
Breakfast: 15 € s.i.
Dogs: allowed (extra cost)
Golf: 18 holes (on the premises)
Accepted cards: AE, DC, JCB, MC, VS

More info on www.relaischateaux.com/waldschloss

Germany

Hotel Villa Hammerschmiede

SINCE 1996

Hauptstrasse 162
D-76327 Pfinztal-Söllingen
(Baden-Württemberg) • Germany

Tel. : (49) (07240) 601 0
Fax : (49) (07240) 601 60
hammerschmiede@relaischateaux.com

Enjoy the hospitality of the Schwalbe family at the beautiful Villa Hammerschmiede, located between Heidelberg and Baden-Baden. 30 guestrooms and suites, some decorated in Italian Art Deco style, with luxurious bathrooms. Relax in the extraordinary swimming pool carved out of the rock. Gourmet cuisine served in the warm atmosphere of the English winter garden or beneath the restaurant's superb vaulted ceiling.

(Other activities P. 629)

Access: From Frankfurt, A5 towards Basle, exit Karlsruhe-Durlach, B10 towards Pforzheim, 500 m after exit Pfinztal-Söllingen.

Airports: Baden-Baden (Intl) 50 km, Stuttgart (Intl) 70 km
Train station: Karlsruhe 12 km

Owner: Norbert Schwalbe
General Managers: Annette Schwalbe-Feldmann, Sebastian Feldmann and Markus Nagy
Open all year
Currency: Euro (€)
Rates: Menus 38-84 € s.i. Carte 41-56 € s.i.
25 rooms: 160-230 € s.i.
5 suites: 260-440 € s.i.
Breakfast: 15 € s.i.
Dogs: allowed (extra cost)
Golf: 8 km
Accepted cards: AE, DC, MC, VS

More info on www.relaischateaux.com/hammerschmiede

Restaurant Bareiss

SINCE 1984

Hotel Bareiss, Gärtenbühlweg 14
D-72270 Baiersbronn-Mitteltal
(Baden-Württemberg) • Germany

Tel. : **(49) (07442) 473320**
Fax : (49) (07442) 47320
bareiss@relaischateaux.com

Germany

In one of the most beautiful and elegant restaurants in Germany, the chef Claus-Peter Lumpp offers inventive and sun-drenched cuisine. You will appreciate the charming and efficient service of Thomas Brandt and his team as well as the excellent advice of Jürgen Fendt, best German sommelier. A superb culinary experience not to be missed.

(Other activities P. 629)

Access: A 5, exit Rastatt, Murg valley, Baiersbronn. A 81, exit Horb, Freudenstadt.

Airports: Strasbourg (Intl) 70 km, Stuttgart (Intl) 120 km
Train station: Baiersbronn 3 km

Owner: Hermann Bareiss
Weekly closing: Monday and Tuesday
Annual closing: From January 6th to February 7th and from July 13th to August 15th
Currency: Euro (€)
Rates: Menus 95-110 € s.i.
Carte 62-72 € s.i.
Dogs: not allowed
Golf: 12 km
Accepted cards: AE, DC, MC, VS

Claus-Peter Lumpp

More info on www.relaischateaux.com/bareiss

Germany

Restaurant Schwarzwaldstube

SINCE 1984

Hotel Traube Tonbach,
Tonbachstrasse 237
D-72270 Baiersbronn-Tonbach
(Baden-Württemberg) • Germany

Tel. : **(49) (07442) 492665**
Fax : (49) (07442) 492692
schwarzwaldstube@relaischateaux.com

Gourmets flock to this sumptuous restaurant to savour Harald Wohlfahrt's culinary marvels, inspired by the finest French tradition. The «rosette de coquilles Saint-Jacques sur un chutney de mangue et d'ananas, bisque de crustacés aromatisée au curry thaï» is sublime and the «mijoté de joues de veau et croustillants de ris de veau sur une polenta de légumes, sauce merlot» a veritable masterpiece. With an exceptional wine list and impeccable service, the Schwarzwaldstube is a gastronomic experience you will never forget.

(Other activities P. 629)

Access: From Strasbourg, Karlsruhe highway, exit Achern, Ruhestein pass, Baiersbronn.

Airports: Strasbourg (Intl) 80 km, Stuttgart (Intl) 100 km
Train station: Baiersbronn 3 km

Owner: Heiner Finkbeiner
Weekly closing: Monday and Tuesday (except bank holidays)
Annual closing: From January 7th to 31st and from July 28th to August 26th
Currency: Euro (€)
Rates: Menus 98-120 € s.i. Carte 55-65 € s.i.
Dogs: not allowed
Golf: Freudenstadt 10 km
Accepted cards: AE, MC, VS

Harald Wohlfahrt

More info on www.relaischateaux.com/schwarzwaldstube

Kur-und Sporthotel Dollenberg

SINCE 1997

Dollenberg 3
D-77740 Bad Peterstal - Griesbach
(Baden-Württemberg) • Germany

Tel. : (49) (07806) 78-0
Fax : (49) (07806) 1272
dollenberg@relaischateaux.com

Germany

In Meinrad Schmiederer's charming and friendly hotel, which perpetuates the tradition of German hospitality and where the scenery of the surrounding Black Forest is relaxing for both body and soul, guests are looked after with exceptional care and courtesy. The chef light gourmet cuisine, based on seasonal regional produce, is a festival of flavours and aromas.

Beauty treatment, outdoor chessboard, petanque ground.
(Other activities P. 629)

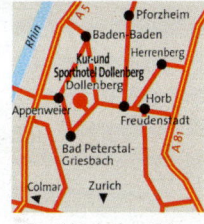

Access: From Frankfurt or Basel: A5 - exit Appenweier towards Freudenstadt, then turn left after Bad Griesbach. From Stuttgart: A81- exit Horb, then B28 towards Strasbourg and turn right before Bad Griesbach.
Airports: Strasbourg (Intl) 50 km, Stuttgart (Intl) 100 km
Train station: Bad Peterstal 2,5 km

Owner: Meinrad Schmiederer
Open all year
Currency: Euro (€)
Rates: Menus 19-72 € s.i. Carte 17-30 € s.i.
28 rooms: 142-170 € s.i.
60 suites: 186-220 € s.i.
Breakfast: included
Dogs: allowed (extra cost) **Golf:** 15 km
Accepted cards: AE, DC, JCB, MC, VS

More info on www.relaischateaux.com/dollenberg

Schwarzwald - Hotel Adler

Germany — SINCE 1998

St. Fridolinstrasse 15
D-79837 Häusern
(Baden-Württemberg) • Germany

Tel. : (49) (07672) 4170
Fax : (49) (07672) 417150
adler@relaischateaux.com

This charming hotel, set in the south of the Black Forest, has been managed for five generations by the Zumkeller family. A high quality cuisine to delight gourmets and those who love regional specialities, a redesigned landscape of ornamental ponds and swimming pools, a health and beauty centre, tastefully decorated rustic-style rooms and the wide variety of sports available all explain why the Adler is a favourite holiday venue.

(Other activities P. 629)

Access: From Frankfurt A 5 exit Freiburg Mitte, B 31 to Titisee, then continue on B 500. From Stuttgart A 81 exit Donaueschingen, B 31 to Titisee and continue on B 500.
Airport: Zurich (Intl) 60 km
Train station: Seebrugg 8 km

Owner: Winfried Zumkeller
Weekly closing: Rest.: Monday and Tuesday
Annual closing:
Rest.: from November 10th to December 18th
Hotel: from November 24th to December 18th
Currency: Euro (€)
Rates: Menus 30-80 € s.i. Carte 18-32 € s.i.
28 rooms: 140-180 € s.i.
17 suites: 200-250 € s.i.
Breakfast: included
Dogs: allowed (extra cost) **Golf:** 25 km
Accepted cards: MC, VS

More info on www.relaischateaux.com/adler

Hotel Schwarzmatt

SINCE 1994

Schwarzmattstrasse, 6a
D-79410 Badenweiler
(Baden-Württemberg) • Germany

Tel. : (49) (07632) 8201 0
Fax : (49) (07632) 8201 20
schwarzmatt@relaischateaux.com

Germany

You will be enchanted with the hospitality of the Mast-Bareiss family and the refined, rustic atmosphere. The comfortable rooms open out onto large sunkissed balconies. The dining-rooms, with their delicately coloured decor, are finished off with floral compositions. The cuisine gives pride of place to fresh market produce, combining traditional dishes with the flavoursome creations of nouvelle cuisine. Baden, French and Italian wines.

Thermal baths. (Other activities P. 629)

Access: A5 - exit Müllheim, Badenweiler, follow signs to centre.

Airports: Basel (Intl) 35 km, Zurich (Intl) 150 km
Train station: Müllheim 10 km

Owner: Heidemarie Mast-Bareiss
Open all year
Currency: Euro (€)
Rates: Menus 33-55 € s.i.
Carte 20-28 € s.i.
24 rooms: 230-280 € s.i.
14 suites: 290-320 € s.i.
Breakfast: included
Dogs: allowed (extra cost)
Golf: 12 golf courses between 9 and 40 km
Accepted cards (Rest., shop): AE, MC, VS

More info on www.relaischateaux.com/schwarzmatt

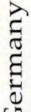

Germany

Seehotel Siber

SINCE 1986

Seestrasse 25
D-78464 Konstanz
(Baden-Württemberg) • Germany

Tel. : (49) (07531) 996699-0
Fax : (49) (07531) 996699-33
siber@relaischateaux.com

The Mediterranean-style terraces and gardens of this villa are located directly on the plane tree-lined lakeside promenade. The numerous excursions or wonderful walks are the best way to work up an appetite for the creative and highly appraised cuisine. A large selection of top European and international wines are the perfect accompaniment. Renowned summer attractions like the Bregenz Festival and the Lake Festival.

Water sports, dancing... (Other activities P. 629)

Access: From Stuttgart, A 81 towards Singen, to Constance, opposite the Constance «Casino».

Airports: Zurich (Intl) 65 km, Stuttgart (Intl) 120 km
Train station: Konstanz 1 km

Owner: Bertold Siber
Annual closing: 10 days in February
Currency: Euro (€)
Rates: Menus 59-95 € s.i. Carte 15-38 € s.i.
11 rooms: 169-235 € s.i.
1 suite: 337 € s.i.
Breakfast: 18-26 € s.i.
Dogs: allowed (extra cost)
Golf: 18 km
Accepted cards: AE, MC, VS

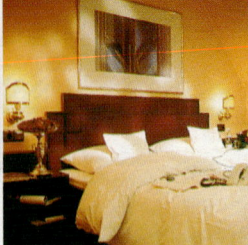

More info on www.relaischateaux.com/siber

Villino

SINCE 2000

Hoyerberg 34
D-88131 Lindau-Bodensee
(Bayern) • Germany

Tel. : (49) (08382) 93 450
Fax : (49) (08382) 93 4512
villino@relaischateaux.com

Germany

If you travel in the lovely region of lake Constance, you must stop at the flower-bedecked and idyllic country residence of Villino. Enjoy the hosts' warm welcome, the comfortable rooms and savour the pleasures of the cuisine inspired by Italian and Asian culinary art. The proverb «A lake, three countries and thousands of possibilities» is a perfect description: there is a myriad of activities to discover.

Biking, tennis, cooking classes, gardens, massage. (Other activities P. 629)

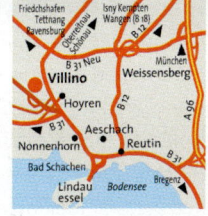

Access: From the A 96, towards Wasserburg-Nonnenhorn. After the hospital, turn right towards Oberreitnau-Schönau. After 200 m, turn left at the lights. Villino is 500 m away.
Airports: Zurich (Intl) 130 km, Friedrichshafen 20 km
Train station: Lindau 4 km

Owners: Sonja and Reiner Fischer
Weekly closing: Restaurant: Monday
Annual closing: From January 10th to 30th
Currency: Euro (€)
Rates: Menus 68-78 € s.i. Carte 18-32 € s.i.
8 rooms: 140-170 € s.i.
8 suites: 180-220 € s.i.
Breakfast: included
Dogs: allowed (extra cost)
Golf: 4 km
Accepted cards: MC, VS

More info on www.relaischateaux.com/villino

Alpenhof Murnau

Germany · SINCE 1972

Ramsachstrasse 8
D-82418 Murnau
(Bayern) • Germany

Tel. : (49) (08841) 4910
Fax : (49) (08841) 491100
murnau@relaischateaux.com

Situated between Munich and Garmisch, the Alpenhof, an elegant chalet-hotel, with a restaurant renowned for the excellence of its cuisine and remarkable wine list, is a veritable oasis of hospitality. In summer months, but also in the winter, this property, with its magnificent sun-drenched terrace looking out across Upper Bavaria, is an absolute must.

Royal Palaces, art and culture, biking. (Other activities P. 629)

Access: A 95 Munich-Garmisch, take Murnau exit, turn right on to U 21 towards Murnau. In Murnau, straight on to the main crossroads, then left towards Garmisch.
Airport: Munich Franz Josef Strauss (Intl) 110 km
Train station: Murnau 2 km

Owner: Erivan Haub
General Manager: Didier Morand
Open all year
Currency: Euro (€)
Rates: Menus 39-80 € s.i. Carte 8-28 € s.i.
60 rooms: single 107-162 € s.i.
double 148-260 € s.i.
17 suites: starting at 271 € s.i.
Breakfast: included
Dogs: allowed (extra cost)
Golf: 20 km
Accepted cards: AE, JCB, MC, VS

More info on www.relaischateaux.com/murnau

Residenz Heinz Winkler

SINCE 1994

Kirchplatz 1
D-83229 Aschau
(Bayern) • Germany

Tel. : (49) (08052) 1799 0
Fax : (49) (08052) 1799 66
winkler@relaischateaux.com

Germany

To the south of Munich, near Chiemsee and the fairytale castle of Ludwig II of Bavaria and the great backdrop of the Alps, legendary cuisine awaits you at the «Residenz», where you can sample Heinz Winkler's fine game specialities enhanced by rare vintages. The ideal place to stay, complete with a health and beauty centre. Visit the Salzburg Festival and the international famous Riedel glassworks.

Opera Festival of Munich, festival of Salzburg. (Other activities P. 629)

Access: From Munich, A 8 towards Salzburg, Chiemsee, exit Frasdorf-Aschau.

Airports: Salzburg (Intl) 60 km,
Munich Franz Josef Strauss (Intl) 120 km
Train station: Aschau 0,8 km

Owner: Heinz Winkler
Open all year
Currency: Euro (€)
Rates: Menus 79-130 € s.i.
Carte 9-23 € s.i.
19 rooms: 150-250 € s.i.
13 suites: 250-317 € s.i.
Breakfast: 19 € s.i.
Dogs: allowed (extra cost) hotel only
Golf: 8 km
Accepted cards: AE, DC, JCB, MC, VS

More info on www.relaischateaux.com/winkler

Czech Republic

Property	Nearest major city	Relais & Châteaux	Relais Gourmands	Page
Hoffmeister (Hotel)	Praha	⚜		333

Equivalent in euros for information only (rate of 1/06/02). Application of the exchange rate valid on the day of transaction.

Hotel Hoffmeister

SINCE 1995

Pod Bruskou 7
CZ-11800 Praha 1
Czech Republic

Tel. : (420) 251 017 111
Fax : (420) 251 017 120
hoffmeister@relaischateaux.com

Czech Republic

An oasis of relaxation and refinement, in the centre of magical Prague, one of history's capital cities. Our beautiful residence, restored in the style of the 1920's, features portraits and collages by A. Hoffmeister, friend of Max Ernst, Cocteau and Picasso. European elegance, footsteps away from Prague castle and all the unforgettable attractions, exquisite regional cuisine and wines – one of the best in Prague.

(Other activities P. 629)

Access: Located in the Malà Strana quarter near the Malostranska Metro, the Vltava river and the Mánes bridge.

Airport: Prague (Intl) 16 km
Train station: Masaryk 3 km

Owner/General Manager: Martin Hoffmeister
Open all year
Currency: Czech crown (CZK)
Rates: Menus 800-1200 CZK s.i. - 27-40 €
Carte 800-2500 CZK s.i. - 27-83 €
17 rooms: 5000-8000 CZK s.i. - 166-265 €
8 suites: 7000-11200 CZK s.i. - 232-371 €
Breakfast: 330 CZK s.i. - 11 €
Dogs: allowed (small)
Golf: 20 km
Accepted cards: AE, DC, JCB, MC, VS

More info on www.relaischateaux.com/hoffmeister

Austria

Properties	Nearest major city	Relais & Châteaux	Relais Gourmands	Page
Arlberg Hospiz	Innsbruck	✦		337
Der Bär (Hotel)	Innsbruck	✦		343
Deuring Schlössle	Zürich	✦	●	336
Gasthof Post	Bludenz	✦		338
Grüner Baum (Hotel)	Salzburg	✦		348
Hubertus (Hotel)	Salzburg	✦	●	344
Landgut Luxnachmule (Hotel)	Reutte in Tirol	✦		339
Schloss Dürnstein (Hotel)	Wien	✦		345
Schloss Seefels (Hotel)	Klagenfurt	✦		349
Schlosshotel Igls	Innsbruck	✦		342
Sporthotel Singer	Innsbruck	✦		340
Steirereck (Restaurant)	Wien		●	346
Taubenkobel	Wien	✦	●	347
Top Hotel Hochgurgl	Obergurgl	✦		341

More info on www.relaischateaux.com

Austria — SINCE 1992

Deuring Schlössle

Ehre-Guta-Platz 4
A-6900 Bregenz
(Vorarlberg) • Austria

Tel. : (43) (05574) 47800
Fax : (43) (05574) 4780080
deuring@relaischateaux.com

A meal fit for a king awaits you in this romantic castle whose 15 magnificent rooms and suites, decorated with antique furniture, offer superb vistas of Lake Constance. Elected «Best chef in Austria 1998», Heino Huber reinvents classic cuisine with creative flair. With immense charm, Bernadette Huber, the castle's owner and wine waiter will serve you superb vintages from the well-stocked wine cellar.

Trout fishing, events, cooking classes, tasting of rare vintages. (Other activities P. 629)

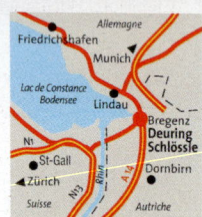

Access: Exit A 14 at Bregenz, take Bahnhofstraße, Montfortstraße, Kirchstraße, and follow signs to Altstadt.

Airport: Zurich (Intl) 110 km
Train station: Bregenz 3 km

Owners: Bernadette and Heino Huber
Annual closing: 1 week in February
Currency: Euro (€)
Rates: Menus 25-71 € s.i.
Carte 23-47 € s.i.
10 rooms: single 153-211 € s.i.
double 182-276 € s.i.
5 suites: 305-427 € s.i.
Breakfast: included
Dogs: allowed (extra cost)
Golf: 15 km
Accepted cards: AE, DC, MC, VS

More info on www.relaischateaux.com/deuring

Arlberg Hospiz

A-6580 St-Christoph 118
(Tirol) • Austria

Tel. : (43) (05446) 2611
Fax : (43) (05446) 3773
arlberg@relaischateaux.com

Austria

SINCE 1976

At the foot of the ski area of Arlberg, this hotel has a tradition of hospitality that is as legendary as its six centuries of history. Intimate and comfortable rooms and suites. Relaxation and entertainment are guaranteed thanks to the wide selection of sports activities, a fitness centre and varied daily programme. Savour delicious food and fine vintages from one of the world's biggest Bordeaux wine cellars.

Childcare, cross-country skiing, alpine skiing, snowboard, trekking, bowling, sledge, snowshoeing. (Other activities P. 629)

Altitude: 1800 metres.
Access: From Innsbruck, towards Arlberg, exit St-Anton. From Switzerland, towards Innsbruck. Exit Arlberg.
Airports: Innsbruck Kranebitten 100 km (Intl) , Zurich (Intl) 200 km
Train station: St-Anton 5 km

Owner: Gerda Werner
General Managers: Florian Werner, Daniela Pfefferkorn
Annual closing: From May 1st to Nov. 30th
Currency: Euro (€)
Rates: Menus 35-80 € s.i. Carte 18-33 € s.i.
35 rooms: 420-750 € s.i.
60 suites: 545-1990 € s.i.
Breakfast: included
Dogs: allowed (extra cost) **Golf:** 15 km
Accepted cards: AE, DC, MC, VS

More info on www.relaischateaux.com/arlberg

Gasthof Post

Austria — SINCE 1976

A-6764 Lech am Arlberg
(Vorarlberg) • Austria

Tel. : (43) (05583) 22060
Fax : (43) (05583) 220623
postlech@relaischateaux.com

Historic inn in the heart of a picturesque alpine village. Rural, warm and cosy atmosphere. Rooms with hand-painted furniture, antiquities and hunting trophies. Spacious guest rooms looking onto spectacular mountains or the idyllic garden. Highly acclaimed restaurant with excellent wine list. Indoor swimming pool and spa. Many cultural and sporting activities. A paradise for hiking enthusiasts.

(Other activities P. 629)

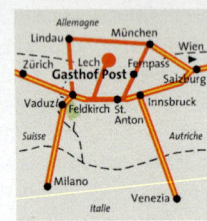

Altitude: 1450 metres.
Access: From Zurich towards Innsbruck, exit Arlberg. From Innsbruck, towards Arlberg, exit St. Anton.
Airports: Zurich (Intl) 180 km, Munich Franz Josef Strauss (Intl) 240 km
Train station: Langen 15 km

Owners: Moosbrugger Family
Annual closing: From beginning of May to mid-June and from beginning of October to end of November
Currency: Euro (€)
Rates: Menus 45-80 € s.i. Carte 25-55 € s.i.
21 rooms: summer 200-300 € s.i. winter 300-590 € s.i.
18 suites: summer 260-420 € s.i. winter 380-740 € s.i.
Breakfast: included
Dogs: allowed (extra cost) **Golf:** 20 km

More info on www.relaischateaux.com/postlech

Hotel Landgut Luxnachmühle

SINCE 2001

Luxnach 4
A-6651 Häselgehr-Lechtal
(Tirol) • Austria

Tel. : (43) (05634) 6100-0
Fax : (43) (05634) 6100-7
landgut@relaischateaux.com

Austria

This XIIth century Tyrolean chalet offers comfort and refined taste. Its period country furniture, the big fireplaces, the many precious-cloth draperies combine to create an ambience of unequalled well-being in a perfect blend of style and tradition. Gourmets will enjoy the Austrian and French specialities, and art and nature lovers the private hunting, the royal Bavarian castles and the pre-Alpine landscape.

Climbing, parapenting. (Other activities P. 629)

Altitude: 1050 metres.
Access: From Innsbruck: Reutte (Tyrol), Lech valley, Häselgehr. From Munich: Garmisch-Partenkirchen, Reutte, Lech valley. From Ulm: Kempten, Reutte, Lech valley, Häselgehr
Airport: Innsbruck Kranebitten (Intl) 115 km
Train station: Reutte 20 km

Owner: Barbara v. Frankenberg-Unmüssig
General Manager: Michaela Fricke
Open all year
Currency: Euro (€)
Rates: Menus 33-47 € s.i. Carte 23-45 € s.i.
4 rooms: 244-347 € s.i.
5 suites: 331-672 € s.i.
Breakfast: included
Dogs: allowed (extra cost) except. restaurant
Golf: 40 km
Accepted cards (Restaurant): AE, DC, MC, VS

More info on www.relaischateaux.com/landgut

Austria

Sporthotel Singer

SINCE 1986

A-6622 Berwang
(Tirol) • Austria

Tel. : (43) (05674) 8181
Fax : (43) (05674) 818183
singer@relaischateaux.com

Set in a stunning mountain landscape, this elegant hotel seems to have been purpose-built for your pleasure, with a warm cordial atmosphere and tastefully furnished comfortable rooms. Relax in either of the two bars or in the large, original Tyrolean-style lounge with its roaring log fire and enjoy a wonderful candlelit dinner in the restaurants or on the terrace, savouring the best European vintage wines. Visit the castles of King Ludwig II of Bavaria nearby.

Trout fishing, alpine skiing, cross-country skiing, child minding. (Other activities P. 629)

Altitude: 1340 metres.
Access: From Stuttgart, Ulm, A7 towards Füssen, then B 179 Reutte, Bichlbach or via Fernpass, Berwang.
Airports: Innsbruck Kranebitten (Intl) 75 km, Munich Franz Josef Stauss (Intl) 160 km
Train station: Bichlbach-Berwang 4 km

Owners: Günter and Gerti Singer
Annual closing: From March 30th to May 25th and from September 28th to December 19th
Currency: Euro (€)
Rates: Menus 27-58 € s.i.
Carte 26-45 € s.i.
27 rooms: 120-228 € s.i.
27 suites: 142-358 € s.i.
Breakfast: buffet included
Dogs: allowed (extra cost) only rooms
Golf: 32 km
Accepted cards: AE, DC, MC, VS

More info on www.relaischateaux.com/singer

Top Hotel Hochgurgl

SINCE 2001

Hochgurgl 60
A-6456 Hochgurgl
(Tirol) • Austria

Tel. : (43) (05256) 6265
Fax : (43) (05256) 6265-10
hochgurgl@relaischateaux.com

Austria

The Tyrolean resort of Hochgurgl, one of Europe's highest, owes its success to its magnificent location (twenty peaks over 3000 metres!). The vast, modern chalet-style hotel of the same name started its prestigious career in 1961. The services offered by this fine family-run establishment have continually improved, the pleasures of the mountains and fitness at their peak! Excellent hospitality and facilities.
Hiking. (Other activities P. 629)

Altitude: 2150 metres.
Access: Motorway A12 (Inntalautobahn) towards Bregenz. Take exit «Ötztal» (25 km west of Innsbruck).
Hochgurgl is at the end of the Ötztal valley.
Airports: Innsbruck Kranebitten (Intl) 100 km, Munich Franz Josef Strauss (Intl) 250 km
Train station: Ötztal Bahnhof 50 km

Owner: Alban Scheiber
General Manager: Gerhard Schwendner
Annual closing: From May to November
Currency: Euro (€)
Rates: Carte 33-42 € s.i.
28 rooms: 312-451 € s.i.
36 suites: 436-625 € s.i.
Breakfast: 11 € s.i.
Dogs: allowed (extra cost)
Golf: 80 km
Accepted cards: AE, DC, MC, VS

More info on www.relaischateaux.com/hochgurgl

Austria — SINCE 1985

Schlosshotel Igls

Viller Steig 2
A-6080 Igls
(Tirol) • Austria

Tel. : (43) (0512) 377217
Fax : (43) (0512) 377217-198
schlossigls@relaischateaux.com

This gem of Tyrolean hospitality, in the heart of a splendid park, is situated 5 km above Innsbruck, in an idyllic location far from the hustle and bustle of everyday life. The hotel has luxurious guestrooms and suites, a sauna and bathing areas. An excellent restaurant and pleasant bar with fireplace. Relaxation, rest and sport are on the menu, including golf and skiing with extensive facilities for enthusiasts.

Mountain sports... (Other activities P. 629)

Access: Inntal motorway - Innsbruck-Ost exit. Continue to Olympic Stadium. Turn left. Follow signs to Igls.

Airports: Innsbruck Kranebitten (Intl) 8 km, Munich Franz Josef Strauss (Intl) 160 km
Train station: Innsbruck 4,5 km

Owners: Beck Family
Annual closing: From October 26th to December 19th
Currency: Euro (€)
Rates: Menus 22-51 € s.i.
Carte 23-40 € s.i.
14 rooms: 265-400 € s.i.
6 suites: 317-700 € s.i.
Breakfast: included
Dogs: allowed (extra cost)
Golf: 2 and 7 km
Accepted cards: AE, DC, JCB, MC, VS

342   More info on www.relaischateaux.com/schlossigls

Hotel der Bär

SINCE 1979

Kirchbichl, 9
A-6352 Ellmau
(Tirol) • Austria

Tel. : (43) (05358) 2395
Fax : (43) (05358) 239556
derbar@relaischateaux.com

Austria

Surrounded by 15000 m² of gardens, this hotel looks like a village. Relax in a comfortable suite, then enjoy a sauna, swim, massage and thalassotherapy. You will appreciate the cosy atmosphere and the restaurant's impeccable service, while savouring delicious cuisine. Enjoy walks in the natural surroundings of the Wilder Kaiser region. Activities include golf, hiking, ski and «Bären» miniclub during holidays.

Golf academy, climbing courses and tours, canyoning, paragliding, snowboard, cross-country skiing. (Other activities P. 629)

Altitude: 830 m.
Access: From Innsbruck: A 12, Wörgl-Ost exit, B 178 to Ellmau. From Munich: A 8/E 45, Kufstein-Sud exit, B 173 and then B 178 to Ellmau.
Airports: Innsbruck Kranebitten (Intl) 80 km, Salzburg (Intl) 80 km, Munich Franz Josef Strauss (Intl) 130 km
Train station: Kufstein 23 km

Owners: Windisch Family
Annual closing: From March 23rd to end of May and from the end of October to mid-December
Currency: Euro (€)
Rates: Menus 31-55 € s.i.
31 rooms: 170-400 € s.i.
26 suites: 230-590 € s.i.
Breakfast: included
Dogs: allowed (extra cost) except restaurant
Golf: Ellmau (9 and 18 holes)
Accepted cards: AE, MC, VS

More info on www.relaischateaux.com/derbar

Austria

Hotel Hubertus

SINCE 2002

Am Dorfplatz 1
A-5532 Filzmoos
Austria

Tel. : (43) (06453) 8204
Fax : (43) (06453) 82046
hubertus@relaischateaux.com

The Hotel Hubertus is situated in the idyllic mountain region at the foot of the Dachstein and yet only half an hour drive from Salzburg. A festival for all the senses is staged by Johanna Meier. Her unparalleled cuisine offers gourmets paradise on earth. Many leisure activities close to the tastefully decorated hotel.

**Cooking classes with Johanna, Salzburg Festival, Fly Fishing.
(Other activities P. 629)**

Altitude : 1070 metres.
Access: From Salzburg, A10 exit Eben towards Filzmoos; at the roundabout turn left.

Airport: Salzburg (Intl) 70 km
Helipad: N 47° 25' 940'' O 13° 31' 220''
Train station: Eben 10 km

Owners: Johanna and Dietmar Maier
Weekly closing: Restaurant: Monday, Tuesday
Annual closing: November
Currency: Euro (€)
Rates: Menus 60-120 € s.i. Carte 36-80 € s.i.
12 rooms: 160-240 € s.i.
2 suites: 240-320 € s.i.
Breakfast: included
Dogs: allowed except restaurant (extra cost)
Golf: 15 km
Accepted cards: AE, MC

Johanna Maier

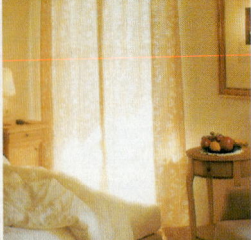

More info on www.relaischateaux.com/hubertus

Hotel Schloss Dürnstein

SINCE 1979

A-3601 Dürnstein
(Niederösterreich) • Austria

Tel. : (43) (02711) 212
Fax : (43) (02711) 212-30
durnstein@relaischateaux.com

Austria

Dürnstein castle, now an elegant 5-star hotel, was built in 1630. The guestrooms, suites and reception rooms are decorated with beautiful traditional furniture. Lunches and dinners are served on the famous terrace overlooking the Danube. The hotel offers one of the finest indoor swimming pools in Austria. Enjoy the sauna, steam bath and fitness room on rainy days.

Winery visits, river boating to Melk monastery. Biking, jogging, rowing, spa with steam bath. (Other activities P. 629)

Access:
From Salzburg, A1 exit Melk, cross the Danube, N3 towards Krems.

Airport: Vienna (Intl) 100 km
Train station: Dürnstein 0,6 km

Owners: Johann and Rosemarie Thiery
General Manager: Rosemarie Thiery
Annual closing: From November 5th to April 5th
Currency: Euro (€)
Rates: Menus 30-45 € s.i.
Carte 30-50 € s.i.
36 rooms: 90-340 € s.i. per person
4 suites: 290-360 € s.i. per person
Breakfast: included
Dogs: allowed (extra cost)
Golf: 15 km
Accepted cards: AE, DC, JCB, MC, VS

More info on www.relaischateaux.com/durnstein

Austria

Restaurant Steirereck

SINCE 1986

Rasumofskygasse 2
Ecke Weissgerberlände
A-1030 Wien • Austria

Tel. : (43) (01) 713 31 68
Fax : (43) (01) 713 51 68 2
steirereck@relaischateaux.com

For some years now the Steirereck has been the trailblazer in Austrian cuisine. A flower-filled setting with attentive service makes everyone feel immediately at home. Helmut Österreicher's tasty, light cuisine cannot fail to please with its emphasis on culinary specialties from Austria. Extraordinary wines in a vaulted cellar which can be visited by the guests.

Opera, festivals... (Other activities P. 629)

Access: A23 Vienna centre, Pratercity, Schüttel Strasse, Donaukanal, Rotunden Brücke bridge.

Airport: Vienna (Intl) 11 km
Train station: Wien Mitte 2 km

Owners: Reitbauer Family
Weekly closing: Saturday, Sunday and bank holidays
Open all year
Currency: Euro (€)
Rates: Menus 33-69 € s.i. Carte 35-49 € s.i.
Dogs: allowed
Golf: 3 km
Accepted cards: AE, DC, MC, VS

Helmut Österreicher

More info on www.relaischateaux.com/steirereck

Taubenkobel

SINCE 2003

Hauptstrasse 27-33
A-7081 Schützen/Gebirge
Austria

Tel. : (43) (02684) 22 97
Fax : (43) (02684) 2297-18
tauben@relaischateaux.com

Austria

In the heart of a village in Burgenland, close to Eisenstadt, the white façade of a beautiful, harmonious residence built in 1864. Walter and Eveline Eselböck chose minimalist aesthetics, a pureness of lines and flavours culminating in creativity and elegance. The sophistication is completely natural. The décor is as light as the pastries prepared by Walter Eselböck who cooks the freshly caught fish from the lake.
(Other activities P. 629)

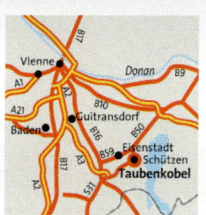

Access: From Vienna, motorway A2 to Guitransdorf. Motorway A3 to end of motorway. Follow B16 and B59 for 6 km. Near Eisenstadt follow B50 for 6.5 km. First village on the right.
Airport: Schwechat (Intl) 35 km
Train station: Schützen 1 km

Owner: Walter Eselböck
General Manager: Eveline Eselböck
Weekly closing: Monday, Tuesday
Annual closing: January
Currency: Euro (€)
Rates: Menus 58-88 € s.i. Carte 47-58 € s.i.
2 rooms: 140-180 € s.i.
5 suites: 195-210 € s.i.
Breakfast: included
Dogs: allowed (extra cost)
Golf: 5 km
Accepted cards: AE, DC, JCB, MC, VS

More info on www.relaischateaux.com/tauben

Austria

Hotel Grüner Baum

SINCE 1983

Kötschachtal 25
A-5640 Bad Gastein
(Salzburg) • Austria

Tel. : (43) (06434) 25160
Fax : (43) (06434) 251625
grunerbaum@relaischateaux.com

On the fringes of the national park, the hotel village with its 5 buildings in the Salzburg style is the ideal setting to relax and experience nature. Comfortable rooms with flower-filled balconies and a view of the mountains, restaurants, bars, spa and beauty centre, open-air pool with lawn, tennis, pétanque, hiking trails, alpine and cross-country skiing, miniclub and, above all, Austrian hospitality!
Miniclub, children's activities. (Other activities P. 629)

Altitude: 1080 metres.
Access: From Salzburg Bischofshofen via A 10, then B 311 towards Gasteinertal, and B 167 to Bad Gastein. From Innsbrück: via Wörgl B 312-311 to Lend, then B 167.
Airports: Salzburg (Intl) 95 km, Munich Franz Josef Strauss (Intl) 280 km
Helipad: 13° 09,80 47° 07,70
Train station: Bad Gastein 3 km

Owners: Hannes and Monica Blumschein
Annual closing: November
Currency: Euro (€)
Rates: Menus 19-54 € s.i. Carte 21-54 € s.i.
37 rooms: 190-258 € s.i.
21 suites: 230-290 € s.i.
Breakfast: buffet included
Dogs: allowed (extra cost)
Golf: 3 km
Accepted cards: AE, DC, MC, VS

More info on www.relaischateaux.com/grunerbaum

Hotel Schloss Seefels

Töschling 1
A-9210 Pörtschach
(Kärnten) • Austria

Tel. : (43) (04272) 2377
Fax : (43) (04272) 3704
seefels@relaischateaux.com

SINCE 1979

Austria

The Seefels, a miniature paradise reflected in the clear blue waters of Lake Wörther, is sure to enchant you with its charm, its refined luxury and its beautiful new decor. Air-conditioned suites, fine dining in the restaurants «Orangerie», «La Terrasse» and «Porto Bello», spa, beauty farm, play area for the children, private beach with marina as well as state-of-the-art seminar rooms which meet the highest demands.

Miniclub, water sports, private beach, marina, events. (Other activities P. 629)

Access: From Klagenfurt airport, A 2 towards Villach, exit Pörtschach-West.

Airport: Klagenfurt (Intl) 23 km
Train station: Pörtschach 2,5 km

Owners: Hotel Schloss Seefels Besitz-und Management GmbH
General Manager: Egon Haupt
Annual closing: From Nov. to December 23rd
Currency: Euro (€)
Rates: Menus 40-80 € s.i.
Carte 23-52 € s.i.
37 rooms: 240-450 € s.i.
20 suites: 360-1200 € s.i.
Breakfast: included
Dogs: allowed (extra cost) except restaurants
Golf: 5 km
Accepted cards: AE, DC, JCB, MC, VS

More info on www.relaischateaux.com/seefels

Slovenia

Properties	Nearest major city	Relais & Châteaux	Relais Gourmands	Page
Kendov Dvorec	Postojna Caves	⚜		351
Vila Bled (Hotel)	Ljubljana	⚜		353

Kendov Dvorec

SINCE 2001

Na Griču 2;
SI-5281 Spodnja Idrija
Slovenia

Tel. : (386) (05) 372 5100
Fax : (386) (05) 375 6475
kendov@relaischateaux.com

Slovenia

This XIVth century house is a cultural monument in the 800-year-old village of Spodnja Idrija. Between the alpine massif and the plateaus of the Karst, with its caves and swallow holes, this is a healthy and peaceful holiday retreat in the heart of romantic, unspoilt valleys where time has stood still. It has inherited the local traditions of sculpted wood and lacework. You will enjoy the warm welcome of this haven of peace and savour the local cuisine enhanced by Slovene wines.

(Other activities P. 629)

Access:
From Ljubljana airport: E63 towards south, E70 after Ljubljana, exit Logatec, route 10-10, north-west towards Spodnja Idrija. From Trieste: E70, direction north-east, exit Logatec.
Airport: Ljubljana (Intl) 90 km
Train station: Logatec 40 km

Owner: Ivi Svetlik
Open all year
Currency: Euro (€)
Rates: Menus 30-50 € s.i.
Carte 25-45 € s.i.
11 rooms: 75-155 € s.i.
Breakfast: included
Dogs: allowed
Golf: 80 km
Accepted cards: AE, DC, MC, VS

More info on www.relaischateaux.com/kendov

DISCOVER THE UNIVERSE OF RELAIS & CHÂTEAUX

www.relaischateaux.com

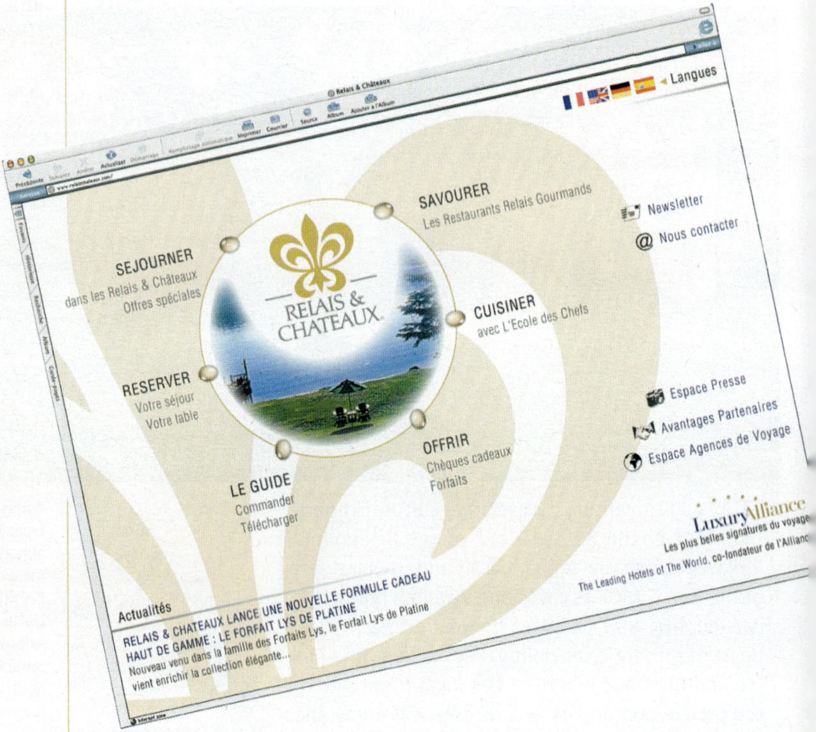

- Order or download the guide
- Visit, select... reserve on-line
- Offer a gift certificate or package Relais & Châteaux
- Learn to cook like a master chef
- Discover Relais Gourmands*

*in partnership with «Saveurs du Monde» at **www.theworldwildegourmet.com/**

Hotel Vila Bled

Cesta Svobode 26
SI-4260 Bled
Slovenia

Tel. : (386) (04) 5791 500
Fax : (386) (04) 5741 320
vilabled@relaischateaux.com

SINCE 1987

Slovenia

Set amidst 12 acres of luxuriant foliage and dazzling flowers on the picturesque shore of Lake Bled, this elegant Marshal Tito's residence is bathed in soft Alpine sunshine throughout the year. The comfortable rooms offer superb vistas of the lake. The pure air of the surrounding forests will do wonders to your health. Enjoy your days rowing on the lake and swimming from the private lido and the light, refined cuisine on the waterside terrace.

Private beach, cross-country skiing, special golf rates... (Other activities P. 629)

Access:
Austrian border
Karawanken-
tunnel
E 61/A1.

Airport: Ljubljana (Intl) 35 km
Train station: Lesce-Bled 5 km

Owner: G.H.T. Bled
General Manager: Janez Fajfar
Open all year
Currency: Euro (€)
Rates: Menus 23-31 € s.i.
Carte 36-46 € s.i.
10 rooms: 140-160 € s.i.
20 suites: 160-360 € s.i.
Breakfast: included
Dogs: allowed (approval needed)
Golf: 5 km
Accepted cards: AE, DC, MC, VS

More info on www.relaischateaux.com/vilabled

# Scandinavia

Properties Denmark	Nearest major city	Relais & Châteaux	Relais Gourmands	Page
Falsled Kro	Odense	⚜	◉	357
Sønderho Kro	Esbjerg	⚜		356

Sweden				
Kattegat Gastronomi	Båstad	⚜	◉	358
Krägga Herrgård	Stockholm	⚜		359
Leijontornet & Victory Hotel	Stockholm	⚜	◉	361
Thoresta Herrgård	Stockholm	⚜		360

Norway				
Bagatelle (Restaurant)	Oslo		◉	362
Eng Gård	Tonsberg	⚜		363

Iceland				
Holt (Hotel)	Reykjavík	⚜		364

Lithuania				
Stikliai Hotel	Trakai	⚜		365

Equivalent in euros for information only (rate of 2/07/01 and 1/06/02). Application of the exchange rate valid on the day of transaction.

Denmark

Sønderho Kro

SINCE 1979

Kropladsen 11
DK-6720 Fanø
Denmark

Tel. : (45) (75) 164009
Fax : (45) (75) 164385
sonderho@relaischateaux.com

On the southern tip of the North Sea Isle of Fanø, Birgit and Niels Sørensen have built their hotel in the gardens of the oldest inn in Denmark (1722). The 13 guestrooms, which are named after boats, bear witness to the extremely close ties existing between this listed building and the sea. Before or after going horseback riding along the beaches, savour tasty dishes in the inn's cosy age-old restaurant.

Museums, swimming (in summer). Discovery of nature: dunes and moors, pebble beaches. (Other activities P. 629).

Access: In Esbjerg, ferry (12 mn) to Fanø; take the Sønderho road (13 km).

Airports: Hamburg Fuhlsbüttel (Intl) 270 km, Esbjerg 17 km
Train station: Esbjerg 15 km

Owners: Birgit and Niels Steen Sørensen
Annual closing: Christmas and one week in January and February
Currency: Danish krone (DKK)
Rates: Menus 360-470 DKK s.i. - 48-63 €
Carte 396-450 DKK s.i. - 53-60 €
13 rooms: 940-1290 DKK s.i. - 126-173 €
Breakfast: 110 DKK s.i. - 15 €
Dogs: allowed (50 DKK - 7 € per night)
Golf: 12 km
Accepted cards: AE, DC, MC, VS

More info on www.relaischateaux.com/sonderho

Falsled Kro

SINCE 1973

Assensvej 513
Falsled DK-5642 Millinge
(Fyn) • Denmark

Tel. : (45) 6268 1111
Fax : (45) 6268 1162
falsled@relaischateaux.com

Denmark

Lulled by the Fionie mermaids' song, your stay at Falsled Kro will be a magical experience. This idyllic haven set in the midst of beautiful countryside is the ideal place to enjoy Jean-Louis Lieffroy's culinary marvels, prepared with forest game, delicacies from the sea and fruit and vegetables from the garden. Savour «aiglefin fumé au caviar d'aubergine», «pigeon en pot-au-feu à la scandinave» and exquisite «crêpes caramélisées».

(Other activities P. 629)

Access: From Odense, route 43 towards Faaborg, then routes 8 and 329 towards Falsled.
Airports: Billund (Intl) 130 km, Copenhagen (Intl) 200 km
Helipad: N 55° 09' 12" E 10° 08' 55"
Train station: Odense 35 km

Owners: Grønlykke Family and Jean-Louis Lieffroy
Weekly closing: Restaurant: Monday (except dinner from May to October)
Open all year
Currency: Danish krone (DKK)
Rates: Menus 480-800 DKK s.i. - 64-107 €
Carte 650 DKK s.i. - 87 €
11 rooms: 1100-2100 DKK s.i. - 148-282 €
8 suites: 2400-2700 DKK s.i. - 322-363 €
Breakfast: 150 DKK s.i. - 20 €
Dogs: allowed **Golf:** Faaborg 7 km
Accepted cards: AE, DC, JCB, MC, VS

More info on www.relaischateaux.com/falsled

Sweden — SINCE 1999

Kattegat Gastronomi

Storgatan 46
S-26093 Torekov
Sweden

Tel. : (46) (0431) 36 30 02
Fax : (46) (0431) 36 30 03
kattegat@relaischateaux.com

At Kattegat, you will bathe in the sumptuous natural decor of a picturesque old port and fascinating mountains where you can enjoy extraordinary views. Around Torekov, enthusiasts will be delighted to discover no less than fifteen golf courses. Have a drink at the bar while watching the chef hard at work in the kitchen. Enjoy your meals in the beautiful setting of the hundred-year-old restaurant – voted one of the best in Sweden in 1999.

(Other activities P. 629)

Access: From South E6 towards Margaretetorp, then Torekov (24 km).
From North E6, towards Ostra Karup, then Torekov (17 km) or route 115.
Airports: Sturup (Intl) 130 km, Angelholm 20 km
Train station: Båstad 20 km

Owners: Rikard and Robert Nilsson
Annual closing: From August 31st to May 15th
Currency: Swedish krone (SEK)
Rates: Menus 565-920 SEK s.i. - 61-100 €
Carte 480-920 SEK s.i. - 52-100 €
11 rooms: 1195-1695 SEK s.c. - 129-184 €
Breakfast: Included
Dogs: not allowed
Golf: 1 km (18 holes)
Accepted cards: AE, DC, MC, VS

Rikard Nilsson

More info on www.relaischateaux.com/kattegat

Krägga Herrgård

S-74693 Bålsta
(Uppsala län) • Sweden

Tel. : (46) (0171) 532 80
Fax : (46) (0171) 532 65
kragga@relaischateaux.com

SINCE 1996

Sweden

This charming XIXth century manor is an idyllic setting in which to enjoy country rambles along the shore of Lake Mälaren, a picnic lunch in the rose gardens or a game of tennis on the manicured lawn. The rooms are exquisitely comfortable, and the old library a haven of calm. Here, the seasons not only determine the pace of life, they also inspire the cuisine. Visit Skokloster Castle, Linné's House and Ekolsundsviken Bay.
Boat rides. (Other activities P. 629)

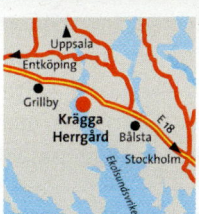

Access: From Stockholm, E18 towards Enköping, 2nd exit Bålsta, straight to Krägga, follow signs.

Airport: Stockholm (Intl) 51 km
Helipad: N 59° 36' 30" E 17° 22' 00"
Train station: Bålsta 8 km

Owner: Leif Bonér
General Manager: L. Bonér
Weekly closing: Restaurant: Sunday
Annual closing: From Dec. 26th to January 2nd
Currency: Swedish krone (SEK)
Rates: Menus 475-695 SEK s.i. - 51-75 €
Carte 280-580 SEK s.i. - 30-63 €
39 rooms: 1200-2000 SEK s.i. - 130-217 €
4 suites: starting at 2900 SEK s.i. - 314 €
Breakfast: included
Dogs: allowed
Golf: 15 km
Accepted cards: AE, DC, JCB, MC, VS

More info on www.relaischateaux.com/kragga

Sweden

Thoresta Herrgård

S-19793 Bro
(Uppland) • Sweden

SINCE 2001

Tel. : **(46) (08) 582 426 00**
Fax : (46) (08) 582 426 07
thoresta@relaischateaux.com

40 kilometres from Stockholm, amidst the charm of the Swedish countryside. Thoresta Herrgård's woodland setting, near a lake, makes this XVIIIth century manor house with its classic lines and intense colours a haven of peace. It has a simple elegance, like the fresh flowers gracing the interior. The countryside is an invitation to fish and hunt. The extensive Skokloster castle collections are also worth a visit.

(Other activities P. 629)

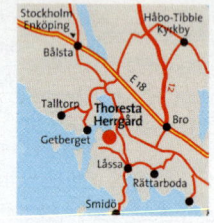

Access: From Stockholm E18 towards Enköping, exit Bro, towards Bålsta, turn left Bt sign after Golf course.

Airport: Stockholm Arlanda (Intl) 40 km
Helipad: N 59° 31' 40'' E 17° 34' 30''
Train station: Bålsta 7 km

Owner: Leif Bonér
General Manager: Pär Bonér
Weekly closing: Hotel: Sunday Restaurant: Sunday evening
Annual closing: From July 1st to 30th and from December 20th to January 2nd
Currency: Swedish krone (SEK)
Rates: Menus 150-350 SEK s.i. - 16-38 €
Carte 515-695 SEK s.i. - 56-75 €
35 rooms: 1200-2200 SEK s.i. - 130-238 €
1 suite: 2900 SEK s.i. - 314 €
Breakfast: included
Dogs: allowed **Golf:** on the premises
Accepted cards: AE, DC, JCB, MC, VS

More info on www.relaischateaux.com/thoresta

Leijontornet & Victory Hotel

SINCE 1990

Lilla Nygatan 5, Gamla Stan
S-11128 Stockholm
Sweden

Tel. : (46) (08) 506 400 00
Fax : (46) (08) 506 400 10
leijontornet@relaischateaux.com

Sweden

This magnificent XVIIth century residence in the heart of Stockholm's Old City offers sumptuous guestrooms and warm hospitality. In the restaurant you will find the remains of Stockholm's medieval fortification wall and on the crude limestone tables, Per Nilsson's kitchen serve the specialities of shellfish, game and fowl from Scandinavia's best suppliers. The wine cellar is one of the finest in Scandinavia.
(Other activities P. 629)

Access: In Stockholm, follow signs to the centre of the city and Gamla Stan.
Airports: Stockholm-Arlanda (Intl) 42 km, Stockholm-Bromma 16 km
Train station : Stockholm Central 1 km

Owners: Bengtsson Family, Peter Östlund and Per Nilsson
General Manager: Rickard Bengtsson
Weekly closing: Rest.: Sunday and bank holidays
Annual closing: Restaurant: July
Currency: Swedish krone (SEK)
Rates: Menus 750 SEK s.i. - 81 €
Carte 435-635 SEK s.i. - 47-69 €
41 rooms: 1850-3590 SEK s.i. - 200-389 €
4 suites: 2800-5600 SEK s.i. - 303-607 €
Breakfast: included
Dogs: not allowed **Golf:** 20 km
Accepted cards: AE, DC, MC, VS

More info on www.relaischateaux.com/leijontornet

Norway

SINCE 2000

Restaurant Bagatelle

Bygdoy Alle 3
N-0257 Oslo
Norway

Tel. : (47) 221 21 440
Fax : (47) 224 36 420
bagatelle@relaischateaux.com

Eyvind Hellstrøm's «Bagatelle» offers the best of contemporary Norwegian cuisine in a modern decor with superb bouquets by Hege Hellstrøm. Savour the products of Norway's forests —grouse and roedeer, and sea— turbot, scallops and Norway lobster. You will marvel at Eyvind's seven course fish and game menu prepared with flair. The wine cellar is one of the best in Scandinavia, with fine French and Italian vintages.

Access: From the south: E6 or E18, exit Oslo V in the Oslo tunnel. From the north: E18, exit Oslo V before the tunnel. The restaurant is next to the National Library opposite the Hydro Park.
Airport: Oslo (Intl) 50 km
Train station: National Teater 0,5 km

Owners: Christen Sveaas, Eyvind Hellstrøm
General Manager: Eyvind Hellstrøm
Weekly closing: Sunday
Annual closing: Easter, three weeks late July/early August and Christmas
Currency: Norvegian krone (NOK)
Rates: Menus 650-1250 NOK s.i. - 82-158 €
Carte 500-850 NOK s.i. - 63-107 €
Dogs: not allowed
Accepted cards: AE, DC, JCB, MC, VS

Eyvind Hellstrøm

More info on www.relaischateaux.com/bagatelle

Engø Gård

SINCE 2003

GML. Engovei 25, BP 104
N-3145 Tjøme
Norway

Tel. : (47) 333 90 048
Fax : (47) 333 90 045
engogard@relaischateaux.com

Norway

Built in 1845, in the heart of a park on the Oslo Fjord coastline, Engø Gård has been an idyllic country inn since the twenties. With the old barn converted and an indoors swimming pool it reopened in June 2000, transformed into a superb country house hotel. The old inn building offers its guests a covered gallery and the intimacy of a cottage. A harmonious setting and an interior decorated with warm, vibrant colours. Tranquil charm.

(Other activities P. 629)

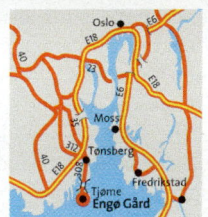

Access: From Oslo, motorway E18. Exit Tønsberg, towards Tjøme, route 308. 3,5 km after Vrengen Bro bridge, Grimestad on your left. Follow Engø on the left next to Rimi shop.
Airport: Oslo (Intl) 160 km **Helipad:** N 59° 07' W 10° 25' **Train station:** Tønsberg 20 km

Owners: Harald Andersen and Nina Felling
G. Managers: Per Hallundbaek and Randi Schmidt
Weekly closing: Sunday and Monday (from Jan. 24th to June 15th and from August 17th to Dec. 22nd)
Annual closing: From December 22nd to January 24th, Easter
Currency: Norwegian krone (NOK)
Rates: Menus 500-800 NOK s.i. - 63-101 €
Carte 125-325 NOK s.i. - 16-41 €
7 rooms: 1300-2550 NOK s.i. - 164-321 €
5 suites: 1830-2550 NOK s.i. - 231-321 €
Breakfast: included
Dogs: not allowed **Golf:** 3 km
Accepted cards: AE, DC, MC, VS

More info on www.relaischateaux.com/engogard

Iceland

Hotel Holt

SINCE 1991

Bergstadastræti 37
IS-101 Reykjavík
Iceland

Tel. : **(354) 552 5700**
Fax : (354) 562 3025
holt@relaischateaux.com

This splendid hotel in the heart of Reykjavík not only offers the ultimate in modern comfort, it also presents 300 works by Icelandic artists. The stylish «Gallery» is Iceland's most renowned restaurant. The Gallery's superb cuisine offers a variety of delicacies from Iceland's pristine fishing grounds as well as an impressive selection of fine wines. After visiting the sights, linger over an aperitif and gaze out across the sea glittering under a summer sun that never sets.

Walks... (Other activities P. 629)

Access: In the heart of Reykjavík, a few minutes from the Parliament and Government House.

Airports: Reykjavík (Intl) 5 km, Keflavik 50 km

Owner: Skuli Thorvaldsson
General Manager: E. Ingi Fridgeirsson
Annual closing: From December 24th to 26th
Currency: Icelandic crown (ISK)
Rates: Menus 2400-5600 ISK s.i.
Carte 1400-7400 ISK s.i.
30 rooms: 17400-23200 ISK s.i.
12 suites: 25600-33100 ISK s.i.
Breakfast: 1625 ISK s.i.
Dogs: allowed
Golf: 10 km
Accepted cards: AE, DC, MC, VS

More info on www.relaischateaux.com/holt

Stikliai Hotel

SINCE 2000

Gaono Str. 7
2024 Vilnius
Lithuania

Tel. : (370) (5) 262 79 71
Fax : (370) (5) 212 38 70
stikliai@relaischateaux.com

Lithuania

In the centre of the historic city of Vilnius, listed as belonging to the Unesco World Heritage, this beautiful XVIIth century residence lovingly restored is named after the glass blowers who worked in the narrow streets where it is located. The decoration highlights the warm colours of Lithuania. The elegant comfort of the rooms, the winter garden and the remarkable hospitality of the hosts will leave you captivated.

Access: Straight from the airport to the town centre to Basanauicius street. Go to the end of this street to the hotel via Traku street and Domininkonu street.
Airport: Vilnius (Intl) 10 km
Train station: Vilnius 5 km

Owners: Aleksandras and Anna Ciupij, Romualdas Zakarevicius
General Manager: Alfreda Mikulskiene
Open all year
Currency: Litas (LTL)
Rates: Carte 120-280 LTL s.i. - 35-81 €
18 rooms: 660-840 LTL s.i. - 191-243 €
11 suites: 840-1400 LTL s.i. - 243-406 €
Breakfast: 40 LTL s.i. - 12 €
Dogs: not allowed
Accepted cards: AE, JCB, MC, VS

More info on www.relaischateaux.com/stikliai

United Kingdom

Properties	Nearest major city	Relais & Châteaux	Relais Gourmands	Page
Bodysgallen Hall	Chester	⚜		385
Buckland Manor Hotel	Cheltenham	⚜		381
Chewton Glen Hotel	Bournemouth	⚜		375
Farlam Hall Hotel	Carlisle	⚜		388
Gavroche (Le)	London		◉	368
Gidleigh Park	Exeter	⚜	◉	378
Glenapp Castle	Ayr	⚜		389
Gravetye Manor	East Grinstead	⚜		374
Hambleton Hall	Leicester	⚜		383
Hartwell House	Oxford	⚜		372
Inverlochy Castle	Fort William	⚜		390
Kinnaird	Perth	⚜		391
Longueville Manor	St-Hélier	⚜		379
Lucknam Park	Bath	⚜		380
Mallory Court	Leamington Spa	⚜		382
Manoir aux Quat' Saisons (Le)	Oxford	⚜	◉	371
Middlethorpe Hall	York	⚜		386
Sharrow Bay Country House	Penrith	⚜		387
Stock Hill Country House	Salisbury	⚜		376
Summer Lodge	Dorchester	⚜		377
Tante Claire (La)	London		◉	369
Vineyard at Stockcross (The)	Newbury	⚜		373
Waterside Inn (The)	Windsor	⚜	◉	370
Ynyshir Hall	Aberystwyth	⚜		384

More info on www.relaischateaux.com

Le Gavroche

SINCE 1999

United Kingdom

43 Upper Brook Street
London W1K 7QR
United Kingdom

Tel. : (44) (020) 7 408 0881
Fax : (44) (020) 7 491 4387
gavroche@relaischateaux.com

Situated in the heart of London, the Gavroche is the ambassador of classical and modern French cuisine. Following the tradition of his father, Michel Roux Jr. proposes a seasonal menu which has the «Gavroche touch». All wine lovers will be amazed by the selection of prize-winning vintages offered on the wine list. Thanks to the comfort of the surroundings and to the impeccable service of the dedicated staff, guests can entirely relax and savour their meal.

Jacket required.

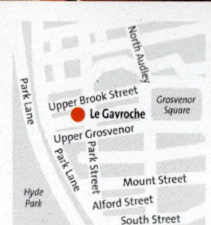

Access: In the centre of London, near Hyde Park and Marble Arch.

Airports: London City Airport (Intl) 23 km, London Heathrow (Intl) 25 km
Train station: Paddington 1 km

Owner: Michel Roux Jr.
General Manager: Silvano Giraldin
Weekly closing: Sunday
Annual closing: From December 21st to January 5th
Currency: Pound sterling (GBP)
Rates: Menus 42-85 GBP t.17.5% s.12.5%
Carte 60-100 GBP t.17.5% s.12.5%
Dogs: not allowed
Accepted cards: AE, DC, JCB, MC, VS

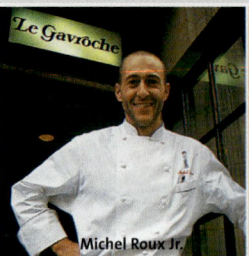

Michel Roux Jr.

More info on www.relaischateaux.com/gavroche

La Tante Claire

SINCE 1987

Wilton Place, Knightsbridge
London SW1X 7RL
United Kingdom

Tel. : (44) (020) 7823 20 03
Fax : (44) (020) 7823 20 01
tanteclaire@relaischateaux.com

United Kingdom

La Tante Claire's in Knightsbridge, where Pierre Koffmann remains at the helm, still shows a strong influence from Gascony, with some interesting departure from the south west of France traditions. Gourmets will appreciate his «tranche de foie gras au chocolat amer», «pied de cochon farci aux morilles», «turbot en croûte de sel aux pousses de légumes» and «croustade aux pommes caramélisées».

Jacket required.

Access: In Knightsbridge, on Wilton Place, to the right of the main entrance of the «Berkeley».

Airport: London Heathrow (Intl) 23 km
Train station: Victoria 1 km

Owner/Chef: Pierre Koffmann
Weekly closing: Saturday noon and Sunday
Annual closing: From December 24th to January 1st and bank holidays
Currency: Pound sterling (GBP)
Rates: Menu 28 GBP s.n.i.
Carte 75 GBP s.n.i.
Dogs: not allowed
Accepted cards:
Access, AE, DC, JCB, MC, VS

Pierre Koffman

More info on www.relaischateaux.com/tanteclaire

The Waterside Inn

SINCE 1976

Ferry Road, Bray
Berkshire SL6 2AT
United Kingdom

Tel. : (44) (01628) 620691
Fax : (44) (01628) 784710
waterside@relaischateaux.com

United Kingdom

Wide bay windows frame a picturesque view of the Thames. Michel and Alain Roux uphold a French tradition which has made their inn one of the temples of the very best in grande cuisine: «tronçonnettes de homard poêlées minute au porto blanc», «filets de lapereau grillés aux marrons glacés» and a divine «péché gourmand selon Michel». Excellent wine list and delightful rooms for heavenly relaxation.

(Other activities P. 629)

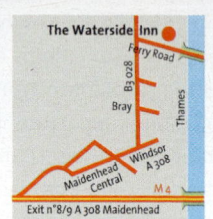

Access: M4, exit 8/9, Maidenhead Central; towards Windsor (A 308); B 3 028 Bray.

Airport: London Heathrow (Intl) 25 km
Train station: Maidenhead 3 km

Owners: Michel Roux and Alain Roux
General Manager: Diego Masciaga
Weekly closing: Monday, Tuesday (from Sept. 1st to May 31st), Monday all day, Tuesday lunch (from June 1st to August 31st)
Annual closing: From December 26th to January 30th included
Currency: Pound sterling (GBP)
Rates: Menus 36-53-76 GBP s.n.i.
Carte 100 GBP s.n.i.
8 rooms: 160-185 GBP s.i.
1 suite: 290 GBP s.i.
Breakfast: included
Dogs: not allowed **Golf:** 3 km
Accepted cards: AE, DC, JCB, MC, VS

Michel Roux

More info on www.relaischateaux.com/waterside

Le Manoir aux Quat' Saisons

SINCE 1987

Church Road, Great Milton
Oxford, OX44 7PD
United Kingdom

Tel. : (44) (01844) 278881
Fax : (44) (01844) 278847
4saisons@relaischateaux.com

United Kingdom

Raymond Blanc's contemporary classic is set in elegant gardens in the Oxfordshire countryside and provides an idyllic setting in which to savour his magical cuisine: «trois bouchées printanières». Dishes to delight the palate are created from the freshest of foods, using as many organic products as possible and vegetables from the Manoir's garden when in season. The thirty-two rooms are each a unique example of the best in design and comfort. Home to Raymond Blanc's famous Ecole de Cuisine.

Cookery School. Fishing, clay pigeon shooting, hunting...
(Other activities P. 629)

Raymond Blanc

Access: From London, M 40 towards Oxford, exit 7 Wallingford, A 329 towards Great Milton.

Airport: London Heathrow (Intl) 60 km
Helipad: N 51° 42' 92" W 001° 05' 48"
Train station: Oxford 12 km

Owners: O-E Hotels Ltd - Raymond Blanc
General Manager: Philip Newman-Hall
Open all year
Currency: Pound sterling (GBP)
Rates: Menus 45-95 GBP s.n.i.
Carte 80-110 GBP s.n.i.
19 rooms: 260-405 GBP s.n.i.
13 suites: 435-825 GBP s.n.i.
Breakfast: 7-25 GBP s.n.i.
Dogs: not allowed
Golf: 10 km
Accepted cards: AE, DC, MC, VS

More info on www.relaischateaux.com/4saisons

United Kingdom

Hartwell House

SINCE 1993

Oxford Road (near Aylesbury)
Buckinghamshire HP17 8NL
United Kingdom

Tel. : (44) (01296) 747444
Fax : (44) (01296) 747450
hartwell@relaischateaux.com

This beautifully restored XVIIIth century stately home is set in a large park in the countryside only one hour from London. The magnificent rooms, once lived in by exiled Louis XVIII and his court, are now superbly furnished with antiques and hung with fine paintings. Enjoy tennis, or relax in the spacious indoor pool or sauna. Dine on delicious food in the elegant setting of the Soane dining room overlooking the garden.

Croquet, hot-air ballooning, walking, Oxford, Waddesdom Manor. Blenheim Palace, Stowe landscape gardens. (Other activities P. 629)

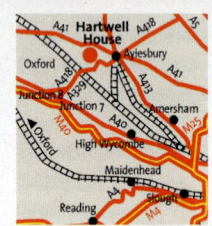

Access: From London, M40 to junction 7, then A329/A418 towards Thame/Aylesbury.

Airports: London Heathrow (Intl) 56 km, London Gatwick (Intl) 99 km
Helipad: N 51° 48' 43" W 000° 50' 88"
Train station: Aylesbury 5 km

Owner: Richard Broyd
Director: Jonathan Thompson
Open all year
Currency: Pound sterling (GBP)
Rates: Menus 22-29 GBP s.i. Carte 46 GBP s.i.
34 rooms: 235-395 GBP s.i.
13 suites: 335-700 GBP s.i.
Breakfast: 13-17 GBP s.i.
Dogs: allowed (only in Hartwell Court)
Golf: 2 km
Accepted cards: AE, MC, VS

More info on www.relaischateaux.com/hartwell

The Vineyard at Stockcross

SINCE 2003

Newbury
Berkshire RG20 8JU
United Kingdom

Tel. : (44) (01635) 528 770
Fax : (44) (01635) 528 398
vineyard@relaischateaux.com

United Kingdom

Owner of a renowned vineyard in northern California, Sir Peter Michael created «The Vineyard at Stockcross» in order to fulfil a dream in Berkshire, just one hour from London, in an exceptional setting where the arts of fine dining and excellent wines are carried to new heights. Everything is spacious; the rooms, suites, private dining rooms and the restaurant are the epitome of elegance. The hotel has its own spa and there is an 18 hole golf course nearby.

(Other activities P. 629)

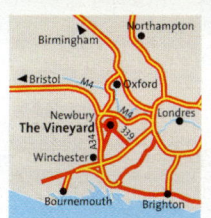

Access: The hotel is just off junction 13 of the M4 motorway. Take A34 south towards Winchester and then the A4 (3rd exit) towards Hungerford and then Stockcross (B4000)
Airport: London Heathrow (Intl) 70 km
Train station: Newbury 2 km

Owner: Sir Peter Michael
General Manager: Nick Hanson
Open all year
Currency: Pound sterling (GBP)
Rates: Menus 23-49 GBP s.i.
Carte 23-49 GBP s.i.
16 rooms: 160-285 GBP t.17.5 % s.i.
15 suites: 285-600 GBP t.17.5 % s.i.
Breakfast: 15 GBP s.i.
Dogs: not allowed
Golf: 3 km
Accepted cards: AE, DC, JCB, MC, VS

More info on www.relaischateaux.com/vineyard

United Kingdom

Gravetye Manor

SINCE 1976

Near East Grinstead
West Sussex, RH19 4LJ
United Kingdom

Tel. : (44) (01342) 810567
Fax : (44) (01342) 810080
gravetye@relaischateaux.com

This peaceful XVIth century Elizabethan manor in William Robinson's Natural English garden is surrounded by a forest, yet only 30 miles from London. Relax in oak panelled sitting rooms warmed by open log fires and furnished with antiques. Every bedroom enjoys vistas of the tranquil gardens. Dine by candlelight, savouring classical British dishes, home-grown vegetables and fruits, with wines from one of Britain's finest cellars.

Trout fishing, croquet. (Other activities P. 629)

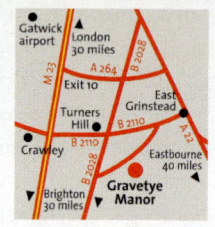

Access: From M23, J10 East Grinstead, A264 The Dukes Head, B2028 towards Turners Hill.

Airports: London Gatwick (Intl) 16 km, London Heathrow (Intl) 76 km
Train station: Esat Grinstead 6 km

Owners: Herbert Family
General Manager: Andrew Russell
Open all year
Currency: Pound sterling (GBP)
Rates: Menus 19-37 GBP s.i.
Carte 36-52 GBP s.i.
18 rooms: 100-320 GBP s.i.
Breakfast: 10-16 GBP s.i.
Dogs: not allowed
Golf: Royal Ashdown 8 km
Accepted cards: MC, VS

More info on www.relaischateaux.com/gravetye

Chewton Glen

SINCE 1971

Christchurch Road
New Milton
Hampshire, BH25 6QS
United Kingdom

Tel. : (44) (01425) 275341
Fax : (44) (01425) 272310
chewton@relaischateaux.com

United Kingdom

This splendid residence, set in a tranquil landscape of gardens and woodlands, 145 km from London, is imbued with the generous hospitality of its owners. Dine on the finest seasonal fish and game, and savour delicious local produce. Body and soul are rejuvenated in the gym, indoor pool, spa and sauna at the Health Club, where treatments include facials and aromatherapy. Enjoy long sea and country walks, fishing and golf.

Children from the age of 6. Putting green, croquet, 2 indoor and outdoor tennis courts. (Other activities P. 629)

Access: From London, M3 then M27 West, Jct. 1 A337 Lyndhurst A35 towards Christchurch then Walkford.
Airports: Southampton (Intl) 30 km, London Heathrow (Intl) 120 km
Helipad: N 50° 45' W 01° 40'
Train station: New Milton 2 km

Owners: Martin and Brigitte Skan
Director : Peter Crome
Open all year
Currency: Pound sterling (GBP)
Rates: Lunch 35 GBP s.i. Dinner 55 GBP s.i.
43 rooms: 250-425 GBP s.i.
22 suites: 405-720 GBP s.i.
Breakfast: English breakfast 20 GBP s.i. continental 14 GBP s.i.
Dogs: not allowed **Golf:** on the premises (9 holes) 10 courses in 30 km
Accepted cards: AE, DC, MC, VS

More info on www.relaischateaux.com/chewton

Stock Hill Country House

United Kingdom

SINCE 1995

Gillingham
Dorset SP8 5NR
United Kingdom

Tel. : (44) (01747) 823626
Fax : (44) (01747) 825628
stockhill@relaischateaux.com

Stock Hill House is a late Victorian mansion set in 11 acres of beautifully wooded grounds. Peter Hauser and his wife Nita have spent over a decade refurbishing the house and gardens to exacting standards, so that today, Stock Hill's serenity and acclaimed cuisine have been recognised internationally. From the moment you enter the beech-tree-lined drive, you are about to experience exceptional hospitality.

Fishing (trout, carp...) in a private lake, flying club, sauna. (Other activities P. 629)

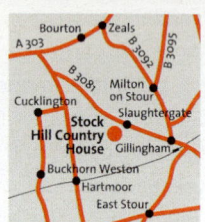

Access: London M3, exit 8 - A 303 towards Exeter turn off B 3081 towards Gillingham.

Airports: Bristol (Intl) 50 km, London Heathrow (Intl) 140 km
Helipad: N 51° 2' 23'' W 2° 18' 23''
Train station: Gillingham 0,5 km

Owners: Peter and Nita Hauser
Open all year
Currency: Pound sterling (GBP)
Rates: Menus
lunch 22-24 GBP s.i.
dinner 32-35 GBP s.i.
8 rooms: half board 240-300 GBP s.i.
Breakfast: included
Dogs: not allowed
Golf: 30 km, putting green on the premises
Accepted cards: MC, VS

More info on www.relaischateaux.com/stockhill

Summer Lodge

SINCE 1992

Evershot-Dorchester
Dorset DT2 OJR
United Kingdom

Tel. : (44) (01935) 83424
Fax : (44) (01935) 83005
summer@relaischateaux.com

United Kingdom

Summer Lodge, a beautiful manor built in the heart of Thomas Hardy's Dorset in 1789, certainly lives up to its name. Everything from the elegant white façade and grey slate roof, to the pretty pastel rooms and the magnolias in the garden is imbued with summer splendour. Hosts Nigel, Margaret Corbett and Family offer generous hospitality. Enjoy a classic English afternoon tea and refined cuisine enhanced by vintage Bordeaux.

Clay pigeon shooting, croquet... (Other activities P. 629)

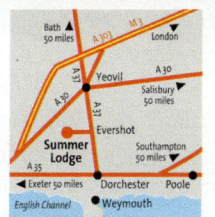

Access: From London, M3, exit 8, A 303 then A 37 towards Dorchester then Evershot, Summer Lane.

Airports: London Heathrow (Intl) 160 km, Bournemouth 50 km
Helipad: N 50° 50' 1" W 2° 36' 3"

Owners: Nigel and Margaret Corbett
General Manager: Thierry Lepinoy
Open all year
Currency: Pound sterling (GBP)
Rates: Menu 40 GBP s.i.
Carte 25-45 GBP s.i.
16 rooms: 145-305 GBP s.i.
1 suite: 195-315 GBP s.i.
Breakfast: included
Dogs: allowed (extra cost)
Golf: 5 km
Accepted cards: AE, DC, JCB, MC, VS

More info on www.relaischateaux.com/summer

Gidleigh Park

SINCE 1984

Chagford
Devon TQ13 8HH
United Kingdom

Tel. : (44) (01647) 432367
Fax : (44) (01647) 432574
gidleigh@relaischateaux.com

United Kingdom

Kay and Paul Henderson's idyllic manor house stands in the midst of Dartmoor National Park, renowned for its wealth of prehistoric remains. Enjoy rambling and horse-riding in the beautiful Devon countryside or fishing in the North Teign River. Savour the delights of Devon cuisine, prepared with the finest local produce and fish from the nearby sea, and relish one of the 500 fine wines from Europe and the New World.

Hunting, croquet... (Other activities P. 629)

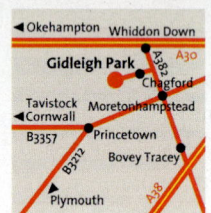

Access: From London, M4 and M5; after Exeter, take the A30, then the A382 towards Chagford.

Airports: London Heathrow (Intl) 300 km, Exeter 35 km
Helipad: N 50° 40' 58" W 3° 52' 36"
Train station: Exeter 35 km

Owners: Kay and Paul Henderson
General Manager: Catherine Endacott
Open all year
Currency: Pound sterling (GBP)
Rates: Menus 35-70 GBP s.i. (lunch) 70-75 GBP s.i. (dinner)
12 rooms: Half board 410-525 GBP s.i.
3 suites: Half board 450-525 GBP s.i.
Breakfast: included
Dogs: allowed
Golf: 15 km
Accepted cards: MC, VS

More info on www.relaischateaux.com/gidleigh

Longueville Manor

SINCE 1972

Longueville Road
St Saviour, Jersey JE2 7WF
United Kingdom

Tel. : (44) (01534) 725501
Fax : (44) (01534) 731613
longueville@relaischateaux.com

United Kingdom

Sitting at the foot of its private wooded valley, this XIIIth century manor offers all the natural charms of Jersey and adds many of its own. Its elegant interior, fine antique furniture and carved oak panelling is tastefully combined with the height of modern comfort, while outside a heated swimming pool and lawn tennis courts await you. Enjoy impeccable service and delicious local cuisine.

Walks, water sports... (Other activities P. 629)

Access:
St Helier,
A3 for 1.25 miles
towards Gorey.

Airport: Jersey 10 km

Owners: Malcolm Lewis and Susan Dufty
General Manager: Malcolm Lewis
Open all year
Currency: Pound sterling (GBP)
Rates: Menus 27-42 GBP s.i. Carte 48-75 GBP s.i.
28 rooms: 200-340 GBP s.i.
3 suites: 410-600 GBP s.i.
Breakfast: included
Dogs: allowed
Golf: 3 km
Accepted cards: AE, DC, JCB, MC, VS

More info on www.relaischateaux.com/longueville

United Kingdom

Lucknam Park

SINCE 2001

Lucknam Park,
Colerne-near Bath
Wiltshire, SN14 8AZ
United Kingdom

Tel. : (44) (01225) 742777
Fax : (44) (01225) 743536
lucknam@relaischateaux.com

A warm & personal welcome awaits you at this magnificent XVIIIth century Palladian mansion. Lucknam Park sits in a 500 acre parkland only 6 miles from the historic city of Bath. This country house offers relaxation in the Spa, Health & Beauty Salon, superb gardens or walks and horse riding in the park. Enjoy excellent cuisine using only the freshest local produce.

Fishing, croquet, ballooning, clay pigeon shooting. (Other activities P. 629)

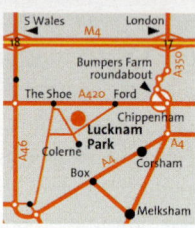

Access: M 4, exit at junction 17, towards Chippenham, via A 350. At «Bumpers Farm» round-about, take A 420 towards Bristol. After 7 km, turn left for Colerne & Lucknam Park.
Airports: Bristol (Intl) 50 km, London Heathrow (Intl) 144 km
Hélipad : N 51° 27' 27" W 00° 215' 61"
Train station: Bath 13 km

Owner: Lucknam Park Hotel Ltd
Director: Harry Murray
Open all year
Currency: Pound sterling (GBP)
Rates: Menus 20-28 GBP s.i. (lunch)
Carte 48 GBP s.i. (dinner)
28 rooms: 205-335 GBP s.i. **13 suites:** 445-700 GBP s.i.
Breakfast: 12-18 GBP s.i.
Dogs: not allowed **Golf:** 6 km
Accepted cards: AE, DC, JCB, MC, VS

More info on www.relaischateaux.com/lucknam

Buckland Manor Hotel

SINCE 1995

Buckland near
Broadway
Worcestershire WR12 7LY
United Kingdom

Tel. : (44) (01386) 852626
Fax : (44) (01386) 853557
buckland@relaischateaux.com

United Kingdom

This historic and beautiful XIIIth century manor, mentioned in William the Conqueror's Domesday Book, lies amidst 10 acres of idyllic and tranquil gardens, in a peaceful valley in the Cotswolds. Lounges are decorated with antique furniture and warming log fires. 13 luxury bedrooms, four-poster beds, bathrooms use water from spring. The elegant restaurant with stunning views, serves award-winning cuisine with an extensive wine list of 762 selections.

Hunting. Stratford-upon-Avon and Shakespeare. (Other activities P. 629)

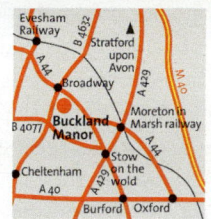

Access: 1 1/2 miles from Broadway, Worcestershire, on the B4632; Broadway to Winchcombe road.

Airports: Birmingham (Intl) 72 km, London Heathrow (Intl) 136 km
Helipad: N 52° 01' 27" W 1° 52' 90"
Train station: Moreton in Marsh 16 km

Owners: Roy and Daphné Vaughan
General Manager: Nigel Power
Open all year
Currency: Pound sterling (GBP)
Rates: Menus 29 GBP s.i. (lunch)
48 GBP s.i. (dinner)
13 rooms: 225-360 GBP s.i.
Breakfast: included
Dogs: not allowed
Golf: Putting green on the premises, 3 km
Accepted cards: AE, DC, MC, VS

More info on www.relaischateaux.com/buckland

Mallory Court

SINCE 1983

Harbury Lane
Bishops Tachbrook, Leamington Spa
Warwickshire CV33 9QB
United Kingdom

Tel. : (44) (01926) 330214
Fax : (44) (01926) 451714
mallory@relaischateaux.com

United Kingdom

This magnificent manor, surrounded by ten acres of landscaped gardens, lies in the heart of the Warwickshire countryside. You might begin the evening sipping champagne on the terrace before setting off for nearby Stratford-upon-Avon to visit the Royal Shakespeare Theatre. Or you may prefer to enjoy the manor's fine restaurant after a busy day roaming around the Cotswold villages and browsing in the antique shops.

Trout fishing, Warwick Castle, Cotswolds, Shakespeare Theatre.
(Other activities P. 629)

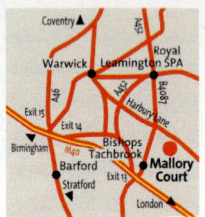

Access: M40, from London J13, from Birmingham J14, 2 miles on B4087, to Leamington Spa.

Airports: Birmingham (Intl) 30 km, London Heathrow (Intl) 175 km
Train station: Leamington Spa 4 km

Owners: Peter Rigby and Jeremy Mort
Open all year
Currency: Pound sterling (GBP)
Rates: Menu 38 GBP s.i. Carte 48-60 GBP s.i.
18 rooms: 185-325 GBP s.i.
Breakfast: Continental: included
English breakfast: à la carte
Dogs: not allowed
Golf: 3 km
Accepted cards: AE, DC, MC, VS

More info on www.relaischateaux.com/mallory

Hambleton Hall

SINCE 1984

Hambleton
Oakham - Rutland LE15 8 TH
United Kingdom

Tel. : (44) (01572) 756991
Fax : (44) (01572) 724721
hambleton@relaischateaux.com

United Kingdom

A spectacular setting on a peninsula in the middle of Rutland Water, a sumptuous and welcoming interior and glorious cooking are three key elements in the Hambleton formula. Tim Hart's enthusiasm for wine and the gardens is obvious. Visit charming villages and great houses in the Rutland area.

(Other activities P. 629)

Access: From London, A1 to Stamford, then A 606; Whitwell then Hambleton.

Airports: East Midlands (Intl) 45 km, London Heathrow (Intl) 170 km
Helipad: N 52° 39' 4'' W 000° 40' 1''
Train station: Oakham 6 km

Owners: Tim and Stefa Hart
Open all year
Currency: Pound sterling (GBP)
Rates: Menus 17-60 GBP s.i. Carte 30-60 GBP s.i.
15 rooms: 180-340 GBP s.i.
1 suite: 500-600 GBP s.i.
Breakfast: included
Dogs: allowed
Golf: 15 km
Accepted cards: DC, MC, VS

More info on www.relaischateaux.com/hambleton

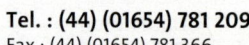

Ynyshir Hall

SINCE 2002

Eglwysfach, Machynlleth
Powys SY20 8TA
United Kingdom

Tel. : (44) (01654) 781 209
Fax : (44) (01654) 781 366
ynyshir@relaischateaux.com

United Kingdom

This beautiful XVIth century manor, bearing the same name as the splendid bird reserve on its doorstep, has been cherished by many illustrious owners including Queen Victoria who was instrumental in making the gardens even more beautiful. Artist Rob Reen and his wife Joan, the current owners, have created a setting unlike any other in the land of the Celts. The decor of each room reveals the painter's love of colour.

Bird watching... (Other activities P. 629)

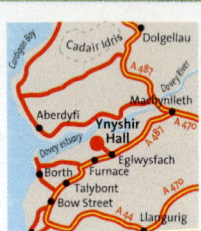

Access: From Aberystwyth: take the A487 for 11 miles (towards Machynlleth) to Eglwysfach. Turn left in the village and Ynyshir Hall is on your right after half a mile.
Airports: Manchester (Intl) 168 km, Cardiff 200 km
Helipad: N 52° 32' 686" W 03° 56' 623"
Train station: Machynlleth 10 km

Owners: Rob and Joan Reen
Annual closing: From January 5th to 25th
Currency: Pound sterling (GBP)
Rates: Menus lunch 28-30 GBP s.i. dinner 42-55 GBP s.i.
6 rooms: 160-215 GBP s.i.
3 suites: 215-275 GBP s.i.
Breakfast: included
Dogs: allowed, extra cost (in some rooms)
Golf: 10 km
Accepted cards: AE, DC, JCB, MC, VS

More info on www.relaischateaux.com/ynyshir

Bodysgallen Hall

SINCE 1998

Llandudno
North Wales LL30 1RS
United Kingdom

Tel. : (44) (01492) 584 466
Fax : (44) (01492) 582 519
bodysgallen@relaischateaux.com

United Kingdom

This magnificent XVIIth century residence, set amidst luxuriant parkland in North Wales, has been beautifully restored. Bodysgallen Hall offers 19 spacious rooms decorated with antique furniture, while 16 charming cottages with private gardens await you in the park. Stroll through the elegant gardens, relax in the spa or indoor pool, play tennis and savour superb cuisine. The views of Snowdonia are breathtaking.

Historic Houses, Bodnant Gardens, Snowdon National Park, Caernarfon Castle, Conwy Castle, Swallow Falls, preserved railways and mountain scenery. (Other activities P. 629)

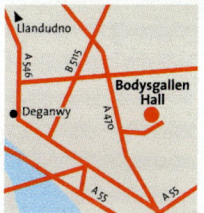

Access:
A55 to its intersection with A470 and exit at junction 19. Follow A470 towards Llandudno. The hotel is 2 miles on the right.

Airports: Manchester (Intl) 128 km, Chester 72 km
Train station: Llandudno 3 km

Owner: Richard Broyd
Director: Matthew Johnson
Open all year
Currency: Pound sterling (GBP)
Rates: Menu 35 GBP s.i.
19 rooms: 150-245 GBP s.i.
16 suites: 170-245 GBP s.i.
Breakfast: 12-15 GBP s.i.
Dogs: allowed (cottages only)
Golf: 5 km
Accepted cards: JCB, MC, VS

More info on www.relaischateaux.com/bodysgallen

Middlethorpe Hall

Bishopthorpe Road, York
North Yorkshire YO23 2GB
United Kingdom

Tel. : **(44) (01904) 641 241**
Fax : (44) (01904) 620 176
middlethorpe@relaischateaux.com

SINCE 1998

United Kingdom

This distinguished William III house, set in gardens and parkland, was built in 1699. Now restored with many antiques and pictures, its individually designed bedrooms are both in the house and nearby classical courtyard. Superb cuisine in the oak-panelled dining-room. Health and beauty spa. Only 5 minutes from the historic city of York, and ideally situated for the many other attractions of Yorkshire.

Country Houses, abbey-church ruins, city of York, museums. (Other activities P. 629)

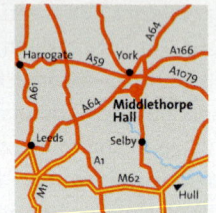

Access: From A1, join the A64, following signs to York West (A1036). Follow signs to Bishopthorpe, then Middlethorpe.

Airports: Leeds-Bradford (Intl) 40 km, Manchester (Intl) 113 km
Helipad: N 53° 55' 80" W 00° 105' 60"
Train station: York 2 km

Owner: Richard Broyd
General Manager: Milton J.D. Hussey
Open all year
Currency: Pound sterling (GBP)
Rates: Menus starting at 36 GBP s.i.
23 rooms: 160-265 GBP s.i.
7 suites: 230-340 GBP s.i.
Breakfast: 12-15 GBP s.i.
Dogs: not allowed
Golf: 8 km
Accepted cards: MC, VS

More info on www.relaischateaux.com/middlethorpe

Sharrow Bay Country House

SINCE 1967

Lake Ullswater, Howtown
Penrith Cumbria CA10 2LZ
United Kingdom

Tel. : (44) (017684) 86301
Fax : (44) (017684) 86349
sharrow@relaischateaux.com

United Kingdom

Sharrow Bay has been in existence for 54 years. The terrace of this elegant family mansion, built in 1840, offers breathtaking views of Lake Ullswater. This idyllic country retreat is impeccably run on very personal lines by the proprietor, assisted by his caring staff. Savour traditional English cuisine. Sharrow is an oasis where one can escape the cares of the world and you will love the intimate relaxed atmosphere.

Water sports. (Other activities P. 629)

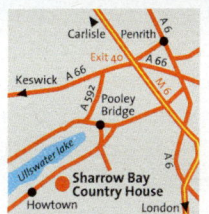

Access: M6, exit 40; A 66 West; A 592; Pooley Bridge; turn right after the church, towards Howtown.

Airport: Manchester (Intl) 160 km
Train station: Penrith 2 km

Owner/General Manager: Nigel Lightburn
Annual closing: From December to March
Currency: Pound sterling (GBP)
Rates: Menus 30-47 GBP s.i.
19 rooms:
Half board/2 persons 300-400 GBP s.i.
7 suites:
Half board/2 persons 380-410 GBP s.i.
Breakfast: included
Dogs: not allowed
Golf: 12 km
Accepted cards: AE, MC, VS

More info on www.relaischateaux.com/sharrow

United Kingdom

Farlam Hall Hotel

SINCE 1985

Brampton
Cumbria CA8 2NG
United Kingdom

Tel. : (44) (016977) 46234
Fax : (44) (016977) 46683
farlam@relaischateaux.com

The elegant façade of this XVIIth century manor, set in beautiful green parkland studded with hundred-year-old trees, is reflected in the waters of the ornamental lake and fountain. The 12 comfortable guestrooms in its interior are charming, and the seasonal cuisine a feast for the senses. Stroll through the magnificent countryside or visit Hadrian's Wall and the region's historic castles, abbeys and stately homes.

Fishing, hiking on Hadrian's Wall, flying club-pilot on staff. (Other activities P. 629)

Access: From the A 69 towards Newcastle, take the A 689 towards Alston for 2 miles to Farlam Hall (not Farlam Village).

Airports: Newcastle (Intl) 75 km, Manchester (Intl) 170 km
Helipad: N 54° 56' 08" W 002° 40' 28"
Train station: Brampton 3 km

Owners: Quinion and Stevenson Families
General Manager: Alastair Stevenson
Annual closing: From December 26th to 30th
Currency: Pound sterling (GBP)
Rates: Menus 33-34 GBP s.n.i.
12 rooms: Half board 235-270 GBP s.n.i.
Breakfast: included
Dogs: allowed
Golf : Brampton 5 km
Accepted cards: MC, VS

More info on www.relaischateaux.com/farlam

Glenapp Castle

SINCE 2002

Ballantrae
Ayrshire KA26 ONZ
United Kingdom

Tel. : (44) (01465) 831 212
Fax : (44) (01465) 831 000
glenapp@relaischateaux.com

United Kingdom

Set amid magnificent gardens and woodland, this spectacular castle built in 1870, with its Victorian greenhouses and views across the Irish Sea to the island of Arran, is the perfect setting for a delightful stay. Its regained splendour is the work of Graham and Fay Cowan who have selected period furniture for their gracious rooms. A family dwelling of rare elegance. Tariff includes all meals, Castle wines and spirits.

Biking, horseback riding. (Other activities P. 629)

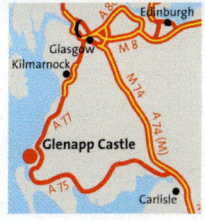

Access: From Glasgow: take A77 South. From Carlisle: take A75 to Stranraer, then take A77 North. Glenapp Castle is one mile south of the village of Ballantrae.
Airport: Glasgow (Intl) 90 km
Helipad: N 55° 04' 6'' W 004° 58' 8''
Train station: Girvan 25 km

Owners/General Managers:
Graham and Fay Cowan
Annual closing: From November to April
Currency: Pound sterling (GBP)
Rates: Menu 80 GBP s.n.i. (drinks included)
15 rooms: 440-550 GBP s.n.i.
2 suites: 480 GBP s.n.i.
Breakfast: included
Dogs: allowed
Golf: 30 km
Accepted cards: AE, JCB, MC, VS

More info on www.relaischateaux.com/glenapp

Inverlochy Castle

United Kingdom

SINCE 1977

Torlundy-Fort William
Scotland PH33 6SN
United Kingdom

Tel. : (44) (01397) 702177
Fax : (44) (01397) 702953
inverlochy@relaischateaux.com

Inverlochy Castle built in 1863 near the site of the original XIIIth century fortress, nestles in the foothills of Ben Nevis, sitting amidst some of Scotland's finest scenery once enjoyed by Queen Victoria herself. The beauty and tranquillity of the castle's setting is remarkable, and in keeping with the grandeur of its surroundings.

Pheasant, shooting, stalking for red deer, guided hill walking...
(Other activities P. 629)

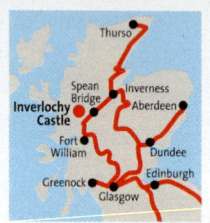

Access: Inverlochy is situated 3 miles north of Fort William on the main A82 towards Inverness.

Airports: Glasgow (Intl) 160 km, Inverness 110 km

Owner: Inverlochy Castle Ltd
General Manager: Niall Edmondson
Annual closing: From mid January to February 12th
Currency: Pound sterling (GBP)
Rates: Menus 40-55 GBP s.i.
Carte 30-50 GBP s.i.
16 rooms: 290-435 GBP s.i.
1 suite: 440-550 GBP s.i.
Breakfast: included
Dogs: allowed
Golf: 2 km
Accepted cards: AE, JCB, MC, VS

More info on www.relaischateaux.com/inverlochy

Kinnaird

SINCE 1993

Kinnaird Estate, By Dunkeld
Perthshire PH8 OLB
United Kingdom

Tel. : (44) (01796) 482440
Fax : (44) (01796) 482289
kinnaird@relaischateaux.com

United Kingdom

This elegant family home, built in 1770 near the River Tay, offers a majestic view of the Scottish Highlands. Set in the midst of its own 9000 acre estate, Kinnaird offers salmon and loch fishing, deer stalking and country walking. After an invigorating day in the outdoors, relax beside a fire in your lovely room and enjoy a fine malt whisky in preparation for an excellent dinner.

Walking, rafting, clay pigeon shooting, billiards... (Other activities P. 629)

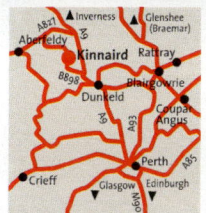

Access: From Perth, A9 towards Inverness, do not enter Dunkeld, continue North, then B898 towards Dalguise.

Airports: Edinburgh (Intl) 95 km, Glasgow (Intl) 130 km
Helipad: N 56° 38' W 3° 38'
Train station: Dunkeld 6 km

Owner: Constance Ward
General Manager: Douglas Jack
Weekly closing: Monday, Tuesday, Wednesday from January 13th to March 31st
Open all year
Currency: Pound sterling (GBP)
Rates: Carte 45 GBP s.i.
8 rooms: 275-345 GBP s.i.
1 suite: 385 GBP s.i.
Breakfast: included
Dogs: heated kennels **Golf:** 6 km
Accepted cards: AE, MC, VS

More info on www.relaischateaux.com/kinnaird

Ireland

Properties	Nearest major city	Relais & Châteaux	Relais Gourmands	Page
Ballylickey Manor House	Cork	⚜		395
Cashel House Hotel	Clifden	⚜		397
Longueville House	Cork	⚜		396
Marlfield House	Wexford	⚜		399
Newport House	Wesport	⚜		398
Sheen Falls Lodge	Kenmare	⚜		394

More info on www.relaischateaux.com

Ireland

Sheen Falls Lodge

SINCE 1994

Kenmare
Co. Kerry
Ireland

Tel. : (353) (064) 41600
Fax : (353) (064) 41386
sheenfalls@relaischateaux.com

When the first stones were laid in 1691, the famous Sir William Petty could not have imagined that this magnificent lodge would become so renowned. A 300-acre haven of woodland and cascading waterfalls, with its luxurious rooms, extensive cellar of fine wines, and rare books, the lodge retains the welcoming atmosphere of a country manor house. Outstanding service and cuisine combine to make your stay as unique as Ireland itself.

Vintage car excursions, billiard room, library, clay pigeon shooting, health spa. (Other activities P. 629)

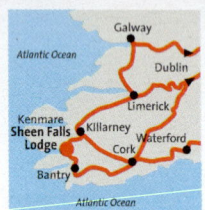

Access: From Kenmare, N 71 direction Glengarriff, left after the suspension bridge.

Airports: Kerry (Intl) 48 km, Cork (Intl) 96 km
Helipad: N 51° 50' W 09° 35'
Train station: Killarney 40 km

Owner: Bent Hoyer
General Manager: Adriaan Bartels
Annual closing: From Jan. 2nd to Feb. 7th and from Dec. 2nd to 4th, 9th to 11th, 16th to 18th
Currency: Euro (€)
Rates: Menu 60 € s.i.
52 rooms: 250-510 € s.i.
9 suites: 435-620 € s.i.
Breakfast: starting at 15 € s.i.
Dogs: not allowed
Golf: Kenmare 2 km, Ring of Kerry 6 km
Accepted cards: AE, DC, MC, VS

More info on www.relaischateaux.com/sheenfalls

Ballylickey Manor House

SINCE 1967

Ballylickey
Bantry bay
Co. Cork • Ireland

Tel. : (353) (027) 50071
Fax : (353) (027) 50124
ballylickey@relaischateaux.com

Ireland

Set against a backdrop of wild moors, mountains and sweeping coastlines, Ballylickey offers breathtaking views, and its gleaming white façade opens onto magnificent ornamental gardens winding down to the sea. After a day's fishing or golfing, unwind beside a log fire and enjoy a gourmet meal by candlelight. Choose between a comfortable, sunny room in the manor or a charming cottage hidden in the gardens.

Salmon and trout fishing, walks, croquet, library. (Other activities P. 629)

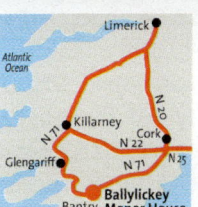

Access: N 71 between Bantry and Glengariff, exit T 64 Ballylickey.

Airport: Cork (Intl) 80 km
Train station: Cork 80 km

Owners: Mr and Mrs George Graves
Annual closing: From November to mid-March
Currency: Euro (€)
Rates: Menus 45-51 € Carte 45-60 €
5 rooms: 203-220 €
5 suites: 254-341 €
Breakfast: included
Dogs: allowed
Golf: 2 km and 7 km (2 golf courses)
Accepted cards: AE, DC, MC, VS

More info on www.relaischateaux.com/ballylickey

Longueville House

Ireland — SINCE 1984

Mallow
Co. Cork • Ireland

Tel. : (353) (022) 47156
Fax : (353) (022) 47459
longuehouse@relaischateaux.com

This 1720 Georgian Heritage Mansion is set on a 500-acre wooded estate in the heart of the Blackwater Valley. The O'Callaghan Family have preserved their beautiful home with loving care. William O'Callaghan's cuisine is served in the Victorian conservatory with fine wines. Private fishing, shooting game and walks on the estate. Ideal venue for prestigious gatherings and business meetings.

Horse racing (2 km), salmon and trout fishing on estate, shooting on estate (November-mid. February). Ideal venue for residential wedding parties. (Other activities P. 629)

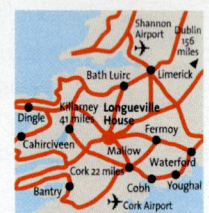

Access: 3 miles west of Mallow via N 72 road to Killarney. Follow signs. Cork Ferry 35 km.

Airports: Cork (Intl) 35 km, Shannon (Intl) 85 km
Train station: Mallow 5 km

Owners: O'Callaghan Family
Annual closing:
From mid-December to the end of February (except for groups: January/February)
Currency: Euro (€)
Rates: Menus 50-65 € s.n.i.
18 rooms: 180-335 € s.i.
2 suites: 290-355 € s.i.
Breakfast: included
Dogs: not allowed
Golf: Mallow 6 km
Accepted cards: AE, DC, MC, VS

More info on www.relaischateaux.com/longuehouse

Cashel House Hotel

SINCE 1979

Cashel
Connemara, Co. Galway
Ireland

Tel. : (353) (095) 31001
Fax : (353) (095) 31077
cashel@relaischateaux.com

Ireland

General and Madame de Gaulle were enchanted by this elegant mid XIXth century house, nestling amidst the most beautiful garden in Ireland. Its Georgian guestrooms offer superb views of the Atlantic coastline and the rolling green hills of Connemara. After an invigorating walk through the magnificent Connemara wilderness, recline by a traditional peat fire, then savour delicious regional cuisine accompanied by vintage wine.

(Other activities P. 629)

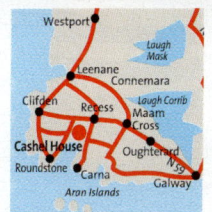

Access: From Galway, take N 59 towards Recess, then take Cashel (1 mile West of Recess).

Airports: Shannon (Intl) 152 km, Galway 72 km
Train station: Galway 72 km

Owner: Dermot McEvilly
General Manager: Kay McEvilly
Annual closing: From January 3rd to February 3rd
Currency: Euro (€)
Rates: Menus 45-48 € s.12.5%
Carte 31-47 € s.12.5%
19 rooms: 160-250 € s.12.5%
13 suites: 215-300 € s.12.5%
Breakfast: included
Dogs: allowed (from G.B. only)
Golf: Connemara 20 km
Accepted cards: AE, DC, MC, VS

More info on www.relaischateaux.com/cashel

Ireland

Newport House

SINCE 1986

Newport
Co. Mayo • Ireland

Tel. : (353) (098) 41222
Fax : (353) (098) 41613
newport@relaischateaux.com

The O'Donnell family, princes of Tir Connell, built their historic home in 1720. Its classical façade looks out across the Newport river, which is famous for its salmon fishing. The house with its charming interior is decorated with elegant furniture and fine artwork. The delicious cuisine features freshly caught fish and fine garden produce. It is an idyllic haven in County Mayo.

Secnic walks. (Other activities P. 629)

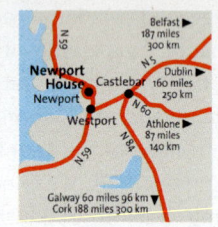

Access: Main roads to Westport, N 59 from Newport village (9.5 km).

Airports: Shannon (Intl) 200 km, Knock 70 km
Train station: Westport 10 km

Owners: Kieran and Thelma Thompson
Annual closing: From October 6th to March 18th
Currency: Euro (€)
Rates: Menu (6 courses) dinner, 46 € s.i.
18 rooms: 208-320 € s.i.
Breakfast: included
Dogs: not allowed
Golf: 10 km
Accepted cards: AE, DC, MC, VS

More info on www.relaischateaux.com/newport

Marlfield House

Gorey
Co. Wexford • Ireland

SINCE 1984

Tel. : (353) (055) 21124
Fax : (353) (055) 21572
marlfield@relaischateaux.com

Ireland

This elegant XIXth century house, formerly the residence of the Earls of Courtown, is set amidst stunning flower gardens and woodland walks. Superbly renovated by hosts Mary and Ray Bowe, Marlfield's sumptuous interior is adorned with gleaming antiques, blazing fires and captivating paintings. The blooming conservatory, overlooking the garden, provides a most romantic setting in which to enjoy superb modern Irish cuisine.

Horseback riding, beaches nearby. (Other activities P. 629)

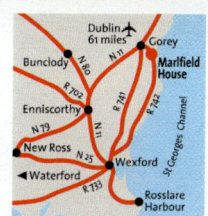

Access: From Dublin, N 11 towards Wexford. Before Gorey, left towards Courtown Harbour.

Airports: Dublin (Intl) 80 km, Shannon (Intl) 160 km
Helipad: N 52° 39' 50" W 06° 16' 00"
Train station: Gorey 1,5 km

Owners: Mary and Ray Bowe
General Manager: Margaret Bowe
Annual closing: From mid-December to end January
Currency: Euro (€)
Rates: Menus 55-60 € s.i.
13 rooms: 240-265 € s.i.
6 suites: 440-750 € s.i.
Breakfast: included
Dogs: allowed upon request
Golf: Courtown 2 km
Accepted cards: AE, DC, VS

More info on www.relaischateaux.com/marlfield

Italy

Properties	Nearest major city	Relais & Châteaux	Relais Gourmands	Page
Albereta et Rest. G. Marchesi (L')	Bergamo	⚜	❦	410
Ambasciata (Ristorante)	Mantova		❦	419
Antica Osteria del Ponte	Milano		❦	408
Bellevue (Hotel)	Aosta	⚜		404
Borgo Paraelios	Roma	⚜		433
Bottaccio di Montignoso (Il)	Pisa	⚜		422
Cala del Porto (Hotel)	Roma	⚜		431
Calandre (Ristorante Le)	Padova		❦	416
Certosa di Maggiano (Hotel)	Siena	⚜		426
Da Vittorio (Ristorante)	Bergamo		❦	409
Dominik (Hotel)	Bolzano	⚜		413
Don Alfonso 1890	Napoli		❦	437
Duchessa Isabella (Hotel)	Ferrara	⚜		420
Enoteca Pinchiorri (Restaurant)	Firenze		❦	421
Gallia Palace Hotel	Grosseto	⚜		429
Hermitage (Hotel)	Aosta	⚜		403
La Collegiata (Hotel)	San Gimignano	⚜		425
Locanda l'Elisa	Lucca	⚜		424
Melograno (Il)	Bari	⚜		439
Meridiana (La)	Genova	⚜		418
Parkhotel Villa Grazioli	Roma	⚜		434
Pellicano (Il)	Roma	⚜		432
Pescatore (Restaurant dal)	Mantova		❦	417
Posta Vecchia (La)	Roma	⚜		435
Relais Borgo San Felice (Hotel)	Siena	⚜		427
Relais Il Falconiere	Cortona	⚜		428
Rosa Alpina	Cortina d'Ampezzo	⚜		414
San Pietro (Hotel)	Napoli	⚜		438
Sole di Ranco (Il)	Milano	⚜	❦	407
Sorriso (Al)	Borgomanero	⚜	❦	405
Villa Abbazia	Treviso	⚜		415
Villa Del Quar (Hotel)	Verona	⚜		412
Villa Fiordaliso	Brescia	⚜		411
Villa la Massa	Firenze	⚜		423

More info on www.relaischateaux.com

Hotel Hermitage

SINCE 1994

I-11021 Breuil Cervinia
(Valle d'Aosta) • Italy

Tel. : (39) 0166 94 89 98
Fax : (39) 0166 94 90 32
hermitage@relaischateaux.com

Italy

At the foot of the Matterhorn, built in true Alpine style, the Hermitage is a magnificent residence at an altitude of 2000 m! Under its white blanket you will discover a cosy and elegant universe in which Aosta valley decor reaches perfection. All guest rooms have breathtaking vistas of the valley or the Matterhorn. Regional cuisine and fine wines. Beauty centre. Summer ski.
Heli-skiing, climbing, flying club. (Other activities P. 629)

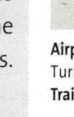

Altitude: 2000 metres.
Access: From Turin, A 5 towards Aosta, Châtillon exit, RR 46 towards Breuil-Cervinia.

Airports: Milan Malpensa (Intl) 170 km, Turin 110 km
Train station: Châtillon 27 km

Owners: Neyroz Family
General Manager: Corrado Neyroz
Annual closing: From beg. May to beg. July and from beginning September to end November
Currency: Euro (€)
Rates: Menu 50 € s.i. Carte 60 € s.i.
33 rooms: 220-440 € s.i.
7 suites: starting at 450 € s.i.
Breakfast: Buffet included
Dogs: not allowed
Golf: 9 holes / 1 km
Accepted cards: AE, DC, MC, VS

More info on www.relaischateaux.com/hermitage

Italy

Hotel Bellevue

SINCE 2000

Rue Grand Paradis 22
I-11012 Cogne
(Valle d'Aosta) • Italy

Tel. : **(39) 0165 74825**
Fax : (39) 0165 749192
bellevue@relaischateaux.com

Situated on the edge of the Sant' Orso meadows, opposite a glacier in the Gran Paradiso national Park, the Hotel Bellevue welcomes you to this delightful family-run property. You will be enchanted by the unique décor of the rooms, the regional cuisine, a wonderful selection of fine wines and the new fitness centre. The charm of its antique furniture makes this hotel a true museum of popular art.

Hiking in the national park (in winter with snowshoes), cross-country skiing, alpine skiing, climbing, fitness. (Other activities P. 629)

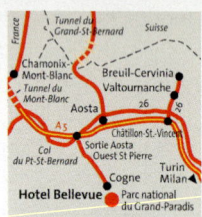

Altitude : 1534 m.
Access: From Turin take the A5 towards Aosta/Mont-Blanc, exit at Aosta west / Saint-Pierre, RR 47 towards Cogne.
Airports: Geneva (Intl) 150 km, Turin 112 km
Train station: Aosta 28 km

Owners: Jeantet-Roullet Family
Annual closing: From beginning of October to mid-December
Currency: Euro (€)
Rates: Menus 40-50 € s.i. Carte 35-60 € s.i.
19 rooms: 149-260 € s.i.
16 suites: 209-350 € s.i.
Breakfast: included
Dogs: allowed (subject to conditions)
Golf : 37 km (9 holes)
Accepted cards: AE, DC, JCB, MC, VS

More info on www.relaischateaux.com/bellevue

Al Sorriso

SINCE 1999

Via Roma 18
I-28018 Soriso
(Piemonte) • Italy

Tel. : (39) 0322 983 228
Fax : (39) 0322 983 328
sorriso@relaischateaux.com

Italy

Once you stay at Al Sorriso, you are certain to have an unforgettable holiday. The calm, peaceful rooms open out onto the green hills surrounding Lake Orta. In the restaurant, the chef proposes true Piedmont cuisine: «les fagots de lapin aux truffes d'Alba» and «le filet de bœuf du Piémont au vin rouge». As for the wine cellar, enjoy the selection of excellent regional wines, such as the sublime Barbaresco.
Skiing, horseback riding. (Other activities P. 629)

Access: From Switzerland, take Simplon motorway exit Arona, then continue 11 km on the trunk road. From France, take Fréjus, Mont-Blanc motorway and Ventimiglia, exit Borgomanero then take trunk road for 11 km.
Airport: Milan-Malpensa (Intl) 30 km
Train station: Borgomanero 8 km

Owners: Valazza Family
Weekly closing: Monday and Tuesday noon
Annual closing: From August 5th to 25th and from January 9th to 25th
Currency: Euro (€)
Rates: Menus 110-130 € s.n.i.
Carte 100-140 € s.n.i.
8 rooms: single 120 € s.n.i. double 200 € s.n.i.
Breakfast: 10 € s.n.i.
Dogs: not allowed
Golf: 15 km (18 holes)
Accepted cards: AE, DC, JCB, VS

Louisa Valazza

More info on www.relaischateaux.com/sorriso

L'Art de Vivre. Dans le cœur de l'Europe, dans le cœur de la Vallée d'Aoste.

Dans le cœur de la Vallée d'Aoste, entouré des sommets les plus élevés des Alpes: le Casino de la Vallée de Saint-Vincent, un des plus grands d'Europe.

Profitez d'une soirée unique avec émotions toutes différentes: aux tables des Salles de Jeu, aux tables de la Brasserie et en vous amusant dans le DiscoSlotClub.

On arrive facilement dans la Vallée d'Aoste et à Saint-Vincent: les aéroports de Aoste (25 km), de Turin (90 km), de Milan (180 km) et de Genève (150 km) ne sont pas loin.

Vallée d'Aoste

Tel. +39 0166 5221 Fax +39 0166 511616 · e-mail: marketing@casinodelavallee.it · internet: www.casinodelavallee.it

Il Sole di Ranco

SINCE 1992

Piazza Venezia 5
I-21020 Ranco-Varese
(Lombardia) • Italy

Tel. : **(39) 0331 97 65 07**
Fax : (39) 0331 97 66 20
soleranco@relaischateaux.com

Italy

Il Sole celebrated its 150th anniversary in the year 2000. Managed, as always, by the Brovelli family, cleverly perpetuating tradition. Andrea will offer you one of the 14 rooms, some of them overlook the lake so that you can fully appreciate your stay in this fragrant, pastoral setting. Then enjoy the delicate flavours of Carluccio's cuisine with many seafood specialities, followed by Davide's delicious desserts.

Excursions on the lake, visits of the botanical gardens, tennis nearby... (Other activities P. 629)

Access: Milan-Laghi motorway or Turin. Alessandria-Gravellona, Sesto Calende exit, towards Angera.
Airports: Milan-Malpensa (Intl) 20 km, Milan-Linate (Intl) 50 km
Helipad: N 45° 48.00 E 008° 34.134
Train station: Sesto Calende 10 km

Owners: Brovelli Family
General Manager: Andrea Brovelli
Weekly closing: Monday and Tuesday from Nov. to March, Monday noon and Tuesday from April to October
Annual closing: From Dec. 1st to February 14th
Currency: Euro (€)
Rates: Menu 70 € s.i. Carte 57-72 € s.i
4 rooms: 181-207 € s.i. **10 suites:** 232-362 € s.i.
Breakfast: 10-15 € s.i.
Dogs: not allowed **Golf:** 10 km
Accepted cards: AE, DC, MC, VS

More info on www.relaischateaux.com/soleranco

Italy

Antica Osteria del Ponte

SINCE 1998

Piazza G. Negri 9
I-20080 Cassinetta di Lugagnano
(Lombardia) • Italy

Tel. : (39) 02 942 00 34
Fax : (39) 02 942 06 10
osteriaponte@relaischateaux.com

Food lovers flock to this select restaurant near Milan to savour Ezio Santin's innovative gourmet cuisine. Sitting on the picturesque veranda or in the elegant white-walled dining-room, resplendent with polished wood, sumptuous carpets and antique furniture, savour the exquisite «tarte de pâtes fraîches à la courge et truffes blanches» and «oie de ferme à la royale», accompanied by the finest Italian vintages.

Certosa di Pavia 22 km, piazza di Vigevano 16 km.

Access: From Milan take the main road to Abbiategrasso, then follow signs for the next 2 km. From Turin exit Aut. Casello di Arluno, then Corbetta, then Cassinetta di Lugagnano.
Airports: Milan Malpensa (Intl) 20 km, Milan Linate (Intl) 25 km
Train station: Abbiategrasso 3 km

Owners: Santin Family
General Manager: Renata Santin
Weekly closing: Rest.: Sunday and Monday
Annual closing: From December 25th to January 12th and in August
Currency: Euro (€)
Rates: Menu 98 € s.i. Carte 80-110 € s.i.
Dogs: not allowed
Accepted cards: AE, DC, MC, VS

Ezio Santin

More info on www.relaischateaux.com/osteriaponte

Ristorante Da Vittorio

SINCE 2002

Viale Papa Giovanni XXIII n°21
I-24121 Bergamo
(Lombardia) • Italy

**Tel. : (39) 035 21 80 60
(39) 035 21 32 66**
Fax : (39) 035 21 08 05
davittorio@relaischateaux.com

Italy

Bergamo, the birthplace of Donizetti, is home to Lombardy's most precious assets: culture in all respects. Da Vittorio, a beautiful property run by the Cerea family, lives up to this heritage. Chef Enrico-Roberto Cerea proposes a flavourful cuisine: «risotto avec coquilles en carpaccio de scampi», «confit de thon avec capponata de légumes et fruits», «canard épicé et purée de fruits secs». Excellent wine list.

Access: Milan-Venice motorway: exit Bergamo, towards city centre. Follow direction «Bonomelli» then «viale Papa Giovanni XXIII» to N° 21.
Airports: Milan Malpensa (Intl) 45 km, Bergamo Orio al Serio 5 km
Train station: Bergamo 0,5 km

Owner/General Manager: Vittorio Cerea
Weekly closing: Wednesday
Annual closing: 3 weeks in August
Currency: Euro (€)
Rates: Menus 93-103 € s.i. Carte 103-114 € s.i.
Dogs: not allowed
Accepted cards: AE, DC, MC, VS

Enrico-Roberto Cerea

More info on www.relaischateaux.com/davittorio

409

L'Albereta et Restaurant Gualtiero Marchesi

Italy — SINCE 1999

Via Vittorio Emanuele n°11
I-25030 Erbusco-Franciacorta
(Lombardia) • Italy

Tel. : (39) 03077 605 50
Rest. : (39) 03077 605 62
Fax : (39) 03077 605 73
albereta@relaischateaux.com

This ancient manor, home of the Moretti family, is located in the Alpine forelands in the heart of the Franciacorta vineyards, famous for their sparkling wines. The estate, transformed into a hotel, is a privileged setting whose every detail ensures you an absolutely charming stay. The restaurant too has been skilfully transformed by Gualtiero Marchesi, a master in combining Italian savour and inventiveness.

Sailing, visits to Bellavista and Contadi Castaldi cellars, trips on the lake. (Other activities P. 629)

Access: Turn left at the toll. At crossroads towards Sarnico. After 3 km turn right. Albereta is on top of Bellavista Hill.
Airports: Milan Malpensa (Intl) 65 km, Verona 60 km, Bergamo 30 km
Helipad: N 045° 36.440' E 009° 58.781'
Train station: Rovato 4 km

Owner: Carmen Moretti de Rosa
General Manager: Rachele Belladelli
Weekly closing: Rest.: Sunday evening, Monday noon (from Februar 16th to March 31st and from November 2nd to December 22nd)
Annual closing: Rest.: from Jan. 6th to Feb. 11th
Currency: Euro (€)
Rates: Menus 103-135 € s.i. **Breakfast:** 22 € s.i.
40 rooms: starting at 210 € t.10% s.i.
15 suites: starting at 510 € t.10% s.i.
Dogs: all. (small dogs) **Golf:** 3 km (18 and 9 holes)
Accepted cards: AE, DC, JCB, MC, VS

More info on www.relaischateaux.com/albereta

Villa Fiordaliso

SINCE 1997

Via Zanardelli 150
I-25083 Gardone Riviera
(Lombardia) • Italy

Tel. : (39) 0365 201 58
Fax : (39) 0365 290 011
fiordaliso@relaischateaux.com

Italy

Nestling amidst cypresses, pine trees and olive trees, near a private beach, Villa Fiordaliso offers idyllic surroundings and absolute calm. Its elegant neo-classical façade looks out across the tranquil waters of Lake Garda, and it was here that the poet Gabriele D'Annunzio used to gaze out through the villa's beautiful stained glass windows. The seasonal Italian cuisine is excellent and the hospitality exquisite.

(Other activities P. 629)

Access: From Milan, A4, Brescia East, exit 45 bis towards Lago di Garda West. From Venice A4, Desenzano, towards Salo.

Airports: Verona (Intl) 45 km, Milan Linate (Intl) 100 km
Train station: Desenzano/Garda 20 km

Owner: Rosa Tosetti
General Manager: Max Tosetti
Weekly closing: Rest.: Monday (all day) and Tuesday noon
Annual closing: From November 20th to February 10th
Currency: Euro (€)
Rates: Menu 85 € s.i. Carte 39-57 € s.i.
6 rooms: 200-400 € s.i.
1 suite: 540 € s.i.
Breakfast: included
Dogs: not allowed
Golf: 3 km
Accepted cards: AE, DC, MC, VS

More info on www.relaischateaux.com/fiordaliso

Italy

Hotel Villa del Quar

SINCE 1996

Via Quar n°12
I-37020 Pedemonte, Verona
(Veneto) • Italy

Tel. : (39) 045 680 06 81
Fax : (39) 045 680 06 04
delquar@relaischateaux.com

This elegant Renaissance villa on the outskirts of Verona has been converted into a luxurious hotel. Encircled by an old stone wall, the villa is set on a vast estate, looking across vineyards, meadows and emerald lawns where a pool sparkles in the sun. Enjoy exquisite calm in the guestrooms, decorated with oak beams and antique furniture and savour exceptional Italian vintages in the ancient cellar. Tea-room. Jogging course. (Other activities P. 629)

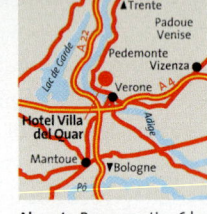

Access: A22 exit Verona north, take the Valpolicella motorway all the way to the end, then take a right towards S. Floriano; Pedemonte.
Airports: Boscomantico 6 km, Catullo 18 km
Helipad: N 45° 29' 48'' E 010° 55' 49''
Train station: Verona 7 km

Owners: Montresor Family
General Manager: M. Evelina Acampora
Weekly closing: Rest.: Monday (from March to April)
Annual closing: From January 1st to March 14th
Currency: Euro (€)
Rates: Menu-carte 44-77 € s.i.
18 rooms: 235-285 € s.i.
4 suites: 290-390 € s.i.
Breakfast: included
Dogs: allowed (ground floor only) **Golf:** 18 km
Accepted cards: AE, DC, MC, VS

More info on www.relaischateaux.com/delquar

Hotel Dominik

SINCE 1981

I-39042 Bressanone/Brixen
(Südtirol) • Italy

Tel. : (39) 0472 83 01 44
Fax : (39) 0472 83 65 54
dominik@relaischateaux.com

Italy

Set in the magnificent countryside of the South Tyrol, in the ancient town of Brixen-Bressanone, this comfortable hotel is the ideal base for exploring the Dolomite Alps. The quiet, spacious guestrooms, decorated with traditional Tyrolian furniture and featuring loggias or private terraces, offer superb panoramic views of the nearby mountains. The traditional cuisine is delicious and the regional wines superb.

The Dolomite Alps, Archeology museum, wine and food excursions, wine tasting. (Other activities P. 629)

Altitude: 560 metres.
Access: Exit: from North Brixen/Bressanone, from South Klausen/Chiusa.

Airports: Innsbruck (Intl) 80 km, Bolzano 40 km
Train station: Bressanone 1,5 km

Owners: Demetz Family
General Manager: Uli Demetz
Weekly closing: Rest.: Tuesday (except August)
Annual closing: March
Currency: Euro (€)
Rates: Menus 40-50 € s.i. Carte 35-55 € s.i.
30 rooms: 165-210 € s.i.
5 suites: 270-340 € s.i.
Breakfast: included
Dogs: allowed (extra cost)
Accepted cards: AE, DC, VS

More info on www.relaischateaux.com/dominik

Rosa Alpina

Italy — SINCE 2000

Str. Micura de Rü
I-39030 S. Cassiano
(Südtirol) • Italy

Tel. : (39) 0471 84 95 00
Fax : (39) 0471 84 93 77
alpina@relaischateaux.com

The Rosa Alpina is an ideal stopping place for those who seek fitness and relaxation. In a typical 1535 m-high Dolomite village, this hotel has planned everything for invigorating holidays. After a wonderful day of skiing, enjoy beauty treatments, cures and relaxation in this temple of well-being, decorated with XVIIth and XIXth centuries style Tyrolean furniture. Excellent regional cuisine and superb wine list.

Climbing, cross-country skiing, heliskiing, snow shoeing. (Other activities P. 629)

Altitude: 1535 m
Access: From Venice, A27 exit Belluno, SS51 towards Cortina, SS48 Passo Falzarego, S. Cassiano. From Verona, A22 exit Bressanone, SS49 Val Pusteria, SS244 Val Badia, S. Cassiano.
Airports: Venice Marco Polo (Intl) 180 km, Bolzano 80 km **Train station:** Brunico 30 km

Owners/General Managers: Pizzinini Family
Weekly closing: Restaurant: Tuesday and Wednesday for lunch
Annual closing: From Easter to mid-June and from October 1st to Dec. 4th
Currency: Euro (€)
Rates: Menus 40-70 € s.i. Carte 35-70 € s.i.
31 rooms: 210-385 € s.i. **20 suites:** 310-480 € s.i.
Breakfast: included
Dogs: allowed (extra cost) **Golf:** 10 km (9 holes)
Accepted cards: MC, VS

More info on www.relaischateaux.com/alpina

Villa Abbazia

SINCE 2002

Plazza IV Novembre, 3
I-31051 Follina
(Veneto) • Italy

Tel. : (39) 0438 97 12 77
Fax : (39) 0438 97 00 01
abbazia@relaischateaux.com

Italy

In the village of Follina, on the Prosecco wine route (a delicious white wine from the region), the Villa Abbazia is a prime example of the XVIIth century palatial-like summer residences of the Venetian aristocracy. It enjoys a romantic, tranquil and intimate setting. The ideal base from which to explore the surrounding countryside, savour Venetian cuisine in the restaurant La Corte and visit Treviso, Asolo and Venice.

(Other activities P. 629)

Access:
From Venice airport take motorway A27, exit Vittorio Veneto north. Turn right. After 2 km, turn again right and continue for 15 km, the hotel is in the centre of Follina.
Airports: Treviso (Intl) 40 km, Venice Marco Polo (Intl) 60 km
Train station: Conegliano 20 km

Owners: Zanon and De Marchi Families
General Manager: Giovanni Zanon
Weekly closing: Restaurant: Sunday
Annual closing: From January 7th to February 9th
Currency: Euro (€)
Rates: Menus 45-60 € s.i. Carte 45-65 € s.i.
12 rooms: 190-220 € s.i.
6 suites: 285-500 € s.i.
Breakfast: included
Dogs: allowed upon request
Golf : 24 km
Accepted cards: AE, DC, MC, VS

More info on www.relaischateaux.com/abbazia

Italy

SINCE 1999

Ristorante Le Calandre

Via Liguria 1
I-35030 Sarmeola di Rubano, Padova
(Veneto) • Italy

Tel. : (39) 049 63 03 03
Fax : (39) 049 63 30 00
calandre@relaischateaux.com

5 minutes from Padua, Raffaele and Massimiliano will ask you to share in their passion. Massimiliano, with his creativity, will introduce you to the culinary traditions of his region such as «l'escalope de tomates et glace au basilic»; «les cannellonis croustillants de ricotta et mozzarella de buffle»; «les spaghettis avec foie de seiches», while Raffaele will invite you to visit the wine cellar with its 600 vintages.

Conference room. (Other activities P. 629)

Access: From Milano, A4 exit Grisignano, take SS 11 towards Padua. From Venice, A4 exit Padua West.

Airport: Venice Marco Polo (Intl) 20 km
Train station: Padua 8 km

Owners: Alajmo Family
General Manager: Raffaele Alajmo
Weekly closing: Sunday and Monday
Annual closing: From January 1st to 20th and from August 3rd to 25th
Currency: Euro (€)
Rates: Menus 89-104 € s.i. Carte 70-128 € s.i.
Dogs: not allowed
Golf: 6 km (27 holes)
Accepted cards: AE, DC, MC, VS

Massimiliano Alajmo

More info on www.relaischateaux.com/calandre

Restaurant dal Pescatore

SINCE 1990

Loc. Runate 17
Canneto S/O - I-46013 Mantova
(Lombardia) • Italy

Tel. : (39) 0376 72 30 01
Fax : (39) 0376 703 04
pescatore@relaischateaux.com

Italy

Between Cremona and Mantova, the picturesque village of Canneto in the reserve of the Oglio Park provides an idyllic setting for this elegant restaurant opened in 1920 by Antonio Santini's grandparents. Today chef Nadia rejuvenates regional cuisine with innovative flair and talent. Savour her «tortelli de chèvre et truffe blanche» or «brochet sauce de Mantova». The cellar is a treasure trove of rare vintages.

Historical XVth century cities of Cremona and Mantova.
(Other activities P. 629)

Access: From Parma, Brescia or Mantova towards Piadena.

Airports: Verona (Intl) 65 km, Milan Malpensa (Intl) 100 km
Train station: Canneto 3 km

Owner: Antonio Santini
Weekly closing: Monday, Tuesday and Wednesday noon
Annual closing: From January 2nd to 26th and from August 6th to Sept. 5th
Currency: Euro (€)
Rates: Menu 120 € s.i. Carte 100-140 € s.i.
Dogs: not allowed
Golf: 40 km
Accepted cards: AE, DC, JCB, MC

Nadia Santini

More info on www.relaischateaux.com/pescatore

Italy

La Meridiana

SINCE 1979

Via Ai Castelli
I-17033 Garlenda
(Liguria) • Italy

Tel. : (39) 0182 58 02 71
Fax : (39) 0182 58 01 50
meridiana@relaischateaux.com

Nestling between Monaco and Portofino, La Meridiana is renowned for its traditional Italian hospitality and its magnificent 18 hole golf course. Gourmets will be enchanted by the «Il Rosmarino» restaurant where the finest seafood, infused with the delicate aroma of garden herbs, is enhanced by exceptional vintages. Enjoy a romantic stroll through the ancient Roman villages or relax on the magnificent beach at Alassio.

Tennis (nearby), biking, ping-pong; roman and medieval villages... (Other activities P. 629)

Access:
A 10 Genova Ventimiglia, exit Albenga, towards Garlenda (9 km).
Airports:
Nice Côte d'Azur (Intl) or Genova Cristoforo Colombo (Intl) 90 km, Villanova 2 km
Helipad: N 44° 02' 41" E 08° 07' 35"
Train station: Albenga 6 km

Owners: Segre Family
General Managers:
Edmondo and Alessandra Segre
Annual closing: From Nov. to the beg. of March
Currency: Euro (€)
Rates: Menus 50-80 € s.i.
Carte 60-90 € s.i.
14 rooms: 220-330 € s.i. **16 suites:** 330-800 € s.i.
Breakfast: 20-24 € s.i.
Dogs: allowed (upon request)
Golf: on the premises (18 holes)
Accepted cards: AE, DC, MC, VS

More info on www.relaischateaux.com/meridiana

Ristorante Ambasciata

SINCE 2000

Via Martiri di Belfiore, 33
I-46026 Quistello-Mantova
(Lombardia) • Italy

**Tel. : (39) 0376 61 91 69
(39) 0376 61 90 03**
Fax : (39) 0376 61 82 55
ambasciata@relaischateaux.com

Italy

In the Lombardy county village of Quistello, only 20 minutes from Mantua, Francesco and Romano Tamani have transformed their home into a stopping place for superb gastronomy. They will delight gourmets with their regional cuisine. Savour the «tagliatelles aux saucisses fraîches» and the sublime «millefeuille de tripes de bœuf à la polenta grillées aux feuilles de laurier». Excellent international vintages.

Access: Modena-Brennero motorway, exit at Mantova south or Pegognaga.

Airport: Verona (Intl) 50 km

Owners: Francesco and Romano Tamani
General Manager: Francesco Tamani
Weekly closing: Sunday evening and Monday
Annual closing: From January 1st to 22th and from August 6th to 29th
Currency: Euro (€)
Rates: Menus 57-88 € s.i. Carte 46-77 € s.i.
Dogs: not allowed
Accepted cards: AE, DC, JCB, MC, VS

Francesco Tamani

More info on www.relaischateaux.com/ambasciata

Italy

Hotel Duchessa Isabella

SINCE 1996

Via Palestro 68/70
I-44100 Ferrara
(Emilia-Romagna) • Italy

Tel. : (39) 0532 20 21 21/20 21 22
Fax : (39) 0532 20 26 38
isabella@relaischateaux.com

Nestling in the heart of Ferrara, the picturesque town built by the dukes of Este, this elegant XVIth century residence is resplendent with coffered ceilings, ancient frescos and a collection of antique clocks. The sumptuous rooms, overlooking the park, are havens of comfort and the cuisine, inspired by the gastronomical traditions of Este, is a sheer delight. The magnificent Ferrara Palio is the oldest in the world.

(Other activities P. 629)

Access: From Bologna or Padua, A13 exit Ferrara-North, straight ahead; Via Palestro and right after Massari Park.

Airports: Bologna (Intl) 50 km, Venice Marco Polo (Intl) 90 km
Train station: Ferrara 1 km

Owner: Evelina Bonzagni
Weekly closing: Restaurant: Sunday and Monday evening
Annual closing: From August 1st to 31st
Currency: Euro (€)
Rates: Menus 67-83 € s.i. Carte 77-88 € s.i.
21 rooms: 234-296 € s.i.
6 suites: 400-828 € s.i.
Breakfast: included
Dogs: allowed (extra cost)
Golf: 1 km
Accepted cards: AE, DC, JCB, MC, VS

More info on www.relaischateaux.com/isabella

Restaurant Enoteca Pinchiorri

SINCE 1984

Via Ghibellina, 87
I-50122 Firenze
(Toscana) • Italy

Tel. : (39) 055 24 27 77
Fax : (39) 055 24 49 83
enoteca@relaischateaux.com

Italy

European gourmets flock to this restaurant set in a magnificent Renaissance palace. Giorgio Pinchiorri himself will help you choose from the 150000 wines in his prestigious cellar, stocked with French, Italian and Californian vintages. In the kitchens, French chef Annie Féolde adds innovative flair to Tuscan cuisine with her «gnocchis parfumés à la Trévise» and her superb «filet d'agneau, aubergines, tomates séchées au soleil».

Uffizi museum, Duomo... (Other activities P. 629)

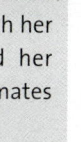

Access: Piazza Santa Croce, Via Verdi, and turn right into Via Ghibellina.

Airports: Firenze Peretola (Intl) 2 km, Pisa Galileo Galilei (Intl) 85 km
Train station: Santa Marta Nuova 2 km

Owners: Giorgio Pinchiorri and Annie Féolde
Weekly closing: Sunday, Monday and Tuesday for lunch
Annual closing: August and Christmas
Currency: Euro (€)
Rates: Gourmet menu served at dinner 145 € s.i. Carte 180 € s.i.
Dogs: allowed
Golf: Grassina 10 km
Accepted cards: AE, JCB, MC, VS

Annie Féolde

More info on www.relaischateaux.com/enoteca

Il Bottaccio di Montignoso

Italy

SINCE 1988

Via Bottaccio 1
I-54038 Montignoso
(Toscana) • Italy

Tel. : **(39) 0585 34 00 31**
Fax : (39) 0585 34 01 03
bottaccio@relaischateaux.com

This beautiful XVIIth century oil mill, nestling in the hills sloping down to the Tyrrhenian Sea, offers a perfect balance between authentic tradition and modern comfort. The guestrooms, resplendent with old oak beams, varnished floors and period furniture, are veritable havens of calm. As for the sunny Mediterranean cuisine, enhanced by fine Italian vintages and grappas, it is a sheer delight. Welcome to la dolce vita!

(Other activities P. 629)

Access:
From the north, A-12, Massa, seafront towards Viareggio, Cinquale, towards Montignoso.

Airport: Pisa Galileo Galilei (Intl) 30 km
Helipad: N 43° 59' 07" E 10° 08' 35"
Train station: Forte di Marmi 5 km

Owner: Stefano d'Anna
General Manager: Sossio Mosca
Open all year
Currency: Euro (€)
Rates: Menus 49-67 € s.i. Carte 49-67 € s.i.
4 rooms: starting at 232 € s.i.
4 suites: 284-620 € s.i.
Breakfast: 13-18 € s.i.
Dogs: allowed
Golf: 3 km
Accepted cards: AE, MC, VS

More info on www.relaischateaux.com/bottaccio

Villa La Massa

SINCE 2000

Via della Massa, 24
I-50012 Candeli, Firenze
(Toscana) • Italy

Tel. : (39) 055 62 611
Fax : (39) 055 63 31 02
lamassa@relaischateaux.com

Italy

With its riverside parkland on the banks of the Arno river, this XVIth century villa is located in the heart of the Tuscany countryside. From its XVIIth century period furniture, refined decoration and inspired Tuscany cuisine to its superb cellar with its excellent regional vintages, it offers all the ingredients for an idyllic stay. For lovers of Italy and its flamboyant Renaissance.

Biking... (Other activities P. 629)

Access: Milan-Florence-Rome motorway, exit Florence south, after 3 km, towards Pontassieve till you reach Candeli. Follow signs.
Airports: Firenze Peretola (Intl) 18 km, Pisa Galileo Galilei (Intl) 50 km
Helipad: N 43° 45' 53" E 11° 20' 18"
Train station: Firenze 8 km

Owner: Villa d'Este SPA
General Manager: Giampaolo Ottazzi
Annual closing: From December to March
Currency: Euro (€)
Rates: Menus 67-93 € s.i. Carte 69 € s.i.
19 rooms: 230-550 € s.i.
18 suites: 550-1100 € s.i.
Breakfast: included
Dogs: allowed
Golf: 11 km
Accepted cards: AE, DC, JCB, MC, VS

More info on www.relaischateaux.com/lamassa

Locanda l'Elisa

Italy — SINCE 1994

Via Nuova per Pisa 1952
I-55050 Lucca
(Toscana) • Italy

Tel. : (39) 0583 37 97 37
Fax : (39) 0583 37 90 19
elisa@relaischateaux.com

This sumptuous mauve and white villa was restored during the Napoleonic era for one of Princess Elisa's civil servants. The soft Tuscan light floods through the windows of its elegant suites, decorated with marble fireplaces, luxurious damask fabrics, canopy beds and beautiful antique furniture. Enjoy a romantic dinner on the «Belle Epoque» veranda overlooking the park and savour one of the exceptional local vintages.

(Other activities P. 629)

Access: From Rome or Bologna, A 1 exit Firenze, A 11 exit Lucca, follow signs to «Locanda l'Elisa».

Airports: Pisa Galileo Galilei (Intl) 18 km, Florence Peretola (Intl) 65 km
Train station: Lucca 4 km

Owner: Alessandro Del Grande
Weekly closing: Restaurant: Sunday
Annual closing: From November 1st to February 12th
Currency: Euro (€)
Rates: Menus 46-59 € s.i.
Carte 49-67 € s.i.
2 rooms: 180-285 € s.i.
8 suites: 285-450 € s.i.
Breakfast: 17 € s.i.
Dogs: allowed (small dogs)
Golf: 20 km
Accepted cards: AE, DC, JCB, MC, VS

More info on www.relaischateaux.com/elisa

Hotel La Collegiata

SINCE 1999

Loc. Strada 27
I-53037 San Gimignano
(Toscana) • Italy

Tel. : **(39) 0577 943 201**
Fax : (39) 0577 940 566
collegiata@relaischateaux.com

Italy

Originally a Franciscan convent built in 1587, this magnificent hotel overlooks the heart of the Chianti wine region and is only a few kilometres away from the medieval city of San Gimignano. The guestrooms are located in the former cloister. You will dine under the Roman vaulting of the ancient chapel richly decorated in the sumptuous red so reminiscent of the Siennese Renaissance. From the uppermost floors, you can discover the 13 towers of San Gimignano.

Horseback riding, whirlpool... (Other activities P. 629)

Access: From Firenze, follow Firenze-Siena motorway, exit Poggibonsi north. Follow signs to San Gimignano. The hotel is 1.5 km from the city's historic centre.
Airport: Pisa Galileo Galilei (Intl) 65 km
Train station: Poggibonsi 12 km

Owner: Société Parco dei Cipressi
General Manager: Silvia Perko
Annual closing: From January 2nd to February 28th
Currency: Euro (€)
Rates: Menus 50-80 € s.i. Carte 60-110 € s.i.
20 rooms: starting at 360 € s.i.
1 suite: starting at 670 € s.i.
Breakfast: 18-25 € s.i.
Dogs: allowed (small only)
Golf: 20 km (18 holes)
Accepted cards: AE, DC, MC, VS

More info on www.relaischateaux.com/collegiata

Italy
SINCE 1978

Hotel Certosa di Maggiano

Strada di Certosa 82
I-53100 Siena
(Toscana) • Italy

Tel. : **(39) 0577 28 81 80**
Fax : (39) 0577 28 81 89
certosa@relaischateaux.com

In the XIVth century, St. Bruno's disciples used to meditate in the cloisters of this beautiful Carthusian monastery. Today, gourmets gather here to savour superb local cuisine and fine wines. The panoramic view from the guestrooms encompasses medieval Siena and its magnificent cathedral, museums and fountains. Visit the site of the Palio, the Chianti vineyards and castles and explore Volterra, Pienza and San Quirico.

Biking, thermal baths, visit of cellars and gardens, winetasting, cooking classes, outings on the Argentario sailing boat. (Other activities P. 629)

Access: From Florence, Siena South, towards «Porta Romana»; right in front of the Porta, 200 m.

Airports: Firenze Peretola (Intl) 50 km,
Pisa Galileo Galilei (Intl) 120 km
Helipad: N 43° 18′ 56″ E 011° 21′ 01″
Train station: Siena 3 km

Owner: I.T.A.R. S.P.A.
General Managers:
Anna Recordati, Anna Claudia Grossi
Open all year
Currency: Euro (€)
Rates: Menus 67-83 € s.i. Carte 62-83 € s.i.
6 rooms: starting at 380 € s.i.
11 suites: starting at 620 € s.i.
Breakfast: 31 € s.i.
Dogs: not allowed **Golf:** 7 km
Accepted cards: AE, MC, VS

Hotel Relais Borgo San Felice

SINCE 1992

San Felice
I-53019 Castelnuovo Berardenga (Siena)
(Toscana) • Italy

Tel. : (39) 0577 39 64
Fax : (39) 0577 35 90 89
borgofelice@relaischateaux.com

Italy

This charming inn is set in the medieval village of San Felice, nestled in the hills of the Chianti Classico, in the heart of the magnificent Tuscan countryside. The inn's elegant stone façade looks out across a labyrinth of winding alleyways and shaded piazzas, and its beautifully decorated rooms are havens of comfort and charm. The superb regional cuisine will complete your experience of authentic Italian dolce vita.

Visit of the wine cellars of our S. Felice agricultural property. (Other activities P. 629)

Access: From Firenze, expressway towards Siena North, and towards Arezzo-Monteaperti San Felice.

Airport: Firenze Peretola (Intl) 90 km
Train station: Siena 16 km

Owner: RAS S.p.A
General Manager: Birgit Fleig
Annual closing: From Nov. 1st to March 31st except for seminar facilities
Currency: Euro (€)
Rates: Menus 55-75 € s.i. Carte 65-95 € s.i.
29 rooms: 336 € s.i.
14 suites: 570 € s.i.
Breakfast: included
Dogs: not allowed
Golf: 55 km
Accepted cards: AE, DC, MC, VS

More info on www.relaischateaux.com/borgofelice

Italy

SINCE 1998

Relais Il Falconiere

Localita S. Martino 370
I-52044 Cortona (Arezzo)
(Toscana) • Italy

Tel. : (39) 0575 612 679
Fax : (39) 0575 612 927
falconiere@relaischateaux.com

Set between Tuscany and Umbria, this elegant residence, built in 1600, was home to poet Antonio Guadagnoli in the XIXth century. Today, Il Falconiere, which retains all the splendour of its historical past, has been magnificently restored. 13 guestrooms and 6 suites, resplendent with beautiful antique furniture, offer exquisite comfort. Savour regional cuisine while enjoying superb views of the idyllic Tuscan countryside.

Cooking classes (November-March), wine-tasting, exhibition of antique dealers. (Other activities P. 629)

Access: A1, exit «Valdichiana» towards Perugia, exit 2, Cortona. Arrival Camucia, towards Arezzo (SS71). Go 2 km and turn right at first crossroad.
Airports: Perugia Sant Egidio (Intl) 45 km, Florence Peretola (Intl) 100 km
Helipad: N 43° 17' 47" E 011° 58' 16"
Train station: Camucia Cortona 2 km

Owners: Baracchi Family
Weekly closing:
Rest.: Monday from Nov. to March
Open all year
Currency: Euro (€)
Rates: Menus 52-62 € s.i. Carte 52-77 € s.i.
13 rooms: 238-300 € s.i.
6 suites: 398-542 € s.i.
Breakfast: buffet included
Dogs: allowed (small) extra cost **Golf:** 25 km
Accepted cards: AE, DC, MC, VS

More info on www.relaischateaux.com/falconiere

Gallia Palace Hotel

SINCE 1973

Via delle Sughere
I-58040 Punta Ala, Grosseto
(Toscana) • Italy

Tel. : **(39) 0564 92 20 22**
Fax : (39) 0564 92 02 29
gallia@relaischateaux.com

Italy

Clear blue skies, fine sand beaches and the turquoise waters of Punta Ala Bay... Experience the dolce vita at the Gallia Palace pool or in the shade of the century-old pine trees on the private beach. After a massage or steam bath at the beauty centre, savour seafood specialities and Tuscan wines. Explore medieval villages and Etruscan ruins and enjoy Grosseto's summer festivities such as the famous Rodeo of the Rose.

Beauty centre, Turkish bath, candlelit dinners in the garden (Saturdays)... (Other activities P. 629)

Access: Rome, A16 Civitavecchia, Aurelia SS1 Grosseto, towards Castiglione della Pescaia.

Airports: Pisa Galileo Galilei (Intl) 110 km, Rome Fiumicino (Intl) 220 km
Train station: Follonica 20 km

Owners: Gallia Family
General Manager: Luciano Bonfanti
Annual closing: From October 1st to April 18th
Currency: Euro (€)
Rates: Menus 50-60 € s.i. Carte 45-75 € s.i.
75 rooms: 240-400 € s.i.
8 suites: 460-610 € s.i.
Breakfast: buffet included
Dogs: allowed (extra cost) only in rooms
Golf: Club Punta Ala 2 km, Club Toscana 28 km
Accepted cards: AE, DC, JCB, MC, VS

More info on www.relaischateaux.com/gallia

CASTELLO DI RESCHIO - UMBRIA / TUSCANY BORDERS

"More than a house, it is a continuous service that you buy" - *Egon Ronay, London*

Castello di Reschio is a unique 2,000-acre estate dating back to medieval times and preserving some 30 ancient farmhouses scattered across protected land. Purchasers enjoy custom-renovated homes designed with Italian gardens and interiors to highest standards. The state-of-the-art maintenance, security and full concierge services, the sports and leisure facilities combined with a professional purchase process contribute to Reschio's eight years of proven success. In the cultural heart of central Italy Count Antonio Bolza and his family have created and continue to provide the perfect hideaway for the most exclusive international clientele. Turn-key projects including freehold acquisition of a farmhouse with some three acres of land, complete renovation and landscaped garden with pool start from Euro 2,4 million.

Contact: Count Benedikt Bolza CdR s.r.l.
TEL.: +39-075-844 362 FAX: +39-075-844 363
info@castellodireschio.com / www.castellodireschio.com

Hotel Cala del Porto

SINCE 2003

Via del Pozzo
I-58040 Punta Ala
(Toscana) • Italy

Tel. : (39) 0564 922 455
Fax : (39) 0564 920 716
delporto@relaischateaux.com

Italy

Built on a slope covered with pine trees which gently winds its way down towards the sea, the hotel Cala del Porto enjoys an enchanting location, overlooking a beautiful bay, white sandy beaches and a marina. This setting cannot fail to enthral upscale guests for whom the property provides the very best services (shuttle to the private beach and golf course) and an elegant interior. The décor is both contemporary and warm.

(Other activities P. 629)

Access: From Pisa, motorway A12 to Rosignano. Take SS1 Aurelia towads Rome. Exit Follonica north. Follow signs to Punta Ala.

Airports: Pisa Galileo Galilei (Intl) 110 km, Rome Fiumicino (Intl) 220 km
Train station: Follonica 15 km

Owner: Roberto Polito
General Manager: Giovanni Di Carmine
Annual closing: From end of September to Easter
Currency: Euro (€)
Rates: Menus 40-50 € s.i. Carte 45-70 € s.i.
34 rooms: 240-505 € s.i.
6 suites: 380-590 € s.i.
Breakfast: included
Dogs: not allowed
Golf: 2 km
Accepted cards: AE, DC, JCB, MC, VS

More info on www.relaischateaux.com/delporto

Italy

Il Pellicano

SINCE 1982

Cala dei Santi
I-58018 Porto Ercole, Grosseto
(Toscana) • Italy

Tel. : (39) 0564 85 81 11
Fax : (39) 0564 83 34 18
pellicano@relaischateaux.com

This elegant villa, set on the picturesque Argentario peninsula overlooking the Tyrrhenian Sea, is built on several levels. Wander down through flower-bedecked patios to the private beach and the pool by the sea or relax in a spacious room, secluded beneath the cypresses and pine trees. Dine al fresco at the barbecue buffet while contemplating the sunset or enjoy a romantic candlelit dinner at the panoramic restaurant.

Shop, water sports, cooking classes (March, April, October). (Other activities P. 629)

Access: From Rome, A 12 towards Civitavecchia, exit Orbetello towards Porto Ercole.

Airport: Rome Fiumicino (Intl) 150 km
Train station: Orbetello 15 km

Owner: Roberto Sciò
General Manager: Cinzia Fanciulli
Annual closing: From January 1st to the end of March and from end of October to December 31st
Currency: Euro (€)
Rates: Menu 74-93 € s.i. Carte 55-81 € s.i.
31 rooms: 300-647 € s.i.
19 suites: 466-1417 € s.i.
Breakfast: included
Dogs: not allowed
Golf: 50 km
Accepted cards: AE, MC, VS

More info on www.relaischateaux.com/pellicano

Borgo Paraelios

SINCE 1993

I-02040 Poggio Catino, Rieti
(Lazio) • Italy

Tel. : (39) 0765 26 267
Fax : (39) 0765 26 268
borgo@relaischateaux.com

Italy

This magnificent XIXth century villa, surrounded by a beautiful park, is an idyllic haven of calm in which the architect has lovingly preserved the period furniture and marvellous vaulted ceilings of bygone days. The villa's elegant rooms are hung with masterpieces by Canaletto and Attardi and its restaurant pays tribute to the finest Italian gastronomy. The Borgo offers a special minibus service to Rome.

Water colour painting courses, ceramics courses, wine tasting, visits to roman museums, skiing. (Other activities P. 629)

Access: From Rome, A 1 Roma-Firenze, exit Ponzano Romano-Soratte. Follow Poggio Mirteto for approx. 11 km.

Airports: Rome Fiumicino (Intl) 70 km, Urbe 30 km
Train station: Poggio Mirteto Scalo 3 km

Owners: Salabé Family
General Manager: Lorenzo Righi
Open all year
Currency: Euro (€)
Rates: Menus 57-72 € s.i.
13 rooms: 200-270 € s.i.
2 suites: 340 € s.i.
Breakfast: included
Dogs: allowed (small dogs only), extra cost
Golf: on the premises (9 holes)
Accepted cards: AE, DC, JCB, MC, VS

More info on www.relaischateaux.com/borgo

Italy

SINCE 2001

Parkhotel Villa Grazioli

Via Umberto Pavoni 19
I-00046 Grottaferrata, Roma
(Lazio) • Italy

Tel. : (39) 06 945 40 01
Fax : (39) 06 941 35 06
grazioli@relaischateaux.com

After ten years of restoration work, one of the finest patrician villas on the outskirts of Rome has regained its history and beauty, reflected in a vast series of XVIIIth century frescoes, painted decors and trompe-l'œil. The star attraction is the Pannini Gallery: an exceptional feature. A holiday hotel again, the Villa Grazioli offers its guests a haven of peace in its gardens and simplicity of decoration in the rooms.

Mountain-biking, flying club, hiking... (Other activities P. 629)

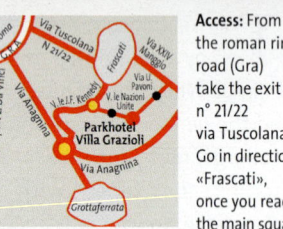

Access: From the roman ring road (Gra) take the exit n° 21/22 via Tuscolana. Go in direction «Frascati», once you reach the main square of Frascati follow the road indications «Villa Grazioli».
Airports: Rome Ciampino (Intl) 10 km, Rome Fiumicino (Intl) 45 km
Train station: Frascati 1,5 km

Owners: Ceribelli Family
General Manager: Rolf Rampf
Open all year
Currency: Euro (€)
Rates: Menus 30-45 € s.i. Carte 45-55 € s.i.
56 rooms: 240-266 € s.i.
2 suites: 380-450 € s.i.
Breakfast: included
Dogs: allowed
Golf: 10 km
Accepted cards: AE, DC, JCB, MC, VS

434   More info on www.relaischateaux.com/grazioli

La Posta Vecchia

SINCE 1992

Palo Laziale
I-00055 Ladispoli, Roma
(Lazio) • Italy

Tel. : **(39) 06 994 95 01**
Fax : (39) 06 994 95 07
posta@relaischateaux.com

Italy

This elegant residence, overlooking the Tyrrhenian Sea, was once the home of Paul Getty, who transformed La Posta Vecchia into a temple of art. Many of the guestrooms, lavishly decorated with Carrara marble bathtubs, Venetian lamps and Gobelins tapestries, are luxuriously comfortable. Laze on the terrace, savour traditional Italian cuisine or visit the sights of Rome (just 35 minutes away). La dolce vita is guaranteed.

Massage, cooking classes in October and November. (Other activities P. 629)

Access: Aurelia-SS 1 at 37 km take exit Ladispoli. First overpass turn left, then straight.

Airport: Rome Fiumicino (Intl) 20 km
Train station: Ladispoli 2 km

Owner: Roberto Sció
General Manager: Franco Ottaviani
Annual closing: From November to March
Currency: Euro (€)
Rates: Menu 72 € s.n.i.
Carte 46-77 € s.n.i.
12 rooms: 346-542 € t.n.i., s.n.i.
7 suites: 868-1317 € t.n.i., s.n.i.
Breakfast: included
Dogs: not allowed
Golf: 20 km
Accepted cards: AE, DC, MC, VS

More info on www.relaischateaux.com/posta

435

Learn to Cook Like a Chef!

The secrets of foie gras...a perfect beurre blanc... the only way to hold a chef's knife... Stir, chop, mix, taste... live your culinary dream.

Our unique program allows the passionate amateur cook to go behind the scenes as a kitchen intern in nearly 100 Relais Gourmands restaurants worldwide. Put on your chef's coat and step into the kitchen, where you will work side-by-side with the chef and kitchen team as you learn the secrets of the masters. Your dinner parties will never be the same.

For more information, please visit us at www.ecoledeschefs.com or call toll-free (North America) 877-334-6464.

L'Ecole des Chefs

11 East 44th Street, Suite 707 New York, NY 10017
212-856-0115 Tel • 212-856-0193 Fax • info@ecoledeschefs.com

33, boulevard Malesherbes 75008 Paris
Tel. (33) (0)1 45 72 90 00 • Fax (33) (0)1 40 06 04 35 • contact@ecoledeschefs.com
www.ecoledeschefs.com

Don Alfonso 1890

SINCE 1993

Corso S. Agata 11
I-80064 S. Agata Sui Due Golfi
(Campania) • Italy

Tel. : (39) 081 878 00 26
Fax : (39) 081 533 02 26
donalfonso@relaischateaux.com

Italy

A panoramic road on the Gulf of Naples and Salerno leads to the restaurant Don Alfonso where family tradition is at the service of a brilliant cuisine, centred around vegetables and oil which are produced on the premises: «espadon aux pois chiches et au thym», «rougets au romarin et au concombre», «pâtes aux clovisses et courgettes». Everything deserves mention. Built into rock, the cellar has a remarkable selection of the world's wines.

Pompei theatre festival (July-September). Chamber music in Sorrento.

Access: From Naples A 3, exit Castellammare di Stabia towards Sorrento, Positano.

Airport: Naples (Intl) 60 km
Train station: Sorrento 8 km

Owners: Iaccarino Family
Weekly closing: Monday and Tuesday (except Tuesday evening from June 1st to September 30th)
Annual closing: From Jan. 10th to March 6th
Currency: Euro (€)
Rates: Menus 83-110 € s.i. Carte 84-110 € s.i.
Dogs: not allowed
Accepted cards: AE, DC, MC, VS

Alfonso Iaccarino

More info on www.relaischateaux.com/donalfonso

Italy

SINCE 1988

Hotel San Pietro

Via Laurito 2, Campania
I-84017 Positano
(Campania) • Italy

Tel. : (39) 089 87 54 55
Fax : (39) 089 81 14 49
sanpietro@relaischateaux.com

Overlooking the stunning Amalfi coastline, the San Pietro's decor is designed to blend in with its idyllic natural surroundings. The terraced gardens cascading down the rocks to the private beach are resplendent with Neapolitan ceramics and luxuriant foliage which spills through the windows of the elegant rooms. The cuisine, a tribute to the flavours of the South, is enhanced by excellent French and Italian vintages.

Private beach, whirlpools, fishing... (Other activities P. 629)

Access: From Naples A3 exit Castellammare di Stabia towards Sorrento, Positano.

Airport: Naples (Intl) 60 km
Helipad: N 40° 37' 25" E 14° 30' 00"

Owner: Virginia Attanasio
Annual closing: From November 18th to April 1st
Currency: Euro (€)
Rates: Carte 46-62 € s.i.
45 rooms: 400-470 € s.i.
15 suites: 580-900 € s.i.
Breakfast: included
Dogs: allowed (only in the hotel)
Accepted cards: AE, DC, MC, VS

More info on www.relaischateaux/sanpietro

Il Melograno

SINCE 1993

Contrada Torricella 345
I-70043 Monopoli-Bari
(Puglia) • Italy

Tel. : (39) 080 690 90 30
Fax : (39) 080 74 79 08
melograno@relaischateaux.com

Italy

This beautiful XVIth century estate, set in the heart of the breathtaking Puglia countryside near the Adriatic beaches, has been restored by antique collector Camillo Guerra. The elegant rooms, decorated with Persian rugs and period furniture, offer vistas of olive groves, orchards and pomegranate trees. Relax on the private beach, located in an ancient Roman fishpond, then savour regional cuisine and fine wines.
Private beach (15-06/15-09) nearby. (Other activities P. 629)

Access: From Bari, SS16; towards Monopoli then Alberobello, towards Rizzitello-Tormento, Melograno.

Airports: Bari (Intl) 60 km, Naples (Intl) 300 km
Helipad: N 40° 55' E 17° 16'
Train station: Monopoli 3 km

Owners: Guerra Family
General Manager: Camillo Guerra
Annual closing: From January to March (except seminars)
Currency: Euro (€)
Rates: Menus 35-45 € s.i. Carte 40-55 € s.i.
30 rooms: starting at 190 € s.i.
7 suites: starting at 560 € s.i.
Breakfast: included
Dogs: allowed, upon request
Golf: 30 km
Accepted cards: AE, DC, MC, VS

More info on www.relaischateaux.com/melograno

Malta

Property	Nearest major city	Relais & Châteaux	Relais Gourmands	Page
Xara Palace (The)	Rabat	⚜		441

Equivalent in euros for information only (rate of 1/06/02). Application of the exchange rate valid on the day of transaction.

The Xara Palace

SINCE 2001

Mdina-RBT 12
Malta

Tel. : (356) 21 450 560
Fax : (356) 21 452 612
xara@relaischateaux.com

Malta

One of Malta's most romantic and secret places, set in the fortified city of Mdina, the island's capital until 1598. Far from the hustle and bustle, The Xara Palace is a refined oasis of peace, totally in keeping with its XVIIth century architecture. Tasteful decoration and a splendid view from the roof terrace where lunch and dinner are served. The seclusion of this historic place ensures your privacy is preserved.

Cultural tours of all major sites accompanied by personalized professional guide in a private limousine. Visits to the neighbouring island of Gozo also arranged. Fishing, hiking... (Other activities P.629)

Access: Coming through front gate of Mdina, take first left, second right to cathedral, right to St-Paul's Street. Straight to Misrah Il-Kunsill.

Airport: Luqa (Intl) 8 km

Owners: Zammit-Tabona Family
General Manager: Justin Zammit-Tabona
Open all year
Currency: Maltese pound (MTL)
Rates: Menus 12-28 MTL s.n.i. - 30-70 €
Carte 15-22 MTL s.n.i. - 37-55 €
17 suites: 115-250 MTL s.n.i. - 287-623 €
Breakfast: 8 MTL s.n.i. - 20 €
Dogs: not allowed
Golf: 8 km
Accepted cards: AE, DC, JCB, MC, VS

More info on www.relaischateaux.com/xara

Portugal
Spain

Properties Portugal	Nearest major city	Relais & Châteaux	Relais Gourmands	Page
Casa Velha do Palheiro	Funchal	⚜		444
Estalagem Casa Melo Alvim	Oporto	⚜		445
Fortaleza do Guincho	Cascais	⚜		448
Quinta Das Lagrimas (Hotel)	Coimbra	⚜		447

Spain				
Akelaŕe (Restaurant)	San Sebastián		◉	454
Arzak (Restaurante)	San Sebastián		◉	456
Berasategui (M.) - Restaurante	San Sebastián		◉	455
Cala Sant Vicenç (Hotel)	Pollença	⚜		475
Can Fabes	Barcelona		◉	463
Casa de Carmona	Sevilla	⚜		449
El Castell de Ciutat	Andorra	⚜		458
El Cenador de Salvador	Madrid	⚜		451
«El Montiboli» (Hotel)	Villajoyosa	⚜		469
Girasol	Alicante		◉	466
Gran Hotel Son Net	Palma	⚜		474
Hacienda Na Xamena (Hotel)	Ibiza	⚜		471
Mas de Torrent	Gerona	⚜		460
Neichel (Restaurant)	Barcelona		◉	464
Orfila (Hotel)	Madrid	⚜		450
Peregrino (Hotel el)	Puente la Reina	⚜		457
Posada de la Casa del Abad	Valladolid	⚜		452
Read's	Santa Maria	⚜		473
Rodat (El)	Jávea	⚜		467
San Román de Escalante (Hotel)	Santander	⚜		453
Sant Pau (Restaurant)	Barcelona		◉	462
Santa Marta (Hotel)	Gerona	⚜		461
Torre del Remei	Andorra	⚜		459
Torre del Visco (La)	Tortosa	⚜		465

More info on www.relaischateaux.com

Casa Velha do Palheiro

Palheiro Golf, São Gonçalo
P-9050-296 Funchal
(Ilha da Madeira) • Portugal

Tel. : (351) (291) 794 901
Fax : (351) (291) 794 925
casavelha@relaischateaux.com

Portugal — SINCE 2001

A former hunting lodge consisting of three houses, built around 1800, the Casa Velha enjoys a quiet location on an island devoted to tourism. A few kilometres north of Funchal, between the golf course of Palheiro (preferential access to guests) and the gardens of the same name offering superb views, the fine residence displays classicism, elegance and discretion amidst the surrounding legendary luxuriance of Madeira.

Gardens, badminton, croquet, billards, deep-sea fishing. (Other activities P. 629)

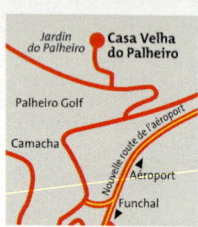

Access: From the airport, towards Funchal. After about fifteen minutes, follow sign Funchal/ Camacha/ Portela. Leave motorway and turn right. Follow sign Golf de Palheiro.
Airport: Funchal (Intl) 16 km

Owners: Blandy Family
General Manager: James T. Scott
Open all year
Currency: Euro (€)
Rates: Menus 38-70 € s.i. Carte 44-60 € s.i.
32 rooms: 144-299 € s.i.
5 suites: 294-358 € s.i.
Breakfast: included
Dogs: allowed (extra cost)
Golf: on the premises
Accepted cards: AE, DC, MC, VS

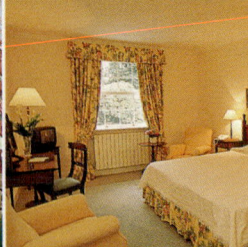

More info on www.relaischateaux.com/casavelha

Estalagem Casa Melo Alvim

SINCE 2001

Av. Conde da Carreira, 28
P-4900-343 Viana do Castelo
(Minho) • Portugal

Tel. : **(351) (258) 808 200**
Fax : (351) (258) 808 220
alvim@relaischateaux.com

Portugal

The Casa Melo Alvim is the oldest house in the heart of the historical Viana do Castelo and was named after the original owner's son-in-law who extended the building, doubling its size. The various architectural and furnishing styles contribute to the charm of this stately residence with its oriental crenellation, Baroque staircase and beds of different Portuguese styles. The holiday resort itself is particularly interesting.

Hiking, karting, marina (nearby). (Other activities P. 629)

Access: From Porto or Vigo (Spain), take IC1 dir. Viana do Castelo center (close to town hall). Alternatively take A3 and exit also to same direction.

Airport: Porto (Intl) 70 km
Train station: Viana do Castelo 50 m

Owners: Laranjeira Family
General Manager: José Laranjeira
Open all year
Currency: Euro (€)
Rates: Menus 27-35 € s.i.
Carte 27-35 € s.i.
16 rooms: 130-160 € s.i.
4 suites: 160-220 € s.i.
Breakfast: 6-7 € s.i.
Dogs: not allowed
Golf: 22 km
Accepted cards: AE, DC, MC, VS

More info on www.relaischateaux.com/alvim

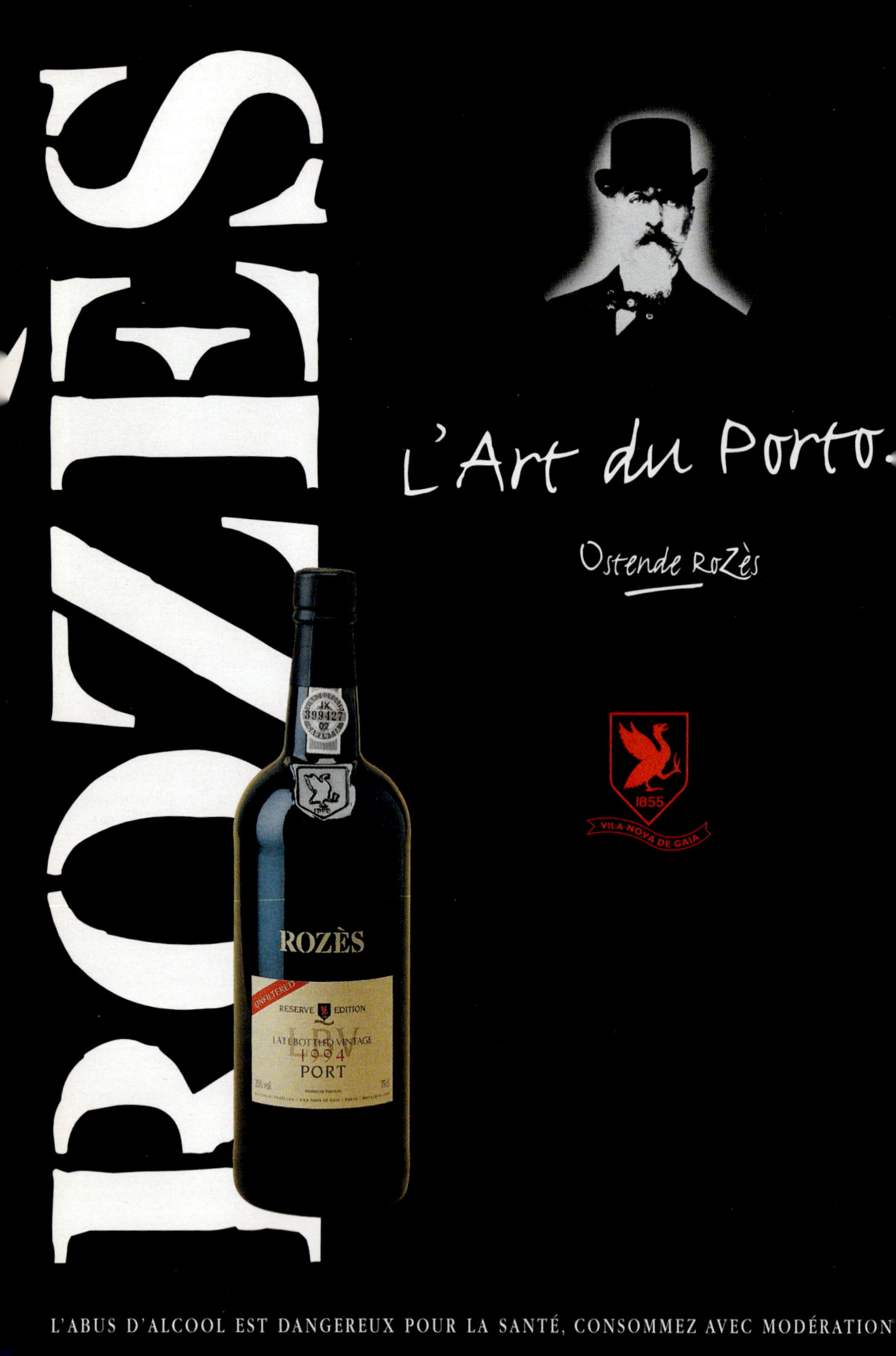

L'Art du Porto.

Ostende RoZès

L'ABUS D'ALCOOL EST DANGEREUX POUR LA SANTÉ, CONSOMMEZ AVEC MODÉRATION

SINCE 1999

Hotel Quinta das Lagrimas

Santa Clara - Apartado 5053
P-3041-901 Coimbra
(Beira Litoral) • Portugal

Tel. : (351) (239) 802 380
Fax : (351) (239) 441 695
lagrimas@relaischateaux.com

Portugal

This XVIII{th} century palace surrounded by magnificent gardens still vibrates with the memory of the famous romance between Prince Pedro and Inès de Castro. Today, this property has been transformed into a superb hotel, beautifully decorated in the traditional colours of Portugal. Enjoy the charm of its elegant guestrooms with inlaid furniture and savour the innovative cuisine prepared with the finest local produce.

Water-skiing, drive in 4x4. (Other activities P. 629)

Access: Take exit Lousa-Condeixa or A1, towards Coimbra. Continue 12 km, turn left.

Airports: Porto (Intl) 100 km, Lisbon (Intl) 180 km
Helipad: N 40° 11' 59.4'' W 008° 25' 57.3''
Train station: Coimbra 1 km

Owner: Jose-Miguel Alarcão Júdice
General Manager: Mário Stromp de Morais
Open all year
Currency: Euro (€)
Rates: Menu 42 € s.i. Carte 35-50 € s.i.
35 rooms: 133-189 € s.i.
4 suites: 300-375 € s.i.
Breakfast: included
Dogs: allowed (except in restaurant and rooms)
Golf : Driving-range, pitch and putt
Accepted cards: AE, DC, JCB, MC, VS

More info on www.relaischateaux.com/lagrimas

Fortaleza do Guincho

Portugal — SINCE 2000

Estrada do Guincho
P-2750-642 Cascais
Portugal

Tel. : (351) (21) 487 0491
Fax : (351) (21) 487 0431
guincho@relaischateaux.com

Perched on a hilltop overlooking the ocean, this entirely renovated XVIIth century fortress will astound and enchant you with its myriad charms. You will appreciate the winter garden in an ancient cloister and the rooms with their balconies that open onto a breathtaking view. The cuisine draws its inspiration from regional French and Portuguese culinary tradition. A privileged site in a main tourist region.

Sailing, tennis. (Other activities P. 629)

Access: A5 to Cascais. Take EN91, at first roundabout follow signs to Birre. At second roundabout, follow signs to Torre until you reach the sea. On the right, continue for 6 km till you reach the fortress on the left.
Airport: Lisbon (Intl) 30 km
Helipad: N 38° 43' 54" W 009° 21' 55"
Train station: Cascais 10 km

Owner: Guinchotel Ltd
General Manager: Gabriel Lousada
Open all year
Currency: Euro (€)
Rates: Menus 38-53 € s.i. Carte 45-75 € s.i.
26 rooms: 165-330 € s.i.
3 suites: 295-385 € s.i.
Breakfast: included
Dogs: allowed
Golf: 5 km
Accepted cards: AE, DC, JCB, MC, VS

More info on www.relaischateaux.com/guincho

Casa de Carmona

SINCE 2003

Plaza de Lasso, 1
E-41410 Carmona
(Sevilla) • Spain

Tel. : (34) 95 41 91 000
Fax : (34) 95 41 90 189
carmona@relaischateaux.com

Spain

20 minutes from Seville on the way to Cordoba, a Renaissance palace transformed into a hotel that has retained the uniqueness and opulence of its roots: luxurious patios with fountains, distinguished rooms with period furniture and objets d'art, exquisite décor. An elegant restaurant with amiable service. An ideal setting to sample the life of a Spanish aristocrat in Carmona, which is full of palaces, monasteries and churches.

(Other activities P. 629)

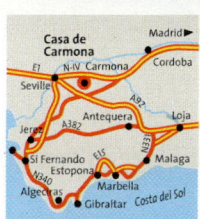

Access: From Sevilla, take motorway N-IV towards Cordoba / Madrid. Exit Carmona, towards city centre. Follow signs «Centro Historico» and «Casa de Carmona».
Airport: Sevilla San Pablo (Intl) 25 km
Train station: Santa Justa 30 km

Owner/General Manager: Felipe Guardiola
Open all year
Currency: Euro (€)
Rates: Menus 17-29 € t.7% s.i.
Carte 17-36 € t.7% s.i.
31 rooms: 135-310 € s.i.
1 suite: 600-900 € s.i.
Breakfast: included
Dogs: allowed
Golf: 35 km
Accepted cards: AE, DC, MC, VS

More info on www.relaischateaux.com/carmona

Spain

Hotel Orfila

SINCE 2001

c/Orfila N°6
E-28010 Madrid
Spain

Tel. : (34) 91 702 77 70
Fax : (34) 91 702 77 72
orfila@relaischateaux.com

This impressive house built in 1886 in a residential area of Madrid, close to the centre, has not only preserved its elegant, classic façade but also its very essence. Space has been gained without affecting the privacy and undeniable comfort of a high-class establishment. The decoration is light and harmonious with period furniture, wallpaper and soft furnishings, polychrome marble floors and clever trompe-l'oeil.

Hunting, skiing. (Other activities P. 629)

Access: Centrally located in the cultural and business centre of Madrid. Five minutes from the Prado museum and Thyssen Bornemisza museum.
Airport: Madrid Barajas (Intl) 20 km
Train station: Atocha 2 km

Owner: Gabriel García
General Manager: Elena Bravo
Open all year
Currency: Euro (€)
Rates: Menus 24-30 € t.7% s.i.
Carte 36-60 € t.7% s.i.
28 rooms: 283-348 € t.7% s.i.
4 suites: 390-700 € t.7% s.i.
Breakfast: 13-21 € t.7% s.i.
Dogs: not allowed
Golf: 5 km
Accepted cards: AE, DC, JCB, MC, VS

More info on www.relaischateaux.com/orfila

El Cenador de Salvador

SINCE 2002

Avda de España, n°30
E-28411 Moralzarzal
Madrid • Spain

Tel. : (34) 91 857 77 22
Fax : (34) 91 857 77 80
elcenador@relaischateaux.com

Spain

To the north-east of Madrid at the foot of the Guadarrama mountains, the village of Moralzarzal shelters a beautiful family residence which has enhanced this location since it opened in 1985. The chef and his wife Toñi set out and succeeded in creating an atmosphere where guests feel at home. A warm welcome and romantic atmosphere in the restaurant and in the chalet with its highly comfortable rooms.
(Other activities P. 629)

Altitude: 1200 metres.
Access: A6 exit 36. At first roundabout, turn right, continue to village of Moralzarzal.

Airport: Madrid (Intl) 45 km
Train station: Cercanias 6 km

Owners: Salvador Gallego and Toñi Antolínez
General Manager: Margarita Gallego
Weekly closing: Sunday, Monday
Open all year
Currency: Euro (€)
Rates: Menus 46-69 € t.7% s.n.i.
7 suites: 150-301 € t.7% s.n.i.
Breakfast: 15 € t.7% s.n.i.
Dogs: not allowed
Golf: 20 km
Accepted cards: AE, DC, MC, VS

More info on www.relaischateaux.com/elcenador

Spain

Posada de la Casa del Abad

SINCE 2000

Plaza Francisco Martín Gromaz, 12
E-34191 Ampudia-Palencia
(Castilla y León) • Spain

Tel. : (34) 979 768 008
Fax : (34) 979 768 300
abad@relaischateaux.com

At the heart of historic Ampudia in the vast Castilla y León region, the Posada brings a touch of colour and beauty to a serene and calm atmosphere. Built in the XVIIth century, this former seigniorial residence was lovingly transformed into the luxurious hotel it is today. The inventive regional cuisine gives pride of place to freshly-grown vegetables, game, milk-fed lamb served with superb Ribero del Duero wines.

(Other activities P. 629)

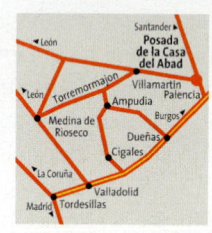

Access: From Madrid: motorway N-VI towards La Coruña and Tordesillas, then N-620 to Valladolid. After Valladolid, towards Palencia-Burgos to Dueñas. Then take P-903 to Ampudia.
Airport: Madrid Barajas (Intl) 220 km
Train station: Valladolid 30 km

Owners: Garcia Puertas Family
General Manager: Jorge Garcia Puertas
Open all year
Currency: Euro (€)
Rates: Menu 37 € s.i. Carte 40 € s.i.
13 rooms: Off-season 107 € s.i. season 123 € s.i.
4 suites: Off-season 150 € s.i. season 171 € s.i.
Breakfast: 11 € s.i.
Dogs: allowed
Golf: 30 km
Accepted cards: AE, MC, VS

More info on www.relaischateaux.com/abad

Hotel San Román de Escalante

SINCE 1996

Carretera Escalante, Castillo km 2
E-39795 Escalante
(Cantabria) • Spain

Tel. : (34) 942 67 77 28
Fax : (34) 942 67 76 43
escalante@relaischateaux.com

Spain

San Román de Escalante, a historic site, has everything to please: a beautiful setting, hospitality – all imbued with the desire to anticipate our guests' every wish. We know how to make them happy by truly understanding them. We know what makes life agreeable: tranquillity and an oasis to delight and reawaken long forgotten yearnings – all with the delicious flavours of our cuisine and our excellent wine cellar.

Hunting, skiing, flying club, water sports. (Other activities P.629)

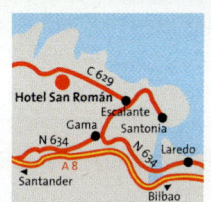

Access: From Bilbao, A8 towards Santander, exit 182, towards Gama-Santona C629.
In Escalante, towards Castillo C402, km 2.

Airports: Bilbao (Intl) 65 km, Santander 35 km
Train station: Gama 5 km

Owners: Mr Juan Melis, Mr Juan A. Iribarnegaray and Mrs Victoria Reynes
General Manager: Juan Melis
Annual closing: From Dec. 21st to January 21st
Currency: Euro (€)
Rates: Menus 36-40 € t.7% s.i.
Carte 36-40 € t.7% s.i.
13 rooms: 96-139 € t.7% s.i.
3 suites: 145-157 € t.7% s.i.
Breakfast: 10 € t.7% s.i.
Dogs: allowed (extra cost)
Golf: 18 km
Accepted cards: AE, DC, MC, VS

More info on www.relaischateaux.com/escalante

Spain

SINCE 1999

Restaurant Akelaŕe

P° Padre Orcolaga 56
E-20008 San-Sebastián
(Guipúzcoa) • Spain

**Tel. : (34) 943 31 12 09
(34) 943 21 40 86**
Fax : (34) 943 21 92 68
akelare@relaischateaux.com

In Igueldo, only five minutes away from the centre of Saint-Sebastian, the bay windows of the Akelare overlook the Cantabrian Sea, offering an idyllic panorama. Pedro Subijana delights guests with an ever changing gourmet menu prepared with the seasonal garden-grown vegetables and aromatic herbs he so lovingly grows, as well as the wide choice of superb vintages. A visit to the Akelare will ensure you a moment of pure bliss.

(Other activities P. 629)

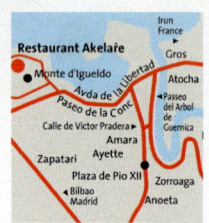

Access: A8 Bilbao/Behobia, exit Ondarreta. Follow the route all along the University area. On arrival in the city, take direction «Monte Igueldo»

Airports: Biarritz (Intl) 40 km,
Saint-Sebastian 20 km
Train station: Saint-Sebastian 5 km

Owner: Pedro Subijana
Weekly closing: Sunday evening, Monday and Tuesday (from January to June), Sunday evening and Monday (from July to December)
Annual closing: February and first half of October
Currency: Euro (€)
Rates: Menu 84 € t.7% s.i.
Carte 84-100 € t.7% s.i.
Dogs: not allowed
Golf: 6 km (18 holes)
Accepted cards: AE, DC, MC, VS

Pedro Subijana

More info on www.relaischateaux.com/akelare

Restaurante Martin Berasategui

SINCE 1999

Calle Loidi, 4
E-20160 Lasarte-Oria
(Guipúzcoa) • Spain

Tel. : (34) 943 36 64 71
Fax : (34) 943 36 61 07
berasategui@relaischateaux.com

Spain

In this elegant restored residence, located in the heart of the countryside, guests will be amazed by Martin Berasategui's imagination and brilliance. By combining typical Basque cuisine with regional and traditional products, he offers a wide range of novel recipes such as the superb «mille-feuille au caramel d'anguille fumée au fois gras, à l'oignon et à la pomme verte». The wines and the service are exceptional.

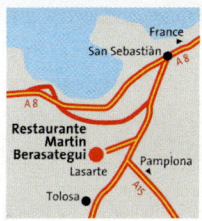

Access: From San-Sebastian, take N1 towards Toulouse, then exit Lasarte and continue 5 km.

Airports: Bilbao (Intl) 100 km, Hondarribia 20 km
Train station: San Sebastian-Donastia 11 km

Owner: Martin Berasategui
Weekly closing: Sunday evening, Monday, Tuesday
Annual closing: From mid-December to mid-January
Currency: Euro (€)
Rates: Menu 85 € t.7% s.i.
Carte 90 € t.7% s.i.
Dogs: not allowed
Accepted cards: AE, DC, MC, VS

Martin Berasategui

More info on www.relaischateaux.com/berasategui

Spain

Restaurante Arzak

SINCE 1979

Alto de Miracruz 21
E-20015 San Sebastián
(Guipúzcoa) • Spain

Tel. : (34) 943 28 55 93
(34) 943 27 84 65
Fax : (34) 943 27 27 53
arzak@relaischateaux.com

The elegant seaside resort of San Sebastian is home to one of Spain's finest chefs. Indeed, international gourmets flock to this picturesque town to savour the gastronomic delights created by Juan-Mari Arzak «Donostiarra» and his daughter Elena. Discover quintessential Basque cuisine and choose from a superb list of vintage wines in this charming restaurant hung with old paintings.
(Other activities P. 629)

Access: From France, motorway until exit 5, from Bilbao, highway until exit 6.

Airports: Bilbao (Intl) 90 km, Pamplona 90 km
Train station: San Sebastian 0,2 km

Owners: Juan-Mari Arzak and Maite Espina
Weekly closing: Sunday evening, Monday and Tuesday (from January to June), Sunday evening and Monday (from July to December)
Annual closing: From June 15th to July 2nd and from November 2nd to 27th
Currency: Euro (€)
Rates: Menus 86-100 € s.i.
Carte 96-120 € s.i.
Dogs: not allowed
Golf: Basozabal 2 km, Jaizquibel 20 km
Accepted cards: AE, DC, MC, VS

Juan-Mari Arzak

More info on www.relaischateaux.com/arzak

Hotel el Peregrino

SINCE 2003

Crta. Pamplona a Logroño
Km 23
E-Puente la Reina
(Navarra) • Spain

Tel. : (34) 948 34 00 75
Fax : (34) 948 34 11 90
peregrino@relaischateaux.com

Spain

At the crossroads of the official paths to Santiago de Compostela, the House of the Pilgrim welcomes passing guests who are immediately enchanted. A stone architecture broken down into different spaces and levels with impressive wooden constructs creates a décor that is both minimalist and audacious. Originality and comfort in a unique setting where the cuisine of Nina Sedano is yet another highlight.
(Other activities P. 629)

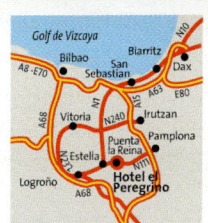

Access: From San Sebastian, motorway A15, towards Pamplona. In Pamplona, N111 towards Logroño. The hotel is on the outskirts of Puente la Reina.
Airport: Pamplona 15 km
Train station: Pamplona 15 km

Owner/General Manager: Angelo Cambero
Weekly closing: Restaurant: Sunday evening, Monday
Annual closing: From December 24th to January 20th
Currency: Euro (€)
Rates: Menu 60 € t.7% s.i.
Carte 50-80 € t.7% s.i.
15 rooms: 150-190 € t.7% s.i.
Breakfast: 15 € s.i.
Dogs: allowed **Golf:** 10 km
Accepted cards: AE, DC, MC, VS

More info on www.relaischateaux.com/elmeson

Spain

El Castell de Ciutat

SINCE 1983

Route N-260 km 229, Apto. 53
E-25700 Seu d'Urgell
(Lérida) • Spain

Tel. : (34) 973 35 00 00
Fax : (34) 973 35 15 74
elcastell@relaischateaux.com

Perched at 650 metres in the Pyrenees, this elegant modern hotel offers breathtaking views of the mountain landscape. The rooms, spacious and comfortable, open out onto private terraces where guests will enjoy magical breakfasts basking in the morning sunlight. The renowned cuisine, inspired by the finest produce from the local rivers and huertas, is enhanced by a wine list featuring over 650 vintages.

Private concerts, archery, trips with all-wheel drive vehicles, hot-air balloons, rafting, romanesque art, hunting, fishing... (Other activities P. 629)

Access: Barcelona - Igualada - Jorba via the N-II. Jorba - Ponts via the C-1412. Ponts - Adrall via the C-1313. Adrall - Seu d'Urgell via the N-260.

Airports: Barcelona (Intl) 200 km, Seu d'Urgell 5 km
Helipad: N 42° 21' 30'' E 001° 26' 40''
Train station: Puigcerdá 45 km

Owners: Tápies Family
General Manager: Jaume Tápies Ibern
Open all year
Currency: Euro (€)
Rates: Menu 60 € t.7% s.i. Carte 55 € t.7% s.i.
32 rooms: 160-190 € t.7% s.i.
6 suites: 240-325 € t.7% s.i.
Breakfast: included
Dogs: allowed except restaurant (extra cost 6 €)
Golf: 5 and 40 km
Accepted cards: AE, DC, MC, VS

More info on www.relaischateaux.com/elcastell

Torre del Remei

SINCE 1993

Cami Reial s/n
E-17539 Bolvir
(Girona) • Spain

Tel. : **(34) 972 14 01 82**
Fax : (34) 972 14 04 49
torreremei@relaischateaux.com

Spain

Shaded by sequoias and nestling in the Pyrenees amidst an 8-acre forest near the Cadi National park, this magnificent summer palace has been transformed into an elegant hotel. Enjoy peace and calm in one of the 11 marvellously comfortable guestrooms, offering superb vistas of the mountain landscape. Savour refined regional cuisine, enjoy golf and horseback riding or venture into the Pyrenees with an experienced mountain guide.

Airfield with different aeronautic activities, mountain guide, excursions, climbing, cross-country skiing, wine tasting. (Other activities P. 629)

Altitude: 1100 metres.
Access: Perpignan, N116 Prades-Andorra; Barcelona, C-16 Tunel del Cadi-Berga-Puigcerdá.

Airports: Perpignan (Intl) 80 km, Barcelona (Intl) 150 km
Helipad: N 42° 25' 16'' E 01° 53' 27''
Train station: Puigcerdá 3 km

Owners: José Maria Boix and Loles Vidal de Boix
Open all year
Currency: Euro (€)
Rates: Menus 50-60 € t.7% s.i.
Carte 50-65 € t.7% s.i.
13 rooms: starting at 190 € t.7% s.i.
9 suites: starting at 280 € t.7% s.i.
Breakfast: 18 € t.7% s.i.
Dogs: allowed (extra cost) **Golf:** 1 km
Accepted cards: AE, DC, MC, VS

More info on www.relaischateaux.com/torreremei

Spain

Mas de Torrent

SINCE 1990

E-17123 Torrent
(Girona) • Spain

**Tel. : (34) 972 30 32 92
(34) 972 30 11 50**
Fax : (34) 972 30 32 93
mastorrent@relaischateaux.com

Near the Costa Brava's beaches and golf courses, discover this beautifully restored XVIIIth century farmhouse. Relax in a superb guestroom, decorated in rustic style or in the garden of an independent bungalow, or in one of the 7 suites, each with a heated private pool. In the restaurant decorated with contemporary Spanish paintings in homage to Picasso, enjoy savoury cuisine prepared with fresh local seafood.

(Other activities P. 629)

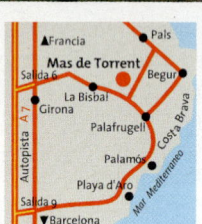

Access: From France, A 7 towards Girona, exit 6 (C-66 - Palamós), follow the Gi 652 Pals-Begur road.

Airports: Barcelona (Intl) 125 km, Girona 35 km
Helipad: N 41° 57' 28" E 00° 307' 55"
Train station: Flaçà 30 km

Owners: Figueras Family
General Managers: Xavier Rocas, Oriol Casas
Weekly closing: Rest.: Sunday evening, Monday (except July, August and bank holidays)
Open all year
Currency: Euro (€)
Rates: Menu starting at 48 € t.7% s.i.
Carte starting at 41 € t.7% s.i.
22 bungalows: starting at 280 € t.7% s.i.
17 suites: starting at 320 € t.7% s.i.
Breakfast: 17 € t.7% s.i.
Dogs: not allowed
Golf: 6 km
Accepted cards: AE, DC, MC, VS

More info on www.relaischateaux.com/mastorrent

Hotel Santa Marta

SINCE 1960

Playa Santa Cristina
E-17310 Lloret De Mar
(Girona) • Spain

Tel. : (34) 972 36 49 04
Fax : (34) 972 36 92 80
santamarta@relaischateaux.com

Spain

The magnificent coastline and fine sand beach of Santa Cristina seem to have been specially designed for this elegant modern hotel, nestling amidst a 15-acre park. Its spacious, sunny rooms open onto terraces overlooking the ocean and the pine forests. After an afternoon playing tennis or relaxing by the marvellous pool, enjoy the «sweet and savoury» flavours of traditional Catalan cuisine at the waterside restaurant.

(Other activities P. 629)

Access: From Barcelona, E15, exit 9 Vidreres, Lloret de Mar.

Airport: Barcelona (Intl) 80 km
Helipad: N 41° 41' 378'' E 02° 49' 003''
Train station: Blanes 6 km

Owners: Noguera Family
General Manager: Jorge Noguera
Annual closing: Rest.: From Dec. 1st to March 1st
Currency: Euro (€)
Rates: Menu 42 € t.n.i., s.i.
Carte 34-50 € t.n.i., s.i.
52 rooms: 131-217 € t.n.i., s.i.
8 suites: 208-348 € t.n.i., s.i.
Breakfast: 12 € t.n.i., s.i.
Dogs: allowed (extra cost) except restaurant
Golf: 5 clubs less than 40 km away
Accepted cards: AE, DC, MC, VS

More info on www.relaischateaux.com/santamarta

Spain

SINCE 2001

Restaurant Sant Pau

Nou 10,
E-08395 Sant Pol de Mar
(Catalunya) • Spain

Tel. : (34) 93 760 0662
Fax : (34) 93 760 0950
santpau@relaischateaux.com

North of Barcelona, in the old Catalan town of Sant Pol de Mar, Carme Ruscalleda cooks in a contemporary style, using products fresh from the region's orchards and vegetable gardens. Not forgetting the fish and seafood from the Mediterranean. In an old house, with a pleasant garden overlooking the sea, the cuisine follows the seasons, emphasising unusual combinations of flavours. Finest Spanish and International wines.

(Other activities P. 629)

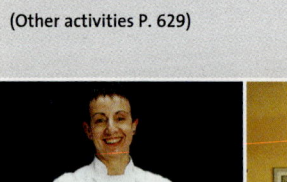

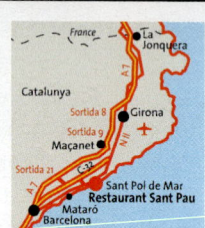

Access:
From Barcelona, take the C-32 motorway, exit 21 (Sant Pol de Mar).

Airport: Barcelona (Intl) 45 km
Train station: Sant Pol 0,2 km

Owners: Carme Ruscalleda and Toni Balam
Weekly closing: Sunday evening, Monday, Thursday noon
Annual closing: From May 6th to 22nd and from November 4th to 20th
Currency: Euro (€)
Rates: Menu 85 € s.7%
Dogs: not allowed
Golf: 19 km, Pitch and put 2 km
Accepted cards: AE, DC, MC, VS

More info on www.relaischateaux.com/santpau

Can Fabes

SINCE 1992

Sant Joan 6
E-08470 Sant Celoni
(Barcelona) • Spain

Tel. : **(34) 93 867 28 51**
Fax : (34) 93 867 38 61
raco@relaischateaux.com

Spain

All the aspects of present-day Catalonia –diverse, dynamic, artistic and progressive– are reflected in the modern, inventive cuisine proposed with brio by Santi and Àngels Santamaria, in the admirable setting of the Montseny Natural Park. Close to perfection, the culinary creations display the talent of a genius.
Food workshops: mushrooms and truffles.

Access: From Barcelona, A 7, exit 11 Sant Celoni; located 200 m behind the town hall.

Airports: Barcelona (Intl) 50 km, Gerona 50 km
Train station: Sant Celoni 1 km

Owners: Santi and Àngels Santamaria
Weekly closing: Sunday evening and Monday
Annual closing: From February 3rd to 17th and from July 1st to 14th
Currency: Euro (€)
Rates: Menus 95-120 € s.i.
Carte 95-120 € s.i.
Dogs: allowed
Accepted cards: AE, DC, JCB, MC, VS

Santi Santamaria

More info on www.relaischateaux.com/raco

Spain

Restaurant Neichel

SINCE 1990

Beltrán i Rózpide 1-5
(antes Av. de Pedralbes)
E-08034 Barcelona • Spain

Tel. : **(34) 93 203 84 08**
Fax : (34) 93 205 63 69
neichel@relaischateaux.com

Restaurant looking onto a small, southern garden full of lavender, lemon trees and rosemary. Discover the Mediterranean cuisine of Jean-Louis Neichel with imaginative and creative dishes using seafood, mushrooms, milk-fed lamb, vegetables, herbs and desserts based on lavender, thyme and orange blossom. Menus to savour the delicious flavours of this exceptional and inspiring region.
Private salon (for 12 and 16).

Access: From the Southern entrance to Barcelona (A 2), take the avenue Diagonal to Pie XII plaza.

Airport: Barcelona (Intl) 10 km

Owners: Evelyn and Jean-Louis Neichel
Weekly closing: Sunday and Monday
Annual closing: August
Currency: Euro (€)
Rates: Menus 53-60 € s.i.
Carte 50-70 € s.i.
Dogs: allowed (small)
Accepted cards: AE, DC, MC, VS

Jean-Louis Neichel

La Torre del Visco

SINCE 2000

Fuentespalda
E-44587 Teruel
(Bajo Aragón) • Spain

**Tel. : (34) 978 76 90 15
(34) 978 76 90 56**
Fax : (34) 978 76 90 16
torrevisco@relaischateaux.com

Spain

The most remote hotel in Spain. Solitary and romantic, this labyrinthine XVth century estate house surrounded by lovely gardens, overlooks its own extensive farm in the beautiful and undiscovered region of Bajo Aragón. Utterly peaceful and relaxing, excellent mediterranean cuisine, home-grown produce, game, black truffles and medieval wine cellar. Library, hundreds of CDs, grand piano and open fires. No television.

Restaurant reservations are required for non-hotel guests. Trips with all-wheel drive vehicles. (Other activities P. 629)

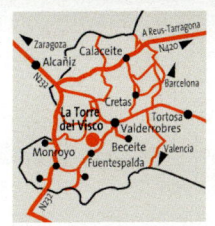

Access: From Barcelona, A7 south to junction 34 Reus east. N420 through Falset to Calaceite. A1413/A231 towards Valderrobres. A1414 towards Fuentespalda. After 6.2 km take right onto track to hotel (5 km).
Airports: Barcelona (Intl) 250 km, Zaragoza 150 km

Owners: Piers Dutton, Jemma Markham
Annual closing: From January 7th to 16th
Currency: Euro (€)
Rates: Menu 45 € t.7% s.i.
11 rooms: Half board 200-240 € t.7% s.i.
3 suites: Half board 300 € t.7% s.i.
Breakfast: included
Dogs: not allowed
Accepted cards: MC, VS

More info on www.relaischateaux.com/torrevisco

Spain

Girasol

SINCE 1997

Ctr. Moraira-Calpe, KM 1,5
E-03724 Moraira
(Alicante) • Spain

Tel. : (34) 96574 4373
Fax : (34) 96649 0545
girasol@relaischateaux.com

A delightful villa with an elegant decor, suffused in Mediterranean light. This same light illuminates the culinary creations of Joachim Koerper. His reputation is characterised by sophisticated dishes using very high quality seafood such as gambas and redmullet, enhanced by the treasures of a royal cellar. An essential place to stay for the most demanding epicureans.

(Other activities P. 629)

Access: From Alicante, A 7 towards Valencia, exit 63, RN 332 towards Teulada, route N° AV 1342 towards Moraira, at the roundabout take a right, route N° AP 1391, Moraira-Calpe.
Airports: Alicante (Intl) 90 km, Valencia (Intl) 120 km
Train station: Gandia 40 km

Owners: Joachim and Victoria Koerper
Weekly closing: Monday (except in summer)
Nov. to March: Sunday evening and Monday
Summer: closed at noon (except Sunday)
Annual closing: From November 10th to 30th
Currency: Euro (€)
Rates: Menus 70-110 € t.7% s.i.
Carte 84-108 € t.7% s.i.
Dogs: allowed
Golf: 5 between 1.5 and 30 km
Accepted cards: AE, DC, JCB, MC, VS

Joachim Koerper

More info on www.relaischateaux.com/girasol

El Rodat

SINCE 2003

Ctra. al Cabo de la Nao S/N
E-03730 Jávea
(Alicante) • Spain

Tel. : **(34) 966 470 710**
Fax : (34) 966 471 550
elrodat@relaischateaux.com

Spain

Close to Javea, between Valencia and Alicante, nestled between the capes of San Antonio and Nao, El Rodat boasts a beautiful ensemble of suites and bungalows hidden away amongst pine trees, palm trees and flowers. This superb residence is brimming over with charm and gaiety. Its earthen colours mix with the yellow and blue décor that draws inspiration from wonderful southern Spain. El Rodat, with its wellness centre, is the ideal place to regenerate your energies in an environment of peace and tranquillity.

(Other activities P. 629)

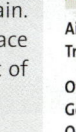

Airport: Valencia (Intl) 90 km
Train station: Gandía 25 km

Access: From Valencia or Alicante, motorway A 7. Exit 62 towards Denia-Xavea (Javea). Follow cape Nao. The hotel is located next to El Tosalet.

Owner: Mery de Madrigal
General Manager: Christian Kremers
Open all year
Currency: Euro (€)
Rates: Menus 21-26 € s.i.
Carte 29-34 € s.i.
8 rooms: 149-175 € s.i.
34 suites: 150-300 € s.i.
Breakfast: 10-13 € s.i.
Dogs: allowed (extra cost)
Golf: 5 km
Accepted cards: AE, DC, MC, VS

More info on www.relaischateaux.com/elrodat

Costa Blanca

PATRONATO PROVINCIAL DE TURISMO

ALICANTE - SPAIN

www.costablanca.org

Hotel «El Montiboli»

SINCE 1999

Partida Montiboli S/N
E-03570 Villajoyosa
(Alicante) • Spain

Tel. : (34) 96 589 02 50
Fax : (34) 96 589 38 57
montiboli@relaischateaux.com

Spain

The Arabs believed that the chosen souls flew up to heaven from these very cliffs, a natural frontier between El Montiboli and the Mediterranean Sea. Indeed, the hotel, nestled in the midst of Moorish gardens, has a paradisiac charm. In this pleasant setting, the chef enhances the flavours of an innovative Mediterranean cuisine with talent and finesse.

Climbing, skiing. (Other activities P. 629)

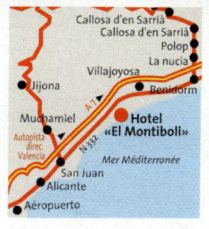

Access: From the airport: A7 towards Valence, exit Villajoyosa, towards Alicante, after 4 km, turn left at the roundabout, follow signs for hotel.

Airport: Alicante (Intl) 40 km
Train station: Alicante 30 km

Owner: José Maria Caballé
General Manager: José Manuel Castillo
Open all year
Currency: Euro (€)
Rates: Menu 37 € t.7% s.i.
Carte 42-60 € t.7% s.i.
38 rooms: 146-222 € t.7% s.i.
12 suites: 208-322 € t.7% s.i.
Breakfast: included
Dogs: not allowed
Golf: 15 km (18 holes)
Accepted cards: AE, DC, MC, VS

More info on www.relaischateaux.com/montiboli

Hotel Hacienda Na Xamena

SINCE 1981

E-07815 San Miguel - Ibiza
(Baleares) • Spain

Tel. : (34) 971 33 45 00
Fax : (34) 971 33 45 14
xamena@relaischateaux.com

Spain

Relax and unwind in the unique, multi-ethnic atmosphere of a hotel situated on a wild cliff at the seaside. Diverse and refined cuisine, individual therapeutic and cosmetic treatments. Enjoy lunch in a natural setting and at the seaside to discover beauty in its pure state. Unforgettable experiences, only 20 minutes away from the high life of Ibiza.

52 private whirlpools with view of the sea, concerts...
(Other activities P. 629)

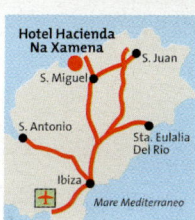

Access: 22 km northwest of Ibiza town, towards San Miguel

Airport: Ibiza (Intl) 25 km

Owner: Na Xamena - Hotel Hacienda S.A
General Manager: Sabine Lipszyc
Annual closing:
From November 1st to April 15th
Currency: Euro (€)
Rates: Menu 44 € t.7% s.i.
Carte 27-59 € t.7% s.i.
52 rooms: 196-308 € s.i.
9 suites: 436-1300 € s.i.
Breakfast: 16 € t.7% s.i.
Dogs: allowed (rooms only)
Golf: 18 km
Accepted cards: AE, DC, JCB, MC, VS

More info on www.relaischateaux.com/xamena

Read's

SINCE 2003

E-07320 Santa Maria del Cami
(Mallorca) • Spain

Tel. : (34) 971 140 262
Fax : (34) 971 140 762
reads@relaischateaux.com

Spain

In the heart of Majorca lies a magnificent 18th century manor house which took seven years to lovingly restore. Vivian Read has turned this house into a luxurious hotel set in lush gardens surrounded by peaceful countryside. With its collection of antique furniture and fantasy murals, it offers the elegance of a refined property coupled with an invitation to savour a truly special cuisine.

(Other activities P. 629)

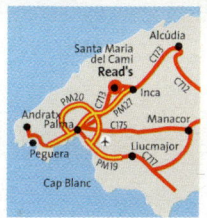

Access: From Palma airport, motorway PM19 towards Palma. Exit Via Cintura, towards Inca via motorway PM27. Exit Santa Maria del Carmi. Follow Hotel Read's signs.
Airport: Palma (Intl) 20 km
Train station: Santa Maria 2 km

Owner: Vivian Read
General Manager: Marcus Read
Open all year
Currency: Euro (€)
Rates: Menu 69 € t. 7% s.n.i.
Carte 46-58 € t. 7% s.n.i.
10 rooms: 160-270 € t. 7% s.n.i.
15 suites: 225-445 € t. 7% s.n.i.
Breakfast: included
Dogs: not allowed
Golf: 10 km
Accepted cards: AE, DC, MC, VS

More info on www.relaischateaux.com/reads

Spain

SINCE 2000

Gran Hotel Son Net

E-07194 Puigpunyent-Mallorca
(Baleares) • Spain

Tel. : (34) 971 1470 00
Fax : (34) 971 1470 01
sonnet@relaischateaux.com

Set in a hidden valley surrounded by lush green mountains, Son Net is poised above a charming mountain village just 20 minutes from Palma's finest golf courses, beaches and cultural attractions. You will be captivated by Son Net's elegant rooms, spacious marble baths, luxurious swimming pool and tranquil gardens. Enjoy superb Mediterranean cuisine in L'Orangerie, one of Spain's most elegant and emblematic restaurants.

Spa, trekking. (Other activities P. 629)

Access: From the airport, take PM19 towards Palma, after 5 km take PM20 towards Andraitz exit Puigpunyent. After the roundabout, continue straight on for 11 km. The Son Net is on top hill.
Airport: Palma (Intl) 25 km

Owners: David Stein, Norman and Lyn Lear
General Manager: Angel Luis Alonso
Open all year
Currency: Euro (€)
Rates: Tasting menu 63 € t.7% s.i.
Carte 60-72 € t.7% s.i.
17 rooms: 269-420 € t.7% s.i.
7 suites: 850-990 € t.7% s.i.
Breakfast: 19 € s.i.
Dogs: not allowed
Golf: 15 km
Accepted cards: AE, DC, MC, VS

More info on www.relaischateaux.com/sonnet

Hotel Cala Sant Vicenç

SINCE 1998

2, rue Maressers
E-07469 Cala Sant Vicenç-Mallorca
(Baleares) • Spain

Tel. : (34) 971 530 250
Fax : (34) 971 532 084
calasantvicenc@relaischateaux.com

Spain

Set on the northern coast of Majorca, this family-run hotel offers impeccable service and exceptional hospitality. Its 38 elegant rooms are fully refurbished and beautifully decorated. Relax in the calm, cool interior of Italian sandstone, swim in the pool, surrounded by palm trees, 200 metres from a limpid, turquoise sea. Savour Mediterranean cuisine at the «Cavall Bernat» restaurant.

Indoor gym, beauty salon. Special winter activities. (Other activities P. 629)

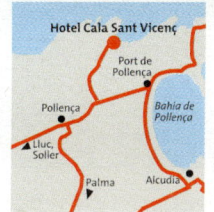

Access: From the airport, go to Palma, then Inca, then Pollença.

Airport: Palma (Intl) 60 km

Owners: Suau Family
Annual closing:
From December 1st to February 1st
Currency: Euro (€)
Rates: Menus 48-65 € s.i.
Carte 50-70 € s.i.
23 rooms: 119-230 € s.n.i.
15 suites: 189-270 € s.n.i.
Breakfast: included
Dogs: not allowed
Golf: 8 km
Accepted cards: AE, DC, MC, VS

More info on www.relaischateaux.com/calasantvicenc

Greece (Crete)

Property	Nearest major city	Relais & Châteaux	Relais Gourmands	Page
Elounda Mare Hotel	Aghios Nikólaos			477

Elounda Mare Hotel

SINCE 1988

GR-720 53 Elounda
Crete
Greece

Tel. : (30) (08410) 411 02/03
Fax : (30) (08410) 413 07
elounda@relaischateaux.com

Greece

Built in Cretan style, the Elounda Mare enjoys an elegant setting surrounded by lush greenery bathed in the muted turquoise of the sea. The tranquility of this hotel, tucked away on a private sandy beach, is further enhanced by its orthodox chapel and its art gallery. Each bungalow has air conditioning and a private garden with swimming pool. Three restaurants draw their inspiration from regional cuisine with the emphasis on fish and the very best wines.

(Other activities P. 629)

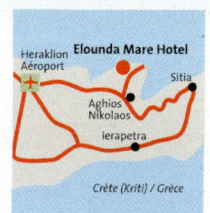

Access: North of Aghios Nikolaos (9 km), on the north-eastern coast of the island.

Airport: Iraklion (Intl) 70 km
Helipad: N 35° 14' 84" E 25° 43' 94"

Owners: Spyros and Eliane Kokotos
General Manager: Chris Tzianos
Annual closing: From Nov. to the end of March
Currency: Euro (€)
Rates: Menu 35 € s.i. Carte starting at 45 € s.i.
37 rooms: 220-440 € s.i.
42 bungalows: 245-2000 € s.i.
Breakfast: buffet included
Dogs: not allowed
Golf: 500 m (9 holes par-3)
Accepted cards: AE, DC, MC, VS

More info on www.relaischateaux.com/elounda

Turkey - Lebanon Israel - Dubai

Properties Turkey	Nearest major city	Relais & Châteaux	Relais Gourmands	Page
Ada Hotel	Bodrum	✦		481

Lebanon				
Albergo (Hotel)	Beyrouth	✦		482

Israel				
American Colony (The)	Jerusalem	✦		484
Mizpe-Hayamim	Rosh-Pina	✦		483

Dubai				
Hatta Fort Hotel	Dubaï	✦		485

Ada Hotel

SINCE 2001

PO Box 350
Türkbükü köyü
48400 Bodrum • Turkey

Tel. : (90) (252) 377 59 15
Fax : (90) (252) 377 53 79
ada@relaischateaux.com

Turkey

Located in the historical village of Gôltürkbükü on the Bodrum peninsula, the Ada Hotel offers refined comfort in the unique setting of an Ottoman palace. The marble hammam, the period furniture with its sculpted wood, the splendid rugs and art works all contribute to creating an unparalleled atmosphere. Discover the Bosphorus or sail to the Antalya coast on a superb yacht.
(Other activities P. 629)

Access: From Milas-Bodrum Airport, Bodrum motorway. After Güvercinlik, towards Torba, continue to Yalikavak. After 11 km, turn right towards Gôltürkbükü. Ada Hotel after 5 km.
Airports: Milas-Bodrum (Intl) 40 km, Izmir (Intl) 240 km

Owner: Vedat Semiz
General Manager: Ayse Nur Azrak
Open all year
Currency: US dollar (USD)
Rates: Carte 25-45 USD s.i.
8 rooms: 245-310 USD s.i.
6 suites: 285-545 USD s.i.
Breakfast: included
Dogs: not allowed
Accepted cards: AE, DC, MC, VS

More info on www.relaischateaux.com/ada

Lebanon

Hotel Albergo

SINCE 1999

137, rue Abdel Wahab El Inglizi
Beyrouth
Lebanon

Tel. : (961) (01) 339 797
Fax : (961) (01) 339 999
albergo@relaischateaux.com

Situated in the heart of the oldest quarter of Beirut, the secret of the splendid facade of the Hotel Albergo combines the enchantment of supreme comfort with the magic of a refined setting. This residence is a unique experience where the subtle hospitality and the friendly atmosphere make this a privileged hotel. The Albergo will soon become one of your favourite places to enjoy a unique and memorable stay.

Climbing, sailing, whirlpools, thalassotherapy. (Other activities P. 629)

Access: From the airport, take av. de l'aéroport; at the roundabout, take av. Jamel Abdel Nasser; at 2nd roundabout, take av. de Novembre, continue straight on towards av. Béchara El Khoury; after 2 km, take bd de l'Indépendance to the right and turn left after Sodeco Square.
Airport: Beirut (Intl) 5 km

Owner: Sté Hôtelière de Vinci
General Manager: Michel Chardigny
Open all year
Currency: US dollar (USD)
Rates: Carte 25-60 USD t.10% s.16%
33 suites: 215-650 USD t.10% s.16%
Breakfast: 15-20 USD t.10% s.16%
Dogs: allowed
Golf: 5 km (18 holes)
Accepted cards: AE, DC, MC, VS

More info on www.relaischateaux.com/albergo

Mizpe-Hayamim

SINCE 2001

PO 27
12000 Rosh-Pina
(Upper Galilee) • Israel

Tel. : (972) (04) 699 4555
Fax : (972) (04) 699 9555
mizpe@relaischateaux.com

Israel

A magnificient setting near Rosh-Pina overlooking the sea of Galilee. A unique concept created with one theme in mind: a delicate balance between man and his environment. By combining a charming hotel, health spa, biological vegetable gardens and dairy farm, a private winery into an artistic vision, created a realm of serenity, charm, distinctive rooms and natural ambience.

Mountain-biking, fishing, sailing... (Other activities P. 629)

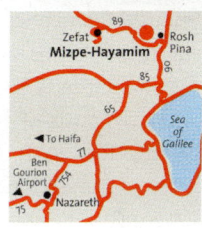

Access: Ben-Gurion airport: road n°1, Morash-Glilot junction. Turn left into road n°2, Zichron junction. Turn right into road n°70, Yokneam junction, road n° 722, 75, 77, 65, 85, 90 and 89.
Airports: Tel-Aviv (Intl) 180 km, Rosh-Pina 5 km

Owner: Sammy Chazan
General Manager: Anita Blom
Weekly closing: Restaurant: Sunday
Open all year
Currency: US dollar (USD)
Rates: 25 USD s.15%
60 rooms: 197-290 USD s.15%
23 suites: 324-385 USD s.15%
Breakfast: included
Dogs: not allowed
Accepted cards: AE, DC, MC, VS

More info on www.relaischateaux.com/mizpe

Israel

The American Colony Hotel

SINCE 1997

Nablus Road - PO BOX 19215
97200 Jerusalem
Israel

Tel. : (972) (2) 627 9777
Fax : (972) (2) 627 9779
americancolony@relaischateaux.com

Spend a thousand and one magical nights in historic Jerusalem. This authentic Middle-Eastern mansion built in 1860 and with a fascinating history is an oasis of tranquility in this vibrant city. It offers various categories of rooms, each full of atmosphere and charm and three high-class restaurants. The hotel is a ten-minute walk from the Old City and other major tourist sites.

Antiques, art galleries, historical tours of the city, business centre, car hire, souvenir shop, book shop, travel agency. (Other activities P. 629)

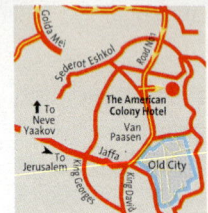

Access:
From Tel-Aviv, turn left at first lights in Jerusalem to «T» junction. Left then right at lights. Next lights right, continue for 1,500 m to 6th lights. Hotel on the left.
Airports: Tel-Aviv (Intl) 45 km, Jerusalem 15 km

Owner: Valentine Vester
General Manager: Pierre Berclaz
Open all year
Currency: US dollar (USD)
Rates: Menus 15-29 USD s.i.
Carte 15-40 USD s.i.
71 rooms: 175-340 USD t.17% s.i.
13 suites: 360-700 USD t.17% s.i.
Breakfast: 18 USD s.i.
Dogs: allowed
Golf: 120 km
Accepted cards: AE, DC, MC, VS

More info on www.relaischateaux.com/americancolony

Hatta Fort Hotel

SINCE 1983

PO Box 9277
Dubaï
United Arab Emirates

Tel. : (971) (04) 85 23 211
Fax : (971) (04) 85 23 561
hattafort@relaischateaux.com

United Arab Emirates

This extraordinary hotel set in the foothills of the magnificent Hajar mountains is an hour's drive from Dubai. Relax in one of the comfortably furnished chalets or stroll through 80 acres of gardens overlooking the Hatta oasis. Enjoy clay pigeon shooting, archery, 9 hole fun golf and mountain safaris or take a dip in the temperature-controlled swimming pool. The superb restaurants serve traditional Arab delicacies and international cuisine.

Clay pigeon shooting, archery. Helicopter and limousine services. (Other activities P. 629)

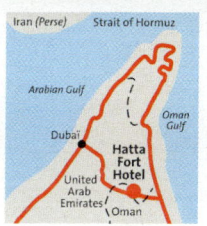

Access: From Dubai, direct highway to Hatta (105 km).

Airport: Dubaï (Intl) 105 km

Owner: Dutco Hotels L.L.C.
General Manager: Claudio Campolucci
Open all year
Currency: Dirham (AED)
Rates: Menus 75-250 AED t.10% s.10%
Carte 100-250 AED t.10% s.10%
50 rooms: 440-650 AED t.10% s.10%
3 suites: starting at 1200 AED t.10% s.10%
Breakfast: 35-46 AED t.10% s.10%
Dogs: not allowed
Golf: on the premises (9 holes)
Accepted cards: AE, DC, MC, VS

More info on www.relaischateaux.com/hattafort

Morocco

Property	Nearest major city	Relais & Châteaux	Relais Gourmands	Page
Villa des Orangers	Marrakech	⚜		487

La Villa des Orangers

SINCE 2001

6, rue Sidi Mimoun
40000 Marrakech
Morocco

Tel. : (212) (044) 384 638
Fax : (212) (044) 385 123
orangers@relaischateaux.com

Morocco

At the crossroads of the souks and the Royal Palace, who could have imagined that a former palace with beautiful patios adorned with fragrant orange trees lies tucked away behind a huge gate fashioned out of cedar wood. You can enjoy the pool on the roof overlooking the old town or relax in marocain salons soothed by the sound of the fountains. A magical setting from which to explore the red city of Marrakech.

(Other activities P. 629)

Access: Cross the ramparts at the «Bab Jdid» gate. At the 1st traffic light, turn right. Go 100 meters. The hotel is the first building on the left side of the road.
Airports: Marrakech-Menara (Intl) 5 km
Train station: Marrakech 2 km

Owners: Véronique and Pascal Beherec
General Manager: Pascal Beherec
Annual closing: From july 21st to august 14th
Currency: Dirham (MAD)
Rates: Menu 450 MAD s.i. (dinner)
Carte 450 MAD s.i.
5 rooms: 2900-3600 MAD s.i.
11 suites: 3800-4800 MAD s.i.
Breakfast: included
Dogs: not allowed
Golf: 6 km
Accepted cards: AE, MC, VS

More info on www.relaischateaux.com/orangers

Southern Africa
Mauritius
Seychelles

Properties South Africa	Nearest major city	Relais & Châteaux	Relais Gourmands	Page
Bushmans Kloof Wilderness Reserve	Cape Town	⚜		500
Cellars - Hohenort (The)	Cape Town	⚜		510
Clearwater Lodges	Johannesburg	⚜		504
Cybele Forest Lodge and Spa	White River	⚜		498
Ellerman House	Cape Town	⚜		509
Grande Roche	Cape Town	⚜	●	503
Hunter's - Tsala	Port Elizabeth	⚜		501
Kwandwe Private Game Reserve	Grahamstown	⚜		505
Londolozi Private Game Reserve	Johannesburg	⚜		497
Marine Hermanus (The)	Cape Town	⚜		508
Plettenberg (The)	George	⚜		502
Quartier Français (Le)	Cape Town	⚜		507
Singita Private Game Reserve	Skukuza	⚜		496
Tswalu Kalahari Reserve	Kimberley	⚜		499

Namibia

Heinitzburg (Hotel)	Windhoek	⚜		511

Tanzania

Sultan Palace	Zanzibar	⚜		490

Zimbabwe

Imba Matombo Lodge	Harare	⚜		494
Pamushana	Masvingo	⚜		495

Mauritius

Prince Maurice (Le)	Port Louis	⚜		493

Seychelles

Château de Feuilles	Praslin	⚜		491
Lemuria Resort	Praslin	⚜		492

More info on www.relaischateaux-sa.co.za

Sultan Palace

Tanzania

SINCE 2001

Pierre Ltd
4074 Zanzibar
Tanzania

Tel. : (255) 24 2240 173
Fax : (255) 24 2240 188
sultan@relaischateaux.com

On the untouched East Coast of the legendary Spice Island of Zanzibar, Sultan Palace evokes an exotic past of mystery and adventure. Overlooking the warm turquoise waters of the Indian Ocean, Sultan Palace's fifteen cottages with their castellated walls and private gardens offer an elegant and romantic ambience reminiscent of an era unchanged.

Sailing, mountain-biking, excursions. (Other activities P. 629)

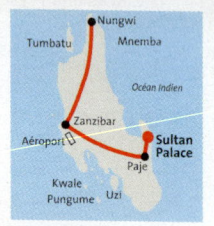

Access: From the airport, towards Paje (local drivers).

Airport: Zanzibar (Intl) 60 km

Owner: Pierre LTD
General Manager: Laurence Parkman
Annual closing: From March 30th to July 15th
Currency: US dollar (USD)
Full board
10 rooms:
150-250 USD s.i. per person
5 suites:
250-350 USD s.i. per person
Breakfast: included
Dogs: not allowed
Accepted cards: MC, VS

More info on www.relaischateaux.com/sultan

Château de Feuilles

SINCE 1999

Pointe Cabris - Baie Sainte-Anne
Ile de Praslin
Seychelles

Tel. : (248) 290 000
Fax : (248) 290 029
feuilles@relaischateaux.com

Seychelles

This privileged place with its breathtaking view of the ocean and the islands has ten rooms, divided between the château and the outbuildings with their splendid local architecture in the shade of the mango and coconut trees. The light inventive cuisine is a homage to sea and sun. Enjoy this charming place with its bougainvilleas and relax to the sound of exotic birds singing. A unique experience.

Excursion to its private island «Grande Sœur» (weekend), snorkelling, casino. (Other activities P. 629)

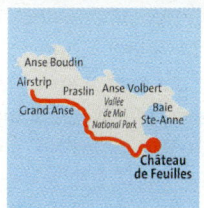

Access: From Praslin airport, follow the route along the beaches.

Airports: Mahé (Intl) 45 km, Praslin 10 km
Helipad: S 04° 21' 21" E 055° 45' 99"

Owner: Château LTD
General Manager: Cédric Morel
Annual closing: June
Currency: Euro (€)
Rates: Menus 53-60 € s.i.
Carte 20-60 € s.i.
5 rooms: 370-435 € s.i.
4 suites: 435-525 € s.i.
Breakfast: included
Dogs: not allowed
Golf: Praslin 20 km
Accepted cards: AE, MC, VS

More info on www.relaischateaux.com/feuilles

Seychelles

SINCE 2002

Lemuria Resort

Anse Kerlan
Ile de Praslin
Seychelles

Tel. : (248) 281 281
Fax : (248) 281 001
lemuria@relaischateaux.com

Along three white sandy beaches, the 110 hectare domain hugs the cove of Kelan. The Lemuria is a first rate resort offering the most diverse activities: tennis courts, 18 hole golf course, fitness centre, diving centre, spacious, light-filled suites. The special feature of this resort, whose main building is perched over three cascading swimming pools, is that it blends harmoniously into a luxuriant and rare vegetation.

(Other activities P. 629)

Access:
In Mahé, take plane to Praslin (15 min. flight). After leaving Praslin airport, turn right, the entry of the Lemuria Resort is 3 km away.

Airports: Mahé (Intl) 45 km, Praslin 3 km
Helipad: S 04° 18.59' E 055° 41.09'

Owner: LRP Ltd
General Manager: Peter Wynne
Open all year
Currency: US dollar (USD)
Rates: Menus 45-60 USD s.n.i.
Carte 37-75 USD s.n.i.
88 suites: 600-1800 USD s.n.i.
Breakfast: 14-22 USD s.n.i.
Dogs: not allowed
Golf: on the premises
Accepted cards: AE, DC, MC, VS

More info on www.relaischateaux.com/lemuria

Le Prince Maurice

SINCE 2001

Poste de Flacq
Mauritius

Tel. : **(230) 413 91 00**
Fax : (230) 413 91 29
maurice@relaischateaux.com

Mauritius

One of a new generation of luxury hotels, The Prince Maurice, located on the north east part of the island, reflects the haven of peace that most first class clients cherish. Surrounded by the turquoise ocean, the Prince Maurice offers you four beaches where you can enjoy swimming. The entire property perfectly blends into the beauty and genuine simplicity of the setting.

Squash... (Other activities P. 629)

Access: Plaisance Airport: towards military quarter, then Flacq post.

Airport: Plaisance (Intl) 45 km

Owner: Hotels Constance
General Manager: Andrew Milton
Open all year
Currency: US dollar (USD)
Rates: Carte 60-100 USD s.i.
89 suites: 520-2100 USD s.i.
Breakfast: included
Dogs: not allowed
Golf: 3 km
Accepted cards: AE, DC, MC, VS

More info on www.relaischateaux.com/maurice

Zimbabwe

Imba Matombo Lodge

SINCE 1997

3, Albert Glen Close
Glen Lorne
Harare • Zimbabwe

Tel. : (263) (4) 499013/4
Fax : (263) (4) 499071
imbamatombo@relaischateaux.com

Perched on a hill on the edge of Harare, this elegant lodge offers supreme comfort, impeccable service and one of the capital's finest restaurants. Imba Matombo is just a short flight from Zimbabwe's famous game reserves and the magnificent Victoria Falls. It is also a golfers' paradise, offering eight first-class courses within a 40 minute drive. Savour warm African hospitality, superb cuisine and undisturbed calm.

Gymnasium, whirlpools. (Other activities P. 629)

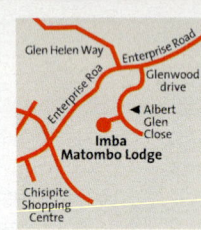

Access: Leave central Harare, take Enterprise Road. 10 km drive to Chisipite, 5 km further on turn right into Glenwood drive, follow signs.
Airport: Harare (Intl) 20 km

Owners: John and Charlotte Ford
Open all year
Currency: US dollar (USD)
Rates: Menus 25-50 USD t.5% s.i.
Carte 30-50 USD t.5% s.i.
7 rooms: 210-350 USD t.5% s.i.
3 suites: 300-360 USD t.5% s.i.
Breakfast: included
Dogs: not allowed
Golf: 6 at 20 km
Accepted cards: AE, MC, VS

More info on www.relaischateaux.com/imbamatombo

Pamushana

SINCE 2001

Private Bag 7085
Chiredzi
Zimbabwe

Tel. : **(263) (4) 870 265**
Fax : (263) (4) 884 759
pamushana@relaischateaux.com

Zimbabwe

Perched on top of an escarpment with spectacular panoramic views, is a luxurious and unrivalled celebration of the glory of the African bush – that is Pamushana! The 44000 hectares of Malilangwe Private Wildlife Reserve allows you to experience the wild in the most intimate and uncrowded way. Day and night safaris and walks enable you to view the «Big Five», including both black and white Rhino, at your leisure.

Guided game drives and walks (by day and night), photographic safaris, birding safaris, sundowner cruises, visit to San bushman paintings, gymnasium, curio shop. (Other activities P. 629)

Access: A4 from Harare to Chivhu, towards Triangle via Gutu and Zaka. Towards «T» junction at Buffalo Range, left onto Chiredzi/Chisumbanje Road. Right at Chipinda Pools. Follow Pamushana signs.
Airport: Buffalo Range (Intl) 45 km
Helipad: S 21° 911' E 31° 52.183'

Owner: The Malilangwe Trust
General Manager: Terry Ryan
Open all year
Currency: US dollar (USD)
Full board
6 suites: 650 USD s.i. per person
Breakfast: included
Dogs: not allowed
Golf: 70 km
Accepted cards: MC, VS

More info on www.relaischateaux.com/pamushana

South Africa

Singita Private Game Reserve

SINCE 1996

PO Box 650881
Benmore, 2010
South Africa

Tel. : (27) (11) 234 0990
Fax : (27) (11) 234 0535
singita@relaischateaux.com

This magnificent 18000 hectare reserve overlooking the Sand River offers 18 superb suites, nestling beneath giant ebony trees, each with its own swimming pool. Safaris in an open Land Rover enable you to discover, by day and by night, lion, leopard, rhino, elephant, buffalo and cheetah. Enjoy traditional evenings in the «Boma» and savour refined cuisine accompanied by the finest vintage South African wines from the 12000 bottles underground wine cellar.

Curio shop, bush walks, game drives by day and night with rangers and trackers, bird watching. Health Spa. (Other activities P. 629)

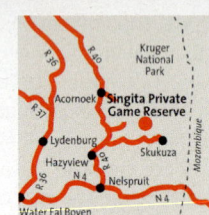

Access: From Skukuza airport, R536 towards Hazyview, sign board to the left 1 km before Lisbon Store, follow signs to Singita (28 km).
Airports: Johannesburg (Intl) 500 km, Singita 3 km (private airstrip)
Helipad: S 24° 48' 18" E 31° 25' 34"

Owner: Luke Bailes
General Manager: Mark Witney
Open all year
Currency: US dollar (USD)
Full board
18 suites: 650 USD s.i. per person
Breakfast: included
Dogs: not allowed
Accepted cards: AE, DC, MC, VS

More info on www.relaischateaux.com/singita

Londolozi Private Game Reserve

SINCE 1993

PO Box 6
Skukuza, 1350
South Africa

Tel. : (27) (011) 809 4300
Fax : (27) (011) 809 4511
londolozi@relaischateaux.com

South Africa

Londolozi, the Zulu word meaning «protector of living things», has been acclaimed by President Nelson Mandela as «the model of the dream I cherish for the future of nature preservation in our country». For over 70 years, the Varty family have welcomed guests to experience Africa's most magical safari and wildlife reservation while offering luxury, personalised service and superb Pan-African cuisine.

Game drives in open 4x4 safari vehicles, guided nature walks. Professional photographic safaris. Bush banqueting. (Other activities P. 629)

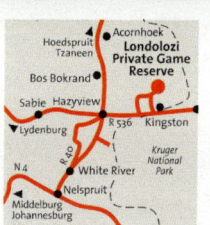

Access: Kruger Mpumalanga International airport to Hazyview. 8 km from Paul Kruger Gate, right towards Shaws Gate. Follow signs.
Airports: Johannesburg (Intl) 500 km, Londolozi Airstrip 1,2 km
Helipad: S 24° 48' 37" E 31° 30' 27"

Owners: David and Shan Varty
General Manager: Chris Kane Berman
Open all year
Currency: US dollar (USD)
Full board
36 rooms: 475 USD s.i. per person
Breakfast: included
Dogs: not allowed
Golf: Hazyview 65 km
Accepted cards: AE, DC, JCB, MC, VS

More info on www.relaischateaux.com/londolozi

South Africa

Cybele Forest Lodge and Spa

SINCE 1996

PO Box 346
White River 1240
(Mpumalanga) • South Africa

Tel. : **(27) (013) 764 1823**
Fax : (27) (013) 764 1810
cybele@relaischateaux.com

A secluded farmhouse-retreat of rare distinction, tucked away in a breathtaking African paradise. The lavish personalised accommodation includes cosy log fireplaces and some rooms have private gardens and pools. The spacious Paddock Suites offer exceptional comfort and undisturbed privacy with magnificent views. Delicious meals and Cape wines can be enjoyed in the candlelit award-winning restaurant or in the garden.

Trout fishing, walks. (Other activities P. 629)

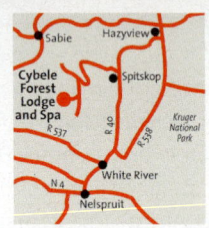

Access: From White River, along the R40 towards Hazyview; left towards Spitskop.

Airports: Johannesburg (Intl) 400 km, Nelspruit 50 km
Helipad: S 25° 09' 15" E 30° 58' 77"

Owners: Rupert and Barbara Jeffries
Open all year
Currency: South African rand (ZAR)
Half-board
6 cottages: 1790-2190 ZAR t.14% s.n.i.
6 suites: 3300-3980 ZAR t.14% s.n.i.
Breakfast: included
Dogs: not allowed
Golf: 15 km
Accepted cards: AE, DC, MC, VS

More info on www.relaischateaux.com/cybele

Tswalu Kalahari Reserve

SINCE 1999

PO Box 1081
Kuruman 8460
(The Kalahari, Northern Cape Province) • South Africa

Tel. : (27) (0) 21 426 4139
Fax : (27) (0) 21 426 4150
tswalu@relaischateaux.com

South Africa

Tswalu... where the Kalahari Bushmen once roamed... is an exquisite place where time seems to stand still. Set in a malaria free area of South Africa, this privately owned, luxurious, game reserve is home to many and varied species of wildlife. Motse sits at the foot of the Korannaberg mountains amidst nine individual, sumptuously furnished, air-conditioned legaes each with wonderful views across the spectacular Kalahari plains. Tswalu's unique setting and standard of excellence places it first amongst equals.

Day and night game drives, bush walks, bird watching, African open air boma dining, sundowners on the sand dunes. (Other activities P. 629)

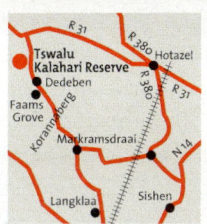

Access:
From Upington, N14 to Olifantshoek, then towards Barton then towards Sonstraal. After Healthcare Centre continue 10 km further. Tswalu is on the left.
Airports: Johannesburg (Intl) 700 km, Upington Riviere Au Tonner 255 km, Tswalu
Helipad: S 27° 13' 30'' E 22° 28' 70''

Owners: Oppenheimer Family
Open all year
Currency: South African rand (ZAR)
Full board
9 suites: 4400 ZAR s.n.i. per person
Breakfast: included
Dogs: not allowed
Golf: Sishen 70 km
Accepted cards: AE, DC, MC, VS

More info on www.relaischateaux.com/tswalu

Bushmans Kloof Wilderness Reserve

SINCE 2000

PO Box 53405 - Kenilworth 7745
(Cederberg Mountains-
Western Cape) • South Africa

Tel. : (27) (021) 797 09 90
Fax : (27) (021) 761 55 51
bushmans@relaischateaux.com

South Africa

Spectacular 18000 acres wilderness reserve situated in the famous Cederberg Mountains. This oasis lies in a valley surrounded by gigantic rock formations, rivers and exquisite indigenous gardens. The reserve is world famous for its 130 ancient rock art sites and boasts a rich diversity of wildlife and birds. Stylish contemporary cuisine, award winning wine list and Cape hospitality.

755 plant species, 34 mammals, and 135 bird varieties. Guided Rock Art walks and game drives, bird watching... (Other activities P. 629)

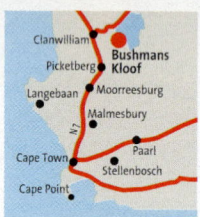

Access: From Capetown (3 hours): follow N1, then N7 to Clanwilliam. Follow R364 for 35 km over the Parkhuis Pass to the lodge. Road transfers on request and air shuttle from Capetown.
Airport: Cape Town (Intl) 278 km
Helipad: S 39° 02' 00" E 19° 02' 32"
Train station: Cape Town 278 km

Owners: Bill and Penny McAdam
General Manager: Mark McAdam
Annual closing: June
Currency: South African rand (ZAR)
Full board
7 rooms: 3100 ZAR s.i.
9 suites: 5000 ZAR s.i.
Breakfast: included
Dogs: not allowed
Golf: 36 km
Accepted cards: AE, DC, MC, VS

More info on www.relaischateaux.com/bushmans

Hunter's - Tsala

SINCE 1998

PO Box 454
Plettenberg Bay 6600
(Cape Province) • South Africa

Tel. : (27) (044) 532 7818
Fax : (27) (044) 532 7878
hunters@relaischateaux.com

South Africa

Set in a 90 hectare estate, overlooking indigenous forest, the Country House, nestling in beautiful gardens, offers accommodation in luxurious thatched cottages. «Tsala Treetop Lodge», set high in the forest canopy, speaks of adventure and romance, each suite with private pool suspended above the forest floor. Intimate, candle-lit dining, cellars of fine wines, warm hospitality. Private weddings in the Chapel.

Garden walks, forest trails, water sports, beaching. (Other activities P. 629)

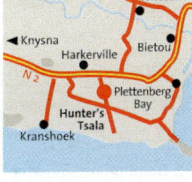

Access: From Plettenberg Bay, take N2 West. 10 km until you see the sign.

Airports: Cape Town (Intl) 530 km, Port Elizabeth 240 km
Train station: Knysna 20 km

Owners: Hunter Family
General Managers: Colin Morris and Julie Smith
Open all year
Currency: South African rand (ZAR)
Rates: Menus 165-185 ZAR s.n.i.
Carte 140-250 ZAR s.n.i.
15 rooms: 1740-2760 ZAR s.n.i.
18 suites: 2510-4290 ZAR s.n.i.
Breakfast: included
Dogs: not allowed
Golf: 10 km
Accepted cards: AE, DC, MC, VS

More info on www.relaischateaux.com/hunters

South Africa

SINCE 1992

The Plettenberg

Look out Rocks - PO Box 719
Plettenberg Bay 6600
(Cape Province) • South Africa

Tel. : (27) (044) 5332 030
Fax : (27) (044) 5332 074
plettenberg@relaischateaux.com

Built on the rocky headland overlooking the Indian Ocean, this exclusive hotel provides elegant accommodation, furnished in impeccable taste. Enjoy diving, tennis or golf, or simply laze on the terraces, enjoying the Tsitsikamma mountains and watching the whales and dolphins in the Bay. Dine at «Sand at the Plettenberg» on seafood delicacies and Karoo lamb, accompanied by the finest selection of wines.

Dolphin and whale watching, scenic flights, wine cellar. (Other activities P. 629)

Access: From Cape Town, N2 exit Plettenberg Bay, Marine Way, Main Street, Church Street.

Airports: Cape Town (Intl) 550 km, Port Elizabeth 220 km, Plettenberg Bay 10 km

Owner: Liz McGrath
General Manager: Nigel Pace
Open all year
Currency: South African rand (ZAR)
Rates: Menus 140-250 ZAR s.n.i.
Carte 160-280 ZAR s.n.i.
24 rooms: 1750-3500 ZAR s.n.i.
13 suites: 3600-8500 ZAR s.n.i.
Breakfast: included
Dogs: not allowed
Golf: 2 km
Accepted cards: AE, DC, MC, VS

More info on www.relaischateaux.com/plettenberg

Grande Roche

SINCE 1995

PO Box 6038
7622 Paarl
(Western Cape) • South Africa

Tel. : (27) (021) 863 27 27
Fax : (27) (021) 863 22 20
granderoche@relaischateaux.com

South Africa

South Africa's most hedonistic property, with a white-washed XVIIIth century Cape Dutch manor house, historic and new vine-clad suites is in the heart of the Cape Winelands surrounded by vineyards and exquisite gardens. Renowned «Bosman's» offers an extensive Cape wine cellar to complement Cape delicacies such as Tandoori Flavoured Yellowtail on vegetable chutney with curry sauce or Cutlet and Loin of Karoo Lamb.

Cycling, hot-air balloon, parachuting, wine tasting, squash, massage. (Other activities P. 629)

Access: Airport, N 2, towards Somerset West, R 300, towards N 1 to Paarl, exit Paarl Main Road - 5 km to the left.

Airport: Cape Town (Intl) 40 km
Helipad: S 33° 44' E 18° 58'

Owner: Hans Georg Allgaier
General Manager: Horst W. Frehse
Annual closing: From the beginning of June to the end of August
Currency: South African rand (ZAR)
Rates: Menus 130-450 ZAR s.n.i.
Carte 45-110 ZAR s.n.i.
5 rooms: 1500-2050 ZAR s.n.i.
30 suites: 1750-4125 ZAR s.n.i.
Breakfast: included
Dogs: not allowed
Golf: 5 km
Accepted cards: AE, DC, MC, VS

More info on www.relaischateaux.com/granderoche

South Africa

Clearwater Lodges

SINCE 2002

Welgevonden
Private Game Reserve
(Waterberg, Limpopo Province)
South Africa

Tel. : (27) (021) 889 5514
Fax : (27) (021) 889 5514
clearwater@relaischateaux.com

In the Waterberg mountains, a merely two-and-a-half hours' drive from Johannesburg, the private Welgevonden Game Reserve, 34000 hectares of magnificent landscapes, malaria-free, is the setting for two charming havens of peace, Clearwater Lodges: Kudu set out on the open savannah overlooking a waterhole and Tshetshepi, amongst lush indigenous trees, next to a stream. Colonial elegance combined with warm hospitality.

Game drives day and night, bush walks. (Other activities P. 629)

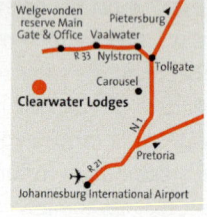

Access: From Johannesburg, R21 towards Pretoria, exit Pietersburg (N1). N1 towards toll gate, then towards Nylstroom. Cross Nylstroom and Vaalwater. Reserve approx. 25 km from Vaalwater.
Airports: Johannesburg (Intl) 260 km, Welgevonden Reserve (private) on the premises
Helipad: S 24° 12' 29" E 27° 54' 14"

Owner: Anne Cointreau-Huchon
General Managers: Anina Venter, Annie-Claude Bergonzoli
Open all year
Currency: South African rand (ZAR)
Full board
10 rooms: 2375-3738 ZAR per person
Breakfast: included
Dogs: not allowed
Golf: Nylstroom 85 km
Accepted cards: AE, DC, MC, VS

More info on www.relaischateaux.com/clearwater

Kwandwe Private Game Reserve

SINCE 2003

Private Bag X27
Benmore 2010
South Africa

Tel. : (27) (011) 809 4300
Fax : (27) (011) 809 4400
kwandwe@relaischateaux.com

South Africa

A 90-minute drive from Port Elizabeth in the heart of the Xhosa region, Kwandwe Private Game Reserve has organised safaris since October 2001. Accommodation-wise, there is a choice of nine sumptuous suites in the lodge or for six people in the exclusive villa, Uplands Homestead. Impeccable service, architecture that blends in with the magnificent bush landscape and an opportunity to experience the «Big Five» and much more.

(Other activities P. 629)

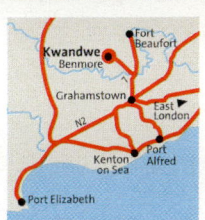

Access: From Port Elizabeth, N2 to Grahamstown. Take R67 to Fort Beaufort. Follow signs to Kwandwe.

Airports: Cape Town (Intl) 800 km, Kwandwe (private)
Helipad: S 33° 08' 59'' E 26° 31' 36''

Owner: Carl Desantis
General Manager: Yvonne Short
Open all year
Currency: US dollar (USD)
Full board
12 suites: 600-1060 USD s.i.
Breakfast: included
Dogs: not allowed
Golf: 90 km
Accepted cards: AE, DC, MC, VS

More info on www.relaischateaux.com/kwandwe

Le Quartier Français

SINCE 2000

CNR Berg-Wilhelmina Str.
Franschhoek 7690
(Cape Winelands) • South Africa

Tel. : (27) (021) 876 2151
Fax : (27) (021) 876 3105
quartier@relaischateaux.com

South Africa

83 kms from Cape Town, Le Quartier Français is in the heart of the vineyards of the famous Franschhoek valley of the French Huguenots. Located in the village centre, this Victorian residence is an exquisite stopping place on the wine trail and the trace of the history of the Huguenot settlers, between Mont Rochelle, Haute Provence, Môreson. Impeccable decoration and service. Eclectic cuisine by Margot Janse and regional wine, of course!

Fly fishing, health treatments (aromatherapy and massages). (Other activities P. 629)

Access: R45 to Franschhoek, down Huguenot Rd, police station on the left, Restaurant Le Quartier on the right. Right into Berg St and into Wilhelmina St for the Auberge.
Airports: Cape Town (Intl) 83 km
Stellenbosch 26 km

Owners: Susan Huxter, Richard Friedman and Pauline Friedman
General Manager: Linda Coltart
Open all year
Currency: South African rand (ZAR)
Rates: Menus 120-400 ZAR s.n.i.
Carte 120-300 ZAR s.n.i.
15 rooms: 1950-2200 ZAR t.1% s.n.i.
2 suites: 3900-4100 ZAR t.1% s.n.i.
Breakfast: 45-80 ZAR s.n.i.
Dogs: not allowed
Golf: 26 km
Accepted cards: AE, DC, JCB, MC, VS

More info on www.relaischateaux.com/quartier

The Marine Hermanus

South Africa — SINCE 2000

Marine Drive
Hermanus 7200
South Africa

Tel. : (27) (028) 313 10 00
Fax : (27) (028) 313 01 60
hermanus@relaischateaux.com

In the famous coastal village of Hermanus, the hotel overlooks Walker Bay with its hues of blue; The Marine, a totally renovated turn of the century colonial marvel is well named. Everything about it is marine, clear and luminous and decorated in contemporary style. Fresh seafood is served at «The Seafood at the Marine» and «The Pavilion» restaurants accompanied by the finest regional wines.

Whale watching, diving, squash, tennis. (Other activities P. 629)

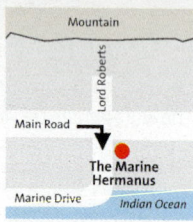

Access: Shortly after the main shopping centre on the Marine road.

Airport: Cape Town (Intl) 100 km
Helipad: S 34° 25' 00" E 19° 15' 00"

Owner: Liz McGrath
General Manager: Peter Kunz
Open all year
Currency: South African rand (ZAR)
Rates: Menus 110-185 ZAR s.n.i.
31 rooms: 1750-3500 ZAR s.n.i.
14 suites: 3600-8500 ZAR s.n.i.
Breakfast: included
Dogs: not allowed
Golf: 1 km
Accepted cards: AE, DC, VS

More info on www.relaischateaux.com/hermanus

Ellerman House

SINCE 1996

180 Kloof Road
Bantry Bay - 8005 Cape Town
(Western Cape) • South Africa

Tel. : (27) (021) 439 91 82
Fax : (27) (021) 434 72 57
ellerman@relaischateaux.com

South Africa

In 1962, Sir John Ellerman fell in love with Bantry Bay and undertook the renovation of this beautiful aristocratic villa. Ellerman House has nine elegant rooms and two sumptuous suites, decorated in Edwardian style, which offer superb views of the ocean. Linger over an evening aperitif on the terrace under the deep blue starry night of the southern hemisphere, then savour excellent seafood cuisine and local vintages.
(Other activities P. 629)

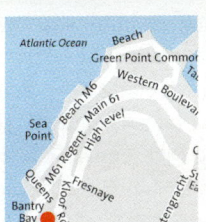

Access: From the airport, N2 towards Cape Town, via Eastern Blvd; Strand Street, High Level Rd, Av. Fresnaye.

Airport: Cape Town (Intl) 19 km
Train station: Cape Town 5 km

Owners: Peter Bayly and Paul Harris
General Manager: Justin Arenhold
Open all year
Currency: South African rand (ZAR)
Rates: Carte 100-175 ZAR s.n.i. (residents only)
9 rooms: 3100-5100 ZAR s.n.i.
2 suites: 7250 ZAR s.n.i.
Breakfast: included
Dogs: not allowed
Golf: 20 km
Accepted cards: AE, DC, JCB, MC, VS

More info on www.relaischateaux.com/ellerman

The Cellars-Hohenort

SINCE 1993

93, Brommersvlei Rd
Constantia - 7800 Cape Town
(Western Cape) • South Africa

Tel. : (27) (021) 794 21 37
Fax : (27) (021) 794 21 49
cellars@relaischateaux.com

South Africa

This elegant hotel situated in the heart of the Constantia Valley boasts beautiful gardens with sweeping views across False Bay and Table Mountain. A Beauty Spa awaits you. Enjoy swimming and tennis, or golf on the one hole golf green designed by Gary Player. Dine at the «Restaurant at the Cellars» or «The Cape Malay Restaurant» both are complimented by our award winning wine list.

Excursions, mountain walks, boules, biking, wine tasting, hair salon, gift shop. (Other activities P. 629)

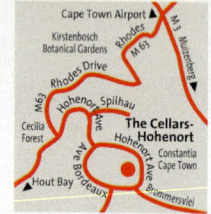

Access: Airport, Cape Town (N2), Muizenberg (M3), Kirstenbosch (M63) and towards Hout Bay.

Airport: Cape Town (Intl) 20 km

Owner: Liz McGrath
General Manager: Fredrik Aspegrén
Open all year
Currency: South African rand (ZAR)
Rates: Menus 190-350 ZAR s.i.
Carte 130-210 ZAR s.i.
36 rooms: 1750-3500 ZAR s.i.
17 suites: 3600-8500 ZAR s.i.
Breakfast: 60-70 ZAR s.i.
Dogs: not allowed
Golf: 5 km
Accepted cards: AE, DC, MC, VS

More info on www.relaischateaux.com/cellars

Hotel Heinitzburg

SINCE 2002

Heinitzburg Str. 22
Box 458, Windhoek
Namibia

Tel. : (264) (61) 249 597
Fax : (264) (61) 249 598
heinitzburg@relaischateaux.com

Namibia

This castle, built at the turn of the nineteenth century by Count von Schwerin for his fiancée Margarethe von Heinitz, offers accommodation in plush romantic elegance. Perched high above Windhoek, «Leo's» Restaurant offers spectacular vistas of the city lights below, not to mention unrivalled African sunsets. Savour masterfully prepared game dishes and relish fine wines from the country's largest private wine cellar.

(Other activities P. 629)

Street» on the left.
Airport: Windhoek (Intl) 40 km

Altitude: 1620 metres.
Access: From the airport: take «Sam Nujoma Drive», pass «Berg Street» and take «Heinitzburg

Owners: Jürgen and Beate Raith
General Manager: Beate Raith
Open all year
Currency: Euro (€)
Rates: Menus 20-35 € s.i.
Carte 17-27 € s.i.
16 rooms: single 110-130 € s.i.
double 165-190 € s.i.
Breakfast: 6-8 € s.i.
Dogs: not allowed
Golf: 4 km
Accepted cards: AE, DC, MC, VS

More info on www.relaischateaux.com/heinitzburg

Australia
New Zealand

Properties Australia	Nearest major city	Relais & Châteaux	Relais Gourmands	Page
Chateau Yering	Yarra Glen	⚜		513

New Zealand				
Kauri Cliffs	Bay of Islands	⚜		515

More info on www.relaischateaux.com

Chateau Yering

SINCE 2001

Melba Highway,
Yering, Yarra Valley
Victoria 3775 • Australia

Tel. : (61) (03) 9237 3333
Fax : (61) (03) 9237 3300
chateauyering@relaischateaux.com

Australia

This stunningly restored mansion located in the heart of the Yarra Valley, Victoria's premier wine growing region, an easy one-hour drive from Melbourne. Featuring 20 luxurious suites individually decorated with antiques and fine furnishings. This welcoming property in the European tradition is surrounded by historically significant gardens. It is a fitting tribute to Paul de Castella, a Swiss immigrant who established this superb residence in 1854.

Hunting, fishing, flying club, hiking, wineries. (Other activities P. 629)

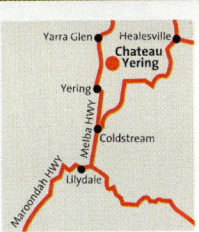

Access: 50 kilometres from Central Melbourne, East along the Maroondah Highway thru Lilydale turn left at Coldstream onto the Melba Highway.
Airport: Melbourne Tullamarine (Intl) 60 km
Helipad: S 37° 41.550' E 37° 14.522'
Train station: Lilydale 15 km

Owners: Len Milner & partners
General Manager: Sue O'Brien
Open all year
Currency: Australian dollar (AUD)
Rates: Menus 50-75 AUD s.i.
20 suites: starting at 435 AUD s.i.
Breakfast: 27-50 AUD s.i.
Dogs: not allowed
Golf: 20 km
Accepted cards: AE, DC, JCB, MC, VS

More info on www.relaischateaux.com/chateauyering

Kauri Cliffs

SINCE 2003

Matauri Bay Road,
Matauri Bay
Northland • New Zealand

Tel. : (64) (09) 405 1905
Fax : (64) (09) 405 1901
kauricliffs@relaischateau.com

New Zeaand

In the far north of New Zealand lies an unspoilt peninsula. High cliffs and a few ranches on this welcoming island which won the hearts of Julian and Josie Robertson. After designing a magnificent 18-hole golf course, the couple created a splendid colonial residence with outlying cottages. Space is the real luxury, the suite an apartment, the bathroom a spa. The epitome of refinement in a distant corner of the world.

(Other activities P. 629)

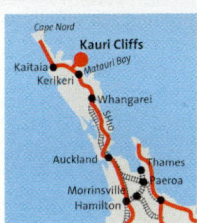

Access: From Kerikeri take State Hwy 10 towards the north. Exit Matauri Bay. Take Matauri Bay road and follow Kauri Cliffs signposting.
Airports: Auckland (Intl) 280 km, Kerikeri 30 km
Helipad: S 35° 04' 92" E 173° 55' 08"

Owner: Julian Robertson
General Manager: Richard Nauck
Annual closing: From July 1st to 21st
Currency: New Zealand dollar (NZD)
Rates: Menus 10-25 NZD s.i. Carte 150 NZD s.i.
16 suites: 1200-2200 NZD s.i.
Breakfast: 40 NZD s.i.
Dogs: allowed (extra cost)
Golf: on the premises
Accepted cards: AE, DC, MC, VS

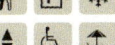

More info on www.relaischateaux.com/kauricliffs

Indonesia

Properties	Nearest major city	Relais & Châteaux	Relais Gourmands	Page
Matahari Beach Resort & Spa	Lovina	⚜		519
Tugu Bali (Hotel)	Kuta	⚜		517

Hotel Tugu Bali

SINCE 2002

J1 Pantai Batu Bolong
80351-Canggu Beach
(Bali) • Indonesia

Tel. : (62) (0361) 731 701
Fax : (62) (0361) 731 704
tugubali@relaischateaux.com

Indonesia

A setting of rare elegance, Tugu Bali celebrates Asian art. Created by Anhar Setjadibrata, a lawyer and art lover, the hotel, with its own private beach, was designed to accommodate the Dutch, Chinese, Javanese and Balinese furniture of its owner. The reception and services are on a par with the art collections. The spa ensures that all the traditions of beauty are represented here.

Cooking class, flower arrangement class, dancing lessons and performance. (Other activities P. 629)

Access: A8. 10 km north of Kuta, follow direction Tanah Lot, then turn left (signposts) to the end of the street, after approximately 2 km.

Airport: Denpasar (Intl) 17 km
Helipad: S 08° 43' 290'' E 115° 11' 016''

Owner: Anhar Setjadibrata
General Manager: Wedya Julianti
Open all year
Currency: US dollar (USD)
Rates: Menus 25-40 USD t.11% s.10%
Carte 20-40 USD t.11% s.10%
21 suites: 300-750 USD t.11% s.10%
Breakfast: 10-15 USD t.11% s.10%
Dogs: not allowed
Golf: 10 km
Accepted cards: AE, DC, JCB, MC, VS

More info on www.relaischateaux.com/tugubali

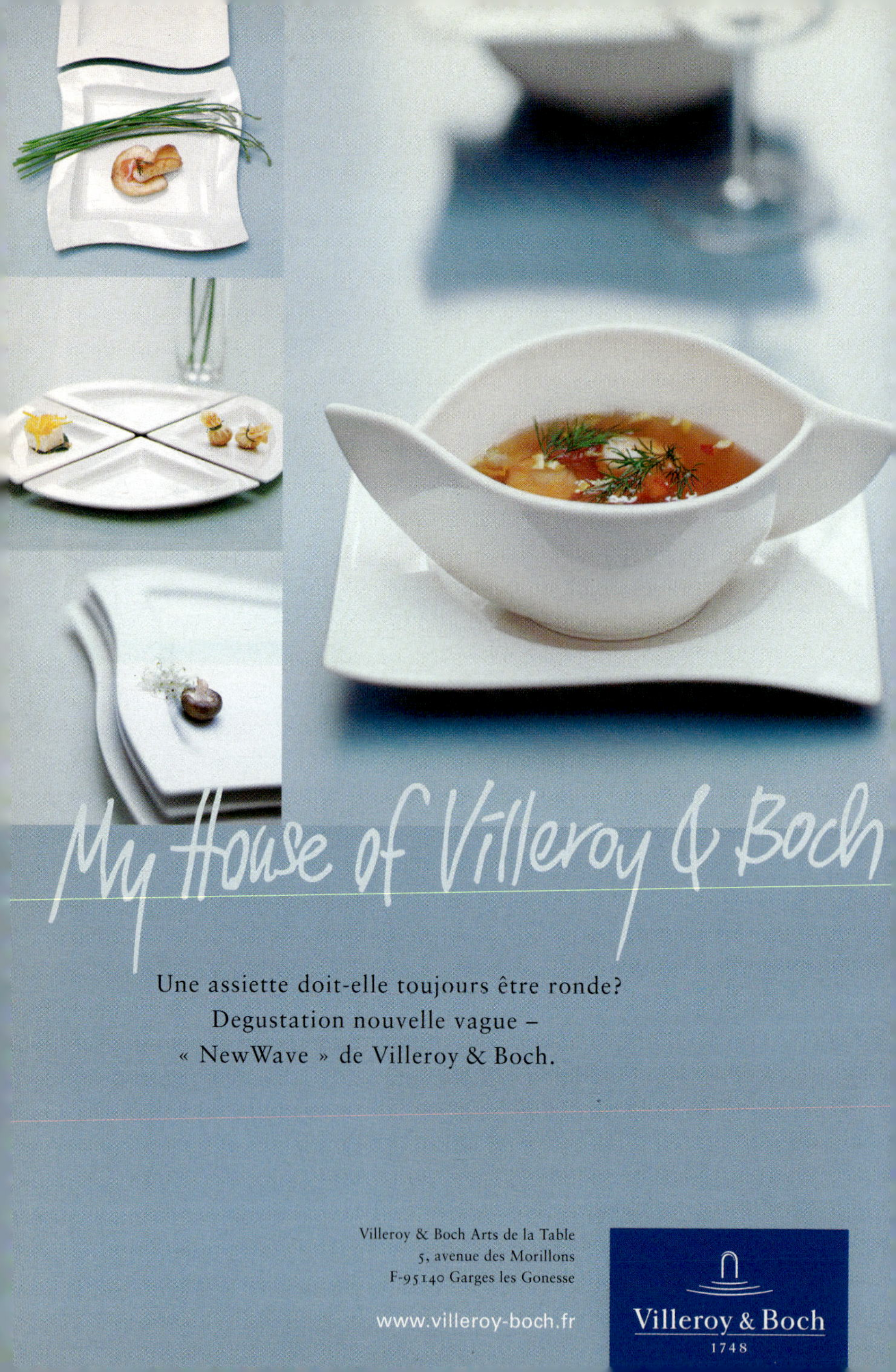

My House of Villeroy & Boch

Une assiette doit-elle toujours être ronde?
Dégustation nouvelle vague –
« NewWave » de Villeroy & Boch.

Villeroy & Boch Arts de la Table
5, avenue des Morillons
F-95140 Garges les Gonesse

www.villeroy-boch.fr

Matahari Beach Resort & Spa

PO Box 194
Pemuteran
(Bali) • Indonesia

Tel. : **(62) (362) 92 312**
Fax : (62) (362) 92 313
matahari@relaischateaux.com

SINCE 2002

Indonesia

On the northern coast of the island, set amongst fragrant lotus and frangipani flowers, this splendid village consisting of Balinese pavilions overlooks the sea. Each ornate bungalow has hand-carved wooden folding doors, a tropical garden and an outdoor shower with a stone dragon: pure nirvana. Just like the sense of wellbeing imparted from the spa with its massage and other treatments in the best Balinese tradition.

Snorkeling, badminton, volleyball, wood and stone carving courses. (Other activities P. 629)

Access: From the airport: take hotel bus (3 hour drive)

Airport: Denpasar (Intl) 150 km

Owners: Parwathi and Magnus Bauch
General Manager: Jany-Michel Fourré
Open all year
Currency: US dollar (USD)
Rates: Menus 30-37 USD t.10% s.10%
Carte 5-16 USD t.10% s.10%
30 rooms: 194-319 USD t.10% s.10%
2 suites: 424-466 USD t.10% s.10%
Breakfast: included
Dogs: not allowed
Golf: 60 km
Accepted cards: AE, DC, JCB, MC, VS

More info on www.relaischateaux.com/matahari

Japan
South Korea

Properties Japan	Nearest major city	Relais & Châteaux	Relais Gourmands	Page
Anaga (Hotel)	Kobe City	⚜		522
Asaba	Tokyo	⚜		529
Bécasse (La)	Osaka		◉	524
Enoteca Pinchiorri	Tokyo		◉	531
Gôra Kadan	Tokyo	⚜		530
Hiramatsu (Restaurant)	Tokyo		◉	527
Horai	Tokyo	⚜		525
Mikuni	Tokyo		◉	532
Seiryuso	Tokyo	⚜		528
Tosen Goshobo	Kobe City	⚜		523

South Korea				
Paradise Hotel Jeju	Jeju-City	⚜		533

More info on www.relaischateaux.com

Japan

Hotel Anaga

SINCE 1993

Anaga, Seidan-cho
Mihara-gun, Hyogo-ken 656-0661
Japan

Tel. : (81) (0799) 39 11 11
Fax : (81) (0799) 39 11 91
anaga@relaischateaux.com

Hotel Anaga, a veritable jewel of modern luxury and comfort, is set on the tip of Awaji island. After breakfast on a flower-bedecked balcony overlooking the sea, stroll to the beach or the Sumoto golf course or enjoy a cruise through the Strait of Naruto. Linger over cocktails in the elegant Lounge Bar, then savour French seafood specialities at the «Cadeau de la mer» or Japanese cuisine at the «Anaga Restaurant».

Fishing, cruise, whirlpool. (Other activities P. 629)

Access: From Tokushima airport, towards Naruto then Anaga (30 mn).

Airports: Kansai (Intl) 60 km, Tokushima 20 km
Helipad: N 34° 16' 12" E 134° 40' 15"

Owner: Sadao Iue
General Manager: Hidekatsu Matsuoka
Open all year
Currency: Yen (JPY)
Rates: Menus 6000-12000 JPY t.5% s.10%.
Carte 2500-8000 JPY t.5% s.10%
55 rooms: 18000-35000 JPY t.5% s.10%
6 suites: starting at 60000 JPY t.5% s.10%
Breakfast: 2000-3000 JPY t.5% s.10%
Dogs: not allowed
Golf: private 25 km
Accepted cards: AE, DC, JCB, MC, VS

More info on www.relaischateaux.com/anaga

Tosen Goshobo

SINCE 2001

858 Arima Onsen kita-ku
Kobe Hyogo 651-1401
Japan

Tel. : (81) (078) 904 0551
Fax : (81) (078) 904 3601
goshobo@relaischateaux.com

Japan

Goshobo was founded 800 years ago and is the oldest inn in the spa town of Arima, an exceptional spot with astonishing brick-coloured waters. «Gosho», which means «imperial palace», is an echo of the long, feudal era when the establishment was reserved for the nobility. It has maintained its renown and high quality. The region's excellent Kobe beef is also served here.

Walking... (Other activities P. 629)

Access: Take a Taxi from Shinkobe station (Shinkansen) or Osaka international airport, via driveways Hanshin Kosoku Kita Kobesen (Arimaguchi I.C.) or Chugoku Do (Nishinomiyakita I.C.).
Airports: Kansai (Intl) 105 km, Osaka 28 km
Train station: Arima Onsen 0,3 km

Owner: Hironobu Kanai
General Manager: Kimiko Kanai
Open all year
Currency: Yen (JPY)
Lunch on request
20 Japanese style rooms-suites:
half-board 64000-80000 JPY t.5%. s.10%
Breakfast: included
Dogs: not allowed
Golf: 5 km
Accepted cards: AE, DC, JCB, VS

More info on www.relaischateaux.com/goshobo

Japan — SINCE 1993

La Bécasse

ARK Bldg. 1F, 1-1-10 Kitahorie
Nishi-ku Osaka 550-0014
Japan

Tel. : (81) (06) 6543 4165
Fax : (81) (06) 6543 1268
becasse@relaischateaux.com

Yoshinori Shibuya, one of the highest stars in the firmament of Japanese gastronomy, is renowned for his original Franco-Japanese cuisine, inspired by Robuchon and Chapel, who taught him «never to be satisfied». This lesson has certainly borne fruit. Savour Shibuya's exquisite «salade de homard à la coriandre», «paupiettes de sole au foie gras» and «piccata d'agneau» in a tastefully decorated restaurant in the heart of Osaka.

Tenjinmatsuri Festival (July), Osaka Palace visit.

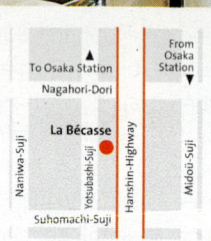

Access: From Osaka train station, towards Midoü-Suji, Namba, Suhomachi-Suji, towards Yotsubashi and Umeda.

Airport: Kansaï (Intl) 30 km
Train station: Osaka 3 km

Owner: Yoshinori Shibuya
Weekly closing: Sunday
Open all year
Currency: JPY (Yen)
Rates: Menus 4000-10000 JPY t.5% s.10%
Carte 10000-15000 JPY t.5% s.10%
Dogs: not allowed
Golf: 30 km
Accepted cards: AE, DC, JCB, VS

Yoshinori Shibuya

More info on www.relaischateaux.com/becasse

Horai

SINCE 1986

750-6 Izusan
Atami-shi, Shizuoka-ken 413-0002
Japan

Tel. : (81) (0557) 80 51 51
Fax : (81) (0557) 80 02 05
horai@relaischateaux.com

Japan

The only sound that you will hear in this idyllic haven, bathed in the aromas of ancient Japan, is the wind murmuring in the cherry trees or the waves rolling onto the sands. The minimalist «sukiya» style apartments, decorated with fresh flowers, open out directly onto the ocean. Relax in the open-air hot springs, then enjoy Japanese seafood in your room or savour French cuisine at the «Nanki Bunko» restaurant.

Sailing... (Other activities P. 629)

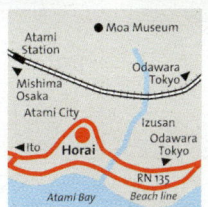

Access: From Tokyo, Super Bullet Train (50 mn) until Atami Station; 5 mn from Horai.

Airports: Tokyo-Narita (Intl) 170 km, Tokyo-Haneda 100 km
Train station: Atami 2,5 km

Owner: Seiyu Furutani
General Manager: Ryozo Tayama
Open all year
Currency: Yen (JPY)
Lunch on request
13 Japanese-style rooms-suites:
half board 80000-120000 JPY t.5%
3 Japanese-style apartments:
half board 160000-200000 JPY t.5%
Breakfast: included
Dogs: not allowed
Golf: 5 km
Accepted cards: AE, DC, JCB, MC, VS

More info on www.relaischateaux.com/horai

Restaurant Hiramatsu

SINCE 2003

5-15-13 Minamiazabu
Minato-ku, 106-0047 Tokyo
Japan

Tel. : (81) (03) 3444 3967
Fax : (81) (03) 3444 3991
hiramatsu@relaischateaux.com

Japan

In the cosmopolitan district of Hiroo in Tokyo, the chef Hiroyuki Hiramatsu welcomes you to a very elegant location, the walls devoted to the great masters of painting. Eyes and taste buds are wide awake. Exceptional wine list. Just try the: «terrine en gelée de poireaux et foie gras épicé au vieux Xérès», «pigeonneau rôti au miel, sauce vin rouge liée au foie» or the «demi-deuil de carrelet aux truffes blanches».

Access: Hiroo underground station, Hibya line, exit A1. At the junction of the Tokyo Mitsubishi Bank and the Kobeya bakery. Towards Arisugawa memorial park.
Airports: Tokyo Narita (Intl) 80 km, Tokyo Haneda 13 km
Train station: Hiroo/Hibiya 0,3 km

Owner/Chef: Hiroyuki Hiramatsu
Weekly closing: Monday
Annual closing: One week in Summer and from December 30th to January 6th
Currency: Yen (JPY)
Rates: Menus 6000-18000 JPY t.5% s.10%
Carte 6000-7500 JPY t.5% s.10%
Dogs: not allowed
Accepted cards: AE, DC, JCB, MC, VS

Hiroyuki Hiramatsu

More info on www.relaischateaux.com/hiramatsu

Japan

Seiryuso

SINCE 1986

2-2 Kochi
Shimoda-Shi
(Shizuoka-ken 415-0011) • Japan

Tel. : (81) (0558) 22 13 61
Fax : (81) (0558) 23 20 66
seiryuso@relaischateaux.com

Serenity and calm reign in this vast park bathed in Izu's light. A flagstone walk flanked by 100-year-old willows and a lovely stone lantern leads to six pavilions admirably arranged in the purest Japanese style. Pure water from on-site hotsprings replenish the external pool, which is open all year long. Casa Vino, renowned for its refined cuisine, offers primarily fish and wines from around the world.

(Other activities P. 629)

Access: 3.5 km from the Shimoda train station; from Tokyo via the Tomei highway and Rte 135.

Airport: Tokyo-Narita (Intl) 250 km
Train station: Shimoda 3,5 km

Owner: Kenichi Tanaka
General Manager: Hideo Tanaka
Open all year
Currency: Yen (JPY)
Rates: Menus 12000-25000 JPY t.8% s.i. Dinner on request
24 Japanese style rooms-suites:
half board 56000-90000 JPY t.8% s.i.
6 Japanese style suites:
half board 110000 JPY t.8% s.i.
Breakfast: included
Dogs: not allowed
Golf: 8 km
Accepted cards: AE, DC, JCB, VS

More info on www.relaischateaux.com/seiryuso

Asaba

SINCE 1989

3450-1 Shuzenji-Machi
Shizuoka-ken 410-2416
Japan

Tel. : (81) (0558) 72 70 00
Fax : (81) (0558) 72 70 77
asaba@relaischateaux.com

Japan

Asaba was built in 1675, amidst the oldest hotsprings on the Izu Peninsula. Its crowning feature is a bamboo forest bordering a magnificent pond. A series of sumptuous buildings seems to float along this stretch of water. Opposite them is the stage of the «No» Theatre, a little bridge, a room of mirrors... Outdoor or family bathing facilities are made of cypress wood. Festive Japanese cuisine.

(Other activities P. 629)

Access: From Mishima, R 136 towards Shuzenji; right after Kokey bridge in front of the Shuzenji Temple, 200 m farther on the left.

Airports: Tokyo-Narita (Intl) 200 km, Tokyo-Haneda 130 km
Train station: Shuzenji 2,5 km

Owner: Aiko Asaba
General Manager: Kazuhide Asaba
Open all year
Currency: Yen (JPY)
Half-board
15 rooms: 66000-84000 JPY t.5% s.i.
4 suites: 96000-110000 JPY t.5% s.i.
Breakfast: included
Dogs: not allowed
Golf: 3 km
Accepted cards: AE, DC, JCB, VS

More info on www.relaischateaux.com/asaba

Japan

SINCE 1992

Gôra Kadan

1300 Gôra, Hakone-Machi
Ashigara-Shimogun, Kanagawa-ken,
250-0408 • Japan

Tel. : (81) (0460) 2 3331
Fax : (81) (0460) 2 3334
gora@relaischateaux.com

Discover the wonders of an ancient Japanese hideway at Gôra Kadan, the former relaxing retreat of the «Kanin-no-miya» imperial family. This noble residence set in beautiful surroundings in the national park of Hakone, offers authentic Tatami style rooms with cypress bath, open-air bath or whirlpool bath. After a visit to the nearby botanical gardens or art and tradition museum, savour traditional «Kaiseki cuisine».

Beauty spa, thermal baths, open-air thermal bath. Limousine service available on request. (Other activities P. 629)

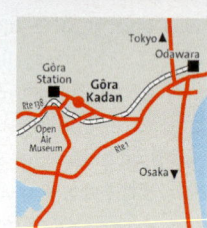

Access: 90 km South West of Tokyo, via the Tomei motorway then Atsugi-Odawara way and route 1.

Airports: Tokyo-Narita (Intl) 170 km, Tokyo-Haneda 100 km
Train station: Gôra 1 km

Owners: Miwako and Yuji Fujimoto
Open all year
Currency: Yen (JPY)
Rates: starting at 20000 JPY t.5% s.i.
26 Japanese style rooms-suites:
half-board 100000-124000 JPY t.5% s.i.
12 Japanese style apartments:
half-board 140000-150000 JPY t.5% s.i.
Breakfast: included
Dogs: not allowed
Golf: 5 km
Accepted cards: AE, DC, JCB, MC, VS

More info on www.relaischateaux.com/gora

Enoteca Pinchiorri

SINCE 2002

Ginza Core Bldg - 7th floor
8-20 Ginza 5 Chome, Chuo-Ku, Tokyo
Japan

Tel. : (81) (03) 3289 8081
Fax : (81) (03) 3289 8019
pinchiorri@relaischateaux.com

Japan

In the district of Ginza, a warm, elegant restaurant in classic European style. Besides exquisite Italian and French wines, guests can savour the wonderful Italian cuisine of Annie Féolde and her chef Toshikasu-Tsuji: «coquilles Saint-Jacques panées aux cèpes séchés, avec une purée de pois chiches et sauge frite aux anchois», «tortellis de brocolis sautés à l'huile d'olive et gousse d'ail, avec ragoût de pigeon au vinaigre balsamique».

Access: From the Ginza underground station, take exit A3. Enter the 2nd building on the left.

Airports: Tokyo-Narita (Intl) 80 km, Tokyo-Aneda 15 km
Train station: Ginza 1 km

Owner: A Table Matsuya
General Manager: Hideaki Sakama
Open all year
Currency: Yen (JPY)
Rates: Menus 12000-18000 JPY t.5% s.10%
Carte 12000-16000 JPY t.5% s.10%
Dogs: not allowed
Accepted cards: AE, DC, JCB, MC, VS

Toshikasu-Tsuji

More info on www.relaischateaux.com/pinchiorri

Mikuni

Japan

SINCE 1991

1-18 Wakaba
Shinjuku-ku Tokyo 160-0011
Japan

Tel. : **(81) (03) 33 51 38 10**
Fax : (81) (03) 32 25 13 24
mikuni@relaischateaux.com

Kiyomi Mikuni is one of Tokyo's highest rated chefs. Drawing on Girardet, Troisgros and Chapel, he has created his own «cuisine spontanée», blending French and Japanese tradition with innovative flair. Savour his exquisite «Japanized» «salade de homard d'Alain Chapel», and «platinium et menthe fraîche Kiyomi Mikuni», and choose from an excellent selection of French wines.

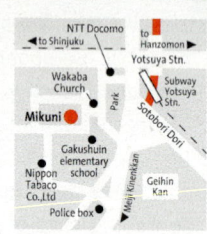

Access: From the Yotsuya railway station, cross Sotobori-Dori, then the park. Go straight on to the left of the church. Turn left at the first crossroads, then right to the very end.
Airports: Tokyo-Narita (Intl) 80 km, Tokyo-Haneda 12 km
Train station: Yotsuya 0,2 km

Owner/Chef: Kiyomi Mikuni
Annual closing: From Dec. 31st to January 7th and from August 9th to 16th
Currency: Yen (JPY)
Rates: Lunch 6500-10000 JPY t.5% s.15%
Dinner 15000 JPY t.5% s.15%
Carte 4200-18000 JPY s.i.
(Possibility of half portions for tasting)
Dogs: not allowed
Accepted cards: AE, DC, JCB, MC, VS

Kiyomi Mikuni

More info on www.relaischateaux.com/mikuni

Paradise Hotel Jeju

SINCE 2002

511 Topyong-dong
Seogwipo-City
(Jeju Province) • South Korea

Tel. : (82) (64) 763 2100
Fax : (82) (64) 732 9355
jeju@relaischateaux.com

South Korea

The semi-tropical island of Jeju, the largest in Korea, was formed by Mount Halla, an extinct volcano of legendary beauty. In this area with its abundant waterfalls, forests and canyons, the Paradise Group has created a luxurious resort and spa: a white building in the shape of an unusual circle with an enormous landscaping and terrace. Each room has its own distinct style: Korean, Mediterranean, Scandinavian, African, American…

(Other activities P. 629)

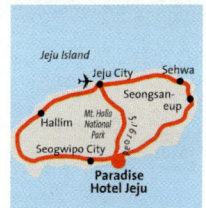

Access: From Jeju airport, take route 11 (5.16 roads), pass through the new town of Jeju and stay on the road crossing Mt. Halla, at 45 km, two streets cross, continue straight for 1 km.
Airport: Jeju (Intl) 50 km

Owner: Rak-Won Chun
General Manager: Young-Kwan ROH
Open all year
Currency: Korean Won (KRW)
Rates: Menus 15000-60000 KRW t.10% s.10%
Carte 20000-135000 KRW t.10% s.10%
46 rooms: 275000-385000 KRW t.10% and 2% s.10%
10 suites: 560000-800000 KRW t.10% and 2% s.10%
Breakfast: 12000-25000 KRW t.10% s.10%
Dogs: not allowed **Golf:** 25 km
Accepted cards: AE, DC, JCB, MC, VS

More info on www.relaischateaux.com/jeju

North America

Canada

Properties	Nearest major city	Relais & Châteaux	Relais Gourmands	Page
Aerie (The)	Victoria	⚜		550
Auberge Hatley	Montréal	⚜	◉	541
Eau à la Bouche (Hôtel L')	Montréal	⚜	◉	543
Hastings House	Vancouver	⚜		549
Inn at Manitou (The)	Toronto	⚜		544
Kingsbrae Arms	Saint-John	⚜		538
Langdon Hall	Toronto	⚜		545
Little Beaver Creek Ranch	Vancouver	⚜		547
Lumière	Vancouver		◉	548
Pinsonnière (La)	Québec	⚜		539
Post Hotel	Calgary	⚜		546
Trois Tilleuls & Spa (Les)	Montréal	⚜		540
Wickaninnish Inn (The)	Tofino	⚜		551

Kingsbrae Arms

Canada — SINCE 1998

219 King Street
St Andrews
New Brunswick E5B 1Y1 • Canada

Tel. : (1) (506) 529 1897
USA/Can Toll free : (1) (877) 529 1897
Fax : (1) (506) 529 1197
kingsbrae@relaischateaux.com

Set amidst 27 acres of Kingsbrae Garden, this XIXth century enclave offers the ultimate private country house experience. Romantic suites with draped canopy beds, marble bathrooms, fireplaces, and balconies with sweeping ocean views. An historic seaside resort with golf, galleries, enchanting harbor, and the world's highest tides. Each evening the house party gathers for superb regional cuisine and fine wine.

Massage, garden tours, museums, deep sea and fly fishing, whale watching, biking. (Other activities P. 629)

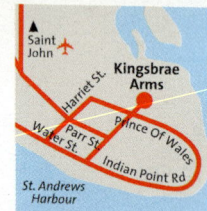

Access: From the Fundy Coastal Drive, Hwy 1, exit St Andrews. Turn up King St. and go to the top of the hill.

Airports: Saint John (Intl) 100 km, Bangor (Intl) 145 km

Owners: Harry Chancey Jr. and David Oxford
General Manager: Harry Chancey
Annual closing: Mid-winter
Currency: Canadian dollar (CAD)
Dinner included
5 rooms: 550-750 CAD t.15% s.15%
3 suites: 700-1000 CAD t.15% s.15%
Breakfast: included
Dogs: on request
Golf: 1 km
Accepted cards: AE, MC, VS

More info on www.relaischateaux.com/kingsbrae

La Pinsonnière

SINCE 1985

124 Saint-Raphaël - La Malbaie
(secteur Cap-à-l'Aigle)
Québec G5A 1X9 • Canada

Tel. : (1) (418) 665 4431
USA/Can Toll free : (1) (800) 387 4431
Fax : (1) (418) 665 7156
pinsonniere@relaischateaux.com

Canada

Perched high above the majestic St. Lawrence River, La Pinsonnière embraces the changing seasons and natural splendours of the Charlevoix region, a UNESCO World Biosphere Reserve. The rooms, with four-poster beds, fireplaces and whirlpool baths, offer idyllic views. Outdoor activities include skiing, dog-sledding and whale watching cruises. Award-winning cuisine is complemented by an impressive wine cellar.

Massotherapy, trapping, snowmobile outings, concerts, casino. (Other activities P. 629)

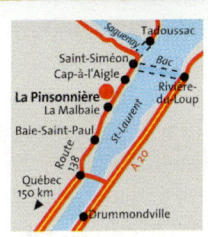

Access: From Québec, route 138 East to Cap-à-l'Aigle, or by 362 East, the scenic route.

Airports: Québec (Intl) 150 km, Montreal (Intl) 400 km
Train station: Québec 150 km

Owners: Authier Family
General Manager: Valérie Andrée Authier
Open all year
Currency: Canadian dollar (CAD)
Rates: Menus 60-125 CAD t.15% s.15%
25 rooms: 160-550 CAD t.15% s.i.
1 suite: 550 CAD t.15% s.i.
Breakfast: 18 CAD t.15% s.15%
Dogs: not allowed
Golf: 5 km (2)
Accepted cards: AE, MC, VS

More info on www.relaischateaux.com/pinsonniere

Canada

Les Trois Tilleuls & Spa

SINCE 1983

290 Richelieu
St-Marc-sur-Richelieu
Québec JOL 2EO • Canada

Tel. : (1) (514) 856 7787
USA/Can Toll free : (1) (800) 263 2230
Fax : (1) (450) 584 3146
tilleuls@relaischateaux.com

Deep in the heart of Quebec, maple groves, manors, churches and mills bear witness to the birth of a nation. On the tranquil banks of the Richelieu River, discover a magnificent setting where the comfortable rooms (decorated with fresh bouquets) open onto terraces and the beautiful riverfront garden. After hunting and sleigh riding in unspoiled natural surroundings, relax in the Givenchy spa, savour superb cuisine and exceptional wines.

Hiking, cross-country skiing. (Other activities P. 629)

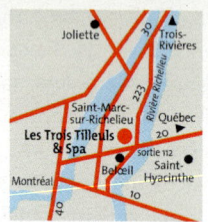

Access: From the airport, A20 towards Quebec City, exit 112; route 223 north, 7 km.

Airports: Dorval (Intl) 60 km, Mirabel (Intl) 100 km
Helipad: N 39° 12' W 45° 73'
Train station: Montréal 50 km

Owner: Michel Aubriot
Open all year
Currency: Canadian dollar (CAD)
Rates: Menus 55-76 CAD t.15% s.15%
Carte 40-76 CAD t.15% s.15%
23 rooms: 95-125 CAD t.15% s.i.
18 suites: 275-450 CAD t.15% s.i.
Breakfast: 4-13 CAD t.15% s.15%
Dogs: not allowed
Golf: 15 km
Accepted cards: AE, DC, MC, VS

More info on www.relaischateaux.com/tilleuls

Auberge Hatley

SINCE 1985

325 Chemin Virgin, C.P. 330
North Hatley
Québec J0B 2C0 • Canada

Tel. : (1) (819) 842 2451
Fax : (1) (819) 842 2907
hatley@relaischateaux.com

Canada

A charming country house with magnificent views overlooking Lake Massawippi and surrounding forests tinged with purple and gold during the Indian summer. Bright and intimate rooms, many with fireplace, balconies. One of the most celebrated restaurants in Quebec. The Hatley grows its salads and herbs in its own greenhouse. Super wine cellar with over 1100 vintages. Enjoy private access to the lake.

Alpine and cross-country skiing, snowmobiling, dog sleighing, cycle paths, massage therapy. (Other activities P. 629)

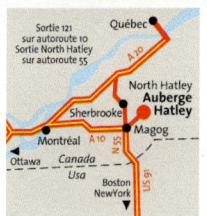

Access: From Montreal, highway n° 10, exit 121; follow signs to «Auberge Hatley».

Airports: Dorval (Intl) 140 km, Mirabel (Intl) 180 km
Train station: Montréal 140 km

Owners: Robert and Liliane Gagnon
Annual closing: From January 5th to 24th
Currency: Canadian dollar (CAD)
Rates: Menus 60-110 CAD t.16% s.n.i.
Carte 60-110 CAD t.16% s.n.i.
24 rooms: 175-400 CAD t.16% s.i.
Breakfast: 15 CAD t. 16% s.n.i.
Dogs: not allowed
Golf: 3 km
Accepted cards: AE, MC, VS

Alain Labrie

More info on www.relaischateaux.com/hatley

Learn to Cook Like a Chef!

The secrets of foie gras...a perfect beurre blanc... the only way to hold a chef's knife...
Stir, chop, mix, taste... live your culinary dream.

Our unique program allows the passionate amateur cook to go behind the scenes as a kitchen intern in nearly 100 Relais Gourmands restaurants worldwide. Put on your chef's coat and step into the kitchen, where you will work side-by-side with the chef and kitchen team as you learn the secrets of the masters. Your dinner parties will never be the same.

For more information, please visit us at www.ecoledeschefs.com or call toll-free (North America) 877-334-6464.

L'Ecole des Chefs

11 East 44th Street, Suite 707 New York, NY 10017
212-856-0115 Tel • 212-856-0193 Fax • info@ecoledeschefs.com

33, boulevard Malesherbes 75008 Paris
Tel. (33) (0)1 45 72 90 00 • Fax (33) (0)1 40 06 04 35 • contact@ecoledeschefs.com
www.ecoledeschefs.com

Hôtel L'Eau à la Bouche

SINCE 1989

3003 Bd Ste-Adèle
Sainte-Adèle
Québec J8B 2N6 • Canada

Tel. : (1) (450) 229 2991
USA/Can Toll free : (1) (888) 828 2991
Fax : (1) (450) 229 7573
eaubouche@relaischateaux.com

Canada

In the Laurentides mountains, less than 45 minutes from Montreal and Mount Tremblant, time stands still. As you cross the threshold of this inn, backing onto maple and pine-clad mountains, the courtesy of the staff works its magic. Let yourself be tempted by Anne Desjardins' cuisine, inspired by the fine regional produce, and the harmony between wine and food, which her team of wine waiters will help you achieve.

52 golf courses in the region, snowmobiling, alpine skiing, cross-country skiing, concerts, art gallery, antiquing, cycle track... (Other activities P .629)

Access: Laurentides motorway (15 North), exit 67, route 117 North (blvd. Sainte-Adèle).

Airports: Mirabel (Intl) 35 km, Dorval (Intl) 75 km

Owners: Pierre Audette and Anne Desjardins
Open all year
Currency: Canadian dollar (CAD)
Rates: Menus 70-140 CAD t.15% s.15%
Carte 37-47 CAD t.15% s.15%
25 rooms: 225-330 CAD t.15% s.i.
Breakfast: 15 CAD t.15% s.15%
Dogs: not allowed
Golf: 1 km
Accepted cards: AE, DC, MC, VS

Anne Desjardins

More info on www.relaischateaux.com/eaubouche

Canada

The Inn at Manitou

SINCE 1986

Center Road
McKellar
Ontario POG 1CO • Canada

Tel. : (1) (705) 389 2171
USA/Can. Toll free : (1) 800 571 8818
Fax : (1) (705) 389 3818
manitou@relaischateaux.com

Charming resort of 220 hectares nestled along the shores of unspoiled Lake Manitou-wabing. Outstanding programmes in golf, tennis and a full service spa. Most guest rooms and suites with spectacular views. Comfortable sitting areas in front of log burning fireplaces. With its renowned restaurant, exceptional wine list, this wonderful resort is created with utmost care and managed by Ben and Sheila Wise.

Water sports, tennis clinics. (Other activities P. 629)

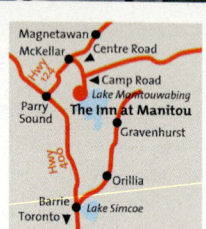

Access: Toronto, Highway 401, 400 North towards Parry Sound, Highway 124 Sundridge.

Airports: Toronto (Intl) 250 km, Lake Manitouwabing 1 km
Train station: Parry Sound 40 km

Owners/General Managers: Ben and Sheila Wise
Annual closing: From October 21st to May 8th
Currency: Canadian dollar (CAD)
Rates: Carte 31-65 CAD t.8% and 7% s.16%
22 rooms: pp/pd includes all meals
250-418 CAD t.8% and 7% s.16%
11 suites: pp/pd includes all meals
336-441 CAD t.8% and 7% s.16%
Breakfast: 21 CAD t.8% and 7% s.16%
Dogs: allowed
Golf: Golf Academy on the premises
Accepted cards: AE, DC, MC, VS

More info on www.relaischateaux.com/manitou

Langdon Hall

SINCE 1990

Country House Hotel & Spa
RR n°33 Cambridge
Ontario N3H 4R8 • Canada

Tel. : (1) (519) 740 2100
Fax : (1) (519) 740 8161
langdon@relaischateaux.com

Canada

Set amidst 200 acres, our house was built for a descendant of legendary financier John Jacob Astor. Most guestrooms have a fireplace, and all are decorated with period furniture, crisp white linens and the most comfortable feather beds. The dining-room offers outstanding cuisine featuring local products and our garden's bounty. Indulge at the Spa, visit Mennonite countryside and enjoy theatre at the Stratford Festival or visit Niagara Falls.

Croquet, walking trails. (Other activities P. 629)

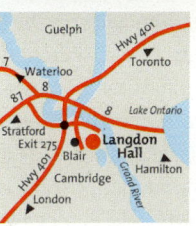

Access: Hwy 401, exit 275 travel South on Fountain Street Take 2nd right- Blair Road, then 4th right Langdon Drive.

Airport: Toronto (Intl) 85 km
Train station: Kitchener 10 km

Owners: Beaton and Bennett Families
General Manager: Jill McGoey
Open all year
Currency: Canadian dollar (CAD)
Rates: Menus 75-95 CAD t.15% s.n.i.
Carte 65-85 CAD t.15% s.n.i.
40 rooms: 289-400 CAD s.i.
13 suites: 450-650 CAD s.i.
Breakfast: 15 CAD t.15% s.n.i.
Dogs: allowed (extra cost)
Golf: public 2 km
Accepted cards: AE, DC, MC, VS

More info on www.relaischateaux.com/langdon

Post Hotel

PO Box 69
Lake Louise
Alberta TOL 1EO • Canada

SINCE 1991

Tel. : (1) (403) 522 3989
USA/Can Toll free : (1) (800) 661 1586
Fax : (1) (403) 522 3966
posthotel@relaischateaux.com

Canada

Summer and winter, the Canadian Rockies at their finest. Perched at 1500 metres amidst the natural wonders of Banff National Park, you will find this cherished Alpine chalet. Canada's largest ski area is just minutes away and the abundance of snow is just one reason a growing number of European skiers visit the area each winter. The dining-room features fresh market cuisine complemented by an 1300 label, 28500 bottle award-winning wine cellar.

Hiking... (Other activities P. 629)

Altitude: 1500 metres.
Access: From Calgary, take the Trans Canada Highway (#1), via Banff
Airport: Calgary (Intl) 190 km
Owners: André and Georges Schwarz
General Manager: Geoffrey Booth
Annual closing: From October 19th to December 11th
Currency: Canadian dollar (CAD)
Rates: Menu 95 CAD t.7% s.15%
Carte 60-80 CAD t.7% s.15%
71 rooms: 320-450 CAD t.12% s.i.
27 suites: 500-750 CAD t.12% s.i.
Breakfast: 17 CAD t.7% s.15%
Dogs: not allowed
Golf: 55 km
Accepted cards: AE, MC, VS

More info on www.relaischateaux.com/posthotel

Little Beaver Creek Ranch

SINCE 1998

Quilchena
Glimpse Lake Box 37
British Columbia V0E 2R0 • Canada

Tel. : (1) (250) 371 76 64
Fax : (1) (250) 372 48 93
littlebeaver@relaischateaux.com

Canada

The spirit of the Wild West still lives on this ranch, built at the turn of the century. Between the Pacific coast and the Rockies, this authentic ranch is set on the shores of Glimpse Lake amidst stunning countryside where beavers, bears and elk still roam. Explore the region on horseback and then enjoy the comfort of the superb guest suites. Savour a hint of freedom and adventure combined with luxury and refined cuisine.
Horseback riding, fishing. (Other activities P. 629)

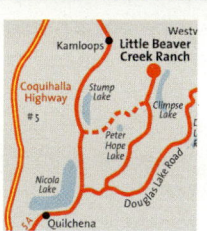

Altitude: 1100 metres.
Access: From Vancouver, Hwy 1 to Hope. Coquihalla, Hwy 5 towards Merritt – exit 290 – Quilchena, Hwy 5A to Douglas Lake Road intersection – follow signs.
Airports: Vancouver (Intl) 300 km, Kamloops 80 km
Helipad: N 50° 15' 27" W 120° 15' 44"

Owners: Alex and Nathalie Schütz-Meissner
Annual closing: From October 15th to May 1st
Currency: Canadian dollar (CAD)
Full board
7 suites: 450-650 CAD t.15%
per person and per day
Breakfast: included
Dogs: allowed
Golf: 22 km
Accepted cards: AE, DC, MC, VS

More info on www.relaischateaux.com/littlebeaver

Lumière

Canada

SINCE 2001

2551 West Broadway
Vancouver
British Columbia, V6K 2E9 • Canada

Tel. : (1) (604) 739 8185
Fax : (1) (604) 739 8139
lumiere@relaischateaux.com

This award winning restaurant is a combination between European elegance, North American flair and Asian minimalism. Robert Feenie's cuisine reflects this eclectic style. For this young Canadian chef, the simplest cuisine is the most complex. Savour: «salade d'asperges blanches et d'asperges vertes», «ragoût de champignons sauvages», «braisé de homard» and «sorbet au marscapone». The vegetable menu is a feast of flavours.

(Other activities P. 629)

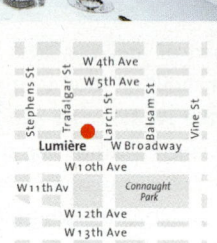

Access: From Downtown: over the Granville Street Bridge, turn right on West Broadway for 3 km. Between Larch Street and Trafalgar Street.

Airport: Vancouver (Intl) 5 km
Train station: CPR 5 km

Owner/Chef: Robert Feenie
General Manager: Mark Steenge
Weekly closing: Monday
Open all year
Currency: Canadian dollar (CAD)
Rates: Menus 90-110 CAD t.7% and 10% s.n.i.
Tasting bar 25-40 CAD t.7% and 10% s.n.i.
Dogs: not allowed
Golf: 2 km
Accepted cards: AE, DC, MC, VS

Robert Feenie

More info on www.relaischateaux.com/lumiere

Hastings House

SINCE 1986

160 Upper Ganges Rd
Salt Spring Island
British Columbia V8K 2S2 • Canada

Tel. : (1) (250) 537 2362
USA/Can. Toll free : (1) (800) 661 9255
Fax : (1) (250) 537 5333
hastings@relaischateaux.com

Canada

Return to an era of grace and simplicity. This magnificent half-timbered English manor nestles amidst the forests of Salt Spring Island beside a peaceful harbor. Enjoy acres of vibrant lawns and gardens, breathtaking vistas, abundant wildlife, and a lively arts community. Savor exquisite cuisine prepared with the finest local products, and relax in the comfort of your individually appointed fireplace suite.

Galleries, crafts market, bird watching, spa, croquet, bocce ball. (Other activities P. 629)

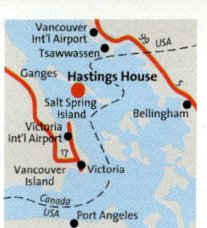

Access: By car-ferry from Vancouver or Victoria, or by seaplane from Vancouver, Victoria or Seattle.

Airports: Vancouver (Intl) 47 km, Seattle 117 km

Owners: Jerry Parks and Bonny O'Connor
General Managers: Marcel Kauer, Shirley McLaughlin
Annual closing: From January 1st to March 19th and from November 17 th to December 31st
Currency: Canadian dollar (CAD)
Rates: Menu 90 CAD t.7% s.n.i.
3 rooms: 350-450 CAD t.15% s.n.i.
15 suites: 420-700 CAD t.15% s.n.i.
Breakfast: included
Dogs: not allowed
Golf: 4 km (2 courses)
Accepted cards: AE, MC, VS

More info on www.relaischateaux.com/hastings

Canada

The Aerie

SINCE 1996

600 Ebadora Lane - Box 108
Malahat - Vancouver Island
British Columbia, VOR 2LO • Canada

Tel. : (1) (250) 743 7115
USA/Can. toll free : (1) (800) 518 1933
Fax : (1) (250) 743 4766
aerie@relaischateaux.com

Nestled high above the Malahat summit viewpoint, yet only 20 minutes north of Victoria, The Aerie's exquisite setting, Mediterranean-style elegance and awe-inspiring vistas are simply unforgettable. A sanctuary for body and soul, the inn will offer you options as varied as your mood. Soak up the atmosphere in the pool, sauna and magnificent outdoor hot tub. Or simply rejuvenate your spirit at the Wellness and Beauty Centre.

Whale watching, bird watching, wine tours, garden tours, city tours, shopping. (Other activities P. 629)

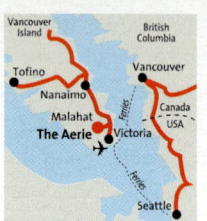

Access: From Victoria Airport, Trans Canada Highway, exit at Spectacle Lake; follow road signs.

Airport: Victoria (Intl) 40 km
Helipad: N 48° 34' 13" O 123° 32' 06"

Owner: Maria Schuster
General Manager: Markus Griesser
Annual closing: From January 6th to 24th
Currency: Canadian dollar (CAD)
Rates: Menus 55-85 CAD t.7% s.n.i.
Carte 30-40 CAD t.7% s.n.i.
10 rooms: 195-295 CAD t.15% s.n.i.
19 suites: 325-525 CAD t.15% s.n.i.
Breakfast: included
Dogs: not allowed
Golf: 3 golf courses (20 mn)
Accepted cards: AE, DC, MC, VS

More info on www.relaischateaux.com/aerie

The Wickaninnish Inn

SINCE 1998

Osprey Lane at Chesterman Beach
Tofino
British Columbia V0R 2Z0 • Canada

Tel. : (1) (250) 725 31 00
Fax : (1) (250) 725 31 10
wickaninnish@relaischateaux.com

Canada

Nature lovers will adore this idyllic retreat nestled on the West Coast of Vancouver Island. Imagine a fine sand beach, surrounded by a forest of giant conifers, and a charming residence, built of cedar wood, whose wide bay windows offer breathtaking views of the open ocean and the islands. Imagine savoring delicious seafood then relaxing in a tranquil room, lulled by the sound of the waves. Wickaninnish Inn: the answer to your dreams.

Whale watching, sea kayaking, birding, surfing, storm-watching. (Other activities P. 629)

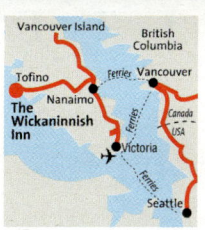

Access: From Nanaimo Highway 19, then Hwy 4 West until Port Alberni then Tofino. Turn left on Lynn Road and right on Osprey Lane.

Airports: Vancouver (Intl) 250 km, Long Beach Airport 15 km
Helipad: N 49° 7' 406" W 125° 54' 22"
Train station: Parksville 171 km

Owners: McDiarmid Family
Director: Charles McDiarmid
Open all year
Currency: Canadian dollar (CAD)
Rates: Menu 85 CAD t.15% s.n.i.
Carte 60-80 CAD t.15% s.n.i.
46 rooms: 230-480 CAD t.15% s.n.i.
Breakfast: 7-18 CAD t.15% s.n.i.
Dogs: allowed (extra cost 25 CAD)
Golf: 10 km
Accepted cards: AE, DC, JCB, MC, VS

More info on www.relaischateaux.com/wickaninnish

United States (East)

Properties	Nearest major city	Relais & Châteaux	Relais Gourmands	Page
Auréole	New York		●	557
Bernardin (Le)	New York		●	560
Blackberry Farm	Knoxville	⚜		579
Blantyre	Boston	⚜		565
Canoe Bay	Minneapolis	⚜		588
Charlie Trotter's	Chicago		●	584
Charlotte Inn (The)	Boston	⚜		573
Daniel	New York		●	559
Everest	Chicago		●	585
Fearrington House (The)	Chapel Hill	⚜		578
Gastonian Inn	Savannah	⚜		582
Glendorn	Buffalo	⚜		575
Home Hill	Hanover	⚜		571
Homestead Inn	New York	⚜	●	563
Inn at Little Washington (The)	Washington	⚜	●	577
Inn at Sawmill Farm (The)	Albany	⚜		572
Jean Georges	New York		●	561
Lake Placid Lodge	Albany	⚜		567
Mayflower Inn (The)	New York	⚜		564
Morrison House	Washington	⚜		576
Nomades (Les)	Chicago		●	587
Old Drovers Inn	New York	⚜		566
Pitcher Inn (The)	Burlington	⚜		570
Planters Inn	Charleston	⚜		581
Point (The)	Albany	⚜		568
Ryland Inn (The)	New York		●	562
Seeger's	Atlanta		●	583
Tru	Chicago		●	586
Wauwinet (The)	Nantucket Town	⚜		574
White Barn Inn	Boston	⚜	●	569
Woodlands Resort & Inn	Charleston	⚜	●	580

More info on www.relaischateaux.com

United States (West)

Properties	Nearest major city	Relais & Châteaux	Relais Gourmands	Page
Auberge du Soleil	San Francisco	⚜		597
Château du Sureau	Fresno	⚜	●	600
French Laundry (The)	San Francisco		●	595
Gary Danko	San Francisco		●	598
Goldener Hirsch Inn	Park City	⚜		591
Home Ranch (The)	Steamboat Springs	⚜		592
Knob Hill Inn	Ketchum	⚜		590
Little Nell (The)	Aspen	⚜		593
Meadowood Napa Valley	San Francisco	⚜		596
Orangerie (L')	Los Angeles		●	603
Patina Restaurant	Los Angeles		●	604
Rancho de San Juan	Española	⚜		594
Rancho Valencia Resort	San Diego	⚜		605
San Ysidro Ranch	Los Angeles	⚜		601
Sherman House (The)	San Francisco	⚜		599
Triple Creek Ranch	Missoula	⚜		589

More info on www.relaischateaux.com

Aureole

SINCE 1997

34, East 61st Street
New York
New York 10021 • USA

Tel. : (1) (212) 319 1660
Fax : (1) (212) 750 8613
aureole@relaischateaux.com

USA

Behind the huge two-storey glass façade of an Upper East Side brownstone is the original showcase of great American cooking founded by Charlie Palmer. Upon entering you are immediately surrounded by warm attention in an elegant setting. The carefully selected wine list is offered electronically by e-wine book. Diners return to savour the popular tasting menus that change monthly to reflect the season's best ingredients.

Access: On Manhattan's Upper East Side, between Madison and Park Avenues, just one block from 5th Avenue and Central Park.
Airports: New York J.F.K. (Intl) 35 km, New York La Guardia 29 km

Owner: Charlie Palmer
General Manager: Richard Lo Pozzo
Weekly closing: Sunday
Open all year
Currency: US dollar (USD)
Rates: Week lunch: Menu 35 USD s.20%
Carte 30-50 USD s.20%
Dinner: Menus 69-85 USD s.20%
Dogs: not allowed
Accepted cards: AE, MC, VS

Charlie Palmer

More info on www.relaischateaux.com/aureole

Daniel

SINCE 1995

60 East 65th Street
New York
New York 10021 • USA

Tel. : (1) (212) 288 0033
Fax : (1) (212) 396 9014
daniel@relaischateaux.com

USA

Daniel, New York's most fashionable gourmet destination, enchants you with a warm and welcoming bar & lounge and elegant Venetian renaissance dining-room. Chef Daniel Boulud's French cuisine inspired by the finest American products features «Oregon morel stuffed with squab and foie gras» and «Maine sea scallop seviche with oscetra caviar and oysters». The renowned wine cellar is filled with over 1200 world class vintages.

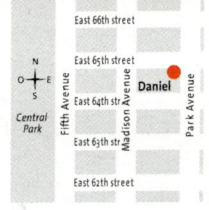

Access: At Park Avenue and E 65th Street. Near the Upper East Side's fashionable art galleries and boutiques, and minutes from midtown.

Airports: New York J.F.K. (Intl) 25 km, New York La Guardia 15 km
Train station: Grand Central Station 2 km

Owners: Daniel Boulud and Joël Smilow
Weekly closing: Sunday
Open all year
Currency: US dollar (USD)
Rates: Dinner 85-160 USD s.n.i.
Dogs: not allowed
Accepted cards: AE, DC, MC, VS

Daniel Boulud

More info on www.relaischateaux.com/daniel

USA

Le Bernardin

SINCE 1998

155 West 51st Street
New York
New York 10019 • USA

Tel. : (1) (212) 554 15 15
Fax : (1) (212) 554 11 00
bernardin@relaischateaux.com

Chef Eric Ripert and Maguy Le Coze preside over Le Bernardin, innovation and luxury in dining located in Midtown Manhattan. Ripert's interpretations of seafood such as Striped Bass Baked with Shaved Celery Root Perigord Truffles and Salsify have been lauded by critics and diners alike, while the exceptional wine list and beautiful dining-room provide the perfect setting for an unforgettable experience.

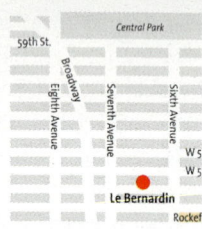

Access: Between Rockefeller Center and Broadway. Two streets away from the Museum of Modern Art (MoMA).

Airports: New York J.F.K. (Intl) 40 km, New York La Guardia 24 km

Owners: Maguy Le Coze and Eric Ripert
Weekly closing: Saturday for lunch and Sunday
Annual closing: Bank holidays
Currency: US dollar (USD)
Rates: Menus Lunch 47 USD t.8.25% s.n.i.
Dinner 79 USD t.8.25% s.n.i.
Tasting 95-130 USD t.8.25% s.n.i.
Dogs: not allowed
Accepted cards: AE, DC, VS

Eric Ripert

More info on www.relaischateaux.com/bernardin

Jean Georges

SINCE 2000

One Central Park West
New York
New York 10023 • USA

Tel. : (1) (212) 299 3900
Fax : (1) (212) 299 3914
jeangeorges@relaischateaux.com

USA

The unconventional Jean-Georges Vongerichten has set up his restaurant inside the Trump International Hotel, at Central Park West. Excessively fond of wild herbs and oriental flavours, he prepares a multitude of inventive French new cuisine style dishes, including an excellent «thon blanc et rouge mariné à l'huile d'olive et citron», in a resolutely restrained, contemporary setting. Excellent wine cellar.

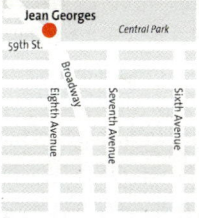

Access: First building of Central Park West, at the corner of Columbus Circle (ground floor of the Trump International Hotel).
Airports: New York J.F.K. (Intl) 25 km, New York La Guardia 20 km

Owners: Jean-Georges Vongerichten, Phil Suarez and Bob Giraldi
General Manager: Patrick Gioannini
Weekly closing: Saturday for lunch and Sunday
Nougatine: open every day
Open all year
Currency: US-Dollar (USD)
Rates: Menus
Lunch 35-45-60 USD t.8.25% s.18-20%
Dinner 87 USD t.8.25% s.18-20%
Tasting 118 USD t.8.25% s.18-20%
Dogs: not allowed
Accepted cards: AE, DC, MC, VS

Jean-Georges Vongerichten

More info on www.relaischateaux.com/jeangeorges

USA

SINCE 1999

The Ryland Inn

Route 22 West - Box 284
Whitehouse
New Jersey 08888 • USA

Tel. : (1) (908) 534 4011
Fax : (1) (908) 534 6592
ryland@relaischateaux.com

15 minutes from the New York City Center by helicopter, enter a totally different universe at The Ryland Inn. Located in the very heart of the New Jersey hunting region, this famous restaurant is surrounded by 50 acres of hills and magnificent landscape. Its organic garden produces vegetables and herbs which provide the inspiration behind the French-American cuisine of the owner-chef, Craig Shelton. A refined cuisine, full of elegance, giving pride of place to local American products.
(Other activities P. 629)

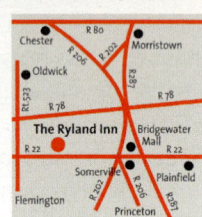

Access:
From Princeton, R 206 north until R 28 west. Follow R 28 to R 22 west for 10 km. At sign «Whitehouse», turn right exit off R 22 east and continue for 180 m.
Airport: Newark (Intl) 35 km
Helipad: N 40° 36' 33'' O 74° 44' 30''

Owner: Craig C. Shelton
General Manager: David Merves
Weekly closing: Monday
Open all year
Currency: US dollar (USD)
Rates: Menus 90-110 USD t.6% s.15%
Carte 65-75 USD t.6% s.15%
Dogs: not allowed
Golf: 2 km
Accepted cards: AE, DC, MC, VS

Craig Shelton

More info on www.relaischateaux.com/ryland

Homestead Inn - Thomas Henkelmann

SINCE 2002

420 Field Point Road
Greenwich
Connecticut 06830 • USA

Tel. : (1) (203) 869 7500
Fax : (1) (203) 869 7502
homestead@relaischateaux.com

USA

Forty minutes from New York City this exquisite Victorian mansion has gracefully embraced the XXIst century. Sophisticated guest chambers artfully display a vast array of treasures from the Henkelmann's world travels. The Inn's shaded verandas are surrounded by extensive gardens. Chef Thomas Henkelmann showcases his award winning cuisine and excellent wine list.

Mountain-biking, hiking... (Other activities P. 629)

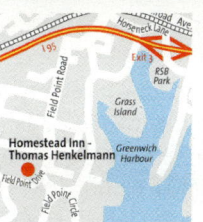

Access: North I 95 to exit 3 Arch St. Left at bottom of ramp, 2nd light left on Horseneck Lane, left onto Field Point Road, 1/4 mile on right.
Airports: New York J.F.K. (Intl) 55 km, New York La Guardia 40 km
Train station: Metro North 1 km

Owners/General Managers:
Theresa and Thomas Henkelmann
Weekly closing: Sunday
Annual closing: Restaurant: from February 23rd to March 10th
Currency: US dollar (USD)
Rates: Menus 75-95 USD t.6% s.20%
Carte 55-75 USD t.6% s.20%
12 rooms: 250-395 USD t.12% s.i.
7 suites: 395-495 USD t.12% s.i.
Breakfast: 11-18 USD t.6% s.20%
Dogs: not allowed
Golf: 2 km
Accepted cards: AE, DC, MC, VS

More info on www.relaischateaux.com/homestead

USA

SINCE 1995

The Mayflower Inn

118 Woodbury Road
Washington
Connecticut 06793 • USA

Tel. : (1) (860) 868 9466
Fax : (1) (860) 868 1497
mayflower@relaischateaux.com

Adriana and Robert Mnuchin have lovingly restored this elegant residence, transforming it into a superb country-house hotel full of traditional charm. The elegant rooms, overlooking manicured lawns and gardens, are decorated with XVIIIth and XIXth century furniture, sumptuous Tabriz rugs and canopy beds, and most rooms feature magnificent fireplaces and balconies. Gourmet cuisine is enhanced by an excellent wine list.

(Other activities P. 629)

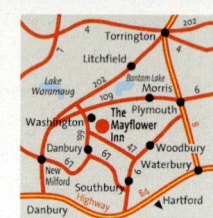

Access: From Hartford: Rte 84 (West), exit 15 Southbury. Right on rte 6 (North) - Woodbury, 5 miles, to the left, rte 47: 8 miles.

Airports: Bradley (Intl) 70 km, New York J.F.K. (Intl) 130 km
Train station: Browster 60 km

Owners: Adriana and Robert Mnuchin
General Manager: John Trevenen
Open all year
Currency: US dollar (USD)
Rates: Menus 40-45 USD t.6% s.18%
17 rooms: 400-700 USD t.12% s.i.
8 suites: 725-1300 USD t.12% s.i.
Breakfast: 6-12 USD t.6% s.18%
Dogs: not allowed
Golf: 2 km
Accepted cards: AE, MC, VS

More info on www.relaischateaux.com/mayflower

Blantyre

SINCE 1984

Blantyre Road, P.O. Box 995
Lenox
Massachusetts 01240 • USA

Tel. : **(1) (413) 637 3556**
Fax : (1) (413) 637 4282
blantyre@relaischateaux.com

USA

Built in 1902 in the Berkshire hills, just 200 kilometres from Boston, this elegant Tudor-style residence is set amidst 100 acres of lawns and woodland. Its aristocratic interior, resplendent with four-poster beds, magnificent fireplaces and luxurious bathrooms, is decorated with impeccable taste. The country house cuisine, served in the oak-panelled dining-room, is delicious, and the cellar's 450 vintages outstanding.

(Other activities P. 629)

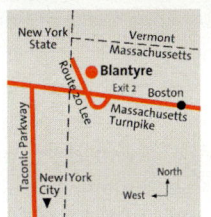

Access: From Boston, Massachusetts Turnpike West, exit 2 Lee; Rte 20 West, 3 miles, then turn right into Blantyre Road.

Airports: Hartford (Intl) 100 km, Boston (Intl) 200 km
Helipad: N 44° 46' W 69° 22'
Train stations: Hudson, N.Y. 70 km

Owner: Ann Fitzpatrick Brown
General Manager: Katja Henke
Weekly closing: Restaurant: Monday
Annual closing: From November 4th to May 8th
Currency: US dollar (USD)
Rates: Menu 80 USD t.5% s.18%
15 rooms: 350-610 USD t.9.7% s.10%
9 suites: 420-1200 USD t.9.7% s.10%
Breakfast: included
Dogs: not allowed **Golf:** 0,5 km
Accepted cards: AE, DC, MC, VS

More info on www.relaischateaux.com/blantyre

USA

Old Drovers Inn

SINCE 1993

196 East Duncan
Hill Road - PO Box 100
Dover Plains
New York 12522 • USA

Tel. : (1) (845) 832 9311
Fax : (1) (845) 832 6356
droversinn@relaischateaux.com

This authentic Colonial house is steeped in American history. Indeed, it is one of the oldest inns in the United States, serving as a stopover from 1750 for cowboys herding their cattle to the city markets. You don't have to reserve the entire Inn, as Elizabeth Taylor and Richard Burton once did, to indulge in its charm and hospitality, and savour superb regional cuisine accompanied by the finest French and American vintages.

Biking, antique dealers, Hyde Park Museums... (Other activities P. 629)

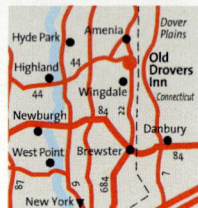

Access: From New York, take the Saw Mill River Parkway towards I 684 Brewster, Route 22 North.

Airports: New York J.F.K. (Intl) 140 km, New York La Guardia 130 km
Train station: Dover Plains 5 km

Owner: Alice Pitcher
Weekly closing: Tuesday and Wednesday
Annual closing: From January 2nd to February 1st
Currency: US dollar (USD)
Rates: Menus 14-38 USD t.7.25%
Carte 25-60 USD t.7.25%
4 rooms: 150-450 USD t.10.25% s.15%
Breakfast: included
Dogs: allowed (extra cost)
Golf: 12 km
Accepted cards: AE, DC, MC, VS

More info on www.relaischateaux.com/droversinn

Lake Placid Lodge

PO Box 550
Lake Placid, New York
New York 12946 • USA

Tel. : (1) (518) 523 2700
Fax : (1) (518) 523 1124
lakeplacid@relaischateaux.com

USA

SINCE 1997

This magnificent Lodge, nestled on the secluded wood-lined shore of Lake Placid, affords breathtaking views of the age-old Adirondack Mountains. A romantic and rustically elegant retreat, the Lodge offers warm and comfortable decor, stone fireplaces, deep soaking tubs and endless outdoor recreation. The highly acclaimed restaurant artfully blends the cuisines of Southeast Asia, the Caribbean and Latin America.

Yoga, Taichi, Kick boxing, whitewater rafting, swimming, biking, skiing (alpine, nordic and water), boating, rock climbing, ice skating, snowmobiling, olympic venues. (Other activities P. 629)

Access: From N. Y. City - I 87 N, exit 30 route 73 NW. At Lake Placid take route 86 west, then Whiteface Inn Road and follow signs to Lake Placid Lodge.

Airports: Albany (Intl) 200 km, Saranac Lake 30 km
Train stations: Westport, New York 56 km

Owners: David and Christie Garrett
Open all year
Currency: US dollar (USD)
Rates: Menu 65 USD t.7% s.15%
Carte 10-36 USD t.7% s.15%
10 rooms: 400-500 USD t.7% s.15%
24 suites: 600-1200 USD t.7% s.15%
Breakfast: included
Dogs: allowed (extra cost)
Golf: direct access
Accepted cards: AE, MC, VS

More info on www.relaischateaux.com/lakeplacid

USA — SINCE 1983

The Point

P.O. Box 1327
Saranac Lake
New York 12983 • USA

Tel. : (1) (518) 891 5674
Fax : (1) (518) 891 1152
point@relaischateaux.com

Nestled in the Adirondack mountains on a pristine lake, this former Rockefeller estate offers the ultimate civilized wilderness experience. Log architecture, stone fireplaces, sumptuous beds and antique furniture recreate the historic Great Camp Era. A refined and relaxed houseparty atmosphere, superb cuisine and the feeling of total escape have earned this idyllic retreat the rating of «Number One Resort Hotel».

Boating, picnics, nature walks, antiqueing, skiing, snowmobiling, skating. (Other activities P. 629)

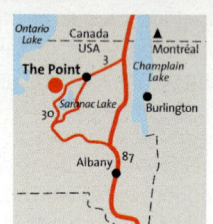

Access: From the airport, take roads 186 and 30, Lake Clear, Saranac Inn Golf Club, 16 km to the left.

Airports: Montreal (Intl) 240 km, Saranac Lake 17 km

Owners: David and Christie Garrett
General Manager: Tim Thuell
Annual closing: From March 15th to April 15th
Currency: US dollar (USD)
Full board
11 rooms: 1200-2300 USD t.7% s.18%
Breakfast: included
Dogs: allowed
Golf: 4 km
Accepted cards: AE, MC, VS

More info on www.relaischateaux.com/point

The White Barn Inn

SINCE 1991

P.O. Box 560 C
Kennebunkport
Maine 04046 • USA

Tel. : (1) (207) 967 2321
Fax : (1) (207) 967 1100
whitebarn@relaischateaux.com

USA

Since the 1800's, travellers have made their way to the White Barn Inn. Today, not only is the welcome just as warm, but the famous old inn has been transformed into a luxury hotel. Each of the elegant suites and guestrooms are individually decorated, many with fireplaces and whirlpools. Our restaurant, set in the original farmhouse Barn, serves imaginative New England cuisine and enjoys a national reputation.

Boating, beach, water sports, tennis, cross-country skiing.
(Other activities P. 629)

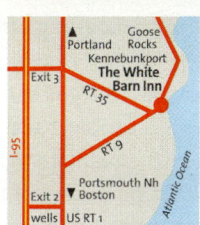

Access: From Boston, I 95 North to the Maine Turnpike; exit 3, Rte 35, 7 miles to Kennebunkport.

Airports: Portland (Intl) 30 km, Boston (Intl) 100 km
Train station: Amtrak, Wells 7 km

Owner: Laurence Bongiorno
General Managers: Roderick Anderson and Jonathan Cartwright
Annual closing: Rest.: from January 5th to 22nd
Currency: US dollar (USD)
Rates: Menu 85 USD t.7% s.i.
16 rooms: 350-460 USD t.7% s.i.
9 suites: 425-650 USD t.7% s.i.
Breakfast: included
Dogs: not allowed
Golf: 3 km
Accepted cards: AE, MC, VS

Jonathan Cartwright

More info on www.relaischateaux.com/whitebarn

USA

The Pitcher Inn

SINCE 1999

275 Main Street - PO Box 347
Warren
Vermont 05674 • USA

Tel. : (1) (802) 496 6350
USA Toll free : (1) (888) 867 4824
Fax : (1) (802) 496 6354
pitcher@relaischateaux.com

Located in a picturesque New England village, the Pitcher Inn provides its guests with the very best of Vermont tradition. In each room, there is a certain harmony between the antiques and the hidden «treasures» of today. The restaurant proposes contemporary American cooking, spiced with regional influences and one of the region's best-stocked wine cellars.

Climbing, cross-country skiing, downhill skiing, snow shoeing, biking, antiquing. (Other activities P. 629)

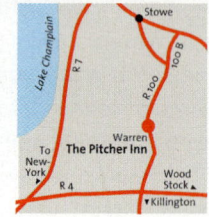

Access: From New York: take I 95N, then I 91N, then I 89N, exit 9. Take R 2E, then R 100B, continue on R 100S. Exit Warren Village. The Pitcher Inn is on the left.

Airport: Burlington (Intl) 75 km
Train station: Montpelier 45 km

Owners: Winthrop and Margaret Smith
General Managers: Heather Smith Carino and John Carino
Weekly closing: Restaurant: Tuesday
Open all year
Currency: US dollar (USD)
Rates: Menus 8-39 USD t.9% s.n.i.
Carte 45-55 USD t.9% s.n.i.
9 rooms: 330-600 USD t.9% s.n.i.
2 suites: 660 USD t.9% s.n.i.
Breakfast: included
Dogs: not allowed **Golf:** 5 km (18 holes)
Accepted cards: AE, MC, VS

More info on www.relaischateaux.com/pitcher

Home Hill

SINCE 2003

703 River, Plainfield
New Hampshire 03781
USA

Tel. : (1) (603) 675 6165
Fax : (1) (603) 675 5220
homehill@relaischateaux.com

USA

Just two hours from Boston, experience Provence in New Hampshire. The story line: the marriage between a native of Provence, Stéphane du Roure, and an American Victoria – and a 19th century country house overlooking Connecticut River. The rich, warm colours of the Mediterranean and the cosy comfort of New England are a truly marvellous combination. Savour the fabulous sunny cuisine of Victoria. Boules guaranteed.

(Other activities P. 629)

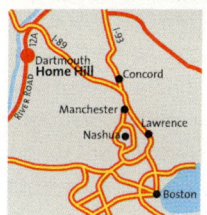

Access: From I-89N, exit n° 20. Road 12A, left after the ramp on 12AS. Continue until River Road. Home Hill is on the left after 3,5 miles.

Airport: Boston (Intl) 224 km
Helipad: N 43° 33' W 072° 22'
Train station: White River 12 km

Owners: Victoria and Stéphane du Roure
Weekly closing: Restaurant: Monday, Tuesday
Annual closing: From January 2nd to 15th
Currency: US dollar (USD)
Rates: Menus 59-89 USD t.8% s.20%
Carte 56-67 USD t.8% s.20%
9 rooms: 175-295 USD t.8% s.10%
3 suites: 315-325 USD t.8% s.10%
Breakfast: included
Dogs: not allowed
Golf: 20 km
Accepted cards: AE, DC, JCB, MC, VS

More info on www.relaischateaux.com/homehill

USA

SINCE 1984

The Inn at Sawmill Farm

Route 100 - Crosstown Road
P.O. Box 367
West Dover
Vermont 05356 • USA

Tel. : (1) (802) 464 8131
USA Toll free : (800) 493 1133
Fax : (1) (802) 464 1130
sawmill@relaischateaux.com

Tucked away in the scenic foothills of Southern Vermont's Green Mountains lies an extraordinary treasure for the discriminating traveler. With elegant guestrooms, inspired cuisine and a cellar boasting 34,000 bottles, the Inn is noted for its warmth and courtesy. Accolades from Dirona, the Grand Award from Wine Spectator, and the Mobil Four-Star Award have affirmed the Inn's pronounced reputation for excellence.

Downhill & cross-country skiing, biking, antiquing. (Other activities P. 629)

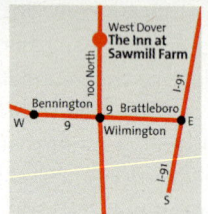

Access: I-91 North to exit 2 (Brattleboro), 9 West to Wilmington (approx. 18 miles), right at traffic light in Wilmington, 100 North 6 miles to West Dover, first left after church.
Airports: Albany (Intl) 121 km, Bradley (Intl) 180 km
Train station: Albany 121 km

Owner: Rodney Williams Jr.
General Manager: Bobbie Dee Molitor
Annual closing: April and May
Currency: US dollar (USD)
Full board (2 persons)
10 rooms: 360-420 USD t.9% s.15%
11 suites: 420-850 USD t.9% s.15%
Breakfast: included
Dogs: not allowed
Golf: 1 km
Accepted cards: AE, DC, MC, VS

More info on www.relaischateaux.com/sawmill

Charlotte Inn

SINCE 1992

27 South Summer St.
Edgartown
Massachusetts 02539 • USA

Tel. : (1) (508) 627 4151
Fax : (1) (508) 627 4652
charlotte@relaischateaux.com

USA

In the heart of a village on Martha's Vineyard island, this beautiful XIXth century inn, surrounded by manicured gardens, is decorated in the best English style. The elegant rooms, each individually decorated, could be in a museum but the ambience is decidedly comfortable. In the restaurant, the crystal, porcelain and silver glisten in soft candlelight. Savour light, refined French cuisine accompanied by the finest wines.

Children from the age of 14. (Other activities P. 629)

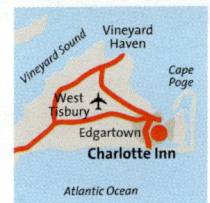

Access: From Boston, Rte 3 to Woods Hole (Massachusetts), ferry to Vineyard Haven.

Airports: Boston (Intl) 120 km, Martha's Vineyard 5 km

Owners: Gerret and Paula Conover
General Manager: Carol Read
Weekly closing: Rest.: Wednesday, Thursday, Friday, Saturday, Sunday (low season)
Annual closing: Rest.: from January 2nd to February 13th
Currency: US dollar (USD)
Rates: Menu starting at 75 USD t.5% s.i.
23 rooms: 325-595 USD t.9.7% s.i.
2 suites: 450-895 USD t.9.7% s.i.
Breakfast: 16 USD t.5% s.i.
Dogs: not allowed
Golf: 6,5 km
Accepted cards: AE, MC, VS

More info on www.relaischateaux.com/charlotte

USA

The Wauwinet

SINCE 2000

120 Wauwinet Road - PO Box 2580
Nantucket, MA 02584
(New England) • USA

Tel. : (1) (508) 228 01 45
Fax : (1) (508) 228 67 12
wauwinet@relaischateaux.com

It is on the New England island of Nantucket with its unique whaling history that you will find this lovely grey-shingled building built in 1860 nestled between the bay and Atlantic Ocean. Its luminous and cozy rooms, warm hospitality, private beaches, walks and the infinite blue ocean, all combine to making your stay a truly magical one, ideal for nature lovers. Refined cuisine at Topper's restaurant featuring an award-winning wine list.

Jacket requested for dinner. Biking, croquet, nature excursions. (Other activities P. 629)

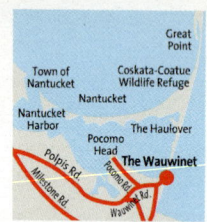

Access: At the roundabout, take Milestone Road for about 1/4 mile. Turn left on Polpis Road and continue for 5 miles, then turn left on Wauwinet Road to the end of the road (about 2 miles). The Wauwinet is on your left.
Airport: Nantucket 13 km

Owners: Stephen and Jill Karp
General Managers: Eric and Bettina Landt
Annual closing: From November through April
Currency: US dollar (USD)
Rates: Menus 25-40 USD (lunch) s.n.i.
50-80 USD (dinner) s.n.i.
26 rooms: 250-950 USD s.n.i.
5 suites: 570-1500 USD s.n.i.
Breakfast: included
Dogs: not allowed
Golf: 6 km
Accepted cards: AE, DC, MC, VS

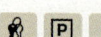

More info on www.relaischateaux.com/wauwinet

Glendorn

SINCE 1999

1032 West Corydon Street
Bradford
Pennsylvania 16701 • USA

Tel. : (1) 814 362 6511
USA toll free : (1) (800) 843 8568
Fax : (1) 814 368 9923
glendorn@relaischateaux.com

USA

Tucked away in the mountains, our 1280 acre private estate is yours to enjoy. The antique furniture, wood panelling and quality linens enhance the beauty of the rooms. Suites and cabins are veritable havens of tranquillity where you will hear the mountain streams outside your window and nothing else to disturb the peace. Meals are served in the Great Hall with a two-story sandstone fireplace as a backdrop.

Boating, guided fishing trips, fly fishing, trap and skeet shooting, massages. (Other activities P. 629)

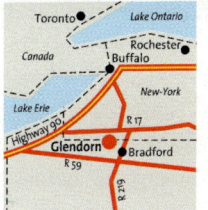

Access: From Buffalo, take I-90 towards Erie. After Seneca West exit, take 219 South to Salamanca, then follow 219 to Bradford.

Airports: Buffalo (Intl) 135 km, Bradford 35 km
Train station: Erie, PA 100 km

Owners: Dorn Family
General Manager: Daniel J. Abrashoff
Open all year
Currency: US dollar (USD)
Full board
2 rooms: 395-495 USD t.6% s.17.5%
8 suites: 525-715 USD t.6% s.17.5%
Breakfast: included
Dogs: allowed (extra cost)
Golf: 18 km (18 holes)
Accepted cards: AE, DC, MC, VS

More info on www.relaischateaux.com/glendorn

USA

SINCE 2002

Morrison House

116 South Alfred St.
Washington, DC/Alexandria
Virginia 22314 • USA

Tel. : (1) (703) 838 8000
Fax : (1) (703) 684 6283
morrisonhouse@relaischateaux.com

A striking reproduction of a brick colonial-style XVIIIth century manor house with period furniture, and located moments from the White House, Morrison House represents the best of the European holiday tradition. Peter Greenberg, the owner, has ensured that Morrison House combines the elegance of a private home with relaxed hospitality and service.

(Other activities P. 629)

Access: From DC or Reagan Nat'l Airport : G. Washington Pkwy S, right on King St. 2 blks, left on S. Alfred. From all other points : Capital Bltw 495, exit US 1 N, right on King St. 1 blk, right on S. Alfred.
Airports: Dulles (Intl) 63 km, Reagan 5 km
Train station: Amtrak 5 km

Owners: Peter Greenberg, Richard J. Puleo
Open all year
Currency: US dollar (USD)
Rates: Menus 67-75 USD t.7.5% s.18%
Carte 27-58 USD t.7.5% s.18%
42 rooms: 225-400 USD t.10% s.n.i.
3 suites: 450-600 USD t.10% s.n.i.
Breakfast: 20-30 USD t.7.5% s.18%
Dogs: not allowed
Golf: 10 km
Accepted cards: AE, DC, MC, VS

More info on www.relaischateaux.com/morrisonhouse

The Inn at Little Washington

SINCE 1987

Middle and Main Streets, PO Box 300
Washington
Virginia 22747 • USA

Tel. : (1) (540) 675 3800
Fax : (1) (540) 675 3100
washington@relaischateaux.com

USA

This magnificent inn, one of America's most renowned country retreats, lies in a romantic village in the foothills of the Blue Ridge Mountains. For two decades, Patrick O'Connell and Reinhardt Lynch have welcomed guests with exquisite hospitality. Savour fine wines and gourmet delicacies such as «Medaillons of veal sauté with local morels, Sauternes and Virginia country ham» in idyllic natural surroundings.

Hot air balloon, vineyard visits, massage, antiquing. (Other activities P. 629)

Patrick O'Connell

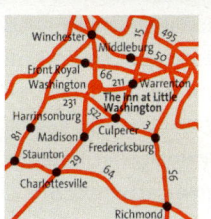

Access: Washington D.C., 66 West, exit 43 A, (Gainesville), Warrenton, Rte. 211 West.

Airport: Washington DC (Intl) 70 km

Owners: Patrick O'Connell and Reinhardt Lynch
Open all year
Currency: US dollar (USD)
Rates: Menus 98-148 USD t.7% s.18%
9 rooms: 340-865 USD t.7% s.i.
5 suites: 550-940 USD t.7% s.i.
Breakfast: 25 USD t.7% s.18%
Dogs: not allowed
Golf: 30 km
Accepted cards: MC, VS

More info on www.relaischateaux.com/washington

USA

SINCE 1988

The Fearrington House

2000 Fearrington Village
Pittsboro
North Carolina 27312 • USA

Tel. : (1) (919) 542 2121
Fax : (1) (919) 542 4202
fearrington@relaischateaux.com

Traditional Southern hospitality awaits you at this elegant country inn set amidst floral gardens in the heart of a picturesque village. Relax in the beautiful suites and guestrooms, each individually decorated with antique furniture, original artwork and bouquets of fresh flowers. Experience the charm of regional cuisine by soft candlelight and enjoy poetry readings, wine tastings and garden visits throughout the year.
Biking. (Other activities P. 629)

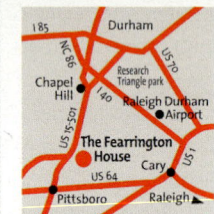

Access: Take I 40 until Chapel Hill, then 15-501 south towards Pittsboro. The hotel is 13 km to the south of Chapel Hill.

Airport: Raleigh-Durham (Intl) 30 km
Train station: Cary 30 km

Owners: Fitch Family
General Manager: Richard Delany
Open all year
Currency: US dollar (USD)
Rates: Menu 79 USD t.6% s.n.i.
16 rooms: 220-290 USD t.9% s.i.
17 suites: 290-450 USD t.9% s.i.
Breakfast: included
Dogs: not allowed
Golf: 10 km
Accepted cards: AE, MC, VS

More info on www.relaischateaux.com/fearrington

Blackberry Farm

SINCE 1994

1471, West Millers Cove
Walland
Tennessee 37886 • USA

Tel. : (1) (865) 984 8166
Fax : (1) (865) 681 7753
blackberry@relaischateaux.com

USA

This 1,100-acre Great Smoky Mountain luxury resort is ranked among the world's best hotels. Best known for exceptional service, gorgeous mountain views and extraordinary cuisine, Blackberry offers a unique atmosphere of relaxed luxury. Rooms offer English-style antiques and fluffy feather beds. Relax in the spa, fly fish on Hesse Creek or simply enjoy the view from a rocker on the veranda. Rates include all meals.

Fly fishing (instruction and guided trips), hiking, cooking school. (Other activities P. 629)

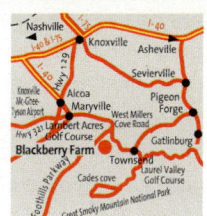

Access: From Knoxville, Hwy. 129 S. to Hwy. 321 N towards Townsend. Past the Foothills Parkway. First right after parkway on Millers Cove Rd. Entrance is 3 miles down on the left.
Airports: Atlanta (Intl) 340 km, Knoxville 25 km
Helipad: N 35° 41' 15'' W 83° 51' 92''
Train station: Knoxville 25 km

Owners: Kreis and Sandy Beall
General Manager: Matt Alexander
Open all year
Currency: US dollar (USD)
Full board
23 rooms: 395-745 USD t.12% s.15%
16 suites: 695-895 USD t.12% s.15%
Breakfast: included
Dogs: not allowed
Golf: nearby
Accepted cards: AE, MC, VS

More info on www.relaischateaux.com/blackberry

Woodlands Resort & Inn

USA

SINCE 1997

125 Parsons Road
Summerville
South Carolina 29483 • USA

Tel. : (1) (843) 875 2600
Fax : (1) (843) 875 2603
woodlands@relaischateaux.com

Charleston's luxury getaway, this magnificently restored 1906 revival home is famous for luxurious, individually decorated guest rooms, a beautiful rural setting amidst moss-draped live oaks and magnolias and regionally inspired, New American cuisine accompanied by award winning wine list. This romantic retreat's charming atmosphere and dreamy Southern pace of life beckons relaxation.

Day spa service, bikes, croquet lawn, clay tennis courts, afternoon tea on property. Historic Charleston, homes, gardens, museums. (Other activities P. 629)

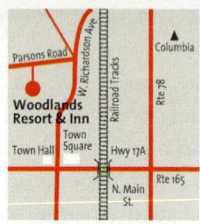

Access: From Interstate I-26, exit 199-A 1.8 miles to West Richardson. On West Richardson, turn right, after 1.25 miles, left onto Parsons Road.

Airport: Charleston 35 km
Train station: Amtrak 20 km

Owner: Joe Whitmore
General Manager: Marty Wall
Annual closing: From January 2nd to 14th
Currency: US dollar (USD)
Rates: Menus lunch 18-24 USD t.5% s.20%
Dinner 59-69 USD t.5% s.20%
Tasting 89-135 USD t.5% s.20%
19 rooms: 295-395 USD t.7% s.n.i.
Breakfast: 10-15 USD t.5% s.20%
Dogs: allowed
Golf: 10 km
Accepted cards: AE, DC, MC, VS

More info on www.relaischateaux.com/woodlands

Planters Inn

SINCE 1999

112 North Market Street
Charleston
South Carolina 29401 • USA

Tel. : (1) (843) 722 2345
Fax : (1) (843) 577 2125
planters@relaischateaux.com

USA

Located in the heart of the largest historic district in the United States, Planters Inn, built in 1844, is the ideal starting point for your visit to Charleston. Its rooms echo the noble accents of the local landscape, by recreating a calm, peaceful, yet luxurious decor. The courtyard and verandas, with their ornate fountains, create an urban oasis. The renowned Peninsula Grill proposes regional American cooking and an award-winning wine list.

Spa and fitness center, water sports, historic tours nearby. (Other activities P. 629)

Access: Follow Meeting Str. south; turn left on Hayne Str. then right on Church Str. and right on North Market Str.

Airport: Charleston 19 km
Train station: Charleston 10 km

Owner: Hank Holliday
General Manager: Larry Spelts
Open all year
Currency: US dollar (USD)
Rates: Menus 45-90 USD t.8% s.i.
Carte 20-29 USD t.8% s.i.
56 rooms: 195-350 USD t.12% s.i.
6 suites: 400-600 USD t.12% s.i.
Breakfast: 8-15 USD t.8% s.i.
Dogs: not allowed
Golf: 5 km (18 holes)
Accepted cards: AE, DC, MC, VS

More info on www.relaischateaux.com/planters

Gastonian Inn

SINCE 2001

220 East Gaston Street
Savannah
Georgia 31401 • USA

Tel. : (1) (912) 232 2869
Fax : (1) (912) 232 0710
gastonian@relaischateaux.com

One of the finest residences in a cultural and historical southern town, marked by the War of Secession. Built in 1868 in the Italian Regency style, the two wings of the building are linked by a footbridge which overlooks a verdant garden. Anne Landers, who acquired the Gastonian in 1996 has kept the spirit alive of a special, affluent, elegant house, with period furniture. Every attention is given to guests.
Water-skiing. (Other activities P. 629)

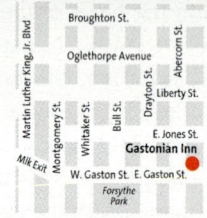

Access: From I-16 exit at W. Martin L. King Blvd. Cross MLK and continue straight ahead with no turns which becomes Gaston St.
Continue to Inn at 220 E. Gaston St.
Airport: Savannah (Intl) 15 km
Train station: Amtrak 6 km

Owner: Anne Landers
General Manager: Mélanie Bliss
Weekly closing: Restaurant: Sunday and Monday
Open all year
Currency: US dollar (USD)
Rates: Carte 18-36 USD (lunch) t.6% s.i.
14 rooms: 250-365 USD t.12% s.i.
3 suites: 405-435 USD t.12% s.i.
Breakfast: included
Dogs: not allowed
Golf: 3 km
Accepted cards: AE, MC, VS

More info on www.relaischateaux.com/gastonian

Seeger's

SINCE 2001

111 West Paces Ferry Road
Atlanta, GA 30305
USA

Tel. : (1) (404) 846 9779
Fax : (1) (404) 846 9217
seegers@relaischateaux.com

USA

You absolutely must discover Guenter Seeger's restaurant in Atlanta, set in a renovated 1920's house, with its elegant modern decor and perpetually innovative cuisine. Here, you will savour such culinary creations as «filets de rouget servis sur un lit d'oranges confites» and «roulade de foie gras avec marmelade d'oignons et purée de pommes fruits au vin rouge».

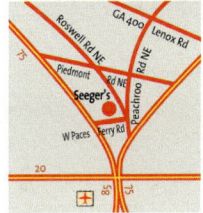

Access: From I-75, take West Paces Ferry east to intersection of East Andrews Drive and West Paces Ferry. Self parking is available behind the restaurant.

Airport: Hartsfield (Intl) 15 km

Owner/Chef: Guenter Seeger
General Manager: Peter Krehan
Weekly closing: Sunday
Open all year
Currency: US dollar (USD)
Rates: Menus 64-80 USD t.7% s.18-20%
Dogs: not allowed
Accepted cards: AE, DC, MC, VS

Guenter Seeger

More info on www.relaischateaux.com/seegers

USA

Charlie Trotter's

SINCE 1996

816 W. Armitage Avenue
Chicago
Illinois 60614 • USA

Tel. : (1) (773) 248 6228
Fax : (1) (773) 248 6088
charlie@relaischateaux.com

Charlie Trotter, one of the brightest stars of American gastronomy, is renowned for his innovative cuisine, which embraces organically raised seasonal products. Experience Chef Trotter's brilliant flavor combinations, such as Rabbit Loin, Liver and Kidney with Morel Mushrooms, Vidalia Onion Puree and Oven Roasted Tomato Cracker. The award-winning cellar, stocked with over 2000 vintages, is superb.

Visits to the kitchen, private salon, great museums: Art Institute, Field Museum of Natural History...

Access: In Lincoln Park, 1/2 block west of Halsted St., on the northern side of the street.

Airports: O'Hare (Intl) 20 km, Midway Airport 17 km

Owner: Charlie Trotter
Weekly closing: Sunday and Monday
Annual closing: Last two weeks in March
Currency: US dollar (USD)
Rates: Carte 115 USD t.9.75%
Dogs: not allowed
Accepted cards: AE, MC, VS

Charlie Trotter

More info on www.relaischateaux.com/charlie

Everest

SINCE 2002

440 South LaSalle Street
Chicago
Illinois 60605 • USA

Tel. : (1) (312) 663 8920
Fax : (1) (312) 663 8802
everest@relaischateaux.com

USA

Jean Joho opened Everest in 1984, in the financial district of Chicago. The view from this restaurant on the 40th floor of Chicago Stock Exchange is simply breathtaking. An ambassador of Alsace wines, Jean Joho offers refined cuisine reminiscent of his native Alsace: «filet de bœuf poché en pot-au-feu au raifort et légumes», «homard du Maine rôti au beurre de Gewurztraminer», «filet de loup de mer en backaofa»...

Access: The parking garage is located on Financial Place street, one block west of LaSalle. Financial Place is a two-way street with access either from Congress or Van Buren.
Airport: O'Hare (Intl) 20 km
Train station: Metro 0,2 km

Owner: Jean Joho
General Manager: Chris Lister
Weekly closing: Sunday and Monday
Open all year
Currency: US dollar (USD)
Rates: Menus 79-110 USD s.n.i.
Carte 70-120 USD s.n.i.
Dogs: not allowed
Accepted cards: AE, DC, JCB, MC, VS

Jean Joho

More info on www.relaischateaux.com/everest

585

USA

Tru

SINCE 2003

676 North Saint Clair
Chicago
Illinois 60611 • USA

Tel. : (1) (312) 202 0001
Fax : (1) (312) 202 0003
trurest@relaischateaux.com

Executive Chef/Partner Rick Tramonto and culinary partner Executive Pastry Chef/Partner Chef Gale Gand opened this gourmet temple, contemporary yet tranquil interior, in 1999. Boundless creativity leading to daring and whimsical cuisine: they offer a 7 course Vegetable Collection or Seafood Collection and a 10 course Chef Tramonto's Collection, with a «carrot and ginger cappuccino», signature «Caviar Staircase with four caviars», «roasted rack of lamb with truffle bread and butter pudding» and «Fromage Blanc Mousse with Strawberry Gelée and Blueberry Stew».

(Other activities P. 629)

Access: Leaving the O'Hare International Airport, take the Kennedy 1.90 expressway towards Chicago to Ohio St. East. Take Ohio St. one block east of Michigan Av. Turn left on St. Clair.
Airport: O'Hare (Intl) 25 km
Train station: Union station 5 km

Owners: Rick Tramonto and Gale Gand
General Manager: Adam Seger
Weekly closing: Sunday
Open all year
Currency: US dollar (USD)
Rates: Menus 75-150 USD t.9.75% s.20%
Dogs: not allowed
Accepted cards: AE, DC, JCB, MC, VS

Gale Gand - Rick Tramonto

More info on www.relaischateaux.com/trurest

Les Nomades

SINCE 2000

222 East Ontario Street
Chicago
Illinois 60611 • USA

Tel. : (1) (312) 649 9010
Fax : (1) (312) 649 0608
nomades@relaischateaux.com

USA

In a charming turn-of-the-century brownstone of downtown Chicago, Les Nomades offers gastronomic cuisine signed Roland Liccioni. Savor: «duo de foie gras sauté et tarte de foie gras à l'orange sanguine et ananas rôti à la vanille», «raviolis aux truffes», «consommé de canard relevé», «trio de ris de veau rôti», «oie de veau sauté et filet de veau grillé, sauce Périgueux».
(Other activities P. 629)

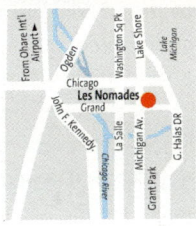

Access: Located just steps from Chicago's famed «Magnificent Mile», Les Nomades is a 25 minutes drive from both local airports and a block and a half east of Michigan Avenue.
Airport: O'Hare (Intl) 50 km
Train station: Chicago 5 km

Owner: Roland Liccioni
General Manager: Mary-Beth Liccioni
Weekly closing: Sunday and Monday
Open all year
Currency: US dollar (USD)
Rates: Menu 72 USD t.9.75% s.n.i.
Tasting menu 85 USD t.9.75% s.n.i.
Dogs: not allowed
Golf: 15 km
Accepted cards: AE, DC, MC, VS

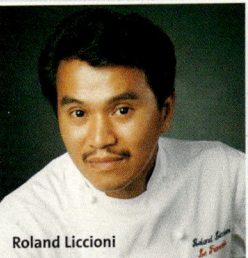

Roland Liccioni

More info on www.relaischateaux.com/nomades

USA

Canoe Bay

SINCE 1998

P.O. Box 28
Chetek
Wisconsin 54728 • USA

Tel. : (1) (715) 924 4594
Fax : (1) (715) 924 2078
canoebay@relaischateaux.com

Set on a beautiful wilderness estate, this premier romantic hideaway in the Midwest has long enchanted guests. Couples enjoy true privacy and spectacular views in luxurious accommodations, with year-round activities on crystal-clear lakes and wooded trails. Superb service, excellent cuisine and an award-winning wine list accent the breathtaking setting. Wine Cellar dining available – an unforgettable experience.

Whirlpool, snow-shoeing, massage therapy, extensive library... (Other activities P. 629)

Access: From Minneapolis, follow I-94 E to 53 N, exit Chetek.

Airports: Minneapolis (Intl) 192 km, Eau Claire 72 km
Train station: Minneapolis 192 km

Owners: Dan and Lisa Dobrowolski
Open all year
Currency: US dollar (USD)
Rates: Menu 55 USD t.5.5% s.n.i.
6 rooms: 350 USD t.5.5% s.n.i.
13 suites: 400-850 USD t.5.5% s.n.i.
Breakfast: included
Dogs: not allowed
Golf: 19 km
Accepted cards: AE, MC, VS

More info on www.relaischateaux.com/canoebay

Triple Creek Ranch

SINCE 1996

5551 West Fork Road
Darby
Montana 59829 • USA

Tel. : (1) (406) 821 4600
Fax : (1) (406) 821 4666
triplecreek@relaischateaux.com

USA

The American dream lives on in this spectacular landscape in the heart of Montana. Enjoy fishing in the lakes and rivers, or skiing on the mountain slopes. Explore the magnificent valley, resplendent with pine trees and wild flowers, on foot or on horseback. Relax in the ranch's comfortable private lodges, which feature a full range of amenities, before savouring a delicious candlelit dinner accompanied by superb vintages.

Downkill and cross-country skiing. (Other activities P. 629)

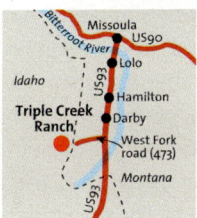

Altitude: 1535 metres.
Access: 75 miles south of Missoula via Highway 93; after Darby, right onto West Fork Rd (Highway 473) for 7 miles. Follow signs.
Airports: Hamilton 45 km, Missoula 115 km
Helipad: N 45° 52' 87" W 114° 12' 46"

Owners: Craig and Barbara Barrett
General Managers: Wayne and Judy Kilpatrick
Open all year
Currency: US dollar (USD)
Meals included
19 suites: 510-995 USD t.11.25 USD, s.15%
Breakfast: included
Dogs: allowed (subject to conditions)
Golf: Putting green on the premises
18 holes 45 km
Accepted cards: AE, MC, VS

More info on www.relaischateaux.com/triplecreek

USA

Knob Hill Inn

SINCE 1996

960 North Main Street, PO Box 800
Ketchum
Idaho, 83340 • USA

Tel. : (1) (208) 726 8010
Fax : (1) (208) 726 2712
knobhill@relaischateaux.com

Located in Sun Valley, America's first destination ski resort, Knob Hill Inn is also a heaven for summer activities – world class fly fishing, tennis, golf, hiking and mountain biking; summer symphony, ballet and art galleries abound. Guestrooms at the Austrian style Inn open onto balconies with stunning mountain views. After a full day of activity, savour luxury comfort cuisine and fine wine at Place Restaurant.

(Other activities P. 629)

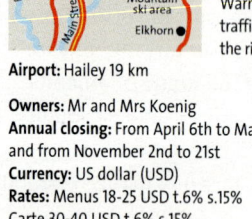

Altitude: 1750 m.
Access: From Hailey Airport, the hotel is 12 miles N. on Highway 75, 2 blocks after the Warm Springs traffic light on the right.

Airport: Hailey 19 km

Owners: Mr and Mrs Koenig
Annual closing: From April 6th to May 23rd and from November 2nd to 21st
Currency: US dollar (USD)
Rates: Menus 18-25 USD t.6% s.15%
Carte 30-40 USD t.6% s.15%
16 rooms: 195-260 USD t.9% s.15%
8 suites: 310-400 USD t.9% s.15%
Breakfast: included
Dogs: not allowed
Golf: 1 km
Accepted cards: AE, MC, VS

More info on www.relaischateaux.com/knobhill

Goldener Hirsch Inn

SINCE 2001

PO Box 859
Park City
Utah 84060 • USA

Tel. : (1) (435) 649 7770
Fax : (1) (435) 649 7901
goldener@relaischateaux.com

USA

Located mid-mountain in Deer Valley, and featuring ski-in, ski-out access, the Hirsch is elegant yet relaxed. All rooms and suites are uniquely furnished with hand-made Austrian furniture and Frette linens. Most have a fireplace and private balcony. Enjoy the character and service of a fine European inn combined with the grandeur of the Rockies.

Cross-country skiing, snowmobiling, snowshoeing, ballooning. (Other activities P. 629)

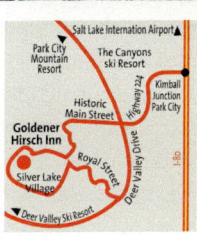

Altitude: 2550 m.
Access: Take I-80 East from Salt Lake to Park City exit (Highway 224). Drive 10 miles to Deer Valley Drive. Turn left and follow road for 2 miles to Royal Street. Turn right. Follow signs to Goldener Hisch Inn.
Airport: Salt Lake (Intl) 50 km

Owners: Spencer F. Eccles Family
General Managers: C. Hope Eccles and Trent Rogers
Annual closing: From April to June and November
Currency: US dollar (USD)
Rates: Menus 18-34 USD t.8.35% s.15-20%
Carte 32-56 USD t.8.35% s.15-20%
8 rooms: 100-590 USD t.10.35% s.10%
12 suites: 200-950 USD t.10.35% s.10%
Breakfast: 8-15 USD t.8.35% s.15-20%
Dogs: not allowed **Golf:** 10 km
Accepted cards: AE, MC, VS

More info on www.relaischateaux.com/goldener

USA

SINCE 1986

The Home Ranch

PO Box 822
Clark
Colorado 80428 • USA

Tel. : (1) (970) 879 1780
Fax : (1) (970) 879 1795
homeranch@relaischateaux.com

The Home Ranch combines the activities of a World Class Equestrian Center with the qualities of western ranch life and the 5C's of the Relais & Châteaux into one great location in the Rocky Mountains. There is something for everyone, hiking, fishing, swimming, and fine dining. In winter, skiing at Steamboat Springs, a world class ski resort is combined with cross-country skiing, snowshoeing and equestrian classes.

World Class Western Equestrian Center. (Other activities P. 629)

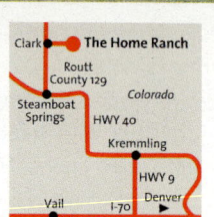

Access: Denver, I-70 West, Hwy 9 North, Hwy 40 West, Steamboat Springs; Rte 129 towards Clark.

Airports: Denver (Intl) 350 km, Yampa Valley 70 km
Train station: Granby 130 km

Owner: Kendrick Jones
Annual closing: April and November
Currency: US dollar (USD)
Full board
6 rooms: 500-600 USD t.4% s.15%
8 suites: 570-660 USD t.4% s.15%
Breakfast: included
Dogs: not allowed
Golf: 25 km
Accepted cards: AE, MC, VS

More info on www.relaischateaux.com/homeranch

The Little Nell

SINCE 1993

675 East Durant Avenue
Aspen
Colorado 81611 • USA

Tel. : (1) (970) 920 4600
USA toll free : (888) 843 6355
Fax : (1) (970) 920 4670
littlenell@relaischateaux.com

USA

Nestled in the heart of the Colorado Rockies, Aspen is one of America's finest ski resorts and in summer the town is a centre of music and cultural activities. «The Little Nell», ideally situated at the foot of Aspen mountain, is a haven of comfort and elegance. Its superb rooms, featuring contemporary architecture, open onto gardens, waterfalls and a private pool. Hospitality is generous and the food impeccable.

Cross-country skiing, rafting, spa, concerts. (Other activities P. 629)

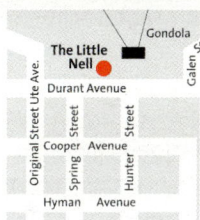

Airports: Aspen (Intl) 6 km, Denver (Intl) 360 km

Owner: Aspen Skiing Company
General Manager: Eric Calderon
Open all year
Currency: US dollar (USD)
Rates: Carte 25-45 USD t.8.6% s.i.
77 rooms: 400-550 USD (summer) t.9.6% s.i.
600-750 USD (winter) t.9.6% s.i.
15 suites: 950-2800 USD (summer) t.9.6% s.i.
1125-4400 USD (winter) t.9.6% s.i.
Breakfast: 6-11 USD t.8.6% s.i.
Dogs: allowed
Golf: 1 km
Accepted cards: AE, DC, MC, VS

Altitude: 2600 metres.
Access: From Denver, take the I-70 towards Glenwood Springs, then Highway 82 towards Aspen.

More info on www.relaischateaux.com/littlenell

USA

SINCE 1996

Rancho de San Juan

PO Box 4140
Española
New Mexico 87533 • USA

Tel. : (1) (505) 753 6818
USA toll free : (1) (800) 726 7121
Fax : (1) (505) 753 6818
sanjuan@relaischateaux.com

Discover sophisticated elegance in the majestic desert overlooking the Ojo Caliente River Valley. The Rancho's luxurious suites and guestrooms are decorated with antiques, art and fireplaces and offer private terraces for outdoor enjoyment. Its elegant restaurant serves award-winning cuisine, enhanced by fine custom porcelain and family silver for candlelight dining: a feast for the senses.
Hunting, rafting, water-skiing. (Other activities P. 629)

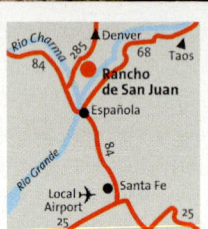

Access: From Santa Fe, Hwy. 84/285 north; 7 miles after Española, right on Hwy. 285, Rancho 3.5 miles after the intersection.

Airports: Albuquerque (Intl) 160 km, Denver (Intl) 520 km

Owners: David G. Heath and John H. Johnson III
Weekly closing: Rest.: Sunday and Monday
Annual closing: January
Currency: US dollar (USD)
Rates: Menus 45-95 USD t.6% s.i.
9 rooms: 175-250 USD t.9% s.18%
8 suites: 300-400 USD t.9% s.18%
Breakfast: included
Dogs: not allowed
Golf: 11 km
Accepted cards: AE, MC, VS

More info on www.relaischateaux.com/sanjuan

The French Laundry

SINCE 1998

6640 Washington Street
Yountville
California 94599 • USA

Tel. : (1) (707) 944 2380
Fax : (1) (707) 944 1974
laundry@relaischateaux.com

USA

This elegant turn-of-the-century stone residence in the heart of California's famous Napa Valley is set amidst a charming country garden. This idyllic haven is the setting for Chef Thomas Keller's innovative, award-winning cuisine. His contemporary dishes feature a subtle blend of classic French traditions and regional fare. The prix-fixe menus are accompanied by over 600 selections of all world wines.

Visit of the Napa Valley.

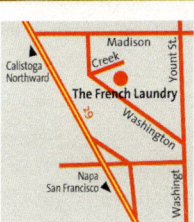

Access: From Napa, take Highway 29 North, exit Yountville/ Veterans Home, turn right at the stop sign. Go left on Washington St. Stay left, a half mile north to 6640 Washington at Creek St.
Airports: Oakland (Intl) 100 km, San Francisco (Intl) 120 km
Train station: Albany 50 km

Owner: Thomas A. Keller
General Manager: Laura Cunningham
Annual closing: From 1st to 18th January
Currency: US dollar (USD)
Rates: Menus 105-120 USD t.7.25% s.n.i.
Dogs: not allowed
Accepted cards: AE, VS

Thomas Keller

More info on www.relaischateaux.com/laundry

USA

SINCE 1987

Meadowood Napa Valley

900 Meadowood Lane
St. Helena
California 94574 • USA

Tel. : (1) (707) 963 3646
Fax : (1) (707) 963 3532
meadowood@relaischateaux.com

Surrounded by pristine vineyards and hills roamed by Robert Louis Stevenson, this superb Meadowood Napa Valley estate nestles in a private 250-acre valley. Expect understated elegance with a tradition of intimacy, discreet service and refined comfort. Idyllic setting for golf, tennis, hiking, swimming or pampering at the full-service spa. Savour California wine country cuisine and discover Napa Valley wine with Meadowood's wine tutor.

Croquet, bicycling, musical events, lectures, wine education classes. (Other activities P. 629)

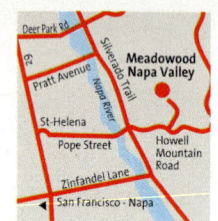

Access: From the Golden Gate Bridge, take Hwy 101 towards Marin County; Hwy 37, Hwy 121, Hwy 29 North.

Airports: San Francisco (Intl) 110 km, Napa 35 km

Owners: William Harlan and John Montgomery
Open all year
Currency: US dollar (USD)
Rates: Carte 35-55 USD t.7.75% s.15%
38 rooms: 385-810 USD t.10.5% s.i.
47 suites: 580-3675 USD t.10.5% s.i.
Breakfast: 9-18 USD t.7.75% s.15%
Dogs: not allowed
Golf: on the premises (9 holes)
Accepted cards: AE, DC, JCB, VS

More info on www.relaischateaux.com/meadowood

Auberge du Soleil

SINCE 1988

180 Rutherford Hill Road, PO Drawer B
Rutherford
California 94573 • USA

Tel. : (1) (707) 963 1211
Fax : (1) (707) 963 8764
soleil@relaischateaux.com

USA

Nestled amidst olive trees, on a hillside, above a mosaic of vineyards – this superb setting inspired Claude Rouas to open his magnificent restaurant here in 1981. The superb cuisine, which features the full splendor of the region's flavours and colours, is enhanced by 15000 bottles in the cellar. The romantic guest-rooms, each with fireplace and private terrace, are housed in country cottages.
Buisness center. (Other activities P. 629)

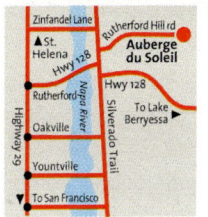

Access: Napa, towards St. Helena (Hwy 29) to Rutherford, take Hwy 128 towards Silverado Trail.

Airports: San Francisco (Intl) 120 km, Santa Rosa 60 km

Owners: Claude Rouas and Robert Harmon
General Managers: George A. Gœggel and Philippa J. Perry
Open all year
Currency: US dollar (USD)
Rates: Menus 29-120 t.7.25% s.n.i.
31 rooms: 500-700 USD s.i.
19 suites: 850-3500 USD s.i.
Breakfast: 16-24 USD t.7.25% s.20%
Dogs: not allowed
Golf: 15 km
Accepted cards: AE, DC, MC, VS

More info on www.relaischateaux.com/soleil

Gary Danko

USA

SINCE 2002

800 North Point
San Francisco
California 94109 • USA

Tel. : (1) (415) 749 2060
Fax : (1) (415) 775 1805
danko@relaischateaux.com

Located in San Franciso, this elegant cosmopolitan restaurant offers diners a warm, sophisticated atmosphere accented with beautiful wood, fabrics and modern art. Gary Danko, whose subtle cuisine epitomizes contemporary American gastronomy, conjures up «caille rôtie farcie aux morilles, poireaux et pignons», «crustacés cuits à la vapeur avec un curry thaï», «coquilles Saint-Jacques juste poêlées aux légumes de printemps»...

Access: Follow Van Ness to North Point St, turn right. Follow North Point 3 blocks to Hyde St. Gary Danko is located left, at the corner of Hyde and North Point.
Airport: San Francisco (Intl) 26 km
Train station: San Francisco 20 km

Owner/Chef: Gary Danko
General Manager: Patrick Skovran
Annual closing: July 4th, Thanksgiving, December 25th and 31st
Currency: US dollar (USD)
Rates: Menus 55-74 USD t.8.5% s.i.
Carte 55-74 USD t.8.5% s.i.
Dogs: not allowed
Accepted cards: AE, DC, MC, VS

Gary Danko

More info on www.relaischateaux.com/danko

The Sherman House

SINCE 1987

2160 Green Street
San Francisco
California 94123 • USA

Tel. : (1) (415) 563 3600
Fax : (1) (415) 563 1882
sherman@relaischateaux.com

USA

Just minutes from Fisherman's Wharf, stands a magnificent Victorian residence, built in 1876, where Leander Sherman once played host to the greatest names in music, art and literature. Sherman House is still imbued with the splendour of bygone days, and guests will be enchanted by the exquisite gardens and magnificent rooms, many with superb views of San Francisco Bay. The eclectic menus are wonderfully imaginative.

Water sports. (Other activities P .629)

Access: South of Golden Gate Bridge, from Lombard Street, turn right on Fillmore St., turn left on Green St.

Airport: San Francisco (Intl) 26 km
Train station: Amtrak 28 km

Owners: Manou and Vesta Mobedshahi
General Manager: Christine Berlin
Open all year
Currency: US dollar (USD)
Rates: Menus 55-65 USD t.8.5% s.20%
Carte 42-48 USD t.8.5% s.20%
8 rooms: 460-545 USD t.14% s.i.
6 suites: 600-1200 USD t.14% s.i.
Breakfast: included
Dogs: not allowed
Golf: 10 km
Accepted cards: AE, DC, MC, VS

More info on www.relaischateaux.com/sherman

Château du Sureau

USA — SINCE 1994

48688 Victoria Lane, PO Box 577
Oakhurst, Yosemite National Park
California 93644 • USA

Tel. : (1) (559) 683 6860
Fax : (1) (559) 683 0800
sureau@relaischateaux.com

This beautiful Provençal château lies in the heart of the Sierra Nevada forest. Its ten elegant guestrooms and the 2-bedroom Parisian Villa, decorated with sumptuous antique furniture, open onto balconies which offer stunning views of the Californian countryside. After a glass of champagne in the gardens, owner and renowned cordon-bleu Erna Kubin-Clanin will delight you with superb regional cuisine and an award-winning wine list.

Water sports, rock climbing, sporting clay shooting and cross-country skiing. (Other activities P. 629)

Access: Near Yosemite National Park.

Airports: San Francisco (Intl) 320 km, Fresno 68 km
Train station: Fresno 68 km

Owners: Erna Kubin-Clanin, Dr. René Clanin
General Manager: Lucy Royse
Annual closing: January 5th to 24th
Currency: US dollar (USD)
Rates: Carte 53-85 USD t.7.75% s.18%
10 rooms: 350-550 USD t.7.75% s.12%
1 villa: 2800 USD t.7.75% s.12%
Breakfast: included
Dogs: not allowed
Golf: 5 km
Accepted cards: AE, MC, VS

More info on www.relaischateaux.com/sureau

San Ysidro Ranch

SINCE 1988

900 San Ysidro Lane
Montecito, Santa Barbara
California 93108 • USA

Tel. : (1) (805) 969 5046
Fax : (1) (805) 565 1995
sanysidro@relaischateaux.com

USA

Vivien Leigh and Laurence Olivier were married at San Ysidro and the Kennedys spent their honeymoon here. You too will be enchanted by this beautiful ranch built in 1893. Nestled beneath orange trees, its bungalows look out over the Santa Ynez hills and the scent of eucalyptus and jasmin will make you forget that Los Angeles is less than an hour away. Enjoy regional cuisine, an ocean view pool and exercise room.
Biking, kayaking, surfing, boce ball. (Other activities P. 629)

Access: On Highway 101, along the coast, San Ysidro Ranch exit.

Airports: Los Angeles (Intl) 150 km, Santa Barbara 20 km
Train station: SB Railway Stn 10 km

Owner: Ty Warner
Open all year
Currency: US dollar (USD)
Rates: Menus 30-50 USD t.8% s.i.
13 rooms: 375-595 USD t.10% s.i.
25 suites: 695-3995 USD t.10% s.i.
Breakfast: 10 USD t.8% s.i.
Dogs: allowed (extra cost)
Golf: 30 km
Accepted cards: AE, DC, MC, VS

More info on www.relaischateaux.com/sanysidro

RELEASE THE SPIRIT OF THE MANDARINE

L'Orangerie

SINCE 1987

903 N La Cienega Bd
Los Angeles
California 90069 • USA

Tel. : (1) (310) 652 9770
Fax : (1) (310) 652 8870
lorangerie@relaischateaux.com

USA

For 25 years now, the most renowned French restaurant in Los Angeles has enchanted guests with gourmet cuisine. Faithful to the epicurean principles of simplicity, freshness and flavour, the chef, Christophe Émé, at L'Orangerie practices his art with passion. Savour «John Dory brocolli cream sauce with mixed herbs». Finest French and Californian wines.

Access: Between Melrose Avenue (North) and Santa Monica Boulevard (South).

Airport: Los Angeles (Intl) 10 km

Owners: Gérard and Virginie Ferry
Director: Stéphane Clasquin
Weekly closing: Monday
Open all year
Currency: US dollar (USD)
Rates: Menu 85 USD s.15%
Carte 49-75 USD s.15%
Dogs: not allowed
Accepted cards: AE, DC, JCB, MC, VS

Christophe Émé

More info on www.relaischateaux.com/lorangerie

Patina Restaurant

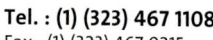

SINCE 2002

5955 Melrose Avenue
Los Angeles
California 90068 • USA

Tel. : (1) (323) 467 1108
Fax : (1) (323) 467 0215
patina@relaischateaux.com

German-born and French-trained chef Joachim Splichal and his wife Christine have created a chic restaurant in the heart of Hollywood's studio district. Refined Franco-Californian cuisine with dishes such as «queue de homard du Maine rôtie et fettucine en bolognaise de homard», «agneau du Colorado grillé aux deux lasagnes» and three tasting menus. Award winning wine list with over 2000 selections from around the world.

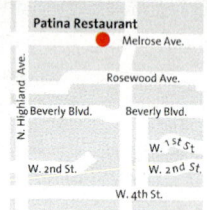

Access: From L A International Airport: Fwy 405 South, Fwy 105 East, Fwy 110 North, Fwy 10 West, exit La Brea. North on La Brea Av. to Melrose Av., turn right on Melrose Av.
Airport: Los Angeles (Intl) 21 km

Owners: Christine and Joachim Splichal
General Manager: Christophe Thomas
Open all year
Currency: US dollar (USD)
Rates: Menus 75-85 USD t.8% s.15%
Carte 52-75 USD t.8% s.15%
Dogs: not allowed
Accepted cards: AE, DC, JCB, VS

Joachim Splichal

More info on www.relaischateaux.com/patina

Rancho Valencia Resort

SINCE 1993

P.O. Box 9126
Rancho Santa Fe
California 92067 • USA

Tel. : (1) (858) 756 1123
Fax : (1) (858) 756 0165
valencia@relaischateaux.com

USA

Set amidst 40 acres of hills and orange trees north of San Diego, this magnificent resort is imbued with Mediterranean style. Ideally located near the beaches of La Jolla and Del Mar, Rancho Valencia is the perfect place to practice your tennis and improve your golf swing on the nearby championship course. Enjoy the comfort of the beautiful «casitas», and savor the delights of the renowned restaurant and wine cellar.

Spa, croquet and tennis tournaments... (Other activities P. 629)

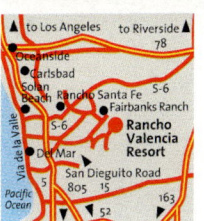

Access: San Diego, Interst. 5, Del Mar Heights Road, El Camino Real, San Dieguito Road.

Airport: San Diego (Intl) 37 km
Train station: Amtrak 11 km

Owner: Harry Collins
General Manager: Michael J. Ullman
Open all year
Currency: US dollar (USD)
Rates: Menus 17-29 USD t.7.75% s.15%
Carte 27-44 USD t.7.75% s.15%
49 suites: 450-875 USD t.9% s.i.
Breakfast: 9-15 USD t.7.75% s.15%
Dogs: not allowed
Golf: Champion 2 km
Accepted cards: AE, DC, MC, VS

More info on www.relaischateaux.com/valencia

Mexico Caribbean Bermuda

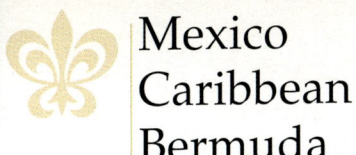

Properties Mexico	Nearest major city	Relais & Châteaux	Relais Gourmands	Page
Champs-Elysées (Restaurant)	Mexico City		◉	609
Puerto Rico				
Horned Dorset Primavera (The)	Mayagüez	⚜		610
Virgin Islands				
Biras Creek	Spanish Town	⚜		611
French West Indies				
Eden Rock	Gustavia	⚜		613
Toiny (Le)	Saint-Barthélemy	⚜		614
Barbados				
Coblers Cove	Speightstown	⚜		615
Bermuda				
Horizons and Cottages	Hamilton	⚜		616
Waterloo House	Hamilton	⚜		617

More info on www.relaischateaux.com

LES JARDINS
AU BOUT DU MONDE

Mobilier en teck

Manufacturer - Exclusive furniture
Tél. Paris (33) 01 34 50 83 22
Tél. Aix-en-Provence (33) 04 42 90 45 30

www.jardinsauboutdumonde.com

Restaurant Champs-Elysées

SINCE 1997

Paseo de la Reforma
316-Col. Juarez
Ciudad de México • Mexico

Tel. : (52) 5514 0450
Fax : (52) 5208 2302
champselysees@relaischateaux.com

Mexico

Set on the Paseo de la Reforma, Mexico City's equivalent of the Champs-Elysées, this elegant restaurant is renowned for its remarkable gourmet cuisine. François and Paquita Avernin welcome guests with exquisite courtesy and serve them gastronomical surprises such as «soupe de foie gras aux morilles», «canard rôti aux olives et sa pissaladière» or «gâteau chocolat à l'estragon». Excellent wines.
(Other activities P. 629)

Access: In the centre of the Rose zone, across from the Independence monument (Angel).

Airports: Mexico Juarez (Intl) 15 km, Toluca (Intl) 25 km

Owners: Paquita and François Avernin
Weekly closing: Sunday
Annual closing: Easter week
Currency: Mexican peso (MXP)
Rates: Carte 400-600 MXP s.15%
Dogs: allowed
Golf: 25 km
Accepted cards: AE, DC, JCB, MC, VS

François Avernin

More info on www.relaischateaux.com/champselysees

Puerto Rico

The Horned Dorset Primavera

SINCE 1993

Apartado 1132, route 429
00677 Rincon
Puerto Rico

Tel. : (1) (787) 823 40 30
USA toll free : (800) 633 18 57
Fax : (1) (787) 823 55 80
horneddorset@relaischateaux.com

The veranda of this neo-colonial style hacienda opens out onto the azure waters of the Caribbean. The guestrooms, furnished with impeccable taste, are exquisite havens of calm and all feature air-conditioning and luxurious marble bathrooms. Linger over an apéritif at the poolside and contemplate the spectacular Puerto Rican sunset, then enjoy delicious seafood and freshly-caught lobster by romantic candlelight.

Water sports, fishing, massage, fitness centre, concerts. (Other activities P. 629)

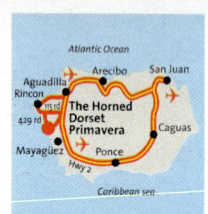

Access: Mayaguez, rte. 2 north, rte. 115 towards Rincon at the Anasco intersection, then route 429.

Airports: San Juan Luis Munoz Marin (Intl) 200 km, Mayagüez Eugenio M. de Hastos 10 km

Owners: Harold Davies, Kingsley Wratten, Wilhelm Sack
Open all year
Currency: US dollar (USD)
Rates: Menus 64-88 USD s.15%
Carte 56-80 USD s.15%
30 rooms: 280-800 USD t.7% + 3%
Breakfast: 15-20 USD s.15%
Dogs: not allowed
Golf: 25 km
Accepted cards: AE, VS

More info on www.relaischateaux.com/horneddorset

Biras Creek

SINCE 1999

P.O. Box 54
Virgin Gorda
British Virgin Islands

Tel. : (1) (284) 494 3555
Fax : (1) (284) 494 3557
biras@relaischateaux.com

A low key hideaway, located on a private 140 acre estate that is only accessible by boat. Overlooking three bodies of water with spectacular views, the resort offers extensive water sport activities or total relaxation. Spacious suites are situated on the ocean and are decorated with hand painted West Indian fabrics. All feature separate lounge, bedroom, outdoor living area, many with garden showers and bicycles.

Private beach with windsurfing, sailing, Hobie Cats, motor-rigged dinghies, snorkelling, boats charters, picnics, billiard table and massage. (Other activities P. 629)

Access: Complimentary boat transfers arranged from Beef Island Airport (Tortola) and Virgin Gorda Airport. Both are accessible via San Juan (Puerto Rico), Antigua and St. Martin.
Airports: Virgin Gorda 10 km, Beef Island 30 km
Helipad: N 18"29 W 64"21

Owner: Bert Houwer
General Managers: Michael and Luciana Nijdam
Annual closing: From September to October
Currency: US dollar (USD)
Full board
33 suites: Off-season: 525-1125 USD t.7% s.10%
Season: 750-1650 USD t.7% s.10%
Breakfast: included
Dogs: not allowed
Accepted cards: AE, MC, VS

More info on www.relaischateaux.com/biras

The Relais & Châteaux Gift Certificate: happiness à la carte!

To offer the Relais & Châteaux gift certificate is to provide your loved one with the key to 459 Relais & Châteaux hotels and restaurants worldwide. Gift certificates are available in US dollars or Euros.

The Relais & Châteaux gift certificate -- a gift of everlasting memories.

For more information, call **(1) (212) 856 0115 (USA)** or **(44) (0)20 7978 5842 (UK)**, or visit **www.relaischateaux.com**

Eden Rock

SINCE 2002

St Jean Baie
97133 Saint-Barthélemy
French West Indies

Tel. : (590) 05 90 29 79 99
Fax : (590) 05 90 27 88 37
edenrock@relaischateaux.com

French West Indies

In the beautiful Bay of Saint-Jean, Eden Rock is like an island set in the turquoise sea. David & Jane Matthews with Jane's sister, Pamela Parker, have created an English country house atmosphere in the tropical sunshine, with beautifully decorated rooms and exciting restaurant choices. A perfect sandy beach and health giving Spa complement the full range of services.

Motorboat, deep sea fishing, wind surfing, surfing, catamaran, tennis... (Other activities P. 629)

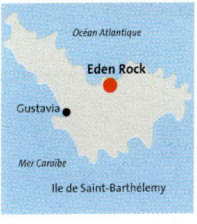

Access: From airport: straight ahead on main road (2 minutes).

Airport: Saint-Barthélemy 2 km

Owners: Jane and David Matthews
General Manager: Pamela Parker
Annual closing: From September 1st to October 18th
Currency: Euro (€)
Rates: Carte 35-90 € s.i.
6 rooms: 310-815 € s.i.
10 suites: 760-1095 € s.i.
Breakfast: included
Dogs: allowed (small dogs)
Accepted cards: AE, MC, VS

More info on www.relaischateaux.com/edenrock

French West Indies

Le Toiny

SINCE 1996

Anse de Toiny
97133 Saint-Barthélemy
French West Indies

Tel. : (059) 05 90 27 88 88
Fax : (059) 05 90 27 89 30
toiny@relaischateaux.com

Discover Caribbean paradise in your own colonial-style villa surrounded by lush tropical gardens. Relax in your private pool overlooking the ocean and enjoy the utmost in modern amenities (personal fax, satellite TV, DVD, video and air conditioning). After a day on the sun-drenched beaches, dine by romantic candlelight at «Le Gaïac», which offers refined French cuisine with a local Caribbean flair and a superb panoramic ocean view.

Boat and plane trips, game fishing. (Other activities P. 629)

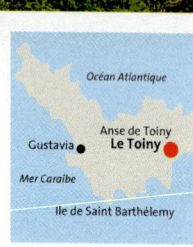

Access: Complimentary transport to and from the airport.

Airports: Saint-Martin (Intl) 20 km, Saint-Barthélemy 6 km

Owner: Michael Shen
General Manager: David P. Henderson
Annual closing: From Sept. 1st to October 19th
Currency: Euro (€)
Rates: Carte 60 € (lunch) s.i. 110 € (dinner) s.i.
14 villas: low season: 750 € s.i.
high season: 1550 € s.i.
Breakfast: included
Dogs: allowed
Accepted cards: AE, DC, MC, VS

More info on www.relaischateaux.com/toiny

Cobblers Cove

SINCE 1990

St. Peter, Barbados
West Indies
Barbados

Tel. : (1) (246) 422 2291
Fax : (1) (246) 422 1460
cobblers@relaischateaux.com

Barbados

Imagine the elegance of an English country house combined with the charms of a tropical island paradise. Cobblers Cove, nestled beneath palm trees and overlooking fine sand beaches and turquoise waters, offers exceptional hospitality and luxurious accommodation. Relax on the terrace of a sumptuous suite, secluded in the hotel's landscaped gardens, then savour fine wines and cuisine at the «Terrace Restaurant».

Water sports, golf trips... (Other activities P. 629)

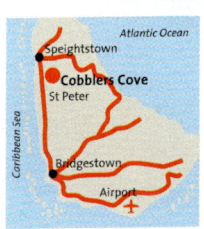

Access: From the airport, take the ABC Highway, then on to Highway 1, travelling North along the West Coast.

Airport: Barbados Grantley Adams (Intl) 29 km

Owner: Hayton Ltd.
General Manager: Hamish Watson
Annual closing: From September 1st to October 15th
Currency: US dollar (USD)
Rates: Menus 45-70 USD t.15% s.10%
Carte 45-70 USD t.15% s.10%
40 suites: 306-1927 USD s.i.
Breakfast: 15 USD t.7.5% s.10%
Dogs: not allowed
Golf: Sandy Lane 8 km
Accepted cards: AE, MC, VS

More info on www.relaischateaux.com/cobblers

Horizonsand Cottages

Bermuda — SINCE 1985

33 South Shore Road
Paget PG 04
Bermuda

Tel. : (1) (441) 236 0048
USA Toll free : 800 468 0022
Fax : (1) (441) 236 1981
horizons@relaischateaux.com

This XVIIIth century Plantation Estate offers idyllic natural surroundings and traditional island hospitality. Sporting enthusiasts will enjoy the wide range of leisure pursuits such as golf, putting and tennis, while guests seeking sun and relaxation will adore the coral sand beaches of the South Shore. Enjoy an apéritif in the shade of the hibiscus, then savour fine wines and seafood delicacies on the «Ocean Terrace».

Private Beach Club, European spa, fitness center, horticulturist tours, water sports, Coral Beach Club 500 m. (Other activities P. 629)

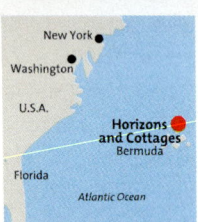

Access: From Bermuda airport, follow the south coast towards Paget.

Airport: Bermuda (Intl) 15 km

Owners: Elfrida Wardman Chappell and George Wardman
General Manager: Brian Crook
Open all year
Currency: US dollar (USD)
Rates: Menus included Carte 55 USD s.15%
45 rooms: 400-550 USD t.7.25% s.10%
3 suites: 580-780 USD t.7.25% s.10%
Breakfast: included
Dogs: allowed (extra cost)
Golf: on the premises
Accepted cards: AE, MC, VS

More info on www.relaischateaux.com/horizons

Waterloo House

SINCE 1993

100 Pitts Bay Road
Hamilton HM 08 • Bermuda

Tel. : (1) (441) 295 4480
USA toll free : 800 468 4100
Fax : (1) (441) 295 2585
waterloo@relaischateaux.com

Bermuda

Views of shimmering blue water and pink coral beaches stretch to the horizon and the scent of frangipani wafts on the breeze. Paradise awaits you at this manor house which offers luxurious accommodation and an outstanding restaurant. Cruise aboard the private launch, picnic on a deserted island, or snorkel with the tropical fish. After cocktails by the pool, enjoy a romantic dance in the moonlight with a local band.

Tennis, European spa, snorkelling. Private beach club.
(Other activities P. 629)

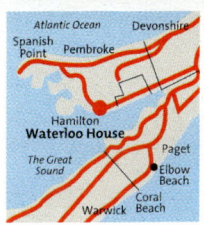

Access: From Bermuda Airport, towards Hamilton, then Outskirts via Front Street, the hotel is indicated.

Airport: Bermuda (Intl) 15 km

Owners: Elfrida Wardman Chappell and George Wardman
General Manager: Trudy Mulder
Open all year
Currency: US dollar (USD)
Rates: Menus 40-45 USD s.15%
Carte 50-60 USD s.15%
20 rooms: 330-460 USD t.7.25% s.10%
10 suites: 430-780 USD t.7.25% s.10%
Breakfast: included
Dogs: allowed (extra cost)
Golf: Mid Ocean Club 10 km
Accepted cards: AE, MC, VS

More info on www.relaischateaux.com/waterloo

South America

Properties Colombia	Nearest major city	Relais & Châteaux	Relais Gourmands	Page
Casa Medina	Bogota	⚜		621

Ecuador				
Mirage - Garden Hotel & Spa (La)	Quito	⚜		622

Brazil				
Rosa dos Ventos (Hotel e Fazenda)	Teresópolis	⚜		623

Uruguay				
Bourgogne (La)	Punta del Este		◉	624

Argentina				
Bondoux (Jean-Paul) (Restaurant)	Buenos Aires		◉	625
Las Balsas (Hosteria)	Villa La Angostura	⚜		627
Posada de los Pájaros - Spa & Hotel	Mar del Plata	⚜		626

More info on www.relaischateaux.com

GRAND CRU CLASSÉE EN 1855

APPELLATION PAUILLAC CONTRÔLÉE

MIS EN BOUTEILLE AU CHÂTEAU

Château
Pontet-Canet
Pauillac

Casa Medina

SINCE 1997

Carrera 7 N° 69 A-22
Bogota
(Cundinamarca) • Colombia

Tel. : (57) (1) 3120 299
Fax : (57) (1) 2126 668
casamedina@relaischateaux.com

Colombia

The elegant Casa Medina, set in the heart of Bogota's new business district, has become one of Colombia's national monuments. Nothing is left to chance in this splendid hotel, where guests will enjoy impeccable service and exquisite hospitality. Relax in the luxuriously comfortable suites and guestrooms, tastefully decorated with remarkable works of art, and savour classical cuisine in the split-level restaurant.
(Other activities P. 629)

Access: From the airport, follow Eldorado Ave. until carretera 7 North then carretera 69A.

Airport: Bogota Eldorado (Intl) 10 km

Owner: Charleston S.A.
General Manager: Carmen Gonzalez
Annual closing:
Hotel: from December 20th to January 8th
Rest.: from December 21st to January 14th
Currency: US dollar (USD)
Rates: Menu 25 USD t.15% s.i.
32 rooms: 165 USD s.i.
26 suites: 190-230 USD s.i.
Breakfast: 16 USD t.15% s.i.
Dogs: not allowed
Golf: 15 km
Accepted cards: AE, DC, VS

More info on www.relaischateaux.com/casamedina

Ecuador

La Mirage - Garden Hotel & Spa

SINCE 1997

Cotacachi - Imbabura
Ecuador

Tel. : (593) (6) 91 52 37
Fax : (593) (6) 91 50 65
lamirage@relaischateaux.com

La Mirage is a contemporary resort built on the grounds of a 200 year old hacienda. Wander through the extraordinary fragrant hummingbird-filled gardens, watching peacocks strolling by. Enjoy delightful regional and international cuisine. Relax in the unique and elegant spa for a variety of 11 different treatments.

Aromatherapy, massages, mountain climbing, fishing, festivals. (Other activities P. 629)

Altitude: 2450 metres.
Access: Pan American highway north. 8 km after Otavalo, turn left at the sign Cotacachi, take main road, 300 m after second traffic light, turn left.
Airport: Quito Mariscal Sucr (Intl) 120 km

Owner: Jorge Espinosa
General Manager: Patricio Hidrovo
Open all year
Currency: US dollar (USD)
Rates: Menus 20-30 USD t.12% s.10%
Carte 25-35 USD t.12% s.10%
9 rooms: half-board 220-260 USD t.12% s.10%
14 suites: half-board 270-550 USD t.12% s.10%
Breakfast: 10-15 USD t.12% s.10%
Dogs: not allowed
Accepted cards: DC, MC, VS

More info on www.relaischateaux.com/lamirage

Hotel e Fazenda Rosa dos Ventos

SINCE 1991

Km 22, Estrada Teresópolis-Nova Friburgo
25977-400 Teresópolis-R.J.
Brazil

Tel. : (55) (021) 2644 99 00
(55) (021) 2532 11 97
Fax : (55) (021) 2240 81 25
(55) (021) 2642 81 74
fazenda@relaischateaux.com

Brazil

Perched at 1250 metres, this elegant hotel is set amidst 250 acres of luxuriant foliage in the heart of the Serra dos Orgaos National Park. Its marvellously comfortable guestrooms are housed in three alpine-style chalets overlooking flower gardens, stables and a mountain lake. Savour regional specialities or classic international cuisine and enjoy exquisite hospitality in this haven of peace and eternal sunshine.

Lake fishing, steam bath. Trekking: 5 miles of internal paths inside 120 acres in an environmentally preserved area. (Other activities P. 629)

Altitude : 1250 metres.
Access: Exit Rio, Linha Vermelha, BR 040 towards Petrópolis, BR 116 towards Teresópolis, RJ 130.

Airports: Rio-Galeao (Intl) 110 km, Rio-Santos Dumont (Intl) 130 km
Helipad: S 22° 17' 53.6'' W 42° 47' 46.7''

Owner: Hotel e Fazenda Rosa dos Ventos Ltda
General Manager: Elizabeth Waddington Agra
Open all year
Currency: US dollar (USD)
Rates: Menu 20 USD s.10%
Carte 25-35 USD s.10%
35 rooms: 155-182 USD s.10%
5 suites: 195-214 USD s.10%
Breakfast: included
Dogs: not allowed
Golf: 27 km
Accepted cards: AE, DC, MC, VS

More info on www.relaischateaux.com/fazenda

Uruguay

La Bourgogne

SINCE 1992

Pedragosa Sierra,
20100 Punta del Este
(Maldonado) • Uruguay

Tel. : (598) (042) 4820 07
Fax : (598) (042) 4878 73
bourgogne@relaischateaux.com

This elegant restaurant, set in a cool jasmine-scented garden near magnificent beaches and the local yacht club, is renowned for its superb French cuisine. Jean-Paul Bondoux is a true perfectionist, cultivating fresh vegetables, herbs and spices on his own farm. Savour «terrine de jeunes poireaux aux langoustines» and «gigot d'agneau rôti aux herbes du jardin», accompanied by the finest French and South American vintages.

Museums and galleries. (Other activities P. 629)

Access:
From Parada 5 straight ahead, intersection: av. del Mar and Pedragosa Sierra.

Airports: Montevideo Carrasco (Intl) 120 km, Laguna del Sauce 22 km

Owners: Evelyne and Jean-Paul Bondoux
Weekly closing: Monday, Tuesday, Wednesday (from April to November)
Annual closing: July
Currency: US dollar (USD)
Rates: Menus
Lunch 35 USD t.23% s.i.
Dinner 55-75 USD t.23% s.i.
Dogs: allowed
Golf: 4 km
Accepted cards: MC

Jean-Paul Bondoux

More info on www.relaischateaux.com/bourgogne

Restaurant Jean-Paul Bondoux

SINCE 1995

c/o Alvear Palace
2027 Ayacucho, Buenos Aires
(Río de la Plata) • Argentina

Tel. : (54) 11 4805 3857
Fax : (54) 11 4808 2158
bondoux@relaischateaux.com

Argentina

Jean-Paul Bondoux has chosen this elegant restaurant, tastefully decorated in contemporary style, to showcase his gourmet delicacies inspired by Burgundy tradition. The menu features a superb «faisan en deux cuissons au muscat de Beaumes de Venise», a «merluza au coulis de petits pois» and an extraordinary «carré de veau service voiture aux sauces de votre choix», accompanied by Argentine wines or an exceptional pommard.

Access: In the centre of Buenos Aires, at the corner of avenue Alvear and Ayacucho.

Airport: Buenos Aires (Intl) 40 km

Owner: APHSA
General Managers:
Evelyne and Jean-Paul Bondoux
Weekly closing:
Saturday noon and Sunday
Open all year
Currency: US dollar (USD)
Rates: Menus 45-65 USD s.i.
Carte 50-80 USD s.i.
Dogs: not allowed
Accepted cards: AE, DC, MC, VS

More info on www.relaischateaux.com/bondoux

Posada de los Pájaros - Spa Hotel

Argentina — SINCE 2001

Av. Don Bosco y Ceferino Namuncurá
7000 Tandil
(Provincia de Buenos Aires)
Argentina

Tel. : (54) (2293) 43 2013
Fax : (54) (2293) 43 1108
lospajaros@relaischateaux.com

A few kilometres away from Tandil, on the oldest hills in South America, at a height of 300 meters, this spa hotel offers its guests a devoted service and refined spa cuisine. Within 50 hectares, groves and gardens for walking, sports and riding. The comfortable, elegantly decorated rooms overlooking the hills will give you the rest and relaxation you are looking for. Saunas, swimming pools, a whirlpool and the spa centre will round off your stay.

Hunting, climbing... (Other activities P. 629)

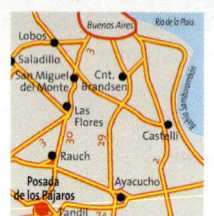

Access: From Buenos Aires take motorway 2 to Las Armas which then connects to national motorway 74 straight to Tandil.

Airports: Buenos Aires (Intl) 350 km, Tandil 14 km
Helipad: S 37° 22' 40'' W 59° 6' 38''
Train station: Tandil 12 km

Owner: Ricardo Giovannetti
General Manager: Gustavo Di Giorgio
Open all year
Currency: US dollar (USD)
Full board
15 rooms: 170 USD s.n.i. per person
2 suites: 210 USD s.n.i. per person
Breakfast: included
Dogs: not allowed
Golf: 800 metres
Accepted cards: AE, MC, VS

More info on www.relaischateaux.com/lospajaros

Hosteria Las Balsas

SINCE 1995

Villa La Angostura
8407 Neuquen
Argentina

Tel. : (54) (2944) 49 4308
Fax : (54) (2944) 49 4308
lasbalsas@relaischateaux.com

Argentina

Magnificent forests and snow-capped peaks surround the sparkling waters of Lake Nahuel Huapi. In the midst of these idyllic natural surroundings, the blue wooden walls and octagonal tower of Las Balsas overlook a peaceful cove. Relax in one of the fifteen beautiful rooms and enjoy the exquisite hospitality of Las Balsas. Enjoy riding, hiking, or a boat tour and savour delicious cuisine and fine wines.
Water sports, walks. (Other activities P. 629)

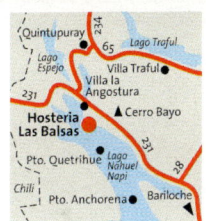

Access:
From Bariloche, Route 231 towards Villa La Angostura. After Cerro Bayo signs, 300 m to the left.

Airport: San Carlos de Bariloche 80 km

Owners: Hosteria Las Balsas S.A.
General Manager: Romina Cambiasso
Annual closing: From May to September
Currency: US dollar (USD)
Rates: Menu 40 USD s.i. Carte 40 USD s.i.
13 rooms: 200 USD s.i.
2 suites: 300 USD s.i.
Breakfast: included
Dogs: not allowed
Accepted cards: AE, MC, VS

More info on www.relaischateaux.com/lasbalsas

Discover the universe of Relais & Châteaux

www.relaischateaux.com

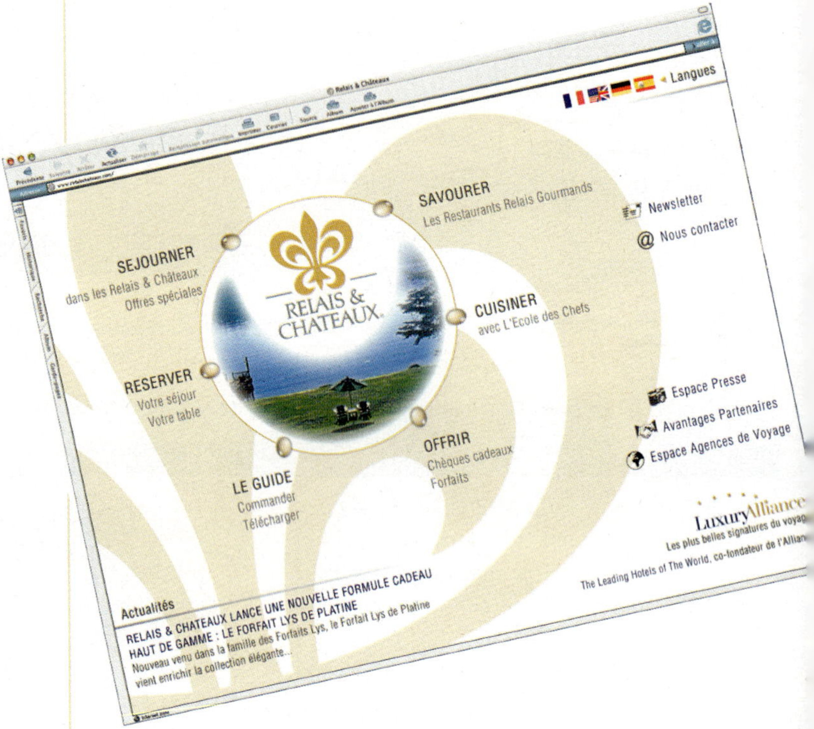

- Order or download the guide
- Visit, select... reserve on-line
- Offer a gift certificate or package Relais & Châteaux
- Learn to cook like a master chef
- Discover Relais Gourmands*

*in partnership with «Saveurs du Monde» at **www.theworldwildegourmet.com/**

INDEX
Sports and Leisure, Fitness and Beauty, Meeting Facilities

This index describes the leisure and meeting facilities of each Relais & Châteaux. It also provides comprehensive and rapid visual information.

• Sports and leisure
Swimming, tennis, golf course nearby, biking and mountain biking, riding, polo, hunting, fishing, sailing, water skiing, canoeing, kayaking and rafting, skiing, aeroclub.

• Fitness
Steam baths, sauna, hammam, solarium, fitness, spa, beauty centre.

• Meeting facilities
Receptions or cocktails, number of meeting rooms available, availability or not of audiovisual equipment, presence or not of a secretariat, number of guest rooms.

Sports and Leisure

Properties	Page	Seaside	Swimming-pool on site	Tennis on site	9/18 holes golf course	Mountain-biking	Hiking	Horseback riding - Polo	Diving	Hunting	Fishing	Sailing	Water-Skiing	Canoeing Kayaking-Rafting	Skiing	Flying club
France																
Paris - Paris Region (page 51)																
Ambassadeurs (Les)	53															
Apicius	60															
Arpège (L')	63															
Auberge des Templiers	75		●	●	25 km	●		●		●	●					
Bas-Bréau (Hôtellerie du)	74		●	●	5 km	●	●	●								
Boyer «Les Crayères»	81			●	5 km	●	●	●		●	●					●
Carré des Feuillants	67															
Cazaudehore et «La Forestière»	73				2 km	●	●									
Château de Courcelles	83		●	●	18 km	●		●				●				
Clos (Hostellerie Le)	77				7 km	●		●				●				
Darroze (Hélène)	65															
Faugeron (Restaurant)	54															
Gagnaire (Pierre)	57															
Grand Véfour (Le)	69															
Le Divellec - La Cuisine de la Mer	61															
Rostang (Michel) - Restaurant	55															
Royal Champagne	79				25 km	●	●	●		●						●
Savoy (Guy) - Restaurant	59															
Vigny (Hôtel De)	56															
Brittany - Normandy - Pas-de-Calais (page 85)																
Auberge Bretonne (L')	100				15 km	●	●	●	●			●		●		
Bretagne et sa Résidence (Le)	97				15 km											
Castel Clara	96	●	●	●	7 km	●	●	●	●			●	●	●		●
Castel Marie-Louise	101	●			7 km				●			●				
Château d'Audrieu	90		●		15 km	●	●					●				●
Château de Locguénolé	95	●	●	●	16 km	●	●	●			●	●	●	●		●
Château de Montreuil	86		●		12 km	●	●	●			●		●			
Chaumière (La)	89	●		●	6 km											
Domaine de la Bretesche	99		●	●	100 m	●	●	●		●						
Ferme St-Siméon (La)	88	●	●		10 km											
Gill (Restaurant)	87															
Maisons de Bricourt	91	●			3 km		●	●				●				
Manoir de Lan-Kerellec	92	●			5 km	●	●	●			●	●		●		●
Plage (Hôtel de la)	93	●		●	35 km						●	●				●
Loire Valley (page 103)																
Bardet (Jean) - Château Belmont	106		●		12 km	●	●	●				●	●	●		●

Fitness	Spa	Beauty Salon	Swimming-pool covered	Whirlpool	Sauna	Hammam	Solarium	Meeting	Conference	Reception	Cocktail party	Number of conference rooms	Audio-visual equipment	Secretarial Services	Number of rooms	Properties
																France
																Paris - Paris Region (page 51)
								40	140	130	450	10		●		Ambassadeurs (Les)
																Apicius
											15					Arpège (L')
								25	60	80	120	4	●	●	30	Auberge des Templiers
								25	30	40	40	3	●	●	20	Bas-Bréau (Hôtellerie du)
								15		50		1	●		19	Boyer «Les Crayères»
																Carré des Feuillants
								25		130	160	3	●		30	Cazaudehore et «La Forestière»
				●				30	60	100	150	2	●		20	Château de Courcelles
●					●			20	30			1	●		10	Clos (Hostellerie Le)
																Darroze (Hélène)
																Faugeron (Restaurant)
																Gagnaire (Pierre)
																Grand Véfour (Le)
																Le Divellec - La Cuisine de la Mer
										60		4		●		Rostang (Michel) - Restaurant
								25	40	40	60	4	●	●	25	Royal Champagne
																Savoy (Guy) - Restaurant
															37	Vigny (Hôtel De)
																Britanny - Normandy - Pas-de-Calais (page 85)
															8	Auberge Bretonne (L')
								10	30	30	30				9	Bretagne et sa Résidence (Le)
●	●	●			●	●	●	25	25			1	●	●	40	Castel Clara
								25	40	50	60		●		31	Castel Marie-Louise
								20	50	100	100	2	●	●	29	Château d'Audrieu
				●	●			40	140	240	300	3	●		28	Château de Locguénolé
								12		40		1	●		14	Château de Montreuil
															9	Chaumière (La)
								35	60	80	120	4	●	●	31	Domaine de la Bretesche
●	●	●		●	●	●	●	50	60	100	200	3	●	●	29	Ferme St-Siméon (La)
																Gill (Restaurant)
								20		20	20				19	Maisons de Bricourt
								20	30	50	70	4	●	●	19	Manoir de Lan-Kerellec
								15	30	100		2	●		30	Plage (Hôtel de la)
																Loire Valley (page 103)
								35	45	150	150	3	●		21	Bardet (Jean) - Château Belmont

More info on **www.relaischateaux.com**

Sports and Leisure

Properties	Page	Seaside	Swimming-pool on site	Tennis on site	9/18 holes golf course	Mountain-biking	Hiking	Horseback riding - Polo	Diving	Hunting	Fishing	Sailing	Water-Skiing	Canoeing Kayaking - Rafting	Skiing	Flying club
Château de Curzay	113		●		10 km	●	●	●			●					
Château de Marçay	105		●	●	20 km	●	●	●			●			●		
Château de Noirieux	104		●	●	20 km	●	●	●			●			●		●
Château de Noizay	108		●	●	28 km	●	●	●			●			●		
Domaine des Hauts de Loire	109		●	●	5 km	●	●									
Hautes Roches (Les)	107		●		15 km	●	●	●		●	●	●	●	●		●
Lion d'Or (Grand Hôtel du)	112				28 km	●	●	●			●					●
Robin (Bernard) - Le Relais	111				9 km											
The Greater South-West (page 117)																
Bras (Michel)	130				10 km		●			●	●					
Centenaire (Hôtel du)	125		●		20 km	●								●		
Chapelle Saint-Martin (La)	120		●	●	15 km	●	●	●			●			●		●
Château Cordeillan-Bages	130		●		25 km					●						
Château de Castel-Novel	122		●	●	10 km	●	●	●			●			●		
Château de la Treyne	126		●	●	10 km	●	●	●		●	●			●		
Château de Mercuès	129		●	●	30 km			●			●		●	●		
Château de Puy Robert	124		●		28 km	●								●		
Château de Riell	143		●	●	15 km	●	●	●			●			●		
Château de Roumégouse	128		●		30 km	●		●		●	●					●
Coutanceau (Richard) (Restaurant)	119	●			12 km											
Domaine d'Auriac	142		●	●	on site											
Domaine de Bassibé	137		●		7 km											●
Guérard (M.) «Les Prés d'Eugénie»	138		●		1,5 km	●	●	●		●	●			●		
Hauterive (Hôtel)	135		●		15 km	●	●				●					
Loges de l'Auberade (Les)	131		●		10 km	●	●				●		●			
Moulin de l'Abbaye	123				25 km	●					●			●		
Moulin de la Gorce (Au)	121				30 km	●	●	●			●					
Parc Victoria (Le)	139		●		2 km			●	●		●	●	●			
Plaisance (Hostellerie de)	134				30 km	●	●				●					●
Pyrénées (Les)	140		●		50 km		●				●					
Relais de la Poste	136		●		20 km	●	●	●			●	●				
Réserve (La)	141		●	●	6 km	●	●	●			●	●	●	●		
Richelieu (Le)	118	●	●	●	20 km	●		●					●			●
Vieux Logis (Le)	127		●		20 km	●	●	●			●			●	●	
Alsace - Lorraine (page 145)																
Abbaye La Pommeraie	153				20 km		●							●		
Arnsbourg (L')	149				15 km											
Bas Rupts et Chalet Fleuri	146		●	●	50 km	●	●	●		●	●	●			●	●

Fitness	Spa	Beauty Salon	Swimming-pool covered	Whirlpool	Sauna	Hammam	Solarium	Meeting	Conference	Reception	Cocktail party	Number of conference rooms	Audio-visual equipment	Secretarial Services	Number of rooms	Properties
								40				2	●		22	Château de Curzay
								60	90	80	150	4	●	●	34	Château de Marçay
								50	60	60	120	2	●		19	Château de Noirieux
								21	30	36	50	2	●		19	Château de Noizay
								30	40	80		2	●		35	Domaine des Hauts de Loire
								30	50	120	200	2	●	●	15	Hautes Roches (Les)
								10		30		1			16	Lion d'Or (Grand Hôtel du)
										60		1				Robin (Bernard) - Le Relais

The Greater South-West (page 117)

Fitness	Spa	Beauty Salon	Swimming-pool covered	Whirlpool	Sauna	Hammam	Solarium	Meeting	Conference	Reception	Cocktail party	Number of conference rooms	Audio-visual equipment	Secretarial Services	Number of rooms	Properties
								20	20	60	60	1	●	●	15	Bras (Michel)
●															24	Centenaire (Hôtel du)
								100	60	200	300	3	●	●	13	Chapelle Saint-Martin (La)
								15		24	50	1		●	29	Château Cordeillan-Bages
								80	150	200	250	3			37	Château de Castel-Novel
			●					50	70	60	80	1	●	●	16	Château de la Treyne
								60	120	110	120	2	●	●	30	Château de Mercuès
								30	45	30	60	2	●		38	Château de Puy Robert
●	●	●			●		●	20	150	100	120	5	●		22	Château de Riell
								20		250		1	●		15	Château de Roumégouse
								30	50	120	120	1		●		Coutanceau (Richard) (Restaurant)
								40	65	120	120	9	●	●	26	Domaine d'Auriac
								20	35	120	200	4	●	●	17	Domaine de Bassibé
●	●	●		●		●	●	80	120	120	150	7		●	40	Guérard (M.) «Les Prés d'Eugénie»
				●				26	120	120	200	2	●		18	Hauterive (Hôtel)
								25	40	100		2	●	●	10	Loges de l'Aubergade (Les)
								25	30		40	1	●		19	Moulin de l'Abbaye
								30	45			1			10	Moulin de la Gorce (Au)
								25	15	20	30	2	●		17	Parc Victoria (Le)
								50	100	70	150	1	●	●	19	Plaisance (Hostellerie de)
								25				2	●		21	Pyrénées (Les)
			●					20	40	100	150	2	●	●	12	Relais de la Poste
								80	120	200	400	4	●	●	24	Réserve (La)
●	●	●	●	●	●		●	40	100	300	500	2	●	●	40	Richelieu (Le)
								80	100	80	100	2	●	●	26	Vieux Logis (Le)

Alsace - Lorraine (page 145)

Fitness	Spa	Beauty Salon	Swimming-pool covered	Whirlpool	Sauna	Hammam	Solarium	Meeting	Conference	Reception	Cocktail party	Number of conference rooms	Audio-visual equipment	Secretarial Services	Number of rooms	Properties
								18	36	40	60	1			14	Abbaye La Pommeraie
																Arnsbourg (L')
								15	25	50	60	4	●	●	24	Bas Rupts et Chalet Fleuri

More info on www.relaischateaux.com

Sports and Leisure

Properties	Page	Seaside	Swimming-pool on site	Tennis on site	9/18 holes golf course	Mountain-biking	Hiking	Horseback riding - Polo	Diving	Hunting	Fishing	Sailing	Water-Skiing	Canoeing Kayaking - Rafting	Skiing	Flying club
Buerehiesel (Restaurant)	151				10 km											
Château d'Adoménil	147		●				●									
Cheneaudière (Hostellerie La)	152		●	●	45 km		●	●			●				●	
Crocodile (Au)	150				10 km											

Burgundy - Franche-Comté (page 155)

Properties	Page	Seaside	Swimming-pool on site	Tennis on site	9/18 holes golf course	Mountain-biking	Hiking	Horseback riding - Polo	Diving	Hunting	Fishing	Sailing	Water-Skiing	Canoeing Kayaking - Rafting	Skiing	Flying club
Blanc (Georges)	167		●	●	12 km	●		●			●					
Château de Germigney	163				30 km	●	●			●	●			●		
Château d'Igé	165				12 km	●	●									
Côte St-Jacques (La) (J.-M.) Lorain	156		●	●	18 km						●		●			●
Espérance (L')	157		●			●	●	●		●	●		●			
Greuze (Restaurant)	164				15 km											
Lameloise	162				15 km											
Levernois (Hostellerie de)	161			●	100 m											●
Loiseau (Bernard) - La Côte d'Or	159		●		20 km	●	●	●		●	●	●		●		

Lyon - Rhone Valley (page 169)

Properties	Page	Seaside	Swimming-pool on site	Tennis on site	9/18 holes golf course	Mountain-biking	Hiking	Horseback riding - Polo	Diving	Hunting	Fishing	Sailing	Water-Skiing	Canoeing Kayaking - Rafting	Skiing	Flying club
Auberge et Clos des Cimes	175				15 km		●				●					
Chapel (Alain)	171				2 km											
Château de Codignat	173		●	●	35 km	●					●		●			
Château de Faverges-de-la-Tour	182		●	●	on site			●		●	●			●		
Léon de Lyon	177				20 km											
Orsi (Pierre) (Restaurant)	179				20 km											
Pic	183		●		10 km	●		●		●	●	●				
Poularde (Hostellerie La)	174		●		3 km	●										●
Pyramide (La)	181				25 km											●
Troisgros (La Maison)	172				2 km											●
Villa Florentine	180		●		15 km	●	●				●	●	●			●

Savoy - Mont Blanc (page 185)

Properties	Page	Seaside	Swimming-pool on site	Tennis on site	9/18 holes golf course	Mountain-biking	Hiking	Horseback riding - Polo	Diving	Hunting	Fishing	Sailing	Water-Skiing	Canoeing Kayaking - Rafting	Skiing	Flying club
Alpes Hôtel du Pralong	195		●												●	
Auberge du Bois Prin	187				3 km	●	●	●			●	●			●	●
Auberge du Père Bise	190				2 km	●	●	●	●			●	●	●	●	
Chalet du Mont d'Arbois	193		●	●	300 m	●	●	●							●	●
Grand Cœur (Le)	197														●	
Hameau Albert 1er (Le)	188		●		4 km	●	●				●				●	
Ombremont	194		●		10 km	●	●				●	●	●	●		
Verniaz et ses chalets (La)	186		●	●	2 km	●	●				●	●	●	●		
Veyrat (M.) - Auberge de l'Eridan	189				2 km	●	●	●				●			●	
Veyrat (M.) - La Ferme de mon Père	191				2 km	●	●	●			●			●	●	●

Fitness	Spa	Beauty Salon	Swimming-pool covered	Whirlpool	Sauna	Hammam	Solarium	Meeting	Conference	Reception	Cocktail party	Number of conference rooms	Audio-visual equipment	Secretarial Services	Number of rooms	Properties
								26		100		3	•			Buerehiesel (Restaurant)
								20	40	50		2			12	Château d'Adoménil
		•	•	•	•			25	40		70	1	•		29	Cheneaudière (Hostellerie La)
										120	250	3				Crocodile (Au)

Burgundy - Franche-Comté (page 155)

Fitness	Spa	Beauty Salon	Swimming-pool covered	Whirlpool	Sauna	Hammam	Solarium	Meeting	Conference	Reception	Cocktail party	Number of conference rooms	Audio-visual equipment	Secretarial Services	Number of rooms	Properties
								120	150	400	600	3	•		30	Blanc (Georges)
								40	60	100	200	4	•	•	20	Château de Germigney
								50	100	100		1	•		14	Château d'Igé
			•		•			30	45	80	80	4			32	Côte St-Jacques (La) (J.-M.) Lorain
								80	120	150	200	4		•	27	Espérance (L')
										30		2				Greuze (Restaurant)
								20		20					16	Lameloise
								20	50	100	100	1	•		16	Levernois (Hostellerie de)
•	•			•	•	•		19	30	40	40	3	•	•	32	Loiseau (Bernard) - La Côte d'Or

Lyon - Rhone Valley (page 169)

Fitness	Spa	Beauty Salon	Swimming-pool covered	Whirlpool	Sauna	Hammam	Solarium	Meeting	Conference	Reception	Cocktail party	Number of conference rooms	Audio-visual equipment	Secretarial Services	Number of rooms	Properties
															12	Auberge et Clos des Cimes
									30	60	40				12	Chapel (Alain)
								40	70	100	120	1	•	•	19	Château de Codignat
								80	100	150	200	6	•	•	36	Château de Faverges-de-la-Tour
																Léon de Lyon
								40	50	100	100	5	•	•		Orsi (Pierre) (Restaurant)
								50	80	80	100	2	•		15	Pic
								40	40	50	50	2	•		14	Poularde (Hostellerie La)
								28		75	120	1	•	•	24	Pyramide (La)
								25							18	Troisgros (La Maison)
•					•	•	•	16	30	70	100	2			28	Villa Florentine

Savoy - Mont Blanc (page 185)

Fitness	Spa	Beauty Salon	Swimming-pool covered	Whirlpool	Sauna	Hammam	Solarium	Meeting	Conference	Reception	Cocktail party	Number of conference rooms	Audio-visual equipment	Secretarial Services	Number of rooms	Properties
•			•	•	•			40	50	45	60	3			64	Alpes Hôtel du Pralong
				•	•			40	60	50	80	2	•	•	11	Auberge du Bois Prin
								30	45	100	120	2	•	•	34	Auberge du Père Bise
	•	•	•	•	•			15		100	150	1	•	•	32	Chalet du Mont d'Arbois
•								15	15	15	25	1	•		40	Grand Cœur (Le)
•	•	•	•	•	•	•		15	25			1	•		42	Hameau Albert 1er (Le)
								40	60	60	80	1	•	•	17	Ombremont
								15	20	60	60	2	•		32	Verniaz et ses chalets (La)
															11	Veyrat (M.) - Auberge de l'Eridan
			•												8	Veyrat (M.) - La Ferme de mon Père

More info on **www.relaischateaux.com**

Sports and Leisure

Properties	Page	Seaside	Swimming-pool on site	Tennis on site	9/18 holes golf course	Mountain-biking	Hiking	Horseback riding - Polo	Diving	Hunting	Fishing	Sailing	Water-Skiing	Canoeing Kayaking - Rafting	Skiing	Flying club
Provence (page 199)																
Abbaye de Sainte Croix	215				10 km	●	●	●		●	●					●
Auberge de Noves	210		●	●	20 km	●	●	●		●	●			●		
Auberge La Regalido	207				10 km	●	●	●								
Cabro d'Or (La)	212		●	●	2 km											
Cardinale et sa Résidence (La)	200		●		25 km					●	●			●		
Château de Montcaud	203		●	●	22 km						●					
Château de Rochegude	201		●		10 km	●	●	●								
Clos de la Violette	217				5 km											
Crillon-le-Brave (Hostellerie de)	202		●		30 km	●	●	●						●		
Domaine de Châteauneuf	219		●	●	on site	●	●	●			●					
Frênes (Hostellerie Les)	209		●		5 km	●	●	●		●	●			●		●
Jardin des Sens (Le)	205		●		10 km							●	●			
Jules César (Hôtel)	206		●		20 km		●									
Mas des Herbes Blanches (Le)	213		●	●	23 km	●	●									
Oustau de Baumanière	211		●	●	3 km											
Petit Nice-Passédat (Le)	216	●			10 km		●	●	●		●	●	●	●		
Phébus (Hostellerie Le)	214		●	●	20 km						●					
Prieuré (Le)	208		●	●	12 km											●
Vieux Castillon (Le)	204		●		15 km								●			
Villa Gallici	218		●		5 km	●	●									●
French Riviera - Corsica (page 221)																
Bonne Etape (La)	222		●		18 km	●	●	●			●					●
Cagnard (Le)	232				8 km	●	●	●	●			●	●	●		
Cala Rossa (Grand Hôtel de)	237	●			40 km	●	●	●				●	●			
Château de la Chèvre d'Or	236		●		7 km	●	●	●				●	●	●		
Château de Trigance	223				20 km	●	●	●			●			●		
Château du Domaine St Martin	233		●	●	20 km	●	●	●				●	●			
Chibois (J.) - Bastide St-Antoine	230	●	●		2 km	●	●	●		●						●
Club de Cavalière (Le)	225	●	●	●	18 km	●	●			●		●	●			
Métropole (Le)	235	●	●		16 km	●							●			
Moulin de Mougins (Le)	229				2 km											
Oasis (Restaurant L')	228	●			1 km											
Réserve de Beaulieu (La)	234	●	●		12 km	●		●			●	●	●			
Résidence de la Pinède	226	●	●		5 km			●					●			
Saint-Paul (Le)	231				12 km											
Villa (La)	239	●	●		10 km	●	●	●			●	●	●			●
Villa Belrose (La)	227	●	●		15 km		●	●		●	●	●	●			●

Fitness and Beauty / Meeting Facilities

Fitness	Spa	Beauty Salon	Swimming-pool covered	Whirlpool	Sauna	Hammam	Solarium	Meeting	Conference	Reception	Cocktail party	Number of conference rooms	Audio-visual equipment	Secretarial Services	Number of rooms	Properties
																Provence (page 199)
								80	200	150	200	3			25	Abbaye de Sainte Croix
								40	60	100	120	2	●	●	23	Auberge de Noves
															15	Auberge La Regalido
								50	80	120	120	2	●	●	31	Cabro d'Or (La)
								20	30	50	80	2	●	●	10	Cardinale et sa Résidence (La)
●					●	●		40	60	80	100	5	●	●	29	Château de Montcaud
								25	50	120	180	2			27	Château de Rochegude
								20	50	70						Clos de la Violette
								20	30	75	100	2	●		32	Crillon-le-Brave (Hostellerie de)
								35		60	90	2	●	●	30	Domaine de Châteauneuf
				●	●			20		25	30	1	●	●	18	Frênes (Hostellerie Les)
								20		40		2			14	Jardin des Sens (Le)
								100	130	100	180	3	●		54	Jules César (Hôtel)
								28	40	25	30	1			19	Mas des Herbes Blanches (Le)
								25	25	80	100	1	●	●	30	Oustau de Baumanière
								20	25	50		1			16	Petit Nice-Passédat (Le)
								25	50	70	100	2	●	●	26	Phébus (Hostelllerie Le)
								25	40	90	120	2			36	Prieuré (Le)
					●			40	90	100		2	●		35	Vieux Castillon (Le)
							●								22	Villa Gallici
																French Riviera - Corsica (page 221)
								40	60	90	100	3	●		18	Bonne Etape (La)
								20	25	30	45	2	●	●	25	Cagnard (Le)
●	●	●	●	●	●	●	●	20				1	●	●	48	Cala Rossa (Grand Hôtel de)
●				●	●	●		25	45	50	100	2	●		34	Château de la Chèvre d'Or
															10	Château de Trigance
								45	65	150	80	2	●		40	Château du Domaine St Martin
								80	200	200	350	3	●	●	11	Chibois (J.) - Bastide St-Antoine
								25	25	100	100	2	●	●	42	Club de Cavalière (Le)
							●	8		25	40	1			40	Métropole (Le)
															7	Moulin de Mougins (Le)
								16	25	100	20	3	●			Oasis (Restaurant L')
●	●	●		●		●	●	40	40	40	50	2	●		37	Réserve de Beaulieu (La)
															40	Résidence de la Pinède
															19	Saint-Paul (Le)
		●						40			40		●		53	Villa (La)
●		●						15	20	60	100	1	●	●	38	Villa Belrose (La)

More info on **www.relaischateaux.com**

Sports and Leisure

Properties	Page	Seaside	Swimming-pool on site	Tennis on site	9/18 holes golf course	Mountain-biking	Hiking	Horseback riding-Polo	Diving	Hunting	Fishing	Sailing	Water-Skiing	Canoeing Kayaking-Rafting	Skiing	Flying club
Benelux Countries																
Belgium (page 241)																
Auberge du Moulin Hideux	250		●	●	40 km	●	●	●			●			●		●
Barbizon (Restaurant)	245				9 km											
Clos St. Denis	246															
De Snippe (Hôtel)	242				10 km											
Hof Van Cleve	244				5 km											
Lafarque (Hostellerie)	249				15 km											
Moulin des Ramiers (Le)	248				16 km		●									
Saint-Roch (Hostellerie)	247				18 km	●	●	●						●		
Shamrock (Hostellerie)	243				15 km											
Luxembourg (page 241)																
Bergerie (La)	251				10 km											
Gaichel (La)	253			●	on site		●									
Table des Guilloux (La)	252															
Netherlands (page 241)																
Kasteel Wittem	254				7 km	●	●							●		
Manoir «Inter Scaldes»	255				11 km			●			●	●		●		
Switzerland - Liechtenstein																
Switzerland (page 257)																
Albergo Giardino	284		●		1 km	●	●					●	●			
Auberge du Raisin	273				8 km		●									
Bruderholz (Restaurant)	258				8 km											
Castello del Sole	283		●	●	3 km	●	●	●				●	●			
Cerf (Restaurant du)	271															
Chalet d'Adrien	279				1 km		●								●	
Cigogne (Hôtel de la)	268				8 km											
Débarcadère (Hostellerie du)	269				20 km	●	●	●			●	●	●			●
Domaine de Châteauvieux	267				15 km	●	●	●	●		●	●	●	●		●
Ermitage Am See	261				10 km	●			●		●	●	●			
Grandhotel Schönegg	282					●	●								●	
Gygax (Nick) - Gasthof Löwen	264				18 km											
Haus Paradies (Hotel)	292				15 km	●	●		●			●				
Hostellerie Alpenrose	276				3,5 km	●	●							●	●	
Kunststuben (Restaurant)	262				3 km											
Park Hotel Weggis	263				8 km	●	●		●		●	●	●		●	
Pas de l'Ours (Hostellerie du)	277		●		1 km	●	●	●			●				●	

Fitness and Beauty / Meeting Facilities

Fitness	Spa	Beauty Salon	Swimming-pool covered	Whirlpool	Sauna	Hammam	Solarium	Meeting	Conference	Reception	Cocktail party	Number of conference rooms	Audio-visual equipment	Secretarial Services	Number of rooms	Properties
																Benelux Countries
																Belgium (page 241)
			●					12		20	20	1			12	Auberge du Moulin Hideux
								20	40	55		2				Barbizon (Restaurant)
																Clos St. Denis
										80	40				8	De Snippe (Hôtel)
																Hof Van Cleve
				●				10		40		1			8	Lafarque (Hostellerie)
								16				1	●		6	Moulin des Ramiers (Le)
								15	25	110	200	3	●		15	Saint-Roch (Hostellerie)
								20		35	40	2			5	Shamrock (Hostellerie)
																Luxembourg (page 241)
												1				Bergerie (La)
					●		●								13	Gaichel (La)
								30								Table des Guilloux (La)
																Netherlands (page 241)
								20	40	50	150	1	●		12	Kasteel Wittem
								16	35	65	130	2	●		12	Manoir «Inter Scaldes»
																Switzerland - Liechtenstein
																Switzerland (page 257)
●	●	●	●	●	●	●	●	30	50	70	70	3	●		72	Albergo Giardino
								20	35	32	40	1			9	Auberge du Raisin
								35	80	120	150	2				Bruderholz (Restaurant)
●	●	●	●	●	●	●	●	16	40	100	100	2			79	Castello del Sole
																Cerf (Restaurant du)
	●	●		●	●	●		25	45	50	70	1	●		25	Chalet d'Adrien
								25	35	25	40	1	●	●	52	Cigogne (Hôtel de la)
								20	20	80	180	3			15	Débarcadère (Hostellerie du)
										65					17	Domaine de Châteauvieux
								20	30	45	100	3	●	●	26	Ermitage Am See
●				●	●	●	●					1	●		36	Grandhotel Schönegg
								25	50	80	100	3	●			Gygax (Nick) - Gasthof Löwen
			●	●	●		●	20	20	60	60	3		●	24	Haus Paradies (Hotel)
			●	●			●	20	40	70	100	2			18	Hostellerie Alpenrose
																Kunststuben (Restaurant)
●	●	●		●			●	120	200	170	200	3	●		43	Park Hotel Weggis
			●		●	●	●			100	100				9	Pas de l'Ours (Hostellerie du)

More info on www.relaischateaux.com

Sports and Leisure

Properties	Page	Seaside	Swimming-pool on site	Tennis on site	9/18 holes golf course	Mountain-biking	Hiking	Horseback riding - Polo	Diving	Hunting	Fishing	Sailing	Water-Skiing	Canoeing Kayaking - Rafting	Skiing	Flying club
Pont de Brent (Le)	274				15 km											
Ravet (Bernard) (L'Ermitage de)	272				25 km	●	●	●		●	●		●			
Rheinhotel Fischerzunft	259				20 km	●	●									
Rochat (Ph.) - Rest. de l'Hôtel de Ville	270				5 km											
Rosalp (Hôtel)	278				3 km	●		●								
Santabbondio	287				5 km											
Schlosshotel Chastè	293				6 km		●	●								
Sources des Alpes (Les)	281		●		22 km		●	●							●	
Splügenschloss (Hotel)	260				3 km											
Talvo (Jöhri's) (Restaurant)	289				10 km											
Victoria (Hôtel)	275		●	●	18 km	●	●	●		●	●	●	●			
Vieux Manoir au Lac (Le)	266				8 km	●	●				●	●	●			
Villa Margherita	285		●		10 km	●	●	●	●		●	●	●			●
Villa Principe Leopoldo & Resid.	288		●	●	5 km		●	●			●	●	●			
Walserhof (Hotel)	294				10 km	●				●	●				●	●
Walther (Hotel)	291		●	●	6 km	●	●	●		●	●	●			●	●
Wenger (Georges)	265				5 km	●	●			●	●				●	●

Liechtenstein (page 257)

Properties	Page	Seaside	Swimming-pool on site	Tennis on site	9/18 holes golf course	Mountain-biking	Hiking	Horseback riding - Polo	Diving	Hunting	Fishing	Sailing	Water-Skiing	Canoeing Kayaking - Rafting	Skiing	Flying club
Parkhotel Sonnenhof	295		●		20 km		●	●		●	●				●	●

Germany (page 297)

Properties	Page	Seaside	Swimming-pool on site	Tennis on site	9/18 holes golf course	Mountain-biking	Hiking	Horseback riding - Polo	Diving	Hunting	Fishing	Sailing	Water-Skiing	Canoeing Kayaking - Rafting	Skiing	Flying club
Abtei (Hotel)	300				17 km						●					
Alpenhof Murnau	330		●		20 km	●								●	●	
Bareiss (Restaurant)	323				12 km											
Brandenburger Hof (Hotel)	303				12 km			●			●	●				●
Bülow Residenz (Hotel)	305				12 km											
Burg Schlitz	301		●		15 km	●				●	●					
Burg Wernberg (Hotel)	317				10 km		●	●			●				●	
Burghotel Hardenberg	308				5 km	●	●				●	●				
Deidesheimer Hof (Hotel)	320				10 km	●	●	●			●					
Fürstenhof Celle	306		●		8 km		●			●	●			●		●
Gutshaus Stolpe	302			●	25 km	●	●			●	●	●		●		
Hohenhaus (Hotel)	314		●	●	10 km	●	●	●		●				●		
Jagdhof Glashütte (Hotel)	315		●		30 km	●	●								●	
Johann Lafer's Stromburg	316				1 km		●	●		●	●		●			
Kur-und Sporthotel Dollenberg	325		●	●	15 km	●	●				●				●	
Landhaus Ammann (Hotel)	307				5 km		●			●	●	●		●		
Landhaus «Zu den Rothen Forellen»	309		●		on site	●		●		●	●	●		●	●	●
Pflaums Posthotel Pegnitz	319		●		9 km	●	●	●		●	●			●	●	●

Fitness	Spa	Beauty Salon	Swimming-pool covered	Whirlpool	Sauna	Hammam	Solarium	Meeting	Conference	Reception	Cocktail party	Number of conference rooms	Audio-visual equipment	Secretarial Services	Number of rooms	Properties
																Pont de Brent (Le)
								35	35	70		3			9	Ravet (Bernard) (L'Ermitage de)
												2			10	Rheinhotel Fischerzunft
																Rochat (Ph.) - Rest. de l'Hôtel de Ville
			●	●	●			20	30			1	●		21	Rosalp (Hôtel)
										50	100					Santabbondio
			●	●	●	●									21	Schlosshotel Chastè
●	●	●	●	●	●	●	●								30	Sources des Alpes (Les)
								18	30	60	100	1	●	●	50	Splügenschloss (Hotel)
										70	80					Talvo (Jöhri's) (Restaurant)
			●	●			●	100	130	120	150	3	●		59	Victoria (Hôtel)
								30	100	80	200	3	●	●	33	Vieux Manoir au Lac (Le)
	●	●	●		●	●	●	24	34	80	100	3			33	Villa Margherita
●				●			●	140	240	160	250	7	●	●	75	Villa Principe Leopoldo & Resid.
						●									15	Walserhof (Hotel)
●	●	●	●	●	●		●	15	20	200	300	5			73	Walther (Hotel)
															5	Wenger (Georges)
																Liechtenstein (page 257)
			●		●		●	16		50	150		●		29	Parkhotel Sonnenhof
																Germany (page 297)
										18	18				11	Abtei (Hotel)
●	●	●	●	●	●		●	140	200	180	300	6	●		77	Alpenhof Murnau
																Bareiss (Restaurant)
	●	●					●	26	40	120	350	5	●	●	82	Brandenburger Hof (Hotel)
								18	30	60	75	1	●		30	Bülow Residenz (Hotel)
●	●	●		●	●	●	●	40	70	60	200	9	●	●	20	Burg Schlitz
								150	300	120	160	9	●	●	30	Burg Wernberg (Hotel)
●				●	●		●	70	150	220	220	8	●	●	44	Burghotel Hardenberg
				●				100	150		500	6	●	●	28	Deidesheimer Hof (Hotel)
			●		●		●	50	80	100	250	7	●	●	76	Fürstenhof Celle
●				●	●	●	●	40	100	200	250	3			33	Gutshaus Stolpe
			●		●		●	40	60	70		2			26	Hohenhaus (Hotel)
			●		●		●	30	80	80	120	5	●	●	29	Jagdhof Glashütte (Hotel)
								100	150	120	150	4	●	●	14	Johann Lafer's Stromburg
●	●	●	●	●				50		200	200	2			71	Kur-und Sporthotel Dollenberg
								60	160	180	250	5	●	●	14	Landhaus Ammann (Hotel)
		●	●	●	●		●	60	120	120	250	8	●	●	52	Landhaus «Zu den Rothen Forellen»
●	●	●	●	●	●		●	50	100			5	●	●	50	Pflaums Posthotel Pegnitz

Sports and Leisure

Properties	Page	Seaside	Swimming-pool on site	Tennis on site	9/18 holes golf course	Mountain-biking	Hiking	Horseback riding - Polo	Diving	Hunting	Fishing	Sailing	Water-Skiing	Canoeing Kayaking - Rafting	Skiing	Flying club
Residenz Heinz Winkler	331				8 km		●	●		●	●	●		●	●	
Schloss Hubertushöhe	304				10 km		●	●		●	●	●		●		
Schloss Hugenpœt (Hotel)	311			●	5 km	●	●	●								
Schloss Wilkinghege (Hotel)	310			●	on site											
Schlosshotel Lerbach	313		●	●	5 km		●	●			●					
Schwarzmatt (Hotel)	327		●		9 km	●	●	●		●	●					
Schwarzwald - Hotel Adler	326		●	●	25 km	●	●	●				●			●	
Schwarzwaldstube (Restaurant)	324				10 km											
Seehotel Siber	328				18 km	●	●				●	●	●			●
Stadt Hamburg (Hotel)	299		●		5 km	●	●	●	●		●	●	●			●
Villa Hammerschmiede (Hotel)	322		●		8 km		●	●								
Villino	329				4 km	●	●	●		●	●	●	●			●
Wald & Schlosshotel Friedrichsruhe	321		●	●	on site	●	●	●		●	●			●		
Zur Traube (Hotel Restaurant)	312				2 km											
Czech Republic (page 332)																
Hoffmeister (Hotel)	333				20 km											
Austria (page 335)																
Arlberg Hospiz	337		●		15 km	●	●			●	●			●	●	●
Der Bär (Hotel)	343		●	●	1 km	●	●									
Deuring Schlössle	336				15 km	●	●			●	●	●	●	●	●	●
Gasthof Post	338		●		20 km	●	●			●	●				●	
Grüner Baum (Hotel)	348		●	●	3 km	●	●			●	●				●	
Hubertus (Hotel)	344		●	●	15 km	●	●			●	●			●	●	
Landgut Luxnachmühle (Hotel)	339				40 km	●	●			●	●				●	
Schloss Dürnstein (Hotel)	345		●		15 km	●	●							●		
Schloss Seefels (Hotel)	349		●	●	5 km	●	●	●	●		●	●	●		●	
Schlosshotel Igls	342		●		2 km	●	●	●							●	
Sporthotel Singer	340				32 km		●	●					●		●	
Steirereck (Restaurant)	346				3 km											
Taubenkobel	347		●		5 km	●	●	●		●	●	●	●			●
Top Hotel Hochgurgl	341		●		80 km										●	
Slovenia (page 350)																
Kendov Dvorec	355			●	80 km	●	●			●	●				●	
Vila Bled (Hotel)	353			●	5 km	●	●	●		●	●	●		●	●	●
Scandinavia																
Denmark (page 355)																
Falsled Kro	357	●			7 km	●					●					

Fitness	Spa	Beauty Salon	Swimming-pool covered	Whirlpool	Sauna	Hammam	Solarium	Meeting	Conference	Reception	Cocktail party	Number of conference rooms	Audio-visual equipment	Secretarial Services	Number of rooms	Properties
●	●	●		●	●	●	●	24	40	80	120	4	●	●	32	Residenz Heinz Winkler
								20	30	60	100	2	●	●	22	Schloss Hubertushöhe
								60	120	120	350	5	●	●	25	Schloss Hugenpœt (Hotel)
								50	90	130	200	4	●		35	Schloss Wilkinghege (Hotel)
	●	●	●		●		●	60	110	100	150	3	●	●	54	Schlosshotel Lerbach
		●	●				●	25	60	40	100	1			38	Schwarzmatt (Hotel)
●	●	●	●	●	●	●	●			60					45	Schwarzwald - Hotel Adler
								36	50	40	40	5	●	●		Schwarzwaldstube (Restaurant)
								25		50			●		12	Seehotel Siber
●	●	●	●		●		●	50	100	100	100	5	●	●	72	Stadt Hamburg (Hotel)
		●	●	●	●			30	60	70	100	5	●		30	Villa Hammerschmiede (Hotel)
	●	●			●	●	●								16	Villino
●	●	●	●	●	●		●	60	120	72	100	3	●		43	Wald & Schlosshotel Friedrichsruhe
															6	Zur Traube (Hotel Restaurant)
Czech Republic (page 332)																
								25	40	100	180	2	●	●	25	Hoffmeister (Hotel)
Austria (page 335)																
	●		●	●	●	●	●	60	200	300	400	5	●		95	Arlberg Hospiz
●	●	●	●	●	●		●	70	120	120	150	3	●		57	Der Bär (Hotel)
								60	120	80	150	4	●	●	15	Deuring Schlössle
●	●	●	●		●	●	●	40	150	150	150	6	●		39	Gasthof Post
●	●	●	●	●	●		●	30	50	200	200	5	●		58	Grüner Baum (Hotel)
				●	●	●	●			30	30	2	●		14	Hubertus (Hotel)
				●	●	●	●								9	Landgut Luxnachmühle (Hotel)
		●		●	●		●	30	40	100	150	3	●		40	Schloss Dürnstein (Hotel)
●	●	●	●	●	●		●	30	80	140	350	4	●		57	Schloss Seefels (Hotel)
			●	●	●		●	30	40	50	90	2		●	20	Schlosshotel Igls
●				●	●		●	30		180	100	2			54	Sporthotel Singer
																Steirereck (Restaurant)
				●	●	●									7	Taubenkobel
●	●	●	●	●	●		●	10		300	150				64	Top Hotel Hochgurgl
Slovenia (page 350)																
								30	60	80	100	3	●	●	11	Kendov Dvorec
								60	80	80	120	2	●		30	Vila Bled (Hotel)
Scandinavia																
Denmark (page 355)																
								25	40	100	100	2	●	●	19	Falsled Kro

More info on www.relaischateaux.com

Sports and Leisure

Properties	Page	Seaside	Swimming-pool on site	Tennis on site	9/18 holes golf course	Mountain-biking	Hiking	Horseback riding - Polo	Diving	Hunting	Fishing	Sailing	Water-Skiing	Canoeing Kayaking - Rafting	Skiing	Flying club
Sønderho Kro	356	●			12 km		●	●			●					
Sweden (page 355)																
Kattegat Gastronomi	358	●			1 km											
Krägga Herrgård	359	●		●	15 km	●	●	●		●	●	●	●	●		
Leijontornet & Victory Hotel	361	●			20 km						●	●				
Thoresta Herrgård	360	●			on site	●	●	●		●	●		●	●		
Norway (page 355)																
Bagatelle (Restaurant)	362															
Engø Gård	363	●	●		3 km		●	●	●	●	●	●	●			
Iceland (page 355)																
Holt (Hotel)	364				10 km		●			●	●					●
Lithuania (page 355)																
Stikliai Hotel	365	●														
United Kingdom (page 367)																
Bodysgallen Hall	385		●	●	5 km	●	●	●		●	●	●			●	
Buckland Manor Hotel	381		●	●	3 km		●	●		●						
Chewton Glen Hotel	375	●	●	●	on site	●	●	●				●	●			●
Farlam Hall Hotel	388				5 km		●									●
Gavroche (Le)	368															
Gidleigh Park	378			●	15 km		●	●			●					
Glenapp Castle	389	●		●	30 km	●				●	●					
Gravetye Manor	374				8 km						●					
Hambleton Hall	383		●	●	15 km					●	●	●	●			
Hartwell House	372		●	●	2 km	●		●		●	●					●
Inverlochy Castle	390			●	2 km	●	●	●		●	●	●			●	●
Kinnaird	391			●	6 km	●	●			●	●					
Longueville Manor	379		●	●	3 km				●	●	●	●	●			●
Lucknam Park	380		●	●	6 km	●	●	●		●				●		
Mallory Court	382		●	●	3 km	●	●	●		●	●					
Manoir aux Quat' Saisons (Le)	371				10 km	●										
Middlethorpe Hall	386			●	8 km											
Sharrow Bay Country House	387				12 km	●				●						
Stock Hill Country House	376			●	30 km			●		●						
Summer Lodge	377		●	●	5 km		●	●		●	●					
Tante Claire (La)	369															
Vineyard at Stockcross (The)	373		●		30 km	●		●			●					
Waterside Inn (The)	370				3 km											

Fitness	Spa	Beauty Salon	Swimming-pool covered	Whirlpool	Sauna	Hammam	Solarium	Meeting	Conference	Reception	Cocktail party	Number of conference rooms	Audio-visual equipment	Secretarial Services	Number of rooms	Properties
								20		60		2	●		13	Sønderho Kro
																Sweden (page 355)
								14	25	100	100	3	●	●	11	Kattegat Gastronomi
			●				●	80	80	300	300	6	●	●	43	Krägga Herrgård
			●					49	89	90	90	14	●	●	45	Leijontornet & Victory Hotel
			●				●	60	60	60	80	4	●	●	36	Thoresta Herrgård
																Norway (page 355)
																Bagatelle (Restaurant)
				●	●			28		64	64	2	●		12	Engø Gård
																Iceland (page 355)
								40	70	60	120	1			42	Holt (Hotel)
																Lithuania (page 355)
●			●		●			20	30	150	150	3			29	Stikliai Hotel
																United Kingdom (page 367)
●		●		●				24	50	40	60	3	●	●	35	Bodysgallen Hall
															13	Buckland Manor Hotel
●	●	●	●	●				40	130	100	200	6	●		59	Chewton Glen Hotel
								12	30	40	100	1	●	●	12	Farlam Hall Hotel
																Gavroche (Le)
								22		22		1	●		15	Gidleigh Park
								20	20	34	34	2			17	Glenapp Castle
								12				1		●	18	Gravetye Manor
								20	40	40	50	3	●	●	16	Hambleton Hall
●	●	●	●		●	●	●	40	90	60	100	4	●	●	47	Hartwell House
				●	●	●	●								17	Inverlochy Castle
								20	30	36	40	2	●		9	Kinnaird
								25	45	65	100	3	●	●	31	Longueville Manor
●		●	●	●	●		●	24	50	80	80	4	●	●	41	Lucknam Park
								20	35	50	30	3	●		18	Mallory Court
								24	40	50	100	2	●		32	Manoir aux Quat' Saisons (Le)
●		●	●	●	●			25	56	45	45	2	●		30	Middlethorpe Hall
								15	24	40	100	2	●		26	Sharrow Bay Country House
								12							8	Stock Hill Country House
			●	●	●			20	30	50	100	3	●	●	17	Summer Lodge
								14		10						Tante Claire (La)
●			●	●	●	●	●	40	120	150	150		●		16	Vineyard at Stockcross (The)
								8		8	24				9	Waterside Inn (The)

More info on **www.relaischateaux.com**

Sports and Leisure

Properties	Page	Seaside	Swimming-pool on site	Tennis on site	9/18 holes golf course	Mountain-biking	Hiking	Horseback riding - Polo	Diving	Hunting	Fishing	Sailing	Water-Skiing	Canoeing Kayaking - Rafting	Skiing	Flying club
Ynyshir Hall	384				10 km	●	●	●			●	●				
Ireland (page 393)																
Ballylickey Manor House	395	●	●		2 km	●	●	●			●	●				
Cashel House Hotel	397			●	20 km		●									
Longueville House	396				6 km		●	●		●	●					
Marlfield House	399			●	2 km											
Newport House	398				10 km			●	●		●	●	●			●
Sheen Falls Lodge	394		●	●	2 km	●	●	●			●		●	●		
Italy (page 401)																
Albereta et Rest. G. Marchesi (L')	410		●	●	2 km			●					●			
Ambasciata (Ristorante)	419															
Antica Osteria del Ponte	408															
Bellevue (Hotel)	404		●		37 km	●	●				●					●
Borgo Paraelios	433		●	●	on site	●	●	●		●						
Bottaccio di Montignoso (Il)	422				3 km	●	●	●	●		●	●	●			●
Cala del Porto (Hotel)	431	●	●		on site			●	●	●	●	●	●			
Calandre (Ristorante Le)	416				6 km											
Certosa di Maggiano (Hotel)	426		●	●	7 km	●		●			●	●				●
Da Vittorio (Ristorante)	409															
Dominik (Hotel)	413		●				●	●			●			●	●	
Don Alfonso 1890	437															
Duchessa Isabella (Hotel)	420				1 km	●										●
Enoteca Pinchiorri (Restaurant)	421				10 km											
Gallia Palace Hotel	429	●	●	●	2 km	●		●			●	●	●			
Hermitage (Hotel)	403		●		1 km	●	●				●				●	
La Collegiata (Hotel)	425		●		20 km											
Locanda l'Elisa	424		●		20 km						●					
Melograno (Il)	439		●	●	30 km		●				●	●				
Meridiana (La)	418		●		on site	●	●	●	●		●	●	●			●
Parkhotel Villa Grazioli	434				10 km			●			●	●				
Pellicano (Il)	432	●	●	●	50 km	●	●	●	●		●	●	●			
Pescatore (Restaurant dal)	417				40 km											
Posta Vecchia (La)	435	●	●		20 km											
Relais Borgo San Felice (Hotel)	427		●	●	55 km											
Relais il Falconiere	428		●		25 km		●	●								
Rosa Alpina	414		●		10 km	●					●	●			●	
San Pietro (Hotel)	438	●	●	●	on site				●			●				
Sole di Ranco (Il)	407				10 km	●		●	●		●	●	●	●		

Fitness and Beauty | Meeting Facilities

Fitness	Spa	Beauty Salon	Swimming-pool covered	Whirlpool	Sauna	Hammam	Solarium	Meeting	Conference	Reception	Cocktail party	Number of conference rooms	Audio-visual equipment	Secretarial Services	Number of rooms	Properties
								15	20	20	25	1			9	Ynyshir Hall
																Ireland (page 393)
								15		15	15		●		10	Ballylickey Manor House
															32	Cashel House Hotel
								26	50	110	110	8		●	20	Longueville House
					●			20	40	60	60	2	●	●	19	Marlfield House
															18	Newport House
●		●	●	●	●		●	45	100	120	140		●		61	Sheen Falls Lodge
																Italy (page 401)
			●	●				40	190	180		4	●	●	55	Albereta et Rest. G. Marchesi (L')
																Ambasciata (Ristorante)
																Antica Osteria del Ponte
	●		●	●	●	●		22	18	80	100	2	●		35	Bellevue (Hotel)
●	●	●	●		●	●		20	50	80	120	3	●	●	15	Borgo Paraelios
								30	30	160	50	1	●	●	8	Bottaccio di Montignoso (Il)
		●						40	60	110	200	2	●	●	40	Cala del Porto (Hotel)
								20	20	30	30	2				Calandre (Ristorante Le)
●									20	30	40	1	●		17	Certosa di Maggiano (Hotel)
								40		40	40	1				Da Vittorio (Ristorante)
			●		●		●	30	130	80	200	3	●	●	35	Dominik (Hotel)
																Don Alfonso 1890
															27	Duchessa Isabella (Hotel)
																Enoteca Pinchiorri (Restaurant)
		●			●			50	90	180	250	2	●		83	Gallia Palace Hotel
●	●	●	●		●	●		15	30	30	30	1	●	●	40	Hermitage (Hotel)
								30	30	60	80	2	●		21	La Collegiata (Hotel)
															10	Locanda l'Elisa
								40	300	400	400	6	●	●	37	Melograno (Il)
					●			30	50	120	150	2	●	●	30	Meridiana (La)
								45	100	170	250	5	●		58	Parkhotel Villa Grazioli
●	●	●		●		●		30	60	60	80	1	●	●	50	Pellicano (Il)
																Pescatore (Restaurant dal)
			●	●											19	Posta Vecchia (La)
●	●						●	40	100	120	100	4	●	●	43	Relais Borgo San Felice (Hotel)
															19	Relais il Falconiere
●	●	●	●	●	●	●				100	150				51	Rosa Alpina
●		●			●										60	San Pietro (Hotel)
								15					●	●	14	Sole di Ranco (Il)

More info on www.relaischateaux.com

Properties	Page	Seaside	Swimming-pool on site	Tennis on site	9/18 holes golf course	Mountain-biking	Hiking	Horseback riding - Polo	Diving	Hunting	Fishing	Sailing	Water-Skiing	Canoeing Kayaking - Rafting	Skiing	Flying club
Sorriso (Al)	405				15 km					●	●	●		●		
Villa Abbazia	415				24 km	●	●	●			●	●				
Villa Del Quar (Hotel)	412		●		18 km	●		●					●			●
Villa Fiordaliso	411				3 km						●	●				
Villa la Massa	423		●		11 km	●		●			●		●			
Malta (page 440)																
Xara Palace (The)	441				8 km		●	●			●	●				●
Portugal - Spain																
Portugal (page 443)																
Casa Velha do Palheiro	444		●	●	on site	●	●	●			●		●			
Estalagem Casa Melo Alvim	445				22 km						●	●	●			
Fortaleza do Guincho	448	●			5 km		●	●	●		●					●
Quinta Das Lagrimas (Hotel)	447		●		on site	●					●					
Spain (page 443)																
Akelaŕe (Restaurant)	454	●			6 km											
Arzak (Restaurante)	456				20 km											
Berasategui (M.) - Restaurante	455															
Cala Sant Vicenç (Hotel)	475	●	●		8 km	●	●	●	●		●	●	●			
Can Fabes	463															
Casa de Carmona	449		●		35 km		●									
El Castell de Ciutat	458		●		5 km	●	●				●			●		●
El Cenador de Salvador	451				20 km	●	●								●	
«El Montiboli» (Hotel)	469	●	●	●	15 km	●	●		●	●	●	●	●			
Girasol	466				2,5 km											
Gran Hotel Son Net	474		●	●	15 km	●	●					●				
Hacienda Na Xamena (Hotel)	471	●	●	●	18 km	●					●	●				●
Mas de Torrent	460			●	6 km	●						●				●
Neichel (Restaurant)	464															
Orfila (Hotel)	450				5 km		●									
Peregrino (Hotel el)	457		●		10 km					●						●
Posada de la Casa del Abad	452		●	●	30 km	●	●	●		●						
Read's	473		●		10 km		●	●				●				
Rodat (El)	467		●	●	30 km		●	●			●					
San Román de Escalante (Hotel)	453				18 km	●	●	●	●		●	●				
Sant Pau (Restaurant)	462	●			19 km											
Santa Marta (Hotel)	461	●	●	●	40 km	●	●				●		●			
Torre del Remei	459		●		1 km	●	●	●			●	●			●	●

Fitness	Spa	Beauty Salon	Swimming-pool covered	Whirlpool	Sauna	Hammam	Solarium	Meeting	Conference	Reception	Cocktail party	Number of conference rooms	Audio-visual equipment	Secretarial Services	Number of rooms	Properties
								20	20	20	20	1			8	Sorriso (Al)
								20	30	70	30	2	●		18	Villa Abbazia
●					●			25	80	70	70	1	●		22	Villa Del Quar (Hotel)
								16	200	300	700	1	●		7	Villa Fiordaliso
								35	60	80	90	4	●		37	Villa la Massa

Malta (page 440)

Fitness	Spa	Beauty Salon	Swimming-pool covered	Whirlpool	Sauna	Hammam	Solarium	Meeting	Conference	Reception	Cocktail party	Number of conference rooms	Audio-visual equipment	Secretarial Services	Number of rooms	Properties
●					●				36	40	60	1	●		17	Xara Palace (The)

Portugal - Spain

Portugal (page 443)

Fitness	Spa	Beauty Salon	Swimming-pool covered	Whirlpool	Sauna	Hammam	Solarium	Meeting	Conference	Reception	Cocktail party	Number of conference rooms	Audio-visual equipment	Secretarial Services	Number of rooms	Properties
					●	●		14	24	80	150	3			37	Casa Velha do Palheiro
								20	50	80	100	2	●	●	20	Estalagem Casa Melo Alvim
								40	200	120	300	1	●		29	Fortaleza do Guincho
								22	200	200	250	4	●	●	39	Quinta Das Lagrimas (Hotel)

Spain (page 443)

Fitness	Spa	Beauty Salon	Swimming-pool covered	Whirlpool	Sauna	Hammam	Solarium	Meeting	Conference	Reception	Cocktail party	Number of conference rooms	Audio-visual equipment	Secretarial Services	Number of rooms	Properties
																Akelaŕe (Restaurant)
																Arzak (Restaurante)
																Berasategui (M.) - Restaurante
●		●		●	●					60	100				38	Cala Sant Vicenç (Hotel)
																Can Fabes
●					●			36	100	100	120	5	●	●	32	Casa de Carmona
●	●	●	●	●	●	●		60	300	300	300	3	●		38	El Castell de Ciutat
				●				250	300	250	350				7	El Cenador de Salvador
●	●		●	●	●	●		60	80	200	200	6	●		50	«El Montiboli» (Hotel)
								30		65	70	4				Girasol
		●		●	●			45	45	120	120		●		24	Gran Hotel Son Net
●	●	●	●	●	●	●	●	100		150	200	7	●		61	Hacienda Na Xamena (Hotel)
								30	50	80	100	1			39	Mas de Torrent
																Neichel (Restaurant)
								60	80	100	140	1	●	●	32	Orfila (Hotel)
								50	50	100	200	1	●		15	Peregrino (Hotel el)
●			●	●	●			30	40	50	80	3			17	Posada de la Casa del Abad
●			●	●	●		●	24	30	90	90	5	●	●	25	Read's
●	●	●	●	●	●		●	100	130	120	150	3	●		42	Rodat (El)
								30	50	150	200				16	San Román de Escalante (Hotel)
										45	45					Sant Pau (Restaurant)
								80	140	200	200	5	●		60	Santa Marta (Hotel)
●					●		●	22	44	250	250	3	●	●	22	Torre del Remei

More info on www.relaischateaux.com

Sports and Leisure

Properties	Page	Seaside	Swimming-pool on site	Tennis on site	9/18 holes golf course	Mountain-biking	Hiking	Horseback riding-Polo	Diving	Hunting	Fishing	Sailing	Water-Skiing	Canoeing Kayaking-Rafting	Skiing	Flying club
Torre del Visco (La)	465					●	●	●		●	●					
Greece (Crete) (page 476)																
Elounda Mare Hotel	477	●	●		●	500 m			●			●	●			
Turkey - Lebanon - Israel - Dubai																
Turkey (page 479)																
Ada Hotel	481		●			●	●	●	●		●	●	●			
Lebanon (page 479)																
Albergo (Hotel)	482		●		5 km		●	●	●				●		●	
Israel (page 479)																
American Colony (The)	484		●		120 km			●								
Mizpe-Hayamim	483		●	●			●	●								
Dubai (page 479)																
Hatta Fort Hotel	485		●	●	on site	●	●									
Morocco (page 486)																
Villa des Orangers (La)	487		●		6 km	●	●	●								
Southern Africa - Mauritius - Seychelles																
South Africa (page 489)																
Bushmans Kloof Wilderness Reserve	500		●		45 km	●	●				●			●		
Cellars - Hohenort (The)	510		●	●	5 km	●	●									
Clearwater Lodges	504		●		85 km		●									
Cybele Forest Lodge and Spa	498		●		15 km			●			●					
Ellerman House	509		●		20 km		●	●	●		●	●	●	●		●
Grande Roche	503		●	●	5 km		●	●								
Hunter's - Tsala	501		●		10 km		●	●	●		●	●	●	●		●
Kwandwe Private Game Reserve	505		●		90 km		●						●			
Londolozi Private Game Reserve	497		●		65 km		●									
Marine Hermanus (The)	508	●	●		1 km	●	●		●		●	●	●			
Plettenberg (The)	502	●	●		2 km	●	●	●	●		●	●	●	●		
Quartier Français (Le)	507		●		26 km	●	●				●					
Singita Private Game Reserve	496		●		40 km						●					
Tswalu Kalahari Reserve	499		●		70 km		●	●								
Namibia (page 489)																
Heinitzburg (Hotel)	511		●		4 km	●	●	●								
Tanzania (page 489)																
Sultan Palace	490	●							●		●					

Fitness	Spa	Beauty Salon	Swimming-pool covered	Whirlpool	Sauna	Hammam	Solarium	Meeting	Conference	Reception	Cocktail party	Number of conference rooms	Audio-visual equipment	Secretarial Services	Number of rooms	Properties
								20	30	36	36	2	•	•	14	Torre del Visco (La)
																Greece (Crete) (page 476)
								60	90	100	150	3	•		79	Elounda Mare Hotel
																Turkey - Lebanon - Israel - Dubai
																Turkey (page 479)
•				•	•	•		26		100	140	3	•		14	Ada Hotel
																Lebanon (page 479)
															33	Albergo (Hotel)
																Israel (page 479)
•					•			12	100	150	200	2		•	84	American Colony (The)
•	•	•	•	•	•			50	80			2	•		83	Mizpe-Hayamim
																Dubai (page 479)
•		•						60	200	150	200	4	•	•	53	Hatta Fort Hotel
																Morocco (page 486)
															16	Villa des Orangers (La)
																Southern Africa - Mauritius - Seychelles
																South Africa (page 489)
	•	•		•				20	20	32	32	1	•	•	16	Bushmans Kloof Wilderness Reserve
	•	•		•				20	30	38	50	2	•	•	53	Cellars - Hohenort (The)
								12		12	20	1			10	Clearwater Lodges
		•	•												12	Cybele Forest Lodge and Spa
•				•											11	Ellerman House
•				•	•	•		80	150	4	160	4			35	Grande Roche
								24	30	70	100	6			33	Hunter's - Tsala
															12	Kwandwe Private Game Reserve
															36	Londolozi Private Game Reserve
		•						26	48	40	60	2	•		45	Marine Hermanus (The)
		•						20	30	80	100	2	•	•	37	Plettenberg (The)
								8				1			17	Quartier Français (Le)
•															18	Singita Private Game Reserve
								12		22	22				9	Tswalu Kalahari Reserve
																Namibia (page 489)
									30	40	150	3			16	Heinitzburg (Hotel)
																Tanzania (page 489)
															15	Sultan Palace

More info on www.relaischateaux.com

Sports and Leisure

Properties	Page	Seaside	Swimming-pool on site	Tennis on site	9/18 holes golf course	Mountain-biking	Hiking	Horseback riding - Polo	Diving	Hunting	Fishing	Sailing	Water-Skiing	Canoeing Kayaking - Rafting	Skiing	Flying club
Zimbabwe (page 489)																
Imba Matombo Lodge	494		●	●	6 km											
Pamushana	495		●	●	70 km	●	●				●			●		
Mauritius (page 489)																
Prince Maurice (Le)	493	●	●	●	3 km	●	●		●		●	●	●	●		
Seychelles (page 489)																
Château de Feuilles	491	●	●		20 km				●		●	●				
Lemuria Resort	492	●	●		on site				●		●	●				
Australia - New Zealand																
Australia (page 512)																
Chateau Yering	513		●	●	20 km		●				●	●				
New Zealand (page 512)																
Kauri Cliffs	515	●	●	●	on site		●	●	●	●	●	●		●		
Indonesia (page 516)																
Matahari Beach Resort & Spa	519	●	●	●	60 km	●	●	●	●			●				
Tugu Bali (Hotel)	517	●	●	●	10 km	●	●		●		●	●	●			
Japan - South Korea																
Japan (page 521)																
Anaga (Hotel)	522	●	●	●	25 km											
Asaba	529				3 km		●		●							
Bécasse (La)	524				30 km											
Enoteca Pinchiorri	531															
Gôra Kadan	530		●		5 km		●									
Hiramatsu (Restaurant)	527															
Horai	525	●			5 km						●					
Mikuni	532															
Seiryuso	528		●		8 km		●				●					
Tosen Goshobo	523		●	●	5 km	●					●	●			●	
South Korea (page 521)																
Paradise Hotel Jeju	533	●	●		25 km		●	●	●		●					
North America																
Canada (page 537)																
Aerie (The)	550		●	●	15 km	●	●				●	●	●			
Auberge Hatley	541		●		3 km		●	●				●			●	
Eau à la Bouche (Hôtel L')	543		●		1 km						●	●				
Hastings House	549	●			4 km						●					
Inn at Manitou (The)	544		●	●	on site	●	●		●		●	●	●	●	●	

Fitness	Spa	Beauty Salon	Swimming-pool covered	Whirlpool	Sauna	Hammam	Solarium	Meeting	Conference	Reception	Cocktail party	Number of conference rooms	Audio-visual equipment	Secretarial Services	Number of rooms	Properties
																Zimbabwe (page 489)
								30	50	48	60	3	●		10	Imba Matombo Lodge
					●			20	50	20	50	1	●		6	Pamushana
																Mauritius (page 489)
●		●			●	●		16	16	50	50		●		89	Prince Maurice (Le)
																Seychelles (page 489)
				●											9	Château de Feuilles
●		●			●	●		16	16	50	50	1	●		88	Lemuria Resort
																Australia - New Zealand
																Australia (page 512)
		●						30	120	120	250	5	●	●	20	Chateau Yering
																New Zealand (page 512)
●				●				20		100	100	1			16	Kauri Cliffs
																Indonesia (page 516)
●	●			●		●		30	100	40	100	1	●		32	Matahari Beach Resort & Spa
●	●			●			●	30	50	200	300	2	●	●	21	Tugu Bali (Hotel)
																Japan - South Korea
																Japan (page 521)
								40	80	80	120	1			61	Anaga (Hotel)
								50	80	70		3			19	Asaba
										32						Bécasse (La)
								40		100	100	1				Enoteca Pinchiorri
●		●	●	●	●	●		25	60	80	100	1			38	Gôra Kadan
								16		60		2	●			Hiramatsu (Restaurant)
								30	60	60		2		●	16	Horai
										80	150	1				Mikuni
					●			40	50			5	●		30	Seiryuso
										20					20	Tosen Goshobo
																South Korea (page 521)
●				●	●			80	120	100	400	3	●	●	56	Paradise Hotel Jeju
																North America
																Canada (page 537)
		●	●	●	●			35	50	80	150	3	●		29	Aerie (The)
								24	30	50	50	3	●		24	Auberge Hatley
								25	40	80	60	4	●	●	25	Eau à la Bouche (Hôtel L')
								40	30	40	50	4	●		18	Hastings House
●	●	●		●	●			30	60	100	120	4	●	●	33	Inn at Manitou (The)

Sports and Leisure

Properties	Page	Seaside	Swimming-pool on site	Tennis on site	9/18 holes golf course	Mountain-biking	Hiking	Horseback riding - Polo	Diving	Hunting	Fishing	Sailing	Water-Skiing	Canoeing Kayaking - Rafting	Skiing	Flying club
Kingsbrae Arms	538	●	●		1 km		●	●		●	●	●		●		
Langdon Hall	545		●	●	2 km	●	●	●						●	●	
Little Beaver Creek Ranch	547		●		22 km	●	●	●		●	●					
Lumière	548				2 km											
Pinsonnière (La)	539	●	●	●	2 km		●	●		●	●			●	●	
Post Hotel	546		●		55 km	●	●	●			●			●	●	
Trois Tilleuls & Spa (Les)	540		●	●	15 km		●									●
Wickaninnish Inn (The)	551	●			10 km	●	●		●	●	●			●		
United States (page 553)																
Auberge du Soleil	597		●	●	15 km		●									
Aureole	557															
Bernardin (Le)	560															
Blackberry Farm	579		●	●	20 km	●	●	●			●			●		
Blantyre	565		●	●	0,5 km						●	●				
Canoe Bay	588				19 km	●	●				●				●	
Charlie Trotter's	584															
Charlotte Inn (The)	573				6,5 km											
Château du Sureau	600		●		5 km	●	●	●			●	●	●			
Daniel	559															
Everest	585															
Fearrington House (The)	578		●	●	10 km	●					●	●	●			
French Laundry (The)	595															
Gary Danko	598															
Gastonian Inn	582				3 km		●	●			●	●		●		
Glendorn	575		●	●	18 km	●	●	●		●	●			●		
Goldener Hirsch Inn	591				10 km	●	●				●	●			●	
Home Hill	571		●	●	20 km	●					●			●	●	
Home Ranch (The)	592				25 km	●	●	●			●				●	
Homestead Inn	563				2 km			●								
Inn at Little Washington (The)	577				30 km	●	●	●			●					
Inn at Sawmill Farm (The)	572		●	●	1 km						●			●		
Jean Georges	561															
Knob Hill Inn	590		●		1 km	●	●	●		●	●				●	
Lake Placid Lodge	567				on site	●	●			●	●			●	●	
Little Nell (The)	593		●		1 km						●				●	
Mayflower Inn (The)	564		●	●	2 km	●		●			●			●	●	
Meadowood Napa Valley	596		●	●	on site		●									
Morrison House	576				10 km		●					●				

Fitness	Spa	Beauty Salon	Swimming-pool covered	Whirlpool	Sauna	Hammam	Solarium	Meeting	Conference	Reception	Cocktail party	Number of conference rooms	Audio-visual equipment	Secretarial Services	Number of rooms	Properties
				●				12	24	24	40	3	●	●	8	Kingsbrae Arms
●	●	●		●	●	●		60	120	84	150	7	●	●	53	Langdon Hall
●			●	●			●	16		30	40	7	●	●	7	Little Beaver Creek Ranch
																Lumière
	●	●	●		●			40	60	140	140	3	●	●	26	Pinsonnière (La)
			●	●				45	64	64	64	2	●		98	Post Hotel
●	●	●	●	●	●		●	60	100	120	200	7	●	●	41	Trois Tilleuls & Spa (Les)
	●			●		●	●	24	60	50	75	2	●		46	Wickaninnish Inn (The)

United States (page 553)

Fitness	Spa	Beauty Salon	Swimming-pool covered	Whirlpool	Sauna	Hammam	Solarium	Meeting	Conference	Reception	Cocktail party	Number of conference rooms	Audio-visual equipment	Secretarial Services	Number of rooms	Properties
●	●	●		●		●	●	30	50	100	150	3	●	●	50	Auberge du Soleil
																Aureole
								40	110	100	175	3	●			Bernardin (Le)
●	●	●		●			●	28	50	125	80	5	●	●	39	Blackberry Farm
				●	●			35	50	150	200		●	●	24	Blantyre
●								30	30	30	30	2			19	Canoe Bay
								20	30	20	30	1	●			Charlie Trotter's
															25	Charlotte Inn (The)
								12		120	120	1	●		11	Château du Sureau
								50	80	80	150	1	●	●		Daniel
								20		125	125	6				Everest
●								100	200	300	400	5	●	●	33	Fearrington House (The)
																French Laundry (The)
																Gary Danko
								8	20		35	1			17	Gastonian Inn
●								35	50	75	100	3	●		10	Glendorn
				●	●			20	25	100	125	3	●		20	Goldener Hirsch Inn
●								20	30	80	80	3			12	Home Hill
				●	●			25		25	25	1	●		14	Home Ranch (The)
								20	24	30		1	●		19	Homestead Inn
															14	Inn at Little Washington (The)
●								20		65	35	2			11	Inn at Sawmill Farm (The)
																Jean Georges
●			●	●	●										24	Knob Hill Inn
								50	75	60	75	2	●		34	Lake Placid Lodge
●				●		●		20	180	130	180	2	●		92	Little Nell (The)
●								40	60			1		●	25	Mayflower Inn (The)
●	●	●		●	●		●	50	140	110	200	5	●		85	Meadowood Napa Valley
								24	50	150	40	5	●		45	Morrison House

Sports and Leisure

Properties	Page	Seaside	Swimming-pool on site	Tennis on site	9/18 holes golf course	Mountain-biking	Hiking	Horseback riding - Polo	Diving	Hunting	Fishing	Sailing	Water-Skiing	Canoeing Kayaking - Rafting	Skiing	Flying club
Nomades (Les)	587				15 km											
Old Drovers Inn	566				12 km		●				●				●	
Orangerie (L')	603															
Patina Restaurant	604															
Pitcher Inn (The)	570				5 km	●	●	●		●	●			●	●	●
Planters Inn	581				5 km			●			●	●	●			
Point (The)	568			●	4 km	●	●	●			●	●	●			
Rancho de San Juan	594				11 km	●	●	●			●				●	
Rancho Valencia Resort	605			●	2 km			●								
Ryland Inn (The)	562				2 km											
San Ysidro Ranch	601		●		30 km	●	●	●				●				
Seeger's	583															
Sherman House (The)	599				10 km											
Triple Creek Ranch	589		●	●	45 km	●	●	●			●		●			
Tru	586															
Wauwinet (The)	574	●		●	6 km	●	●				●	●	●			
White Barn Inn	569		●		3 km	●	●	●			●	●				
Woodlands Resort & Inn	580		●	●	10 km					●	●					●

Mexico - Caribbean - Bermuda

Mexico (page 607)

Properties	Page	Seaside	Swimming-pool on site	Tennis on site	9/18 holes golf course	Mountain-biking	Hiking	Horseback riding - Polo	Diving	Hunting	Fishing	Sailing	Water-Skiing	Canoeing Kayaking - Rafting	Skiing	Flying club
Champs-Elysées (Restaurant)	609				25 km											

Puerto Rico (page 607)

Properties	Page	Seaside	Swimming-pool on site	Tennis on site	9/18 holes golf course	Mountain-biking	Hiking	Horseback riding - Polo	Diving	Hunting	Fishing	Sailing	Water-Skiing	Canoeing Kayaking - Rafting	Skiing	Flying club
Horned Dorset Primavera (The)	610	●	●		25 km				●							

Virgin Islands (page 607)

Properties	Page	Seaside	Swimming-pool on site	Tennis on site	9/18 holes golf course	Mountain-biking	Hiking	Horseback riding - Polo	Diving	Hunting	Fishing	Sailing	Water-Skiing	Canoeing Kayaking - Rafting	Skiing	Flying club
Biras Creek	611	●	●	●		●	●		●		●	●	●	●		

French West Indies (page 607)

Properties	Page	Seaside	Swimming-pool on site	Tennis on site	9/18 holes golf course	Mountain-biking	Hiking	Horseback riding - Polo	Diving	Hunting	Fishing	Sailing	Water-Skiing	Canoeing Kayaking - Rafting	Skiing	Flying club
Eden Rock	613	●	●				●	●			●	●	●			●
Toiny (Le)	614	●	●													

Barbados (page 607)

Properties	Page	Seaside	Swimming-pool on site	Tennis on site	9/18 holes golf course	Mountain-biking	Hiking	Horseback riding - Polo	Diving	Hunting	Fishing	Sailing	Water-Skiing	Canoeing Kayaking - Rafting	Skiing	Flying club
Cobblers Cove	615	●	●	●	8 km			●	●		●	●	●			●

Bermuda (page 607)

Properties	Page	Seaside	Swimming-pool on site	Tennis on site	9/18 holes golf course	Mountain-biking	Hiking	Horseback riding - Polo	Diving	Hunting	Fishing	Sailing	Water-Skiing	Canoeing Kayaking - Rafting	Skiing	Flying club
Horizons and Cottages	616	●	●	●	on site	●	●	●	●		●	●	●	●		
Waterloo House	617	●	●		10 km	●	●	●	●		●	●	●	●		

South America

Colombia (page 619)

Properties	Page	Seaside	Swimming-pool on site	Tennis on site	9/18 holes golf course	Mountain-biking	Hiking	Horseback riding - Polo	Diving	Hunting	Fishing	Sailing	Water-Skiing	Canoeing Kayaking - Rafting	Skiing	Flying club
Casa Medina	621				15 km											

Fitness	Spa	Beauty Salon	Swimming-pool covered	Whirlpool	Sauna	Hammam	Solarium	Meeting	Conference	Reception	Cocktail party	Number of conference rooms	Audio-visual equipment	Secretarial Services	Number of rooms	Properties
								20	40	40	40					Nomades (Les)
								12		24	24	1			4	Old Drovers Inn
												2				Orangerie (L')
								28		90	110	4	●			Patina Restaurant
	●	●						30	40	70	80	3	●		11	Pitcher Inn (The)
								50	150	100	150	2	●	●	62	Planters Inn
								10		22	22	1	●		11	Point (The)
								25		50	100	1			17	Rancho de San Juan
●				●	●				100	120	160	2	●		49	Rancho Valencia Resort
								30	50	75	120		●			Ryland Inn (The)
●								25	40	50	60	2			38	San Ysidro Ranch
										85	200					Seeger's
								25	35	35	35		●		14	Sherman House (The)
●								20	20	20	20	1	●		19	Triple Creek Ranch
								18	36	36	50	3				Tru
															31	Wauwinet (The)
								15	45	45	45	3	●		25	White Barn Inn
			●					30	120	80	125	3	●	●	19	Woodlands Resort & Inn

Mexico - Caribbean - Bermuda

Mexico (page 607)

Fitness	Spa	Beauty Salon	Swimming-pool covered	Whirlpool	Sauna	Hammam	Solarium	Meeting	Conference	Reception	Cocktail party	Number of conference rooms	Audio-visual equipment	Secretarial Services	Number of rooms	Properties
								50	50	80	140	2				Champs-Elysées (Restaurant)

Puerto Rico (page 607)

Fitness	Spa	Beauty Salon	Swimming-pool covered	Whirlpool	Sauna	Hammam	Solarium	Meeting	Conference	Reception	Cocktail party	Number of conference rooms	Audio-visual equipment	Secretarial Services	Number of rooms	Properties
								60	100	100	250	1	●	●	30	Horned Dorset Primavera (The)

Virgin Islands (page 607)

Fitness	Spa	Beauty Salon	Swimming-pool covered	Whirlpool	Sauna	Hammam	Solarium	Meeting	Conference	Reception	Cocktail party	Number of conference rooms	Audio-visual equipment	Secretarial Services	Number of rooms	Properties
										10	10				33	Biras Creek

French West Indies (page 607)

Fitness	Spa	Beauty Salon	Swimming-pool covered	Whirlpool	Sauna	Hammam	Solarium	Meeting	Conference	Reception	Cocktail party	Number of conference rooms	Audio-visual equipment	Secretarial Services	Number of rooms	Properties
	●			●			●								16	Eden Rock
●															14	Toiny (Le)

Barbados (page 607)

Fitness	Spa	Beauty Salon	Swimming-pool covered	Whirlpool	Sauna	Hammam	Solarium	Meeting	Conference	Reception	Cocktail party	Number of conference rooms	Audio-visual equipment	Secretarial Services	Number of rooms	Properties
●										20	40				40	Cobblers Cove

Bermuda (page 607)

Fitness	Spa	Beauty Salon	Swimming-pool covered	Whirlpool	Sauna	Hammam	Solarium	Meeting	Conference	Reception	Cocktail party	Number of conference rooms	Audio-visual equipment	Secretarial Services	Number of rooms	Properties
								24	50	100	200	6	●	●	48	Horizons and Cottages
●								24	50	100	200	6	●	●	30	Waterloo House

South America

Colombia (page 619)

Fitness	Spa	Beauty Salon	Swimming-pool covered	Whirlpool	Sauna	Hammam	Solarium	Meeting	Conference	Reception	Cocktail party	Number of conference rooms	Audio-visual equipment	Secretarial Services	Number of rooms	Properties
●								80	100	50	100	5	●	●	58	Casa Medina

More info on www.relaischateaux.com

Sports and Leisure

Properties	Page	Seaside	Swimming-pool on site	Tennis on site	9/18 holes golf course	Mountain-biking	Hiking	Horseback riding - Polo	Diving	Hunting	Fishing	Sailing	Water-Skiing	Canoeing Kayaking - Rafting	Skiing	Flying club
Ecuador (page 619)																
Mirage - Garden Hotel & Spa (La)	622		●	●		●	●	●								
Brazil (page 619)																
Rosa dos Ventos (Hotel e Fazenda)	623		●		●	27 km	●		●			●				
Uruguay (page 619)																
Bourgogne (La)	624	●				4 km										
Argentina (page 619)																
Bondoux (Jean-Paul) (Restaurant)	625															
Las Balsas (Hosteria)	627		●				●	●	●			●	●			●	
Posada de los Pájaros - Spa & Hotel	626		●		●	800 m	●	●	●				●	●	●		●

Fitness	Spa	Beauty Salon	Swimming-pool covered	Whirlpool	Sauna	Hammam	Solarium	Meeting	Conference	Reception	Cocktail party	Number of conference rooms	Audio-visual equipment	Secretarial Services	Number of rooms	Properties
																Ecuador (page 619)
●	●		●	●	●		●	26	35	100		1	●		23	Mirage - Garden Hotel & Spa (La)
																Brazil (page 619)
●		●		●	●			60	150	100	120	5	●		40	Rosa dos Ventos (Hotel e Fazenda)
																Uruguay (page 619)
									120	150						Bourgogne (La)
																Argentina (page 619)
								30	45	60	100	2	●	●		Bondoux (Jean-Paul) (Restaurant)
●	●	●	●	●	●		●	30	45	40	55		●		15	Las Balsas (Hosteria)
●	●	●		●	●			28	50	50	80	1	●	●	17	Posada de los Pájaros - Spa & Hotel

Une finesse incomparable, un Champagne d'exception

CHAMPAGNE
DEPUIS 1843
BESSERAT de BELLEFON
PRODUIT DE FRANCE
Cuvée des Moines
BRUT
ELABORE PAR S.A. BESSERAT DE BELLEFON · 51200 EPERNAY · FRANCE
12%vol

www.besseratdebellefon.com

L'ABUS D'ALCOOL EST DANGEREUX POUR LA SANTÉ, À CONSOMMER AVEC MODÉRATION

"Who can provide you with the key to 800 of the most luxurious hotels and restaurants on the planet?"

Introducing the new **Relais & Château Gift Certificate**, available in US dollars. Accepted around the world at all Relais & Châteaux and select Leading Hotels of the World. For more information, call (1) (212) 856 0115 (USA) or (44) (0)20 7978 5842 (UK).

THE SMARTEST LUGGAGE YOU CAN CARRY.

Cards

www.americanexpress.fr

Relais & Châteaux Lys packages: A collection of exceptional experiences.

An intimate dinner for two? A romantic weekend retreat in a hidden paradise? A country drive from Relais to Châteaux? Make your dreams come true with the specially-created Relais & Châteaux "Lys Collection" of packages.

Lys de Cristal, Lys d'Argent, Lys Liberté – all offer you a choice that suits your tastes. The hardest part will be choosing one!

For more information, call **(1) (212) 856 0115 (USA)**
or **(44) (0)20 7978 5842 (UK)**, or visit **www.relaischateaux.com**

OUR PARTNERS ARE ON YOUR SIDE

Relais & Châteaux has selected eight internationally renowned partners to guarantee you high-quality service: American Express, AT&T, Hertz, Mastercard, Silversea, Karen Brown, Wine Spectator and Cigar Aficionado.

With each of our partners, we have established exclusive offers: reduction on your stay, preferential rates on cruises or car rentals...

To obtain more information about these offers, please contact us (see page 9) or consult our Website: www.relaischateaux.com

Marianne, maître de chai à Listrac.

Bénéficiant de 57 appellations,
les vins de Bordeaux sont seuls au monde
à offrir une telle diversité de vins fins.

BORDEAUX
tout un monde de finesse

L'ABUS D'ALCOOL EST DANGEREUX POUR LA SANTÉ. A CONSOMMER AVEC MODERATION.